Stress Reduction and Prevention

Stress Reduction and Prevention

Edited by
Donald Meichenbaum
University of Waterloo
Waterloo, Ontario, Canada
and
Matt E. Jaremko
University of Mississippi
University, Mississippi

Springer Science+Business Media, LLC

Library of Congress Cataloging in Publication Data

Main entry under title:

Stress reduction and prevention.

Bibliography: p.
Includes index.
1. Stress (Psychology) I. Meichenbaum, Donald. II. Jaremko, Matt E. [DNLM: 1. Stress, Psychology—Prevention and control. 2. Stress, Psychological—Therapy. WM 172 S9156]
BF575.S75S7737 1982 155.9 82-18926
ISBN 978-1-4899-0410-2

ISBN 978-1-4899-0410-2 ISBN 978-1-4899-0408-9 (eBook)
DOI 10.1007/978-1-4899-0408-9

First Printing—February 1983
Second Printing—April 1984
Third Printing—March 1989

To

RICHARD S. LAZARUS

whose work on stress and coping has influenced
much of the research reported in this volume
and
to my former students
and present colleagues

ROY CAMERON, MYLES GENEST, and DENNIS TURK

whose collaboration and friendship
have continually enriched me.

D. M.

To

CHARLES D. SPIELBERGER

who was a source of encouragement
from the beginning of this project.

M. E. J.

Contributors

FRANK ANDRASIK, Department of Psychology, State University of New York, Albany, New York

MARGARET A. APPEL, Department of Psychology, Ohio University, Athens, Ohio

OFRA AYALON, Department of Education, University of Haifa, Haifa, Israel

ROY CAMERON, Department of Psychology, University of Saskatchewan, Saskatoon, Saskatchewan, Canada

THOMAS M. COOK, Program of Social Ecology, University of California at Irvine, Irvine, California

SEYMOUR EPSTEIN, Department of Psychology, University of Massachusetts, Amherst, Massachusetts

EVA L. FEINDLER, Department of Psychology, Adelphi University, Garden City, New York

WILLIAM J. FREMOUW, Department of Psychology, West Virginia University, Morgantown, West Virginia

KENNETH A. HOLROYD, Department of Psychology, Ohio University, Athens, Ohio

IRVING L. JANIS, Department of Psychology, Yale University, New Haven, Connecticut

MATT E. JAREMKO, Department of Psychology, University of Mississippi, University, Mississippi

PHILIP C. KENDALL, Department of Psychology, University of Minnesota, Minneapolis, Minnesota

DEAN G. KILPATRICK, Department of Psychiatry and Behavioral Sciences , Medical University of South Carolina, Charleston, South Carolina and People Against Rape, Charleston, South Carolina

HOWARD LEVENTHAL, Department of Psychology, University of Wisconsin, Madison, Wisconsin

DONALD MEICHENBAUM, Department of Psychology, University of Waterloo, Waterloo, Ontario, Canada

DAVID R. NERENZ, Department of Psychology, University of Wisconsin, Madison, Wisconsin

RAYMOND W. NOVACO, Program of Social Ecology, University of California at Irvine, Irvine, California

ETHEL ROSKIES, Department of Psychology, University of Montreal, Montreal, Quebec, Canada

IRWIN G. SARASON, Department of Psychology, University of Washington, Seattle, Washington

LOIS J. VERONEN, Department of Psychiatry and Behavioral Sciences, Medical University of South Carolina, Charleston, South Carolina and People Against Rape, Charleston, South Carolina

ROBERT L. WERNICK, Departments of Psychology and Psychiatry, University of Saskatchewan, Saskatoon, Saskatchewan, Canada

Preface

Since 1950, when Hans Selye first devoted an entire book to the study of stress,professional and public concern with stress has grown tremendously. These concerns have contributed to an understanding that has implications for both prevention and treatment. The present book is designed to combine these data with the clinical concerns of dealing with stressed populations. In order to bridge the gap between research and practice, contributions are included by major researchers who have been concerned with the nature of stress and coping and by clinical researchers who have developed stress management and stress prevention programs.

The book is divided into *three* sections. The goal of the first section is to survey the literature on stress and coping and to consider the implications for setting up stress prevention and management programs. Following some introductory observations by the editors are the observations of three prominent investigators in the field of stress and coping. Irving Janis, Seymour Epstein, and Howard Leventhal have conducted seminal studies on the topic of coping with stress. For this book they have each gone beyond their previous writings in proposing models and guidelines for stress prevention and management programs. While each author has tackled his task somewhat differently, a set of common suggestions has emerged.

In the second section of the book, a cognitive-behavioral perspective on stress and coping as well as general guidelines for setting up training programs are considered. This section concludes with a description of a cognitive-behavioral stress inoculation training program. Several of the authors in Section III have used this stress inoculation training program in their work.

The third section of the book, which is divided into three parts, focuses on specific stress prevention and management programs. The papers in Part A describe programs for a variety of medical problems, including hospitalized patients (Philip Kendall), burn patients (Robert Wernick), patients with psychophysiological disorders (Ken Holroyd, Margaret Appel, and Frank Andrasik), and Type A individuals (Ethel Roskies). Each of these authors provides descriptions of demonstration projects and reports on research in progress. We hope that the description of these projects will further stimulate research and clinical practice.

Part B focuses on the stress related to being a victim. Ofra Ayalon discusses the stress related to being a victim of terrorist attacks in Israel. Lois Veronen and Dean Kilpatrick examine the plight of the female rape victim and what can be done to reduce subsequent stress reactions.

Part C considers the application of stress management programs to specific populations. The chapter by Ray Novaco, Thomas Cook, and Irwin Sarason considers the stress accompanying military training and the various ways intervention may be undertaken. The socially anxious (Matt Jaremko) and adolescents acting out problems (Eva Feindler and William Fremouw) are two additional populations for whom stress reduction programs have been developed. In conclusion, some summary observations and comments on needed future directions are offered.

In each of the chapters in Section III on specific applications, authors have been asked to review the literature for their population in terms of

1. the data that indicated the need for a stress management program;
2. performance and social analyses of their stressed population that indicate the role played by cognitive and affective factors and interpersonal support systems in the coping process;
3. a critical evaluation of the training data for their specific populations;
4. a description of how one may conduct a coping-skills training program on both a treatment and preventative basis;
5. a concluding brief discussion of needed future directions.

The editors have provided comments and summaries throughout on the various programs. The editors believe that the authors have described interesting and provocative demonstration projects that reflect the current knowledge about stress and coping. The editors and the chapter authors recognize the limitations of the reported interventions; but nevertheless, there is a feeling of optimism and encouragement. It is in the spirit of critical-mindedness and enthusiasm that we offer this volume. It is dedicated to those who will critique and build on the efforts offered.

DONALD MEICHENBAUM
MATT E. JAREMKO

Contents

I

The Stress Literature

Implications for Prevention and Treatment

The stress-reduction and stress-prevention marketplace is burgeoning. Books, workshops, television programs, advertisements, and so forth bombard us with advice on how to combat stress. The term *stress* has become a rallying cry and the anti-stress industry has become immense. The current vogue of stress-reduction clinics, physical fitness classes, yoga sessions, meditation lectures, various forms of psychotherapy, prescription drugs, and so forth—each with its unique view of stress and coping—is ever expanding.

Our objective is *not* to add another book to the increasing number of so-called antistress books, or to provide a cookbook on "how to cope." The object instead is to help the reader become a more critical consumer of the antistress marketplace.

In order to accomplish this goal we have invited three prominent researchers to consider the implications of their work for setting up stress prevention and management programs. Following the discussion by each of these contributors we will offer our own observations. At this point some brief comments on each of the three chapters in this introductory section are in order.

In the first chapter, Howard Leventhal and David Nerenz describe a sequential model of stress and coping. After discussing the perennial problems surrounding the definitions of stress and coping, Leventhal and Nerenz provide a sequential analysis of self-regulatory coping mechanisms, highlighting the levels of response involved in the coping processes. In their analysis they emphasize the role of cognitive, though not always conscious, processes in the determination of stress responses. Whether it is in the form of perceptual representation, attention and elaboration, schemata, or interpretations, Leventhal and Nerenz indicate that the ways in which individuals cope with stress (e.g., with a disease such as cancer) are often influenced by the deeper interpretations of the stressor's meaning for that individual. Leventhal and Nerenz sensitize us to the complexities of the stress and coping processes that must be taken into consideration in any stress-management program.

In their discussion of stress-prevention and management programs, they highlight the important role of (a) analyzing both the stressor and the individual's representation or meaning of the stressor, (b) developing a comprehensive training regimen, and (c) providing preparatory information. The same features are also underscored in the second chapter, by Seymour Epstein.

Epstein has brought together diverse data, including Freud's work on traumatized soldiers, Pavlov's observations on traumatized dogs, and his own work on sport parachutists, in order to emphasize the important role of graded stress inoculation as a general principle in the mastery of stress. Epstein views the stress inoculation as a natural healing process by which individuals maintain an optimum rate of assimilation of stressful events. Epstein argues that in contrast to an "all or none" defensive system that rarely helps to reduce stress (and in fact may often be stress engendering), a more effective approach is to cope with stress in small doses, which is evident from the initial response to more displaced and less intensely threatening stimuli. With experience and by means of self-pacing (or what Epstein calls *proactive mastery*), individuals are able to handle more intensely stressful stimuli. Thus, graduated practice with increasingly stressful events (i.e., stress inoculation) is offered as an important guideline in the development of any stress prevention or management programs.

This process of graduation permits the stressed individual to become increasingly aware of early warning signs and to develop the ability to interrupt these at low intensity. According to Epstein, treatment programs for individuals under stress should encourage graded exposure and repetition to the point where habituation occurs and new coping responses develop. Such terms as *corrective emotional experience, emboldening the individual, fostering assimilation of stressful experiences that occur in-graded increments, and selective attention and inattention to cues of threat* reflect Epstein's suggestion that graded stress inoculation is a natural healing process of the mind.

A similar view about the potential usefulness of a graded inoculation approach toward stress prevention and treatment was offered by David Orne (1965), who stated:

> One way of enabling an individual to become more resistant to stress is to allow him to have appropriate prior experience with the stimulus involved. The biological notion of immunization provides such a model. If an individual is given the opportunity to deal with a stimulus that is mildly stressful and he is able to do so successfully (mastering it in a psychological sense), he will tend to be able to tolerate similar stimulus of somewhat greater intensity in the future. . . . It would seem that one can markedly affect an individual's tolerance of stress by manipulating his beliefs about his performance in the situation. . . and his feeling that he can control his own behavior. (pp. 315–316)

The concept of stress inoculation as a guideline for stress prevention and management programs is also emphasized by Irving Janis. Janis places the concept of stress inoculation in some historical perspective by tracing his own work from World War II to the present. His initial work was on what he called "battle inoculation" in World War II, when he documented the value of gradual exposure to stressful stimuli and the need to make the training experience as similar as possible to the criterion combat situation. A similar set of observations has been offered by Rachman (1978).

Janis's work with patients preparing for surgery contributed to his replacing the concept "battle inoculation" with the more general concept "emotional inoculation." Janis reports on the value of realistic warnings and preparatory information for surgical patients in stimulating the processes of the "work of worrying" as a means of coping with impending stressors. More recently, Janis (like Epstein) has used the term "stress inoculation" to describe those procedures used to help individuals on a preventative basis to avoid the damaging psychological consequences of subsequent stressful experiences, and on a treatment basis to alleviate stress-related disorders from which individuals already suffer.

Janis also considers some of the possible mechanisms by which stress inoculation training may operate, including such processes as engendering in clients a sense of self-confidence, hope, perceived control, commitment, and personal responsibility. The need to tailor stress prevention and management training programs to individual differences is highlighted and prohibitions against setting up standard programs for everyone is underscored. Carefully preparing clients for intervention, providing rationales for each mode of intervention, and helping clients anticipate and prepare for possible failures enhance the efficacy of the stress treatment programs.

REFERENCES

Orne, D. Psychological factors maximizing resistance to stress with special reference to hypnosis. In S. Klausner (Ed.), *The quest for self-control.* New York: Free Press, 1965.

Rachman, S. *Fear and courage.* New York: Pergamon Press, 1979.

1

A Model for Stress Research with Some Implications for the Control of Stress Disorders

HOWARD LEVENTHAL and DAVID R. NERENZ

INTRODUCTION

For the past several years, we have been engaged in a program of research with the aim of understanding how people comprehend and cope with illness threats. Our early studies examined people's beliefs and behavior in response to health communications urging them to stop smoking, use good dental hygiene practices, drive safely, or take inoculations to protect against tetanus (Leventhal, 1970). Later studies dealt with ways of preparing patients to cope with painful or unpleasant medical procedures such as endoscopy, childbirth, and cancer chemotherapy, and preparing students to cope with cold pressor pain in laboratory settings (Leventhal & Everhart, 1979; Leventhal & Johnson, 1982). Although the studies covered a number of different subject populations and health settings and spanned a period of 15 years, they have been linked by a common thread. Throughout, we have attempted to describe how people, as active agents, interpret and represent the information they receive about health threats from outside sources and from their bodies, and how their subsequent actions depend on their understanding of that information.

We have learned a great deal about how patients cope with specific

HOWARD LEVENTHAL and DAVID R. NERENZ • Department of Psychology, University of Wisconsin, Madison, Wisconsin 53706.

illness threats, but it is apparent that what we have learned is not restricted to specific illnesses or even to illness in general. Indeed, we feel that the behavior of patients in our studies can be used as the basis for a model of how people cope with a wide range of stressful events. In this chapter, we will try to show how the model we have developed for patient behaviors(Leventhal, Meyer, & Nerenz, 1980; Leventhal, Nerenz, & Straus, 1980) can serve as a general approach to the problem of stress and stress control.

SOME DEFINITIONS

There is still some ambiguity about the proper use of the term *stress*. It has been used to refer to environmental circumstances that disrupt the normal activity of an organism (Appley & Trumbull, 1967; House, 1972; Kagan, 1971; Kollar, 1961; Whithey, 1962); it has also referred to the responses of the organism, either physiological or psychological, to particular events (Burchfield, 1979; Mason, 1971; Selye, 1973, 1974, 1976) or as a global label for a field of study that examines the processes by which organisms adapt to disruptive events (Averill, 1979; Lazarus, 1971; Mechanic, 1974).

Clearly, in addition to distinguishing the situational and response aspects of stress, a complete model of stress must deal with the problem of the various levels of stress responses. Stress responses can be "psychological" (mental and overt behavioral responses), neurophysiological (neurohumoral, including catecholamine effects on internal organs, heart, adipose fat organ, kidney, etc.), and immunological. We would like to address briefly the problem of levels, distinguishing between what we regard as unsatisfactory methodological solutions and essential theoretical solutions.

Selye has adopted a distinction between physiological stress and emotional "distress," since he holds to a particular view of their relationship, one with which we disagree. Selye (1956, 1976) believes that the same pattern of physiological stress responses (pituitary, adrenal cortex, thymus, visceral) occurs for all stressors. There may be some features to the pattern that are specific to particular stressors, but these are situationally induced variants on a common biological theme (see Selye, 1975). Selye's model is widely accepted. It forms the intellectual substrate for students of life events who relate illness to the total number of life changes and the total amount of behavioral adaptation they demand and not to the unpleasant character of these events or their association with anger, fear, disgust, etc. (Dohrenwend & Dohrenwend, 1974; Holmes & Masuda, 1974; Holmes & Rahe, 1967). The position is widely accepted in social psychology and has provided a powerful heuristic in the cognition-arousal model so elegantly argued by Schachter and his associates (Schacter, 1964; Schachter & Singer, 1962, 1979; Valins, 1966).

Specificity theories of different sorts provide a clear alternative to the Selye model. But they vastly complicate the definitional issue since specificity not only argues for different neurophysiological response patterns for different stressors, but also suggests the need to identify linkages between specific classes of stressor and the emotional and coping reactions to them. As we examine the specificity and levels issues in the following sections, we will find the problem of definition of stress receding into the background, to be replaced by a variety of more specific questions relating to process.

Systems and Levels of Response

Many investigators have made clear the need to differentiate among verbal, expressive motor, and autonomic response (Graham, 1972; Lacey, 1967; Lang, 1977; Leventhal, 1970). A stressor may initiate change at only one, at any two, or at all three levels of response, and the change may occur in different components at a level (heart, kidney, etc.) or at the physiological level. Janis suggested taking measures at all levels to be sure to detect stressor consequences (Janis & Leventhal, 1968). This fairly widely accepted response to the inconsistency problem assumes a certain degree of equivalence among levels and among components at a given level; hence, stressor effects will be manifest some place, and good methodology requires assessment of all possible places to detect them.

As Schwartz (1977, 1979) suggests, however, the issue of levels is a fundamental conceptual issue and is not adequately resolved by the simple addition of measures. One can talk about the very same response from a psychological, physiological, or physical frame of reference (Graham, 1972). A major goal of much stress research has been to establish plausible associations among different levels of description. This is often done to provide accounts of how psychological stress leads to physical illness. It is also done in efforts to reduce or to explain psychological phenomena in biological terms. Whether we find correlation across levels is an empirical issue (Hempel, 1966). If we succeed, it means we can improve our insight into links between psychological states and disease. But even if correlation is achieved, it does not mean that one level of description, the biological, has taken the place of another, the psychological. We must retain concepts and operations at both levels if we are to correlate them.

We feel that it is important not to mix levels of description; the model to be presented in this chapter is psychological, not muscular or physiological, and we attempt to stay with the psychological level of analysis. Even the best of intentions can go awry, however, in stress research. Levels are relatively easy to deal with if one's only aim is their correlation. But when we attempt ot understand the interaction of levels over time, the distinction between levels has a way of disintegrating. For example, subjective fear may by accompanied by increased heart rate and increased systolic blood pressure, while subjective anger is accompanied by increased heart rate and increased diastolic blood pressure (Ax, 1953; Schachter, 1957). If the correlation is consistent, we learn of an association with subjective state (psychological level) and autonomic response. There are two factors that can upset this picture. First, heart rate and systolic blood pressure may arise with psychological states we had not assessed. Hence, increased heart rate and blood pressure can have multiple meanings. A potential solution is to find indicators other than blood pressure that will distinguish the states.

The second problem generated by the interest of levels is more difficult to deal with; it concerns variables that seem to "move" across levels. For example, if I saw a snake and responded with mild subjective fear and a rapid increase in heart rate but no change in overt expression, you would conclude that I had responded at two of three levels, subjective and autonomic. But if I then noticed my increased heart rate and jumped to my feet and reported that I am terrified of snakes, ***heart rate*** would have moved from a dependent to an independent variable; it is now an antecedent determinant of motor activity and subjective emotional states. Effects of this sort can no longer be handled by simple cross level correlation.

Problems of this kind are seen throughout the study of emotion (e.g., Schachter & Singer, 1962). It appears in attribution studies of phobia where investigators use the term ***arousal*** to refer to physiological activity and the psychological experience of arousal (e.g., Valins, 1966). Actually, there is no intrinsic reason to despair because some measures can be regarded from a dual perspective, as long as we retain our wits and are clear about the levels we are working at.

Differentiation and Organization of Stress Responses

The multilevel nature of distress responses is but one of the complexities confronting investigator and therapist. The other is the differentiation of stress reactions into specific emotional responses. This differentiation occurs at the phenomenological level—the experience of the emotion of distress, anxiety, fear, depression, anger, guilt, disgust, and so on

(Izard, 1971) and at the expressive motor and physiological levels (Ekman, Friesen, & Ellsworth, 1972; Graham, 1972; Izard, 1971, 1977; Mason, 1971; Tomkins, 1962). Differential emotions theory provides one major way of organizing reactions across levels (Izard, 1977). Our adoption of a specificity position (Leventhal, 1974, 1979, 1980) reflects a marked departure from Selye's unidimensional approach.

Differentiation of emotions also presents an opportunity to link particular situations to specific emotions. For example, Lazarus (Folkman & Lazarus, 1980; Lazarus, 1966) distinguishes between threat (a future-oriented stressor) and current injury damage, and differentiates both from loss. The distinction is of empirical and theoretical significance. In their important study of life events, Brown and Harris (1978) identify threats of long-term loss as the key antecedents of depression. These losses can be as diverse as separation due to death, life-threatening illness in a loved one, major material loss, or a loss of felt closeness due to another person's behavior, for instance, marital infidelity. Crises that do not involve loss do not precipitate depressive disorders; they may, however, precipitate schizophrenic breakdowns in those so predisposed (Brown & Harris, 1978). Specificity has also been reported in laboratory situations (Schwartz & Weinberger, 1980; Sternbach, 1966). For example, Schwartz and Weinberger find that undergraduates report specific emotional experiences when imagining each of a series of situations associated with particular emotions by a standardization group. The Brown and Harris and Schwartz data point to an impressive degree of situation–emotional specificity.

The linkage of specific situations to particular emotional states holds out hope for a substantial degree of simplification in what would otherwise be a field of overwhelming complexity. But it is clear that the relationship between situation and emotion is not the complete story. The individual's style of coping and his ability to locate and use coping resources may also have specific impact on the pattern of physiological stress response (Folkman & Lazarus, 1980; Graham, 1972; Kasl & Cobb, 1970; Seligmann, 1975; Weiss, 1972). An essential ingredient for understanding stress responses, therefore, is the development of a psychological model connecting the individual to situations and describing his/her ongoing efforts at adaptation. That, of course, is the goal of this chapter.

MODEL OF EMOTION AND ADAPTATION TO STRESSFUL EVENTS

We have incorporated our ideas on coping and adaptation into a formal model partially described in earlier publications (Leventhal, 1970,

1974, 1979, 1980; Leventhal & Everhart, 1979; Leventhal, Meyer, & Nerenz, 1980; Leventhal, Nerenz, & Straus, 1980). The model attempts to describe the steps in the self-regulative process that produce both short- and long-term adaptation to stress settings. The examples used in describing the model come from studies of patient response to illness and disease symptoms, but the same concepts can be applied to a wide range of stressful events.

Overview

The model conceives of the individual as a regulatory system that actively strives to reach specifiable goals (see Carver, 1979; Lazarus, 1966; Leventhal, 1970; Miller, Galanter, & Pribram, 1960; Powers, 1973). This regulatory system is viewed as a feedback system comprised of a set of serially arranged components or stages: an input stage, which represents the stimulus field and sets goals; a response output or coping stage, which provides for planning, selecting, and performing coping responses; and a monitoring stage, which involves attention to the consequences of the action in relation to the initial set of goals. The stage analysis of the regulatory mechanism has been useful for the analysis of pain (see Leventhal & Everhart, 1979), reactions to health threats (Leventhal, 1970, 1975), and the utilization of the medical care system (Mechanic,1978; Mechanic & Greenley, 1976; Safer, Tharps, Jackson, & Leventhal, 1979; Suchman, 1965).

An important feature of this model is the distinction between processing of what are termed *objective features of the environment,* such as the form, location, and function of external objects, and the processing of *emotional reactions to objects,* such as fear or anxiety (Leventhal, 1970, 1975). These two relatively separate, although interacting, regulatory systems are involved in creating a conscious perception and associated feelings about an illness, object, or person. In the area of pain and distress, noxious stimulation is simultaneously processed by an *informational* or *objective system and a distress* or *emotion system* (Leventhal & Everhart, 1979). The systems operate in parallel; both function at stimulus reception and interact with one another as early as stimulus reception, and they continue to act and interact in interpretation, coping, and monitoring.

It has also been hypothesized that these regulatory systems make use of more than a single type of memory and that perceptual memories, as distinct from conceptual or language memory, are central in the storage of emotional experiences (Lang, 1977; Leventhal, 1980; Leventhal & Everhart, 1979). The basic features of the model are described in Figure 1.

As an example of the sequence of stages in the model, one might

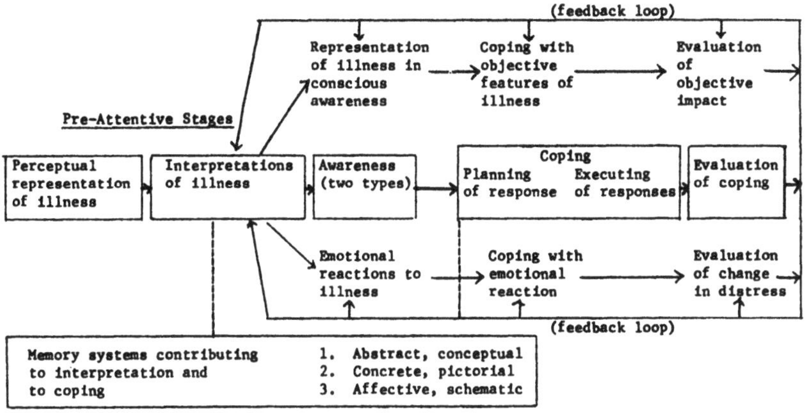

Figure 1. Model of response to illness and treatment.

consider a hypothetical patient with breast cancer who notices a pain in her leg several days after a chemotherapy injection. The pain cues evoke emotional and perceptual memory images of her mother, who had similar pain from bone metasteses of breast cancer. The knowledge of her mother's decline and death, particularly the perceptual memories of the change in her physical appearance, is extremely fear-provoking. The patient becomes agitated and concerned that the pain may represent a spread of the cancer, even though she knows that cancer only occasionally produces pain similar to what she is experiencing.

After a brief period, the patient takes two aspirins in hopes that the pain will diminish. She still remains upset about the possible meaning of her pain, however, and calls two friends, describing her experience and soliciting advice. When these calls fail to calm her, she goes to see her local doctor, who examines the site of pain and suggests the pain is muscular and not due to cancer. After some reassurance and instructions to use aspirin and try muscle relaxation, the visit is concluded.

The patient then becomes more relaxed, comforted by the doctor's lack of worry. After she returns home, she decides that the pain really is much less severe than it was before she took the aspirin. She chides herself for becoming so upset by a minor pain and decides that in the future, she will take aspirin for such pain and continue her daily routine.

This example highlights several major components of the proposed theoretical model: symptom experience, interpretation, coping with the objective (pain) and emotional (fear of cancer) factors, monitoring, and feedback. In the following discussion, each aspect of the model will be explained in detail.

Steps in Processing

We will describe each of the steps of the processing system in serial order, since the system often functions in just that way. But this descriptive ordering is also one of convenience because the system is circular, and the stages can best be thought of as a processing loop. Sometimes one might prefer to begin at a different point, for instance, with coping or with monitoring and evaluation when describing or attempting to influence the system.

Perceptual Representation: The Primary Appraisal

The term *cognitive encoding* was the first label for the initial step of self-regulation in stressful settings (Leventhal, 1970). This concept was similar to what Lazarus meant by initial appraisal of threat: "The appraisal of threat is not a simple perception of the elements of the situation, but a judgment, an inference in which the data are assimilated to a constellation of ideas and expectations" (Lazarus, 1966, p. 44).

Our concept differed in one important respect, however, from that defined by Lazarus; we believed a substantial portion of the appraisal process to be automatic and nonconscious (see Mandler, 1975). Our work on pain (Leventhal, Brown, Shacham, & Enquist, 1979; Leventhal & Everhart, 1979) and our studies of patient behavior in stress settings (Johnson, 1975; Johnson & Leventhal, 1974; Leventhal & Johnson, 1982) have further persuaded us of the importance of recognizing the automatic, nonvoluntary components of appraisal. Conscious judgment is not irrelevant to appraisal, but it is not always the most important aspect.

The second major idea is that the appraisals occur in at least two parallel channels; appraisals are both problem-oriented and emotional (Folkman & Lazarus, 1980; Leventhal, 1970). Emotion, a separable aspect of the appraisal system, seems to be more fully automatic in function (Leventhal, 1974, 1975, 1980; Zajonc, 1980).

Sensory Registration

The first step in responding to a stimulus involves the registration and representation of the stimulus in the perceptual system. Registration is the capturing of the input by a sense organ and the conduction of this input to the central nervous system for further processing. The inputs processed in illness generally include various types of bodily sensations, such as side effects of treatment, pains or pressures produced by the disease, and other bodily processes. The presence of stress-induced emotions can add to the input, since stress appears to both generate and intensify body sensations (Leventhal & Everhardt, 1979; Pennebaker & Skelton, 1978). The stimuli are then integrated with past memories to generate a perceptual representation.

Attention and Elaboration

Once information reaches the perceptual field, it is available for further processing. Perceptual memories may be stimulated by features of the event, and these memories can guide attention to other features of the stimulus and retrieve additional information from memory. Perception is an active process involving reciprocal activity between the sensory stimulus and the memory system (Broadbent, 1977; Neisser, 1967). At some point in this active processing, the information may enter conscious awareness. Whether information enters awareness depends on how closely one attends to it and that, in turn, depends on the strength of the memory structures (schemata) integrated with the incoming information (Broadbent, 1977; Bruneer, 1957). Emotional schemata will typically have greater strength and access to consciousness. Because of this, emotionally laden images often appear to intrude themselves on awareness even when they are unwelcome (Horowitz, 1970). Hence, the power of the input to dominate consciousness depends on its interpretation; for example a body pain is increasingly likely to become the focus of attention as its interpretation changes from that of "irrelevant muscle cramp" and "side effect of therapy" to "metastatic lesion."

Although interpretation is primarily a preconscious process, people may give retrospective reports of interpretation as if it had been conscious. As an example of preconscious interpretation, one might imagine being in the shower and suddenly feeling a large lump underneath the jaw. The discovery will be followed by a dry sensation in the mouth, a trembling of the hands, a feeling of "butterflies" in the stomach, and *then* a cognition: "It might be cancer." Later, you might report that you thought the lump was cancerous because of its size, sudden appearance, or the fact that it was only on one side. These descriptions may or may not accurately represent the factors that went into the interpretation, but the initial interpretation was not likely on a conscious or verbal level.

Schemata and Interpretation

Our recent studies (e.g., Nerenz, Leventhal, & Love, 1982) have indicated the diverse ways in which patients with lymphoma and breast cancer notice symptoms (e.g., pains) and interpret them. For many patients, a pain that "wanders" and is intermittent is not a sign of cancer, while a pain that is continuous and clearly localized is interpreted as tumor related. The patient attends to the symptom and on the basis of concrete, commonsense rules and his view of cancer (a lump that is equivalent to a mechanical injury), classifies the symptom as meaningless or as a sign of danger. If the symptom is interpreted as a sign of cancer, one is likely to find vivid threat imagery accompanied by strong emotional reactions (Wortman & Dunkel-Schetter, 1979).

Our example makes clear that the meaning of a pain emerges from its coding or interpretation. The schema acts as a template: when the sensory information fits the features of the template, the integration generates the experience of illness. The schema includes concrete sensory features (lumps, burning pain, pulling, or cramping) and the abstract labels linked to them (cancer, ulcer, muscle tear). The schema also has prognostic and temporal features; we expect specific abstract and concrete consequences for particular time periods. And the schema includes specific assumptions about cause, for example, "this pain was caused when I pulled a muscle during racquetball or is due to my flu." The label, symptoms, prognosis, time line, and cause are the critical features that give the schema its meaning. These features are inferred by us as observers and theoreticians; they need not be in the consciousness of the patient. Our concept of features appears similar to Lang's (1979) conceptualization of imagery as defined by propositions.

The symptoms and signs of illness can be integrated with schemata that are medical with reference to specific disease agents and underlying physiological processes, or they can be integrated within a commonsense or layman's schema. Commonsense definitions can be cultural and personal. Cultural concepts are shared ideas about the disease's impact on the individual's ability to work and maintain social relationships, and the obligations of others toward him, etc. (Fabrega, 1975). The individual's personal interpretation of a threat will be an integration of ideas taken from the culture at large, from his personal contacts, including his medical practitioner, and from his personal symptom experience (Leventhal, Meyer, & Nerenz, 1980). The integration reflects the parallel and multiple nature of the underlying schema; it is partly abstract and it is partly perceptual or concrete. The distinction between perceptual and conceptual codes is important because interpretations based on perceptual memory codes lead to automatic responding, while interpretations based on abstract, conceptual memory appear to require conscious intervention prior to action.

It is important to distinguish between a perceptual memory, involving visual, auditory, and tactile features of specific episodes, and a conceptual memory, containing abstractions and verbal representations derived from specific experiences (Gardner, 1975; Posner, 1973; Tulving, 1972.) The distinction between different forms of memory as a basis for interpretation is important because combinations of memory codes seem to be closely linked to certain types of coping reactions. Perceptual memory codes seem to be the basis of highly automatic responding; abstract, conceptual memory appears to require conscious intervention prior to action. Examples of these differences can be seen in a situation where two persons are walking while engaged in animated conversation, pausing to look before crossing streets. If stopped and questioned about their experience, they will report the content of their conversation, which has been guided by abstract conceptual memory and in focal awareness, but they will be unable to report their various reactions to particular features of the terrain, which have been guided by integrations of pictorial and motor memory and did not enter focal awareness.

The operation of both perceptual and conceptual thought is clear in the way hypertensive patients generate private views of their illness episodes. Roughly 90% of the hypertensives in medical treatment believe they are aware of the changes in their blood pressure. They infer blood pressure changes from physical symptoms such as headache, face flushing, and nervousness (Meyer, Leventhal, & Gutmann, in press). They can experience pressure changes even though 80% of the respondents state that (other) people cannot tell when their pressure is up! About 65% quickly suggest that the interviewer not mention any of this to the nurse or physician. These hypertensive patients seem to strive for consistency between their concrete and conceptual thought. When a person has symptoms, he/she seeks a diagnostic label. When a person has a diagnostic label, he/she is likely to seek a symptom (Leventhal, Meyer, & Nerenz, 1980; Pennebaker & Skelton, 1980).

One of the central findings of our studies is that patients have a strong tendency to interpret all illness in terms of a schema for acute or infectious disease. The temporal expectation for acute illness is for symptoms to worsen, followed by a remission; remission occurs either with treatment or simply from its "clearing up." The schema of illness as acute and curable has important effects on both expectations for and adherence to treatment. Newly treated hypertensives are very likely to drop out of treatment when they notice symptom changes that they interpret (erroneously) as the disappearance of their conditions (Meyer, 1980).

Although it may be wrong, the expectation that illness is acute is reassuring. It generates hope for a "100% cure from cancer," for complete remission, and for the discontinuance of treatment for diabetes and hypertension. Accepting the long-term, chronic nature of cancer or hypertension is accepting the threat of death and the limitation of activity; patients resist this outlook (Ringler, 1981).

The labels, concrete symptoms, and temporal features of illness schemata can serve as powerful cues for emotional response. Indeed, the emotional reactions themselves appear to become integrated into the schema along with its perceptual symptomatic, temporal, and causal features. The amalgam of specific events with subjective emotional feeling, emotional expressive patterns, and autonomic response patterns has been labeled *emotional memory schemata* (Leventhal, 1980; Leventhal & Everhart, 1979). These are memory structures that can be activated by situations, by imagery, or by stimulating emotions. If we see someone with chronic cancer, we become depressed; if we become depressed, we have images of pain and death from cancer. Illness can generate moods (Miller, 1964), and mood can generate the memory of illness, if not illness itself. The most dramatic example is the reactivation of phantom pain memories (experiences of pain in amputated limbs) by severe life stress (Melzack, 1973).

Responding based on emotional schemata will share many properties with other automatic behaviors, the most important of which is that much of it is not accessible to awareness. Individuals who respond emotionally are unlikely to be fully aware of their behavior; they are usally unaware of their expressive reactions or the various defensive or instrumental actions taken to control their emotional memory schemata. Emotional schematization *is* likely to bring into awareness the eliciting stimulus, that is, the object that one fears and that makes one angry, and the feelings of fear and anger associated with that object.

The concept of interpretation may be summarized by reiterating basic propositions:

1. Interpretation is a necessary antecedent to action.
2. Automatic responding is produced by a combination of the stimulus with perceptual memory codes; conscious, volitional responding is produced by a combination of the stimulus with abstract, conceptual codes.
3. Schemata are composed of features. They have content (abstract labels and concrete symptom memories), causal features, temporal expectations, and prognostic implications. These features give meaning to stimulation.
4. Emotional schematization of the stimulus leads to automatic responding that may be difficult to bring under volitional control.

The Coping Process: Planning and Action

The development and execution of plans for action are processes as complex as the construction of the representation of the threat. They also draw on complex memory systems, abstract and concrete, and utilize plans developed for affective states and plans developed for problem solution. We can at best sketch out only a very small number of features of planning and action

The Representation Guides Coping

The individual's perceptual representation of his illness problem will *direct* planning and action (Leventhal, Meyer, & Nerenz, 1980). Hence, coping behaviors will reflect the basic features of the representation. Plans and actions will be directed to deal with both the concrete and abstract features of the illness; the content of the illness label will influence seeking care, and the waxing and waning of symptoms will influence evaluation of treatment and disease progress. The presence of emotion will evoke efforts to regulate affect. The perceived time line will set limits on planning and influence the durability of coping efforts. The perceived cause of the problem will lead to the addition of new responses for coping or the subtraction of components of medically recommended regimens (Hayes-Bautista, 1976, 1978). Finally, the similarity of the symptomatology to past illnesses will evoke automatic and deliberate responses associated with prior illness episodes.

Given the large number of events that guide coping, it is clear that effective regulation requires clear differentiation of goals and clear staging or temporal sequencing of behavior. The individual needs to know when emotional goals are uppermost and recognize that in attending to an immediate emotional pressure, he may momentarily sacrifice problem-solving. This also means realizing that controlling emotional pressures can make it possible to be more effective in problem-solving later on. Ability to delay and limit one's field of activity refer to strategies for temporal sequencing of coping.

Health problems appear to place especially heavy demands on emotional coping resources because they provoke substantial levels of threat and require reliance on external, expert sources of help (Folkman & Lazarus, 1980)—hence the need for temporal staging of emotional and objective problem goals. This is clearly seen in the behavior of patients with metastatic breast cancer who show very high levels of tolerance for hours of nausea and vomiting to achieve long-term treatment success. Many people find it difficult to tolerate short-term distress for long-term gain. Part of the problem seems to be the absence of a clear image of the long-term problem and identifying the problem only with the immediate, concrete pain and distress generated by both illness and treatment (Zborowski, 1969).

The Schema: History Repeats Itself

A pervasive feature of coping with illness is the degree to which behaviors designed to manage current illness episodes repeat actions more appropriate to past episodes. This repetitiveness may be due to the directive influence of both concrete symptomatology and emotional reactions of fear, pain, and distress. Affects and symptoms focus the person on immediate gains, and this immediacy of focus seems to enhance the tendency to repeat past illness behaviors. Meyer's (1980) findings with hypertensives illustrate this point. His patients used symptoms as signs of blood pressure, discontinuing medication when symptoms disappeared and increasing medication when symptoms were severe, even they had been told and "believed" that (other) people cannot tell when their blood pressure is high. They treated the disorder as they would treat any minor disorder, and this seems a natural consequence of focusing on *immediate* symptomatology. It requires the mediation of an abstract plan to break the short-term hold of symptoms.

Some of the strategies for coping with a disease such as cancer do depend on deeper interpretations of the meaning of cancer and involve relatively long-term behavioral adaptations. For example, patients in our studies who believed that their cancer was due to stress often cut back on commitments and sought assistance with work from friends and family. They also became indifferent to minor life annoyances, differentiated more sharply between important and trivial events, and refused to become involved in those they regarded as trivial. Patients who defined the illness in mechanical terms, as bad cells and tumors, often engaged in intensive exercise, adopted health-food diets, and made other changes to strengthen their bodily resources. While patients differed in their degree of conviction about the effectiveness of these supportive therapies, they saw the therapies as beneficial in most instances, and performing them seemed to play an important role in minimizing maladaptive emotional reactions. Of course, many of these behaviors are largely repetitions of typical actions taken to strengthen the body.

Resources for Coping

Patients draw on a wide range of resources to meet the demands of severe illness. Central among these is their own ability to generate coping responses, or what Bandura (1977) has labeled a sense of self-effectance. People with a history of effective self-regulation, who can differentiate problems, generate plans, and act, are likely to do so when they confront illness threats. For example, Meyer (1980) found that those hypertensives who developed more elaborate coping plans had also developed more elaborate views of their illness problems.

It is important to note that many patients appear to see their own fear as a sign that they are unable to manage threat. Given time, they may calm down and recapture their ability to generate coping responses. Kornzweig (1967) reported this phenomenon in individuals exposed to threat messages about the dangers of tetanus. Subjects low in esteem seemed temporarily paralyzed by their fearfulness. Given a day to recover, they were quite effective in coping. Recently, Rosen, Terry, and Leventhal (1982) found that low-esteem subjects did an effective job in smoking reduction if they received a self-esteem bolstering message prior to their exposure to a fearsome antismoking film.

The actual dynamics of generating coping responses are not clear, but phrases such as "having ideas about what one might do," "knowing what to do," or "trying things out" express the concept of response generation. Past research on the way students cope with the transition from high school to college suggests that success in coping is strongly related to the ability to project an image of oneself as an active doer, that is, seeing oneself as actively managing a situation (Coelho, Solomon, Wolff, Steinberg, & Hamburg, 1969). Another, though apparently less important variable, is seeing oneself as able to produce positive outcomes (Coelho, Silber, & Hamburg, 1962).

Knowledge and skills acquired in past experiences of coping with illness provide another source for coping with a new illness episode. These knowledge and skill factors may include strategies and specific steps for organizing family routines or dealing with economic threats and organizing work, as well as specific steps and strategies for handling compliance with treatment regimens, controlling emotional reactions, and adjusting to side effects of medications. The relevance of past experience to current experiences will depend on the similarity between the demands of the current treatment situations and past episodes.

Coping and problem management are greatly aided by the opportunity to observe others performing positive coping responses (Bandura, 1969; Meichenbaum, 1977), as well as the opportunity to practice or rehearse these reactions either mentally (Leventhal, Singer, & Jones, 1965) or with guided assistance from an authority or model (Bandura, Blanchard, & Ritter, 1969). Students successful in coping with change sought advice and modeled their behavior on that of successful upper classmen (Coelho *et al.,* 1962, 1969). Observing the way in which patients similar to oneself manage cancer and its treatment, along with specific advice and opportunities to practice coping behavior offered by doctors and nurses, is likely to be critical in successful coping and is related to reduced levels of distress (Ringler, 1981).

Two factors stand out in considering the enhancement of coping through preparation by practitioners. First, the practitioner needs to provide precise information about the sensory experiences of illness and treatment. Individual knowledge about what they will feel in their bodies is essential for effective coping. Sensory information appears critical in permitting neutral or objective interpretations of body symptoms that might otherwise be interpreted within a threat and fear framework (Johnson, 1975; Johnson & Leventhal, 1974; Leventhal & Johnson, 1982). Second, the practitioner needs to provide precise response information and the opportunity to practice specific responses to these sensory cues, for instance, how to breathe during throat swabbing, how to make swallowing motions during an endoscopy examination, etc. (Johnson & Leventhal, 1974). It is the combination of accurate sensory information and behavioral instructions that is effective in achieving self-control (Leventhal, Shacham, Boothe, & Leventhal, 1981).

Our studies of cancer patients also show powerful negative effects of modeling. Ringler (1981) found that patients felt more threatened and were less able to make use of coping resources when their experiences with other cancer patients emphasized the desperate, painful, and implacably destructive nature of cancer. For most patients, however, knowledge of others with illness meant less distress and more effective maintenance of everyday activities.

Finally, the way patients conceive of themselves and their illness appears to be a crucial underlying factor in successful coping. Some patients preserve their sense of being active, alive individuals and maintain their career goals and family relationships. Their long-term self-definitions are of ultimate significance to these individuals, and they are unwilling, indeed unable, to adopt the self-concept of a cancer patient; they are people who have cancer. Investigations of chronic pain show similar effects: those who remain involved in work and life and refuse to focus their existence on pain will not become "chronic pain patients" even though they experience chronic pain (Fordyce, 1976; Wooley, Blackwell, & Winget, 1978). These patients will seek treatment for pain only if it is evident that the treatment has a reasonable probability of effectiveness and if it is clear that there is a low probability that it will disrupt their normal activities (Sternbach, 1974).

The discussion of coping may be summarized in three points:

1. Coping is based on the interpretation of symptoms.
2. Patients attempt to cope either with the objective features of a symptom or with the emotion produced by the symptom. In some cases, the patient is coping with both simultaneously.
3. Ability to generate effective coping strategies depends on dispositions such as self-esteem or self-effectance as well as the availability of successful models and social support.

Appraisal Processes

The final stage of the regulatory process is monitoring and varying the effects of coping so as to achieve desired objctives, a process Lazarus (1966) terms *secondary appraisal.* The conclusions drawn from the appraisal process are dependent on the criteria chosen for evaluating outcomes, the immediacy and nature of the feedback, and the attributions made about coping successes and failures. Coping outcomes can be attributed to the effectiveness (or ineffectiveness) of the specific coping response, the adequacy of the individual's general coping skills or competence, the resources of the individual's disposal, or the nature of the threat ("cancer is treatable," "cancer is a deadly killer"). Appraisal is important because it helps to determine the stability of the self-regulatory process, that is, whether the system is coherent and regulating or incoherent and dysregulating (Schwartz, 1979). A dysregulating or unstable system generates psychological and physiological distress that adds to the total strain on the organism and increases the symptom load and sense of illness (Pennebacker & Skelton, 1978). We will discuss each of these problems before turning to our final comments on the process of stress management.

Setting Goals

Whether a response is seen to succeed or fail is highly dependent on the criteria used for appraisal. Unreasonable goals—excessively abstract or demanding, unclear, and temporally inappropriate—doom the individual to conclude that his efforts cannot produce desired outcomes. Take, for example, the cancer patient whose treatment goal is "complete cure," nothing more or less. If this is the individual's only treatment goal, he/she will lack any criteria for monitoring daily progress. And in the absence of other, specific goals, the individual has nothing to work toward: life becomes an anxious wait for the unlikely pronouncement that one is cured. On the other hand, if an individual sets extremely fine criteria for evaluating ongoing coping reactions, virtually every detectable fluctuation in his/her condition could be interpreted as signs of progress or threat, including perhaps alterations in pain and tension induced by variations in his/her emotional arousal. A patient using such fine criteria will have substantial difficulty achieving a stable, closed coping system as she/he will respond with excessive euphoria to minor positive changes and with excessive disappointment to minor regressions.

The effects of setting remote and abstract goals contrast sharply with those of using concrete goals to evaluate treatment. In our studies, both lymphoma and metastatic breast patients with palpable, observable tumors developed a sense of control over both treatment and illness when they could observe clear and steady shrinkage in their tumors with treatment. The behavior of patients whose lymphatic tumors *disappeared* within days of their initial treatment formed a sharp contrast to those whose tumors disappeared gradually. Some of these patients showing the "best" response (complete disappearance) became extremely anxious because they now lacked any clear sign of their disease condition (Nerenz, 1979). It may, indeed, seem surprising that a good, positive response should arouse distress, but chemotherapy treatment usually does not stop with the disappearance of palpable tumors. It continues for months; if stopped prematurely, it is ineffective (Bonadonna & Valagussa, 1981). When the palpable tumors are gone, so too is the patient's justification for treatment. This could produce a basic uncertainty about the state of one's body. Continued treatment implies the disease is present somewhere, but one can no longer tell where! This thought may be far more uncomfortable than regarding cancer as a concrete, localizable event and then observing its response to treatment. Ringler's (1981) findings with breast cancer cases fully support this interpretation. Women given chemotherapy as a preventative treatment (after surgery has removed all detectable signs of disease) have more difficulty dealing with treatment than women receiving chemotherapy to treat metastatic illness. The findings are also fully compatible with the data showing distress reduction with sensory information. Comfort is maximal with a localizable symptom that one can monitor and that changes in a way that is consistent with an acute interpretation of disease (Johnson, 1975; Leventhal & Johnson, 1982).

Monitoring Affective Information

Our model postulates the availability of two basic types of feedback: objective (abstract or concrete) and emotional. With disruptions in coping with objective problems, the individual is no longer focused on the information needed to modify behavior so as to better regulate objective stressors. Under these conditions he/she will become increasingly aware of strong subjective emotion. Indeed, awareness of affect is most likely a key sign of disruption or dysregulation of problem-solving behavior (Dewey, 1894, 1895; Leventhal, 1970, 1980; Mandler, 1975).

Identifying emotion as a sign of dysregulation does not mean emotion is disorganized or disorganizing. To the contrary, emotional expression and subjective emotional feelings are signs that coping is now regulated by an automatic emotional process. The *expressive* components provide external signals for social support and assistance, as seen when the infant's cry of distress stimulates mothering (Dunn, 1977). The *internal, subjective* experience is a signal for internal readjustment. The experience of overwork or the subjective pain, distress, and confusion from excessive information is a signal to "clear the decks" and stop action. The fear stimulated by unexpected threats to physical or economic security is a signal to seek assistance or to find alternative means of sustenance. The anger at frustrating circumstances is a signal to alter (by attack) external circumstances. If we compare the emotional response of jumping up in irritation from an endless mountain of work and yelling "enough" to the objective process of making a thorough assessment of one's immediate and remote demands and then deciding whether one should press forward despite near exhaustion, we can see the value and efficiency of the automatic affective response in contrast to the objective alternative. The logical alternative adds to the overload; the automatic response ends it.

One serious problem with affective information is its coarseness. Emotional states are vague and are inexact guides for coping. A second difficulty is that emotional responding may imply a variety of causal and outcome expectations that generate adjustment problems. For example, individuals may interpret their emotional outburst as meaning they cannot solve objective problems or may anticipate being rejected by support figures for expressing feelings (e.g., anger) that imply doubt about the support figure's competence or willingness to assist in regulating an illness danger (Janis, 1958).

A major difficulty with affective monitoring is interpreting the cause of the emotional state. Emotions and moods and their associated autonomic sensations appear to be pooled or added together regardless of their source (Bowlby, 1969; Leventhal, 1974, 1979). Hence, it is difficult to assess accurately the determinants of fluctuations in emotions and moods. This confusion is of special interest when we look at illness as a determinant. Since illness may be more or less clearly identified at different times, the individual may readily attribute his mood shifts to illness at some times but erroneously attribute it to internal or external causes at other times. For example, it is easy to label oneself *ill* if one has specific symptoms such as fever, pain, or a running nose. Under these circumstances, the vague signs of fatigue, depression, and irritability that accompany illness are attributed to it. But if depression, irritability, and fatigue persist after the concrete symptoms disappear and one is labeled *well*, it is not improbable that these emotions and moods will be attributed to some irrelevant external factor or to a "permanent" personality disposition. Misattributions of generalized emotional states (see Zillman, 1978, for similar examples) may play a crucial role in the development of chronic pain and illness behavior and the development of long-term dependencies in the elderly.

Stability of Self-Regulatory Systems

It should be made explicit that our model is not static, that is, it is not meant to imply that a single interpretation leads to a single coping response, which is performed a few times until a desired outcome is obtained. Simple negative feedback effects may apply to a few patterns of behavior during illness but they provide a limited picture of the adaptation process. The picture is broadened as we recognize that the adaptive mechanism is recursive. It repeats the cycle of interpretation, coping, and appraisal and changes as it does so. The regulatory system is dynamic in that its characteristics at any one point are dependent on events that have occurred earlier. Hence, later interpretations are influenced by prior interpretations, later coping skills by prior exercise of coping activity, and later appraisals by the consequences of earlier goal-setting, monitoring, and explanation (attribution) of coping outcomes. And as the system repeats its behavior, it becomes automatic; symptoms are interpreted in familiar schemata, coping is stereotyped, and appraisals and explanations fit expectations and ignore minor fluctuations in outcomes (Bruner, Goodnow, & Austin, 1956). At this point the systems are stable; their activity produces negative feedback.

Stable regulatory systems are generally regarded as good and unstable ones as bad. When a coping response repeatedly fails to meet criteria, the system begins to hunt for a new way to regulate. If the new search fails, and/or if the individual lacks a systematic approach to the search process (Bruner, 1957), behavior may become increasingly erratic and random. As this happens, it is less likely that an effective coping response will occur or that the individual will be able to detect its impact if it does. As repeated control efforts fail, the threat may appear more vivid and imminent even though its actual rate of approach is unchanged. The constant changing of responses along with the perception of increased threat is likely to increase emotional arousal and enhance the probability of exhaustion and illness (Weiss, 1972). Hence, unstable systems would be seen as bad because they are closely wedded to distress and dysphoric affects.

Our data show that regulatory systems—the way patients represent themselves and their illnesses and the way they cope with and appraise outcomes—undergo major transitions. A breast cancer patient with advanced metastatic disease may experience substantial joy if chemotherapy produces a reduction in pain and allows her to do simple household chores (Ringler, 1981). To the healthy person or to the person receiving preventive chemotherapy treatment, such a minimal gain may seem no gain at all. But the metastatic patient does not compare her current condition to her pre-illness conditions. Her underlying model is no longer that of acute illness; it is of terminal chronic disease, and she no longer expects to be cured. Within her new "chronic" regulatory framework, gains and losses are measured in terms of change in daily function; small reductions in pain and small gains in mobility and gains in quality time represent positive outcomes.

It is our impression that the most stable components of the regulatory system are the schemata underlying the representation of the illness and the individual's capacity for planning, that is, his/her self-effectance.

Both represent sets of highly generalized or prototypic rules for appraising symptomatic change and response effectiveness. Hence, the individual does not expect specific illness episodes or specific coping sequences to precisely fit the underlying model. Not every infectious, acute disease need have the same symptomatology, precisely the same cause (hypertension can be due to eating salty pork, to overwork, etc.) or exactly the same time line. Not every effort at coping succeeds; one expects to "dream up" alternatives and to experience setbacks. The generality of these prototypes and the anticipation of deviation protect them from rejection! "Fuzzy sets" are not readily disconfirmed.

We also suspect that disconfirming experiences lead the individual to substitute an alternative schema and to store rather than discard the old one. For example, Meyer (1980) found that the longer patients were in treatment for high blood pressure, the less likely they were to operate in terms of an acute illness model. They shifted first to a cyclic model—expecting their hypertension to clear and return at a later occasion—and then to a chronic model. The "old" acute model was very likely still used to interpret and generate representations of other illness episodes. Thus, it is possible that there is a hierarchy or sequence of schemata with rules for their own replacement.

The individual's underlying schemata also gain stability because they are well anchored in cultural beliefs. The assumption that social stress (Croog & Levine, 1969), foods, and/or environmental toxins cause illness are widely shared (Herzlich, 1973; Young, 1978), as are basic assumptions about illness being symptomatic, finite in duration, and so on. Schemata are part of ideological systems. They are also compatible with the individual's history of illness experience; indeed, they are compatible with the history of illness experience of family and friends with whom information on illness is shared.

The individual's sense of self-effectance also appears to be a relatively stable factor. But the levels of this factor remain to be explored. For example, little is known about the individual sense of physical vulnerability. Some people clearly feel more vulnerable than others. And many people feel vulnerable to particular illnesses (Ben-Sira, 1977; Niles, 1964). Indeed, it is not uncommon to find people expressing the belief that they will die of a particular illness within some quite specific time span. These beliefs in one's "organic" effectance may be conditioned by early identifications. One's expectations of resistance to illness may be very different, indeed, if one believes himself "like" a father who died of a heart attack at 55 rather than like a grandfather who succumbed to lung cancer at 90. But this is only one level of self-effectance. There are also beliefs about resistance to everyday afflictions. A youngster can state with very great certainty that he is healthier than most of his friends and report that he was out with colds 12 times last school year! Running noses are everyday malaises; they are not diseases. We also suspect that the individual's history and skill in regulating his internal affective states is also closely related to his/her level of confidence in and stability of effectance in coping with specific disease episodes (Ben-Sira & Padeh, 1978). Much of self-diagnosis seems to center around the question "Are these symptoms signs of physical illness or signs of psychological upset?" The overlap in experience is likely to produce some overlap in the sense of effectiveness in self-management (Balint, 1957; Mechanic, 1972).

SOME IMPLICATIONS FOR DISTRESS CONTROL

It would be ideal if we could generate a list of tactics to be used for distress management by the practicing clinician. Unfortunately, we are not yet prepared to do so. Indeed, we are only now conducting randomized trials in which we experimentally test many of the implications of our model. Hence, what we say in this closing section must be highly tentative. We also want to make clear that it is not our intent to propose a grand system for distress management to replace other generalized strategies for teaching cognitive control of stress. Indeed, much of what we have to say will undoubtedly fit models for stress-management training such as Meichenbaum's (Meichenbaum, 1977; Meichenbaum & Novaco, 1978) three-stage model of Education, Rehearsal, and Application, or the strategies for problem analysis proposed by D'Zurilla and Goldfried (1971) and Mahoney and Arnkoff (1978). There is no need for us to substitute a new structure to organize the stress-management training process. Our strategy, therefore, will be to present some of the most obvious implications of our model and let the reader organize them within the framework of existing, programmatic approaches to stress management.

Preparation Should Be Comprehensive, Not Partial

Our model strongly suggests that stress management requires a comprehensive approach. One needs to target change for each of the three stages of the regulatory process, that is, the interpretation or representation of the stressor, coping skills, and appraisal criteria (see Averill, 1979, for an excellent overview). Given that coping is directed by the representation and appraised against criteria established by the representation, stable self-regulative action requires coherent integration of the three systems. Our past experimental work in changing attitudes and behavior to health threats supports this conclusion. In these studies effective action (e.g., taking tetanus shots, quitting smoking for three months), required both a threat warning (a clear representation of the danger) and an action or coping plan (Leventhal, 1970; Leventhal, Meyer, & Nerenz, 1980). Either element alone was ineffective; the integrated unit was essential for change. Our studies on self-regulation during noxious medical examinations have also shown the importance of a combination of information to construct the representation of the stressor (sensory information) and information to create coping responses (Johnson & Leventhal, 1974; Johnson, Rice, Fuller, & Endress, 1978; Leventhal *et al.*, 1981).

None of these studies specifically focused on goal setting, that is, generating a series of behavioral targets and time lines to evaluate coping activity. The action plan packages, however, did include information that would be classified as relevant to appraisal. More complete attention to this component might well prove to be critical in *sustaining* long-term adaptive sequences. Kanfer's (1977) work suggests that appraisal information (criteria setting) is extremely important, if not sufficient, for behavior change. We suspect that information to change outcome appraisals may well be the most effective starting point for developing guides to select coping responses and to develop a valid representation of illness and stress problems. This is likely to be so because appropriate criteria allow the individual to choose actions appropriate to goals and to examine the outcome of behaviors in ways that can develop valid, causal representations of stressful situations.

Self-Regulation Demands Diagnosis of the External and Affective Environments

Training a patient for stress control requires a careful analysis of both the stressor and the individual's representation of it. Discrepancies between the representation and "reality" form critical points for intervention, since coping based on discrepant representations is unlikely to generate stable feedback. It also is essential to diagnose the affective states ssociated with specific stress situations. Emotional schemata (Leventhal, 1980) carry with them specific attributional expectations (e.g., anger is due to insult or frustration; shame due to foolish mistakes; fear due to threat of bodily injury, etc.) and specific, automatic action patterns (such as attack, hide, or flee). Hence, a profile of affects typically found in a given situation (Izard, 1977; Schwartz & Weinberger, 1980) can provide clues as to the kinds of explanations and kinds of coping responses an individual is likely to generate in that situation (Lazarus & Launier, 1978). Given that a variety of invisible internal physiological changes and relatively nonsalient environmental events can generate emotion, it is likely that inappropriate attributional explanations and coping strategies will appear in many stress settings.

Many examples of such inappropriate reactions are seen in illness settings where the individual no longer has clear guides to the determinants of his behavior. One such setting is *recovery* from illness. While ill, the individual has a clear attribution for mood changes and symptom states. As illness clears and the individual arrives at the ambiguous transition to wellness, he lacks any clear explanation for lingering moods of depression, or for body states such as fatigue or minor pain. The likely consequence is attributing these states to external social causes or drawing inappropriate conclusions about one's emotional condition and ability to manage environments. This poststressor phase, beset with vague affects and no clear direction for attribution, is a likely place for therapeutic intervention. Another excellent example of misattribution is seen in the elderly where there is a strong association between depression and beliefs in failure of memory, even though there is no association between depression and actual decline in memory performance.

Altering the Objective and Affective Representations of the Problem Requires Alteration of Both Abstract and Concrete Schemata

We have emphasized the symmetrical association of illness labels and symptoms. Whatever the stressor, its cognitive representation will include both abstract and concrete components. The abstract notions of insult, failure, injury, and work are associated with a set of concrete, perceptual images. Highly available, concrete perceptual memories of particular and generalized stress and illness episodes appear to serve as basic, organizing schemata for generating coping responses. When one plans to cope with failure, one's plans are directed by a concrete image of particular failures, just as coping with illness is directed by underlying schemata representative of acute, infectious illness. Similarly, emotional states such as anger, fear, and shame are organized around perceptual prototypes that include autonomic and automatic instrumental response patterns (Lang, 1979; Lang, Kozak, Miller, Levin, & McLean, 1980; Leventhal, 1980). Verbal persuasion is clearly insufficient to change these concrete memory structures.

Various techniques for producing behavioral reactions appear to be essential for altering concrete schematic structures. Guided participation in reducing snake phobias, for example, provides direct experience, approach, and contact with the phobia object (Bandura *et al.,* 1969). Our model suggests that gaining detailed information about the object itself (i.e., that it is not slimy and does not strike out in anger) and gaining information about one's ability to approach and to withstand the emotional responses to the snake are as critical for behavior change as the rehearsal of the approach responses (Locke, 1971). In short, approach responding provides new concrete, perceptual experience with the snake and with one's emotional and instrumental response capabilities in its presence. One has approached without disintegrating emotionally; the heart beats did not lead to a stroke nor did they paralyze one's capacity to act and observe. This corrective information is not abstract; it is multisensory, concrete, and ultimately persuasive because it is information about what *is* there with respect to our naive apprehension of external reality.

The hierarchical feature of our model suggests the need to explore the relationship between abstract, volitional processes and concrete, perceptual reactions in self-regulation. The problem appears to be how to make available to the volitional system the specific cues and responses that control the automatic system. For example, in a brilliant study, Bair (1901) taught subjects to contract their retrahens muscles by stimulating the muscle electrically, instructing the subjects to attend to the "feel of the response," and then having them make complex, volitional responses (jaw and facial muscle contractions) while searching for the "feel" of the retrahens response. Eventually, the subjects detected the retrahens response, and proceeded to inhibit the volitional reactions in which it was embedded. Finally, subjects were able to contract only the retrahens muscle and selectively wiggle each ear.

There are many examples of "biofeedback" training that involve similar strategies. Furedy and his collaborators (Furedy & Riley, 1980) suggest there is little evidence that information (in the form of operant procedures) alters automatic reactions that are situationally elicited. For example, they suggest that learning to slow heart-rate responses requires the subject to produce the response by means of a voluntarily controllable action, for instance, taking a deep breath to slow heart rate. If one repeats the voluntary response in the same situation, the involuntary one (in this case, slowing of heart rate) will eventually be conditioned to the same situation and will appear without the performance of the volitional reaction.

From the above examples, we can see that self-control involves being one's own experimenter. It means using volitional-conceptual skills to analyze situations and perform responses in ways that will modify stimuli (external or own command) so as to control reactions that are otherwise automatic. If abstract "folklore" about what controls the automatic response is in error, however, then stress control and reconditioning become a difficult, if not impossible, task.

Establishing a Hierarchy of Criteria and Time Lines

Our model and data strongly suggest the need for establishing a hierarchy of criteria and time lines for a successful program of self-regulation. The cancer chemotherapy patient needs to make a commitment to his or her eight-month course of chemotherapy treatment. But this goal and time line need to be differentiated from shorter term subgoals associated with the management of specific treatment side effects such as vomiting and nausea. For example one is likely to vomit every 20 to 40 minutes for 12 to 24 hours following the start of therapy and there are coping strategies (keep a receptacle nearby, take some kind of lozenge to settle one's taste and gut) and appraisal strategies (vomit regularly, search for gradual changes in the intensity and duration of the response) for the symptom (Nerenz, 1979). Additional time lines and coping and appraisal strategies need to be set for dealing with vague symptomatology such as fatigue and depression, which become particularly salient as the specific side effects settle down. Clear expectations of the likely duration of these vague events can help concretize and reinterpret them as treatment—and not disease—related. Finally, time lines need to be established for returning to daily routines of work, household chores, parenting, and fulfilling responsibilities to family and community. Specification of goals and temporal targets provide an ongoing calendar of objectives and ensure a mix of achievements with likely failures.

Establishing an Experimental Set to Self-Management

Many of our patients entered medical therapies with "magical" expectations: drugs would cure their illness with no effort on their part. These expectations were often rudely disconfirmed either by the results of a medical test or the recurrence of the symptoms that led the person to seek medical care. Many patients who returned for high blood pressure treatment did so because of the appearance of a symptom, even though there was no clear evidence the symptom was related to blood pressure (Meyer, 1980). Patients who returned to treatment under such circumstances were likely to drop out of treatment (the hypertension studies) or experience substantial levels of distress (the cancer studies).

It is our belief that more realistic expectations would lead to less distress and to more effective and persistent coping efforts. This means the individual should be made aware that self-control of distress is a learning process. And he should be aware not only of the responses he is to learn—relaxation—but of the kind of effects the response is supposed to produce, that is, how it should alter his representation and underlying schemata, and how he can appraise whether it is doing so. In short, the patient can learn the model and use it as a guide for organizing his thoughts and interpreting the outcomes of his coping efforts.

An awareness of the recursive nature of adaptive processes, of the separateness of abstract and concrete memory systems, of the parallel nature of affective and problem-oriented self-regulation, etc., prepares the individual for interpreting the successes and failures he will experience in the labor of learning self-regulation of distress. Awareness of the nature of self-control and the difficulty and trial and error needed to achieve it should be a strong inoculant against negative consequences of failure, what Marlatt and Gordon (1980) have called Abstinence Violation Effects. Failures in self-control can be cataclysmic if control is interpreted as an all-or-none process.

Awareness of the Risks of Stability and Instability

Knowledge of the recursive nature of regulatory processes leads naturally to preparation for periods of stability and instability in self-control. Being aware of the feel of instability and the random and aimless behavior accompanying it can reduce the felt pressure to recapture control and dissipate the distress it would otherwise induce. And stability itself poses danger: Risk-taking and excitement-seeking may achieve short-term alleviation of emotional dysphoria and boredom, but produce more intensive long-term environmentally induced stress.

Training in the Use of Environmental Resources

Finally, stress-control training should include substantial emphasis on identifying and making use of environmental resources. But this is more than a matter of utilizing resources for action. It includes increased awareness of the way the environment influences one's representation of stressors. People may be only minimally aware of the degree to which their adherence to acute-illness thinking is supported by an anxious and fearful expectations of family members. Social support for inappropriate representations of illness can lead to substantial delays in seeking care; this is true of inappropriate expectations by practitioners as well as by family members (Safer *et al.*, 1979; Salloway & Dillon, 1973).

Family members may also hold highly inappropriate criteria for evaluating treatment progress. One somewhat unusual example appeared in the sample of women we were studying during the time they were on chemotherapy for breast cancer. Virtually all contact of this patient with the medical care system included her family. The family defined the nature of her illness and the criteria for appraising the adequacy of treatment, and played a major role in stopping chemotherapy when they became convinced the treatment was more dangerous (and symptomatic) than the disease. Although the suspicious, indeed paranoid, family environment proved an insurmountable barrier to treatment, it is interesting to note the patient did *not* fully share the paranoia. On an extraordinary occasion the interviewer chanced to see her alone and she voiced concern about the adequacy of her family's definition of her illness and treatment. But in the absence of prior preparation for coping with the support system and without any specific mechanisms to reinforce independent decision-making, the patient was trapped by a support system that committed her to a speedy death despite the high probability that treatment would have added several disease-free years to her life.

Another extremely important aspect of stress preparation would involve training patients in the art of yielding and then regaining control of the regulation of emotions and environmental problems. There are times during the stress of illness, and such times undoubtedly exist with other stressors, when successful problem-solving requires yielding control to someone else. Adequate self-regulation at the point of surgery means yielding control to an anesthetist and a surgeon. Indeed, inability to yield when yielding is necessary may substantially increase iatrogenic risks. Many moderately invasive diagnostic procedures (e.g., cystoscopy and endoscopy), can be performed in office settings without the risk of total anesthesia or the cost and time loss of hospitalization. Excessive efforts to self-regulated, struggling to stay awake, and excessive efforts to participate where no participation is possible may stimulate the practitioner to make use of more drastic medical interventions. The patient needs to know how to turn over control to the practitioner, and the practitioner needs to know how to accept and again yield control with grace.

CONCLUSION

The model emerging from our studies of coping with stressful illness situations has focused our attention on a host of new questions about self-regulation in stressful situations and helped us to generate new data to clarify our thinking about these processes. As researchers, we wish to conduct objective tests of the specific hypotheses we can generate from the model. But we also strongly believe that much can be learned through clinical application. Sharing the conceptual framework with patients can provide us with an unusual opportunity to observe the use of abstract and concrete notions to generate coping strategies. Mutual sharing, with the patient contributing his/her perception of stress situations, reports of his/her coping strategies, diaries of ongoing situations, representations, coping and appraisals of outcomes, provides the therapist with a window on the rich detail of self-regulative processes and the interplay between emotional and objective problem-solving and conceptual and perceptional thought processes. Sharing the model with the therapist provides the client with a series of opportunities to more sharply structure his/her understanding and a series of occasions to conduct more rigorous tests of the appropriateness of representations, coping strategies, and appraisals.

As Mandler (1975) and Nisbett and Wilson (1977) suggest, it is not easy to understand the conditions that control our behavior nor is it easy to redirect our actions. But where intuition and common sense have failed, experimentation may succeed. We cannot see the processes that generate our experience but we can systematically and selectively expose ourselves to situations and observe changes in our experience. An effective self-regulative therapy should offer the client the opportunity for acquiring better strategies for the long-term diagnosis and regulation of stressors in addition to relief from current disturbance. Hence, a self-regulation therapy should move us toward George Kelly's vision of making therapist and client better scientists.

REFERENCES

Appley, M. H., & Trumbull, R. On the concept of psychological stress. In M. H. Appley & R. Trumbull (Eds.), *Psychological stress: Issues in research.* New York: Appleton-Century-Crofts, 1967.

Averill, J. R. A selective review of cognitive and behavioral factors involved in the regulation of stress. In R. A. Depue (Ed.), *The psychobiology of the depressive disorders: Implications for the effects of stress.* New York: Academic Press, 1979.

Ax, A. F. The physiological differentiation between fear and anger in humans. *Psychosomatic Medicine,* 1953, *15,* 433–442.

Bair, J. H. Development of voluntary control. *Psychological Review,* 1901, *8,* 474–510.

Balint, M. *The doctor, his patient, and the illness.* New York: International Universities Press, 1957.

Bandura, A. *Principles of behavior modification.* New York: Holt, Rinehart & Winston, 1969.

Bandura, A. Self-efficacy: Toward a unifying theory of behavioral change. *Psychological Review,* 1977, *84,* 191–215.

Bandura, A., Blanchard, E. B., & Ritter, B. Relative efficacy of desensitization and modeling approaches for inducing behavioral, affective, and attitudinal changes. *Journal of Personality and Social Psychology,* 1969, *13,* 173–199.

Ben-Sira, Z. The structure and dynamics of the image of diseases. *Journal of Chronic Disease,* 1977, *30,* 831–842.

Ben-Sira, Z., & Padeh, B. "Instrumental coping" and "affective defense": An additional perspective in health promoting behavior. *Social Science and Medicine,* 1978, *12,* 163–168.

Bonadonna, G., & Valagussa, O. Dose-response effect of adjuvent chemotherapy in breast cancer. *New England Journal of Medicine,* 1981, *304,* 10–15.

Bowlby, J. *Attachment.* New York: Basic Books, 1969.

Broadbent, D. E. The hidden preattentive processes. *American Psychologist,* 1977, *32,* 109–118.

Brown, G. W., & Harris, T. *Social origins of depression.* London: Tavistock Publications, 1978.

Bruner, J. S. On perceptual readiness. *Psychological Review,* 1957, *64,* 123–152.

Bruner, J. S., Goodnow, J. A., & Austin, G. A. *A study of thinking.* New York: Wiley, 1956.

Burchfield, S. R. The stress response: A new perspective. *Psychosomatic Medicine,* 1979, *41,* 661–672.

Carver, C. S. A cybernetic model of self-attention processes. *Journal of Personality and Social Psychology,* 1979, *37,* 1251–1281.

Coelho, G. V., Silber, E., & Hamburg, D. A. Use of the student-TAT to assess coping behavior in hospitalized, normal and exceptionally competent freshmen. *Perceptual and Motor Skills,* 1962, *14,* 355–365.

Coelho, G. V., Solomon, F., Wolff, C., Steinberg, A., & Hamburg. D. A. Predicting coping behavior in college. *Journal of Nervous and Mental Disease,* 1969, *149,* 386–397.

Croog, S. H., & Levine, S. Social status and subjective perceptions of 250 men after myocardial infarction. *Public Health Reports,* 1969, *84,* 989–997.

Dewey, J. The theory of emotion: (I) Emotional attitudes. *Psychological Review,* 1894, *1,* 553–569.

Dewey, J. The theory of emotion: (II) The significance of emotions. *Psychological Review.* 1895, *2,* 13–32.

Dohrenwend, B., & Dohrenwend, B. P. (Eds.). *Stressful life events: Their nature and effects.* New York: Wiley, 1974.

Dunn, J. *Distress and comfort.* Cambridge, Massachusetts: Harvard University Press, 1977.

D'Zurilla, T. J., & Goldfried, M. R. Problem solving and behavior modification. *Journal of Abnormal Psychology,* 1971, *78,* 107–126.

Ekman, P., Friesen, W. V., & Ellsworth, P. *Emotion in the human face.* New York: Pergamon Press, 1972.

Fabrega, H., Jr. The need for an ethno-medical science. *Science,* 1975, *189,* 969–975.

Folkman, S., & Lazarus, R. S. An analysis of coping in a middle-aged community sample. *Journal of Health and Social Behavior,* 1980, *21*(3), 219–239.

Fordyce, W. *Behavioral methods for chronic pain and illness.* Saint Louis: C. V. Mosby, 1976.

Furedy, J. J., & Riley, D. M. Classical and operant conditioning in the enhancement of biofeedback: Specifics and speculations. In L. White & B. Tursky (Eds.), *Clinical biofeedback: Efficacy and mechanisms.* New York: Guilford Press, 1980.

Gardner, H. *The shattered mind.* New York: Knopf, 1975.

Graham, D. T. Psychosomatic medicine. In N. S. Greenfield & R. A. Sternbach (Eds.), *Handbook of psychophysiology.* New York: Holt, Rinehart & Winston, 1972.

Hayes-Bautista, D. E. Modifying the treatment: Patient compliance, patient control and medical care. *Social Science and Medicine.* 1976, *10,* 233–238.

Hayes-Bautista, D. E. Chicano patients and medical practitioners: A sociology of knowledge paradigms of lay-professional interaction. *Social Science and Medicine,* 1978, *12,* 83–90.

Hempel, C. G. *Philosophy of natural science*. Englewood Cliffs, New Jersey: Prentice-Hall, 1966.

Herzlich, C. *Health and illness: A social psychological analysis*. New York: Academic Press, 1973.

Holmes, T. H., & Masuda, M. Life change and illness susceptibility. In B. S. Dohrenwend & P. P. Dohrenwend (Eds.), *Stressful life events: Their nature and effects*. New York: Wiley, 1974.

Holmes, T. H., & Rahe, R. J. The social readjustment rating scale. *Journal of Psychosomatic Research*, 1967, *11*, 213–218.

Horowitz, M. J. *Image formation and cognition*. New York: Appleton-Century-Crofts, 1970.

House, J. S. The relationship of intrinsic and extrinsic work motivations to occupational stress and coronary heart disease risk. *Dissertation Abstracts International*, 1972, *33*, 2514-A.

Izard, C. E. *The face of emotion*. New York: Appleton-Century-Crofts, 1971.

Izard, C. E. *Human emotions*. New York: Plenum Press, 1977.

Janis, I. L. *Psychological stress*. New York: Wiley, 1958.

Janis, I. L., & Leventhal, H. Human reactions to stress. In E. Borgotta & W. Lambert (Eds.), *Handbook of personality theory and research*. Boston: Rand McNally, 1968.

Johnson, J. E. Stress reduction through sensation information. In I. G. Sarason & C. D. Spielberger (Eds.), *Stress and anxiety* (Vol. 2). Washington, D. C.: Hemisphere Publishing, 1975.

Johnson, J., & Leventhal, H. Effects of accurate expectations and behavioral instructions on reactions during a noxious medical examination. *Journal of Personality and Social Psychology*, 1974, *29*, 710–718.

Johnson, J. E., Rice, V. H., Fuller, S. S., & Endress, M. P. Sensory information, instruction in coping strategy and recovery from surgery. *Res. Nurs. Health*, 1978, , 4–17.

Kagan, A. Epidemiology and society, stress and disease. In L. Levi (Ed.), *Society, stress and disease* (Vol. 1). London: Oxford University Press, 1971.

Kanfer, F. H. The many faces of self-control, or behavior modification changes its focus. In R. B. Stuart (Ed.), *Behavioral self-management: Strategies, techniques and outcomes*. New York: Brunner/Mazel, 1977.

Kasl, S. V., & Cobb, S. Blood pressure changes in men undergoing job loss. *Psychosomatic Medicine*, 1970, *32*, 19–38.

Kollar, E. J. Psychological stress: A reevaluation. *Journal of Nervous and Mental Disease*, 1961, *132*, 382–396.

Kornzweig, N. D. *Behavior change as a function of fear arousal and personality*. Unpublished doctoral dissertation, Yale University, 1967.

Lacey, J. I. Somatic response patterning of stress: Some revisions of activation theory. In M. Appley & R. Trumbull (Eds.), *Psychological stress*. New York: Appleton-Century-Crofts, 1967.

Lang, P. Imagery in therapy: An information processing analysis of fear. *Behavior Therapy*, 1977, *8*, 862–886.

Lang, P. J. A bio-informational theory of emotional imagery. *Psychophysiology*, 1979, *16*, 495–511.

Lang, P. J., Kozak, M. J., Miller, G. A., Levin, D. N., & McLean, A., Jr. Emotional imagery: Conceptual structure and pattern of somatovisceral response. *Psychophysiology*, 1980, *47*, 179–192.

Lazarus, R. *Psychological stress and the coping process*. New York: McGraw-Hill, 1966.

Lazarus, R. S. The concept of stress and disease. In L. Levi (Ed.), *Society, stress and disease* (Vol. 1). London: Oxford University Press, 1971.

Lazarus, R. S., & Launier, R. Stress-related transactions between person and environment. In L. A. Pervin & M. Lewis (Eds.), *Perspectives in interactional psychology*. New York: Plenum Press, 1978.

Leventhal H. Findings and theory in the study of fear communications. In L. Berkowitz (Ed.), *Advances in social psychology* (Vol. 5). New York: Academic Press, 1970.

Leventhal, H. Emotions: A basic problem for social psychology. In C. Nemeth (Ed.), *Social psychology: Classic and contemporary integrations.* Chicago: Rand McNally, 1974.

Leventhal, H. The consequences of depersonalization during illness and treatment. In J. Howard & A. Strauss (Eds.), *Humanizing health care.* New York: Wiley, 1975.

Leventhal, H. A perceptual-motor processing model of emotion. In P. Pliner, K. Blankstein, & I. M. Spiegel (Eds.), *Advances in the study of communication and affect: Perception of emotions in self and others* (Vol. 5). New York: Plenum Press, 1979.

Leventhal, H. Toward a comprehensive theory of emotion. In L. Berkowitz (Ed.), *Advances in experimental social psychology* (Vol. 13). New York: Academic Press, 1980.

Leventhal, H., & Everhart, D. Emotion, pain, and physical illness. In C. Izard (Ed.), *Emotions and psychopathology.* New York: Plenum Press, 1979.

Leventhal, H., & Johnson, J. E. Laboratory and field experimentation: Development of a theory of self-regulation. In R. Leonard & P. Wooldridge (Eds.), *Behavior science and nursing theory.* St. Louis: C. V. Mosby, 1982.

Leventhal, H., Singer, R. P., & Jones, S. Effects of fear and specificity of recommendations upon attitudes and behavior. *Journal of Personality and Social Psychology,* 1965, *2,* 20–29.

Leventhal, H., Brown, D., Shacham, S., & Engquist G. Effect of preparatory information about sensations, threat of pain and attention of cold pressor distress. *Journal of Personality and Social psychology,* 1979, *37,* 688–714.

Leventhal, H., Meyer, D., & Nerenz, D. The common sense representation of illness danger. In S. Rachman (Ed.), *Medical psychology* (Vol. 2). New York: Pergamon Press, 1980.

Leventhal, H., Nerenz, D. R., & Straus, A. Self-regulation and the mechanisms of symptom appraisal. In D. Mechanic (Ed.), *Psychosocial epidemiology.* New York: Neal Watson, 1980.

Leventhal, H., Shacham, S., Boothe, L. S., & Leventhal, E. *The role of attention in distress and control during childbirth.* Unpublished manuscript, University of Wisconsin, Madison, Wisconsin, 1981.

Locke, E. A. Is "behavior therapy" behavioristic? (A analysis of Wolpe's psychotherapeutic methods). *Psychological Bulletin,* 1971, *76,* 318–327.

Mahoney, M. J., & Arnkoff, D. Cognitive and self-control therapies. In S. L. Garfield & A. E. Bergin (Eds.), *Handbook of psychotherapy and behavior change: An empirical analysis.* New York: Wiley, 1978.

Mandler, G. *Mind and emotion*. New York: Wiley, 1975.

Marlatt, G. A., & Gordon, J. R. Determinants of relapse: Implications for the maintenance of behavior change. In P. O. Davidson & S. M. Davidson (Eds.), *Behavioral medicine: Changing health lifestyles.* New York: Brunner/Mazel, 1980.

Mason, J. W. A reevaluation of the concept of "non-specificity" in stress theory. *Journal of Psychiatric Research,* 1971, *8,* 323–333.

Mechanic, D. Social psychological factors affecting the presentation of bodily complaints. *New England Journal of Medicine,* 1972, *286,* 1132–1139.

Mechanic, D. Discussion of research programs on relations between stressful life events and episodes of physical illness. In B. Dohrenwend & B. Dohrenwend (Eds)., *Stressful life events: Their nature and effects.* New York: Wiley, 1974.

Mechanic, D. *Medical sociology: A selective view* (2nd ed.). New York: Free Press, 1978.

Mechanic, D., & Greenley, J. The prevalence of psychological distress and help-seeking in a college student population. *Social Psychiatry,* 1976, *11,* 1–14.

Meichenbaum, D. *Cognitive-behavior modification: An integrative approach.* New York: Plenum Press, 1977.

Meichenbaum, D., & Novaco, R. Stress inoculation: A preventive approach. In C. Spielberger & I. Sarason (Eds.), *Stress and anxiety* (Vol. 5). Washington, D.C.: Hemisphere Publishing, 1978.

Melzack, R. *The puzzle of pain.* New York: Basic Books, 1973.

Meyer, D. *The effects of patients' representation of high blood pressure on behavior in treatment.* Unpublished doctoral dissertation, University of Wisconsin, 1980.

Meyer, D., Leventhal, H., & Gutmann, M. Symptoms in hypertension: How patients evaluate and treat them. *New England Journal of Medicine,* in press.

Miller, G. A., Galanter, E., & Pribram, K. H. *Plans and the structure of behavior.* New York: Holt, 1960.

Miller, N. E. Some psychophysiological studies of motivation and of the behavioral effects of illness. *Bulletin of the British Psychological Society,* 1964, *17,* 1–20.

Neisser, U. *Cognitive psychology.* New York: Appleton-Century-Crofts, 1967.

Nerenz, D. *Control of emotional distress in cancer chemotherapy.* Unpublished doctoral dissertation, University of Wisconsin, 1979.

Nerenz, D. R., Leventhal, H., & Love, R.R. Factors contributing to emotional distress during cancer chemotherapy. *Cancer,* in press.

Niles, P. *The relationships of susceptibility and anxiety to acceptance of fear arousing communications.* Unpublished doctoral dissertation, Yale University, 1964.

Nisbett, R. E., & Wilson, T. D. Telling more than we can know: Verbal reports on mental processes. *Psychological Review,* 1977, *84,* 231–259.

Pennebaker, J. W., & Skelton, J. A. Psychological parameters of physical symptoms. *Journal of Personality and Social Psychology,* 1978, *4,* 524-530.

Pennebaker, J. W., & Skelton, J. A. *Selective monitoring of bodily sensation.* Unpublished manuscript, University of Virginia, 1980.

Posner, M. I. *Cognition: An introduction.* Glenview, Ill.: Scott, Foresman, 1973.

Powers, W. J. Feedback: Beyond behaviorism. *Science,* 1973, *179,* 351–356.

Ringler, K. *Processes of coping with cancer chemotherapy.* Unpublished doctoral dissertation, University of Wisconsin, 1981.

Rosen, T. J., Terry, N. S., & Leventhal, H. The role of esteem and coping in response to a threat communication. *Journal of Experimental Research in Personality,* 1982, *16,* 90–107.

Safer, M. A., Tharps, Q., Jackson, T., & Leventhal, H. Determinants of three stages of delay in seeking care at a medical clinic. *Medical Care,* 1979, *17*(1), 11–29.

Salloway, J. C., & Dillon, P. B. A comparison of family networks and friend networks in health care utilization. *Journal of Comparative Family Studies,* 1973, *4,* 131–142.

Schachter, J. Pain, fear and anger in hypertensives and normotensives. *Psychosomatic Medicine,* 1957, *19,* 17–29.

Schachter, S. The interaction of cognitive and physiological determinants of emotional state. In L. Berkowitz (Ed.), *Advances in experimental social psychology* (Vol. 1). New York: Academic Press, 1964.

Schachter, S., & Singer, J. E. Cognitive, social and physiological determinants of emotional state. *Psychological Review,* 1962, *69,* 379–399.

Schachter, S., & Singer, J. E. Comments on the Maslach and Marshall-Zimbardo experiments. *Journal of Personality and Social Psychology,* 1979, *37,* 989–995.
Schwartz, G. E. Psychosomatic disorders and biofeedback: A psychobiological model of disregulation. In J. D. Maser & M. E. P. Seligman (Eds.), *Psychopathology: Experimental models.* San Francisco: W. H. Freeman, 1977.
Schwartz, G. E. The brain as a health care system. In G. C. Stone, F. Cohen, & N. E. Adler (Eds.), *Health psychology.* San Francisco: Jossey-Bass, 1979.
Schwartz, G. E. & Weinberger, D. A. Patterns of emotional response to affective situations: Relations among happiness, sadness, anger, fear, depression, and anxiety. *Motivation and Emotion,* 1980, *4,* 175–191.
Seligman, M. E. P. *Helplessness: On depression, development, and death.* San Francisco: W. H. Freeman, 1975.
Selye, H. *The stress of life.* New York: McGraw-Hill, 1956.
Selye, H. The evolution of the stress concept. *American Scientist,* 1973, *61,* 692–699
Selye, H. *Stress without distress.* Philadelphia: J. B. Lippincott, 1974.
Selye, H. Confusion and controversy in the stress field. *Journal of Human Stress,* 1975, *1,* 37–44.
Selye, H. *Stress in health and disease.* London: Butterworth, 1976.
Sternbach, R. *Principles of psychophysiology.* New York: Academic Press, 1966.
Sternbach, R. A. *Pain patients: Traits and treatment.* New York: Academic Press, 1974.
Suchman, E. A. Stages of illness and medical care. *Journal of Health and Social Behavior,* 1965, *6,* 114.
Tomkins, S. S. *Affect, imagery, consciousness* (Vol. 1). New York: Springer Publishing, 1962.
Tulving, E. Episodic and semantic memory. In E. Tulvig & W. Donaldson (Eds.), *Organization of memory.* New York: Academic Press, 1972.
Valins, S. Cognitive effects of false heart-rate feedback. *Journal of Personality and Social Psychology,* 1966, *4,* 400–408.
Weiss, J. M. Psychological factors in stress and disease. *Scientific American,* 1972, *226,* 104–113.
Withey, S. B. Reaction to uncertain threat. In G. W. Baker & D. W. Chapmen (Eds.), *Man and society in disaster.* New York: Basic Books, 1962.
Wooley, S. C., Blackwell, B., & Winget, C. A learning theory model of chronic illness behavior: Theory, treatment, and research. *Psychosomatic Medicine,* 1978, *40,* 379–401.
Wortman, C., & Dunkel-Schetter, C. Interpersonal relationships and cancer. *Journal of Social Issues,* 1979, *35,* 120–155.
Young, J. C. Illness categories and action strategies in a Tarascan town. *American Ethnologist,* 1978, *5,* 81–97.
Zajonc, R.B. Feeling and thinking: Preferences need no inferences. *American Psychologist,* 1980, *35,* 151–175.
Zborowski, M. *People in pain.* San Francisco: Jossey-Bass, 1969.
Zillman, D. Attribution and misattribution of excitatory reactions. In J. H. Harvey, W. Ickes, & R. F. Kidd (Eds.), *New directions in attribution research* (Vol. 2). Hillsdale, New Jersey: Lawrence Erlbaum, 1978.

2

Natural Healing Processes of the Mind

Graded Stress Inoculation as an Inherent Coping Mechanism

SEYMOUR EPSTEIN

There are three broad systems with which humans adapt to the world about them. These are learning, regulation of arousal, and maintenance of an organized conceptual system. Associated with these three systems are three kinds of behavioral disorder: Disorders arising from faulty learning; disorders arising from excessive stimulation, as in the traumatic neurosis; and disorders arising from threats to the integrity of an individual's conceptual system, as in acute schizophrenic reactions. A previous article (Epstein, 1979) examined acute schizophrenic disorganization as a natural healing process with the capacity to effect a constructive reorganization. The present article examines a natural process that I shall refer to as "graded stress inoculation," which facilitates the retroactive and proactive mastery of excessive stimulation.

SEYMOUR EPSTEIN • Department of Psychology, University of Massachusetts, Amherst, Massachusetts 01003. The writing of this article and the research reported in it were supported by NIMH Research Grant MH01293.

AN INHERENT PROCESS FOR COPING WITH STRESS AND OVERSTIMULATION

Freud and the Repetition Compulsion

Freud's observation of the traumatic neurosis in the First World War led him to drastically revise his theory of personality. Before then, he had assumed that wish fulfillment, operating according to the pleasure principle, provided the key to unlocking the meaning of dreams. However, the dreams of soldiers suffering from traumatic neuroses simply reproduced the traumatic incident and could not be accounted for by wish fulfillment. In attempting to account for these dreams, Freud (1959), in his essay *Beyond the Pleasure Principle,* proposed a source of motivation more fundamental than wish fulfillment, namely the "repetition compulsion." He speculated that the traumatic neurosis is produced by stimulation of such magnitude that it breaches a hypothetical "stimulus barrier," which normally protects the brain from overstimulation. In addition to intensity of stimulation, he held that an important parameter that determines whether the stimulus barrier will be breached is surprise. According to Freud, anticipatory anxiety is adaptive because it prevents surprise, and, as a result, is able to foster an "anticathexis" that serves to "bind" stimulation, thereby preventing the brain from being flooded with excitation.

Freud viewed the occurrence of frightening repetitive dreams in the traumatic neurosis as a belated attempt to develop the anticipatory anxiety that was not initially present. He stated, "These dreams are endeavoring to master the stimulus retrospectively, by developing the anxiety whose omission was the cause of the traumatic neurosis" (Freud, 1959, p. 60). He noted that the repetition compulsion is also exhibited in the play of children, in transference reactions in psychotherapy, and in a "daemonic fate" that seems to pursue some individuals throughout their lives. Although Freud believed that the repetition compulsion represented an attempt at mastery, he did not discuss how successful the attempt was, other than to note that, insofar as the transference neurosis is concerned, and in the absence of interpretation, the individual is destined to reenact the past. Presumably, the same explanation would apply to the daemonic fate theme. As to the play of children, Freud believed that mastery was fostered only when what had initially been experienced passively was reexperienced actively. He let the matter rest at that and did not suggest that the terrifying repetitive dreams in the traumatic neurosis succeeded in binding stimulation and in curing the neurosis, and indeed, available evidence does not support the view that the dreams are therapeutic.

Freud's analysis suggests that, while there is an inherent tendency to attempt retroactively to master a stressful experience through repetition in memory, repetition in and of itself is not always successful. It is interesting that repetition of a simple stimulus such as a loud tone results in habituation, if it is not too intense, but if it is intense, it results in sensitization (Sokolov, 1963). Thus, repetition of a strong stimulus can contribute to an increase in stress. It is therefore not surprising that, given the intensity of the fear evoked in the dreams of the traumatic neurosis, repetition is apt to contribute to an increase in anxiety. In a review of the effect of repetitive exposure to complex theatening stimuli such as combat and the bombing of civilian populations, Rachman (1978) observed that either habituation or sensitization could occur, depending on the intensity of the attack. It would appear, then, that if repetition of a stressful experience in memory is to be therapeutic, it must occur at a level of intensity appropriate to facilitate habituation. Why then is not the intensity of the memory reduced to an adaptive level in the traumatic neurosis? As we shall see shortly, other factors can interfere with the process. For now, let us turn to the operation of a natural healing process, as observed in Pavlov's dogs.

Pavlov and the Paradoxical Phase

At the time that Pavlov was conducting his famous experiments on conditioning, a great flood occurred in Leningrad. Many of the dogs nearly drowned as the water rose in their cages. After they were rescued, several dogs exhibited intense fear at the sight of water. On later testing, a number of animals failed to exhibit their customary conditioned responses. Pavlov (1927) attributed the failure to respond to a state of protective or "transmarginal" inhibition. He speculated that there is an upper limit of cortical excitation that an animal can endure, and that when this limit is approached, transmarginal inhibition is evoked, protecting the brain from overstimulation. It is interesting to note the similarity between Pavlov's concept of transmarginal inhibition and Freud's concept of a stimulus barrier. Pavlov considered transmarginal inhibition to be a blanket type of inhibition that diffusely shuts off reactivity of the cortex to all stimulation. Such inhibition can be contrasted with Pavlov's concept of internal inhibition, which, by inhibiting specific reaction tendencies, is responsible for discrimination in perception and behavior. Because transmarginal inhibition can inhibit internal inhibition, it can account for regression, disorganization, release of repressed memories and impulses, and failures in perceptual and behavioral discrimination.

After a period of about 10 days, the dogs that had exhibited the massive inhibitory reaction earlier were brought back to the laboratory. When their conditioned responses were tested once more, they exhibited a remarkable transformation in their response hierarchies. Stimuli that had previously elicited the strongest conditioned responses now elicited the weakest ones, while stimuli that had previously elicited the weakest responses now elicited the strongest ones. Pavlov called this stage, in which the normal hierarchy of response strength was reversed, the "ultraparadoxical phase." After a further resting period, stimuli that had previously been intermediate in strength now became the strongest ones, so that the curve of response strength as a function of the original dimension of stimulus intensity became an inverted V-shape. Pavlov labeled this stage the "paradoxical phase." With increasing time, the peak of the inverted V gradually shifted to stimuli of increasing strength, until the original gradient was restored (see Figure 1). Between the early and late paradoxical phases, an equivalence phase was observed, in which responses to all stimuli were approximately equal.

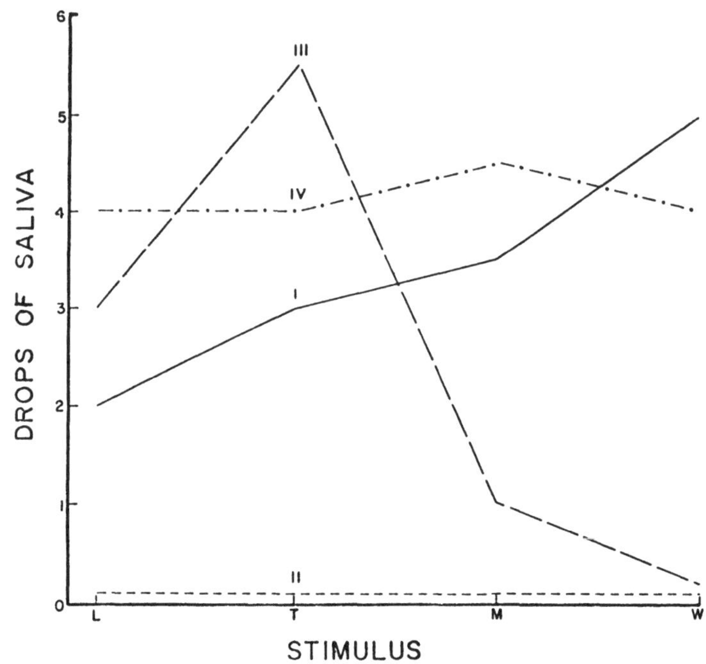

Figure 1. Phases observed by Pavlov in a dog exposed to stress in the laboratory. The curves were plotted from data provided on a single case by Pavlov (1927, p. 271). The ultraparadoxical phase is not included. Phase I is the original gradient, phase II the equivalence phase, an intermediate stage in which responses to all stimuli are equal, and phases III and IV are paradoxical phases (from Epstein, 1967).

Pavlov was later able to produce the same sequence of phases by presenting stressful stimuli in the laboratory. He observed that if the same source of stress were reintroduced following completion of the sequence, the animal again went through the cycle of paradoxical phases, but more rapidly, until, with successive repetitions, the animal could withstand the stress without disruption of the original response hierarchy.

How is this strange sequence of responses to be accounted for? Pavlov attributed it to the dissipation of transmarginal inhibition. He assumed that, as the inhibition lifted, increasingly strong excitatory reactions were released from inhibitory control. The result, accordingly, was that, as the initially overexcited cortex recovered, it was presented with increasingly greater increments in excitation but never with greater stimulation than could be tolerated. That is, the animal at first responded only to weak stimuli but gradually responded to stronger stimuli until its normal reactivity was reestablished. It is noteworthy that this adaptive process is reflexive or passive in nature and is not contingent on active coping.

It is tempting to speculate that the repetition compulsion in traumatized soldiers observed by Freud and the paradoxical responses observed in traumatized dogs by Pavlov are related, the former representing the disruption of a normal process for mastering stress exhibited by the latter. The essence of the process consists of experiencing in memory or reality initially highly displaced and gradually less displaced representatives of a stressful stimulus until the original stimulus can be reacted to without undue disturbance. The process can be viewed as analogous to inoculations with increasing increments of stress (Epstein, 1967). That this process is highly general is suggested by its occurrence in grieving (Lindemann, 1944), as well as by its occurrence in the proactive mastery of stress in combat flying (Bond, 1952) and in sport-parachuting (Epstein, 1967), which we shall turn to next.

Sport-Parachuting and the Mastery of Fear

Sport-parachuting provides an excellent natural laboratory for the study of fear and its mastery. Novice parachutists are almost always fearful before a jump, often to the point that their heart rate rises to double its rate before the jump. In order to perform adequately, the major obstacle that novices have to overcome is their own fear. Because of their inability to control their fear, many novice parachutists perform poorly on their first few jumps, although they were able to go through the same motions without error in training on the ground. Some appear to have forgotten everything they learned and would very likely become casualties if left to their own devices. Fortunately, until they exhibit proficiency, their ripcords are pulled automatically by a "static line" that is attached to the aircraft. With training and experience, the disorganized and frightened novice parachutist becomes a highly skilled, confident jumper who is able to perform complex maneuvers in the air before his chute opens, and who then is able to descend with remarkable accuracy to a small target on the ground.

As a natural laboratory for the study of stress, sport-parachuting permits a degree of experimental control that is normally available only in the laboratory. Parachutists are trained by a relatively standardized procedure, which allows the experimenter to select stimuli that have a common meaning to all parachutists but have no special significance to nonparachutists, who can be used as control subjects. The experimenter can vary the intensity of stress by testing at different points in time from a jump, and can arrange the rate and timing of jumping to meet the requirements of an experimental design. Order and sequence effects can be controlled by testing some subjects first on the day of a jump and second on a control day, and reversing the order for others. The effects of practice and mastery can readily be investigated by comparing parachutists with different amounts of experience and by testing the same parachutists longitudinally as they acquire experience. In all these respects, sport-parachuting has advantages over other real-life stressful situations that have been studied, such as natural disasters, warfare, surgery, criminal interrogation, and academic examinations. Professor Walter Fenz and I have conducted an extensive series of studies of sport-parachuting for the purpose of investigating fear and its mastery. For our present purposes, only those findings will be considered that have special significance for the concept of graded stress inoculation

Not surprisingly, novice parachutists, when presented with a word-association test that contained words that varied according to their relevance to parachuting, produced gradients of increasing GSR reactivity as a function of the stimulus dimension. They produced their smallest reactions to neutral words, larger reactions to words that were moderately related to parachuting, and their largest reactions to words that were strongly related to parachuting. The gradients of novice jumpers were invariably steeper when testing was done shortly before a jump than when it was done on a control day. The situation was quite different for experienced jumpers. When experienced parachutists were tested on a control day, they produced monotonic gradients that were similar to the gradients of the novice parachutists. However, when experienced parachutists were tested shortly before a jump, they invariably produced

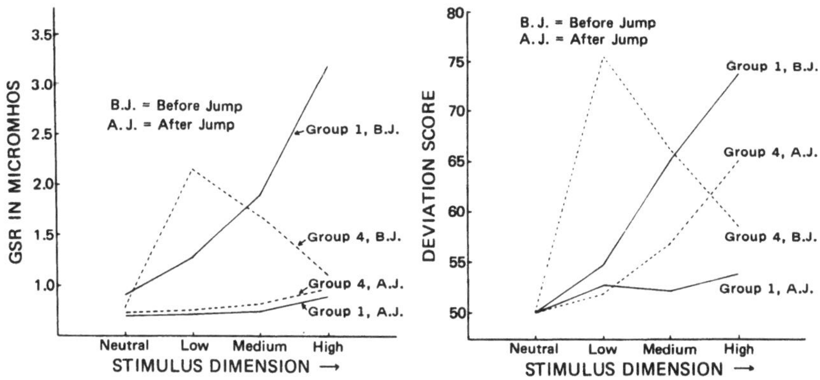

Figure 2. Mean magnitude of GSRs of novice and experienced parachutists to a word-association test containing a built-in stimulus dimension of parachuting relevance. Group 1 subjects had made 1 previous jump and group 4 subjects had made over 100 jumps (from Epstein, 1962).

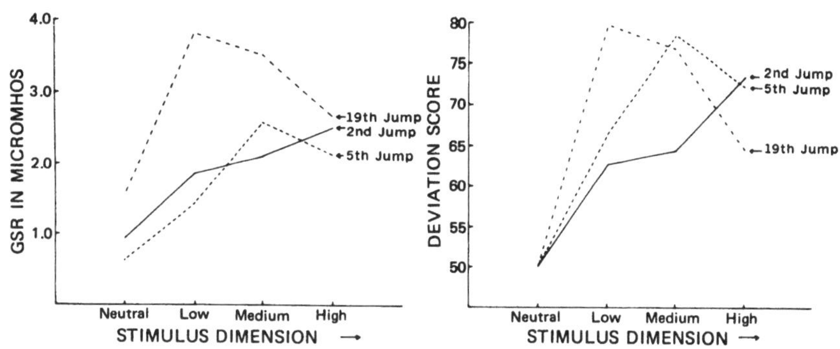

Figure 3. Mean magnitude of the GSRs of a single parachutist tested longitudinally with a word-association test containing a built-in stimulus dimension of parachuting relevance (from Epstein, 1962).

inverted V-shaped curves. That is, they reacted most strongly to words at an intermediate level of relevance to parachuting, so that the curves resembled the responses of Pavlov's dogs in the paradoxical phase. With increasing experience, the peaks of the curves became increasingly displaced toward the low relevant end of the dimension. The phenomenon is illustrated in Figures 2 and 3. As the same experienced parachutist who produced inverted V-shaped curves on the day of a jump produced monotonic gradients on a control day (see Figure 3), the inverted V could not be attributed to increasing familiarity with words associated with parachuting.

The data referred to above were obtained a long time ago. Since then, we have conducted many studies with experienced parachutists and have learned a great deal about the development of inverted V-shaped curves. Experienced parachutists under normal conditions invariably produce inverted V-shaped curves when testing is shortly before a jump and do not do so when testing is on a control day. No novice has yet produced an inverted V-shaped curve. These findings have been found to be widely general across methods and conditions. They occur not only for electrodermal responses to word-association tests but also for ratings of fear along a time dimension (Epstein & Fenz, 1965), as indicated in Figure 4, and for physiological reactions monitored in the aircraft during ascent (Fenz & Epstein, 1967), as indicated in Figure 5.

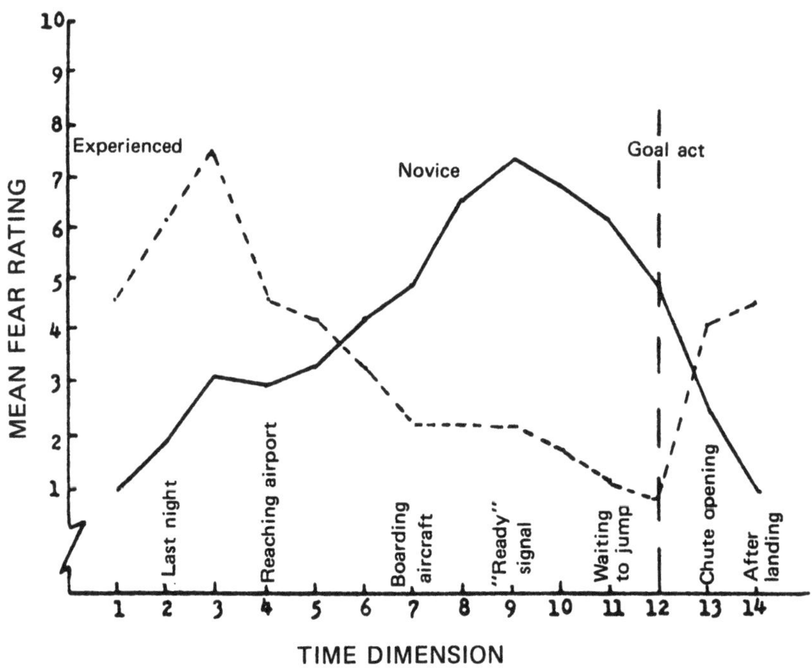

Figure 4. Self-ratings of fear of novice and experienced parachutists as a function of the sequence of events leading up to and following a jump (from Frenz & Epstein, 1967).

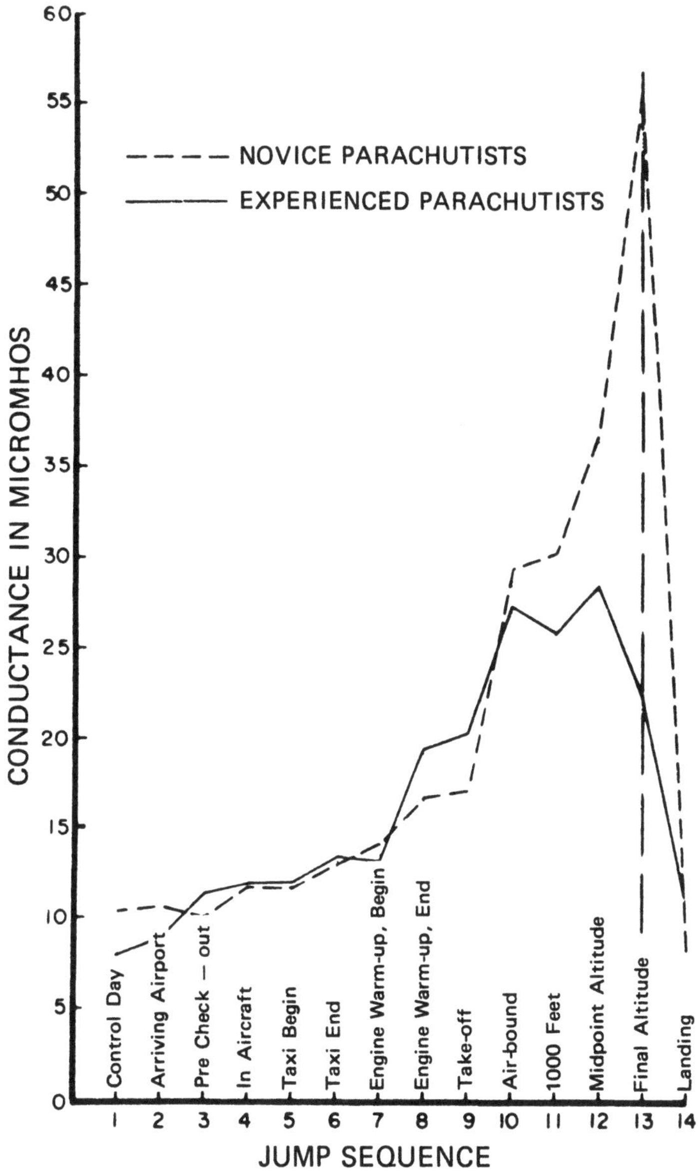

Figure 5. Tonic skin conductance as a function of events leading up to and following a jump for novice and experienced parachutists (from Fenz & Epstein, 1967).

It is instructive to consider the circumstances in which experienced parachutists have failed to produce inverted V-shaped curves. They have failed to do so following events that caused them to be concerned about the safety of jumping, such as after having read about a group of experienced parachutists who drowned when they were blown over Lake Michigan. They have failed to produce inverted V-shaped curves in response to a word-association test when they were threatened with receiving random electric shocks during the test (Fenz, Kluck, & Bankart, 1969). In an investigation (Fenz & Jones, 1972) in which an experienced parachutist volunteered to have a malfunction, which would have required him to use his reserve chute, packed into his chute before any of 10 consecutive jumps, the parachutist produced monotonic gradients instead of inverted V-shaped curves. (Actually, no malfunction was packed into the chute on any occasion.) In a study in progress in which the physiological reactions of experienced parachutists were monitored while they watched a movie that recapitulated the experience of jumping as closely as possible, they did not produce inverted V-shaped curves to the movie. These findings suggest that the inverted V-shaped curve is not passively acquired as the result of repeated exposure to jumping in the manner of a conditioned response but is a consequence of an active coping process that prepares the parachutist for the forthcoming jump. Any experience that interferes with this process will cause the inverted V-shaped curve to be replaced by the monotonic gradient characteristic of novices. An experienced parachutist who did not believe that active mastery of fear was involved in the acquisition of inverted V-shaped curves changed his mind after an experience in which he fell asleep during ascent in the aircraft. Awakened by his comrades shortly before his turn to jump, he felt extremely anxious and made a poor jump that endangered him. He could not attribute the poor performance to drowsiness, because he felt rested and alert. Up to then, he had believed his anxiety had simply dissipated as a result of successful experience. He now concluded his anxiety had been controlled by an active mental process that developed with experience.

The development of the inverted V-shaped curve has considerable adaptive advantages. As a result of the shifting peak of reactivity along stimulus and time dimensions, the experienced parachutist has available to him an increasingly early warning system. In addition, after the anxiety increases to the peak of the inverted-V, the anxiety subsides so that it is relatively low at the moment of critical action. An additional advantage is that the gradual displacement of the peak of reactivity forces attention to be directed to the entire range of relevant cues along both cue and time dimension. The same process of gradually expanding awareness through successive displacement has been reported by Bond (1952) in wartime pilots:

> For practical purposes danger is never treated as an entity, but is divided into segments and each studied individually. Every dangerous event, as it comes up, is broken off and isolated to become the subject of ruination and repetitive conversation. Every possibility is explored, every potential outcome considered, and all defensive action carefully rehearsed. Once mastered, the event drops into the preconscious, and attention is then turned to a new one. (Bond, 1952, p. 84)

How is the development of the inverted V-shaped curve and its successive displacement in parachutists to be explained? I have previously (Epstein, 1967) proposed a two-factor theory of anxiety that assumes that, with experience in effectively coping with a source of threat, two developments take place. An increasing gradient of anxiety and an increasing gradient of inhibition of anxiety develop, with the inhibitory gradient gradually becoming higher and steeper than the anxiety gradient, thereby reducing the higher more than the lower levels of anxiety. The effect is to produce inverted V-shaped curves of anxiety, the peaks of which are increasingly reduced and displaced to more distant points along time and cue dimentions. (For a more detailed description of this process, see Epstein, 1967.) The nature of the inhibitory process will be discussed in greater detail later.

Control of Anxiety through Graded Stress Inoculation

I believe there is a general principle of graded stress inoculation that is exhibited in a variety of forms in the mastery of stress in everyday life. The principle is applicable to both proactive and retroactive mastery of stress and to reactions at various levels of organization, from the reflexive reactions exhibited by Pavlov's dogs to the more complex, cognitively mediated responses exhibited by sport-parachutists. According to the principle, stress is retroactively mastered through repetition of a stressful event in memory or in reality, initially at highly displaced or weak levels of intensity and gradually at less displaced or stronger levels of intensity. In the retroactive mastery of stress, the process permits recovery from, or prevention of, chronic pathology. In the proactive mastery of stress, the process works in the opposite direction, proceeding from the most to the least salient cues. Instead of reducing the anxiety-eliciting cues that are attended to, as in the retroactive mastery of stress, the range of cues is increased. At the same time, level of reactivity is kept within adaptive limits so that anxiety serves as an effective early warning system without reaching disruptive levels. Both processes involve careful pacing of the amount of arousal with which the individual must cope at any moment. Mastery proceeds to less salient stimulation only after it has been accomplished to more salient stimuli.

If there is a natural process of graded stress inoculation for coping with stress in everyday life, the question remains as to why the process does not always operate effectively. It was noted in the discussion of the traumatic neurosis that other factors may interfere. In the traumatic neurosis, repetition occurs in memory at levels too intense for habituation to take place. Given the overwhelming threat that instigates a traumatic neurosis, it is not surprising that there is a prolonged period of intense anxiety that does not readily habituate. This provides the individual with a strong incentive to take whatever steps are necessary to avoid reexposure to the same or similar sources of threat, these steps obviously being adaptive under many circumstances. It follows that one of the conditions that should maintain the disorder and prevent the stressful experience from being assimilated through the natural process of graded stress inoculation is concern over the reoccurrence of the trauma. It is of interest, in this respect, to consider that Freud noted that if a soldier is seriously wounded in combat, he is less likely to suffer from a traumatic neurosis than if he is not. He attributed the protection afforded by the physical injury to a diversion of cathexis from the traumatic event to the wound. A more plausible explanation is that the wound provides insurance against being sent back into combat and therefore reduces the need to retain a state of hyperalertness with respect to the reoccurrence of the traumatic event. A second reason for a traumatic neurosis being retained is that it acquires secondary gain by insuring the continuation of a pension or having dependency needs satisfied. A third reason is the development of an all-or-none defense system.

In the traumatic neurosis, there is a failure of the natural process of graded stress inoculation because the trauma is repeated in memory at excessive levels of intensity. This represents one arm of a maladaptive all-or-none defense system, in which the individual must either completely block out awareness of a stressful event or experience it in overwhelming intensity. In his classic study of grief, Lindemann (1944) described the reactions of people who did and did not recover following severe loss. In the former cases he noted that a working-through process took place in which the individual first grieved in response to displaced cues or reminders of the deceased and gradually reacted to less displaced and stronger reminders. In the cases in which recovery did not take place, there was a general avoidance of all reminders of the loss and a consequent absence of grieving.

An all-or-none defense system is the antithesis of an adaptive defense system, one in which stress is coped with in small doses. The difference between adaptive and maladaptive defenses was well illustrated in the studies of parachuting. Novice parachutists were often observed to exhibit extreme defenses characterized by perceptual denial. For example, novices tended to misperceive anxiety-related words in a word-association test, although the words were loudly and clearly presented by a tape recorder (Epstein & Fenz, 1962). One parachutist was so avoidant of perceiving his own fearfulness that he reported being amazed at how calm he was, until he looked down and saw his knees knocking together. Despite the extremity of such defenses, they are gradually relinquished as mastery progresses. The defenses apparently serve to pace the experience of anxiety. Novice parachutists can cope with only so much anxiety, and it is adaptive for them to avoid awareness of additional sources of anxiety. In this respect, it is particularly instructive to consider a few novice parachutists who exhibited all-or-none defenses. These parachutists were remarkably calm before their first jump, to the point that they were envied by their more frightened comrades. When the jump became imminent, however, they experienced anxiety attacks and were unable to jump, after which they decided to give up jumping forever. Such examples suggest that adaptive defenses are temporary defenses used to pace the experience of stress so that individuals are not exposed to greater anxiety than they can cope with at any one time. These defenses are gradually relinquished as ability to cope with the threatening events increases. It is through this means that defenses facilitate the development of mastery of stressful events. Maladaptive defenses, on the other hand, are all-or-none defenses that result in broad and sustained avoidance reactions to anxiety-producing cues, preventing mastery from occurring. Should the defense fail because of unavoidable stimulation, the defense system collapses and the individual is exposed to overwhelming levels of anxiety.

IMPLICATIONS OF THE PRINCIPLE OF GRADED STRESS INOCULATION FOR PSYCHOTHERAPY

The observation that there is a natural process for the retroactive mastery of stress has obvious implications for psychotherapy. It suggests that stress inoculation in the form of graded exposure to increasing increments of stress should be a widely applicable procedure.

Wolpe's (1958) systematic desensitization therapy provides an excellent example of the principle of graded stress inoculation. Systematic desensitization utilizes a hierarchy of anxiety responses in conjunction with a response incompatible with anxiety, such as eating, sex, or, the one most frequently employed, relaxation. In systematic desensitization in which relaxation is the presumed inhibitor, the patient is usually given training in muscle relaxation. A hierarchy of anxiety-evoking stimuli is established. The anxiety is progressively eliminated by having the patient practice the relaxation response while imagining first the weakest anxiety-eliciting stimulus and gradually progressing to stronger anxiety-eliciting stimuli. When patients demonstrate that they can relax while vividly imagining one level of anxiety, they are advanced to the next level, and so on until the most threatening stimulus in the hierarchy can be imagined without anxiety. The technique has been employed with hierarchies of both real and imagined events. It is evident that the procedure is a remarkably close analog to the one I have described as a natural process for the mastery of stress. Wolpe's theory of why the therapy works, however, is considerably different from the one I presented for the natural mastery of stress. According to Wolpe, "reciprocal inhibition" accounts for the therapeutic effect of systematic desensitization. Reciprocal inhibition refers to an inhibitory effect that a response such as relaxation, sex, or eating is presumed to have on a response such as anxiety, with which it is incompatible. Accordingly, in systematic desensitization in which relaxation is the inhibiting response, specific training in relaxation is deemed essential in order to establish a relaxation response that is sufficiently strong to inhibit an anxiety response. According to the theory presented for the natural mastery of stress, special training in relaxation is not essential (see Rachman, 1978, for a similar conclusion), although it is often helpful. Recovery is assumed to result from the successive habituation of increasingly strong or direct representation of the threat. Inoculation with increasing increments of stress is assumed to result in habituation as long as anxiety is kept limited enough not to evoke excessive arousal and defensiveness. Relaxation in certain cases is useful because it provides a way of reducing defensiveness and ensuring thereby that the stimulus will be fully perceived at a level of arousal that is not excessive. This issue will be discussed in greater detail in a later section.

Once it is recognized that a highly general principle of mastery of stress through graded stress inoculation exists, application of the principle need not be restricted to systematic desensitization. Not only may training in relaxation or in the use of other presumably reciprocally-inhibiting procedures be dispensed with under many circumstances, but the principle of graded stress inoculation can be incorporated into a wide variety of different procedures, including interview types of psychotherapy. The principle is as compatible with psychodynamic approaches to therapy as with behavioral ones. While many psychodynamically oriented therapists informally progress from less to more stressful material, an understinding of the principle of graded stress inoculation can result in its more effective application, such as by encouraging a client to discuss repeatedly a painful memory to the point that habituation occurs. A patient's own momentum for progress cannot always be relied on, since the patient may repeat the same material endlessly or progress too rapidly. The latter is apt to occur when the patient believes there is nothing to be gained by repeating emotionally disturbing memories that have already been reported.

It can be expected that once habituation occurs to displaced anxiety-producing stimuli, there will be a tendency for thoughts and imagery to advance to less displaced ones, until highly stressful past events can be remembered without excessive anxiety. Under such circumstances, the main task of the therapist is to encourage repetition to the point where habituation occurs and then to encourage further progression. Blocks or other defenses that can bring the process to a halt can be dealt with through interpretation or through other techniques, to be discussed later.

IMPLICATIONS OF GRADED STRESS INOCULATION FOR TRAINING IN THE PROACTIVE MASTERY OF STRESS

As observed in the studies of sport-parachuting, graded exposure is as applicable to proactive as to retroactive mastery of stress. This is hardly surprising because exposure to increasing levels of difficulty as mastery progresses is a technique frequently employed in skill acquisition. Learning to deal with stress can be viewed as involving control of thoughts, emotions, and behavior. Too often, attention is paid only to training in manifest behavior and the individual is left to his own devices in learning to control thoughts and emotions. Yet it is evident that emotions and thoughts can affect behavior and may be elements critical to the acquisition of proficiency. According to the Yerkes-Dodson law, the relationship of performance to arousal level forms an inverted V-shape. There is an optimum level of arousal for the performance of different kinds of task. The more complex or abstract the task, the lower the level of arousal that is associated with optimum performance. Further, the more the performance has become a habit–that is, has been overlearned–the more resistant it is to interference from high levels of arousal. There are two practical implications for training that follow from the above considerations. One is that graded levels of task difficulty can be employed to allow individuals to progress at optimum levels of arousal. The other is that individuals need to be taught to control their arousal levels.

In learning a skill, a person should initially be taught under relaxed conditions and should not be expected to learn more than he or she can readily master without becoming anxious or tense. Individuals should not be exposed to increased levels of stress until they have demonstrated the ability to perform well under reduced levels of pressure. Thus, challenges should be increased in increments corresponding to the individual's gain in proficiency. Excessive challenge can be diagnosed by a regression of performance as a result of heightened arousal. A cost of exposing an individual to high levels of stress is that fixations may occur that are difficult to unlearn. The opposite error is to fail to expose an individual to sufficient challenge. In the absence of challenge, the individual will not progress at an optimum rate. Thus, learning a behavioral skill, whether it involves stress associated with physical danger, as in sky diving, fire fighting, and military combat, or stress associated with threats to self-esteem, as in athletic and artistic performances, can be facilitated by taking into account the principle of graded stress inoculation.

As to direct training in the control of arousal, individuals should be taught that their stressful reactions to events are induced not directly by the events but by their interpretations of the events. It remains to be seen to what extent general training can be provided in proactive mastery of stress that will transfer to specific areas of stress. In principle, there is no reason that such a procedure should not be effective, although training in principles of generalization may also have to be provided. Many of the above principles have been taken into account in training programs on stress management by Meichenbaum and his colleagues (Meichenbaum, 1977; Meichenbaum & Novaco, 1975), including, most recently, the addition of procedures involving graded stress inoculation in the management of pain. The results of the program have been reported as highly successful. That the principle of graded stress inoculation is applicable to training in proactive as well as retroactive mastery of stress is also indicated by a series of highly interesting studies by Novaco (1977, 1979, 1980). Novaco has employed the principle of graded stress inoculation in the training of control of anger and aggression in probation officers and in individuals who experienced difficulties as a result of their excessive proneness to anger. Bandura and his colleagues have employed procedures that have used graded stress inoculation in the form of gradually fading out therapist support during participant modeling (Bandura, Jeffery, & Wright, 1974). In summary, graded stress inoculation appears to be a widely applicable procedure that can be incorporated into a variety of techniques or used as a principle form of therapy in its own right.

IMPLICATIONS OF GRADED STRESS INOCULATION FOR IMPULSE CONTROL

By controlling an emotion or impulse at a low level of intensity and then practicing its control at increasingly greater levels of intensity, individuals can acquire finely tuned systems for controlling the emotion or impulse over its entire range of intensity. Such a control system increases freedom, for it permits the individual to experience the emotion or impulse over a wide range of intensity without danger of losing control. A fine-tuned control system can be contrasted with the all-or-none system, in which emotions or impulses must either be completely avoided or experienced with overwhelming intensity.

According to a number of cognitive theorists (e.g., Arnold, 1960; Averill, 1967; Beck, 1976; Ellis, 1962; Epstein, 1967, 1973; Lazarus, 1966), human emotions and impulses are almost invariably mediated by cognitions, often in the form of a chain of verbal responses or images that can accelerate or retard the development of the emotion or impulse. Most people, unaware of this, assume their emotions and impulses are spontaneous, reflexive reactions to situations. They fail to recognize that it is their interpretation of an event and not the event itself that produces their emotion. This point is well illustrated by the following anecdote. John's lawn mower broke down and he decided to borrow his neighbor's. As he walked toward the neighbor's house, it occurred to him that his neighbor might not be willing to loan him the mower. This thought appalled him, because he had freely loaned things to his neighbor in the past. The more he thought about how unfair it would be, the angrier he became. When he came to his neighbor's house, he blurted out, "Keep your damn mower. I wouldn't take it if you begged me."

In Figure 6, the development of an impulse is presented as a function of external and internal impulse-arousing cues. Early in its development, when the impulse is weak, it is easily inhibited. As the impulse becomes stronger, it becomes increasingly difficult to control. When it becomes strong enough to generate a sufficiently high level of arousal to interfere with cortical functioning, it becomes impossible to control. Thus, if one wishes to teach impulse control, it is important to identify the impulse early and to have the individual first learn to control it when it is weak. After this is accomplished, control at increasingly stronger levels can be accomplished. Two curves are presented in Figure 6, one representing a

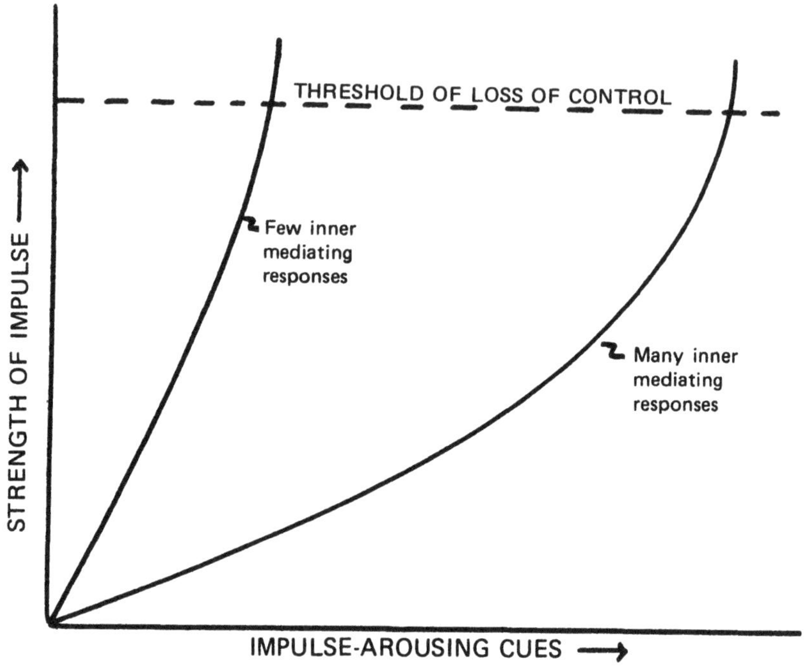

Figure 6. Theoretical curves of strength of an impulse as a function of impulse-arousing cues. The curve on the left describes a situation in which there are few inner mediating responses and the one on the right describes a situation in which there are many inner mediating responses.

small, and the other a considerable degree of internal mediation. The first curve represents the impulses of an individual whose behavior is closely tied to external cues and who is therefore apt to react to a mild insult with immediate rage. The second curve represents the impulses of an individual whose emotional responses are mediated by a long sequence of inner responses, as in the above anecdote. It is obvious that the latter case presents considerable opportunity for control, since once the individual learns to recognize the inner responses that mediate the impulse, he or she can stop the process anywhere in its development. In the former case, because the development of the impulse is contingent on external cues, it is still possible to intercede in the development of the impulse, as will shortly be illustrated in the training of a dog, but it is more difficult than in the latter case.

Some time ago, the author moved to a new town. His dog, a large German shepherd who was used to roaming the countryside, decided to establish territorial rights over the whole town. Invariably, when taken for a walk, he would fight with other dogs. It happened in the following manner. While walking at heel, the dog would see another dog approaching at a distance. Without barking or giving any other signal, he would bolt for the other dog, paying no attention to the author's commands. Under other circumstances, the dog was obedient. Through trial and error, the author learned that if he observed the other dog first, he could abort the runaway reaction by saying "no" firmly whenever he detected an incipient approach response. By following this procedure he was able to lead his dog past other dogs without incident. Interestingly, the dog remained calm throughout the encounters. Apparently, the impulse that could not be inhibited when it was full-blown could easily be inhibited when it was but an incipient tendency.

An illustration of control of an emotion through the inhibition of verbally-mediated responses is provided by a woman in psychotherapy. The patient would burst into tears at the slightest sign of what she interpreted as criticism, which effectively prevented therapy from progressing. Interpretation of the defensive aspect of the reaction was impossible, because it too brought on a flood of tears. Once the weeping occurred, it lasted for the duration of the session. The impasse was broken by the following procedure. The therapist suggested that both he and the patient attempt to identify the incipient cues that elicited the weeping response, and that, when they occurred, the patient should attempt to inhibit the inner response that mediated the weeping. For a while, the therapist would report whenever he was about to say something that he thought might be interpreted as critical, and he would ask the patient to carefully observe her reactions. At times, she would burst into laughter when she caught herself about to react to the most innocuous statement with the sequence of inner verbal responses that instigated the weeping. With practice, she became increasingly adept at recognizing the cues that initiated the weeping response, and once she recognized them, she found she could easily inhibit them. Before long, the weeping disappeared completely. As a by-product, the patient derived additional benefit in the form of learning about the part she played in producing her emotions and in acquiring a technique for controlling impulses, which had been a problem for her.

THE ROLE OF COGNITION IN GRADED STRESS INOCULATION

The view that there is a natural healing process for coping with stress may seem to imply that the process is biologically determined and, therefore, that cognition can play no role in it. This need not be the case. A biological basis need involve no more than making it highly unlikely that a particular pattern of behavior will develop under normal circumstances. Moreover, as I have illustrated elsewhere (Epstein, 1967) a principle that is highly adaptive may be exhibited at various levels of organization, from simple reflexive inhibitory reactions, as exhibited by Pavlov's dogs, to the more complex inhibition of anxiety-producing thoughts, as exhibited by sport-parachutists.

It is hypothesized that graded stress inoculation in humans is, at least in part, mediated by cognitive processes. The development of the cognitive process is based on the operation of two principles. According to the first principle, humans, and possibly other higher-order animals, assimilate significant experiences into coherent conceptual systems. The motive to do so is learned because it is reinforced by the occurrence of pleasurable feelings when assimilation takes place and by the occurrence of anxiety when emotionally significant experiences cannot be assimilated (Epstein, 1976, 1980; Lecky, 1961; McReynolds, 1956, 1960). According to the second principle, assimilation can take place only up to a certain rate and, as this limit is approached, anxiety is increasingly evoked (Epstein, 1967, 1972; Lecky, 1961; McReynolds, 1956, 1960). Given the two principles, it follows that assimilation of stressful experiences will tend to occur in graduated increments, corresponding to graded stress inoculation.

Let us consider how cognitive processes can mediate control of anxiety by examining selected findings from the research on sport-parachuting. Some time ago (Epstein, 1967), I proposed an opponent process theory of anxiety in which an inhibitory gradient interacts with an anxiety gradient. The inhibitory gradient was assumed to increase in height and steepness at a more rapid rate than the anxiety gradient, so that the two gradients ultimately intersected, generating inverted V-shaped curves, the peaks of which became increasingly displaced. As already noted, such a process has adaptive advantages, including forcing awareness to expand over the entire range of threat-relevant cues, providing an early warning signal of danger, reducing anxiety at the critical moment of action, and pacing control of anxiety at an optimum rate. What role does cognition play in this process? With increasing experience, the novice parachutist becomes increasingly aware of new sources of threat, resulting in an increase in anxiety-producing thoughts, which contribute to expansion of the anxiety ingredient. At the same time that the anxiety gradient is expanding, the parachutist is learning to cope with old resources of threat through redirected attention, inhibiting maladaptive self-statements, and learning to make adaptive self-statements. Examples of maladaptive, anxiety-producing statements characteristic of novices shortly before a jump are "I knew I never should have gotten into this'' and ''What if my main chute and my reserve chute both fail to open?'' The experienced parachutist is more apt to think of constructive possibilities for action, such as how to deploy the reserve chute in the event that the main chute fails to open.

It was observed that one of the main obstacles that novice parachutists had to overcome was fear. Attempts at control by novices were relatively crude, often involving perceptual denial. Experienced parachutists controlled their fear in more subtle and adaptive ways. Thus, the cognitive control of anxiety that the novice achieved with crude procedures the experienced parachutist achieved with more adaptive, fine-tuned, procedures. That active inhibition and not a simple dissipation of anxiety was involved in the control of anxiety by the experienced parachutists was supported by the following observations: (1) the development, with experience, of an inverted V-shaped curve of anxiety, rather than a simple decrease in the slope of the initial monotonic gradient; (2) the increasing displacement of the peak of the inverted V-shaped curve as a function of experience; (3) an after-discharge of anxiety following a jump, exhibited only by experienced parachutists; (4) the breakthrough of anxiety when there was reduced opportunity for cognitive control, as in the case of the experienced parachutist who fell asleep during ascent of the aircraft.

In summary, the mastery of anxiety in experienced parachutists appears to be mediated, in part, by selective attention and inattention to cues of threat and by the production of inner responses that facilitate coping with threat and the simultaneous avoidance of unconstructive anxiety-producing thoughts. It is through such cognitive processes that anxiety is paced and attention is directed to new sources of realistic threat as old sources of threat are mastered. A similar process of selective attention and inner verbal responding very likely occurs in the retroactive mastery of stress. The assumption that the process is cognitive is not meant to imply that it is conscious. Much of the process is assumed to occur at a preconscious level of awareness, which is not to suggest that the process cannot be facilitated by making it conscious and by providing specific training in redirecting attention and in replacing maladaptive with constructive inner verbal responses.

COGNITIVE REASSESSMENT AS THE BASIC CONDITION IN THE TREATMENT OF IRRATIONAL FEARS

The basic difference between normal and neurotic anxiety is that the latter is based on unrealistic appraisals of threat. This raises the question of why neurotic anxiety is not extinguished in the course of everyday living when, as an unrealistic fear, it is apt not to be reinforced. From a cognitive perspective, the question is why the realization that the fear is unrealistic is not sufficient reason for giving it up. It must be concluded that appraisals exist at different levels of awareness and conviction and that it is necessary to distinguish intellectual from experiential knowledge, something we know all too little about.

Consciously, the individual knows that it is foolish to be afraid of a mouse or a harmless snake, but at another level the irrational conviction persists. This other level appears to be susceptible to change primarily through corrective experiences that involve nondefensive confrontations with the stimulus in fantasy or reality. If this is true, why, then, do not such corrective experience occur in everyday life? Often, of course, they do, and the fear is then relinquished. There are at least four reasons for extinction of irrational fears failing to occur in everyday life. One is that opportunities for confronting the simulus are simply not available. A second is that individuals develop physical avoidance reactions that keep them from confronting a feared stimulus. A third is that individuals develop defenses, or mental avoidance reactions, that prevent the stimulus from being attended to despite its physical presence. A fourth is that individuals' fear reactions cause the stimulus to be misperceived as threatening, and the fear-inducing hypothesis is thus validated. I venture to submit that the necessary and sufficient conditions for an unrealistic fear of an object to be extinguished is simply for the object to be sufficiently and accurately perceived under conditions in which the anticipated outcome does not materialize. The requirement of therapy, then, is to arrange conditions in which a client can experience a feared stimulus without defenses, and thereby perceive it for what it is and not for what it is feared to be.[1] While this is easily said, it is not so easily done.

According to Rachman (1978), the three major behavioral techniques for treating anxiety disorders are systematic desensitization (e.g., Wolpe, 1958), flooding (e.g., Stampfl, 1970), and modeling (e.g., Bandura *et al.*, 1974). What all three techniques have in common is that they provide an experience in which a client fully faces a threatening stimulus in the absence of defenses and learns thereby that the feared ghost in the closet does not really exist.

[1]It has come to my attention that Bandura (1969) some time ago came to a similar conclusion. He has more recently abandoned this position for one in which he emphasizes a client's belief in "self-efficacy" as the basic condition of therapy (Bandura, 1977). I believe that abandonment of the first position was premature and that it occurred because of a failure to appreciate what is entailed in therapeutically experiencing a stimulus, namely that it must be fully experienced, engaged, or attended to in a manner that permits it to be perceived for what it is and not for what it is feared to be. This is a far cry from simply having the stimulus present in the absence of reinforcement.

In systematic desensitization, the client is initially presented with a minimally threatening stimulus. With a low level of anxiety as the result of training in relaxation or of the presence of pleasant stimulation, the client can risk dropping whatever avoidance reactions had previously been employed and can fully experience the stimulus. The client is thus able to form the cognition based on experience with the stimulus in fantasy or in reality, that the stimulus is not dangerous. Having had this first experience, the client is able to risk confronting the next level of threat without defense, since it involves no greater an increment in threat than the amount already experienced. Through successively relinquishing defenses and fully experiencing stimuli on the hierarchy, realistic appraisals replace the unrealistic ones. Except for the training in relaxation, systematic desensitization is a remarkably close analog to the natural mastery of stress through graded stress inoculation. Returning to the ghost in the closet analogy, the hypothesis that there is a ghost is invalidated in systematic desensitization through successive exposure from subjectively safe distances so that defenses can be relinquished and the contents of the closet can be fully and accurately inspected.

In treatment of fear through flooding, the individual is forced to fully perceive a stimulus by being exposed to it under conditions where defenses are of no avail. The client, for better or worse, has no choice but to fully experience the feared stimulus. The client learns that the fear is unrealistic, because what was feared did not materialize despite optimum conditions for its occurrence. Being able to experience the dreaded situation and living to tell the tale invalidates an unrealistic hypothesis that could not be previously tested because of the operation of avoidance reactions or other defenses. The situation in flooding is analogous to locking the individual in the closet with the feared ghost. Since the ghost does not materialize, the fear-inducing hypothesis is invalidated. When flooding is accomplished with the use of imaginative rather than real situations, the attempt is made to have the individual fully experience in imagination what up to then has been avoided (Stampfl, 1970). As a result, it becomes evident to the client that the fear is ludicrous because what had to be imagined to evoke the fear would not very likely occur in reality. If the imaginative situation does not sufficiently evoke what is feared so that it can be fully confronted, or if the experience does not result in the conviction that was feared is unrealistic, then the flooding experience will not be therapeutic.

It is noteworthy that flooding and systematic desensitization, although manifestly opposite techniques, can be explained by the same principle. The application of the principle to modeling is less direct, but nevertheless, a strong case can be made for it. When an individual observes a model approach and picks up a feared object, such as a snake, it provides far more convincing evidence to the individual that the snake is, in fact, harmless, than if the model were simply to say so. Thus, a convincing demonstration is provided that contributes to the invalidation of the hypothesis that all snakes are dangerous and that awful things would happen if one ever got close to one, let alone picked it up. While observing someone else does not provide as emotionally convincing an experience as picking up the snake onself, it paves the way for the latter action by reducing an individual's fear and indicating how to proceed safely. As a result, it emboldens the individual to discard defenses and approach the snake, something that the individual would not otherwise do. It is the direct experience of handling the snake in the absence of the materialization of what is feared that ultimately contributes most to invalidating the fear-producing hypothesis. Thus, as with systematic desensitization and flooding, an initial fear-producing hypothesis is invalidated by an experience in which defenses are relinquished, a fearful stimulus is fully confronted, and the individual, as a result, has an emotionally convincing experience that invalidates a fear-inducing hypothesis.

The view that overcoming an irrational fear simply involves a change in cognition as the result of appropriate conditions for reassessment may seem little more than common sense dressed up in cognitive metaphors. Such a criticism should be weighed against the consideration that psychologists too often seek explanations that have a pseudoscientific aura about them rather than seeking the simplest ones. There is, accordingly, a proliferation of scientific jargon, a selection of metaphors that imply relationships with biology and physics, and a tendency to treat human beings as lower-order animals or mechanical devices rather than as motivated people who retain at least some responsibility for their emotionally significant experiences. Furthermore, the explanation that was offered does go beyond "common sense," because it stresses the importance of subconscious, irrational cognitions that cannot be invalidated by simply supplying intellectual information but require corrective emotional experiences along prescribed lines. If the argument is correct, it suggests that present procedures often carry ritualistic overloads, and it invites experimentation on how to devise appropriate techniques for applying the proposed principle in various circumstances.

As an illustration of how the principle of graded stress inoculation can be incorporated into different approaches in psychotherapy, let us consider the following example in an approach that emphasizes cognitive processes. Such an approach would be expected to be more effective than standard systematic desensitization, when the anxiety reaction is mediated by implicit cognitions, which I believe it usually is, and less effective than systematic desensitization when the anxiety is the result of accidental conditioning, which Wolpe believes it always is. The therapist explains to the client the principle of graded stress inoculation and how it can facilitate the mastery of anxiety. Examples are given of the natural process of mastery of stress, and it is noted that the same principle will be applied in therapy. It is further explained that one never reacts to a stimulus *per se* but to one's interpretation of the stimulus, which may occur either in the form of inner verbal statements or as implicit, unverbalized beliefs. It is noted that therapy requires fully experiencing the stimulus for what it is rather than for what it is feared to be, and that to accomplish this it is important to attend to the stimulus very carefully or, if it is presented in imagination, to visualize it very clearly. It is emphasized that a change in intellectual thought by itself is not enough. Rather, it is necessary to fully experience the stimulus without defenses, which means suspending inner verbalizations and beliefs that have biased perception of the stimulus in the past. As an aid in accomplishing such perception without defensiveness, clients are told they will be exposed to a hierarchy of increasingly fear-related stimuli, along which they can progress at their own rate. No training in relaxation is provided unless clients are anxious to the extent that they cannot comply with the procedure. A stimulus hierarchy is constructed in the usual manner. The stimulus at the low end of the hierarchy is presented, and the client is encouraged to fully experience it, that is, to imagine or perceive the stimulus as vividly and attentively as possible and to describe his or her reactions, which will, in all likelihood, evoke a mild, manageable degree of anxiety. The client is told to experience the anxiety without resisting it or in any way attempting to defend against it. It is explained that attempts to avoid the anxiety in the past have succeeded only in maintaining it. The client is further urged to describe his or her thoughts and imagery, particularly how the perception or imagination of the stimulus is cognitively embellished so that it is experienced as something more than what it simply is. Through this process, it should become apparent to the client that it is the irrational construal of the stimulus and not the stimulus itself that is responsible for the anxiety. Thus, the problem for the client shifts from having to control the anxiety, which initially appeared to arise automatically from the stimulus, to fully experiencing the stimulus in a way that allows it to be objectively assessed. Once this is accomplished through practice and with the aid of the therapist as necessary, the same procedure is applied to the next stimulus on the hierarchy, and so on, until mastery of anxiety is achieved over the entire hierarchy. Nor does therapy have to end here. A valuable learning experience can be provided by discussing the implications of the symptom, the nature of the thought and behavior that have maintained it, and the general features of the procedure that was used to eliminate it. Once it is recognized that, rather than being a passive victim of accidental conditioning, a person through his or her interpretations and verbal responses plays an active role in acquiring and maintaining symptoms, such knowledge can be of considerable value in coping with other problems.

SUMMARY AND CONCLUSIONS

Evidence was presented for graded stress inoculation as a highly general principle in the mastery of stress in everyday life. According to the principle, stress in everyday life is spontaneously mastered in small doses through repetition of the stressful experience in reality or in memory. Initially the exposure is at highly displaced, or weak, levels of stimulation, but gradually, as mastery progresses, the stimulus is experienced at less displaced, or stronger, levels of stimulation. It was noted that the same principle functions at different levels of organization, from the inhibitory reflexes exhibited by Pavlov's dogs to the cognitively meditated inhibition of fear-producing thoughts by sports-parachutists. The traumatic neurosis in humans was presented as an example of the repetitive process when it is aborted because the repetition occurs at too great a level of intensity for habituation to occur. As a result, the experience is never assimilated and remains a chronic source of disturbance. It was demonstrated in a series of studies on sport-parachuting that the principle of graded stress inoculation is as applicable to proactive as to retroactive mastery of stress. The relevance of the principle for training in impluse control was also discussed.

Graded stress inoculation as a natural healing process is derived from two basic needs, the need to cognitively assimilate emotionally significant experiences and the need to maintain an optimum rate of assimilation. It was noted that the natural process of graded stress inoculation might be aborted by the development of an all-or-none defense system, which requires the individual either to totally avoid the stimulus, physically or psychologically, or to experience the stimulus in overwhelming intensity. In both events, assimilation fails to occur and the problem becomes chronic.

It was noted that the treatment of an irrational fear requires that an accurate cognition replace an inaccurate one, and what is involved, therefore, is a corrective learning experience. The conditions for such an experience were held to be that the stimulus is fully and accurately perceived—it is carefully attended to in the absence of defenses—and that the feared outcome does not materialize. It was argued that this simple principle can account for the successful results of manifestly very different therapies, including systematic desensitization, flooding, and modeling. All of these therapies provide conditions in which a client perceives an irrationally feared stimulus under circumstances in which defenses are relinquished because of low anxiety or are prevented from occurring because the client is forced to confront the stimulus without having an opportunity to employ customary defenses. As a result, the fear-inducing hypothesis that had never been adequately tested before is invalidated by an emotionally convincing experience.

REFERENCES

Arnold, M. B. *Emotions and personality* (2 vols.). New York: Columbia University Press, 1960.

Averill, J. R. Emotion and anxiety: Sociocultural, biological, and psychological determinants. In M. Zuckerman & C. D. Spielberger (Eds.), *Emotion and anxiety: New concepts, methods and applications.* New York: Wiley, 1976.

Bandura, A. *Principles of behavior modification.* New York: Holt, Rinehart & Winston, 1969.

Bandura, A. Self-efficacy: Toward a unifying theory of behavioral change. *Psychological Review,* 1977, *84,* 191–215.

Bandura, A., Jeffrey, R. W., & Wright, C. L. Efficacy of participant modeling as a function of response induction aids. *Journal of Abnormal Psychology,* 1974, *83,* 56–64.

Beck, A. T. *Cognitive therapy and the emotional disorders.* New York: International Universities Press, 1976.

Bond, D. D. *The love and fear of flying.* New York: International Universities Press, 1952.

Ellis, A. *Reason and emotion in psychotherapy.* New York: Lyle Stuart, 1962.

Epstein, S. The measurement of drive and conflict in humans: Theory and experiment. In M. R. Jones (Ed.), *Nebraskas Symposium on Motivation.* Lincoln: University of Nebraska Press, 1962.

Epstein, S. Toward a unified theory of anxiety. In B. A. Maher (Ed.), *Progress in experimental personality research* (Vol. 4). New York: Academic Press, 1967.

Epstein, S. The nature of anxiety with emphasis upon its relationship to expectancy. In C. D. Spielberger (Ed.), *Anxiety, current trends in theory and research* (Vol. 2). New York: Academic Press, 1972.

Epstein, S. The self-concept revisited, or a theory of a theory. *American Psychologist,* 1973, *28,* 404–416.

Epstein, S. Anxiety, arousal, and the self-concept. In I. G. Sarason & C. D. Spielberger (Eds.), *Stress and anxiety* (Vol. 3). Washington, D. C.: Hemisphere Publishing Corporation, 1976.

Epstein, S. Natural healing processes of the mind: I. Acute schizophrenic disorganization. *Schizophrenia Bulletin,* 1979, *5,* 313–321.

Epstein, S. The self-concept: A review and the proposal of an integrated theory of personality. In E. Staub (Ed.), *Personality: Basic issues and current research.* Englewood Cliffs, N.J.: Prentice-Hall, 1980.

Epstein, S., & Fenz, W. D. Theory and experiment on the measurement of approach-avoidance conflict. *Journal of Abnormal and Social Psychology,* 1962, *64,* 97–112.

Epstein, S., & Fenz, W. D. Steepness of approach and avoidance gradients in humans as a function of experience. *Journal of Experimental Psychology,* 1965, *70,* 1–12.

Fenz, W. D., & Epstein, S. Gradients of psychological arousal of experienced and novice parachutists as a function of an approaching jump. *Psychosomatic Medicine,* 1967, *29,* 33–51.

Fenz, W. D., & Jones, G. B. The effect of uncertainty on mastery of stress: A case study. *Psychophysiology,* 1972, *9,* 615–619.

Fenz, W. D., Kluck, B. L., & Bankart, C. P. The effect of threat and uncertainty on mastery of stress. *Journal of Experimental Psychology,* 1969, *79,* 473–479.

Freud, S. *Beyond the pleasure principle.* New York: Bantam, 1959. (First German edition, 1920.)

Lazarus, R. S. *Psychological stress and the coping process.* New York: McGraw-Hill, 1966.

Lecky, P. *Self-consistency: A theory of personality.* Hamden, Conn.: The Shoe String Press, 1961.

Lindemann, E. Symptomatology and management of acute grief. *American Journal of Psychiatry,* 1944, *101,* 141–148.

McReynolds, P. A restricted conceptualization of human anxiety and motivation. *Psychological Reports, Monograph Supplement,* 1956, *2,* 293–312.

McReynolds, P. Anxiety, perception, and schizophrenia. In D. Jackson (Ed.), *The etiology of schizophrenia.* New York: Basic Books, 1960.

Meichenbaum, D. *Cognitive behavior modification.* New York: Plenum Press, 1977.

Meichenbaum, D., & Novaco, R. W. Stress inoculation: A preventive approach. In C. Spielberger & I. Sarason (Eds.), *Stress and Anxiety* (Vol. 5). New York: Wiley, 1975.

Novaco, R. W. Stress inoculation: A cognitive therapy for anger and its application to a case of depression. *Journal of Consulting and Clinical Psychology,* 1977, *45,* 600–608.

Novaco, R. W. The cognitive regulation of anger and stress. In P. Kendall & S. Hollon (Eds.), *Cognitive-behavioral interventions: Theory, research, and procedures.* New York: Academic Press, 1979.

Novaco, R. W. Training of probation counselors for anger problems. *Journal of Consulting Psychology,* 1980, *27,* 385–390.

Pavlov, I. P. *Conditioned reflexes* (G. V. Anrep, trans.),London: Oxford University Press, 1927.

Rachman, S. J. *Fear and courage.* San Francisco: W. H. Freeman, 1978.

Sokolov, Y. N. *Perception and the conditioned reflex* (S. W. Waydenfield, trans.).New York: Macmillan, 1963.

Stampfl, T. "Implosive therapy." In D. Levis (Ed.), *Learning approaches to therapeutic behavior change.* Chicago: Aldine Press, 1970.

Wolpe, J. *Psychotherapy by reciprocal inhibition.* Stanford, Calif.: Stanford University Press, 1958.

3

Stress Inoculation in Health Care

Theory and Research

IRVING L. JANIS

INTRODUCTION

Stress inoculation involves giving people realistic warnings, reommendations, and reassurances to prepare them to cope with impending dangers or losses. At present, stress inoculation procedures range in intensiveness from a single 10-minute preparatory communication to an elaborate training program with graded exposure to danger stimuli accompanied by guided practice in coping skills, which might require 15 hours or more of training. Any preparatory communication is said to function as stress inoculation if it enables a person to increase his or her tolerance for subsequent threatening events, as manifested by behavior that is relatively efficient and stable rather than disorganized by anxiety or inappropriate as a result of denial of real dangers. Preparatory communications and related training procedures can be administered before or shortly after a person makes a commitment to carry out a stressful decision, such as undergoing surgery or a painful series of medical treatments. When successful, the process is called stress inoculation because it may be analogous to what happens when people are inoculated to produce antibodies that will prevent a disease.

IRVING L. JANIS • Department of Psychology, Yale University, New Haven, Connecticut 06525. Preparation of this chapter was supported in part by Grant No. 1R01 MH32995-01 from the National Institute of Mental Health.

OBSERVATIONS DURING WORLD WAR II

The notion that people could be prepared for stress was very much in the air during World War II. I was rather forcibly introduced to that notion shortly after I was drafted into the Army in the fall of 1943. Like millions of other American soldiers who received basic military training at that time, I was put through what was called a "battle inoculation" course. It included not only films, pamphlets, and illustrated lectures about the realities of combat dangers but also gradual exposure to actual battle stimuli under reasonably safe conditions. The most impressive feature of the battle inoculation course was that each of us had to crawl about 80 yards under live machine-gun fire in a simulated combat setting that was all too realistic.

Later on, as a member of an Army research team of social psychologists under the leadership of Samuel Stouffer and Carl Hovland, I had the opportunity to collect and analyze pertinent morale survy data and clinical observations bearing on stress tolerance. In a chapter on fear in combat in *The American Soldier: Combat and Its Aftermath* (1949), I discussed the battle inoculation course. Although its effectiveness had not been systematically investigated during the war, I noted that correlational data from morale surveys indirectly supported the conclusion that "having the experience of escaping from danger by taking successful protective action and having practice in discriminating among [battle] sound cues can be critical factors in the reduction of fears of enemy weapons in combat" (p. 241). In a more speculative vein, I also suggested other ways in which exposure to stress stimuli during basic military training might facilitate coping with the stresses of combat: Battle inoculation training could "increase motivation [of the soldier] to acquire combat skills" and to "develop some personal techniques for coping with his emotional reactions—such as focusing his attention upon the details of his own combat mission as a form of distraction, frequently asserting to himself that he can take it, or some other... verbalization which reduces anxiety" (p. 224).

Battle inoculation training was given only after trainees had received ample training opportunities to build up a repertoire of combat skills. I pointed out that this type of preparation for combat could help to reduce the disruptive effects of fear in two ways:

> (1) the general level of anxiety in combat would tend to be reduced in so far as the men derived from their training a high degree of self-confidence about their ability to take care of themselves and to handle almost any contingency that might threaten them with sudden danger; and (2) the intensity of fear reactions in specific danger situations would tend to be reduced once the man began to carry out a plan of action in a skilled manner. (pp. 222–223)

In a critical review of the evidence bearing on fear in combat, Rachman (1978, p. 64) concludes that, with minor exceptions, the available correlational data support these propositions, which are consistent with Bandura's (1977) recent emphasis on the positive behavioral changes resulting from an improved sense of self-efficacy:

> In sum, troops who expressed a high degree of self-confidence before combat were more likely to perform with relatively little fear during battle; however, a minority who expressed little confidence in themselves also performed well...[and] another minority...expressed a high degree of self-confidence before combat, but experienced strong fear during it. (Rachman, 1978, p. 64)

To some extent, the minor deviant findings may be attributed to the imperfect reliability of the measures of self-confidence and of fear in combat. Further, as Rachman suggests, they may result from the relatively low correlations among subjective fear, physiological disturbances, and avoidance behavior that makes for inadequate performance. Rachman cites evidence that "the physiological aspects of fear are most susceptible to habituation training" and predicts, therefore, "that this component will decline as combat experience increases, provided the soldier succeeds in avoiding traumatic exposures" (Rachman, 1978, pp. 64–65). Although at the time we knew very little about how habituation or related stress inoculation processes work, the data from studies of combat soldiers during World War II clearly highlighted the value of preparatory training experiences for improving men's coping responses when they subsequently encounter danger.

A few years after the end of that war, when reviewing the studies bearing on fear reactions of civilians exposed to air war during World War II, I again encountered indications that realistic warnings and gradual exposure to stress stimuli might have positive effects as "psychological preparation for withstanding the emotional impact of increasingly severe air attacks" (Janis, 1951, p. 155). I was especially impressed by Matte's (1943) observations of Londoners standing for long periods of time silently and solemnly contemplating the bombing damage. These observations, together with his clinical interviews, led him to infer that the Londoners were "working-through" the current air-raid experience in a way that prepared them psychologically for subsequent ones. He surmised that their gradual realization of the possibility of being injured or killed minimized the potentially traumatic effects of a sudden confrontation with air-raid dangers and at the same time heightened their self-confidence about being able to "take it." Rachman's (1978) review of the evidence from wartime research emphasizes the unexpectedly high level of stress tolerance displayed by heavily bombed people in England, Germany, and Japan during World War II. He points out that "some of the strongest evidence pointing to the tendency of fears to habituate with repeated [nontraumatic] exposures to the fear-provoking situation, comes from these [World War II] observations of people exposed to air raids" (p. 39).

The value of psychological preparation was also implied by impressionistic observations of how people reacted to social stresses during World War II. Romalis (1942), for example, reported clinical observations suggesting that the American women who became most upset when their husbands or sons were drafted into the Army tended to be those who had denied the threat of being separated. These women, according to Romalis, were psychologically unprepared because they had maintained overoptimistic beliefs that their husbands or sons would somehow be exempt from the draft. When the threat of being separated actually materialized, they reacted with much more surprise, resentment, and anxiety than those women who had developed realistic expectations.

RESEARCH ON SURGERY

While studying stress reactions in a series of case studies of surgical patients during the early 1950s, I observed numerous indications that preparatory information could affect stress tolerance. My first series of case studies on the surgical wards led me to surmise that the earlier observations on psychological preparation of people exposed to military combat and air-war disasters might have broad applicability to all sorts of personal disasters, including surgery and painful medical treatments. I was able to check on this idea by obtaining survey data from 77 men who had recently undergone major surgical operations (Janis, 1958, pp. 352–394). The results indicated that those surgical patients who had received information beforehand about what to expect were less likely than those given little information to overreact to setbacks during the postoperative period. Although no dependable conclusions about the casual sequence could be drawn from these correlational results, they led to subsequent experiments on the effects of giving patients various kinds of preparatory information intended to increase their tolerance for the stresses of surgery.

Supporting evidence for the effectiveness of anticipatory preparation for stress—information about what to expect combined with various coping suggestions—has come from a variety of controlled field experiments with adult surgical patients (e.g., DeLong, 1971; Egbert, Battit, Welch, & Bartlett, 1964; Johnson, 1966; Johnson, Rice, Fuller, & Endress, 1977; Schmidt, 1966; Schmitt & Wooldridge, 1973; Vernon & Bigelow, 1974). Similarly, positive results on the value of giving psychological preparation have also been reported in studies of childbirth (e.g., Breen,

1975; Dick-Read, 1959; Lemaze, 1958; Levy & McGee, 1975) and noxious medical procedures (e.g., Johnson & Leventhal, 1974).

The research with surgical patients indicates that preparatory information can inoculate people to withstand the disruptive emotional and physical impact of the severe stresses of surgery. Like people traumatized by an overwhelming wartime disaster, those who are not inoculated experience acute feelings of helplessness and react with symptoms of acute fright, aggrievement, rage, or depression. In this respect, the natural tendency of ill people to deny impending threats during the preoperative period is likely to be pathogenic.

A number of interrelated cognitive and motivational processes that may mediate the effects of stress inoculation are suggested by case studies of how hospitalized men and women react to severe setbacks after having decided to accept their physician's recommendation to have an operation (Janis, 1958, pp. 352–394; 1971, pp. 95–102). Most of the case studies deal with surgical patients who for one reason or another were not psychologically prepared. These patients were so overwhelmed by the usual pains, discomforts, and deprivations of the postoperative convalescent period that they manifestly regretted their decision and on some occasions actually refused to permit the hospital staff to administer routine postoperative treatments. Before the disturbing setbacks occurred, these patients typically received relatively little preparatory information and retained an unrealistic conception of how nicely everything was going to work out, which functioned as a blanket immunity type of reassurance, enabling them for a time to set their worries aside. They sincerely believed that they would not have bad pains or undergo any other disagreeable experiences. But then, when they unexpectedly experienced incision pains and suffered from all sorts of other unpleasant deprivations that are characteristic of postoperative convalescence, their blanket immunity reassurance was undermined. They thought something had gone horribly wrong. They could neither reassure themselves nor accept truthful reassurance from physicians and nurses.

Taking account of the surgery findings and the earlier research from World War II, I suggested that it should be possible to prevent traumatic reactions and to help people cope more effectively with any type of anticipated stress by giving them beforehand some form of "emotional inoculation," as I then called it (Janis, 1951, pp. 220–221; 1958, p. 323). (Subsequently, Donald Meichenbaum [1977] called it "stress inoculation," which I now think is a better term.) For people who initially ignore or deny the danger, the inoculation procedure, as I have described it (Janis, 1971, pp. 196–197), includes three counseling procedures: (1) giving "realistic information in a way that challenges the person's blanket immunity reassurances so as to make him aware of his vulnerability" and to motivate him "to plan preparatory actions for dealing with the subsequent crisis"; (2) counteracting "feelings of helplessness, hopelessness, and demoralization" by calling attention to reassuring facts about personal and social coping resources that enable the person "to feel reasonably confident about surviving and ultimately recovering from the impending ordeal"; and (3) encouraging "the person to work out his own ways of reassuring himself and his own plans for protecting himself." The third procedure is important because in a crisis many people become passive and overly dependent on family, friends, and authority figures, such as physicians; they need to build up cognitive defenses involving some degree of self-reliance instead of relying exclusively on others to protect them from suffering and loss. The first two counseling procedures require careful dosage of both distressing and calming information about what is likely to happen in order to strike "a balance between arousal of anticipatory fear or grief on the one hand and authoritative reassurance on the other" (Janis, 1971, p. 196). For persons whose initial level of fear is high, however, only the second and third procedures would be used.

In my theoretical analysis of the psychological effects of preparatory information, I introduced the concept of "the work of worrying" to refer to the process of mentally rehearsing anticipated losses and developing reassuring cognitions that can at least partially alleviate fear or other intense emotions when a crisis is subsequently encountered (Janis, 1958, pp. 374–378). The "work of worrying" is assumed to be stimulated by preparatory information concerning any impending threat to one's physical, material, social, or moral well-being. For example, it may play a crucial role among men and women exposed to the physical and social stresses of tornadoes, floods, and other natural disasters. Wolfenstein (1957) reports having the impression from her review of disaster studies that the people who seemed to cope best and to recover most quickly were those who received unambiguous warnings beforehand and who decided to take precautionary action on the assumption that they could be affected personally. She suggests that among people who deny that any protective measures are necessary up to the last moment, "the lack of emotional preparation, the sudden shattering of the fantasy of complete immunity, the sense of compunction for failing to respond to warnings contribute to the disruptive effect of an extreme event" (1957, p. 29).

RESEARCH ON OTHER POSTDECISIONAL CRISES

Essentially the same adaptive cognitive and emotional changes that were discerned following stress inoculation in surgical patients have been noted in many case studies and in a few field experiments that focus on people who have encountered setbacks and losses when carrying out other decisions, including typical problems arising after choosing a career, taking legal action to obtain a divorce, and making policy decisions on behalf of an organization (Janis & Mann, 1977). Stress inoculation is also pertinent to the problems of backsliding recidivism, which plagues those health-care practitioners who try to help their clients to improve their eating habits, stop smoking, cut down on alcohol consumption, or change their behavior in other ways that will promote physical or mental health (see Janis & Rodin, 1979). Similarly, preparatory communications given prior to relocation of elderly patients to a new nursing home or to a hospital have been found to be effective in reducing protests and debilitation (Schulz & Hanusa, 1978).

Recently stress inoculation has begun to be used in schools to prevent teenaged children from becoming cigarette smokers. A controlled field experiment with seventh graders showed that significantly fewer teenagers became smokers by the end of the school year if they were exposed to an experimental program of stress inoculation designed to counteract the overt and subtle social pressures, such as dares from friends, that frequently induce smoking (McAlister, Perry, & Maccoby, 1979). The stress inoculation procedures, which were given after the students committed themselves to the decision to be nonsmokers, included role-playing skits to represent the various social inducements to smoke, specific suggestions about how to handle difficult situations when confronted with peer-group pressures, and rehearsals of appropriate cognitive responses of commitment to resist the pressures.

All of the various studies just cited on postdecisional crises support the same general conclusion that emerged from the earlier surgery studies, namely, that many people will display higher stress tolerance in response to losses and setbacks when they attempt to carry out a chosen course of action if they have been given realistic warnings in advance about what to expect, together with cogent reassurances that promote confidence about attaining a basically satisfactory outcome despite those losses and setbacks.

CLINICAL USES IN TREATING EMOTIONAL AND PHYSICAL DISORDERS

During the past decade, stress inoculation has been extensively used by clinical practitioners who have developed what they call a "cognitive-behavioral modification" form of therapy (see Goldfried, Decenteco, & Weinberg, 1974; Meichenbaum, 1977; Meichenbaum & Turk, 1976, 1982b). In the earlier work I have just reviewed, stress inoculation was introduced to *prevent* the damaging psychological consequences of subsequent exposures to stress, such as demoralization, phobias, and psychosomatic disorders. In contrast, this new trend in clinical psychology uses stress inoculation to *alleviate* or *cure* the stress-related disorders from which patients are already suffering.

The procedures described by Donald Meichenbaum and his associates for clients suffering from phobic anxiety, such as excessive fear of needles used in injections and blood tests, include three main steps. The first step is to give preparatory information about the stressful situations that evoke the anxiety symptoms. Just as in the surgery cases, the client is told about (a) the negative features of the situations that arouse anxiety, including the possibility of high physiological arousal and feelings of being emotionally overwhelmed, and (b) the positive features that are reassuring and that can lead to the development of more effective ways of managing the situation. A major goal of this initial educational phase, which is usually conducted by means of questions in a type of Socratic dialogue, is to help the clients reconceptualize their anxiety symptoms so that what they say to themselves when confronted with the phobic situation will no longer be self-defeating but will be conducive to effective action. Another somewhat related goal is to enable the client to grasp a more differentiated view of anxiety as comprising both cognitive appraisals of threat and physiological arousal. This differentiation sets the stage for the next phase.

The second phase is intended to help the client develop a new set of coping techniques that modify distressing cognitions and physiological arousal. The client is not only encouraged to make use of coping skills already in his or her repertoire but is also given training in new "direct-action" skills, such as relaxation exercises that can be used to reduce emotional arousal in anxiety-provoking situations. A major goal of this phase is to prepare the client to react in a constructive way to early warning signs, before the full onset of the anxiety symptoms. In addition to direct-action skills, cognitive coping skills are also discussed in collaborative interchanges designed to help the client work out his or her own coping strategies. The counselor gives suggestive examples of positive self-talk that might promote effective coping, such as "I can handle this situation by taking one step at a time." Some of the recommended self-talk is also likely to enhance the client's sense of self-efficacy after each successful trial—for example, "I can do it, it really worked; I can control my fear by controlling my ideas."

The third phase involves applying the new coping skills to a graded series of imaginary and real stress situations. The procedures used in this phase are based on the pioneering work of Seymour Epstein (1967), who emphasized the importance of "self-pacing" and exposure to small doses of threat in the acquisition of coping skills for mastery of stress among men engaging in such dangerous activities as parachuting and combat flying. In the graduated practice phase of stress inoculation, the patient is given role-playing exercises and also a series of homework assignments involving real-life exposures that become increasingly demanding.

Favorable results from using this type of stress inoculation have been reported in clinical studies of clients suffering from a variety of emotional symptoms, including persistent phobias (Meichenbaum, 1977); test anxiety (Goldfried, Linehan, & Smith, 1978; Meichenbaum, 1972); social anxiety and shyness (Glass, Gottman, & Shmurack, 1976; Zimbardo, 1970); speech anxiety (Fremouw & Zitter, 1978; Meichenbaum, Gilmore, & Fedoravicious, 1971); depression (Taylor & Marshall, 1977); and outbursts of anger (Novaco, 1975). Essentially the same procedures have also been used successfully with patients suffering from certain kinds of physical ailments, most notably those involving sporadic or chronic pain (Turk, 1977; Turk & Genest, 1979). From the clinical research that has been done so far, it appears that a package treatment combining the various kinds of intervention that enter into this type of stress inoculation can sometimes be effective with some patients, but it is not yet known which interventions are essential and which are not (see Meichenbaum & Turk, 1982a). Nor do we know very much at present about the conditions under which giving preparatory information or administering any of the other component interventions is likely to succeed or fail.

When Preparatory Information Fails

Here and there in the prior research on stress inoculation one can discern a few rudimentary indications of the conditions under which preparatory information is ineffective or even detrimental. From the very outset of my research on surgery it was apparent that, although preparatory information is advantageous for many patients, it definitely is not for some of them (Janis, 1958, pp. 370–374). In numerous instances of failure, the main source of difficulty seems to be that the message is too meager to influence the patients. Very brief preparatory messages that take only a few minutes to convey information about impending threats are usually too weak to change a patient's expectations or to stimulate the development of effective self-assurances, and therefore have no effect at all. At the opposite extreme, some patients receive very strong preparatory communications from their physicians and friends, which unintentionally stimulate anxiety and feelings of helplessness that decrease rather than increase stress tolerance. Like an overdose of antigens, an overenthusiastic inoculation attempt can produce the very condition it is intended to prevent.

Other sources of detrimental effects have to do with the nature of the stress to which the person is subsequently exposed. For example, I have observed that at least a small minority of surgical patients have become extremely upset when told in advance that they are going to be given certain intrusive treatments such as enemas, catheterization, or injections (Janis, 1958, p. 387). These patients apparently imagine each of these routine treatments as being much worse than it really is. When the time comes to have it, they become so emotionally aroused that they are unresponsive to the physicians' or nurses' reassurances and resist to such an extent that the treatment is either botched or cannot be carried out at all. Some practitioners report that they obtain better cooperation if they give no preparatory information about a disturbing procedure of short duration, such as an enema, until they administer it, at which time they give the patient reassurances along with instructions about what to do (see Janis, 1958, p. 394).

In the instances I have just been discussing, the stress episode itself is relatively mild because the patients do not undergo acute pain or prolonged discomfort and an authority figure is present to reassure them that they are doing fine. Perhaps stress inoculation in most applicable for those episodes of stress that are painful or of long duration and that are likely to occur at times when no one will be around to give reassurances.

More recent research with surgical patients has shown that, as expected, preparatory information is not uniformly effective. (For a review of inconsistent effects of preparatory information given to surgical patients, see Cohen & Lazarus, 1979.) In a number of studies that found no significant effects on psychological or physical recovery, only brief messages were given to the patients, describing what the stressful experiences would be like in the operating room and during convalescence. For example, a field experiment by Langer, Janis, and Wolfer (1975) found that a brief message containing standard preparatory information was ineffective, whereas a special form of psychological preparation that presented detailed instructions about a cognitive coping device (which I shall describe later) proved to be highly effective in helping patients to tolerate postoperative stress.

Johnson, Rice, Fuller, and Endress (1977) found that preparatory information about what to expect was ineffective for patients having one type of operation (herniorraphy) but was highly effective for those having another type (cholecsystectomy). These findings may be in line with the earlier observations suggesting that the success of inoculation attempts will vary depending upon the nature of the stress.

Psychological preparation for childbirth, which for several decades has been extensively applied to hundreds of thousands of women, has often been investigated (e.g., Chertok, 1959; Doering & Entwhistle, 1975; Huttel, Mitchell, Fisher, & Meyer, 1972; Tanzer, 1968). In general, most of the studies of pregnant women, like those of surgical patients, document the value of giving preparatory information and coping suggestions. But occasional failures have also been reported (e.g., Davenport-Slack & Boylan, 1974; Javert & Hardy, 1951). Some women experience severe pains during childbirth despite being given one or another form of psychological preparation. Essentially the same can be said about psychological preparation for other types of pain. Turk and Genest (1979) have reviewed over two dozen systematic evaluation studies of psychological treatments designed to help people suffering from persistent backaches, recurrent headaches, or other chornic pains. Most of the treatments include giving preparatory information about recurrent distressing events that might precipitate or exacerbate the patient's pains, together with suggestions about how to cope more effectively with the stresses. A major conclusion that emerges from all these studies, according to Turk and Genest, is that when the psychological treatments include preparatory information about expected stresses and suggestions about how to cope with the stresses, they are generally effective in helping to alleviate chronic pains, but not with all patients in all situations.

Turk and Genest suggest a number of important factors that may influence the outcome of stress inoculation for patients suffering from chronic pain—the degree of threat perceived by the patient, the perceived effectiveness of the information, the mode or channel used to present the preparatory message, and individual differences in coping style and self-confidence. They point out, however, that these factors await systematic investigation, as do the various ingredients of the treatments that have been found to be effective.

In summary, many findings, both old and new, from studies of psychological preparation for surgery, childbirth, and the stresses associated with chronic pain show that stress inoculation often works but sometimes does not. Obviously, the time has come to move on to a more sophisticated phase of research, to investigate systematically the conditions under which stress inoculation is effective. In this new phase of research, which has just recently begun, the investigators' primary purpose is no longer merely to evaluate the overall effectiveness of stress inoculation procedures, to find out if one or another compound treatment program is successful in building up tolerance for one or another type of stress. Rather, the purpose is to find out which are the *effective com-*

ponents of the stress inoculation treatments that have already been found to be at least partially successful in past research and to determine the conditions under which each component has a positive effect on stress tolerance. This new phase of analytic research on components includes investigating several factors simultaneously in an analysis of variance design so that interaction effects can be determined, which help to specify in what circumstances and for which types of persons certain of the components of stress inoculation are effective. In my opinion, this is where stress inoculation research should have started to go a long time ago; fortunately, this is the direction it is now actually taking.

From prior studies, we have already obtained important clues about what could prove to be the crucial components. The variables that appear to be leading candidates are discussed in the sections that follow.

PREDICTABILITY

According to a number of laboratory investigations, a person's degree of behavioral control is increased by reducing uncertainty about the nature and timing of threatening events (Averill, 1973; Ball & Vogler, 1971; Pervin, 1963; Seligman, 1975; Weiss, 1970). Several experiments indicate that people are less likely to display strong emotional reactions or extreme changes in attitude when confronted with an unpleasant event if they were previously exposed to a preparatory communication that accurately predicted the disagreeable experience (Epstein & Clarke, 1970; Janis, Lumsdaine, & Gladstone, 1951; Lazarus & Alfert, 1964; Staub & Kellett, 1972). These experiments show that advance warnings and accurate predictions can have an emotional dampening effect on the impact of subsequent confrontations with the predicted adverse events. Predictability may therefore be a crucial component in increasing stress tolerance. This hypothesis implies that when a person is given realistic preparatory information about the unpleasant consequences of a decision, he or she will be more likely to adhere to the chosen course of action despite setbacks and losses.

Although the hypothesis has not been systematically investigated with relation to postdecisional behavior, it appears to be plausible in light of a field experiment by Johnson, Morrisey, and Leventhal (1973) on psychological preparation of patients who had agreed to undergo a distressful gastrointestinal endoscopic examination that requires swallowing a stomach tube. In this study one of the preparatory communications was devoted mainly to predicting the perceptual aspects of the unpleasant procedures—what the patient could expect to feel, see, hear, and taste. Photographs of the examining room and the apparatus were also presented. Effectiveness was assessed by measuring the amount of medication required to sedate the patients when the distressing endoscopic procedure was given, which is an indicator of stress tolerance. The preparatory communication that predicted the unpleasant perceptual experiences proved to be highly effective, significantly more so than a control communication that described the procedures without giving any perceptual information. The effectiveness of the preparatory communication with the perceptual information cannot, however, be ascribed unequivocally to the increased predictablity of the unpleasant events, because here and there it also contained reassuring information about the skill of the health-care practitioners and various explanations, which may have involved another variable (discussed in the next section below).

If future research verifies the hypothesis that predictability is a variable crucial to increasing stress tolerance, a subsidiary variable to be considered will be the *vividness* of the perceptual information that is presented, which might make images of expected stressful events more *available,* in the sense that Tversky and Kahneman (1973, 1974) use that term. Psychodramatic role playing, films, and other vividness-enhancing techniques might increase the effectiveness of stress inoculation procedures by increasing the availability of realistic images of the predicted stressful events.

ENHANCING COPING SKILLS BY ENCOURAGING CONTINGENCY PLANS

Another component of standard stress inoculation procedures consists of information about means for dealing with the anticipated stressful event, providing people with more adequate coping skills. If this component is essential, we would expect to find that people will show more adherence to an adaptive course of action, such as following well-established health rules, if they are given preparatory communications containing specific recommendations for coping with whatever adverse consequences of the decision are most likely to occur. In most of the examples of stress inoculation used in the prior research that has already been cited, two different types of coping recommendations are included. One type pertains to *plans for action* that will prevent or reduce objective damage that might ensue if the anticipated stressful events occur. The second type involves *cognitive coping devices*, including attention-diversion tactics, mentally relaxing imagery, and the replacement of self-defeating thoughts with reassuring and optimistic self-talk, all of which can prevent or reduce excessive anxiety reactions.

A good example of the first type is to be found in the highly successful stress inoculation procedure for surgical patients used by Egbert *et al.* (1964), which included giving instruction regarding physical relaxation, positions of the body, and deep-breathing exercises that can help to keep postoperative pains to a minimum. Such instruction can be conceptualized as providing a set of contingency plans for dealing with setbacks, suffering, and other sources of postdecisional regret for a course of action that entails short-term losses in order to obtain long-term gains. For example, surgical patients in the study by Egbert and his associates were encouraged to develop the following contingency plan: "If I start to feel severe incision pains, I will use the relaxation and breathing exercise to cut down on the amount of suffering."

Other investigators also report evidence of the effectiveness of stress inoculation procedures that include instruction about behavioral coping techniques for medical or surgical patients (Fuller, Endress, & Johnson, 1977; Johnson, 1977; Lindeman, 1972; Lindeman & Van Aernam, 1971; Schmitt & Wooldridge, 1973; Wolfer & Visintainer, 1975). In all of these studies, the recommendations about coping actions were presented in compound communications, accompanied by other types of information, such as predictions about what stressful events are likely to be experienced. There is no way of knowing, therefore, whether the coping action recommendations were wholly, partially, or not at all responsible for the successful outcome of the stress inoculation. One major study, however, has attempted to tease out the relative effectiveness of the coping recommendations. In their second study of patients who were about to undergo a distressing endoscopic examination, Johnson and Leventhal (1974) compared a preparatory communication about the discomforts and other sensations most likely to be experienced with one that gave specific behavioral coping instructions about how to use rapid breathing to reduce gagging during throat swabbing and what to do to avoid discomforts while the stomach tube was being inserted into the esophagus. These investigators found that each of these preparatory communications was more effective than a standard (control) communication limited to describing the endoscopic examination procedures (given to all subjects in the experiment), but the combined effect was significantly greater than either alone. Thus, the combination of predicting the adverse events that would be experienced with recommending coping actions proved to be the maximally effective form of stress inoculation. If this outcome is replicated in subsequent analytic research on the effectiveness of different components of stress inoculation, a major controversial issue might be settled. We should be able to find out whether information about coping strategies is essential and which combinations with other components are most effective for various types of individuals.

ENHANCING COGNITIVE COPING CAPABILITIES

We turn next to research on the second type of coping recommendations—those pertaining to positive self-talk and other cognitive changes that might increase stress tolerance without necessarily involving any overt coping actions. A few studies provide evidence that people can be helped by preparatory communications that induce them to reconceptualize in an optimistic way the stresses they will undergo. A coping device developed by Langer *et al.* (1975), which involves encouraging an optimistic reappraisal of anxiety-provoking events, was tested in a field experiment with surgical patients by inserting it in a brief preoperative interview conducted by a psychologist. Each patient was given several examples of the positive consequences of his or her decision to undergo surgery (for example, improvement in health, extra care and attention in the hospital, temporary vacation from outside pressure). Then the patient was invited to think up additional positive examples that pertained to his or her individual case. Finally the patient was given the recommendation to rehearse these compensatory favorable consequences whenever he or she started to feel upset about the unpleasant aspects of the surgical experience. Patients were urged to be as realistic as possible about the compensatory features, so as to emphasize that what was being recommended was not equivalent to trying to deceive oneself. The instructions were designed to promote warranted optimism and awareness of the anticipated gains that outweighed the losses to be expected from the chosen course of action. The findings from the controlled experiment conducted by Langer *et al.* (1975) supported the prediction that cognitive reappraisal would reduce stress both before and after an operation. Patients given the reappraisal intervention obtained lower scores on nurses' blind ratings of preoperative stress and on unobtrusive postoperative measures of the number of times pain-relieving drugs and sedatives were requested and administered.

Additional evidence of the value of encouraging cognitive coping strategies comes from a study by Kendall, Williams, Pechacek, Graham, Shisslak, and Herzoff (1977) on the effectiveness of stress inoculation for patients who had agreed to undergo cardiac catheterization. This is a particularly stressful medical procedure that involves working a catheter up into the heart by inserting it into a vein in the groin. One group of patients was given stress inoculation that included discussion of the stresses to be expected together with suggestions for developing their own cognitive coping strategies, which were encouraged by suggesting various reassurances, modeling cognitive coping strategies, and reinforcing whatever personal cognitive coping responses the patient mentioned. Two other equivalent groups of patients were given different preparatory treatments — an educational communication about the catheterization procedure and an attention–placebo intervention. There was also a no-treatment control group. The patients given the stress inoculation procedure that encouraged them to develop their own cognitive coping strategies showed higher stress tolerance during the cardiac catheterization than those in the other three treatment groups, as assessed by self-ratings and by ratings made by observers (physicians and medical technicians).

One cannot expect, of course, that every attempt to encourage positive thinking among patients facing surgery or distressing treatments will succeed in helping their recovery during convalescence. One such attempt with surgical patients by Cohen (1975), using different intervention procedures from those in the preceding studies, failed to have any effect on indicators of psychological and physical recovery.

Although few studies have been done among patients who are not hospitalized, there is some evidence of favorable effects suggesting that encouraging positive self-talk and related cognitive coping strategies might prove to be successful in many different spheres of health care. In a controlled field experiment, a stress inoculation procedure designed to encourage positive self-talk was found to be effective in helping patients reduce the frequency, duration, and intensity of muscle-contraction headaches (Holroyd, Andrasik, & Westbrook, 1977).

Cognitive coping procedures may also be effective for increasing adherence to such health-related decisions as dieting. That this is a likely prospect is suggested by the findings from a doctoral dissertation by Riskind (1982), which was carried out in the Weight-Reduction Clinic under my research program. In this field study, all the clients were given counseling and information about dieting but only one experimental group was given additional instructions to adopt a day-by-day coping perspective rather than a long-term perspective. Riskind found that the coping instructions resulted in a greater sense of personal control and more adherence to the diet (as measured by weight loss) over a period of two months among clients with a relatively high initial level of self-esteem. The results are similar to those reported by Bandura and Simon (1977) for obese patients being treated by behavior modification techniques. The patients who were instructed to adopt short-term subgoals on a *daily* basis ate less and lost more weight than the patients who were instructed to adopt a longer-term subgoal in terms of *weekly* accomplishments.

From the few systematic studies just reviewed, it seems reasonable to expect that recommendations about coping strategies may prove to be ingredients essential to successful stress inoculation. The evidence is particularly promising, as we have seen, with regard to increasing the stress tolerance of medical and surgical patients by encouraging them to replace self-defeating thoughts with positive coping cognitions. A similar conclusion is drawn by Girodo (1977) after reviewing the positive and negative outcomes of treating phobic patients with the type of stress inoculation procedures recommended by Meichenbaum (1977). Girodo goes so far as to say that the only successful ingredients of stress inoculation are those that induce the person to reconceptualize the threat in nonthreatening terms and that all other ingredients are of limited value, serving to divert attention only temporarily from threat cues. Any such generalization, however, gives undue weight to a limited set of findings and would be premature until we have well-replicated results from a variety of investigations that carefully test the effectiveness of each component of stress inoculation.

SELF-CONFIDENCE, HOPE, AND PERCEIVED CONTROL

Many innovative clinical psychologists who have developed stress inoculation procedures and use them in their practice or research emphasize that teaching patients new cognitive skills is a necessary but not sufficient condition for helping them to deal effectively with stressful situations. They say that the patients not only need to acquire adequate coping skills but also, in order to use them when needed, must feel some degree of self-confidence about being successful (see Cormier & Cormier, 1979; Meichenbaum & Turk, 1982b; Turk & Genest, 1979). Inducing the patients to believe that a recommended course of action will lead to a desired outcome is only one step in the right direction; they must also be able to maintain a sense of personal efficacy with regard to being able to "take it" and to do whatever is expected of them (see Bandura, 1977). Over and beyond the coping recommendations themselves, reassuring social support may be needed to build up the patients' self-confidence and hope about surviving intact despite whatever ordeals are awaiting them (Caplan & Killilea, 1976).

For medical and surgical patients, the key messages include two types of statements along the lines that I have just suggested. One type asserts that the medical treatment or surgery they are about to receive will be successful, which makes them feel it is worthwhile to put up with whatever suffering, losses, and coping efforts may be required. The second type asserts that the patient will be able to tolerate the pain and other sources of stress. Among the "coping thoughts" recommended in the stress inoculation procedure used by Meichenbaum and Cameron

(1973) for fear-arousing situations and by Turk (1977) for chronic pain are some that are specifically oriented toward building a sense of self-confidence and hope—for example, "You can meet this challenge," "You have lots of different strategies you can call upon," and "You can handle the situation." Even the standard recommendations concerning positive self-talk, such as "Don't worry, just think about what you can do about the pain," tend to create an attitude of self-confidence about dealing effectively with the stresses that are anticipated. Similarly, the positive effects of the cognitive coping techniques used with surgical patients by Langer *et al.* (1975) may be at least partly attributable to attitude changes in the direction of increased self-confidence. The patients are encouraged to feel confident about being able to deal effectively with whatever pains, discomforts, and setbacks are subsequently encountered, which may help them to avoid becoming discouraged and to maintain hope about surviving without sustaining unbearable losses.

The crucial role of statements about the efficacy of recommended means for averting or minimizing threats of bodily damage is repeatedly borne out by social psychological studies of the effects of public health messages that contain fear-arousing warnings (see Chu, 1966; Janis, 1971; Leventhal, 1973; Leventhal, Singer, & Jones, 1965; Rogers & Deckner, 1975; Rogers & Thistlethwaite, 1970). A study by Rogers and Mewborn (1976), for example, found that assertions about the efficacy of recommended protective actions had a significant effect on college students' intentions to adopt the practices recommended in three different public health communications dealing with well-known hazards—lung cancer, automobile accident injuries, and venereal disease. The findings from this study and from the other studies just cited are consistent with the hypothesis that when a stress inoculation procedure presents impressive information about the expected efficacy of a recommended protective action, it instills hope in the recipients about emerging without serious damage from the dangers they may encounter, which increases their willingness to adhere to the recommended action.

Obviously, it is difficult to test this hypothesis independently of the hypothesis that information inserted to increase coping skills is a potent ingredient of successful stress inoculation. Nevertheless, as I have already indicated, there are certain types of messages that can induce attitude changes in the direction of increased self-confidence and hope without necessarily changing coping skills, and these messages could be used in field experiments designed to determine whether the postulated attitude changes mediate successful stress inoculation. For example, a patient's self-confidence about surviving the ordeal of a painful medical treatment might be increased by a persuasive communication containing an impressive example of a similar patient who had a successful outcome, possibly counteracting a defeatist attitude and fostering an optimistic outlook without increasing coping skills.

There are theoretical grounds for assuming that communications fostering self-confidence and hope will prove to be effective components of stress inoculation, particularly for preventing backsliding among patients who decide to comply with a troublesome medical regimen. Janis and Mann (1977) describe several basic patterns of coping with realistic threats derived from an analysis of the research literature on how people react to emergency warnings and public health recommendations. They postulate that under conditions in which people are aware of serious risks for whatever alternative actions are open to them, there are three main coping patterns, each of which is assumed to be associated with a specific set of antecedent conditions and a characteristic level of stress:

1. *Defensive avoidance:* The decision-maker evades the conflict by procrastinating, shifting responsibility to someone else, or constructing wishful rationalizations that bolster the least objectionable alternative by minimizing the expected unfavorable consequences and remaining selectively inattentive to corrective information.
2. *Hypervigilance:* The decision-maker searches frantically for a way out of the dilemma and impulsively seizes on a hastily contrived solution that seems to promise immediate relief, overlooking the full range of consequences of his or her choice because of emotional excitement, repetitive thinking, and cognitive constriction (manifested by reduction in immediate memory span and by simplistic ideas). In its most extreme form, hypervigilance is referred to as "panic."
3. *Vigilance:* The decision-maker searches painstakingly for relevant information, assimilates it in an unbiased manner, and appraises alternatives carefully before making a choice.

Defensive avoidance and hypervigilance may occasionally be adaptive but they generally reduce one's chances of averting serious losses. Consequently, they are regarded as defective patterns of decision-making. The third pattern, vigilance, generally leads to careful search and appraisal, effective contingency planning, and the most adequate psychological preparation for coping with unfavorable consequences that might otherwise induce postdecisional regret and backsliding.

According to Janis and Mann's (1977) analysis, the vigilance pattern occurs only when three conditions are met: The person must (1) be aware of serious risks for whichever alternative is chosen; (2) hope to find a satisfactory alternative; and (3) believe that there is adequate time to search and deliberate before a decision is required. If the second condition is not met, the defensive avoidance pattern occurs; if the third condition is not met, the hypervigilance pattern occurs.

Observations from prior studies by my colleagues and I in weight-reduction and antismoking clinics indicate that clients often start carrying out a health-oriented course of action without having engaged in vigilant search and appraisal of the alternatives open to them (Janis, 1982). The dominant coping pattern in many cases appears to be defensive avoidance—deciding without deliberation to adopt the recommended course of action, which appears at the moment to be the least objectionable alternative, and bolstering it with rationalizations that minimize the difficulties to be expected when carrying it out. Defensive avoidance also appears to be a frequent coping pattern among hospitalized surgical and medical patients (see Janis, 1958; Janis & Rodin, 1979)

In order to prevent defensive avoidance, according to Janis and Mann (1977), preparatory communications are needed to meet the second of the three essential conditions for promoting a vigilant coping pattern: Assuming that the clients are already aware of the problems to be expected, interventions are needed that foster hope of solving these problems. Such interventions may also be essential for maintaining a vigilant problem-solving approach to whatever frustrations, temptations, or setbacks subsequently occur when the decision is being implemented.

On the basis of prior studies in clinics for heavy smokers and overweight people, it appears plausible to assume that backsliding occurs when one or more major setbacks make the clients lose hope about finding an adequate solution (Janis, 1982). If this assumption is correct, we would expect stress inoculation to be most effective in preventing patients from reversing their decisions to follow a medical regimen if the preparatory communications contain information or persuasive messages that foster hope of solving whatever problems may arise from that regimen.

Closely related to patients' attitudes of self-confidence and hope are their beliefs about being able to *control* a stressful situation. Stress inoculation may change a patient's expectations of being in control of a dangerous situation, both with regard to the external threats of being helpless to prevent physical damage and the internal threats of becoming panic-stricken and losing emotional control. The stress inoculation procedures used with surgical and medical patients typically include statements designed to counteract feelings of helplessness and to promote a sense of active control. For example, in the stress inoculation procedures designed by Turk (1978) for patients suffering from chronic pain, the coping thoughts that are explicitly recommended and modeled include "Relax, you're in control" and "When the pain mounts, you can switch to a different strategy; you're in control."

There is now a sizable body of literature indicating that perceived personal control sometimes plays an important role in coping with stress (Averill, 1973; Ball & Vogler, 1971; Bowers, 1968; Houston, 1972; Janis & Rodin, 1979; Kanfer & Seiderk, 1973; Lapidus, 1969; Pervin, 1963; Pranulis, Dabbs, & Johnson, 1975; Seligman, 1975; Staud, Tursky, & Schwartz, 1971; Weiss, 1970). Some preparatory interventions may make patients feel less helpless by making them more active participants, increasing their personal involvement in the treatment. Pranulis *et al.* (1975), for example, redirect hospitalized patients' attention away from their own emotional reactions as passive recipients of medical treatments toward information that makes them feel more in control as active collaborators with the staff. Perhaps many of the preparatory communications used for purposes of stress inoculation have essentially the same effect on the patients' perceived control over distressing environmental events, which could increase their self-confidence and hope.

INDUCING COMMITMENT AND PERSONAL RESPONSIBILITY

Another psychological component that may contribute to the positive effects of stress inoculation is the heightening of commitment. As part of the stress inoculation procedure for a new course of action, such as accepting medical recommendations to undergo surgery, painful treatments, or unpleasant regimens, patients are induced to acknowledge that they are going to have to deal with anticipated losses, which is tantamount to making more elaborated commitment statements to the health-care practitioners. Prior psychological research on commitment indicates that each time a person is induced to announce his or her intentions to an esteemed other, such as a professional counselor, the person is anchored to the decision not just by anticipated social disapproval but also by anticipated self-disapproval (Janis & Mann, 1977; Kiesler, 1971; McFall & Hammen, 1971). The stabilizing effect of commitment, according to Kiesler's (1971) research, is enhanced by exposure ot a mildly challenging attack, such as counterpropaganda that is easy to refute. A stress inoculation procedure for medical treatments or surgery might serve this function by first calling attention to the obstacles and drawbacks to be expected (which is a challenging attack) and then providing impressive suggestions about how those obstacles and drawbacks can be overcome (which may dampen the challenging attack sufficiently to make it mild).

Along with inducing increased commitment, stress inoculation tends to build up a sense of personal responsibility on the part of the patient. After hearing about the unpleasant consequences to be expected from undergoing a prescribed treatment and about ways of coping with the anticipated stresses, patients realize all the more keenly that they are personally responsible for the decision to undergo the recommended treatment and for doing their share to help carry it out as effectively as possible, rather than simply being passive recipients of whatever it is that the physician decides to do.

Predictions about each source of stress to be expected and accompanying suggestions convey to the patient the theme "This is yet another problem you must solve yourself; no one else can do it for you." My recent research in weight-reduction and antismoking clinics suggests that such messages may foster long-term adherence to difficult regimens because sticking to it requires that the patients develop attributions of personal responsibility, with a corresponding decline in dependency on the counselor (Janis, 1982). My observations are in agreement with those of Davison and Valins (1969), who conclude from their research in a completely different setting that behavior change is more likely to be maintained when people attribute the cause of the change to themselves rather than to an outside agent. A direct implication of this conclusion is that people who seek help in self-regulation will be more likely to adhere in the long run to a new course of action, such as dieting or stopping smoking, if the counselor stresses the client's own role in whatever behavior change occurs (see Brehm, 1976, p. 168; Rodin, 1978).

A theoretical analysis by Janis (1982, Chapter 2) of supportive helping relationships postulates that when people have the intention of changing to a new course of action that requires undergoing short-term deprivation in order to attain long-term objectives, the incentive value of gaining the approval of a professional advisor or counselor can help to get them started. A supportive norm-setting practitioner can build up and use potential motivating power, according to this analysis, if he or she builds up an image of the helper as a quasidependable source of self-esteem enhancement: The persons who seek help come to realize that they will receive spontaneous acceptance, including times when they reveal weaknesses and shortcomings, *except* when they fail to make a sincere effort to live up to a limited set of norms (see Janis, 1982). This expectation of partly contingent acceptance from the helper allows the client to look forward to receiving genuine acceptance and approval much of the time—and perhaps practically all of the time—provided that he or she makes a sincere effort to follow just a few rules recommended by the helper pertaining to only a limited sphere of personal behavior.

A crisis arises, however, when direct contact between the helper and the client is terminated, as is bound to happen when a counselor arranges for a fixed number of sessions to help a client get started on a stressful course of action such as dieting. When the sessions come to an end, even if prearranged by a formal contract, the client will want to continue the relationship, insofar as he or she has become dependent on the counselor for social rewards that bolster self-esteem. The client is likely to regard the counselor's refusal to comply with his or her demand to maintain contact as a sign of rejection or indifference. If this occurs, the client will no longer be motivated to live up to the helper's norms and will show little or no tendency to internalize the norms during the postcontact period.

In order to prevent backsliding and other adverse effects when contact with the helper is terminated, the person must internalize the norms sponsored by the helper by somehow converting *other-directed* approval motivation into *self-directed* approval motivation. Little is known as yet about the determinants of this process, but it seems plausible to expect that internalization might be facilitated by communications themes in stress inoculation procedures that enhance commitment by building up a sense of personal responsibility.

COPING PREDISPOSITIONS

For certain types of persons, as I mentioned earlier, stress inoculation has been found to have no effect and occasionally even adverse effects. The Janis and Mann (1977) theoretical model of coping patterns has some implications for personality differences in responsiveness to stress inoculation. Certain people can be expected to be highly resistant to communications that attempt to induce the conditions that are essential for a coping pattern of vigilant search and appraisal. The difficulty may be that they generally are unresponsive to authentic information that promotes one or another of the three crucial beliefs (that there are serious risks for whichever alternative course of action is chosen, that it is realistic to be optimistically hopeful about finding a satisfactory solution, and that there is adequate time in which to search and deliberate before a decision is required). Such persons would be expected to show consistently defective coping patterns that often would lead to inadequate planning and overreactions to setbacks. In response to acute postdecisional stress, they would be the ones most likely to reverse their decisions about undergoing painful medical treatments.

Elsewhere (Janis, 1982, Chapter 20), I have more fully elaborated these theoretical assumptions and reviewed the research findings on specific personality variables related to responsiveness to stress inoculation. In the discussion that follows I shall highlight the main findings and conclusions.

A number of studies employing Byrne's (1964) repression–sensitization scale and Goldstein's (1959) closely related coper-versus-avoider test suggest that persons diagnosed as chronic repressors or avoiders tend to minimize, deny, or ignore any warning that presents disturbing information about impending threats. Such persons appear to be predisposed to display the characteristic features of defensive avoidance. Unlike persons who are predisposed to be vigilant, these avoiders would not be expected to respond adaptively to preparatory information that provides realistic forecasts about anticipated stressful experiences along with reassurances. Relevant evidence is to be found in the reports on two field experiments conducted on surgery wards by Andrew (1970) and DeLong (1971). In both studies, patients awaiting surgery were given Goldstein's test in order to assess their preferred mode of coping with stress and then were given preparatory information. The reactions of the following three groups were compared: (1) copers, who tended to display vigilance or sensitizing defenses; (2) avoiders, who displayed avoidant or denial defenses; and (3) nonspecific defenders, who showed no clear preference. In Andrew's (1970) study, preparatory information describing what the experience of the operation and the postoperative convalescence would be like had an unfavorable effect on the rate of physical recovery of avoiders but a positive effect on nonspecific defenders. Copers recovered well whether or not they were given the preoperative information. In DeLong's (1971) study, avoiders were found to have the poorest recovery whether or not they were given preparatory information, and copers showed the greatest benefit from the preparatory information. The findings from the two studies show some inconsistencies but they agree in indicating that persons who display defensive avoidance tendencies do not respond well to preparatory information.

Correlational evidence from studies of surgical patients by Cohen and Lazarus (1973) and Cohen (1975) appears to contradict the implications of the studies just discussed bearing on vigilance versus defensive avoidance. These investigators report that patients who were rated as "vigilant" before the operation showed poorer recovery from surgery than those rated as "avoidant." This finding seems not only to contradict the earlier surgery findings but also to go against the expectation from the conflict-theory model that people who are vigilant will cope better with unfavorable consequences of their decisions than will those whose dominant coping pattern is defensive avoidance. But there are two important considerations to take into account. One is that Sime (1976) attempted to replicate Cohen and Lazarus's (1973) finding using the same categories but was unable to do so. When there are disagreements like this, one suspects that either there are unrecognized differences in the way in which the variables were assessed or that the relationship between the two variables is determined by an uninvestigated third variable, such as severity of the patient's illness. A second consideration has to do with the way Cohen and Lazarus define "vigilance." A careful examination of their procedures reveals that they did not differentiate between hypervigilance and vigilance. The investigators state that they classified as vigilant any patient who sought out information about the operation (which hypervigilant people do even more than vigilant ones) or who were sensitized in terms of remembering the information and displaying readiness to discuss their thoughts about the operation. (Again, the hypervigilant people tend to be much more preoccupied with information about threatening consequences than those who are vigilant.) The one example Cohen and Lazarus give of a so-called vigilant reaction would be classified as "hypervigilant" according to the criteria given in Janis and Mann (1977, p. 74 and pp. 205–206): "I have all the facts, my will is all prepared [in the event of death]. . . you're put out, you could put out too deep, your heart could quit, you can have shock. . . I go not in lightly." Consequently, the correlation observed by these investigators might be attributable to the relationship between preoperative *hypervigilance* and low tolerance for postoperative stress, which has been observed by other investigators (Auerbach, 1973; Janis, 1958; Leventhal, 1963). Auerbach (1973), for example, found that surgical patients who showed a high state of preoperative anxiety relative to their normal or average level (as assessed by the State–Trait Anxiety Inventory developed by Spielberger, Gorsuch, & Lushene, 1970) obtained poorer scores on a measure of postoperative adjustment than did those who showed a relatively moderate level of preoperative anxiety.

In Auerbach's study, the postoperative adjustment of the patients who showed moderate preoperative anxiety was found to be superior to that of the patients who showed relatively low anxiety as well as those who showed relatively high anxiety before the operation. In disagreement with contradictory findings reported by Cohen and Lazarus (1973) and by several other investigators, Auerbach's data tend to confirm Janis's (1958) earlier finding of a curvolinear relationship between the level of preoperative anxiety and postoperative adjustment. Such data are consistent with the "work of worrying" concept, which assumes that inducing vigilance in surgical patients (manifested by a moderate level of preoperative fear or anxiety) is beneficial for postoperative adjustment (Janis, 1958; Janis & Mann, 1977). But it is essential to take note of the disagreements in the correlational results obtained from many nonintervention studies in the research literature on the relationship between level of preoperative fear or anxiety and postoperative adjustment, which can be affected by a number of extraneous variables that are difficult to control even when they can be recognized (see Cohen & Lazarus, 1979). It would not be worthwhile, it seems to me, for investigators to carry out more such correlational studies because even a dozen or two of them cannot be expected to settle the issue. I think it is realistic, however, to hope for dependable conclusions about the postoperative effects of arousal of vigilance before surgery—and also about the interacting effects of such arousal with personality characteristics—if a few more well-controlled *intervention* studies are carried out in which preparatory information designed to induce vigilance is used as an independent variable and is not confounded with social support or with any other potentially potent variable.

Complicated findings on another predispositional attribute were obtained by Auerbach, Kendall, Cuttler, and Levitt (1976) in a study of stress inoculation for dental surgery. Using Rotter's (1966) personality measure of locus of control, these investigators found that "internals" (patients who perceive themselves as having control over the outcome of events) responded positively to specific preparatory information about the surgical experiences to be expected, obtaining higher ratings on behavioral adjustment during surgery than those who were not given the preparatory information. In contrast, "externals" (patients who perceive themselves as primarily under the control of external circumstances) obtained lower adjustment ratings when provided with the specific preparatory information. But subsidiary findings show the reverse outcome when the patients were given general preparatory information that was not directly relevant to their surgical experience.

As is so often the case with the correlational data obtained in personality research, the findings can be interpreted in a number of different ways and it is difficult to determine which interpretation is best. For example, since prior research shows that "externals" tend to be more defensive than "internals," the main finding could be viewed as consistent with the hypothesis that persons who are predisposed to adopt a defensive avoidance coping pattern fail to show increased stress tolerance when given preparatory information about the specific stress experiences that are to be expected. An alternative interpretation would be in terms of the importance of perceived control: Maybe only those patients who are capable of perceiving themselves as influencing what happens develop adequate coping responses when given preparatory information about anticipated stressors. In any case, the complex findings from the many studies of personality variables suggest that, in order to increase the percentage of patients who benefit from stress inoculation, it will be necessary to hand-tailor the preparatory information in a way that takes account of each individual's coping style.

When opportunities for stress inoculation are made available, personality factors may play a role in determining who will choose to take advantage of those opportunities and who will not. A study by Lapidus (1969) of pregnant women indicates that when preparatory information about the stresses of childbirth is offered free of charge, passive-submissive women who are most in need of stress inoculation are unlikely to obtain it if it is left up to them to take the initiative. On various indicators of field dependence–independence, cognitive control, and flexibility, the pregnant women who chose to participate in a program that offered psychological preparation for childbirth differed significantly from those who chose not to participate. The participants were more field-independent and displayed stronger tendencies toward active mastery of stress than the non-participants, many of whom showed signs of strong dependency and denial tendencies.

In order to take account of individual differences in coping style and other personality predispositions, it may be necessary in each clinic or hospital to set up a number of different preparation programs rather than just one standard program. The patients would probably have to be screened in advance for their knowledge about the consequences of the treatment they have agreed to undergo as well as for their capacity to assimilate unpleasant information. At present, health-care professionals have to use their best judgment in selecting what they think will be the most effective ingredients of stress inoculation for each individual facing a particular type of stress. Until more analytic research is carried out on responsiveness to each of the major components of stress inoculation, the hand-tailoring of preparatory information and coping recommendations will remain more of an art than a science.

CONCLUSION

The main point emphasized throughout this chapter is that sufficient research has already been done on the effectiveness of stress inoculation to warrant moving to a new stage of attempting to identify the factors that are responsible for the positive effects. Analytic experiments are needed that attempt to determine the crucial variables by testing hypotheses based on theoretical concepts about basic processes. These can be carried out as field experiments in clinics and hospitals where large numbers of patients are awaiting distressing medical treatments or surgery. With regard to the problems of internal validity and replicability of the findings, investigators can use standard methodological safeguards, such as random assignment of patients to conditions, that have evolved in experimental social psychology and personality research during the past three decades. The major goal should be to pin down as specifically as possible the key variables (and their interactions) that are responsible for the positive effects of stress inoculation on increasing tolerance for adverse events, including those losses that disrupt adherence to health-promoting regimens.

The key variables that should be given priority, in my opinion, are the ones suggested by theory and prior research, as discussed in the preceding sections—(1) increasing the predictability of stressful events, (2) fostering coping skills and plans for coping actions, (3) stimulating cognitive coping responses such as positive self-talk and reconceptualization of threats into nonthreatening terms, (4) encouraging attitudes of self-confidence and hope about a successful outcome with related expectations that make for perceived control, and (5) building up commitment and a sense of personal responsibility for adhering to an adaptive course of action.

ACKNOWLEDGMENTS

I wish to express my thanks to Marjorie Janis, Leah Lapidus, Donald Meichenbaum, and Dennis Turk for valuable criticisms and suggestions on revising earlier drafts.

REFERENCES

Andrew, J. M. Recovery from surgery, with and without preparatory instruction, for three coping styles. *Journal of Personality and Social Psychology,* 1970, *15,* 223–226.

Auerbach, S. M. Trait-state anxiety and adjustment to surgery. *Journal of Consulting and Clinical Psychology,* 1976, *44,* 809–818.

Averill, J. R. Personal control over aversive stimuli and its relationship to stress. *Psychological Bulletin,* 1973, *80,* 286–303.

Ball, T. S., & Vogler, R. E. Uncertain pain and the pain of uncertainty. *Perceptual Motor Skills,* 1971, *33,* 1195–1203.

Bandura, A. Self-efficacy: Toward a unified theory of behavioral change. *Psychological Review,* 1977, *89,* 191–215.

Bandura, D., & Simon, K. The role of proximal intentions in self-regulation of refractory behavior. *Cognitive Therapy and Research,* 1977, *1,* 177–193.

Bowers, K. G. Pain, anxiety, and perceived control. *Journal of Consulting and Clinical Psychology,* 1968, *32,* 596–602.

Breen, D. *The birth of a first child: Towards an understanding of femininity.* London: Tavistock, 1975.

Brehm, S. *The application of social psychology to clinical practice.* New York: Wiley, 1976.

Byrne, D. Repression-sensitization as a dimension of personality. In B. A. Maher (Ed.), *Progress in experimental personality research* (Vol. 1). New York: Academic Press, 1964.

Caplan, G., & Killilea, M. (Ed.). *Support systems and mutual help.* New York: Grune & Stratton, 1976.

Chertok, L. *Psychosomatic methods in painless childbirth.* New York: Pergamon Press, 1959.

Chu, C. C. Fear arousal, efficacy, and imminency. *Journal of Personality and Social Psychology,* 1966, *4,* 517–524.

Cohen, F. *Psychological preparation, coping, and recovery from surgery.* Unpublished doctoral dissertation, University of California, Berkeley, 1975.

Cohen, F., & Lazarus, R. S. Active coping processes, coping disposition, and recovery from surgery. *Psychosomatic Medicine,* 1973, *35,* 375–389.

Cohen, F., & Lazarus, R. S. Coping with the stresses of illness. In G. C. Stone, F. Cohen, & N. E. Adler (Eds.), *Health psychology.* San Francisco: Jossey-Bass, 1979.

Cormier, W. H., & Cormier, L. S. *Interviewing strategies for helpers: A guide to assessment, treatment and evaluation.* California: Brooks/Cole Publishing, 1979.

Davenport-Slack, B., & Boylan, C. H. Psychological correlates of childbirth pain. *Psychosomatic Medicine,* 1974, *36,* 215–223.

Davison, G. C., & Valins, S. Maintenance of self-attributed and drug-attributed behavior change. *Journal of Personality and Social Psychology,* 1969, *11,* 25–33.

DeLong, R. D. Individual differences in patterns of anxiety arousal, stress-relevant information, and recovery from surgery. *Dissertation Abstracts International,* 1971, *32*(3), 554.

Dick-Read, G. *Childbirth without fear: The principles and practices of natural childbirth* (2nd ed. rev.). New York: Harper & Row, 1959.

Doering, S. G., & Entwhistle, D. R. Preparation during pregnancy and ability to cope with labor and delivery. *American Journal of Orthopsychiatry, 1975, 45,* 825–837.

Egbert, L., Battit, G., Welch, C., & Bartlett, M. Reduction of post-operative pain by encouragement and instruction. *New England Journal of Medicine,* 1964, *270,* 825–827.

Epstein, S. Toward a unified theory of anxiety. In B. Maher (Ed.), *Progress in experimental personality research* (Vol. 4). New York: Academic Press, 1967.

Epstein, S., & Clark, S. Heart rate and skin conductance during experimentally induced anxiety: Effects of anticipated intensity of noxious stimulation and experience. *Journal of Experimental Psychology,* 1970, *84,* 105–112.

Fremouw, W. J., & Zitter, R. E. A comparison of skills training and cognitive restructuring–relaxation for the treatment of speech anxiety. *Behavior Therapy,* 1978, *9,* 248–259.

Fuller, S. S., Endress, M. P., & Johnson, J. E. *Control and coping with an aversive health examination.* Paper presented at the annual meeting of the American Psychological Association, San Francisco, 1977.

Girodo, M. Self-talk: Mechanisms in anxiety and stress management. In C. D. Spielberger & I. G. Sarason (Eds.), *Stress and anxiety* (Vol. 4). New York: Wiley, 1977.

Glass, C., Gottman, J., & Shmurack, S. Response acquisition and cognitive self-statement modification approaches to dating skill training. *Journal of Counseling Psychology,* 1976, *23,* 520–526.

Goldfried, M. R., Decenteco, E. T., & Weinberg, L. Systematic rational restructuring as a self-control technique. *Behavior Therapy,* 1974, *5,* 247–254.

Goldfried, M. R., Linehan, M. M., & Smith, J. L. The reduction of test anxiety through

rational restructuring. *Journal of Consulting and Clinical Psychology,* 1978, *46,* 32–39.
Goldstein, M. J. The relationship between coping and avoiding behavior and response to fear-arousing propaganda. *Journal of Abnormal and Social Psychology,* 1959, *58,* 247–252.
Holroyd, K. A., Andrasik, F., & Westbrook, T. Cognitive control of tension headache. *Cognitive Therapy and Research,* 1977, *1,* 121–134.
Houston, B. K. Control over stress, locus of control, and response to stress. *Journal of Personality and Social Psychology,* 1972, *21,* 249–255.
Huttel, F. A., Mitchell, I., Fisher, W. M., & Meyer, A. E. A quantitative evaluation of psychoprophylaxis in childbirth. *Journal of Psychomatic Research,* 1972, *16,* 81.
Janis, I. L. Problems related to the control of fear in combat. In S. A. Stouffer (Ed.), *The American soldier* (Vol. 2) *Combat and its aftermath.* Princeton, N.J.: Princeton University Press, 1949.
Janis, I. L. *Air war and emotional stress.* New York: McGraw-Hill, 1951.
Janis, I. *Psychological stress.* New York: Wiley, 1958.
Janis, I. L. *Stress and frustration.* New York: Harcourt, Brace, & Jovanovich, 1971.
Janis, I. L. (Ed.). *Counseling on personal decisions: Theory and research on short-term helping relationships.* New Haven, Conn.: Yale University Press, 1982.
Janis, I. L., & Mann, L. *Decision making: A psychological analysis of conflict, choice, and commitment.* New York: Free Press, 1977.
Janis, I. L., & Rodin, J. Attribution, control and decision-making: Social psychology in health care. In G. C. Stone, F. Cohen, & N. E. Adler (Eds.), *Health psychology.* San Francisco: Jossey-Bass, 1979.
Janis, I. L., Lumsdaine, A. H., & Gladstone, A. I. Effects of preparatory communications on reactions to a subsequent news event. *Public Opinion Quarterly,* 1951, *15,* 488–518.
Javert, C. T., & Hardy, J. D. Influence of analgesia on pain intensity during labor ("with a note on natural childbirth"). *Anesthesiology,* 1951, *12,* 189–215.
Johnson, J. E. The influence of purposeful nurse-patient interaction on the patients' postoperative course. *A. N. A. Monograph series No. 2.: Exporing medical-surgical nursing practice.* New York: American Nurses' Association, 1966.
Johnson, J. E. *Information factors in coping with stressful events.* Paper presented at the eleventh annual convention of the Association for the Advancement of Behavioral Therapy, Atlanta, December 1977.
Johnson, J. E., & Leventhal, H. Effects of accurate expectations and behavioral instructions on reactions during a noxious medical examination. *Journal of Personality and Social Psychology,* 1974, *29,* 710-718.
Johnson, J. E., Morrissey, J. F., & Leventhal, H. Psychological preparation for endoscopic examination. *Gastrointestinal Endoscopy,* 1973, *19,* 180–182.
Johnson, J. E., Rice, V. H., Fuller, S. S., & Endress, P. *Sensory information, behavioral instruction, and recovery from surgery.* Paper presented at the annual meeting of the American Psychological Association, San Francisco, 1977.
Kanfer, F., & Seider, M. L. Self-control: Factors enhancing tolerance of noxious stimulation. *Journal of Personality and Social Psychology,* 1973, *25,* 381–389.
Kendall, P., Williams, L., Pechacek, T. F., Graham, L. E., Shisslak, C., & Herzoff, N. *The Palo Alto medical psychology project: Cognitive-behavioral patient education interventions in catheterization procedures.* Unpublished manuscript, University of Minnesota, 1977.
Kiesler, C. A. (Ed.). *The psychology of commitment.* New York: Academic Press, 1971.
Langer, E., Janis, I., & Wolfer, J. Reduction of psychological stress in surgical patients. *Journal of Experimental Social Psychology,* 1975, *1,* 155–166.

Lapidus, L. B. Cognitive control and reaction to stress: Conditions for mastery in the anticipatory phase. *Proceedings of the 77th Annual Convention of the American Psychological Association,* 1969, *4.*
Lazarus, R. S., & Alfert, E. The short-circuiting of threat by experimentally altering cognitive appraisal. *Journal of Abnormal and Social Psychology,* 1964, *69,* 195–205.
Lemaze, F. *Painless childbirth: Psychoprophylactic method.* London: Burke, 1958.
Leventhal, H. Patient responses to surgical stress in regular surgery and intensive care units. *Progr. Rep. Div. Hosp. Med. Facilities, U. S. Public Health Service,* 1963 (mimeographed).
Leventhal, H. Changing attitudes and habits to reduce chronic risk factors. *American Journal of Cardiology,* 1973, *31,* 571–580.
Leventhal, H., Singer, R. E., & Jones, S. Effects of fear and specificity of recommendations. *Journal of Personality and Social Psychology,* 1965, 2, 20–29.
Levy, J. M., & McGee, R. K. Childbirth as crisis: A test of Janis' theory of communication and stress resolution. *Journal of Personality and Social Psychology,* 1975, *31,* 171–179.
Lindeman, C. A., Nursing intervention with the presugrical patient: The effectiveness and efficiency of group and individual preoperative teaching. *Nursing Research,* 1972, *21,* 196–209.
Lindeman, C. A., & Van Aernam, B. Nursing intervention with the presurgical patient—The effects of structured and unstructured preoperative teaching. *Nursing Research,* 1971, *20,* 319–332.
Matte, I. Observations of the English in wartime. *Journal of Nervous Mental Diseases,* 1943, *97,* 447–463.
McAlister, A. L., Perry, C., & Maccoby, N. Adolescent smoking: Onset and prevention. *Pediatrics,* 1979, *63,* 650–680.
McFall, R. M., & Hammen, L. Motivation, structure, and self-monitoring: Role of nonspecific factors in smoking reduction. *Journal of Consulting and Clinical Psychology,* 1971, *37,* 80–86.
Meichenbaum, D. Cognitive modification of test anxious college students. *Journal of Consulting and Clinical Psychology,* 1972, *39,* 370–380.
Meichenbaum, D. *Cognitive-behavior modification: An integrative approach.* New York: Plenum Press, 1977.
Meichenbaum, D., & Cameron, R. *An examination of cognitive and contingency variables in anxiety relief procedures.* Unpublished manuscript, University of Waterloo, 1973.
Meichenbaum, D., & Jaremko, M. *Stress prevention and management: A cognitive-behavioral approach.* New York: Plenum Press, 1980.
Meichenbaum, D. H., & Turk, D. C. The cognitive-behavioral management of anxiety, anger and pain. In P. O. Davidson (Ed.), *The behavioral management of anxiety, depression and pain.* New York: Brunner/Mazel, 1976.
Meichenbaum, D., & Turk, D. Stress, coping, and disease: A cognitive-behavioral perspective. In R. Neufeld (Ed.), *Psychological stress and psychopathology* . New York: McGraw-Hill, 1982. (a)
Meichenbaum, D., & Turk, D. Stress inoculation: A preventative approach. In R. Neufeld (Ed.), *Psychological stress and psychopathology.* New York: McGraw-Hill, 1982. (b)
Meichenbaum, D., Gilmore, B., & Fedoravicious, A. Group insight vs. group desensitization in treating speech anxiety. *Journal of Consulting and Clinical Psychology,* 1971, *36,* 410–421.
Novaco, R. *Anger control: The development and evaluation of an experimental treatment.* Lexington, Mass.: Health, 1975.
Pervin, L. A. The need to predict and control under conditions of threat. *Journal of Personality,* 1963, *34,* 570–587.

Pranulis, M., Dabbs, J., & Johnson, J. General anesthesia and the patients' attempts at control. *Social Behavior and Personality,* 1975, *3,* 49–51.
Rachman, S. J. *Fear and courage.* San Francisco: W. H. Freeman, 1978.
Riskind, J. The client's sense of personal mastery: Effects of time perspective and self-esteem. In I. L. Janis (Ed.), *Counseling on personal decisions: Theory and research on short-term helping relationships.* New Haven, Conn.: Yale University Press, 1982.
Rodin, J. R. Somatopsychics and attribution. *Personality and Social Bulletin,* 1978, *4,* 531–540.
Rogers, R. W., & Deckner, W. C. Effects of fear appeals and physiological arousal upon emotion, attitudes, and cigarette smoking. *Journal of Personality and Social Psychology,* 1975, *32,* 220–230.
Rogers, R. W., & Mewborn, C. R. Fear appeals and attitude change: Effects of a threat's noxiousness, probability of occurrence, and the efficacy of coping responses. *Journal of Personality and Social Psychology,* 1976, *34,* 54–61.
Rogers, R. W., & Thistlethwaite, D. L. Effects of fear arousal and reassurance upon attitude change. *Journal of Personality and Social Psychology,* 1970, *15,* 227-233.
Romalis, F. The impact of the war on family life. Part I: Reactions to change and crisis. *The Family,* 1994, *22,* 219–224.
Rotter, J. B. Generalized expectancies for internal versus external control of reinforcement. *Psychological Monographs,* 1966, *80*(1), No. 609.
Schmidt, R. L. *An exploratory study of nursing and patient readiness for surgery.* Unpublished master's thesis , School of Nursing, Yale University, 1966.
Schmitt, F. E., & Woolridge, P. J. Psychological preparation of surgical patients. *Nursing Research,* 1973, *22,* 108–116.
Schulz, R., & Hanusa, B. M. Long term effects of control and predictability enhancing interventions: Findings and ethical issues. *Journal of Personality and Social Psychology,* 1978, *36,* 1194–1201.
Sime, A. M. Relationship of preoperative fear, type of coping, and information received about surgery to recovery from surgery. *Journal of Personality and Social Psychology,* 1976, *34,* 716–724.
Spielberger, C. D., Gorsuch, R. L., & Lushene, R. E. *Manual for the state-trait anxiety inventory.* Palo Alto, Calif.: Consulting Psychologist Press, 1970.
Staub, E., & Kellett, D. Increasing pain tolerance by information about aversive stimuli. *Journal of Personality and Social Psychology,* 1972, *21,* 198–203.
Staub, E., Tursky, B., & Schwartz, G. E. Self-control and predictability: Their effects on reactions to aversive stimulation. *Journal of Personality and Social Psychology,* 1971, *18,* 157–162.
Tanzer, D. Natural childbirth: Pain or peak experience. *Psychology Today,* 1968, *2,* 17–21.
Taylor, F. G., & Marshall, W. L. Experimental analysis of a cognitive-behavioral therapy for depression. *Cognitive Therapy and Research,* 1977, *1,* 59–72.
Turk, D. C. *Cognitive control of pain: A skills-training approach.* Unpublished master's thesis, University of Waterloo, 1977.
Turk, D. Cognitive behavioral techniques in the management of pain. In J. P. Foreyt & D. J. Rathgen (Eds.), *Cognitive behavior therapy: Research and application.* New York: Plenum Press, 1978.
Turk, D. C., & Genest, M. Regulation of pain: The application of cognitive and behavioral techniques for prevention and remediation. In P. Kendall & S. Hollon (Eds.), *Cognitive-behavioral interventions: Theory, research, and practices.* New York: Academic Press, 1979.
Tversky, A., & Kahneman, D. Availability: A heuristic for judging frequency and probability. *Cognitive Psychology,* 1973, *5,* 207–232.

Tversky, A., & Kahneman, D. Judgment under uncertainty: Heuristics and biases. *Science,* 1974, *185,* 1124–1131.

Vernon, D. T. A., & Bigelow, D. A. The effect of information about a potentially stressful situation on responses to stress impact. *Journal of Personality and Social Psychology,* 1974, *29,* 50–59.

Weiss, J. M. Somatic effects of predictable and unpredictable shock. *Psychosomatic Medicine,* 1970, *32,* 397–409.

Wolfenstein, M. *Disaster.* New York: Free Press, 1957.

Wolfer, J. A., & Visintainer, M. A. Pediatric surgical patients' and parents' stress responses and adjustment as a function of psychologic preparation and stress-point nursing care. *Nursing Research,* 1975, *24,* 244–255.

Zimbardo, P. G. The human choice. In W. Arnold & D. Levine (Eds.), *Nebraska Symposium on Motivation* (Vol. 17). Lincoln: University of Nebraska Press, 1970.

Concluding Comments to Section I

Our own observations as well as the discussions in this section suggest that the field of stress and coping is moving toward a *transactional* model of stress as described by Richard Lazarus and his colleagues (Lazarus, 1981; Lazarus & Cohen, 1977; Lazarus & Launier, 1978; Roskies & Lazarus, 1980) and by John Mason (1975). This transactional perspective suggests that stress occurs in the face of "*demands that tax or exceed the resources of the system* or . . . demands to which there are no readily available or automatic adaptive resources" (Lazarus & Cohen, 1977, p. 109; emphasis in original). The transactional model highlights the nature of the fit or misfit between the person's adaptive capacities and the environmental demands. The discrepancy between the perceived demands on a person (whether internal or external, whether challenges or goals) and the way individuals perceive their potential responses to these demands constitutes stress and has an impact on the individual's health.

According to the transactional model, stress resides neither in the situation nor in the person. Instead, stress depends on the transaction of the individual in the situation. The individual plays a critical role in defining how stressful a set of events will be. The individual's perception both of the stressfulness of the event and of his or her ability to cope with events ultimately defines the stress. Thus, according to the transactional model, any attempt to avoid or reduce stress should be directed toward (a) changing the situation by means of direct-action techniques and (b) changing the individual's appraisal processes and his or her ability to cope by cognitive coping and palliative coping procedures (Lazarus, 1981). The model thus emphasizes a complex interplay between the individual and the situation that determines the onset, magnitude, duration, and quality of the stressful episode.

As Lazarus and Launier (1978) indicate, an adequate coping response in some instances may involve direct action to change the situation for the better, to escape from an intolerable situation, or to relinquish certain goals. Direct action may take several forms, such as preparing for a stressor, collecting information and engaging problem-solving, actually avoiding or escaping the stressor, or asserting oneself and trying to change the environment directly or trying to influence significant others in the environment. Such direct actions may prove particularly helpful in situations where one can anticipate the stressor and possibly act to prevent or lessen harm.

In other instances, in which stress cannot be altered or avoided, one may use what Lazarus and Launier call palliative modes of coping, (i.e., ways of responding that make us feel better in the face of threat and harm without resolving the problem). In situations where little or nothing can be done, various techniques may be used to regulate emotional distress. Thus, in some situations, successful coping will *not* always involve active mastery over one's environment. As Lazarus notes, stress prevention and reduction programs must recognize that in some situations retreat, toleration, and disengagement may be the most adaptive responses. In our discussion of stress inoculation training in Chapter 4, we will consider further the direct-action and palliative coping procedures. As described in Chapter 4, there is an affinity between the transactional model of stress and the stress inoculation approach (Cameron & Meichenbaum, 1982; Roskies & Lazarus, 1980). The stress inoculation treatment procedures are designed to facilitate adaptive appraisals, to enhance the repertoire of coping responses, and to nurture the client's confidence in his or her coping capabilities.

Given these brief comments on the transactional model of stress, we can propose several factors or guidelines that should be considered in setting up any stress prevention or treatment program.

1. There is a need to appreciate that coping is neither a single act nor a static process. As Lazarus (1981) notes, *coping is a constellation of many acts* that stretch over time and undergo changes. What may be a useful coping procedure at one time may not be as useful at another time. Similarly, one needs to appreciate that *stress is usually multiply determined and has multiple and often long-term effects.* Silver and Wortman (1980), remind us that in some cases, individuals who have experienced serious life stress events (e.g., death of a child, rape, and so forth) do not recover but instead continue to experience stress.

2. Any training program must be sensitive to the role *individual differences* play in defining what will be appraised as stressful and what is the most adaptive coping response. This point is further underscored by

the conclusions offered by Silver and Wortman, who indicate that there is little evidence that people go through predictable and orderly sets of reactions following a life crisis. Various proposed sequences of how people cope with stress are usually based on subjective interviews with small samples of patients. In most of these reports, there is little detail offered about how the proposed pattern or sequence of reactions was determined. Stress training programs that are based on such hypothetical sequences of coping responses should be viewed with a good deal of caution.

3. Any training program must be sensitive to the important role that *cultural differences* play in defining what will be appraised as stressful and what the nature of the coping process is. In many non-Western cultures, people adopt a fatalistic belief that can serve as a coping function. In some non-Western cultures, people tend to deal with the stresses of life passively by trying to endure them (e.g., see Marsella, Tharp, & Ciborowski, 1979). This may be in a sharp contrast to those in Western societies, who usually look upon stress as a challenge, as a problem-to-be-solved, and who attempt actively to modify the environment in some fashion. Training programs must be sensitive to such cultural differences.

4. Stress prevention and training programs should *foster flexibility* in a client's coping repertoire. One should guard against providing clients with a single or simple formula or a cook-book approach for coping with stress. The individual's ability to tailor his or her particular coping response to situational demands seems critical. An emphasis on the importance of flexibility is consistent with the findings of a number of investigators who have studied coping processes (Mechanic, 1962; Meichenbaum, 1982; Pearlin & Schooler, 1978; Silver & Wortman, 1980; Rachman, 1978). A flexible repertoire seems to be the best resistance to stress. Any training program should attempt to build in such flexibility rather than focusing on a limited set of coping responses (relaxation, problem-solving, etc.).

The stress training program should be *individually tailored* to the individual's or group's needs. As we shall consider in the next section, one way to accomplish such individual tailoring is to *enlist the client as a collaborator,* a someone who adopts a "personal scientist" orientation or engages in what Beck, Rush, Shaw, and Emery (1979) call "collaborative empiricism." In this way the client is actively involved in the development, implementation, and assessment of the usefulness of coping procedures. Clients can be encouraged and guided to perform "personal experiments" in order to determine the adaptive value of specific coping procedures. But how clients view the outcomes of such attempts, what they say to themselves, or how they appraise such efforts will play an important role in influencing the stress reaction. These appraisal processes will be considered as the next important factor to be included in any training program.

5. How we feel and think about events—*how we appraise stressors and our ability to handle them*—will influence our level of stress. Our attitudes toward the stressor, our prior experience with it, our knowledge of its possible effects, and our evaluation of the costs and benefits of our actions will each influence our stress reactions. When a stressor is familiar, when it occurs at a definite time and place, and when we have a sense that we can handle it, then our reactions will be less intense and less debilitating. Insofar as we can prepare for the stressor by means of mental rehearsal or by means of the constructive "work of worrying;" insofar as we can view the stressor as a problem-to-be-solved or a challenge rather than as a personal threat or interpersonal provocation, the stressor will prove manageable. Preparatory communication can often stimulate such constructive "work of worrying," problem-solving, and contingency planning.

6. While the focus on appraisal processes has been primarily on the individual, the coping literature (e.g., see Heller, 1979) has indicated that the nature (number and quality) of the social contacts or *social supports can often act as a buffer to stress.* This literature, as reviewed by Cassel (1976), Cobb (1979), and others indicates that persons with established support network (e.g., close relationships with others) are in better mental and physical health and cope better with stress than those individuals who are unsupported. Individuals who live alone and who are not involved with people or organizations have a heightened vulnerability to a variety of chronic diseases. The availability of such supports may provide individuals with opportunities to express their feelings, find meaning in crises with others, receive material aid, provide information, develop realistic goals, and receive feedback. As Rachman (1978) has noted, people manifest less fear and stress and greater courage in the presence of others than when they are alone. Thus, any training program should assess the nature and quality of the individual's social support system and moreover, should ensure that the individual has the interpersonal skills to nurture and use others in a supportive manner.

In some instances, in order to avoid and reduce stress, the trainer may focus his or her efforts directly on the group or family and not focus on the individual client *per se.* In other cases, the trainer can work on both the individual and group levels simultaneously. As described in Section III, several authors (e.g., Ayalon, Novaco *et al.,* and others) describe the ways in which the spouse, the group, and the community can be employed to act as buffers to stress. In short, in order to avoid and reduce stress *one can intervene at various levels from the individual to the societal level.* Such an observation is consistent with a transactional model of stress.

Parenthetically, it is worth noting that even in the case of social support systems, the influence of individual differences comes into play. There are many instances where the individual may choose *not* to join a group or seek help from significant others. For example, Turk, Meichenbaum, and Genest (1983) report on surgery patients who chose *not* to join patient self-help groups because they felt that they did not wish to be affiliated or identified with such groups. Joining such groups or developing such social supports was viewed a stress-engendering.

Once again the trainer must be sensitive to such individual preferences and should not prejudge such resistance as a maladaptive means of coping; rather, one must individually tailor all interventions. As long as the client is viewed as a collaborator, the trainer and client can collect data to determine what is the most meaningful and effective way to cope with stress.

7. Consistent with a concern about collecting data, the last factor to be considered in setting up stress training programs is the need for including *gradual exposure to more threatening stressful events.* If one looks on the ability to cope with stress as a set of complex intra- and interpersonal skills, then gradual exposure to stressful events can provide individuals with feedback that will bolster their self-confidence. The trainer should keep in mind that there is a need to pace the mastery of stress in order to help individuals cope with limited amounts of stress in a given time. Gradual exposure to small amounts of stress before entering a high-pressure situation can boost the individuals' defenses against stress. Graded assignments can be conducted both in the clinic and in the client's natural environment. Since some of these efforts at coping with increasingly demanding stressful situations will inevitably lead to failures, a major focus in any training program should be on the processes of relapse prevention and treatment generalization (both considered in the next section).

In conclusion, the research on stress and coping has suggested several general guidelines or factors that should be considered in any stress prevention and management program. The next section of the book is designed to describe how these factors can be translated into a general training program. Section III illustrates the ways in which these factors can be employed with specific populations.

REFERENCES

Beck, A., Rush, J., Shaw, B., & Emery, G. *Cognitive therapy of depression.* New York: Guilford Press, 1979.

Cameron, R., & Meichenbaum, D. A cognitive-behavioral model of effective coping processes and the treatment of stress related problems. In L. Goldberger & S. Breznitz (Eds.), *Handbook of stress.* New York: Free Press, 1982.

Cassel, J. The contribution of the social environment to host resistance. *American Journal of Epidemiology,* 1976, *104,* 107–123.

Cobb, S. Social support and health through the life course. In M. Riley (Ed.), *Aging from birth to death: Interdisciplinary perspectives.* Boulder, Colo.: Westview Press, 1979.

Heller, K. The effects of social support: Prevention and treatment implications. In A. Goldstein & F. Kanfer (Eds)., *Maximizing treatment gains.* New York: Academic Press, 1979.

Lazarus, R. The stress and coping paradigm. In C. Eisdorfer (Ed.), *Models for clinical psychopathology.* New York: Spectrum Publications, 1981.

Lazarus, R.S., & Cohen, J. Environmental stress. In I. Altman & J. Wohlwill (Eds.), *Human behavior and the environment.* New York: Plenum Press, 1977.

Lazarus, R. S., & Launier, R. Stress-related transactions between person and environment. In L. Pervin & M. Lewis (Eds.), *Perspectives in interactional psychology.* New York: Plenum Press, 1978.

Marsella, A., Tharp, R., & Ciborowski, T. *Perspectives on cross-cultural psychology.* New York: Academic Press, 1979.

Mason, J. An historical view of the stress field. *Journal of Human Stress,* 1975, *1,* 6–12.

Mechanic, D. *Students under stress.* New York: Free Press, 1962.

Meichenbaum, D. *Coping with stress.* London: Lifestyle Publications, 1982.

Pearlin, L., & Schooler, C. The structure of coping. *Journal of Health and Social Behavior,* 1978, *19,* 2–21.

Rachman, S. *Fear and courage.* San Francisco: W.H. Freeman, 1978.

Roskies, E., & Lazarus, R. Coping theory and the teaching of coping skills. In P. Davidson (Ed.), *Behavioral medicine: Changing health life styles.* New York: Brunner/Mazel, 1980.

Silver, R., & Wortman, C. Coping with undesirable life events. In J. Garber & M. Seligman (Eds.), *Human helplessness: Theory and applications.* New York: Academic Press, 1980.

Turk, D., Meichenbaum, D., & Genest, M. *Pain and behavioral medicine.* New York: Guilford Press, 1983.

II
Guidelines for Training

There are three purposes for this section of the book. First, it is designed to provide a transition from Section I, which reviewed the literature on stress and coping, to Section III, which provides descriptions of specific clinical applications. Second, this section provides a description and clinical guide for the cognitive-behavioral treatment procedure of stress inoculation training. Before considering the specifics of stress inoculation training, however, it is useful first to briefly discuss several procedural guidelines that should be considered in the formulation of a training program. It is this third objective, namely, deciding what should go into stress training programs, that is the focus of our attention in this brief overview.

It is worthwhile to put the comments to be offered about procedural guidelines in some perspective. For a number of years, the senior author has been involved in developing and evaluating various training programs for children, adolescents, and adults (see Meichenbaum, 1977). This experience, as well as content analyses of other training programs, has suggested various guidelines that should be included in any training program in order to increase the likelihood of generalization and durability of treatment effects.

Table I lists procedural guidelines that should be considered in setting up any training program, or conversely, they represent a consumer's guide for evaluating training programs. These guidelines are consistent with advice offered by others who have also been concerned with issues involved in training (Borkowski & Cavanaugh, 1978; Brown & Campione, 1978; Meichenbaum, 1980; Nickerson, Perkins, & Smith, 1980; Stokes & Baer, 1977). Although most of these authors have commented on what is needed to achieve generalizable and durable training effects with children, the issues they raise are equally applicable to setting up stress prevention and management programs with other populations.

Table I. Guidelines to Consider in Developing a Training Program

1. *Analyze* target behaviors. Conduct both a performance and situation analysis. Identify component processes and capacity requirements to perform target behaviors.
2. *Assess* for client's existing strategies, behavioral competencies, and affect-laden thoughts, images, and feelings that may inhibit performance.
3. *Collaborate.* Have client collaborate in the analysis of the problem and in the development, implementation, and evaluation of the training package.
4. *Select* training tasks carefully. Make training tasks similar to the criterion.
5. *Training.* Insure that the component skills needed to perform in the criterion situation are in the client's repertoire and then teach metacognitive or executive planning skills.
6. *Feedback.* Insure that the client receives and recognizes feedback about the usefulness of the training procedures.
7. *Generalize.* Make the need and means for generalizing explicit. Don't expect generalization—train for it.
8. *Multiple trials.* When possible, train in multiple settings with multiple tasks. Have clients engage in multiple graded assignments in clinic and *in vivo.*
9. *Relapse prevention.* Anticipate and incorporate possible and real failures into the training program.
10. *Termination.* Make the termination of training performance-based, not time-based. Include follow-through booster sessions and follow-up assessments.

Their wisdom is incorporated in Table I. We shall briefly consider most of these guidelines and then, in the next chapter, we shall see how these guidelines are incorporated into the stress inoculation training approach.

1. *Analyze target behaviors.* The senior author has worked with impulsive children for a number of years and he has often wondered what happens to these children when they grow up. One tongue-in-cheek answer that he has offered is that many of them became mental health workers and researchers (obviously the present reader is excluded). By this observation it is noted that the field of stress management is often marked by "impulsivity," that is, we tend to intervene before we understand the nature of the problem we are trying to treat.

The first guideline to be considered in setting up stress prevention and management programs is the necessity to identify the population and to conduct performance and situational analyses in order to ascertain exactly what coping skills are in fact needed. While a detailed presentation of the behavior-analytic approach needed to conduct such an analysis is beyond the scope of this book some illustrations can be offered (see discussions by Dewe, Guest, & Williams, 1979, Goldfried & D'Zurilla, 1969, Pearlin & Schooler, 1978, and Turk, Sobel, Fallick, & Youkilis, 1980; Turk, Meichenbaum, & Genest, 1983).

The behavior-analytic approach entails three stages: problem identification, response enumeration, and response evaluation. The first stage of analysis calls for a systematic assessment of the range of problems that confront the targeted group. A number of techniques (questionnaires, interviews, diaries, role-playing, and so forth) can be used with the targeted group, significant others, and health-care providers to compile a comprehensive listing of the variety of stressful problems. For example, Gordon, Feudenberg, Diller, Rothman, Wolf, Ruckdeschel-Hibbard, Ezrachi, and Gerstmann (1980) surveyed 135 cancer patients and identified 122 medical and psychosocial problems covering 13 areas of life functioning (e.g., physical discomfort, medical treatment, vocation, finances, etc.). This list of problems was presented to a new group of cancer patients, who were asked to indicate the perceived severity of each of the problems listed. Gordon *et al.* employed this data to identify major problematic areas for individuals and to pinpoint specific problems. Follick and Turk (1978) used a similar approach to help individuals cope with the stress of undergoing surgery. Follick and Turk emphasize the importance of including significant others and health-care providers—not just patients—in order to generate a more comprehensive list of possible stressors and to identify possible discrepancies between patients' perceptions of problems and perceptions of those involved in their care. Dewe *et al.* (1979) have used a similar problem–identification approach to identify the nature of stress and possible coping mechanisms experienced by middle managers in a transport industry.

The second step to be undertaken before establishing a training program is to identify the range of responses that can be employed to cope with the problems, stressors, and demands cataloged during the initial problem–identification stage. The trainer needs to enumerate both overt and covert, intra- and interpersonal coping responses, as well as any possible organizational changes that may be considered. In the development of stress prevention and management programs, the focus should be not only at the level of the individual, but also at the level of the group or organization.

The final stage of analysis is to determine the relative efficacy of different coping responses in managing stress. The complexities of this task are underscored by Silver and Wortman (1980), who indicated that the potential usefulness of a particular coping respones in reducing stress will be influenced, in part, by which outcome measures one considers and at what point such assessments are conducted. For example, the various indicators of coping, such as vocational adjustment, positive mood, social functioning, and biochemical indicators of stress, often do *not* correlate very strongly. Thus, one should be cautious about identifying an individual as a "good coper" without first qualifying this judgment with statements about which measure of coping was used at a particular time.

What may work in the short run may not be as beneficial in the long run. In each case, different types of coping responses may differentially correlate with different outcome measures.

The knowledge that the relationship among stress, coping, and outcome measures is complex is not new. This knowledge, however, should provide a cautionary reminder to those who set up stress prevention and mangement programs and to those who write prescriptive antistress books. There is a need to make clients and readers aware of the complexity of the processes involved and to enlist them in a collaborative process (see Meichenbaum, 1982).

The assessment strategy that includes problem identification and response enumeration and evaluation should allow a better understanding of problems and coping strategies. This procedure can also be used to develop screening instruments to identify "high-risk" individuals in need of intervention and to pinpoint the content and direction such interventions may take. The behavior-analytic assessment approach should be useful in evaluating the relative efficacy of training programs as well.

Thus, prior to the implementation of a training program, it is necessary to identify the problems posed by the demands of the situation, the range of response options, and the relative efficacy of coping strategies and resources. In other words, just because one stress training program taught a group how to relax (e.g., by means of tensing and relaxing muscle groups), the trainer of another program using a different population should *not* mindlessly incorporate the relaxation with his or her population. It is possible that such relaxation exercises under certain conditions and for certain individuals may exacerbate stress or prove irrelevant to the demands of the situation (as noted in the next chapter). Instead, each trainer must ascertain for his or her population what set of coping responses is most useful. We should be cautious about the supposed transportability of so-called packages of coping techniques.

Finally, it is critical for the trainer to maintain some perspective, keeping in mind that the assessment or behavior analysis should be conducted not only with those who are seeking help or who have failed to cope adequately, but also with those resilient individuals who have adapted and coped adequately with stressful events. The inclusion of such nonclinical populations in the analysis of coping skills should enhance the efficacy of our training programs.

2. *Assess for existing competencies and inhibiting processes.* Closely associated with the first guideline of analyzing target behaviors is the need for the trainer to assess the client's existing coping repertoire in order to determine whether the client has the knowledge and abilities to implement his or her already existing coping skills. Trainers should ascertain if such skills already exist in the client's repertoire or whether

specific affect-laden thoughts (e.g., negative expectations about outcomes, catastrophizing thoughts, etc.) interfere with the implementation of such skills. Moreover, as noted in the discussion of stress inoculation training, it is also necessary to assess the client's attitude about the use of any specific coping response. Negative attitudes may interfere with the acquisition or implementation of specific coping skills.

3. *Collaborate.* A careful assessment conveys to the client the need to establish a collaborative working relationship. The training program should be set up so that the client collaborates in the analysis of the problem and in the development and implementation of the training regimen. Such a collaborative approach reduces the likelihood of client resistence and treatment nonadherence, as discussed in the next chapter.

4. *Selection of training tasks.* The selection of training tasks is critical in bridging the gap between training and the criterion situations. The training should be focused on both component skills (e.g., communication skills, relaxation) and on more executive cognitive skills that apply across stressful situations (e.g., self-interrogation, self-checking, analyzing tasks, breaking problems into manageable steps, and so forth). The training of such *metacognitive* skills will encourage the client to become a better problem-solver when confronting future stressors. Training should *not* be limited to the acquisition and consolidation of specific coping skills, but should also focus on insuring that the client knows when, where, and how to implement his or her coping skills. Training should attend to what clients say or fail to say to themselves about the use of their coping skills.

5. *Feedback.* There is a need to insure that the client receives and attends to the feedback about the natural consequences of his or her efforts at coping. If such efforts at coping are viewed as "personal experiments," then the consequences (e.g., whether the experiments worked or not, how the client felt about the attempt, and so forth) can be viewed as data to improve on. The trainer must insure that the client appreciates that the use of the coping procedure does indeed make a difference.

6. *Generalize.* It is important to appreciate that the training will *not* generalize unless the trainer has built into the regimen explicit efforts at fostering such generalization. It is as if people are "welded" in the use of specific coping skills and do *not* seem readily to apply coping techniques across situations or over time. By discussing with the client exactly how to apply the coping procedures across situations, and by using various imagery and role-playing techniques (as described in the next chapter), one can increase the likelihood of generalization.

7. *Multiple trials.* One means of increasing the chances of achieving generalization and durability of training effects is to expand the training across trainers and settings and over time. But such efforts will most

likely lead to some failures. The trainer should anticipate and incorporate such failures into the training program by employing *relapse prevention* techniques, as described by Marlatt and Gordon (1980). These procedures focus on having the client identify high-risk situations in which he or she may fail and in preparing clients for such possible failures by working on specific coping skills.

8. *Termination*. Finally, consistent with the general theme of individually tailored training programs, there is a need to base the length of training on the client's performance and not on the mere passage of time or on an arbitrarily fixed number of training sessions. One should also build follow-up assessments and booster sessions into training if feasible.

In short, the trainer of any stress prevention and treatment program should ask himself or herself a number of questions before undertaking the training program. These questions include

(a) Have I identified what needs to be trained? How do I know that this is what we should be working on?
(b) Does the client have coping skills within his or her repertoire? Are there processes that are interfering with the use of such skills?
(c) Have I enlisted the client as a collaborator in the analysis, development, implementation, and evaluation of the training regimen?
(d) Why were these particular training tasks and coping skills selected and how will the mastery of these skills help the client in the criterion situations?
(e) What has been done to insure generalization of training effects across situations and over time? Have I arranged for the client to engage in multiple trials or "personal experiments"? Have I reviewed the outcomes with the client in order to make feedback explicit?
(f) What have I done to anticipate and incorporate the client's possible failures? How can I reduce the likelihood of the client's "catastrophizing" and help him or her begin to view stressful events as problems-to-be-solved?
(g) Have I established performance-based criteria for determining the length of training? What have I done to insure follow-up assessment and arrange for booster sessions if necessary?

It is suggested that having trainers attend to such questions or procedural guidelines will increase the efficacy of training programs. The next chapter on stress inoculation training, by Don Meichenbaum and Roy Cameron, is designed to illustrate how these procedural guidelines as well as the observations offered at the end of Section I can be combined and translated into a clinically sensitive training regimen.

REFERENCES

Borkowski, J., & Cavanaugh, J. Maintenance and generalization of skills and strategies by the retarded. In N. Ellis (Ed.), *Handbook of mental deficiency: Psychological theory and research.* Hillsdale, N.J.: Lawrence Erlbaum, 1978.

Brown, A., & Campione, J. Permissible inference from the outcome of training studies in cognitive development research. *Quarterly Newsletter of the Institute for Comparative Human Development,* 1978, *2*, 46–53.

Dewe, P., Guest, D., & Williams, R. Methods of coping with work-related stress. In C. Mackey & T. Cox (Eds.), *Response to stress: Occupational aspects.* Guilford, England: IPC Science and Technology Press, 1979.

Follick, M., & Turk, D. *Problem specificaion by ostomy patients.* Paper presented at the 12th Annual Meeting of the Association for the Advancement of Behavior Therapy, Chicago, 1978.

Goldfried, M., & D'Zurilla, T. A behavior-analytic model for assessment competence. In C. Spielberger (Ed.), *Current topics in clinical and community psychology.* New York: Academic Press, 1969.

Gordon, W., Feudenberg, I., Diller, L., Rothman, L., Wolf, C., Ruckdeschel-Hibbard, M., Ezrachi, O., & Gerstmann, L. The psychosocial problems of cancer patients. *Journal of Consulting and Clinical Psychology,* 1980, *48,* 743–759.

Meichenbaum, D. *Cognitive-behavior modification: An integrated approach.* New York: Plenum Press, 1977.

Meichenbaum, D. *Teaching thinking: A cognitive-behavioral perspective.* Paper presented at the Conference of Thinking and Learning Skills, Pittsburgh, Pa., 1980.

Meichenbaum, D. *Coping with stress.* London: Lifecycle Publications, 1982.

Nickerson, R., Perkins, D., & Smith, E. *Teaching thinking.* Unpublished manuscript, Harvard University, 1980.

Pearlin, L., & Schooler, C. The structure of coping. *Journal of Health and Social Behavior,* 1978, *9,* 2–21.

Silver, R., & Wortman, C. Coping with undesirable life events. In J. Garber & M. Seligman (Eds.), *Human helplessness.* New York: Academic Press, 1980.

Stokes, T., & Baer, D. An implicit technology of generalization. *Journal of Applied Behavior Analysis,* 1977, *10,* 349–367.

Turk, D., Sobel, H., Follick, M., & Youkilis, H. A sequential criterion analysis for assessing coping with chronic illness. *Journal of Human Stress,* 1980, *6,* 35–40.

Turk, D., Meichenbaum, D., & Genest, M. *Pain and behavioral medicine.* New York: Guilford Press, 1983.

4

Stress Inoculation Training

Toward a General Paradigm for Training Coping Skills

DONALD MEICHENBAUM and ROY CAMERON

Stress inoculation training originally referred to a relatively specific set of operations (Meichenbaum & Cameron, 1972). In order to evaluate the efficacy of a skills training approach to anxiety management, a study was conducted using phobia as a target problem. Treatment involved three phases. It began with an *educational phase* that clarified the cognitive, affective, and physiological concomitants of the client's avoidant behavior. The Schachter (1966) model of emotion was presented to the client, who was encouraged to view anxiety as a reaction involving negative self-statements and images and physiological arousal. It was suggested that acquisition of two skills, namely, coping self-statements and self-directed relaxation, would help ameliorate the problem. This initial phase was followed by a *skills training phase*: specific types of coping self-statements and relaxation skills were learned and rehearsed. Finally, during an *application phase,* the client actually tested out the skills in a stressful laboratory situation (unpredictable electric shock was administered). This treatment was found to be more effective than imaginal systematic desensitization, then the standard treatment for phobia.

The general stress inoculation paradigm (i.e., the educational–skills-training–application phase sequence) was soon applied to other prob-

DONALD MEICHENBAUM • Department of Psychology, University of Waterloo, Waterloo, Ontario, Canada N2L 3G1. ROY CAMERON • Department of Psychology, University of Saskatchewan, Saskatoon, Saskatchewan, Canada 57N 0X0.

lems, in both laboratory and clinical setting. However, the specific operations conducted during the course of treatment varied depending on the population treated. That is, the content of the educational phase, the specific skills trained, and the nature of the skills application phase were geared to the target problem. Thus, stress inoculation training became a generic term referring to a general treatment paradigm but not denoting a specific set of operations.

There is striking diversity among treatments that have been conducted within the general stress inoculation paradigm. A wide variety of problems have been treated. They include phobias, other anxiety-related problems, pain, anger, rape trauma, and alcohol abuse. Treatment has been as brief as one hour in the case of acute, situationally specific problems (patients preparing for aversive medical procedures) and as long as 40 treatments sessions for chronic problems (e.g., back pain). Training has been undertaken not only to provide remedial treatment but also in a prophylactic way, with police officers, military recruits, and patients scheduled for stressful medical procedures. Trainers have included a wide range of professionals (e.g., psychiatrists, psychologists, nurses, social workers, and probation oficers) and lay peers of trainees (e.g., policemen and military servicemen). Treatment has been carried out with individuals, couples, and groups, and it is beginning to be applied to larger populations on a "community" basis. Many widely used cognitive behavioral treatment procedures have been incorporated into these programs. The various applications of the stress inoculation paradigm are described in subsequent chapters in this volume and elsewhere (Meichenbaum, 1977; Turk, Meichenbaum, & Genest, 1983).

As the preceding perspective suggests, stress inoculation training is best viewed as an attempt to develop a *framework* for integrating familiar (or innovative) assessment and treatment procedures. The therapist is seen not as a technician who carries out a prescribed, routinized set of operations (although highly structured procedures may be included in the treatment), but rather as a creative problem-solver who is faced with the challenge of developing interventions specifically tailored to the requirements of individual clients.

The purpose of the present chapter is to provide an updated overview of the approach. The discussion will be organized around the three phases of therapy, which we will refer to as the (a) conceptualization, (b) skills acquisition and rehearsal, and (c) application and follow-through phases. Readers interested in detailed information about specific applications should read the recent extended discussion by Turk *et al.* (1983).

Before we consider issues related to the three phases of therapy, we would like to set the stage in two ways. First, we present a brief theoretical perspective. Second, we comment on some general considerations not specific to any of the three core phases of treatment.

Brief Theoretical Perspective

A transactional view of stress appears to be emerging as a broad, integrative framework among stress researchers (Cameron & Meichenbaum, 1982). The transactional model has been developed largely by Richard Lazarus and his colleagues (e.g., Lazarus, 1955; Lazarus & Launier, 1978; Lazarus, Cohen, Folkman, Kanner, & Schaefer, 1980). As noted previously, the transactional perspective suggests that stress occurs in the face of "*demands that tax or exceed the resources of the system* or . . . demands to which there are no readily available or automatic adaptive responses" (Lazarus & Cohen, 1977, p. 109; emphasis in original).

The concepts of *cognitive appraisal* and *coping responses* lie at the heart of the transactional model. A stressful transaction originates with a primary appraisal that a situation demands an effective response to avoid or reduce physical or psychological harm, and a secondary appraisal that no adequate response is available. The person then either attempts a response or fails to respond. The response (or its absence) has environmental repercussions and alters the situation. There is, then, an ongoing series of appraisals, responses, and situational transformations. The transactional sequences ceases to be stressful when the person judges the danger to have passed, either spontaneously or because an effective coping response has neutralized the threat. The model thus emphasizes a complex interplay between the individual and the situation that determines onset, magnitude, duration, and quality of the stressful episode.

There is an affinity between the transactional model of stress and stress inoculation approach (Cameron & Meichenbaum, 1982; Roskies & Lazarus, 1980). The treatment procedures are designed to facilitate adaptive appraisals (conceptualization phase), to enhance the repertoire of coping responses (skills acquisition and rehearsal phase), and to nurture the client's confidence in and utilization of his or her coping capabilities (application and follow-through phase).

It is worth highlighting the fact that the transactional model of stress postulates that people both influence and respond to their environments. Bandura (1977b) has discussed this bidirectional influence process in some detail and coined the term "reciprocal determinism" as a convenient label for it. The concept of reciprocal determinism is central to stress inoculation training. There is a recognition that situational deter-

stress inoculation training. There is a recognition that situational determinants of problems are important and are not to be underestimated. Considerable therapeutic benefit may be derived from restructuring situations and training clients to recognize this for themselves. At the same time, it is postulated that trained coping responses are likely to have an impact on the environment.

The goal of treatment is to bring about change in three domains. First, there is a focus on altering the *behavior* of clients. Maladaptive behaviors are identified and altered, and adaptive behaviors are fostered. It is anticipated that such behavior change will alter transactions with the environment and trigger a therapeutic ripple effect (i.e., have beneficial environmental, cognitive, and affective sequelae).

Self-regulatory activity represents the second domain. Attention is devoted to altering the ongoing self-statements, images, and feelings that interfere with adaptive functioning. The aim is to reduce the frequency and/or impact of maladaptive cognitions (e.g., distorted interpretations, unwarranted catastrophic anticipations, self-denigrating ideation) and disruptive feelings (e.g., anxiety, depression, and hopelessness) that may interfere with effective coping. At the same time, attempts are made to promote adaptive cognitions and affect (e.g., a problem-solving set, facilitative self-regulatory cues, sense of morale, and optimism).

Finally, there is a focus on *cognitive structures*. By cognitive structures we mean tacit assumptions and beliefs that give rise to habitual ways of construing the self and the world. For instance, clients may see themselves as inadequate or unlovable; they may see others as domineering or exploitative. Given such a cognitive set, clients may handicap themselves by misreading situations, avoiding opportunities, or behaving in a maladaptive way. Change in one's cognitive structures is most likely to occur by discovering through enactive experience that old cognitive structures are unwarranted and that the adoption of new, more adaptive structures is rewarding. The data of experience provide a convincing basis for construing the self, the world, and the commerce between the two in a fundamentally different way.

General Considerations

A number of general, practical issues warrant comment before we turn to a discussion of specific phases of therapy. First, one should avoid assuming that intervention should necessarily be directed at the individual experiencing the distress. The social context in which clients operate is an important focus of assessment and intervention. Sometimes the most appropriate target of change is a social environment that engenders or exacerbates stressful reactions: Ayalon (Chapter 9) and Veronen and Kilpatrick (Chapter 10), for example, describe ways in which communities and "caregivers" may actually increase rather than decrease stress levels of victims of terrorist attacks and rape. In cases like these it seems most sensible to attempt to change the social environment that compounds tragedies rather than simply dealing with individual victims. Similarly, Novaco, Cook, and Sarason (Chapter 11) highlight the potential for interventions at the group level for establishing positive morale among military recruits. In short, skills training should not be undertaken without a careful analysis of the problem and consideration of alternative interventions.

At the same time, it should be noted that stress inoculation training may be integrated with other interventions, including those just described. For example, in the case of chronic pain patients, stress inoculation training typically forms only one part of the overall therapy regimen (which may, for instance, also include medical treatments, physiotherapy, vocational counseling, and creating patient self-help groups).

Second, if stress inoculation training is undertaken, it appears to be advantageous to develop a *collaborative relationship* with the client. Since the general approach is relatively structured and action-oriented, it is easy for the trainer to adopt a didactic lecture style that may interfere with effective communication. A collaborative relationship implies that both client and therapist participate in formulating the problem and establishing a plan of action. The therapist offers ideas tentatively and solicits candid reactions from the client. The goal is to create an ambience that encourages free exchange of information, including client expressions of misunderstanding or misgiving.

Third, it is to be remembered that there are many ways to construe and cope with most problems. As the therapist and client explore the problem, the *therapist seeks a conceptual framework and action plan appropriate to the client.* Different clients will come to terms with their situations in different ways. For instance, some may be inclined to exert control over their environment while others may focus on cultivating a sense of subjective serenity. These individual differences seem particularly important when they are embedded in the client's social-cultural milieu. Attempting to train clients to cope in ways that violate cultural norms may actually aggravate stress-related problems (although the client and therapist together may deem it best to risk this in the interests of anticipated long-term benefits).

Fourth, it may be possible to avoid negative client reactions by *attending to the referral and intake process.* If, for instance, a medical patient is referred to a psychologist after physical tests have been completed and proven negative, the patient may infer that the referral implies that the problem is being dismissed as "imaginary." Such an interpretation may result in a hostile presentation that makes it difficult for the psychologist to establish a working relationship with the client. If referring agents can be coached on when and how to refer and prepare clients, this may help circumvent such difficulties. Even variables such as the length of time clients spend waiting before seeing the therapist have been found to be related to treatment adherence (Davidson, 1976; Dunbar, 1980). Turk *et al.* (1983) present detailed suggestions for promoting a smooth referral-intake process.

Fifth, there is a *problem-solving focus.* Throughout stress inoculation training, there is an emphasis on encouraging clients to view stressful situations as problems to be solved. As individual problems are examined, an attempt is made not only to solve the specific problem but also to develop skills that will enhance general problem-solving capabilities as well. More specifically, the client is trained (a) to evaluate those hypotheses in terms of their consistency with available data and their heuristic value, and (d) to regard proposed behavior changes as experiments. An attempt is made to create a sense of curiosity and adventure. This problem-solving, hypothesis-testing, evidential approach views man as a scientist in a way that is reminiscent of Kelly's (1955) model of man, a conceptualization that appears to be central to the cognitive-behavioral treatment approach (Meichenbaum 1977).

THE TREATMENT PROCESS

We turn now to a discussion of the three phases of therapy. Although the model to be presented suggests a linear progression through the various phases, in practice, the phases blend together. For instance, while assessment is the main focus of the first phase, reassessment is is an ongoing process throughout the treatment period. Phases may also be recycled. For example, if there is a shift in the client's circumstances during the second or third phase of therapy, the focus will revert to phase one (assessment) activities. Moreover, it is important to appreciate that the target of intervention also may change over the course of treatment. In the case of a pain patient, for instance, the initial objective may be the reduction of discomfort and medication, but with improvement in these areas, the focus may shift to helping the client meet the demands of resuming normal social and vocational activities. Table I provides a flow chart of the stress inoculation training paradigm that we shall consider.

PHASE ONE: CONCEPTUALIZATION

The initial phase of therapy has two main objectives. The first is to collect and integrate data that allow client and therapist to develop a

Table I. A Flow Chart of Stress Inoculation Training

Phase One: Conceptualization

(a) Data collection–integration
- Identify determinants of problem via interview, image-based reconstruction, self-monitoring, and behavioral observation
- Distinguish between performance failure and skill deficit
- Formulate treatment plan—task anslysis
- Introduce integrative conceptual model

(b) Assessment skills training
- Train clients to analyze problems independently (e.g., to conduct situational analyses and to seek disconfirmatory data)

Phase Two: Skills Acquisition and Rehearsal

(a) Skills training
- Train instrumental coping skills (e.g., communication, assertion, problem-solving, parenting, study skills)
- Train palliative coping skills as indicated (e.g., perspective-taking, attention diversion, use of social supports, adaptive affect expression, relaxation)
- Aim to develop an extensive repertoire of coping responses to facilitate flexible responding

(b) Skills Rehearsal
- Promote smooth integration and execution of coping responses via imagery and role play
- Self-instructional training to develop mediators to regulate coping responses

Phase Three: Application and Follow-Through

(a) Induce application of skills
- Prepare for application using coping imagery, using early stress cues as signals to cope
- Role play (a) anticipated stressful situations and (b) client coaching someone with a similar problem
- "Role play" attitude may be adopted in real world
- Exposure to in-session graded stressors
- Use of graded exposure and other response induction aids to foster *in vivo* responding and build self-efficacy

(b) Maintenance and generalization
- Build sense of coping self-efficacy in relation to situations client sees as high risk
- Develop strategies for recovering from failure and relapse
- Arrange follow-up reviews

General Guidelines for Training

- Attend to referral and intake process
- Consider training peers of clients to conduct treatment. Develop collaborative relationship and project approachability
- Establish realistic expectations regarding course and outcome of therapy
- Foster optimism and confidence by structuring incremental success experiences
- Respond to stalled progress with problem-solving versus labeling client resistant
- Include family members in treatment where this is indicated

mutual understanding of the problem in terms that open the way for the skills acquisition phase that follows. The second objective is to enhance the client's problem-solving skills by training him or her to gather and interpret data with greater sophistication. From the present point of view, then, assessment and treatment are seen as highly interdependent: The therapist not only conducts an assessment but also trains the client to better conduct such assessments autonomously as future problems arise. The kinds of questions the trainer asks, the assessment instruments employed, and the therapy rationale offered are all seen as actively contributing to the training process by providing models for the client. For purposes of explication, however, the data collection–integration and the skills training endeavors will be treated separately, although in practice they are quite interwoven.

Data Collection–Integration

The basic purpose of the assessment is to identify the determinants of the problem. Determinants may be categorized as situational, behavioral, cognitive, affective, and physiological. The essential task of assessment is to identify specific variables in these various domains that appear to contribute to the maladaptive functioning.

This information may be obtained in three ways, namely, client report, reports from persons who have observed the client on a day-to-day basis or during crucial episodes, and direct observation of the client's behavior. A number of methods may be used to collect such verbal reports and behavioral observations. These include (a) interviews with the client and significant others (e.g., the spouse), (b) imagery reconstructions of particularly stressful incidents, (c) self-monitoring reports and (d) observation of spontaneous or contrived behavioral enactments. Each of these methods will be described very briefly.

Interviews

Interviews that focus on a functional analysis of the problem often yield valuable information about the situational determinants of the behavior. Detailed guidelines for conducting functional analyses have been offered by Kanfer and Saslow (1969) and by Peterson (1968). The goal is to identify (a) situations that increase or decrease the probability of adaptive and maladaptive response patterns, (b) factors that relieve or aggravate the problem, and (c) the environmental (especially social) consequences of the behaviors under consideration. Key questions that are considered in these interviews include the following: Under what specific circumstances does the problem occur? What sorts of things seem to make the problem worse or better? What have clients done to alleviate their stress, and what do they believe can be done? What would it take to change?

As the client describes experiencs in specific situations, it is important to encourage detailed description. Ideally, one would like to know what aspects of the situation the client attends to, what thoughts pass through his or her mind, what is experienced emotionally, and what behaviors are produced. In order to collect detailed information and also to avoid misunderstanding, it is important that the therapist have the client clarify the meaning of abstract terms like "anxiety" or "stress" by indicating their referents (behavioral, cognitive, affective, and physiological). We want, in other words, to know how "anxiety" manifests itself in this particular client in this specific situation. Mischel (1981) presents an analysis of classes of information that are important.

People who spend considerable time with the client or have had an opportunity to observe the client in situations of particular interest are often able to provide useful information about the problem. Moreover, these individuals, often family members, may have become enmeshed in the problem. For instance, families of pain patients sometimes encourage dependent behaviors that work to the detriment of both the client and the family. Thus, family members in particular are frequently able to play a valuable role in both understanding and resolving problems.

The interviewer may check with the client to see whether there have been situations in which the client has been able to find adaptive ways of circumventing or surmounting difficulties similar to the presenting problem. The details of such experiences may provide important clues about coping strengths that might be overlooked in an interview focused exclusively on maladaptive functioning.

Image-Based Reconstruction

During the course of an interview, the client may report an important experience but have difficulty recapturing details. In this situation, it may be helpful to encourage the client to reconstruct the experience by means of imagery. The intention here is to have the client generate potential retrieval cues that may facilitate recall of important aspects of the experience. The imagery procedure has proven useful in helping clients attend to apects and details of their stress response that might otherwise have been overlooked or underemphasized in a direct interview. The retrieval of pertinent images, self-statements, and other self-generated stimuli is particularly encouraged. Such subjective data, which are useful for clarifying how the client's own reactions may actively contribute to the problem, sometimes emerge in more detail during image-based reconstruction than during a standard interview.

Some clients may feel strange about engaging in imagery reconstruction. Such discomfort may be minimized by explaining the rationale underlying the procedure and by providing detailed instructions that invite relaxed reflection and detailed responding. For instance, the trainer may say something like this:

> I'm going to ask you to do something a bit different. I'd like you to sit back, relax, and just reflect on that experience. I'd like you to actually relive the experience in your mind's eye. Quite often this sort of imagery replay makes it possible to remember important details of the experience.
>
> If you're all set, then, just settle back, close your eyes, and think about the experience. Take your time, there's no rush. Just replay the experience in your imagination, as if you were rerunning a movie in slow motion. Begin at the point just before you felt distressed and, taking your time, just go through the whole experience, and see what comes to mind.
>
> Describe anything you remember noticing, or thinking, or feeling, or doing. Any thoughts, feelings, or images you had before, during, or after the incident may be important even though they may seem insignificant.

When this procedure has been used in a group setting, each participant has been asked to engage initially in covert recall of a stressful experience. This prevents attention from focusing on a given member and increasing self-consciousness. After covert imaging, one member is asked to report aloud his or her reconstructions, with other group members describing their reconstructions in turn. In the context of a group, clients come to appreciate that they are not alone in having certain types of thoughts and feelings that they may have viewed as idiosyncratic. This "normalization" process is most likely to occur if the group is composed of persons who are experiencing similar stressful demands (e.g., divorcees, policemen, etc.). Once the therapist has solicited the clients' thoughts and feelings surrounding significant events, the therapist can ask clients if they have similar thoughts and feelings in other situations. In short, a situational analysis is conducted of the clients' experiences in a variety of stressful situations.

Not all clients have equal access to their thoughts and feelings, nor are all equally facile in expressing them. Indeed, with some clients, reports of subjective experience are so consistently meager that one is inclined to suspect that perhaps the stressful reaction has played itself out in an automatic, scripted manner (Abelson, 1978; Langer, 1978). On the other hand, a paucity of cognitive or affective reports may reflect client discomfort with self-disclosure, and the therapist may be able to find ways to overcome this by putting the client at ease (e.g., by modeling self-disclosure in an appropriate way). In any case, although reports of subjective experience are often illuminating and useful (e.g., self-generated subjective stimuli may be used to cue coping behaviors), it is not clear that the absence of such reports precludes any of the interventions (including self-instructional training) we describe below. In short, if the client does not appear to be "psychologically minded," the therapist should attempt to create conditions maximally conducive to the production of subjective reports. If attempts to elicit such reports continue to prove futile, the treatment process can nonetheless proceed. (See Turk *et al.*, 1983, for additional discussions of how one might handle some of the problems involved in conducting an imagery-based assessment.)

Self-Monitoring

Asking clients to record ongoing experiences represents an extremely valuable source of information. Since interview and imagery reconstruction methods are only as good as the client's memory, the immediate recording of experience often results in a more fine-grained view of the factors related to target experience. A number of different self-monitoring methods have been used (Nelson, 1977); they include maintaining open-ended diaries, recording details of specific types of reactions, and rating particular behaviors.

Different self-monitoring methods may be appropriate with different clients (e.g., relatively nonverbal clients may balk at keeping open-ended diaries but may faithfully complete checklists). Also, the type of self-monitoring may shift with the same client over the course of assessment and treatment. For instance, an open-ended approach may be used initially to yield maximal information; as the nature of the problem comes into focus, the client may report only on those variables shown to be relevant; and eventually, only frequency counts of specified adaptive and maladaptive behaviors may be used to track therapeutic progress.

The value of self-monitoring reports appears to be proportionate to the immediacy with which they are completed. Clearly, records completed hours or days after an experience are less likely to contain precise information than records completed immediately after (or even during) the experience. Hence, in planning self-monitoring procedures, it is important to find methods that will increase the probability of immediate reporting. For instance, clients are more likely to keep *in situ* records that can be completed inconspicuously in public situations.

Self-monitoring is uniquely suited to identifying low-intensity cues that signal the onset of stressful transactions. Identification of such cues is strongly encouraged as part of the self-monitoring process. As interventions are planned during treatment, these early warning signals may be used to cue coping responses before the client feels too overwhelmed to cope effectively.

A good deal could be said about how one should introduce homework such as self-monitoring assignments (see Turk *et al.*, 1983). The most important points that bear inclusion here are that homework assignments should *not* be given without the therapist providing a rationale for and checking with clients about their comprehension of the assignment (e.g., self-monitoring). The therapist should discuss with the clients any potential problems they may foresee in implementing the self-monitoring produres (e.g., forgetfulness, embarrassment) and collaborate with them to devise suitable strategies for overcoming anticipated difficulties.

Self-monitoring data often help clients become aware of the situational fluctuations in their stress reactions. The therapist can ask clients to compare and contrast those situations in which their distress (or pain or anger) is most intense with those that evoke less intense reactions. By means of reflection, juxtaposition of data (wondering how certain events go together), and Socratic probes, the therapist attempts to foster a self-inquiring attitude in clients. The therapist acts as a good detective, using his or her own befuddlement as a means of stimulating the clients to reappraise the nature of their stress reactions. By such comments as "On the one hand I hear you saying . . . and on the other hand I hear you saying . . . . I wonder how these go together? Correct me if I am wrong, but what I hear you saying is . . . . Am I correct in assuming that . . . ? I get the feeling that . . . ," the therapist guides clients both to view their stress reactions differently and to develop an analytical approach for considering their difficulties.

The trainer nurtures an attitude whereby clients consider such self-queries as

> What are the data? How are my reactions contributing to my stress? If I had those thoughts, what is the evidence for my conclusions? What is the degree of harm to me if . . . ? How serious is . . . ? How do I know he meant that by what he did? If I look at it this way, where will that lead me?

As the reconceptualization process unfolds, clients and therapist consider the heuristic value of looking at the data from various points of view. The goal is to find a way of looking at things that not only fits available data but also points the way to a solution. Note that the solution may not always involve active coping or problem-solving, but could be the adoption of a passive acceptance or even of "denial" (not thinking about it), as discussed below.

By questioning selectively, reviewing information, and suggesting interpretations, the therapist shapes the process of reconceptualization and encourages an attitude of self-inquiry. Another means of shaping this process is to have clients engage in behavioral assessments in the clinic or laboratory, as well as *in vivo*.

Behavioral Assessments

Direct observation of clients is often extremely revealing. This may be accompanying the client as he or she undertakes stressful tasks or by generating behavior samples in the clinic or laboratory. For instance, if the client complains of communication problems, the client's spouse may be invited to come in and discuss contentious topics with the client as the therapist observes. The nature of the problem often becomes evident under such circumstances. Observations of role-playing may substitute for observation of actual interactions where the latter is not logistically feasible. For example, socially anxious individuals have been asked to give a public speech or engage in a stressful social interaction; test-anxious individuals have been asked to take an exam; and policemen and military recruits have participated in role-playing situations that simulate real life stressful encounters. Such contrived behavioral tasks have usually been conducted in the clinic but may also be arranged *in vivo*.

Turk *et al.* (1983) suggest that it can be useful to videotape the client during a stressful experience. For instance, they describe videotaping pain patients as they are exposed to painful stimuli. The videotape is then replayed and the patient is asked to describe ongoing thoughts and feelings during the experience. The aim is to explore with the patient the role that these subjective factors may play in the pain experience. (For a more detailed discussion and critique of this type of videotape reconstruction procedure, see Meichenbaum & Butler, 1979.) As an alternative to videotaping, one could ask clients to report their subjective experiences at intervals as they progress through enactive experiences in order to sample self-regulatory processes and disruptive private events.

Behavioral observations are also extremely important for evaluating the client's coping capabilities. If a client is failing to cope adequately in a particular type of situation, two possibilities must be considered. Either the client is not capable of executing the responses effectively or the person is capable, but fails to deploy the response at the time it is required. *This distinction between capacity and performance is of crucial diagnostic importance,* since the nature of the intervention (basic response training or response activation) hinges on it.

Assessment of cognitive or behavioral competencies (i.e., what the person *can* do as opposed to what he or she typically *does*) demands that the assessor create conditions and incentives conducive to optimal performance (Mischel, 1981; Wallace, 1966). Goldfried and D'Zurilla (1969) and Wallace (1966) have discussed the assessment of competence.

Generation of Data

Assessment is viewed as an *active* process during which data are not only collected but are actively *sought out* or even *generated* by having the client conduct mini-experiments. The client may, for instance, behave differently toward other persons to see how they respond. These preplanned experiments are often designed with a view to generating data that will disconfirm hypotheses held by the client.

For example, a client may report that he sees his wife as sarcastic and belittling. His description suggests that he sees her as quite uniformly "bitchy" when they are interacting in private. His inability to tolerate the strained relationship is a source of considerable distress. If he is willing to entertain the hypothesis that his own behavior toward his wife may be an important determinant of her mood and behavior, he can plan specific behavioral changes that might elicit desired behaviors from his wife. This provides an opportunity for him to disconfirm his anticipation that his wife's private behavior toward him will be invariably negative. Such disconfirmatory experiments must be planned carefully and it may be necessary to run several trials to ensure a fair test. Also, the client should recognize that it is probable that only small positive reciprocal changes may be elicited initially; but such small positive responses are not to be discounted. In some circumstances (e.g., parents learning to interact more effectively with children), it may be possible for the client to undertake such experiments with the therapist present to coach or model, and this too may enhance the probability of an outcome that disconfirms the client's initial assumptions.

Integration of Data

The data that emerge from interviewing, imagery reconstruction, self-monitoring, behavioral observations, and mini-experiments provide extensive information about probable situational, behavioral, cognitive, affective, and physiological determinants of the problem. As the data accumulate, client and therapist must integrate them in a way that is heuristically useful (i.e., in a way that points toward possible solutions).

One strategy for accomplishing this integration is to conduct a *task analysis* of effective coping sequences. This strategy, described in detail elsewhere (e.g., Kinsbourne, 1971; Meichenbaum, 1977), involves specifying situations in which change is desired and analyzing what is required to produce effective coping responses in each of these situations. The assessment data are then reviewed to isolate factors that interfere with adaptive functioning. These factors become the focus of intervention.

For example, does the client respond effectively in the situation under certain conditions (e.g., when well-rehearsed and prepared), and is it possible to create these facilitative conditions more regularly? Does the client tend to make distorted appraisals in this type of situation, and consequently behave inappropriately? Does the client lack the enactive, behavioral competence required to make the response? Is the required response available but inhibited? Does the client behave adequately but experience excessive arousal and require a long time to unwind? The data of the assessment are used to address these questions. The answers lead directly to the formulation of a treatment plan by specifying precisely what needs to be changed.

Up to this point, emphasis has been placed on the importance of evaluating the client's behavior and experience in relation to specific situations. This increases the likelihood of obtaining precise information rather than vague general impressions. As the data are integrated, however, it is important to look for common reactions across a variety of situations. Such prototypic reactions are particularly important targets for interventions. For instance, a recently separated woman resolved never to allow herself to be vulnerable again and made personal control a pervasive concern. Issues like stopping smoking, losing weight, and being assertive at work were important as she became preoccupied with a desire to be in control of all areas of her life and as she magnified the significance of even minor failures to exert control. The major concern appeared to be a central factor in her stress reactions across many situations.

In summary, a major objective of the assessment procedures is to facilitate a *translation* process. Many stressed clients enter treatment with a confused understanding of their problems. They often have a sense of being victimized by circumstances and by feelings and thoughts over which they believe they have little or no control. They may, for instance, view their problems as arising from a lack of willpower, from unattainable interpersonal forces, or from uncontrollable impulses. As they collect and examine data from a variety of sources, they have an opportunity to reconstrue their problems. They can come to recognize how their *own* thoughts, feelings, and behaviors co-create or exacerbate difficulties. The problem, in part, comes to be seen as a question of self-defeating cognitive, affective, and behavioral patterns. This reformulation is more benign and hopeful, for it implies that many of the contributing factors are potentially under their control. This translation process is further highlighted by the therapist's offering a conceptual model of the clients' stress reactions.

Introducing a Conceptual Model.

It may be useful to provide the client with an explicit conceptual model that provides a framework for integrating assessment data and firmly comprehending the treatment rationale. The conceptual model presented will, of course, depend on the presenting problem. For instance, anxious clients may find heuristic value in Schacter's (1966) cognitive-physiological model of emotion or Lang's (1968) tripartite model of fear. Melzack and Wall's (1965) gate-control model of pain may be described to pain patients (Turk *et al.*, 1983). Bandura's (1977a) model of self-efficacy may help a wide range of clients construe their problems in a new and productive way. Lazarus's transactional model of stress is very compatible with stress inoculation training.

There seem to be some advantages to providing clients with conceptual frameworks such as these. The most notable advantage is that an appropriate psychological model may serve to help the client integrate and monitor experiences more effectively by calling attention to relevant dimensions of the problems and the interrelationship among dimensions. For instance, Lazarus's model provides a differentiated view of stress reactions in terms of primary appraisals of threat and secondary appraisals of coping capabilities and coping responses. In situations that don't require rapid responding, the client who has such a model in mind may consciously examine the actual degree of threat, consider response capabilities thoroughly, and develop a plan for action. The model thus provides a blueprint for organized adaptive responding.

A second potential advantage of providing such models is that they may be reassuring. For instance, the pain patient who is suspicious of a psychological interpretation of his or her problem may be reassured by the gate-control model of pain, which integrates psychological and physical variables in a psychophysiological model: Psychological factors may amplify "real" pain and the problem is not being regarded as "imaginary." Or the client complaining of stress may be reassured by construing the problem in transactional terms rather than in terms of basic personal inadequacy.

If a psychological model is introduced, the manner in which it is presented merits consideration. The model is most likely to be comprehensible and convincing if the data of the client's own experience are used to illustrate its component elements (e.g., by referring to appraisal processes that the client has described in the course of introducing the transactional model of stress). Second, care should be taken to present the conceptual model in *lay* terms, at a level appropriate to the client's understanding so as to avoid bewilderment on one hand or condescension on the other. Third, it seems prudent to avoid trying to "sell" the model as scientifically valid but simply to introduce it as a heuristic device. This approach circumvents any necessity for didactic digressions or having to defend the validity of models that may be empirically or theoretically contentious, although heuristically useful.

The aim is *not* to convert clients to a "true" conception of their problems, but simply to encourage them to adopt a way of looking at difficulties that inherently allows for change. As the rationale for training is offered, the trainer solicits clients' feedback, permits interruptions, and reads the clients' reactions to the reconceptualization. Throughout, clients (and their spouses, where possible) collaborate in the generation of this reconceptualization. The reconceptualization evolves gradually over the course of training and it is *not* formally agreed upon. "My problem now fits this reconceptualization." Instead the reconceptualization acts as a working framework that is refined continuously over the course of training.

In reformulating the problem with the client, it is helpful to construe the clients' reactions as involving a series of temporal phases, such as anticipating the preparing for a stressor, confronting or handling a stressor and dealing with the stress reaction, possibly being overwhelmed by a stressor or stress reaction, and finally a period of subsequent reflection on how the stress was resolved or not resolved. In this way, the stress reaction is broken down or chunked into manageable units. For example the trainer might say,

> As I listen to each of you describe your stress experiences, there seem to be a number of different things going on. Correct me if I am wrong or if I am missing something, but it seems that the stress you are experiencing is made of several components and that your reactions involve a series of phases.

At this point, the trainer conveys a conceptual model of stress, using the client's own self-descriptions to illustrate and document each of the proposed components and phases. Written materials describing the model may be given to the client. In order to avoid imposing a model on the client, the trainer can invite the client to review this written material to see how well it fits for him or her, and to discuss reactions with the trainer.

In *summary,* the reconceptualization process often serves a therapeutic as well as a diagnostic function. Clients sometimes come to the clinic with concerns that they may have deep-seated "emotional" or "mental" problems. As they begin to attribute problems to situational determinants in combination with self-defeating ways of thinking feeling, and behaving, and problems seem less sinister. Moreover, a sense of optimism and improved morale is likely to develop as a plan for making concrete changes starts to take shape.

Assessment Skills Training

For many clients, a second type of therapeutic benefit is derived as well. If the client lacks skill in analyzing psychosocial problems (and this deficiency seems common), the therapist attempts to train such skills during the course of the assessment. The goal of the conceptualization phase is not only to analyze presenting problems but also to teach the client to analyze personal and interpersonal problems autonomously.

More specifically, an attempt is made to train the client to collect detailed information about determinants of problem behavior by conducting a functional analysis, self-monitoring, and so forth. Hypothetical thinking is modeled by the therapist and encouraged in the client. The greater heuristic value of situational versus dispositonal attributions is noted, and clients are taught to consider situational determinants of the behavior of other people. The value of actively seeking data that might disconfirm important assumptions or beliefs is emphasized.

To the extent that clients acquire such analytic skills, they are more likely to be able to read situations in a more sophisticated way. Their appraisals are likely to be more "realistic" and heuristically useful. These are clearly therapeutic benefits from the point of view of a transactional model of stress.

Finally, before we move onto phase two of training, it should be noted how much time and effort has been spent on the initial phase of stress inoculation training, all prior to the introduction of any specific training techniques. The need to prepare clients for intevention is seen as a primary objective of the cognitive-behavioral approach. Unfortunately there is little research to evaluate how much change follows from the initial phase alone. When dismantling studies have been conducted (see Meichenbaum, 1977; Turk *et al.*, 1983), the results have indicated that the total stress inoculation training package was more effective than any one component alone. With this observation in mind let us consider the training of specific coping skills.

PHASE TWO: SKILLS ACQUISITION AND REHEARSAL

The objective of this phase is to ensure that the client develops the capacity to effectively execute coping responses. If the assessment reveals a basic skills deficit, skills training is undertaken. This is the first focus of this phase. The second activity associated with this phase is skill rehearsal to ensure that the client is able to integrate and smoothly execute basic coping sequences. These two aspects of the treatment process will be considered in turn.

Skills Training

Coping skills may be classified as instrumental or palliative (Lazarus & Launier, 1978). *Instrumental* coping refers to actions that serve to meet environmental demands or alter stressful situations and transactions. *Palliative* coping involves responding as adaptively as possible in unavoidable stressful situations when instrumental coping is not possible. Palliative coping responses, which focus largely on regulating cognitive, affective, and physiological components of stress reactions, may be used in conjunction with instrumental responses (e.g., the person engages in self-relaxation while producing instrumental responses). For ease of explication, however, they will be discussed separately.

Instrumental Coping Skills

Some direct coping skills are primary *cognitive.* The skills required to analyze psychosocial problems, trained during the conceptualization phase, fall into this category.

Another basic cognitive coping capability of instrumental value in a wide variety of situations involves the capacity to engage in effective problem-solving routines. A number of guidelines for efficient problem solving have been described (e.g., D'Zurilla & Goldfried, 1971; Mahoney, 1977). Although details of problem-solving guidelines vary, all essentially involve teaching the client to (a) analyze the problems, (b) generate possible solution alternatives, (c) evaluate the alternative generated, (d) implement the most promising alternative, and (e) assess the outcome of the change, beginning the process again if the problem has not been resolved adequately.

The client may be coached in the use of such a problem-solving strategy in relation to problems reported to the trainer. Attention may be devoted to discussing and *demonstrating* how each phase of the problem-solving process can be accomplished most effectively. For instance, the value of temporarily suspending critical judgment and of brainstorming during the process of generating potential solutions may be not only described, but actually demonstrated. The therapist can acomplish this by asking the client to enumerate all of the possibilities he or she can think of. Once the client runs out of ideas, the therapist can encourage suspension of critical judgment and begin to become involved in brainstorming with the client to illustrate how additional possibilities emerge under these conditions. It is important for the client to recognize how the process demonstrated in therapy can be set in motion in the "real world" (e.g., by seeking out friends with whom to brainstorm); it should not be assumed that clients will automatically engage in this sort of generalization.

More specifically, the training of problem-solving skills usually occurs in the context of a discussion of how clients' thoughts and feelings contribute to and exacerbate stress reactions. As the trainer and clients review the various phases of the clients' stressful reactions, they consider how the clients' internal dialogue can be changed. If certain thoughts (self-statements and images) contribute to stress, then the question is raised as to what different thoughts, feelings, and behaviors might help reduce and avoid stress. In group treatment, members become collaborators in developing a problem-solving approach toward their stress reactions.

The therapist might ask clients what advice they would have for others who are faced with similar stressful experiences. Quite often, clients offer useful coping strategies that can act as catalysts for a discussion of problem-solving skills. The object of the discussion is to encourage and train clients to

1. define the stressor or stress reaction as a problem-to-be-solved;
2. set realistic goals as concretely as possible by stating the problem in behavioral terms and by delineating steps necessary to reach a goal;
3. generate a wide range of possible alternative courses of action;
4. imagine and consider how others might respond if asked to deal with a similar stress problem;
5. evaluate the pros and cons of each proposed solution and rank-order the solutions from least to most practical and desirable;
6. rehearse strategies and behaviors by means and imagery, behavioral rehearsal, and graduated practice;
7. try out the most acceptable and feasible solution
8. expect some failures, but reward self for having tried; and
9. reconsider the original problem in light of the attempt at problem-solving.

The therapist works with clients to adopt such a problem-solving set. This may entail encouraging clients to (a) talk to others in order to obtain information; (b) review how they coped with past stressful events, with the objective of encouraging clients to recognize that potential coping skills may already exist in their repertoire and that these coping skills may be transferable to the present stressful situation; (c) chunk stressful events into smaller, manageable tasks; (d) make contingency plans for future eventualities, drawing an analogy to the type of "game plans" that sports teams make or contingency planning that astronauts may employ; (e) mentally rehearsing ways of handling each mini-stress; and (f) viewing any possible failures or disappointments as needed feedback to begin the problem-solving process once again.

Many instrumental coping responses require complex *behavioral* as well as cognitive responding. Some classes of enactive skills, such as competence in communicating, time management, and setting priorities, seem universally valuable for meeting important, recurrent demands in our lives. Other skills, such as competencies related to studying or parenting, are significant to particular subpopulations. If the assessment indicates that the client lacks the capacity to produce behaviors required to meet ongoing demands, behavioral skills training is indicated.

It is beyond the scope of the present chapter to review methods for training specific behavioral competencies. An extensive literature, some of which has been reviewed by Goldfried (1980), is available. Modeling processes play a central role in such training. Rosenthal and Bandura (1978) have published a comprehensive review of the modeling literature that is rich with implications for clinical training.

We will restrict ourselves to commenting on only two fundamental issues related to the training of behavioral skills. First, clients who really lack behavioral skills are more likely to acquire these through modeling and practice (with feedback) of relevant coping sequences than by talking or reading about the skills. It is improbable that enactive finesse will be developed without enactive practice. The effectiveness of interpersonal coping responses often hinges on nuances of verbal, paraverbal, and nonverbal elements that are most vividly communicated through modeling and most effectively acquired through practice.

Second, training should focus on developing an extensive repertoire of responses. *Adaptive coping is flexible.* Assertiveness, for instance, is best expressed in different ways in different situations. Since adaptive coping chains are not routinized but integrated in a flexible way to be situationally appropriate, the object of training should be to develop (a) the largest possible repertoire of coping responses appropriate to the full range of target situations and (b) practice in fluid integration of coping elements.

Palliataive Coping Skills

In an aversive situation that can neither be altered substantially nor avoided (e.g., experiencing intense pain that cannot be relieved medically), the goal is to relieve distress as much as possible. The way the client thinks and behaves may to some degree either intensify or moderate the stressful reaction.

There are at least two cognitive strategies that may be useful in coping with unalterable stressful situations. One strategy involves *perspective taking.* When things are objectively bad, they may seem subjectively worse. Depending on the source of the stress, perspective taking may involve reminding oneself that the problem is time-limited, that serious outcomes would be bearable though unwelcome, that there are still sources of satisfaction in other areas of life, and so forth. These strategies have greatest potential value in situations where the subjective distress is magnified by the client's ideation.

Some clients, however, have to deal with unalterable threats that are indeed catastrophic in nature (e.g., life-threatening illness). Attempts to train such clients to keep things in perspective must be handled with sensitivity; a heavy-handed, Pollyanna approach would be both naive and disrespectful. A potentially effective way to deal with such clients is to expose them to persons who have managed to cope well with the same problem. These models, who are likely to be much more credible than the therapist, can be sources of both inspiration and information. Carefully chosen models may help the client move toward a more positive perspective by transmitting attitudes and coping skills that build morale. For instance, a young, athletic ostomy patient may benefit greatly from exposure to a person with an ostomy who is also young and who has resumed athletic activities. Such a model is in a much stronger position than the therapist to provide convincing strategies for minimizing impediments to resuming normal activities and for cultivating a positive perspective.

A second palliative coping strategy is *attention diversion*. Lazarus (1981) has written thoughtfully about the adaptive value of "denial," especially in circumstances over which it is impossible to exert control. Although the psychoanalytic model postulates that "denial" involves an unconscious defensive distortion that is not under voluntary control, it is sometimes possible to create intentionally conditions that increase the probability of diverting attention away from distressing experiences or concerns. To the extent that the person can become absorbed in positive experiences, there may be at least temporary respite.

For example, people experiencing chronic pain may become inactive and reclusive. In extreme cases, we have worked with pain patients who, for a period of years, have seldom gone out of the house, had visitors, or even dressed. One has the impression that such patients are preoccupied almost continuously with their (very real) dolorous condition. Such persons may find that they can sometimes escape from their malaise by establishing or rediscovering activities that are gratifying and engrossing. Imagery-based attention-diversion strategies may also be helpful for palliative coping (Turk *et al.*, 1983).

There is increasing evidence to indicate that appropriate use of *social support networks* may facilitate adaptive coping processes (e.g., Heller, 1979). Other persons may be able to provide physical assistance, valuable information, feedback, or perspective. The therapist may be able to assist clients by helping them find ways to use existing social supports more effectively, or to develop new support systems. For example, a physically incapacitated person may learn how to use marital and extended family support systems to better advantage or to cultivate new support systems in the neighborhood or worksite.

Social skills training, especially that designed to assist the client become more effective in marshalling social supports, may be undertaken if indicated. For example, in working with abusive parents, trainers have focused on ways in which parents could rearrange their environments and martial support systems to reduce and avoid stress. The discussion of the clients' building support systems often leads to a consideration of the clients' communication and assertion skills and the clients' ability to seek help. A number of cognitive-behavioral techniques can be used to facilitate social training. These include role-playing, behavioral rehearsal, imagery rehearsal of possible interactions, and graduated *in vivo* attempts to develop such social supports.

A major goal of this training is to encourage clients to question themselves before acting. How would they feel if someone asked them for help in this particular manner at this particular time? How is someone else likely to look on their request for help? The trainer not only wants clients to adopt such perspective-taking approach, but also works with clients to insure they have the interpersonal skills to state their requests clearly and to identify problems and communicate needs. A good deal of stress that clients experience daily is in the form of personal friction with others. The ways in which clients communicate often play an important role in contributing to the stress they experience and engender in others. Clients who can convey their needs in terms that permit solutions have a greater likelihood of receiving helpful stress-reducing responses.

It is noteworthy that social support systems are not always beneficial. For instance, well-meaning family members may usurp activities that the client is capable of performing. Similarly, "self-help" groups may be detrimental if the focus is on providing mutual sympathy rather than on developing constructive coping strategies.

A fourth palliative coping strategy involves *appropriate expression of affect*. It is widely believed that "ventilation of feelings" or "getting things off one's chest" is adaptive when people experience pressures they cannot control. It is probably true that there can be some advantage in expressing emotion. For instance, an extremely stoical person who refuses to talk about affect-laden problems or concerns may cut him or herself off from useful social supports. Others may not detect the distress or may even exacerbate the client's problem by misinterpreting and reacting negatively to the client's "moodiness" or preoccupation. However, at the other extreme, persistent, dramatic displays of affect over a long period of time may be demoralizing, restrict communication, or even result in abandonment. The way the client expresses (or inhibits) emotion may be an important determinant of the quality of adjustment, and clients may profit from learning how to express emotion in adaptive ways.

Training in *relaxation skills* can facilitate both instrumental and palliative coping. Although progressive relaxation training is used widely, there are many procedural variations. It is not unequivocally clear which methods are best with specific clients or specific problems

(Borkovec & Sides, 1979; Qualls & Sheehan, 1981). It seems reasonable for the therapist and client to experiment with different variations so that the client can select the approach that results in greatest personal benefit.

If relaxation training is conducted, the rationale provided may be as important as the specific induction procedure used. For instance, if it is emphasized that the client is acquiring a skill to be deployed in stressful situations, this may enhance the client's sense of personal control. This perception of control may in itself be therapeutic (e.g., Lefcourt, 1976; Seligman, 1975). Moreover, this conceptualization encourages clients to use relaxation techniques to interrupt established maladaptive cognitive-behavioral chains that occur in stressful situations. Goldfried (1980) and Turk *et al.* (1983) have discussed the use of relaxation skills training in greater detail than is possible here. One point that warrants emphasis here, however, is that the therapist must be sensitive to the issue of treatment generalization. It is *not* sufficient merely to train clients to relax (by whatever means); the trainer also much insure that clients know how, when, and where they will use the relaxation procedures.

Before leaving the topic of relaxation training, it is perhaps worth noting that it is unnecessarily restrictive to think of relaxation skills as being synonymous with deep breathing and the loosening of muscles. Granted, these methods may be useful and have broad application. However, pleasant recreational, social, sensual, athletic, and meditative activities may also be relaxing for many clients. The wider the range of methods considered, the more likely the client will end up with a variety of options, appealing and useful, across a variety of situations.

There is obviously considerable overlap between instrumental and palliative coping skills. It can be useful, however, for the client as well as the therapist to recognize explicitly both generic types of responses so that palliative skills are not overlooked. The client who has a concept of palliative coping has an implicit set to recognize that *some form* of coping response is possible in virtually any situation.

Skills Rehearsal

The second phase of therapy includes an emphasis on skills rehearsal as well as skills acquisition. The goal is to have the client refine newly acquired or previously existing coping skills.

Rehearsal may involve exposing the client to models who demonstrate a range of styles of implementing relevant skills (e.g., making effective assertive responses). Imagery rehearsal may be useful. Role-playing also may be used in a variety of ways. The first and most obvious approach to role-playing is to have the client practice the desired coping response in the clinic. These performances may be videotaped and reviewed.

Rehearsal is intended to nurture the client's confidence in producing responses flexibly and appropriately in "real-world" situations. In the interests of building this confidence, a second type of "role play" may be used: The client may be induced to act out the response sequences in relatively safe, naturally occurring "practice" situations. For example, the client who is awkward about expressing personal feelings may be induced to compliment and express appropriate, personalized appreciation to friends to rehearse for more intimate interchanges.

Self-instructional training is also introduced to facilitate production of coping sequences. Self-instructional training is used to develop self-regulatory processes that will increase the probability that the client will activate, disinhibit, and integrate coping responses.

Thus, another means to help clients develop a problem-solving attitude is to work with them on specific cognitive strategies that they can use at various phases of their stress response. The trainer can state

> We have discussed how your appraisal of your situation, what you think and feel, plays a key role in influencing your stress reaction. [At this point the trainer offers several specific examples from the clients' accounts that illustrates the important role of the appraisal process on their stress reactions.]
>
> In fact, the way we think can affect how we feel in a fairly direct, intentional fashion. We each influence our thoughts by a sort of *internal monologue*—an ongoing series of *statements to ourselves*—in which we tell ourselves what to think and believe, and even how to act.
>
> You may find that speaking about your thoughts as "self-statements" is somewhat unexpected. But there is good reason for using this phrase. Calling a thought a "statement to yourself" emphasizes the deliberateness of that particular thought, and the fact that it is under your control. Let's consider the kinds of thoughts or self-statements and images you had before, during, and after your stress reaction.

At this point, the trainer explores with clients the various phases of the stress reaction (preparatory, confronting stressful event, critical moments of intense stress, and periods of reflecting on how the stressful event went) and the *specific* thoughts and feelings they had at each phase.

This discussion provides the basis for the trainer to make the observation that if such reactions make stress worse, then different thoughts and feelings (self-statements) may be employed at each phase to reduce and avoid stress. In a collaborative manner, client and therapist generate lists of incompatible coping self-statements that can be used. See Table II for a description of such self-statements that were used in a stress inoculation training program for phobic patients (Meichenbaum, 1977) and for

Table II. Examples of Coping Self-statements Used in Stress Inoculation Training

Phobic patient

Preparing for a stressor

What do you have to do?
You can develop a plan to deal with it.
Just think about what you can do about it. That's better than getting anxious.
No negative self-statements: Just think rationally.
Don't worry: Worry won't help anything.
Maybe what you think is anxiety is eagerness to confront the stressor.

Confronting and handling a stressor

Just "psych" yourself up—you can meet this challenge.
You can convince yourself to do it. You reason your fear away.
One step at a time: You can handle the situation.
Don't think about fear, just think about what you have to do.
Stay relevant.
This anxiety is what the doctor said you might feel.
It's a reminder to use your coping exercises.
This tenseness can be an ally, a cue to cope.
Relax, you're in control. Take a slow deep breath. Ah, good.

Coping with the feelings of being overwhelmed

When fear comes, just pause.
Keep the focus on the present; what is it you have to do?
Label your fear from 0 to 10 and watch it change.
You should expect your fear to rise.
Don't try to eliminate fear totally; just keep it manageable.

Reinforcing self-statements

It worked; you did it.
Wait until you tell your trainer (or other group members) about this.
It wasn't as bad as you expected.
You made more out of your fear than it was worth.
Your damn ideas—that's the problem. When you control them, you control your fear.
It's getting better each time you use the procedure.
You can be pleased with the progress you're making.
You did it.

Anger control patient[a]

Preparing for a provocation

This could be a rough situation, but you know how to deal with it.
You can work out a plan to handle this. Easy does it.
Remember, stick to the issues and don't take it personally.
There won't be any need for an argument. You know what to do.

Table II (Continued)

Anger control patient[a]
Impact and confrontation
As long as you keep your cool, you're in control of the situation.
You don't need to prove yourself. Don't make more out of this than you have to.
There is no point in getting mad. Think of what you have to do.
Look for the positives and don't jump to conclusions.
Coping with arousal
Muscles are getting tight. Relax and slow things down.
Time to take a deep breath. Let's take the issue point by point.
Your anger is a signal of what you need to do. Time for problem solving.
He probably wants you to get angry, but you're going to deal with it constructively.
Subsequenct reflection
(a) Conflict unresolved
Forget about the aggravation. Thinking about it only makes you upset.
Try to shake it off. Don't let it interfere with your job.
Remember relaxation. It's a lot better than anger.
Don't take it personally. It's probably not so serious.
(b) Conflict resolved
You handled that one pretty well. That's doing a good job!
You could have gotten more upset than it was worth.
Your pride can get you into trouble, but you're doing better at this all the time.
You actually got through that without getting angry.

[a]As listed in Novaco (1975).

anger control patients by Novaco (1975). Meichenbaum (1977) and Turk *et al.* (1983) provide comparable lists of coping self-statements for other target populations such as anxious clients and pain patients. Clients are encouraged to translate the self-statements into their own words and to personalize them in a meaningful manner.

In perusing the cognitive strategies listed in Table II, it is important to understand that they are not offered as catch-phrases or as verbal palliatives to be repeated mindlessly. There is a difference between encouraging the use of a formula or psychological litany that tends to lead to rote repetition and emotionless patter *versus* problem-solving thinking that is the object of stress inoculation training. Formula-oriented thoughts that are excessively general tend to prove ineffective.

What is important to appreciate about the lists of self-statements, as described in Table II, is that the trainer does *not* suggest, "Here is a list of things to say to yourself that will make stress go away." One should *not* equate the problem-solving training to which clients have actively contributed with the "power of positive thinking" approach as espoused by Norman Vincent Peale, Dale Carnegie, or W. Clement Stone. While there is an element of positive thinking and self-reliance inherent in the self-instructional approach, there is a difference between providing clients with a questionable verbal palliative (e.g., see Miller, 1955) and the active problem-solving training that is being proposed here. The rejection of schools of "positive thinking" should *not* lead trainers to overreact and neglect to consider how cognitive control might be employed to help clients cope with stress.

One way to introduce such coping cognitive strategies is for the trainer to state:

> In the last session we discussed some of the thoughts and feelings you have in stressful situations and some of the possible alternative self statements you might employ at each phase of your stressful reaction. I thought it would be useful if I summarized our discussion. So I have put together a list of self-statements that one can use before, during, and after stressful events. I have included your suggestions, as well as some suggestions that other clients like yourselves have made and have found useful.
>
> What I would like us to do is to take a few minutes to look over this list and then discuss it. In reviewing the list of coping self-statements, keep in mind that each person's situation is slightly different and that each of you is unique. Look over the list with an eye to deciding what might be worth considering in your case.

At this point, the group considers the coping self-statments (such as those described in Table II, but individually tailored to the specific population) and how and when such self-statements may be of use.

In short, the self-instructional training begins by identifying the client's habitual self-statements during various phases of stressful experiences (using assessment methods described prerviously). Therapist and client then consider how these self-statements may exacerbate the stress reaction and interfere with performance of adaptive coping responses. Next, they collaborate in the generation of alternative self-statements (similar to those presented in Table II) that may serve to cue production of adaptive cognitive, affective, and behavioral responses. Clients personalize these self-statements by using their own words in developing self-regulatory mediators. The list of coping self-statements can be extended as treatment continues.

The self-statements are also tailored to the specific target coping-responses pattern and inhibitions of individual clients. Consider, for instance, a man who inhibits assertive responses for fear of offending.

When he does make an assertive response, he tends to do so in an apologetic, extended way that creates discomfort and diminishes the impact of his response. Such a client may develop a series of self-statements such as the following ones to be used when faced with an unreasonable request: "You'll resent it if I just say yes. There you go, just hold on. What exactly do you want, don't just go along. Be polite and friendly, but be firm and crisp." The idea is to link a naturally occurring stimulus event or inhibitory cognition (e.g., the fleeting thought that it's easier just to say "yes") to a set of self-statements that both counteract the inhibitory self-statement and cue production of an effectively delivered coping response.

Self-instructional training may be undermined in a number of ways. Some clients feel uncomfortable about the idea of self-talk, and it is important to normalize the experience, emphasizing that private speech plays a significant (and potentially very adaptive) role in regulating behavior. Also, it seems to be tactically preferable to concentrate on increasing coping positive self-statements. The latter is sometimes difficult to accomplish and the attempt can be frustrating. And, as the example above suggests, it may be possible to neutralize negative self-statements by using them as cues for the production of coping self-statements; the key is to prevent them from disrupting effective coping. Research reviewed by Meichenbaum, Henshaw, and Himel (1981) indicates that "good copers" also have negative self-statements in their repertoire, but these negative thoughts act as cues for coping, while in the case of "poor copers," such negative self-statements lead to heightened emotionality, further negative thoughts, and poor coping behavior. And so the cycle continues.

It has been suggested that self-statements are used in part to overcome the inhibition of coping responses. As these inhibitions (e.g., reluctance to be assertive for fear of hurting someone's feelings) become apparent, they may be taken into account during the process of basic skills training as well. Therapist and client can concentrate on developing response patterns that have the potential to produce the desired effect while simultaneously minimizing the undesired outcome. For instance, special efforts may be made to generate responses that are unequivocally assertive, but also polite, humorous, and friendly so that the client is likely to experience minimal inhibition of the response.

PHASE THREE: APPLICATION AND FOLLOW-THROUGH

After the client has acquired the capacity to respond effectively in target situations, the next step is to actually *implement* coping responses. This transitional point may be regarded as marking the beginning of the third phase of therapy. This phase has two objectives. The first, of course, is to have the client make changes in day-to-day situations. The second is to maximize the probability of generalized, enduring change. These objectives will be discussed separately.

Inducing Application of Skills

Many of the changes that therapy aims to bring about represent stressful demands from the point of view of the client. The phobic is expected to approach objects or situations that have elicited incapacitating distress. The timid person is expected to assert him- or herself in relation to people who have been viewed as intimidating. Clients' expectations about their ability to perform the appropriate responses and the probable outcomes if they do produce the behavior are usually quite negative initially.

These negative expectations cannot be expected to change instantaneously. Although the availability of coping responses developed during the second phase of therapy may increase expectations of effective performance, progressive experiences of success in coping are likely to provide the most convincing basis for shifting expectations (Bandura, 1977a). Early change efforts are almost certain to be accompanied by misgivings and discomfort that make it difficult for the client to initiate and persist in the new response pattern. Old, well-established response habits and expectations must be overcome.

This perspective suggests that it would be naive to assume that the clients will automatically generalize coping skills acquired in therapy to "real-world" situations. Such transfer must be insured by the structure of the training program. The success of therapy will depend in large measure on the adequacy of procedures used to foster new response patterns in day-to-day affairs.

One general strategy for initiating this generalization is to have the client engage in *imagery rehearsal.* The general format for this procedure is derived from Wolpe's (1958) systematic desensitization paradigm. Client and therapist generate a hierarchy of scenes from least to most stressful. As in desensitization, the client is asked to imagine progressively more threatening scenes while relaxed. However, instead of following Wolpe's practice of terminating the scene when the client experiences anxiety, the client is asked to imagine dealing with the situation by producing coping responses (e.g., coping self-statements, self-guided relaxation, appropriate assertive behavior). Goldfried (1980) and Turk *et al.* (1983) provide a more detailed discussion and review of this approach.

During such imagery rehearsal, it may be useful for the client to imagine initiating coping efforts in response to the early, low-intensity cues that signal the onset of a stressful reaction. These cues, a focus of interest during assessment, may be the client's own response-produced stimuli (i.e., cognitive, affective, behavioral, physiological reactions) or they may be external cues (e.g., approaching a threatening situation, a potentially threatening behavior made by another person). The general goal here is to have the client notice early signs of distress or threat and to develop the set of reacting to such cues by initiating coping responses rather than avoiding or "catastrophizing." The client thus uses his or her own reactions and observations (thoughts, feelings, behaviors, physiological reactions, or reactions of others) as signals or cues to produce coping responses (e.g., chunking the stressor into potentially soluble units). In this way, generalization is built into the training program, because the client's own reactions become a constant reminder to use coping skills. Also, by using a coping imagery procedure, clients are providing themselves with a model of how to cope with stressful situations and stressful reactions. The clients are engaging in what has been called the constructive "work of worrying" (Breznitz, 1971; Marmor, 1958; Janis, 1958).

One can also use films of coping models to facilitate the transfer process (Meichenbaum, 1977). A coping model initially demonstrates stressful reactions similar to those experienced by the client, then demonstrates progressively successful coping behaviors until mastering the challenge. In this way coping models demonstrate how the recognition of stressful cues act as reminders to use coping process.

Role playing may be used as a second general strategy for promoting skill application. Client and therapist may role-play anticipated stressful interactions, periodically exchanging roles so that the therapist alternates between modeling situationally specific coping responses (i.e., negative thoughts, images, and feelings the patient is likely to have in particular stressful situations and then the coping strategies and behaviors needed to handle the difficulty) and confronting the client in ways an actual antagonist might. It may also be useful to have the client role-play the trainer, while the latter assumes the role of a novice client. The task is for the actual client to coach the "novice client" on how to cope effectively. The attitude change literature (Janis & Mann, 1977; McGuire, 1964) suggests that such an approach may help promote change as the client is pressed to generate strategies, arguments, illustrations, and motivating appeals that are most personally convincing. This type of role-play also provides an opportunity to assess the client's understanding of the treatment strategies.

Kelly's (1955, 1973) description of fixed role therapy suggests yet another way in which role-playing may be used to promote transfer. The client may be encouraged to assume a role-playing attitude *in the real world* as new response patterns are tried out. The idea is to think of oneself as adopting a certain pattern of behavior on a trial basis, to see what will happen. This set may help to avoid debilitating attitudes of grim determination or desperation as the client initiates change.

What is highlighted in the various role-playing exercises is the need for *flexibility*—coping responses that may work at one time may prove ineffective at a later time. In fact, clients are encouraged to anticipate failure situations and plan ahead for such occasions. Such preplanning lowers the risk of the client becoming overwhelmed at the time of most severe stress.

A third strategy for preparing clients to implement skills *in vivo* is to *allow them to try out their skills under actual stressful conditions during the therapy session.* Turk *et al.* (1983) describe the use of exposure to graded, experimentally induced pain as a means of giving pain patients opportunities to test newly acquired coping skills. Clients also have practiced coping skills as they watched stressful films or experienced unpredictable electric shocks. It is assumed that successful application of coping skills in such situations enhances the client's confidence in the skills, thereby nurturing positive expectations and increasing the probability a client will call on these skills in everyday situations.[1]

Bandura's (1977a) work on self-efficacy suggests some useful guidelines for exposing clients to stressors. Bandura has postulated that the probability of initiating and persisting in coping behavior is determined to a large extent by the degree to which a sense of self-efficacy has been established. A sense of self-efficacy requires confidence that required behaviors can be produced (efficacy expectation) and that the desired outcome will occur when the response is adequately produced (outcome expectation). According to Bandura's model, these expectations can be induced most powerfully if the therapist can arrange for the client to engage in the newly acquired coping response (a) *in vivo,* (b) under circumstances where there is a high probability that the response will produce the desired outcome, and (c) under conditions that allow the client to attribute to personal capability rather than to external factors.

Bandura (1977a) describes a variety of "response induction aids" that may be used to achieve these objectives. These include "preliminary modeling of threatening activities, graduated tasks, enactment over graduated temporal intervals, joint performance with the therapist, protective aids to reduce the likelihood of feared consequences, and variation in the severity of the threat itself" (p. 196). He goes on to note that "as treatment progresses, the supplementary aids are withdrawn so that clients can cope effectively unassisted. Self-directed mastery experiences are then undertaken to reinforce a sense of personal efficacy" (pp. 196–197). Bandura and his colleagues have demonstrated the power of

[1] It should be noted that the exposure to an actual stressor does not necessarily result in greater therapeutic benefit (Horan, Hackett, Buchanan, Stone, & Demchick-Stone, 1978). The conditions under which exposure facilitates therapeutic gain are still being clarified (Klepac, Hauge, Dowling, & MacDonald, 1981).

such an approach with treatment of phobia (e.g., Bandura, Adams, Hardy, & Howells, 1980).

The approach, however, appears to be applicable to the treatment of a wide variety of problems. If, for example, communication skills have been taught, the therapist may use many of the induction aids just enumerated to promote *in vivo* change. To illustrate briefly, the therapist may model the skills during an actual interchange with the client's spouse to demonstrate both the skills and also the spouse's responsiveness to the new communication approach. Graduated tasks may be introduced by initially asking the couple to discuss relatively inocuous topics and moving to progressively more contentious issues over the course of the session(s). The therapist initially may ask the couple to maintain a specified level of communication for a very brief period and may subsequently encourage progressively longer sequences of appropriate interchange, thereby employing graduated temporal intervals as a means of increasing success experiences and building confidence.

Other examples of therapeutic exposure are considered in the next section of the book. For example, burn patients are encouraged to use coping strategies under trainer guidance while undergoing "tanking" (painful bathing) as described by Wernick (Chapter 6); or policemen have been asked to engage in provocative role-playing situations (Meichenbaum & Novaco 1977; Sarason, Johnson, Berberich, & Siegal, 1979).

As the client begins to initiate change in the absence of the therapist between sessions, the latter may nurture the client's sense of self-efficacy by analyzing with the client experiences of success and failure. When clients report successes, it may be valuable to have them analyze how they accomplished these to insure that they attribute the positive outcome to their competency (whenever competence played a role in determining the outcome). If failures are reported, it is important to explore the client's criterion of success: clients may misread partial successes (often the best that can be realistically anticipated) as unmitigated failures. If the client attempted an instrumental coping response that failed, it is important to explore how he or she coped with the failure and what was learned from it: Bouncing back from failures and profiting from them may be construed as successful coping. Goldfried and Robins (in press) have offered additional suggestions for facilitating self-efficacy

Maintenance and Generalization

Inducing changes that are widespread and enduring continues to present a challenge for therapists. There is some evidence that high levels of self-efficacy may be associated with generalized improvement (Bandura *et al.*, 1980) and with maintenance of treatment gains (Condiotte &

Lichtenstein, 1981; DiClemente, 1981). It appears that relapse is most likely to occur in situations where clients are least confident of their ability to cope (Condiotte & Lichtenstein, 1981). Hence, it seems prudent to monitor the client's sense of self-efficacy in the full range of challenging situations he or she faces and to continue to promote efficacy-enhancing experiences until the client has acquired a sense of confidence in each of these situations. Failure to continue treatment until this has been accomplished may increase the probability of relapse.

Marlatt and his colleagues have developed a model of relapse prevention that is compatible with the self-efficacy model (Marlatt & Gordon, 1980) and with stress inoculation training. Marlatt's model, which cannot be reviewed in detail, suggests that it is critical to train the client to cope effectively in situations where relapse is likely.

One aspect of the model that warrants special note is the emphasis it places on identifying high-risk situations and on anticipating the client's reactions to potential coping failures. Both Marlatt and Gordon (1980) and Wilson (1980a) have argued that when a client experiences failure or relapse (a "slip") after successful treatment, the way the "slip" is interpreted is likely to be of critical importance. If the person interprets the "slip" as evidence of inadequate personal efficacy, this appraisal may undermine subsequent coping efforts. The person, in other words, may infer that he or she is not really capable of overcoming the problem after all, and give up. To reduce the risk of this, these authors suggest that therapists encourage clients to anticipate failures and setbacks and have them rehearse how they will respond to such lapses. Marlatt has even suggested that treatment include planned failure experiences ("programmed relapse") to develop appropriate coping responses and to establish a sense of self-efficacy in the face of such slips. Although the concept of programmed relapse may be controversial, clients often experience setbacks "spontaneously" during the course of treatment: These naturally occurring relapses may be welcomed as opportunities to develop resilience (i.e., a sense of confidence one can "get back on track" after setbacks).

These concerns appear to be vitally important in the treatment of stress-related problems. Stress is a normal part of life, and clients should recognize that they will continue to experience stress, even after successful treatment. The goal of treatment is not to eliminate stress, but rather to learn to respond adaptively in stressful situations and to be resilient in the face of failure.

Treatment Follow-through

In general, it has been found useful *not* to have the training terminate abruptly, but instead to thin out sessions during a transitional period. Turk *et al.* (1983) suggest that treatment gains may be consolidated by prearranging to have clients return for review at 2-, 3-, 6-, and 12-month follow-up sessions. The goal is to provide a structure for maintaining the client's momentum despite setbacks or new problems that may develop as the conditions of the client's life change over time. The client may also be invited to contact the therapist if difficult problems arise: Initiating such contact may be construed as an adaptive coping response under many circumstances. In considering follow-through, it is important to remember that the nature of the client's problems may change with time. With client improvement, there may also be a change in the expectations by significant others. The stressful events that brought clients to training are *unlikely* to be the same as those one deals with at follow-up.

FOSTERING CLIENT PARTICIPATION IN THE CHANGE PROCESS

As Wilson (1980b) has noted, the success of therapy "depends in large part on securing the active cooperation and participation of the client in the behavior change process" (p. 300). An otherwise well-conceived treatment program may fail if it is not implemented in a way that evokes client participation. A number of discussions of "non-specific" factors that may influence the course and outcome of cognitive behavior treatments are available (e.g., Meichenbaum & Gilmore, 1982; Turk *et al.*, 1983; Wachtel, 1982; Wilson, 1980b).

We conclude this chapter with a brief discussion of several variables that may well affect the success of stress-inoculation training. It is not feasible to present a comprehensive review and analysis of pertinent literature here. Our purpose is simply to call attention to the general issue of "nonspecific" effects, and to emphasize some factors that may affect the client's involvement in the treatment process.

The first class of variables pertain to the *therapist's manner.* In discussing treatment adherence, Dunbar (1980) has suggested that therapists may be more effective if they are seen as approachable. *Approachability* refers to therapist behaviors that put the clint at ease so that the latter feels free to raise concerns. Therapist warmth, empathy, and general friendliness and spontaneity may enhance perceived approachability. As Dunbar notes, "hurriedness, and not identifying the patient's problems from the patient's own perspective contribute to unwillingness to remain in care" (p. 80). The collaborative approach we have emphasized is likely to contribute to the perceived approachability of the therapist.

Client expectations represent a second class of variables that may affect response to treatment. Unrealistically positive initial expectations that are disconfirmed during the course of therapy may result in demoralization. A client who expects to change in a month well-ingrained patterns of interaction that have been acquired over a lifetime is almost certain to be disheartened by the pace of change. Planning a series of small specific changes that build progressively toward the final objective may help develop realistic expectations and lay the groundwork for maintaining a sense of progress and morale.

Leading the client to expect possible setbacks during treatment, and encouraging a positive response to failures may also be important for maintaining client involvement in treatment. The trainer may indicate that failures are to be expected, as in the case of the scientist who performs an experiment and gets negative results, but that such failures provide useful data. By anticipating failures and setbacks, the trainer can help clients short-circuit overreaction to them. The trainer can indicate that while such setbacks are normal, clients often develop doubts about whether training will work for them or whether they can ever change. In anticipating this negative self-monologue, the trainer can note that it is important for the client to expect this so that when negative thoughts begin, the client recognizes them as a normal part of the training process.

One of the characteristics that typifies the cognitive-behavioral therapists is their problem-solving approach toward "client resistance." For example, Beck, Rush, Hollon, and Shaw (1979) describe the following client reactions that may give rise to resistance: "It's useless to try," "I can't do it," "I am too weak to do anything," "If I try it and it won't work out, I'll only feel worse." Clients usually accept such reasons as valid, while the trainer views these reasons as hypotheses to be tested. Each time the client reports that he or she "failed" or "can't change," this is another occasion for the trainer to have the client reexamine the data that lead to such conclusions. The trainer also should be sensitive to whether the client is inferring from a limited number of failure experiences that he or she will always ("must") fail.

In general, when an impasse occurs, it should serve as a cue for the therapist and client to conduct an analysis to identify the sources of the stalled progress. Assessment activities are reinstituted for this purpose. A failed treatment plan provides the therapist with an opportunity to model the sort of adaptive response to failure that is expected of the clients. Possible sources of impaired progress include an inadequate response repertoire, insufficient incentive (or even disincentives) for engaging in the desired behavior, disruptive physiological arousal, or dysfunctional self-regulatory processes. The assessment of the determinants of the impasse provides a basis for developing an appropriate course of action for instigating renewed progress. Throughout this process, the therapist should take care to avoid appearing to blame the client for lack of progress, but instead should maintain a collaborative, upbeat, problem-solving stance.

Finally, including other family members, especially the spouse, in treatment may enhance client involvement. The importance of involving the spouse in the training program has been noted by a number of authors. Baekeland and Lundwill (1975), for example, reviewed 19 studies that examined the relationship between social support and dropout rate from treatment. In each case, the lack of spouse's participation and investment was related to a high dropout rate. Cobb (1979) concluded that the relationship between social support and cooperateive patient behavior is "one of the best documented relationships in medical sociology." Whenever possible, the trainer in stress inoculation training tries to involve the client's spouse or significant other in the assessment and training, including the implementation of homework assignments. It is important for the trainer to be sensitive to any "hidden agendas" that the client's spouse may hold concerning training. For example, a spouse may sabotage training, fearing that the client's improvement or change may threaten their relationship or the status quo. Thus, the therapist may promote client involvement in the treatment process by remaining "approachable," creating realistic expectations, establishing positive expectations by structuring incremental success experiences, adopting a problem-solving approach to stalled progress, and including other family members in the treatment process.

In *summary,* it is apparent that stress inoculation is a complex, multifaceted intervention designed to meet the intricacies involved in stress and coping. While stress inoculation training can be tailored to the specific population and the goals of training, certain common elements emerge. These include

1. teaching clients the role that cognitions and emotions play in engendering and potentiating stress;
2. training in the self-monitoring of stress-engendering thoughts, images, feelings, and behaviors;
3. training in the fundamentals of problem-solving (e.g., problem definition, anticipation of consequences, evaluating feedback);
4. modeling and rehearsal of instrumental and palliative modes of coping (e.g., relaxation, communication skills, use of social supports, attention-focusing skills, and positive self-evaluation);
5. graded *in vivo* behavioral assignments that become increasingly demanding.

As noted previously, there is a need to further evaluate the importance of these various components, as well as the overall efficacy of the stress inoculation training procedures. Much work is now underway to achieve these goals, as described in the next section of this book.

REFERENCES

Abelson, R. *Scripts.* Paper presented at the meeting of the Midwestern Psychological Association, Chicago, May 1978.

Baekeland, F., & Lundwill, L. Dropping out of treatment: A critical review. *Psychological Bulletin,* 1975, *82,* 738–753.

Bandura, A. Self-efficacy: Toward a unifying theory of behavior change. *Psychological Review,* 1977, *84,* 191–215.(a)

Bandura, A. *Social learning theory.* Englewood Cliffs, N.J.: Prentice-Hall, 1977.(b)

Bandura, A., Adams, N., Hardy, A., & Howells, G. Tests of the generality of self-efficacy theory. *Cognitive Therapy and Research,* 1980, *4,* 39–66.

Beck, A., Rush, J., Hollon, S., & Shaw, B. *Cognitive therapy of depression.* New York: Guilford Press, 1979.

Borkovec, T., & Sides, J. Critical procedural variables related to the physiological effects of progressive relaxation: A review. *Behaviour Research and Therapy,* 1979, *17,* 119–125.

Breznitz, S. A study of worrying. *British Journal of Social and Clinical Psychology,* 1971, *10,* 271–279.

Cameron, R. The clinical implementation of behavior change techniques. In J. Foreyt & D. Ratejan (Eds.), *Cognitive behavior therapy: Research and application.* New York: Plenum Press, 1978.

Cameron, R., & Meichenbaum, D. The nature of effective coping and the treatment of stress related problems: A cognitive-behavioral perspective. In C. Goldberger & A. Breznitz (Eds.), *Handbook of stress.* New York: Free Press, 1982.

Cobb, S. Social support and health through the life course. In M. Riley (Ed.), *Aging from birth to death: Interdisciplinary perspective.* Boulder, Colo.: Westview Press, 1979.

Condiotte, M., & Lichtenstein, E. Self-efficacy and relapse in smoking cessation programs. *Journal of Consulting and Clinical Psychology, 1981, 49,* 648–658.

Davidson, P. Therapeutic compliance. *Canadian Psychological Review,* 1976, *17,* 247–259.

DiClemente, C. Self-efficacy and smoking cessation maintenance: A preliminary report. *Cognitive Therapy and Research,* 1981, *5,* 175–187.

Dunbar, J. Adhering to medical advice: A review. *International Journal of Mental Health,* 1980, *9,* 70–87.

D'Zurilla, T., & Goldfried, M. Problem solving and behavior modification. *Journal of Abnormal Psychology,* 1971, *78,* 107–126.

Goldfried, M. Psychotherapy as coping skills training. In M. Mahoney (Ed.), *Psychotherapy process.* New York: Plenum Press, 1980.

Goldfried, M., & D'Zurilla, T. A behavior-analytic model for assessing competence. In C. Speilberger (Ed.), *Current topics in clinical and community psychology.* New York: Academic Press, 1969.

Goldfried, M., & Robins, C. On the facilitation of self-efficacy. *Cognitive Therapy and Research,* in press.

Heller, K. The effects of social support: Prevention and treatment implications. In A. Goldstein & F. Kanfer (Eds.), *Maximizing treatment gains.* New York: Academic Press, 1979.

Horan, J., Hackett, G., Buchanan, J., Stone, C., & Demchik-Stone, D. Coping with pain: A component analysis. *Cognitive Therapy and Research,* 1978, *1,* 211–221.

Janis, I. *Psychological stress.* New York: John Wiley, 1958.

Janis, I., & Mann, L. *Decision making.* New York: Free Press, 1977.

Kanfer, F., & Saslow, G. Behavioral diagnosis. In C. Franks (Ed.), *Behavior Therapy: Appraisal and status.* New York: McGraw-Hill, 1969.

Kelly, G. *The psychology of personal constructs* (2 vols.). New York: Norton, 1955.

Kelly, G. Fixed role therapy. In R. Jurjevich (Ed.), *Direct psychotherapy* (Vol. 1). Coral Gables, Fla.: University of Miami Press, 1973.

Kinsbourne, M. Cognitive deficit: Experimental analysis. In J. McGaugh (Ed.), *Psychology.* New York: Academic Press, 1971.

Klepac, R., Hauge, G., Dowling, J., & MacDonald, M. Direct and generalized effects of three components of stress inoculation for increased pain tolerance. *Behavior Therapy,* 1981, *72,* 417–424.

Lang, P. Fear reduction and fear behavior: Problems in treating a construct. In J. Shlien (Ed.), *Research in psychotherapy* (Vol. 3). Washington, D.C.: American Psychological Association, 1968.

Langer, E. Rethinking the role of thought in social interaction. In J. Harvey, W. Ickes, & R. Ridel (Eds.), *New directions in attribution research* (Vol. 2). Hillsdale, N.J.: Lawrence Erlbaum, 1978.

Lazarus, R. *Psychological stress and the coping process.* New York: McGraw Hill, 1966.

Lazarus, R. The stress and coping paradigm. In C. Eisdorfer (Ed.), *Models for clincial psychopathology.* New York: Spectrum Press, 1981.

Lazarus, R., & Cohen, J. Environmental stress. In I. Altman & J. Wohlwill (Eds.), *Human behavior and environment* (Vol. 2). New York: Plenum Press, 1977.

Lazarus, R., Cohen, J., Folkman, S., Kanner, A., & Shaefer, C. Psychological stress and adaptation: Some unresolved issues. In H. Selye (Ed.), *Selye's guide to stress research* (Vol. 1). New York: Van Nostrand Reinhold, 1980.

Lazarus, R., & Launer, R. Stress-related transactions between persons and environment. In L. Pervin & M. Lewis (Eds.), *Perspectives in interactional psychology,* New York: Plenum Press, 1978.

Lefcourt, H. *Locus of control: Current trends in theory and research.* Hillsdale, N.J.: Lawrence Erlbaum, 1976.

Mahoney, M. Personal science: A cognitive learning therapy. In A. Ellis & R. Grieger (Eds.), *Handbook of rational-emotive therapy.* New York: Springer Publishing, 1977.

Marlatt, A., & Gordon, J. Determinants of relapse: Implications for the maintenance of behavior change. In P. Davidson & S. Davidson (Eds.), *Behavioral medicine: Changing health lifestyles.* New York: Brunner/Mazel, 1980.

Marmor, J. The psychodynamics of realistic worry. *Psychoanalysis and Social Science,* 1958, *5,* 155–163.

McGuire, W. Inducing resistance to persuasion. Some contemporary approaches. In L. Berkowitz (Ed.), *Advances in social psychology* (Vol. 1). New York: Academic Press, 1964.

Meichenbaum, D. *Cognitive-behavior modification: An integrative approach.* New York: Plenum Press, 1977.

Meichenbaum, D., & Butler, L. Cognitive ethology: Assessing the streams of cognition and emotion. In K. Blankstein, P. Pliner, & J. Polivy (Eds.), *Advances in the study of communication and affect* (Vol. 6). *Assessment and modification of emotional behavior.* New York: Plenum Press, 1979.

Meichenbaum, D., & Cameron, R. *Stress inoculation: A skills training approach to anxiety management.* Unpublished manuscript, University of Waterloo, 1972.

Meichenbaum, D., & Gilmore, B. Resistance: From a cognitive-behavioral perspective. In P. Wachtel (Ed.), *Resistance in psychodynamic and behavioral therapies.* New York: Plenum Press, 1982.

Meichenbaum, D., & Novaco, R. Stress inoculation: A preventive approach. In C. Spielberger & I. Sarason (Eds.), *Stress and anxiety* (Vol. 5). New York: Halstead Press, 1977.

Meichenbaum, D., Henshaw, D., & Himel, N. Coping with stress as a problem-solving process. In W. Krohne & L. Laux (Eds.), *Achievement, stress and anxiety.* Washington, D.C.: Hemisphere Press, 1981.

Melzack, R., & Wall, P. Pain mechanism: A new theory. *Science,* 1965, *150,* 971.

Miller, W. Some negative thinking about Norman Vincent Peale. *The Reporter,* Jan. 13, 1955.

Mischel, W. A cognitive-social learning approach to assessment. In T. Merluzzi, C. Glass, & M. Genest (Eds.), *Cognitive assessment.* New York: Guilford Press, 1981.

Nelson, R. Assessment and therapeutic functions of self-monitoring. In M. Hersen, R. Eisler, & P. Miller (Eds.), *Progress in behavior modification* (Vol. 5). New York: Academic Press, 1977.

Novaco, R. *Anger control: The development and evaluation of an experimental treatment.* Lexington, Mass.: Health & Co., 1975.

Peterson, D. *The clinical study of social behavior.* New York: Appleton-Century-Crofts, 1968.

Qualls, P., & Sheehan, P. Electromyographic biofeedback as a relaxation technique. A critical appraisal. *Psychological Bulletin,* 1981, *90,* 21–42.

Rosenthal, T., & Bandura, A. Psychological modeling: Theory and practice. In S. Garfield & A. Bergin (Eds.), *Handbook of psychotherapy and behavior change* (2nd. ed.). New York: Wiley, 1978.

Roskies, E., & Lazarus, R. Coping theory and the teaching of coping skills. In P. Davidson & S. Davidson (Eds.), *Behavioral medicine: Changing health lifestyles.* New York: Brunner/Mazel, 1980.

Sarason, I., Johnson, J., Berberich, J., & Siegel, J. Helping police officers to cope with stress: A cognitive-behavioral approach. *American Journal of Community Psychology,* 1979, *7,* 593–603.

Schacter, S. The interaction of cognitive and physiological determinants of emotional state. In C. Spielberger (Ed.,), *Anxiety and behavior.* New York: Academic Press, 1966.

Seligman, M. *Helplessness.* San Francisco: W. Freeman, 1975.

Turk, D., Meichenbaum, D., & Genest, M. *Pain and behavioral medicine.* New York: Guilford Press, 1983.

Wachtel, P. *Resistance to psychodynamic and behavioral therapies.* New York: Plenum Press, 1982.

Wallace, J. An abilities conception of personality: Some implications for personality measurement. *American Psychologist,* 1966, *24,* 132–138.

Wilson, G. T. Cognitive factors in life style changes: A social learning perspective. In P. Davidson & S. Davidson (Eds.), *Behavioral medicine: Changing health lifestyles.* New York: Brunner/Mazel, 1980 (a).

Wilson, G. T. Toward specifying the nonspecific factors in behavior therapy: A social learning analysis. In M. Mahoney (Ed.), *Psychotherapy process.* New York: Plenum Press, 1980 (b).

Wolpe, J. *Psychotherapy by reciprocal inhibition.* Stanford: Stanford University Press, 1958.

III
Applications
Part A—Medical Problems

In recent years there has been an increasing interest in the fields of behavioral medicine and health psychology. The four chapters in this section focus on the use of stress management procedures for specific medical populations, namely, hospitalized patients, burn patients, patients with psychophysiological disorders, and coronary-prone Type A individuals. These four projects are illustrative of a cognitive-behavioral stress reduction approach. Many other examples could be offered and are reviewed elsewhere by Turk, Meichenbaum, and Genest (1983).

Cognitive-behavioral stress-management programs have been employed (a) to modify self-imposed risk to health (e.g., obesity, substance abuse, maladaptive lifestyles); (b) to alleviate distress related to aversive diagnostic and noxious therapeutic medical and surgical procedures (e.g., pelvic examinations, cardiac catherization, endoscopic examinations, postsurgical distress and discomfort, debridement of burns); (c) to enhance adaptive coping with stress (e.g., tension and migraine headaches, irritable bowel syndrome, gastric and duodenal ulcers, mucuous colitis); as well as (d) to assist patients to live more satisfactory lives despite chronic medical conditions (e.g., low back pain, diabetes, cancer). Turk *et al.* (1983) review the work in each of these areas.

In the first chapter of this section, Philip Kendall describes how cognitive-behavioral procedures can be used with patients about to undergo stressful medical procedures and with hospitalized patients. Kendall describes the social environment of the hospital and the nature of medical procedures and how they can contribute to patients' stress reactions. Kendall's description of the stressors involved in medical procedures indicates the potential for intervention at various levels. Some interventions designed to reduce stress can focus directly on the patients; other interventions can focus on the staff (doctors and nurses) and on the nature of their communications with patients; and still others may entail intervention at an institution's structural level (e.g., hospital rules, bureaucratic routines, architectural design). Consistent with the theme of this book, Kendall highlights the need for employing multifaceted interventions to solve complex problems.

Kendall also considers the need for being sensitive to individual differences and the value of individually tailoring treatment procedures. For example, the trainer should be sensitive in adapting features of the stress-reduction treatment, such as information-giving, to the patient's cognitive coping style. Given the complexities involved in reducing stress in medical settings, Kendall provides a description of a stress management program directed at patients as well as a description of possible systems-level interventions. While the results offered by Kendall and his colleagues in reducing stress for patients about to undergo cardiac catherization are encouraging, the research requires replication and extension.

A somewhat related project with medical patients is reported by Robert Wernick, who focuses on the stress of burn patients. Although Wernick's study is a very preliminary demonstration project, it has a number of innovative features and promising results. His session-by-session description of the treatment and his use of nurses as therapists can provide the basis for future work with burn patients as well as other medical populations. A more complete account of cognitive-behavioral interventions with pain patients is offered by Turk *et al.* (1983).

Chronic headaches, bronchial asthma, and essential hypertension are disorders that affect a sizable portion of the population. As Holroyd, Appel, and Andrasik indicate, the relationship between such psychophysiological disorders and stress are complex. They trace the pathophysiology of each of these disorders, noting the important role of the client's thoughts, feelings, and life style in contributing to the etiology and maintenance of these disorders. They then consider how cognitive-behavioral interventions can be used in treating psychophysiological disorders. In each case, the goals and techniques of intervention should be tailored to the characteristics of the particular disorder.

In these chapters the contributors focus on how individuals cope with stress related to major health problems (hospitalization, noxious medical examinations, burns, psychophysiological disorders). What happens when the individual's stress is self-imposed, that is, the result of one's life style? This question is further complicated by the fact that in some cases, individuals who are engaging in such potentially stress-engendering behaviors perceive themselves as being "healthy" and "successful" and therefore do not feel they need to change or undergo treatment.

Ethel Roskies considers the problems involved in setting up a stress-reduction training program for Type A individuals. Following a discussion of the coronary risk factors resulting from Type A behavior, (a constellation of hard-driving, striving intensely for achievement, competitive, easily provoked, impatient, driven by deadlines, abrupt in gestures and speech) Roskies considers the complexities involved in altering such behaviors. She provides a very important caveat that the editors wish to underscore; namely, in the absence of understanding the mechanisms involved between the complex pattern of Type A behavior and coronary risk, the therapist must be cautious in setting up such intervention programs.

With this caution in mind, Roskies describes a cognitive-behavioral intervention program designed to help Type A individuals restructure their environments, change the meaning of how they perceive stressful situations, and reduce their emotional responsiveness to stress experiences. This need to include multiple aspects of intervention that focus on direct-action and palliative modes of coping is once again highlighted. As Roskies notes, no single technique nor particular mode of coping can adequately respond to the variety of situations in which stress is experienced and the many forms it takes. As discussed earlier, *flexibility* in coping seems to be the most desirable object of training. The Roskies project provides a promising prototype and a thoughtful consideration of the issues that should guide future research.

REFERENCES

Turk, D., Meichenbaum, D., & Genest, M. *Pain and behavioral medicine: Theory, research and clinical guide.* New York: Guilford Press, 1983.

5

Stressful Medical Procedures

Cognitive-Behavioral Strategies for Stress Management and Prevention

PHILIP C. KENDALL

If you believe in a one-to-one relationship between specific stressors and specific reactions, in personality dispositions that determine the effects of stressors, or in the inevitability of certain events producing stress, then read no further. If, one the other hand, you accept the stress-reducing effects of both successful behavioral experience and informed cognitive processing, then you will find merit in what follows. When considering stress, you will also agree "as I have often said" (the "I" here is Hans Selye), that "it is not what happens to you, but how you take it" (1979, p. 12).

Disproportionate levels of anxiety, tension, worry, apprehension, and general discomfort are often present in patients who are confronted with the potential physical dangers of stressful medical procedures. Some anxiety is legitimate, since the patient is suspected to have a disease (e.g., heart disease). In addition, certain medical assessment procedures are an essential part of proper medical care. Nevertheless, many of the procedures invade the person's physical and psychological boundaries, often while the person is conscious and, at most, minimally sedated. Patients are typically ill-informed about the procedures to be undergone, unclear about the exact effects that the procedures will have on their health, inexperienced at carrying out tasks required during the actual

PHILIP C. KENDALL • Department of Psychology, University of Minnesota, Minneapolis, Minnesota 55455.

procedure, and concerned about both the probability of their death or the likelihood of their subsequent existence in some vegetable state. It is no wonder that the typical patient is not totally calm—the patient can reasonably be considered under stress.

The stressful nature of various medical procedures is further evidenced by the fact that many people who might possibly benefit from certain procedures maintain a pattern of avoidance. Even among those who present themselves for the procedures, many suffer such inordinate anxiety as to interfere with the complete and proper execution of the procedure. Still others suffer from residual distress following the completion of the medical procedures. As clinical psychologists and other behavioral scientists become increasingly involved in the psychology of medicine (e.g., behavioral medicine, medical psychology), the ever-present necessity of assisting these patients under stress becomes increasingly noteworthy.

The general purpose of the present chapter is to describe the cognitive-behavioral intervention strategies relevant for application with stressed medical patients. In so doing, we first examine two stressors that arise in the medical context: the stressful environments and the invasive medical procedures. The results of a survey of patients' self-reported stressors are also detailed. Research and theory bearing on the roles of cognitive and behavioral skills in stress prevention and management are examined. Several cognitive-behavioral intervention programs are described, with research findings demonstrating clinical efficacy. A description of the cognitive-behavioral intervention provides the groundwork for future research and application.

THE STRESSORS

Before considering qualities of the hospital environment and aspects of the medical intervention that are considered stressful, we must first recognize that certain characterisitcs of the psychologist may "stress" the patient, and that frictions within the hospital environment may in turn stress the psychologist.

Clinical psychologists, when in the environs of a mental health service delivery system, are often viewed by clients as helpers whose sensivity, skill, and experience provide relief from psychological distress. In non-mental-health settings, such as a medical ward, clinical psychologists can be seen quite differently. Patients scheduled for examinations to assess the presence or severity of heart disease may well wonder to themselves why the hospital has sent a psychologist ("Do I look crazy to them?"). When patients are not yet experiencing psychological distress and may even be denying the mere existence of the physical problem, they are likely to view the clinician as an intruder rather than a helper. It is essential for the providers of stress management service to try to eliminate any additional stress caused by their own presence. Recognizing the normal-but-stressed nature of the patient's status (as opposed to their being mental health patients) and communicating this directly to the patient often relieves some concern about their mental health. Clear statements to this effect, along with repeated exposure to and interaction with the psychologist, added to the environments' acceptance of the psychologist's role in the medical procedures all combine to transmit a more accepting (and less stressful) perception of the psychologist's involvement.

The clinical psychologist–physician interactions can also be sources of stress. Clinicians are, one hopes, inquisitive, and, coupled with only a cryptic knowledge of the specifics of medical procedures, they are likely to become students of the medical procedure. In an ideal setting, this does not create a problem. In some settings, however, psychologists may be seen as interfering with hospital scheduling, as untrained and therefore unnecessary, and as general nuisances. For example, Braider (1976) describes her experiences as a social scientist on a cancer ward: She was perceived by staff as a threat to their efficiency-oriented hospital system. This dilemma is sometimes exacerbated when physicians themselves have learned to defend against the dehumanizing nature of the patient's treatment and simply see the patient as a physical entity. It is in the human-interest enterprise that the clinician's expertise is most rewarding, and it is this aspect of the patient that physicians can come to bypass. Many of the strategies for stress management and prevention will be successful, but only to the extent that the hospital system is approached sensitively and the patient treated realistically.

The Environments

The hospital, a setting that is often responsible for extending life, has attained an undeserved reputation as the source of pain, discomfort, suffering, and sometimes death. However, part of this reputation may be valid since, after all, hospitalization often occurs when one's illness is past the point when it can be treated at the doctor's office!

Beyond the somewhat general perception of the hospital as threatening, the routine of hospital care probably causes additional stress. Many patients find bedside discussions with physicians and/or a nurse educational and reassuring. However, hearsay information can be distressing. For example, the physicians in charge of patient X, while standing at the foot of patient X's bed, may be discussing among themselves or with interns the status of patient Y. Patient X assumes the discussion concerns her case. Personalizing that which "your" physician says, whether it relates to your case or not, occurs at an alarming rate. Because the physician's conversations are a part of the hospital milieu, they too must be considered part of the stressful environment.

Special hospital settings are likely to be sources of increased patient stress. Kornfeld (1972) noted that as medicine became increasingly specialized, the need arose for specialized hospital settings, and that these unique environments have profound psychological effects. For example, Kornfeld (1972) draws a parallel between a patient's experience in an isolation unit and our understanding of the experience of sensory deprivation. Isolation units have individualized rooms, with masked and gowned attendants and limited visitors. When friends or family do visit, they too must wear masks and gowns. As a result, friends and family members become less familiar in appearance and somewhat more stressful than reassuring. The isolation room often intensifies the patient's anxiety, and, as Kornfeld (1972) noted, an occasional patient will show an acute psychotic reaction.

Reactions to another special hospital environment have been the "intensive care syndrome" (McKegney, 1966). Apparently, the experience of an intensive care unit (ICU) exacerbates a variety of symptoms associated with stress. This description of a "syndrome" resulted from the high rates of delirium (38%–70%) following open heart surgery (e.g., Kornfeld, Zimberg, & Malm, 1965). While in an ICU, patients are relatively immobile: They are attached to monitoring instruments and are often inside an oxygen tent. The instrumentation beeps and flashes and the oxygen tent noisily emits a constant hiss. Kornfeld (1972) describes a typical "intensive care syndrome" patient as one who appears to adjust normally for the first 3 or 4 days but then shows some disorientation in time, place, or person. The patient may think that the sound of the air conditioning is someone calling. Although the stay in the ICU is only part of the entire experience, recommendations for modification of the ICU environment have been emphasized as ways to reduce unwanted psychological reactions. Some reports of ICU modification (e.g., Lazarus & Hagens, 1968) have indicated a lower incidence of post-open-heart surgery delirium. Environmental manipulations have produced positive outcomes in pediatric ICUs as well (e.g., Cataldo, Bessman, Parker, Pearson, & Rogers, 1979).

A final though not unrelated example of a stressful hospital environment is the recovery room. Kornfeld (1972) describes the recovery room as a large open area where patients lie about at various levels of consciousness. One patient may be waiting three hours for an anesthesia to wear off while another may suddenly begin to bleed and require emergency attention. A patient may be brought to the room screaming for relief from pain while another lies quietly awaiting discharge. Suggested environmental adjustments, such as curtains to separate patients, can prevent patients from seeing certain events but cannot block out the sounds. Individual rooms are expensive, and nurses have difficulty keeping an eye on patients when they are so segregated. Other aspects of the hospital environment, such as the "odor" and the presence of "machines," have also been reported by patients to be stressful. As we will discuss, patients can be told what to expect, can be prepared to cope with certain stressors, and can be taught how to interpret constructively the environment that surrounds them. All of these strategies can serve to minimize the stressful nature of the medical procedures and the hospitalization.

The Procedures

Advances in modern medicine continue to offer today's hospital patient greater hope for accurate diagnosis and treatment of physical disorders. This hope can be credited largely to technological advances in medical assessment. The sometimes frightening appearance and nature of the tools of medical assessment aside, these tools help save lives. Nevertheless, the procedures are stressful. Skydell and Crowder (1975) have prepared a reference book that describes diagnostic procedures and mentions, though entirely too briefly, ideas for patient counseling. Consider the following examples as illustrations of stressful medical procedures.

Colonoscopy has been available only since 1969, with its practice often limited to major medical centers. A colonoscopy provides direct visualization of the large intestine through a fiber optic colonoscope. A larger portion of the intestine can be seen than with other procedures barring surgery. The entire length of the colonoscpe is passed, and then withdrawn slowly so that the intestinal mucosa can be examined and suspect tissue removed for further study. Although the time required to perform colonoscopy varies, a procedure as brief as 30 minutes can be extended to 2 or more hours when passage of the colonoscope is difficult.

Patients about to undergo colonoscopy are limited to a fluid diet for 24 hours and are given enemas approximately 2 hours before the test. Medications are used only to produce some relaxation in the patient because the patient's cooperation during the test is important. Colonoscopy is a tiring and trying procedure for many patients. Although it may not be painful, it is difficult to endure because of the body position that is assumed, the experience of cramps, and embarrassment from the face-to-anus juxtaposition of the procedure.

Similar medical procedures seek visualization of the lower portion of the large intestine and are referred to as signoidoscopy, proctoscopy, or anoscopy. These procedures differ in the length of the endoscope that is used and the portion of the intestine that is examined. In all these examinations, however, patients must assume a knee-to-chest position, with the anus protruding. Patients also report experiencing discomfort due to an urge to defecate and dizziness when returning to a standing position.

Endoscopic examinations of gastrointestinal functioning require the inserting of a flexible tube (e.g., 12 mm in diameter, 90 cm in length) through the mouth. Local anesthetic is applied only to the throat. The tube is held down for 15–30 minutes so that the patient's inner track may be transmitted to the physician. The patient must be awake to follow directions and breathe correctly (to prevent gagging), so sedation is unacceptable.

Cardiac catheterization is an invasive medical procedure that provides visualization of the chambers of the heart and of the great vessels. This procedure is likely to be undergone by someone who has been informed that he or she probably has some form of coronary artery disease. The cardiac catheterization procedure is worthwhile since it aids the physician in making determinations about problems in pressure, blood flow and output, and arterial structure. The procedure usually proceeds as follows: The patient, dressed in hospital gown, is escorted to a specialized cardiac catheterization laboratory. The patient assumes a supine position on a "cradle top" platform and is strapped in. Several nurses, technicians, and physicians are independently involved in a variety of tasks. Since it is essential that the patient be able to follow directions throughout the 2- to 3-hour procedure, physicians provide only a mild tranquilizer.

The cardiac catheterization itself involves the following: The catheter, a long and quite narrow tube, is inserted into the patient's femoral artery near the groin. The catheter moves within the artery until it reaches the heart. Physicians make adjustments in placement to assure that the catheter has arrived at the proper location in the heart. A camera suspended above the patient's chest projects the event onto a nearby screen. Once correctly located, the catheter serves to transmit a contrast material (i.e., dye) that will help to show heart functioning and to highlight disease tissue. The dye should not remain in the patient's heart for long, so the physician requires the patient to "cough hard" to help flush the dye. Patients must also take deep breaths on command in order to move the lungs so that clear photographs can be taken. In some settings the screen is visible to the patient. As the patient endures the procedure, medical staff scurry about monitoring equipment, checking physical signs, coaching the patient on following instructions, and commenting on the quality of the pictures that the procedure is producing.

The patient experiences various sensations throughout the catheterization. When the heart is stimulated, patients sometimes feel palpitations or a missed heart beat. When the contrast material is injected, patients experience a sense of warmth and in some cases an overwhelming surge of heat. The procedure produces nausea, some brief but severe spurts of pain due to vasospasm, and discomfort due to the extended period of time the patient spends lying flat on his or her back. As if the procedure itself is not sufficiently stressful, recall the additional pressures due to the implications of the findings.

Patients' Self-Reported Stressors

On an *a priori* basis, both the environments and the procedures associated with medical care are appropriately considered stressful. But how, in fact, do most individuals perceive the experiences of hospitalization? What specific environmental factors are precipitants of the stressful nature of hospitalization? As we will discuss later, knowledge of each individual's specific stress cues is important, yet knowledge of the typically most stressful events can prove equally valuable.

Volicer and Bohannon (1975), while working on the development of a hospital stress rating scale, devised an extensive list of hospital-related stress experiences. By means of a card-sorting strategy, the list was rank-ordered from most to least stressful. A total of 261 patients completed the card sorting; 104 were male and 157 were female, with a mean age of 51.9 years and a mean education of 12.4 years. The list of stressful events, in rank order from least to most stressful, is provided in Table I. The average assigned rank is also provided. As evident in Table I, the most stressful events cluster around (a) the possibility of serious illness or loss of senses and (b) a lack of information about one's condition. That these two clusters do in fact represent the typical stressful factors involved in hospitalization is evident in the degree of similarity of the ranking for different samples of subjects. For example, general medical and surgical patient rankings correlated 0.93, male and female patient rankings correlated 0.92 and for six other subsample comparisons the correlations ranged from 0.90 to 0.96. Apparently, there was a high degree of consensus in the ranking of the stressful nature of the 49 experiences.

Demands of the "Good" Patient

The good patient is obedient. When the physician says, "Turn to the right," the patient is expected to turn immediately. When the patient

Table I. Assigned Rank Order and Mean Rank Score for Events Related to the Stresses of Hospitalization[a]

Assigned Rank	Event	Mean Rank Score
1	Having strangers sleep in the same room with you	13.9
2	Having to eat at different times than you usually do	15.4
3	Having to sleep in a strange bed	15.9
4	Having to wear a hospital gown	16.0
5	Having strange machines around	16.8
6	Being awakened in the night by the nurse	16.9
7	Having to be assisted with bathing	17.0
8	Not being able to get newspapers, radio, or TV when you want them	17.7
9	Having a roommate who has too many visitors	18.1
10	Having to stay in bed or the same room all day	19.1
11	Being aware of unusual smells around you	19.4
12	Having a roommate who is seriously ill or cannot talk with you	21.2
13	Having to be assisted with a bedpan	21.5
14	Having a roommate who is unfriendly	21.6
15	Not having friends visit you	21.7
16	Being in a room that is too cold or too hot	21.7
17	Thinking your appearance might be changed after your hospitalization	22.1
18	Being in the hospital during holidays or special family occasions	22.3
19	Thinking you might have pain because of surgery or test procedures	22.4
20	Worrying about your spouse being away from you	22.7
21	Having to eat cold or tasteless food	23.2
22	Not being able to call family or friends on the phone	23.3
23	Being cared for by an unfamiliar doctor	23.4
24	Being put in the hospital because of an accident	23.6
25	Not knowing when to expect things will be done to you	24.2
26	Having the staff be in too much of a hurry	24.5
27	Thinking about losing income because of your illness	25.9
28	Having medications cause you discomfort	26.0
29	Having nurses or doctors talk too fast or use words you can't understand	26.4
30	Feeling you are getting dependent on medications	26.4
31	Not having family visit you	26.5
32	Knowing you have to have an operation	26.9
33	Being hospitalized far away from home	27.1
34	Having a sudden hospitalization you weren't planning to have	27.2
35	Not having your call light answered	27.3
36	Not having enough insurance to pay for your hospitalization	27.4
37	Not having your questions answered by the staff	27.6
38	Missing your spouse	28.4
39	Being fed through tubes	29.2

Table I (Continued)

Assigned Rank	Event	Mean Rank Score
40	Not getting relief from pain medications	31.2
41	Not knowing the results or reasons for your treatments	31.9
42	Not getting pain medication when you need it	32.4
43	Not knowing for sure what illness you have	34.0
44	Not being told what your diagnosis is	34.1
45	Thinking you might lose your hearing	34.5
46	Knowing you have a serious illness	34.6
47	Thinking you might lose a kidney or some other organ	35.6
48	Thinking you might have cancer	39.2
49	Thinking you might lose your sight	40.6

[a]Adapted from Volicer and Bohannon (1975).

receives instructions to swallow a tube, etc., the "good" patient not only follows directions but also doesn't ask questions. Although this varies from physician to physician, it is generally the case that information-seeking on the part of the patient is considered bothersome. Similarly, it is considered bothersome when patients recognize their current stress and seek emotional support. The good patient does not have any complications. Even though complications may develop outside the control of the patient, the "good" patient still is not supposed to have any.

A major paradox exists in medical treatment—the patient is physically and psychologically in a weak and vulnerable position, yet the treatment staff implicitly expects strength of character and will. The demands of a "good" patient are, indeed, more than one might expect from a physically and psychologically sound person.

Recognition of the stressful nature of invasive medical procedures led Auerbach and Kilmann (1977) to consider them "crises," with the implication that crisis intervention strategies provide an available course of action. Crisis intervention procedures are not designed to reconstruct the client's personality, to change long-standing behavior patterns, or to resolve systems of interpersonal conflict. Crisis intervention strategies are appropriate because there exists a clearly defined crisis, treatment is timeliminted, and the goals of treatment are narrowly defined (Butcher & Maudal, 1976). A recent review of the literature on the psychological preparation of stressed medical patients (Kendall & Watson, 1981) provided additional evidence to endorse such a conceptualization. With the patient seen as "in crisis," the clinician prepares to resolve the crisis.

INFORMATION PROVISION IN STRESS MANAGEMENT AND PREVENTION

Further inspection of Table I serves to highlight the clinical relevance of certain facts. For example, as noted by Volicer and Bohannon (1975), some events that receive high rankings can be altered by stress-management personnel. Items such as "not being told what your diagnosis is," "not knowing for sure what illness you have," "not knowing the results or reasons for your treatments," and "not having your questions answered by staff" demonstrate that a major stess, as perceived by patients, is the lack of communication of information. In general, stress mangement staff would increase their beneficial impact if they could serve as information sources during the patient's hospitalization.

Two types of information are discussed in the literature: procedural and sensory. Providing *procedural* information entails the description of the nature of the medical event (e.g., assessment, surgery) when and where it will take place, why it is being conducted, what the mortality rate is, etc. Providing *sensory* information gives the patient an expectation of the sensations that are likely to be felt during and/or after the procedure.

Vernon and Bigelow (1974) investigated the effectiveness of preoperative procedural information in reducing the anxiety of male patients hospitalized for the repair of inguinal hernias. The treated patients received detailed procedural information two days prior to surgery, while controls received no extra information. Analyses of the patients' anxiety, as measured by an adjective checklist, revealed few significant effects. While these results fail to endorse the utility of providing detailed procedural information in reducing patient anxiety, the authors noted that some of the patients did not seem to find the surgery particularly stressful.

The efficacy of providing patients with sensory information within a physician—patient relationship was investigated by Egbert, Battit, Welch, and Bartlett (1964). Patients scheduled to undergo interabdominal operations were visited the night before surgery and given procedural information about the location, severity, and duration of the pain they might expect to feel postoperatively. Treated patients were also taught some behavioral skills, such as how to relax muscles and turn in bed properly so as to reduce pain. Egbert *et al.*'s (1964) results indicated that although the two groups did not differ in their use of narcotics for pain on the day of their operation, the treatment group had a significantly lower level of use on each of the succeeding five days. Treated patients were released sooner from the hospital and rated blindly as being in less pain. The effects of the special attention and the behavioral skills training cannot be separated from the treatment effects, but the results nevertheless provide some support for the efficacy of sensory informaton provision.

Johnson and Leventhal (1974), employing patients undergoing an endoscopy examination, compared the effectiveness of different interventions in reducing stress. All of the patients were told when the exam would take place, what equipment would be used, etc. (procedural information), but only some of the patients were provided with sensory information. A second intervention proup was given specific breathing instructions and taught specific behaviors to be used during the insertion (behavioral skills training). Both sensory and behavioral skills information were provided to a third group, with the fourth group receiving nothing beyond the procedural information.

The design of the Johnson and Leventhal study allowed for the evaluation of specific components of the treatment, but the results failed to provide clear evidence for the superiority of any component. No group differences were found in tension-related arm movements during the procedure, and only marginal differences in heart rate for patients under 50 years of age. Also, for those under 50, only the sensory information patients took less medication than controls. Both the combined information and sensory only groups gagged less than controls; however, the tube procedure took longer for the combined information group than for the controls.

Moderate support for the effectiveness of information provision was also provided by Mohros (1977) and Johnson, Morissey, and Leventhal (1973). Mohros's gastrointestinal endoscopy patients received different types of information but showed no significant group differences on measures of tranquilizer dosage or avoidant movements. Johnson *et al.*'s (1973) gastrointestinal endoscopy patients also received varying types of information but failed to show group differences in gagging, heart rate, or restlessness. Less medication was required by information groups than controls, and sensory information patients exhibited fewer tension-related movements. Yet these findings provide only a moderate level of support for the utility of information-providing interventions. Recent research by Mills and Krantz (1979) also reported moderate levels of support for the value of information provision. Nevertheless, since information provision is considered an important component of nursing care and good medical practice, many patients routinely receive such treatment. Numerous additional studies evaluating other types of interventions have also routinely included the provision of stress-related information (e.g. Cassell, 1965; Melamed & Siegel, 1975; Wolfer & Visintainer, 1975).

Cognitive Processing and the Effects of Information

Although moderate support for the efficacy of information provision appears in the literature, it is not clear that resolution of stress-related discomfort by means of information takes place in an identical manner for all patients. Indeed, it is erroneous to assume that all patients will respond to any psychological procedure in a uniform fashion. Varying amounts of information, changing specificity of the information, and differing information-receiving and -processing styles among the patients all contribute to the differential effectiveness of information.

The literature provides several examples of how patients' cognitive styles and generalized expectancies interact with information provision in the reduction of stress. The research by Shipley, and his colleagues (Shipley, Butt, Horwitz, & Fabry, 1978; Shipley, Butt, & Horwitz, (1979), for example, demonstrates that a repressing or sensitizing (Byrne, 1964) cognitive style affects informational interventions. Repressors are individuals who characteristically cope with stress by not thinking about it, denying it, and simply not recognizing any potential stressfulness. Repressors appear, then, to be nonanxious. Sensitizers are typically anxious about the impending stress, but they handle the stress through careful attention to threatening cues, information-seeking, and cognitive-coping preparations.

Shipley *et al.*'s (1978) subjects received sensory and procedural information about the coming endoscopy from multiple sources—physician, nurse, and experimenter. On the evening before the endoscopy, patients were shown either a control videotape once, the treatment videotape once, or the treatment videotape three times. The 18-minute treatment tape presented a 35-year-old white male patient actually receiving an endoscopy. The patient showed some distress, with some gagging, and the nurse talked to the patient to calm him. The results indicated that the stress of the endoscopy was reduced as a function of the number of viewings of the treatment videotape. However, the results were not identical for repressors and sensitizers (i.e., heart rate data). The role of this individual cognitive style in the effectiveness of Shipley's treatment was more clearly delineated in his 1979 study.

Employing similar procedures, Shipley *et al.* (1979) reported that when the cognitive coping style (repression–sensitization) variable was ignored, the intervention had *no* effect, but when subjects' coping styles were taken into accout, a significant reduction in anxiety was found for the sensitizers. Stimulus exposure was effective for sensitizers—they deal with anxiety by attending to stress-related cues. Since the intervention was not successful with repressors, Horwitz, Shipley, and McGuire (1977) suggested that a different procedure, consistent with their coping strategy, might be effective. Horwitz *et al.* provided repressors with a distraction intervention. These endoscopy patients were told that people find the procedure easier if they ignore the doctor, close their eyes, and listen to music. Some of the Horwitz *et al.* data suggested the utility of the distractor procedure with repressors, but the findings were not consistent. The accumulated data speak directly to the importance of providing interventions that recognize and allow for individual differences in cognitive processing.

Additional evidence highlights the necessity of examining patients' cognitive coping styles (e.g., Andrew, 1970; Cohen & Lazarus, 1973; see also Turk & Genest, 1979). In the Andrew study, one-half of the minor surgery patients were given surgery-related information, while the other half were not treated. Employing a sentence-completion test, Andrew divided subjects into three coping-style groups. Patients who readily acknowledged negative emotions such as fear and anxiety were classified as "sensitizers," patients who denied and distanced themselves from negative feelings were classified as "avoiders," and those not showing a characteristic pattern were classified as "neutrals." Although the sensitizers showed no significant differences (on length of postsurgery stay and amount of medication needed) as a result of the intervention, neutrals who received the information spent fewer days in the hospital and required less medication. Negative effects were seen in the avoiders who received information, for they required more medication. These iatrogenic effects underscore the importance of individual cognitive coping styles and the effects of stress management interventions.

The effect of general versus specific information has also been reported to interact with individual difference variables such as cognitive-coping style (DeLong, 1971) and generalized expectancy style (Auerbach, Kendall, Cuttler, & Levitt, 1976). DeLong (1971) exposed major abdominal surgery patients to either general or specific information and divided the subjects into three cognitive coping style groups based on responses to a sentence-completion test. "Copers" were those patients who preferred an active, vigilant defense against stress, and "avoiders" were those who preferred a repressive, avoidant defense, with "neutrals" falling in the middle. Patients provided with specific information were discharged from the hospital sooner and had less complicated recoveries than those receiving general information. However, patients' coping styles interacted with the type of information given, with neutrals unaffected, copers preferring specific information, and avoiders preferring general information. In a dental surgery situation, Auerbach *et al.* (1976) found that patients' locus of control (Rotter, 1966) interacted with the type of information (general versus specific) provided. Internal locus of control patients who viewed the specific information tape were rated by dentists as better adjusted than those who viewed the general information tape. The converse was true for the externals, who responded favorably to the general information tape.

How does the provision of information affect adjustment? Why does coping style affect the information intervention? A reasonable conclusion involves the congruence between the patients' typical stress-related response patterns and the intervention strategy. When the intervention focuses on providing specific information and when the subject's typical response pattern involves active information-seeking and vigilant evaluation of stress cues (e.g., sensitizers, copers, internals), the coping styles are *congruent*. Similarly, when patients have adopted a pattern of cognitive denial and behavioral avoidance, the absence of information or the presentation of general nonthreatening information finds a compatible recipient. Averill, O'Brien, and Dewitt (1977) have also demonstrated, in a laboratory situation, that individual differences in cognitive style are predictive of coping in spite of subjects having similar expectations about the outcome. What is being suggested here is that there is no *one* successful intervention strategy for all patients, but that some intervention strategies are successful when individual cognitive-coping styles are considered and when the intervention and individual styles are congruent. In other words, successful stress management strategies play into, subsidize, and reinforce the patient's own coping style. We will return to this issue in a later discussion of the cognitive-behavioral procedures for stress management and prevention.

An example of the effects of cognitive processing on stress appraisal is available from a study that directly altered patients' cognitive processing. The patient, as the receiver of information, processes the new data through a cognitive coping style. As an active processor, a patient may misinterpret environmental or internal events and subsequently experience stress. Langer, Janis, and Wolfer (1975) provided an intervention that focused on the reduction of stress through selective attention and cognition. Patients were taught to process stress-related information by directing their attention to some favorable aspects of the situation. This cognitive reappraisal or coping intervention was compared with (a) information provision, (b) coping training plus information provision, and (c) an interview-only control.

Nurses' ratings of patient's preoperative anxiety and ability to cope showed significant group differences. The two groups receiving the cognitive coping training were rated the lowest in anxiety and the highest in ability to cope. In contrast, the information-only group was rated highest in anxiety and lowest in ability to cope. The coping strategy groups also fared significantly better in postoperative requests for pain relievers and sedatives. The lack of support for information provision is not surprising since patients received only procedural information. The results of the Langer *et al.* study indicate the potential value of a cognitive reappraisal–coping skills intervention, a potential that is more fully described in a later section.

In summary, the literature reviewed thus far indicates the complexity of reducing stress in the medical setting. The impact of any specific technique, whether it be providing information or manipulating the environment, is mediated by the individual's cognitive and coping style. The role of such individual differences is further highlighted in considering the patient's penchant for using denial or avoidance in coping with stress.

Stress can be conceptualized as an imbalance between a person's perceived demand and his or her perceived capability (Lazarus, 1966; McGrath, 1970). Accordingly, demands that are not cognitively attended to should not prove stressful and demands that are cognitively perceived as within the person's response capability are also not stressful. Thus, according to Lazarus, the individual's cognitive appraisal is a key determiner of both psychological stress and effective coping.

This conceptualization has merit when applied to stressful medical procedures. In the first case, when stress does not occur since demands are not perceived, the individual may be employing denial as a coping strategy. The use of denial may prove to be an effective coping technique when there is little or nothing that can be done to reduce the stress. But in other circumstances, denial is likely to be insufficient. The stressor may prove to be difficult if not impossible to deny, and the patient's use of denial will impede his or her ability to cope with stress. Patients must recognize the stressor (reduce denial), but this may not be sufficient without an increase in their response capabilities and sense of self-confidence. While often not the most desirable coping strategy, denial seems to occur at a high rate among normal-but-stressed medical patients. Denial often appears early in the reaction to stress and perhaps represents an initial attempt at coping.

Stress can be prevented if a person appraises that the demands are within his or her own capabilities. Since patients can be taught the cognitive and behavioral skills necessary to perceive the event as within their capability, they can come to cope successfully with the stress.

Information provision, of either a sensory or procedural nature, may serve only to break the denial pattern, bringing into the patient's awareness the nature of the event and its potential harm. Some patients perceive the event as within their capability, and they adjust or cope, using the provided information, while others perceive themselves as incapable and demonstrate stress responses. In the latter case such information may merely exacerbate stress. Any training program must take into consideration such wide individual differences. Before considering one such cognitive-behavioral training program, let us consider other cognitive-behavioral attempts to reduce stress in medical settings.

FILMED MODELING

Based on a literature indicating that exposing a client to a model who demonstrates desired behavior can help the client to engage in the desired behavior, filmed modeling has been successfully employed to help reduce patient stress. Unlike live modeling, where the demonstration by the model is an actual ongoing event, and unlike covert modeling, where the client creates a mental image of the model engaging in the desired behavior, filmed modeling presents the performance of the model by means of film, videotape, or slide show with accompanying audio tape. The filmed model is often a coping model, demonstrating initial fear and stress followed by successful coping. In contrast, a mastery model demonstrates successful coping, but without the initial fear or the strategies for overcoming the fear. Coping models have been found superior to mastery models in several studies (e.g., Kazdin, 1974; Meichenbaum, 1971; Sarason, 1975), and they seem to be most potent with naive as opposed to experienced patients (Klorman, Hilpert, Michael, LaGana, & Sveen, 1980). Such coping models provide not only procedural and sensory information but also response information about how and when to cope.

We have already mentioned the Shipley *et al.* (1978, 1979) studies within the context of the interaction between informational interventions and the patient's cognitive coping style. However, this work can again be mentioned here, because they successfully used coping modeling films. Their films presented a coping model who showed some initial difficulty and distress with the endoscopy and subsequent coping with the procedure.

Another impressive program of research employs filmed models for the reduction of childrens' stress in medical and dental contexts. For instance, Melamed and Siegel (1975) used filmed models to help 4- to 12-year-olds cope with surgery. The films lasted 16 minutes and consisted of coping models who described their feelings and concerns about each event, but who ultimately completed each event in a nonanxious manner. Description of the survey procedures and the operating and recovery rooms were also provided on the film. On both a Hospital Fears Rating Scale and observer ratings of anxiety, the children who saw the filmed models scored significantly lower than children who saw a control film at both pre- and postoperative assessment periods. Although the modeling film initially increased anxiety, as measured by the Palmer Sweat Index, these indices were significantly lower at both pre- and postsurgery. Work by Ferguson (1979) also indicates positive effects from a filmed modeling procedure, but Ferguson did not replicate all of Melamed and Siegel's (1975) findings. However, the discrepancies may be due to the differential effects of the filmed model for different aged children.

Melamed and her colleagues (e.g., Melamed, Weinstein, Hawes, & Katin-Borland, 1975) have also reported on the reduction of fear-related dental management problems through the use of filmed modeling. As these authors noted, while earlier modeling intervention researchers had reported equivocal findings, they had not employed conditions that maximized the effectiveness of the modeling. Melamed *et al.* (1975), in order to maximize the effects of exposure to the filmed model, included praise for cooperative model behavior, coping model characteristics, and showing the modeling film under conditions when the children were aroused in anticipation of the dental work. Children either viewed the modeling film or drew pictures for an equal length of time.

Data from a Behavior Profile Rating Scale, consisting of fear-related disruptive behaviors, and a childrens' fear survey schedule were analyzed. The Behavior Profile Rating Scale indicated the frequency of disruptive behaviors during successive three-minute intervals. Melamed *et al.* (1975) reported that children who viewed the modeling tape showed significantly less disruptive behavior during restorative dental procedures than did the controls. (For a description of other related studies, see Melamed, 1979.)

With both adults and children, filmed modeling interventions have been found to produce positive results in terms of stress reduction and the management of disruptive behavior. In the filmed modeling paradigm, it appears that the efficacy of the treatment lies in the presentation of information about the impending event (both verbally and visually) and in the viewing of an example of successful coping. Evidence suggests that repetition of this exposure is desirable (Shipley *et al.*, 1978) but that there are also individual differences (repression–sensitization) that interact with the success of repeated exposure (Shipley *et al.*, 1979).

The efficacy of the filmed modeling may be enhanced further by including patient–therapist interactions, where the therapist engages the patient in a discussion of the intended message. More importantly, the therapist can require *active* rehearsal of the coping strategies with appropriate feedback. Without such an active interchange between the trainer and patient, there is only a limited performance-based component to the treatment. The efficacy of the filmed modeling procedures could be enhanced through inclusion of a performance-based rehearsal component. The importance of such components is illustrated in the cognitive behavioral approach to which we now turn our attention.

COGNITIVE-BEHAVIORAL STRESS MANAGEMENT

Stress Inoculation Training: Some Beginnings

Stress inoculation training (Meichenbaum & Cameron, 1973) is a cognitive-behavioral intervention that focuses on altering both persons' cognitive processing of the situation and their behavioral skills in order to modify their manner of reacting. Three stages have been outlined for stress inoculation training: client preparation, skills training, and application training. In the client preparation stage, the therapist helps the patient realize how maladaptive thoughts and self-statements can affect behavior. This stage is primarily educational, although the entire training program can be viewed as educational in nature. The trainer presents the client with a rationale for cognitive control of stress and the conceptualization of stress as a controllable force. The therapist works to modify the patient's view of stress through collaborative examination of the client's self-talk.

The second stage involves skills training. Jaremko (1979) described these procedures as including mental and physical relaxation, cognitive restructuring, self-instructional training, and the presentation of a "cafeteria style" array of techniques from which the patient can choose as components of the skills training stage. The cognitive restructuring and self-instructional training focus on the patient's reexamining the stress and learning to develop various cognitive coping strategies.

The final stage involves the patient's actual application and practice of the newly acquired skills in stressful situations. Although the amount of practice will vary, it is essential that the patient have the opportunity to actually engage, either in imagination or *in vivo,* in the use of the coping skills. The stressful experiences can be hierarchically arranged, thus increasing the likelihood that the patient will experience successful coping.

A number of studies have demonstrated the utility of stress inoculation training (e.g., Holcomb, 1979; Holroyd, 1976; Horan, Hackett, Buchanan, Stone, & Demchik-Stone, 1977; Hussian & Lawrence, 1978; Meichenbaum & Cameron, 1973; Turk, 1975; see also other chapters in this volume). For example, Holcomb evaluated the usefulness of stress inoculation procedures with patients hospitalized for severe stress reactions. These "stress reactions" covered a wide range of diagnoses, with 18 depressive neuroses, 4 anxiety neuroses, 4 marital maladjustments, and a few in each of 12 other categories. Twenty-six acute patients were randomly assigned to one of three groups: (a) stress inoculation training, (b) stress inoculation training and chemotherapy, and (c) chemotherapy. Subjects received the stress inoculation training in an average of eight one-hour sessions from one therapist—the experimenter. The stress inoculation training included autogenic training as the relaxation coping skill, cognitive restructuring as a cognitive change procedure, and rehearsal and modeling as performance-oriented behavioral procedures. Dosage level and type of drug for chemotherapy patients were determined by each patient's physician. Seven measures of distress (e.g., MMPI Despression and Psychasthenia scale, subscores of the Sympton Checklist-90, and the State-Trait Anxiety Inventory) were combined by means of multivariate methods to produce one independent measure called the Subjective Distress factor. Following rotation, this factor accounted for 93.5% of the variance. Patients were assessed within two days after their arrival at the hospital, again five days later, and finally after the intervention was completed.

There were no significant differences on the Subjective Distress factor among the three treatment groups on their arrival at the hospital. All three groups showed some decrease in Subjective Distress during the first pretreatment week in the hospital, but the group who received only stress inoculation was significantly superior to the chemotherapy-only group in reducing Subjective Distress over the course of treatment. While these data are preliminary and one would like to see long-term follow-up, they do suggest the utility of stress inoculation training with clinical patients suffering severe stress. Moreover, Holcomb's data suggest that stress inoculation procedures were more effective than chemotherapy in reducing Subjective Distress. Given the heterogeneity of these clinical patients, these data are most encouraging. Future research will need to address the likelihood of change occurring on measures of improvement other than patient self-report.

Cognitive-Behavioral Strategies for Medical Stress Management

Recognition of the environmental, procedural, and personal factors that can contribute to the excessive stress of the hospital patient leads one to a multifactor conceptualization of the stressor. Similarly, recognition of the role of the patient's cognitive coping style in processing stress-related information leads to an individualized stress management pro-

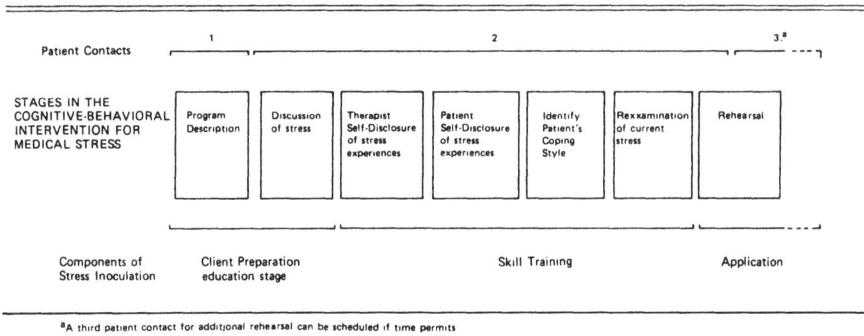

Figure 1. Flowchart illustrating the stages of the cognitive-behavioral intervention for medical stress.

gram. Both of these factors are taken into consideration in the present cognitive-behavioral program for stress management. The program is sensitive to the sources of stress and the program provides an individually tailored intervention. The stages of the cognitive-behavioral intervention are described in Figure 1. Let us consider each of these stages.

Prior to the initiation of the intervention proper, the trainer who may be a psychologist, nurse, or trained volunteer makes initial contact with the patient. This first contact, often at bedside, is very important. Whether a staff person has suggested that the clinician see the patient or even if the clinician routinely provides service for incoming patients it is not uncommon for the *medically* troubled patient to wonder "So they think I'm crazy...why else would they send a psychologist to talk to me?"

A brief initial pretreatment contact contributes to a smooth-running intervention. It provides a chance for patient and clinician to become acquainted with one another. Generating casual conversation, offering suggestions that will enhance comfort, and, most important, being an attentive ear will promote the patient's reception of the clinician's presence and recommendations. A useful technique is to anticipate the patient's concerns and preoccupations and to include these at the same time. During an introduction, for example, one might say

> Hello, I'm Dr.—. I work on this unit as a psychologist and I routinely see all patients to check on how things are going and to see what can be done to make your stay more comfortable. The staff here recognize that a visit to the hospital can be a trying event and that having a chance to talk about how things are going may often prove helpful.

If the patient raises concerns about seeing a psychologist, or if the therapist senses such a concern, he or she might then add,

> Seeing someone like a psychologist may seem odd, but it *doesn't* mean that you are going crazy or that anyone is worried about you. What it does mean is that we have come to appreciate how important stress is to the health process and we'd like to help keep you from feeling unduly stressed.

The exact words are less important than the sentiment that is conveyed. The effort should be on communicating that the psychologist will be a resource that is on call. It is in this context that the description of the intervention program is offered.

The clinician first presents the rationale for the program. The rationale places emphasis on the normal-but-stressed nature of the patient's condition. "Everyone experiences stress" and "You haven't been secretly identified as crazy" are statements that are reassuring for the patient to hear. Describing the role of the psychologist in this setting as one who facilitates the adjustment of normal-but-stressed patients also gives reassurance. Discussing how people cope with stress and practicing how to cope with stress in advance are described as part of the program. The trainer attempts to stimulate an appropriate level of positive expectancy enhanced by mentioning that previous patients have found the discussions interesting and that they reported feeling less stressed as a result.

When operating procedures permit, the intervention proper would begin at a second contact period that had been mutually agreed on by the patient and trainer, giving consideration to the patient's hectic hospital schedule. If scheduling or patient preference dictates, the next training phase can proceed directly following the description of the program. It is more likely, however, that the training will be more enthusiastically received, and perhaps therefore more effective, if the patient has had a chance to think it over and anticipate talking about stress rather than if the intervention follows directly after the program description. This particularly applies when the training is conducted on a group basis.

The discussion of stress begins the intervention (patient contact #2 in Figure 1). The clinician acknowledges the fact that the medical procedures result in varying levels of stress and that stressors may or may not be easily recognized by the patient. The clinician, having done his or her homework, is knowledgeable about the type of medical procedure the patient is scheduled to undergo and discusses the procedure with the patient. The patient is instructed to try to identify what it is about the medical procedure that is discomforting.[1] Specific cues can be identified

[1] Where the swallowing of the endoscope is stressful, for example, the trainer can describe "gagging" as a stress cue. The trainer takes his or her cue from the patient in considering the most stressful features. The trainer should be cautious in invoking excessively emotional topics that might inflate the stress and distance the patient from the clinician (i.e., "I'm not going to listen to this guy, he thinks everything has to do with the fear of death").

by some patients without prompting, but the survey of hospital stress factors discussed earlier in this chapter can be helpful to have the patient talk about stressful cues.

In addition to being an aid in the identification of the patient's stress cues, the clinician serves as a source of sensory, procedural, and response information. Procedural information (and, to a lesser degree, sensory information) can be gleaned from medical texts (e.g., Skydell & Crowder, 1975) and discussions with physicians and nurses. For sensory information, it is more worthwhile to check with recent patients and interview them about their sensory experiences than it is to rely on an observer's retrospective report. The clinician should also observe the procedure personally. Data gathered during these observations serve both to assure that the clinician is not inaccurate when describing events to the patient and to isolate certain "psychological" stress factors that may be overlooked by others. For example, some hospital staff may adopt a cold interpersonal manner in treating patients. This style may be *the* stressful cue for certain patients. The clinician serves as a trained outside observer in the identification of the emotionally stressful components of the medical procedures. Such observations will also provide the trainer with information about the possible coping responses the client might use when experiencing various stressful events.

Skills training proceeds directly from the therapist-patient discussion of stress. Unlike other settings where stress inoculation programs can be implemented in 8, 10, or more sessions, interventions in a hospital setting will often have to take place in a one- or two-hour period. If and when scheduling permits additional sessions, the skills training and rehearsal stages can be extended.

Following the discussion of stress and the identification of stress-related cues, the therapist turns to the consideration of coping with stress. It is often desirable at this time for the clinician to self-disclose a personally stressful experience that had been difficult to cope with. The clinician should have the experience thought through in advance. It is important that the experience was real and that it was difficult to cope with, since the therapist is self-disclosing as a coping model rather than a mastery model (see example in Table II). The therapist, as a coping example, models both the negative thoughts and the aversive arousal associated with the stress and the ways in which the stress was managed. Experiences to be shared with the patient should arise from within the realm of conventionally-acceptable behaviors, as self-disclosures that may be highly personal yet considered "deviant" by the receiver of the information have been shown to result in dislike for the discloser (Derlega, Harris, & Chaikin, 1973).

Table II. Sample Narrative of a Self-Disclosing, Coping Model

One stressful experience for me was going to the dentist. Since I wore braces I had to go in several times a month. Each time the dentist would tighten the braces to help restrain a buck tooth. The pain wasn't all that bad, but it did hurt. Even worse was the dentist's verbal abuse—"You need to brush more, don't you care about your teeth?"—and the fear of his discovering a cavity. When one was found it was filled, but I wasn't given novocain, he just drilled it and filled it. I soon found my dental appointments to be highly stressful. I'd be saying to myself, "I know he's going to find another cavity, and then he'll drill." Fear would mount as I sat in the waiting room imagining the worst thing that could happen. I could feel my heart race and my body become tense.

Worst of all, my dentist's office was on my corner, and each day when I got off the bus from school I had to walk right past it. Though I first looked away and walked quickly, I soon realized that he wasn't going to come running out of his office to check my teeth. In fact, 9 out of 10 days that I walked by I was safe. I began to tell myself "There's the dentist's office, but I'm not scheduled today. Someone else is in there." The office on the corner, the cue for anxiety, soon became less stressful. The stress decreased even further when I realized that the procedures were expensive and that I was lucky that I could afford the opportunity to receive help. I would say these things to myself and soon found that the dentist wasn't so bad; I almost actually tipped him once.

The stage has been set for the therapist to ask the patient to describe a prior stressful experience. The therapist remains nonjudgmental. As in the early phases of brainstorming, in which the generation of alternatives is encouraged without restriction. Encouragement, with shaping, eventuates into a stress-relevant story that will be useful in treatment. The therapist inquires as to how the patient coped with prior stress. This information subsequently becomes an example of how to cope with the present stress.

When time permits, further assessment of the client's own coping style is recommended (Kendall & Williams, in press). For example, a more in-depth interview or use of one of several self-report inventories may be useful, identifying the patient as a repressor or sensitizer or as having an internal or external locus of control would help determine prior coping preferences. When time is brief, however, the therapist will move on to describing and rephrasing the patient's coping style for him or her. For instance, if the patient indicated that in former stress situations he went to the library and read about the medical procedure, then the therapist would describe information-seeking as a valuable stress management and stress prevention strategy. The therapist would then inquire if the patient felt that such a coping response would help in the present situation. In short, the patient is seen as a collaborator in the suggestion of what could be done to cope with the present stressor. It is important that the therapist does *not* merely offer suggestions or tell the patient what should be done, but rather that he or she enlist the patient to view the surgical or medical examination procedures as a problem-to-be solved. This set will permit the implementation of specific suggested coping responses such as providing additional procedural, sensory, and response information and perhaps arranging for reading materials to be left with the patient.

The trainer and patient can now turn to a reexamination of the recently identified stress cues, incorporating certain suggestions for coping that were taken partially from the prior coping experiences of the patient. This portion of the intervention might be called reframing, cognitive restructuring, or strategy retraining. Nevertheless, the central idea is recognizing stress cues and using these cues to trigger cognitive and behavioral coping responses. For example, two cues that were fairly consistently identified as stressful by cardiac catheterization patients were (a) the room full of machinery and (b) how young the doctors looked. In reexamining the stressful nature of the machinery, the therapist might say "a room full of machinery sure is foreign-looking, sort of science fiction. They're especially odd if you don't know what the machines do. What do the machines make you think of?" The patient replies, "Oh, something will go wrong with one of them." The therapist works with the patient to recognize that when "thoughts about the machines and that something is going to go wrong" start to run through the patient's head, it's the cue to seek information about what the machines are for and how they work, in general. Another possibility is to think about the advances in technology and medical science. The therapist might say "as soon as you start thinking about the machines going awry, remember how far technology has come to be able to even perform this test. Your health is in better hands now than before the machines were available. Technology has come a long way to be able to check you out so thoroughly."

"These young doctors make me worry, they're just out of diapers and green all over. What do they know?" Indeed, many physicians do look quite young to patients who are retired or in their later years. Physicians may wear beards or longer hair and appear nonprofessional to older patients. This is certainly not always the case, but it does occur when the stressful medical procedure is performed on predominately older patients.

"You know," the therapist might say, "those young doctors just finished their medical training. They're not bothered by middle age crisis, they're not thinking about their teenage children, and they're not set in their ways. They are trying to show that they're experts, they have a positive view of their abilities, and, most important, they are up on the latest advances in medicine. They're not performing the procedure for the first time, and they're not doing it out of routine either." In both examples, the therapist guides the patient to recognize the stress cues and to use them as reminders to engage in cognitive coping.

Rehearsal of the newly acquired skills constitutes the final stage of the training. Various stress cues are mentioned as the patient rehearses out loud the manner in which these cues can be thought of. Encouragement and social reinforcement are applied to build patient confidence. In some circumstances where extreme muscle tension may plague the patient's ability to adjust, relaxation training can be provided. In such instances, the final stage should also include some rehearsal of the methods of relaxation.

As evident from the stress events provided in Table I, lack of communication (e.g., "not knowing the results or reasons for your treatments") was perceived by patients as very stressful. This stress can be approached from two directions. First, the therapist describes information-seeking to the patient as a desirable behavior. The therapist encourages direct inquiry by the patient and informs physicians that such inquiries are to be supported. In some cases patients may need guidance and encouragement about seeking such information. A second approach is for the clinician to try and work directly with the staff (nurses and doctors) in order to educate them about the role of stress and what they can do to reduce it. In some ways this is easier said than done. The attempt to work directly with the hospital staff is a topic requiring a separate chapter.

Kendall, Williams, Pechacek, Graham, Shisslak, and Herzoff (1979) compared the effectiveness of this cognitive-behavioral treatment and a patient–education treatment in reducing the stress of patients undergoing cardiac catheterization. To control for the effects of the increased attention given to treated patients, an attention–placebo control group was employed. A final control group completed the assessment measures but received only the typical current hospital experiences (i.e., current conditions control). Patients in the cognitive-behavioral treatment group received individual training in the identification of those aspects of the hospitalization that aroused distress in them and in the application of their own cognitive coping strategies to lessen that anxiety. The therapist explained to the patient that stress is typical and that people cope in various ways. The therapist served as a coping model by self-disclosing a source of personal stress and discussing the strategy used to cope. The patient then discussed prior sources of stress and how they were coped with. The therapist next illustrated ways in which the patient's strategies could be used in the current situation. The therapist then helped the patient to rehearse the use of such cognitive and behavioral coping in response to the stress cues.

Subjects in the patient-education group received individual teaching related to heart disease and the catheterization procedures they were to be exposed to. Sample catheters and a heart model were used to display the procedures, and a pamphlet with additional information was provided. Subjects in the attention–placebo control received a nondirective discussion with the therapist who listened and reflected feelings. All three groups (cognitive-behavioral, education, and attention–placebo) received 45- to 50-minute interventions (except those in the control group, who experienced the routine hospital conditions).

The results of the Kendall *et al.*(1979) study indicated that patients' self-reported anxiety was significantly lower for the cognitive–behavioral, patient-education, and attention–placebo groups than for the current hospital conditions controls after the intervention. However, self-reported anxiety levels *during* the catheterization were significantly lower only for the cognitive-behavioral and patient education groups. Physicians and technicians independently rated the patients' behavior during catheterization, and these ratings indicated that the patients

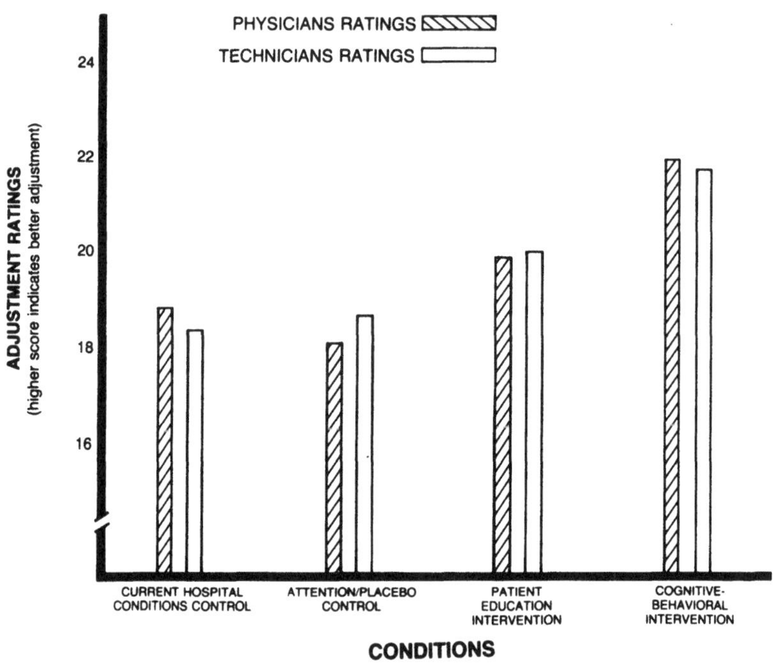

Figure 2. Physician and technician ratings of patient adjustment for the four conditions in the Kendall, Williams, Pechacek, Graham, Shisslak, and Herzoff (1979) study.

receiving the cognitive-behavioral treatment were best adjusted (e.g., least tense, least anxious, most comfortable—see Figure 2). The patient-education group was rated as better adjusted than the two control groups but significantly less well adjusted than the cognitive-behavioral group. While it should be noted that some patients had had prior catheterization experience, prior experience did not interact with treatment and both physician and technician ratings of patient adjustment produced similar findings; namely, the superiority of the cognitive-behavioral treatment.

Kendall *et al.* also examined the thoughts that patients reported having during the catheterization procedure. The authors developed a 20-item self-statement inventory requiring patients to indicate on a 5-point scale how frequently each self-statement characterized their thoughts during the catheterization procedure (see Table III). There are 10 positive and 10 negative self-statements on the inventory. Patients' negative self-statement scores were found to be significantly and negatively correlated with both the physicians' ratings of adjustment, $r = -0.34$, and the technicians' ratings of adjustment, $r = -0.37$. Positive self-statement scores were not significantly related to adjustment. These data are consistent with the results of self-statement assessments across several situations where a negative internal dialogue has been found to be related to poor adjustment. Future cognitive-behavioral intervention research must strive to measure and examine clients' internal dialogues and the self-statement inventory methodology (see Kendall & Hollon, 1981) is a step in that direction.

Systems-Level Involvement

The efficacy of interventions may be maximized to the extent that the patient's natural support systems can be systematically involved. Correspondingly, an intervention program may result in limited success if it remains circumscribed and affects only a restricted portion of the patient's experiences. It is the patient who is central to all experience and therefore justifiable as the center of the intervention focus. But people associated with the patient need also be considered. For example, the patient's spouse can, unwittingly, undermine the intervention by noting unsuccessful aspects of the patient's prior coping efforts, commenting on the lack of proper facilities at the hospital, or simply overemphasizing the level of current stress.

Visitors can bring the patient a sense of relief or a sense of additional stress. While screening visitors is not being suggested, the involvement of the significant others would seem most promising. Some visitors may offer assistance by attempting to find out something about the coming

Table III. Self-Statement Inventory Items and Instructions to Subjects[a]

Listed below are several statements that people make to themselves (their thoughts) during medical procedures. Please read each self-statement and indicate how frequently these self-statements characterized your thoughts during the catheterization procedure. Please read each item carefully and then circle the appropriate number as it relates to your thoughts.

		Hardly ever				Very often
1.	I was thinking that the procedure could save my life.	1	2	3	4	5
2.	I was thinking about the wonders of medical science and how lucky I was that they could do this for me.	1	2	3	4	5
3.	I was thinking about how long I had planned for the procedure and how good it will be to finally know for sure there is nothing wrong with me.	1	2	3	4	5
4.	I was concerned that the doctor looked too young and inexperienced.	1	2	3	4	5
5.	I kept thinking how little pain the procedure caused and how easy it was to go through it.	1	2	3	4	5
6.	I was worried about the bad things that the doctor said might happen to me.	1	2	3	4	5
7.	I was feeling confident in the skills of the doctors and technicians.	1	2	3	4	5
8.	I was listening and expecting them to say something bad about my health.	1	2	3	4	5
9.	I kept thinking that the procedure might cause complications that would never go away.	1	2	3	4	5
10.	I kept reminding myself to just think about pleasant things and take my mind off the procedure.	1	2	3	4	5
11.	I kept reminding myself about all the times in the past when I had been successful in coping with stress and pain and that this was not any worse than these situations.	1	2	3	4	5
12.	Since the procedure wasn't discomforting, I was thinking about other things.	1	2	3	4	5
13.	I kept worrying that the procedure might kill me.	1	2	3	4	5
14.	I kept expecting that the procedure would damage my body.	1	2	3	4	5
15.	I kept thinking that I shouldn't have let them do this procedure on me.	1	2	3	4	5
16.	I kept thinking that once they started I couldn't stop it no matter what.	1	2	3	4	5
17.	I was thinking about the catheter breaking off and sticking into my heart.	1	2	3	4	5
18.	I was thinking about the things I need to do to be a good patient (like staying still and following the doctor's instructions).	1	2	3	4	5
19.	I kept thinking that all this expensive equipment makes me feel more confident that nothing bad is going to happen to me.	1	2	3	4	5
20.	I kept thinking how much I disliked the smell of being in the hospital.	1	2	3	4	5

[a]From Kendall, Williams, Pechacek, Graham, Shisslak, and Herzoff (1979). Positive items (1,2,3,5,7, 10, 11,13,18, & 19) and negative items (4,6,8,9,13,15,17,20) are scored separately by computing separate totals.

event from the staff. In this regard, visitors should be cautioned to avoid spreading hearsay and to let the patient discuss questions directly with the professional staff.

A patient's family members may require involvement in the intervention. A patient's spouse, for instance, may be severely discomforted by the hospitalization and require relaxation training or perhaps sedation. Distressed spouses should be calmed prior to visiting and perhaps encouraged to visit at the same time as nonstressed visitors. In contrast, cooperative and successfully coping family members can facilitate the intervention procedures and can be kept informed and involved.

With pediatric patients, preparation of the child for the medical stress might include both in-hospital and at-home preparations with parental involvement (e.g., Wolfer & Visintainer, 1979). Parents can become fearful of the possibility of a fatal outcome, guilt-ridden as a result of feelings that they "caused" the medical problem, or rejecting since they deny the severity of the child's needs. Indeed, parents as well as their children can benefit from professional consultation regarding the medical procedures, the implications of possible outcomes, and the rehearsal of successful coping strategies.

While we have focused on the stressful nature of the patient's impending medical procedure, there are other related stressors to consider. For example, the outcome of the medical procedure will not always document positive health. Patients being assessed for heart disease or cancer may discover that they have the disease and that it may be at a serious stage. The diagnosis of serious illness also carries with it the possibility of long-term illness and death. Patients who must face these additional stressors require additional interventions with additional coping rehearsal. When faced with the possibility of a lifetime of physical disability, or when the crisis stress of the medical procedure is simply replaced by a more continuous stress, brief coping training will be insufficient and long-range, systems-level involvement becomes essential.

CLOSING COMMENTS

Janis (1969) has cited research suggesting that "if a normal person is given accurate prior warning of impending pain and discomfort, together with sufficient reassurances so that fear does not mount to a very high level, he will be less likely to develop acute emotional disturbances than a person who is not warned" (p. 102). Warburton (1979), while summarizing the contributions to an edited volume on human stress, stated that "psychological stressors must be considered with respect to the individual, and the stress responses will be a function of the person's evaluation of the input" (p. 471). Clearly, the individual's cognitive processing of the stress-related information plays a central role in coping.

The cognitive-behavioral intervention for medical stress management and prevention strives to provide the patient with a realistic sense of control and predictability. Through individualized learning experiences involving information and modeling, the trainer works with the patient in order for the patient to learn that he or she (a) has coped in the past, (b) knows how to cope now, (c) has practiced coping in the face of the present stress, and (d) has planned for additional stressors and has coping strategies prepared for them.

REFERENCES

Andrews, J. Recovery from surgery, with and without preparatory instruction, for three coping styles. *Journal of Personality and Social Psychology,* 1970, *15,* 223–226.

Auerbach, S. M., Kendall, P. C., Cuttler, H. F., & Levitt, N. R. Anxiety, locus of control, types of preparatory information, and adjustment to dental surgery. *Journal of Consulting and Clinical Psychology,* 1976, *44,* 809–818.

Auerbach, S. M., & Kilmann, P. R. Crisis intervention: A review of outcome research. *Psychological Bulletin,* 1977, *84,* 1189–1217.

Averill, J .R., O'Brien, L., & DeWitt, G. W. The influence of response effectiveness on the preference for warning and on psychophysiological stress reactions. *Journal of Psychiatry,* 1977, *45,* 395–418.

Braider, L. Private experience and public expectation on the cancer ward. *Omega,* 1976, *6,* 373–381.

Butcher, J. N., & Maudal, G. R. Crisis intervention. In I. B. Weiner (Ed.), *Clinical methods in psychology.* New York: Wiley, 1976.

Byrne, D. Repression-sensitization as a dimension of personality. In B. A. Maher (Ed.), *Progress in experimental personality research* (Vol. 1). New York: Academic Press, 1964.

Cassell, S. Effect of brief puppet therapy upon the emotional responses of children undergoing cardiac catheterization. *Journal of Consulting Psychology,* 1965, *29,* 1–8.

Cataldo, M. F., Bessman, C. A., Parker, L. H., Pearson, J. E., & Rogers, M. C. Behavioral assessment for pediatric intensive care units. *Journal of Applied Behavior Analysis,* 1979, *12,* 83–98.

Cohen, F., & Lazarus, R. S. Active coping processes, coping disposition, and recovery from surgery. *Psychosomatic Medicine,* 1973, *35,* 375–389.

DeLong, R. D. Individual differences in patterns of anxiety arousal, stress-relevant information, and recovery from surgery (Doctoral dissertation, University of California, Los Angeles, 1970). *Dissertation Abstracts International,* 1971, *32,* 554B.

Derlaga, V. J., Harris, M. S., & Chaikin, A. L. Self-disclosure reciprocity, liking and the deviant. *Journal of Experimental Social Psychology,* 1973, *9,* 277–284.

Egbert, L. D., Battit, G. W., Welch, C. E., & Bartlett, M. K. Reduction of post-operational pain by encouragement and instruction of patients. *New England Journal of Medicine,* 1964, *270,* 825–827.

Ferguson, B. F. Preparing young children for hospitalization: A comparison of two methods. *Pediatrics,* 1979, *64,* 656–664.

Holcomb, W. *Coping with severe stress: A clinical application of stress-inoculation therapy*. Unpublished doctoral dissertation, University of Missouri-Columbia, 1979.
Holroyd, K. Cognition and desensitization in the group treatment of test anxiety. *Journal of Consulting and Clinical Psychology,* 1976, *44,* 991–1001.
Horan, J., Hackett, G., Buchanan, J., Stone, C., & Demchik-Stone, D. Coping with pain: A component analysis. *Cognitive Therapy and Research,* 1977, *1,* 211–221.
Horwitz, E. A., Shipley, R. H., & McGuire, D. *The use of external distractors to reduce pain and anxiety associated with stressful medical and dental procedures.* Paper presented at the Association for Advancement of Behavior Therapy Convention, Atlanta, December 1977.
Hussian, R. A., & Lawrence, P. S. The reduction of test, state, and trait anxiety by test specific and generalized stress inoculation training. *Cognitive Therapy and Research,* 1978, *2,* 25–38.
Janis, I. L. *Stress and frustration.* New York: Harcourt Brace Jovanovich, 1969.
Jaremko, M. E. A component analysis of stress inoculation: Review and prospectus. *Cognitive Therapy and Research,* 1979, *3,* 35–48.
Johnson, J. E., & Leventhal, H. Effects of accurate expectations and behavioral instructions of reactions during a noxious medical examination. *Journal of Personality and Social Psychology,* 1974, *29,* 710–718.
Johnson, J. E., Morrisey, J. F., & Leventhal, H. Psychological preparation for an endoscopic examination. *Gastrointestinal Endoscopy,* 1973, *19,* 180–182.
Kazdin, A. E. Covert modeling, model similarity, and reduction of avoidance behavior. *Behavior Therapy,* 1974, *5,* 325–340.
Kendall, P. C., & Hollon, S. D. Assessing self-referent speech: Methods in the measurement of self-statements. In P. C. Kendall & S. D. Hollon (Eds.), *Assessment strategies for cognitive-behavioral interventions.* New York: Academic Press, 1981.
Kendall, P. C., & Watson, D. Psychological preparation for stressful medical procedures. In L. A. Bradley & C. K. Prokop (Eds.), *Medical psychology: Contributions to behavioral medicine.* New York: Academic Press, 1981.
Kendall, P. C., & Williams, C. L. Preparing patients for stressful medical procedures. In T. J. Coates (Ed.), *Behavioral medicine: A practical handbook.* Champaign-Urbana, Ill.: Research Press, in press.
Kendall, P. C., Williams, L., Pechacek, T. F., Graham, L. E., Shisslak, C., & Herzoff, N. Cognitive-behavioral and patient education interventions in cardiac catheterization procedures. The Palo Alto medical psychology project. *Journal of Consulting and Clinical Psychology,* 1979, *47,* 49–58.
Klorman, R., Hilpert, P. L., Michael, R., LaGana, C., & Sveen, O. B. Effects of coping and mastery modeling on experienced and inexperienced pedodontic patients' disruptiveness. *Behavior Therapy,* 1980, *11,* 156–168.
Kornfeld, D. S. The hospital environment: Its impact on the patient. *Advances in Psychosomatic Medicine,* 1972, *8,* 252–270.
Kornfeld, D. S., Zimberg, S., & Malm, J. R. Psychiatric complications of open-heart surgery. *New England Journal of Medicine,* 1965, *273,* 287–302.
Langer, E. J., Janis, I. L., & Wolfer, J. Reduction of psychological stress in surgery patients. *Journal of Experimental Psychology,* 1975, *11,* 155–165.
Lazarus, H. R., & Hagens, J. H. Prevention of psychosis following open-heart surgery. *American Journal of Psychiatry,* 1968, *124,* 1190–1195.
Lazarus, R. S. *Psychological stress and the coping process.* New York: McGraw-Hill, 1966.
McGrath, J. E. (Ed.). *Social psychological factors in stress.* New York: Holt, Rinehart & Winston, 1970.
McKegney, F. P. The intensive care syndrome. *Connecticut Magazine,* 1966, *30,* 633–636.

Meichenbaum, D. H. Examination of model characteristics in reducing avoidance behavior. *Journal of Personality and Social Psychology,* 1971, *17,* 298–307.
Meichenbaum, D., & Cameron, R. *Stress inoculation: A skills training approach to anxiety management.* Unpublished manuscript, University of Waterloo, 1973.
Melamed, B. G. Behavioral approaches to fear in dental settings. In M. Hersen, R. Eisler, & P. Miller (Eds.), *Progress in behavior modification* (Vol. 7). New York: Academic Press, 1979.
Melamed, B. G., & Siegel, L. J. Reduction of anxiety in children facing hospitalization and surgery by use of filmed modeling. *Journal of Consulting and Clinical Psychology,* 1975, *43,* 511–521.
Melamed, B. G., Weinstein, D., Hawes, R., & Katin-Borland, J. Reduction of fear-related dental management problems with use of filmed modeling. *Journal of the American Dental Association,* 1975, *90,* 822–826.
Mills, R. T., & Krantz, D. S. Information, choice, and reactions to stress: A field experiment in a blood bank with laboratory analogue. *Journal of Personality and Social Psychology,* 1979, *37,*608–620.
Mohros, K. L. L. Effects of reassuring information and sensory information on emotional response during a threatening medical examination (Doctoral dissertation, University of Minnesota, 1976). *Dissertation Abstracts International,* 1977, *38,* 1304–1305A.
Rotter, J. Generalized expectancies of internal versus external control of reinforcement. *Psychological Monographs,* 1966, *80* (Whole No. 609).
Sarason, I. Test anxiety and the self-disclosing model. *Journal of Consulting and Clinical Psychology,* 1975, *43,* 148–153.
Selye, H. Stress without distress. In C. A. Garfield (Ed.), *Stress and survival: The emotional realities of life-threatening illness.* St. Louis: Mosby, 1979.
Shipley, R. H., Butt, J. H., Horwitz, B., & Fabry, J. E. Preparation for a stressful medical procedure. Effect of amount of stimulus preexposure and coping style. *Journal of Consulting and Clinical Psychology,* 1978, *46,* 499–507.
Shipley, R. H., Butt, J. H., & Horwitz, E. A. Preparation to reexperience a stressful medical examination: Effect of repetitious videotape exposure and coping style. *Journal of Consulting and Clinical Psychology,* 1979, *47,* 485–492.
Skydell, B., & Crowder, A. S. *Diagnostic procedures: A reference for health practitioners and a guide for patient counseling.* Boston: Little, Brown, 1975.
Turk, D. *Cognitive control of pain: A skills training approach.* Unpublished manuscript, University of Waterloo, 1975.
Turk, D. C., & Genest, M. Regulation of pain: The application of cognitive and behavioral techniques for prevention and remediation. In P. C. Kendall & S. D. Hollon (Eds.), *Cognitive-behavioral interventions: Theory, research, and procedures.* New York: Academic Press, 1979.
Vernon, D. T. A., & Bigelow, D. A. Effect of information about a potentially stressful situation on responses to stress impact. *Journal of Personality and Social Psychology,* 1974, *29,* 50–59.
Volicer, B. J., & Bohannon, M. W. A hospital stress rating scale. *Nursing Research,* 1975, *24,* 352–359.
Warburton, D. M. Stress and the processing of information. In V. Hamilton & D. M. Warburton (Eds.), *Human stress and cognition.* New York: Wiley, 1979.
Wolfer, J. A., & Visintainer, M. A. Pediatric surgical patients' and parents' stress responses and adjustment as a function of psychologic preparation and stress-point nursing care. *Nursing Research,* 1975, *24,* 244–255.
Wolfer, J. A., & Visintainer, M. A. Prehospital psychological preparation for tonsillectomy patients: Effects on children's and parents' adjustment. *Pediatrics,* 1979, *64,* 646–655.

6

Stress Inoculation in the Management of Clinical Pain

Applications to Burn Pain

ROBERT L. WERNICK

Humankind has long been in search of an effective means of pain relief. Thousands of preparations and procedures have been used in this quest. Perhaps out of desperation, the methods that have been tried have covered the spectrum from the rather primitive to highly sophisticated techniques based on modern technology (Meichenbaum & Turk, 1976; Turk, 1978a; Turk & Genest, 1979). Currently, conventional procedures used are primarily designed to cut or block the "pain pathways" and are of three types: (a) pharmacological agents; (b) anesthetic nerve blocks; and (c) surgical procedures. None of these somatic treatments have proven to be completely satisfactory for adequate or permanent pain relief. Indeed, this search has grown into a multibillion-dollar business.

Most of the current models of pain can be characterized by their unidimensional focus, in which pain is viewed as a direct function of the quality and intensity of sensory input. Treatment follows the assumption that the physical aspects of the input determine the sensations perceived as pain (Turk, 1978a). Psychological variables, if considered at all, are relegated to secondary roles. Recent reviews of the pain literature (e.g., Liebeskind & Paul, 1977), however, have pointed out that pain is not

ROBERT L. WERNICK • Departments of Psychology and Psychiatry, University of Saskatchewan, Saskatoon, Saskatchewan, Canada S7M 0X0.

simply a function of tissue damage. It has been suggested that pain be viewed as a subjective experience, of which sensory input is but one component.

Melzack and Wall (1965, 1975) have proposed a conceptualization of pain in which cognitive and affective factors are viewed as important mediators of the pain experience. Their gate-control theory emphasizes a multidimensional perspective and offers an alternative to the specificity model of pain. From this view, pain perception and response are seen as complex phenomena resulting from the interaction of sensory-discriminative, motivational-affective, and cognitive-evaluative components. The failure to take these components into account can explain the frequent frustration encountered in the treatment of patients with somatic methods designed to block pain pathways (Turk & Genest, 1979). Weisenberg (1977) offers a comprehensive review of the correlates of pain perception and notes that the gate-control theory emphasizes the role of psychological influences in the perception of pain.

While the exact psychological mechanisims and anatomimcal bases for the gate-control theory have been criticized, the multidimensional perspective has received considerable support (Turk & Genest, 1979). Weisenberg (1977) has noted that, regardless of specific inaccuracies, the gate-control theory has been the most influential and important current theory of pain perception. This theory has had considerable influence on pain research and clinical pain control; it has stimulated a multidisciplinary view of pain for research and treatment; and it has been able to demonstrate the importance of psychological variables. The goals of such a multidimensional approach include a decreasing reliance on medical treatments, reducing the incidence of recurring pain after treatment, making pain more bearable when it cannot be eliminated, and increasing tolerance of unavoidable clinical pain (Turk, 1978a).

It is the last goal that provides the focus of this chapter. Unavoidable clinical pain can be viewed as one type of stress that can be managed in much the same way as other stressors. Special emphasis in this area will be placed on the unavoidable pain associated with burn trauma. The main purposes will be to (a) briefly review the psychological literature related to burn patients; (b) describe the sequence of treatment procedures involved in burn care; (c) review the use of cognitive-behavioral interventions for the management of clinical pain; and (d) describe a specific pain management program for burn patients.

PSYCHOLOGICAL ASPECTS OF BURN PATIENTS

Although hundreds of thousands of people are burned yearly, interest in the psychological aspects of burn victims did not appear in the literature until the Cocoanut Grove fire disaster in 1942. In their anecdotal reports, Adler (1943) and Cobb and Lindeman (1943) observed psychological problems in more than 50% of their subjects. While based primarily on interviews and observations, these initial studies identified burn victims as a population at high risk of psychological problems secondary to their injury.

In general, the literature focusing on the psychological aspects of burn victims has remained relatively sparse. It has only been recently that a multidisciplinary team approach has been utilized to meet the many psychosocial needs of these patients and their families (Miller, Gardner, & Mlott, 1976; Morris & McFadd, 1978). It should also be noted that while the pain experience of burn victims has long been identified as a major problem area, very little attention has been paid to its management.

The burn experience has been described as both physically and emotionally devastating (Davidson & Noyes, 1973). Severe burns have been characterized as a catastrophic illness (Andreasen, Norris, & Hartford, 1971), a physical and mental disaster (Miller *et al.,* 1976), and one of the most severe traumas that human beings can survive (Andreasen, Noyes, Hartford, Brodland, & Proctor, 1972). This type of injury is unqiue in exposing patients first to severe pain, delirium, and the threat of death—then later to prolonged convalescence and disfigurement. Thus, the adaptive capacities of the individual are put to a severe test (Noyes, Andreasen, & Hartford, 1971).

The incidence of psychological problems in burn patients has been observed to be quite high during hospitalization. Estimates of both civilian and military adult populations have indicated that from 50 to 100% of severely burned patients have developed at least brief periods of psychological disturbance (Cobb & Lindemann, 1943; Hamburg, Artz, Reiss, Amspacher, & Chambers, 1953; Hamburg, Hamburg, & deGoza, 1953; Lewis, Goolishian, Wolf, Lynch, & Blocker, 1963; Noyes *et al.,* 1971). Additionally, three factors were found to be associated with a poor adjustment: (a) premorbid psychopathology; (b) prior physical problems; and (c) burns covering more than 30% of the body (Andreasen, Noyes, & Hartford, 1972). It should be noted that comparisons between studies have often been difficult to make due to the variability or absence of objective criteria for such factors as psychological disturbance, severity of burn, and adjustment.

The posthospitalization prospects for burn victims appear to be more optimistic. The more favorable long-term prognosis suggested by early reports (e.g., Adler, 1943) has generally received support from more recent studies. Twenty patients without prior psychopathology were evaluated some time between one and five years postburn and only 30%

were observed to have psychological problems (Andreasen & Norris, 1972; Andreasen *et al.,* 1971). Chang and Herzog (1976) studied 51 patients at an average of 25.6 months follow-up and found that 79% had been able to return to work or school. At one-year follow-up, 25 patients without premorbid psychopathology showed general improvement on both the MMPI and the verbal portion of the WAIS (Miller *et al.,* 1976; Mlott, Lira, & Miller, 1977).

Psychological problems frequently encountered with burn patients have been discussed more specifically in the literature. Initially, delirium and fear of death are most common (Andreasen, 1974; Hamburg, Artz, Reiss, Amspacher, & Chambers, 1953; Hamburg, Hamburg, & deGoza, 1953; Kjaer, 1969; Noyes *et al.,* 1971; Steiner & Clark, 1977; Weisz, 1967). Afterward, when survival seemed more likely, fears became those of deformity, handicap, disfigurement, and rejection.

Depression has been identified as the most common type of psychological disturbance during hospitalization. At a minimum, transient episodes of depressive reactions have been noted in all patients with significant burns. Mild to moderate depression of relatively short duration has been observed in a majority of burn patients, while severe depression has been noted in about 20% of those studied (Andreasen, 1974; Andreasen & Norris, 1972; Andreasen *et al.,* 1971; Andreasen, Noyes, & Hartford, 1972; Andreasen, Noyes, Hartford, Brodland, & Proctor, 1972; Chang & Herzog, 1976; Hamburg, Hamburg, & deGoza, 1953; Noyes *et al.,* 1971).

Anxiety reactions, including such symptoms as insomnia, nightmares, and emotional liability, have been cited as common occurrences with most severely burned patients. Several investigators have noted that regression and marked dependence occurred frequently enough to be considered major problems (Andreasen, 1974; Andreasen & Norris, 1972; Davidson & Noyes, 1973; Hamburg, Hamburg, & deGoza, 1953; Steiner & Clark, 1977; Weisz, 1967). Problems related to extreme noncompliance with treatment have been observed less frequently and have been associated with premorbid psychopathology (Andreasen, Noyes, & Hartford, 1972; Davidson & Noyes, 1973; Kjacr, 1969; Wernick, Brantley, & Malcolm, 1980).

It has been observed that since psychological difficulties impede the recovery process and are associated with a poorer prognosis, their treatment should be an integral part of the patient's therapy (Andrasean, 1974; Hamburg, Artz, Reiss, Amspacher, & Chambers, 1953; Morris & McFadd, 1978). In response to this issue, a variety of strategies have been recommended, including (a) the use of appropriate medications, particularly for delirium; (b) the establishment of a close professional relationship between patient and physician; (c) providing accurate and reassuring information; (d) allowing patients to ventilate; (e) providing distractions; and (f) requesting psychiatric consultation (Andreasen, 1974; Andreasen *et al.,* 1971; Andreasen, Noyes, Hartford, Brodland, & Proctor, 1972; Artz, 1965; Cobb & Lindemann, 1943; Hamburg, Artz, Reiss, Amspacher, & Chambers, 1953; Hamburg, Hamburg, & deGoza, 1953; Jorgensen & Brophy, 1975; Kjaer, 1969; Lipowski, 1967; Miller *et al.,* 1976; Weisz, 1967).

Traditionally, psychological intervention with burn patients has taken the form of sometimes vague suggestions or individual consultation for specific problems. More recently, innovative approaches have been employed. Behavioral strategies have been successfully used to manage or modify noncompliant and maladaptive behavior (Jorgensen & Brophy, 1975; Simons, McFadd, Frank, Green, Malin, & Morris, 1978; Wernick *et al.,* 1980; Zide & Pardoe, 1976). Behavioral programs have been carried out by nursing staffs and have often resulted in generalized patient participation in recovery and rehabilitation. Additionally, the multidisciplinary mental health team has been described (Miller *et al.,* 1976; Morris & McFadd, 1978). This approach appears to offer a more effective model for meeting the psychological needs of patients and staff alike.

TREATMENT PROCEDURES IN BURN CARE

Since burn units may be unfamiliar to many professionals, a general description of the procedures involved in patient care will be presented. It should be noted that the various degrees of burn involve increasingly deep tissue damage. First degree burns (e.g., sunburn) involve damage to only the outer layers of skin (epidermis), heal within a week, and leave no permanent scars. Second degree (partial thickness) burns involve from superficial to deep damage to the dermis and will eventually heal by themselves. Third degree (full thickness) burns involve destruction of all the skin and possibily subcutaneous tissue, including the nerve endings, do not generate new skin, and require grafting to cover the wound (Gordon, 1978).

Emergency phase (the first few days post-burn): When a severely burned patient is first admitted to the burn unit, a thorough examination is conducted to determine the percentage of the body burned, as well as the seriousness of the injury. The major concerns include the stabilization of fluids and electrolytes, the maintenance of adequate respiration and circulation, and the prevention of infection. The wounds will be cleaned and dressed, and IVs will be inserted to replace lost fluids. The patient will then be placed in an isolated, intensive care setting.

The intensive care setting can be quite frightening to the patient. The constant activity and the sights and sounds made by monitors, respirators, and other equipment are often bewildering. The patient is likely to have several lines and tubes connected to various parts of his or her body. A compromised mental status is a common occurrence. At this time, second degree burns will be very painful, while third degree burns will be painless since the nerve endings have been destroyed.

Acute phase (until the patient is covered with new skin): This phase may last from several days to several months, depending on the depth and extent of the burn. The acute phase coincides with the remaining period of hospitalization; and while the patient will be transferred out of intensive care early in this phase, his or her condition remains critical. The major concerns are the healing and grafting of the burn wounds and the prevention of infection and contractures (loss of joint function).

Pain is a daily companion of the burn patient during the acute phase (Andreasen, Noyes, & Hartford, 1972). Nerve endings begin to regenerate in third degree burns early in this phase and result in added pain. Fagerhaugh (1974) noted that the outstanding features of burn pain are its intensity and long duration. Primary pain resulting from the burn itself gradually improves, but it is usually not fully relieved until the skin heals or the wounds are completely covered with grafts. The results of a pilot study suggested that the time of hospitalization was identified as the most stressful period by burn patients (Simons, Green, Malin, Suskind, & Frank, 1978).

The most painful experiences of the burn patients often occur as a result of therapeutic procedures (Fagerhaugh, 1974). Suffering is observed to be the greatest during "tankings," in which the patient is lowered on a stretcher into a large tub. The old dressings are removed and the patient is gently scrubbed to remove encrusted medication. Debridement, which is usually necessary during the early weeks of hospitalization, involves the vigorous cutting away of dead tissue in burned areas. The process, which may last for more than an hour and involve several people working on different parts of the body simultaneously, ends when fresh medication and new dressings are applied. Some patients who require skin grafts report severe pain in donor sites (Andreasen, Noyes, Hartford, Brodland, & Proctor, 1972). At these times, analgesics bring only partial and temporary relief (Noyes *et al.*, 1971).

In addition to tanking, debridement, and grafting, other treatment procedures and "demands" involve the infliction of varying degrees of pain or discomfort. Dressing changes other than tankings and blood drawing usually occur at least once a day. Patients are required to eat and drink large quantities in order to obtain the calories necessary to heal. Daily visits by occupational and physical therapists involve exercises and wearing of splints. During this time, the patient is frequently on an emotional roller coaster—wondering when the pain will end and if he or she will ever get well. It is no wonder that the burn team often meets with resistance from the patient.

Rehabilitation Phase (begins when all wounds are covered): This phase is essentially the posthospitalization period. It begins around the time of discharge and ends when the scar tissue has matured. Since all wounds have healed or been grafted, primary pain from the wounds has ended. However, itching can be a source of much discomfort. The main concerns of this phase are the prevention of contractures, the minimizing of scarring, and the return to society.

At the time of discharge, the patient's program is concentrated toward the prevention of secondary complications. In turn, wound care continues at home as in the hospital. Patients are expected to continue exercising to maintain mobility and flexibility. Sometimes Jobst pressure garments are required to minimize scarring. Although these are effective, they are also unsightly and thus, compliance can be a problem. Additional hospitalizations may also be required for reconstructive surgery for functional and/or cosmetic purposes. It may be several years before treatment is completed.

Earlier in the hospitalization, patients often believe that they will look and feel "normal" at the time of discharge. As discharge draws near, the reality of the situation can no longer be denied. While the staff encourages patients to strive for independence, self-care, and a return to society, some patients feel like "freaks," fear rejection, and have a very difficult time separating from the safe and understanding hospital environment. Additionally, there are often limits imposed on the activities of the patient when discharged. For many, adjustment is a constant effort and requires much support and reassurance.

In summary, little research has been conducted related to the psychological aspects of burn patients and the treatment they receive. The research that does exist seems to be primarily anecdotal or descriptive in nature. The few clinical investigations that have been done were mainly case studies. When considering the stressful nature of burn trauma treatment, psychological adjustment becomes very important. Apart from considering use of analgesics, the issue of pain management has received very little attention. Clearly, there is a great need for future research with this population.

COGNITIVE-BEHAVIORAL INTERVENTIONS FOR PAIN MANAGEMENT

In recent years, there has been a growing interest in the application of cognitive and behavioral procedures in the modification of a variety of stress-related problems (Gentry & Bernal, 1977; Jaremko, 1979; Meichenbaum, 1977; Meichenbaum & Turk, 1976; Weisenberg, 1977). Various strategies have been found to be effective, including relaxation training (Bobey & Davidson, 1970), reversal of affect, emotive imagery, refocusing of attention and other forms of distraction (Jaremko, 1978; Spanos, Horton, & Chaves, 1975; Stone, Demchik-Stone, & Horan, 1977; Turk, 1978b), cognitive reappraisal (Meichenbaum & Turk, 1976), and cognitive restructuring (Goldfried, Linehan, & Smith, 1978). Recent evidence has suggested that using multiple strategies is more effective than the use of any one procedure (Jaremko, 1979; Scott & Barber, 1977; Spanos, Radtke-Bodorik, Ferguson, & Jones, 1979; Turk, 1978a).

Among the various packages of cognitive-behavioral techniques, "stress inoculation" has received the most research attention. Stress inoculation was conceived as a flexible, coping-skills approach for the management of stress-related problems (Meichenbaum, 1975). The stress inoculation package has been found to be effective in the management of anger (Novaco, 1976, 1977), experimentally induced pain (Horan, Hackett, Buchanan, Stone, & Demchik-Stone, 1977), test anxiety (Hussian & Lawrence, 1978), and interpersonal anxiety (Meichenbaum & Turk, 1976). While a few recent studies involving the management of clinical pain will be reported here, the interested reader is referred to a recent work for a more complete review of cognitive-behavior modification with pain patients (Turk, Meichenbaum, & Genest, 1983).

Trent (1980) used cognitive relaxation training in the treatment of a single case of chronic back pain. While details of the treatment were not specified, the procedure was reminiscent of various forms of mental relaxation. The results of this study showed a significant increase in the amount of constructive activity, a diminished pain rating, and a decrease in the use of pain medication. These effects were maintained at six-month follow-up. Trent noted several limitations in this study, including the lack of adequate reliability checks and the possibility of placebo effects. In another case report, relaxation training, covert imagery, and cognitive relabeling were used as self-control procedures in the management of chronic abodminal pain (Levendusky & Pankratz, 1975). The subject was trained in deep muscle relaxation and the use of visual imagery. Images were devised that were meaningful to him because of his background. Subsequently, the procedure provided him with new cognitive labels for his psychological cues. While some ethical concerns were raised in regard to the use of deception in drug withdrawal, the results indicated an increase in activity and discontinuation of pain medication usage. These effects were maintained at six-month follow-up.

Chaves and Brown (1978) investigated the use of self-generated strategies for the control of dental pain in 75 patients undergoing either a mandibular block injection or the extraction of one or two teeth. Assessment prior to the dental procedure included gathering demographic data, the State-Trait Anxiety Inventory, the Dental Anxiety Scale, the Internal-External Locus of Control Scale, and Tellegan's Absorption Scale (Tellegan & Atkinson, 1974). After the procedure, a structured interview was conducted to determine whether the patient had used self-generated strategies to control pain. Additionally, patients rated four statements regarding the procedure on 10-point Likert-type scales. While the dental procedures used were not very painful (as dental procedures go), the investigators found that those subjects who employed self-generated coping strategies (44%) rated their experience as significantly less stressful than did subjects who engaged in catastrophizing ideation (37%) during the dental procedures. The use of coping strategies was associated with situational anxiety and high socioeconomic status, while catastrophizing was associated with stress reactivity, increasing age, and nervousness in the dental setting. The authors noted that many patients experiencing clinical pain not only employ self-generated strategies to control their distress, but they also spontaneously tend to use strategies that are quite similar to those taught in studies concerning pain reduction, especially attention diversion and coping self-statements.

Holroyd and Andrasik (1978) treated chronic tension headache subjects using a group format. The 39 subjects were assigned to one of four groups: cognitive self-control, cognitive self-control plus relaxation training, headache discussion, or symptom-monitoring control. Participants in the three treatment groups were taught to monitor their cognitive responses to stress-eliciting situations and were provided with similar rationales emphasizing that disturbing emotional and behavioral responses were a direct function of specifiable maladaptive cognitions. The cognitive self-control group focused on altering manipulative cognitive responses by using cognitive reappraisal, attention diversion, and fantasy. In the combined cognitive self-control and relaxation group, muscle relaxation was also taught as a self-control skill. The headache discussion group focused on the historical roots of symptoms and, while clients were taught to monitor their cognitive responses, no strategies for coping were provided. Participants in the symptom-monitoring control group recorded their headaches but were told that treatment would be available at a later date. The results revealed that the three treatment groups showed significant improvement at posttreatment and follow-up (six weeks) assessments, whereas the control group showed no change. These results complement those obtained in an earlier study, in which cognitive self-control procedures were individually administered (Holroyd, Andrasik, & Westbrook, 1977). Questions could be raised about the effective procedural ingredients since the discussion group did not differ significantly from the two self-control groups. Additional information concerning methods used to control headaches was gathered by means of interviewing subjects in the three treatment groups. The authors noted that all but one participant in the discussion group reported devising cognitive self-control procedures for coping that were similar to those taught to the participants in the two self-control groups. These results provide support for the findings of Chaves and Brown (1978) with dental patients. Additionally, they suggest that the improvements shown by participants in the discussion group may have resulted from their use of cognitive coping strategies of their own devising.

In a more recent study, Rybstein-Blinchik (1979) examined the effects of cognitive strategies on chronic pain. Subjects were 44 rehabilitation patients with a variety of diagnoses involving chronic pain (e.g., amputation, spinal cord injury, rheumatoid arthritis). Patients were assigned to one of four groups: (a) somatization—subjects were told to replace the term *pain* with *a certain feeling* and to concentrate on the sensation itself; (b) irrelevant cognitive strategy—subjects were instructed to replace thoughts accompanying their experience of pain with new ones concerning "important events" in their lives; (c) relevant cognitive strategy—subjects were instructed to replace thoughts accompanying their experience of pain with new ones involving a "reinterpretation of the experience"; and (d) control—subjects shared their personal pain experiences with each other. Subjects in the three treatment groups were provided a conceptualization of their pain, and then trained to be aware of self-statements regarding their pain experience prior to being instructed in the use of a specific cognitive strategy. The results showed that the relevant cognitive strategy group used significantly fewer and milder words to describe their pain and manifested fewer pain behaviors after treatment than did the three other groups. Additionally, this group's pain intensity ratings were significantly lower than those of the somatization and control groups. The author noted that the results, showing greater effectiveness by the relevant strategy group, lent clinical support to the experimental pain literature.

The foregoing data provide a preliminary base of support concerning the efficacy of cognitive-behavioral procedures in the management of pain in general. They suggest that similar procedures would be effective in the management of the pain experience of burn patients.

PAIN MANAGEMENT WITH BURN PATIENTS

The psychological literature on burn patients has identified this group as a high-risk population. One of the harshest problems faced by all burn victims is the stress of an almost continuous encounter with pain. In view of the success achieved in other preliminary studies using cognitive-behavioral approaches to manage pain, Wernick (1980) proposed to test the efficacy of stress inoculation (SI) training in the management of clinical pain experience of burn patients.

The subjects were adult patients from the Burn Unit of the Medical University of South Carolina. This unit is a nine-bed, isolated, critical care facility with its own three-bed intensive care section. Patients with burns to less than 15% of the body, the intellectually impaired, and patients in intensive care were excluded from this study. Sixteen subjects were randomly assigned to the SI or No-Treatment (NT) groups so that eight subjects were in each group.

Nine dependent measures were used in this study. The State-Trait Anxiety Inventory (STAI) was administered three times: during the pretreatment, posttreatment, and follow-up assessment periods (Spielberger, Gorsuch, & Lushene, 1970). A manual with detailed, standardized instructions for assessment and treatment strategies was developed for use in this study (Wernick, Taylor, & Jaremko, 1978). The staff of the Burn Unit obtained several daily measures, including

1. *Pain medication requests:* Each request and administration of analgesic medication was recorded. Unauthorized pain medication requests were defined as the number of requests made, minus the number of administrations of analgesics.

2. *Self-ratings:* All subjects were asked to rate how they felt physically and how they felt emotionally three times per 12-hour shift. Both ratings were obtained on a scale from 0 (worst) to 100 (best), with a rating of 50 representing a neutral point. Ratings were at least 1½ hours apart and were not obtained during any treatment procedure.

3. *Dressing change ratings:* Two ratings were obtained immediately after the tanking or morning dressing change each day. Both employed the same 0–100 scale. One rating was the subject's assessment of the level of pain experienced during the tanking. The other rating was a staff member's assessment of how well the subject tolerated pain during the procedure.

4. *Behavior checklist:* The checklist focused on six behaviors that occurred on request by a staff member. A patient's participation and cooperation with each of these were essential to optimal recovery. Each time a request was made, the subject's response was recorded as compliance, refusal, or delaying. A compliance percentage, defined as the number of compliance responses divided by the total number of responses, was computed to reflect the subject's degree of cooperation with treatment procedures. The six behaviors involved were eating, drinking, wearing splints, physical therapy or exercise, dressing changes and tankings.

5. *Nurses' rating for shift:* At the end of each shift, the nurse assigned to the subject made a global rating of how well the individual coped with stress (pain) during that time interval. This rating also employed the 0–100 scale.

The staff of the Burn Unit were trained by the author in the assessment procedures with the aid of a training manual (Wernick *et al.*, 1978). A one-hour session involved a detailed review of ratings, observations, and the use of the assessment procedures. The registered nurses were trained as therapists in two one-hour sessions. The first training session consisted of a review of the rationale of the study and instructions for the educational phase and physical coping strategies. The second session consisted of procedures for cognitive coping skills, cognitive restructuring, and the application phase of the stress inoculation training. Additionally, the nurses practiced the treatment regimen with each other by means of role-playing.

Three assessment periods were included—pretreatment (five days), posttreatment (five days), and follow-up (three days)—in order to determine the efficacy of a five-day treatment period. Follow-up either took place four weeks after the treatment period or it consisted of the last three days of monitoring for subjects who were transferred or discharged earlier. The same daily monitoring procedures were employed during each assessment period.

For five consecutive days, subjects in the SI group received a 30 to 40-minute treatment session. Treatment, which focused on the management of the pain experience, consisted of three phases: education, skills acquisition, and application. During the first session, subjects were presented with the rationale and goals for treatment. A Schachterian model of emotion (Jaremko, 1979) was used to explain the stress cycle. The next session consisted of a review of the education phase and the beginning of the skills acquisition phase. Subjects were taught physical coping strategies at this time: deep breathing, mental relaxation, and modified muscle relaxation to take account of their physical condition. Cognitive strategies were taught during the third session, which included various forms of attention diversion. Cognitive reappraisal was also taught during this session. The skills acquisition phase was completed and the application phase was begun during the fourth session. At this time, subjects were taught cognitive restructuring and how to combine the various techniques. They mentally rehearsed use of the strategies while imagining themselves being tanked and debrided. The application phase was completed during the last session, in which the therapist served as a coach while the subject used stress inoculation procedures during an actual tanking.

Subjects in the NT group did not receive any particular stress inoculation treatment, but instead, they received the usual services provided to burn patients (e.g., psychiatric consultation, pain medication). In addition, NT subjects were offered a stress inoculation treatment after completing the posttreatment assessment period. For this reason, subjects originally in the NT group were no longer available for a follow-up assessment. The conditions of the study at the hospital required that the NT group be offered treatment prior to their leaving.

The results showed that there were no overall pretest differences in either demographic composition or baseline levels on dependent measures between the SI and NT groups. The data indicate that subjects in the SI group changed significantly on each measure from pretreatment to posttreatment, while the NT group improved significantly on only two variables: physical and emotional self-ratings. Comparisons of the amount of change revealed that the SI group showed significantly greater improvement overall than the NT group in the ability to manage pain. Additionally, significant differences were found on five of the nine dependent measures when analyzed separately. These treatment effects for the SI group were maintained at follow-up. In general, the results of Wernick (1980) supported the efficacy of stress inoculation for the management of clinical pain with burn patients.

While subjects were not asked to reduce their use of pain medications, it was anticipated that those who were better able to manage their pain would request them less frequently. Although both groups were about equal in unauthorized pain medication requests at pretreatment, the SI group showed significant decreases at posttreatment while the NT group nearly doubled their medication requests during this time. This variable clearly differentiated the two groups and appears to be a valuable measure of general pain tolerance.

Tankings are considered the most painful event in the daily lives of burn patients. The primary focus of stress inoculation training was the management of pain during a tanking procedure, and thus, the tanking ratings (subject and staff) were particularly relevant measures of pain experience. The SI group showed significant improvement on both ratings while the NT group did not. These findings further underscore the efficacy of stress inoculation training in the management of the clinical pain of burn patients.

The compliance data indicated the relative degree to which subjects cooperated with essential aspects of their treatment to the Burn Unit. Noncompliance in these areas can ultimately prolong hospitalization, limit recovery of functioning, and render subjects more susceptible to lethal infection. Since parents often identify pain and discomfort as reasons for noncompliance, it was anticipated that those who were better able to manage their pain would be more compliant. Only the SI group showed significant increases on this measure and the difference between the groups was highly significant.

Nurses assigned to each subject were asked to give a general rating based on observations of adaptive and maladaptive behavior. Ratings from pretreatment to posttreatment increased significantly for the SI group but did not change significantly for the NT group. The difference between the groups was also significant.

Since previous research had consistently identified anxiety as a major component of the pain experience, the STAI was administered once during each assessment period to measure levels of anxiety. Significant improvement was found only for the SI group on both A-State and A-Trait. Differences in the amount of improvement between groups were significant for A-State.

The specific focus of the stress inoculation intervention was the management of painful stressors, especially during tankings. While the tanking is perhaps the most prominent stressor during hospitalization, it is only one aspect of a situation that is, in general, extremely stressful. Several of the dependent measures could therefore be considered measures of treatment generalization. For example, the compliance percentage can be viewed as reflecting the general degree to which subjects allow pain behaviors to interfere with active participation in essential components of their treatment program. Similarly, the nurses' overall rating can be considered a global assessment of adaptive coping behavior, while the unauthorized pain medication requests can be viewed as a measure of more general pain management. Therefore, the results reported previously may be interpreted as providing evidence for the generalization of treatment effects beyond specific tanking situations.

While the Wernick (1980) data are very encouraging, several questions can be raised regarding some of the procedures used. No attempt was made to control the analgesic regimen of any subject. Medication was usually available to patients once every four hours and dose levels for different analgesics were generally equivalent. While it was anticipated that stress inoculation subjects would be better able to manage their pain and would request analgesics less frequently, no subjects were asked to limit their medication use.

The nursing staff of the Burn Unit played a dual role in this study—they had primary responsibility for data collection and also served as therapists. They were trained in procedures for both roles by the author, who remained available for consultation throughout the study. Therefore, neither the nursing staff nor the author was blind to subject group assignment. These factors represent potential confounds in the data. Questions can be raised regarding the possibility of experimenter bias, suggestion effects, and interaction effects between therapists and subjects. It is not possible to determine the extent to which these factors may have influenced the outcome of this investigation. The preliminary nature of this study must not be overlooked. Future work in the area would do well to include more adequate controls in an attempt to disentangle the various possible confounds.

There may also be some positive aspects to the dual role of the nurses. Interactions between patients and staff frequently center around painful procedures or control issues. It was felt that the dual role would provide opportunities for interaction in a context that would be neither painful nor threatening. Positive effects, while not directly assessed, were observed to occur with several subjects.

Stress inoculation subjects were interviewed to obtain feedback on the use of the various components in the package. Most subjects found the physical coping skills to be most helpful in preparing for painful procedures and in trying to get comfortable before going to sleep. Cognitive strategies were reported to be most helpful in getting through painful procedures. Cognitive restructuring seemed to be used less frequently than other strategies and was employed by some subjects to deal with the anxiety associated with the anticipation of painful procedures.

SPECIFIC TREATMENT PROCEDURES IN BURN PAIN MANAGEMENT

Let us now consider the stress inoculation training procedure of this study in more detail. These procedures will be presented in session-by-session format and will include comments about the procedure.[1] It should be remembered that members of the nursing staff were trained as therapists and were the ones to conduct the stress inoculation training with the patients.

The treatment phase lasted five days. All treatment sessions lasted 30–40 minutes and were conducted on an individual basis. There were three general guidelines for these instructions: (1) All teaching was Socratic in style—that is, information was elicited from subjects when-

[1] This material is based on a procedure manual and does not include instructions for assessment procedures. The assessment instructions as well as the complete instructions for the treatment procedures, are included in the original manual (Wernick, Taylor, & Jaremko, 1978), which is available from the author on request.

ever appropriate; (2) all sessions began with a review of the previous session; and (3) subjects were asked to practice on their own what they learned at each session.

Session One

Rationale, Goals, and Contract

The subject is told that all burn patients experience pain. The severity of injury is only one of the factors involved in the experience of pain. Other factors include past experiences of pain, what one says to oneself about the experience, and one's ability to tolerate painful sensations by such means as relaxation. In other words, two people with the same degree of burn will have different perceptions of their pain. This pain may be experienced quite differently even though the degree of the injury may be the same.

Patients in Wernick (1980) were told—you are receiving all of the pain medication that your system can tolerate. We know that it is a bad feeling to have little or no control over your pain and to have to depend on others to take care of you. Therefore, the purpose of this treatment is to teach you additional ways to cope with your stress in general, and particularly with your pain. The goal is for you to achieve a greater degree of control over your pain and to increase your ability to cope with stress.

To accomplish this, you will meet with your nurse for about 30 minutes each day this week. During these meetings we will teach you some techniques, help you practice using them, and teach you when to use them. The name of the treatment is Stress Inoculation training and the reason for the name is important. You will be taught a variety of skills that you can use to cope with stress—any stress, but mainly pain. Burn patients, like yourself, have found this procedure to be helpful. We do not

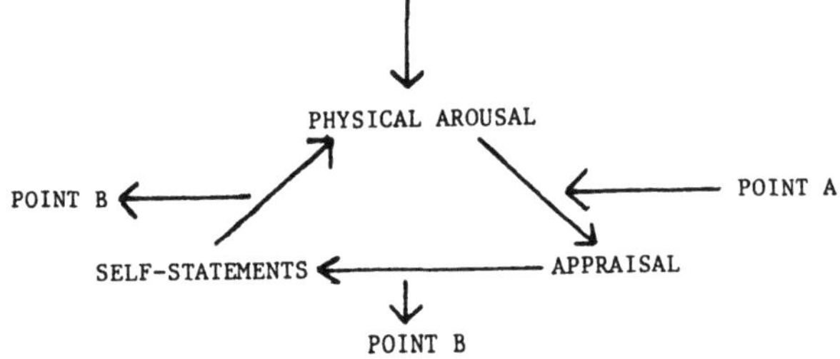

Figure 1. Modified Schachterian model of stress responding (from Jaremko, 1979).

expect it to eliminate your pain, but we do expect it to be able to help you decrease the severity of your pain.

Educational Phase

In order to further describe the nature of the treatment the subject is given a copy of the diagram (Figure 1) illustrating the stress cycle. In presenting the stress cycle, the therapist points out the three phases and asks the subject for his or her own instances of each phase. The therapist should also be prepared to provide one or two additional examples for the subject.

In Wernick (1980) the patients were told—stress can be viewed as a three-phase cycle. The stressor in this case is pain. The first phase is physical arousal and represents what you feel. The second phase is appraisal and represents the way you evaluated the physical sensations. The third phase is called self-statements and represents the specific things you think or imagine to yourself about the situation. This usually serves to keep the cycle going. For instance, let's consider a tanking situation. The stressor is pain and the physical arousal that accompanies it might include an increase in heart rate and blood pressure, shallow and rapid breathing, and general tensing of muscles. These sensations are likely to be evaluated in an automatic fashion with the appraisal being a negative one labeled "painful." The negative self-statements that result might consist of thoughts such as "This is killing me!" or "I can't take any more!" While this cycle might end in much screaming and yelling, treatment involves learning to break the cycle by using adaptive techniques.

Session Two

Skills Consolidation and Acquisition Phase

It is important to find out how subjects have attempted to cope with stress (pain) in the past. This should be elicited by a series of questions such as: "What have you used in the past to help you cope or handle feelings of tenseness, upset, or even pain? What advice would you have for someone else who has burns such as yours to cope with the stress and pain?" It is very important to *listen* for any strategies that subjects have used. Some of these are likely to be similar to those you will be teaching. If this occurs, let the subject know that is one of the strategies to be *taught.* A summary of possible treatment strategies is presented in Table I.

Physical Coping Skills

The subject is told that physical coping strategies are designed to be used at point A of Figure 1 in response to the physical arousal associated

Table I. Treatment Flow-Chart

Physical Coping Strategies

1. Deep breathing
2. Autogenic training
3. Muscle relaxation

Cognitive Strategies

1. Attentive diversion (distraction)
2. Cognitive reappraisal

Cognitive Restructuring

Combining the Techniques

Application Phase

1. *In vitro* (imagery)
2. *In vivo* (in tank)

with stress or pain. The primary purpose of these skills is to relax. It is only by learning the techniques and trying them out that the subject will know which skills are helpful for him or her.

1. Deep Breathing. Subjects are asked to close their eyes and become as comfortable as possible. They are told to take a slow, deep breath and then exhale it slowly. While concentrating on breathing, repeat six to eight times.

2. Autogenic Training. Autogenic training (Schultz & Luthe, 1959) is a form of "mental relaxation." It is preferred that the patient be lying down during the procedure. Relaxation is achieved by having the patient concentrate on various parts of the body and focusing on the "warm" and "heavy" feelings until the entire body has become relaxed. A word such as "calm" can be used in association with this experience so that it later becomes a cue for relaxation. To facilitate teaching and practice, instructions for autogenic training are recorded on a cassette.

3. Muscle Relaxation. Many people, when stressed, tense certain muscles. Burn patients are no exception. While progressive muscle relaxation procedures are usually effective in relaxing tense muscles, conducting this procedure with burn patients would only serve to increase pain due to the nature of the injuries. It was thought that progressive muscle relaxation could be modified for use with burn patients by teaching a tension-release procedure to be used only with muscles in unburned areas that remain tense after autogenic training. While this was accomplished, patients did not find this strategy helpful and tended not to use it.

Session Three

Cognitive Strategies

Subjects are told that cognitive strategies are designed to be used at point B, in response to the appraisal of pain and the focusing of attention on the painful situation. The subject can learn which strategies are most helpful by learning the various techniques and practicing them.

1. Attention Diversion (Distraction). Most subjects already use distraction in one form or another. Therefore, the therapist asked subjects how they distract themselves. If subjects deny using distraction, they can be asked how it was used in the past. For example, most people have been able to distract themselves by such means as going fishing, reading, watching television, playing the piano, or just daydreaming. The purpose of distraction is to divert attention from the painful experience. This can be accomplished either by *thinking* about other things or by *doing* other things. Categories of strategies (Turk, 1978b) include

Focusing on environmental aspects: Subjects can focus on the physical characteristics of the room. For example, they might count ceiling tiles or take inventory of visible objects.

Mental distractions: This involves focusing attention on various thoughts. For example, one can engage in mental arithmetic, make plans for an outing or trip, sing songs, or recite poems to oneself (or aloud if others don't mind).

Somatization: This involves focusing on bodily sensations in painful or nonpainful areas. One may watch and analyze changes in the sensations, comparing them to sensations in other parts of the body.

Imaginative inattention: With this technique, the subject tries to ignore the pain by engaging in a mental image or goal-directed fantasy, which, if real, would be incompatible with the experience of pain. The subject should have the details of this fantasy prepared in advance so that the images can be produced on cue. For example, the subject might fantasize about spending a pleasant day on the beach. The details should be prepared as if a script were being written.

Imaginative transformation of pain: In this strategy, the subject includes the experience of pain in the fantasy, but transforms the sensations. For example, the subject can imagine that a limb is made of rubber or is numb, and thus, is unable to feel the hurt.

Imaginative transformation of context: This technique includes the experience of pain in the fantasy, but transforms the context or situation. For example, subjects might imagine that they are no longer burn patients in the tank, but spies being tortured, or soldiers who have been wounded while saving their buddies.

Activity presents another alternative as a means of distraction. In Wernick (1980), a variety of activites were available on the unit, including watching television, reading, talking with other patients and staff, playing games, writing letters, exercising, making phone calls, and visiting with friends or relatives.

2. *Cognitive Reappraisal.* This technique involves teaching the subject to view the stress (pain) reaction as a series of four phases rather than one overwhelming panic reaction (Meichenbaum, 1977; Meichenbaum & Turk, 1976). Instead of seeing themselves as helpless and having no control, subjects learn to "get ready," to prepare for the pain, confront it, and handle it. While the sample statements listed in Table II are geared toward pain, similar statements can be used for other kinds of stressful situations.

Session Four

Cognitive Restructuring

Cognitive restructuring is designed to be used at point C, in response to the negative self-statements generated by the subject. This technique involves the subject looking at the positive aspects of a threatening (painful) situation. For example, having dressings changed, even though it is painful, will help prevent infection and promote recovery.

The first step is to identify the *specific* negative self-statements emitted when in pain. If subjects respond that they are always in pain, they should be asked to focus on the self-statements that they emit during a tanking. Subjects can close their eyes and use imagery procedures to find out how they had reacted in the past. At least two or three specific negative self-statements should be elicited and written down.

Next, the subject and the therapist together generate positive coping statements for each of the negative self-statements. It is important that the positive statements that are generated be specific and realistic.

After the positive statements have been generated, the subject is instructed to imagine feeling the pain while having his/her dressing changed. At the same time, he/she is instructed to imagine saying the negative self-statement, and then replacing it with the positive coping statement.

Table II. Sample Self-Statements for Pain Control[a]

Preparing for the painful stressor	
	What is it you have to do?
	You can develop a plan to deal with it.
	Just think about what you have to do.
	Just think about what you can do about it.
	Don't worry; worrying won't help anything.
	You have lots of different strategies you can call upon.
Confronting and handling the pain	
	You can meet the challenge.
	One step at a time; you can handle the situation.
	Just relax, breathe deeply, and use one of the strategies.
	Don't think about the pain, just what you have to do.
	This tenseness can be an ally, a cue to cope.
	Relax. You're in control; take a slow deep breath. Ah, good.
	This anxiety is what the trainer said you might feel.
	That's right; it's the reminder to use your coping skills.
Coping with feelings at critical moments	
	When pain comes just pause; keep focusing on what you have to do.
	What is it you have to do?
	Don't try to eliminate the pain totally; just keep it under control.
	Just remember, there are different strategies; they'll help you stay in control.
	When the pain mounts you can switch to a different strategy; you're in control.
Reinforcing self-statements	
	Good, you did it.
	You handled it pretty well.
	You knew you could do it!
	Wait until you tell the trainer about which procedures worked best.

[a]From Meichenbaum (1977).

Combining the Techniques

The subject has now been taught a variety of techniques and skills with which to cope with stress in general and pain in particular. These skills can be used in a "cafeteria-style" format; that is, different techniques can be used in succession to "make it through" the stressful (painful) situation. The subject merely uses one strategy until it stops working and then switches to another. He or she continues to switch to another strategy as each one loses its effectiveness until the stressful event is over.

A subject might first prepare for the painful stressor by getting relaxed. As the painful stimulation begins, the subject can first use one method of distraction and then another as each becomes ineffective. This continual switching to alternate strategies might progress through various imagery scenes that had been prepared until the event has ended.

Application Phase

The subject is asked to imagine that it is time for the morning dressing change. At this point, the subject should be preparing for this stressful event. The therapist can act as a "coach" during the rehearsal. As subjects imagine the beginning of the dressing change, they should start to use the coping strategies. As the rehearsal continues, subjects can use the coping skills in a "cafeteria-style" format, as described previously. Perhaps this method can best be illustrated by presenting a segment of a session in which the therapist (nurse) and patient rehearse for a tanking.

THERAPIST: We are going to practice using the strategies you've learned while imagining that you are being tanked. Close your eyes and imagine that you are being prepared for a tanking.

PATIENT: I've got a clear image now. I can see myself being taken to the tank.

THERAPIST: Good. Begin preparing yourself for the tanking. What will you do first?

PATIENT: I need to get relaxed so I'll start with deep breathing and then use autogenic exercises.

THERAPIST: Fine.... Now you are being lowered into the tank and your old dressings are being removed. Can you visualize this?

PATIENT: Yes. This is not too hard for me to manage. I can count the tiles on the ceiling while they are doing that.

THERAPIST: All your dressings are off now and they are about to begin washing you.

PATIENT: I can visualize this. I'm preparing for this. I know that it is important to have my wounds washed to prevent infection. This will help me get well quicker. They know it is painful and they try to be as gentle as possible. I will plan a family picnic in my mind.

THERAPIST: That's a good approach [pause] It looks like you're having some difficulty now. Is the pain becoming more severe?

PATIENT: Yes. They are washing some very sensitive areas now. This is one of those critical moments we've talked about.

THERAPIST: You're prepared for this. Switch to your beach scene. Imagine yourself at the beach—hear the surf, smell the salt air, notice the people, feel the sun and the breeze. Can you experience that?

The patient and therapist would continue in this fashion through the imagined tanking until it was completed.

Session Five

This session is to begin just prior to the subject's morning tanking. The therapist (nurse) will again serve as a "coach" during this tanking, as was practiced in the preceding session. As the tanking begins, the therapist should suggest that the subject try to relax. The therapist should also remind the subject to view the tanking as a series of four phases and to use the coping strategies in a "cafeteria-style." If the subject appears to have difficulty coping with the pain at any point during the tanking, the therapist should suggest that the subject use another coping technique. At the end of the tanking, the therapist as well as the subject should reinforce the subject for having coped.

Epilogue

A few additional comments are in order before concluding the discussion of Wernick (1980). Although each nurse–therapist was equally capable of conducting a treatment session, providing a patient with the same therapist for each session might prove beneficial. In addition to providing continuity, the therapist might be more familiar with strategy preferences and might also be a more effective coach after having worked with the patient during each session. As a preliminary test of stress inoculation, this study did not attempt to evaluate the various aspects of the treatment procedures. While patient feedback indicated that strategy preference and effectiveness varied a great deal, the task of identifying the effective components of the treatment package for this population is left to future investigations.

It is important to note that the treatment described in this study was limited to the acute phase of the burn patient's treatment. How might stress inoculation training be used to help the patient through the relatively short but traumatic emergency phase? How can these procedures best be adapted to help the patient adjust to the many changes that accompany the return to society during the rehabilitation phase? This latter phase seems particularly important and yet, has not been the focus of any systematic intervention. The case of Ms. B. may stimulate some thought as to the use of stress inoculation for the rehabilitation phase.

> Ms. B. was a 29-year-old married mother of two, who served as a pilot subject in the study just described. She was burned in a house fire along with her two-year-old daughter and sustained second and third degree burns to more than 60% of her body. Her total hospitalization lasted approximately six months.
>
> Ms. B. was taught the stress inoculation procedures and found them

helpful in dealing with her pain. She began to look forward to going home as she recovered. Toward the end of her hospitalization, she realized that she would have a lengthy rehabilitation period after discharge and that she would not "look like new" when released. She became quite anxious and fearful at the thought of having to "face the world". At this time, she requested additional therapy.

It was going to be necessary for Ms. B. to wear her Jobst mask nearly all the time. She anticipated that her different appearance would result in being stared at and the thought of wearing the mask in public resulted in panic attacks. In her sessions, Ms. B. was able to generalize from her stress inoculation training for the management of pain and apply what she had learned to this new problem. Essentially, she was able to prepare for these stressors in much the same way as she was prepared for a tanking. She got relaxed, distracted herself with pleasant imagery and used cognitive restructuring to deal with her negative self-statements. She collected her strategies and rehearsed them. She even requested and obtained a short pass pior to her discharge for additional practice.

Ms. B. returned for follow-up several weeks after discharge. She reported that managing her anxiety was extremely difficult at first and she was often tempted to "just give up." However, she continued to use the strategies she had prepared and gradually was better able to manage her stress. Her success might best be illustrated by an anecdote she told with great relish. Her father drove her to the bank one day and waited in the car while she went inside. She was wearing her Jobst mask and as she waited in line, she thought people were staring at her. She thought that these people might look at her mask and think she was a bank robber. They might even think that her father was waiting in the get-away car. She developed this thought into a rather pleasant fantasy while waiting her turn and was quite proud of herself when she completed her transaction and left the bank.

SUMMARY

The brief review of the psychological literature on burn patients reveals that there is a paucity of research and that most of the existing studies are descriptive in nature. Burn patients represent a high-risk population and the need for controlled investigations is apparent. The results of the present study are consistent with other studies on the treatment of pain (see Turk *et al.*, 1983). Previous investigations have found stress inoculation training to be effective in the management of pain and a variety of stress-related problems.

It is important to note the preliminary nature of the data reported here. While the data are most encouraging, a number of factors moderate the conclusions that can be drawn. These factors include a lack of normative information on the measures used; the absence of blind raters; and possible expectancy effects. Larger samples, longer follow-ups, and tighter controls are needed to obtain more conclusive data.

REFERENCES

Adler, A. Neuropsychiatric complications of victims of Boston's Cocoanut Grove disaster. *Journal of the American Medical Association,* 1943, *123,* 1098–1101.

Andreasen, N. J. C. Neuropsychiatric complications in burn patients. *International Journal of Psychiatry in Medicine,* 1974, *5,* 161–171.

Andreasen, N. J. C., & Norris, A. S. Long-term adjustments and adaptation mechanisms in severely burned adults. *Journal of Nervous and Mental Disease,* 1972, *154,* 352–362.

Andreasen, N. J. C., Norris, A. S., & Hartford, C. E. Incidence of long-term psychiatric complications in severely burned adults. *Annals of Surgery,* 1971, *174,* 785–793.

Andreasen, N. J. C., Noyes, R., & Hartford, C. E. Factors influencing adjustment of burn patients during hospitalization. *Psychosomatic Medicine,* 1972, *34,* 517, 525.

Andreasen, N. J. C., Noyes, R., Hartford, C. E., Brodland, G., & Proctor, S. Management of emotional reactions in seriously burned adults. *New England Journal of Medicine, 1972, 286,* 65–69.

Artz, C. P. The burn patient. *Nursing Forum,* 1965, *4,* 87–92.

Bobey, M. J., & Davidson, P. O. Psychological factors affecting pain tolerance. *Journal of Psychosomatic Research,* 1970, *14,* 371–376.

Chang, F. C., & Herzog, B. Burn morbidity: A follow-up study of physical and psychological disability. *Annals of Surgery,* 1976, *183,* 34–37.

Chaves, J. F., & Brown, J. M. *Self-generated strategies for the control of pain and stress.* Paper presented at the Annual Meeting of the American Psychological Association, Toronto, August 1978.

Cobb, S., & Lindemann, E. Cocoanut Grove burns: Neuropsychiatric observations. *Annals of Surgery,* 1943, *117,* 814–824.

Davidson, S. P., & Noyes, R. Psychiatric nursing consultation on a burn unit. *American Journal of Nursing,* 1973, *73,* 1715–1718.

Fagerhaugh, S. Y. Pain expression and control on a burn care unit. *Nursing Outlook,* 1974, *22,* 645–650.

Gentry, W. D., & Bernal, G. A. A. Chronic pain. In R. B. Williams & W. D. Gentry (Eds.), *Behavioral approaches to medical treatment.* Cambridge, Mass.: Ballinger, 1977.

Goldfried, M. R., Linehan, M. M., & Smith, J. L. Reduction of test anxiety through cognitive restructuring. *Journal of Consulting and Clinical Psychology,* 1978, *46,* 32–39.

Gordon, M. *The burn team and you.* Phoenix, Ariz.: Burn Treatment Skin Bank, 1978.

Hamburg, D. A., Artz, C. P., Reiss, E., Amspacher, W. H., & Chambers, R. E. Clinical importance of emotional problems in the care of patients with burns. *New England Journal of Medicine,* 1953, *248,* 355–359.

Hamburg, D. A., Hamburg, B., & deGoza, S. Adaptive problems and mechanisms in severely burned patients. *Psychiatry,* 1953, *16,* 1–20.

Holroyd, K., & Andrasik, F. Coping and the self-control of chronic tension headache. *Journal of Consulting and Clinical Psychology,* 1978, *46,* 1036–1045.

Holroyd, K., Andrasik, F., & Westbrook, T. Cognitive control of tension headache. *Cognitive Therapy and Research,* 1977, *1,* 121–133.

Horan, J. J., Hackett, H. G., Buchanan, J. D., Stone, C. I., & Demchik-Stone, D. Coping with pain: A component analysis of stress inoculation. *Cognitive Therapy and Research,* 1977, *1,* 211–221.

Hussian, R. A., & Lawrence, P. S. The reduction of test, state, and trait anxiety by test specific and generalized stress inoculation training. *Cognitive Therapy and Research,* 1978, *2,* 25–38.

Jaremko, M. E. Cognitive strategies in the control of pain tolerance. Journal of Behavior Therapy and Experimental Psychiatry, 1978, *9,* 239–244.
Jaremko, M. E. A component analysis of stress inoculation: Review and prospectus. *Cognitive Therapy and Research,* 1979, *3,* 35–48.
Jorgensen, J. A., & Brophy, J. J. Psychiatric treatment modalities in burn patients. *Current Psychiatric Therapies,* 1975, *15,* 85–92.
Kjaer, G. C. D. Psychiatric aspects of thermal burns. *Northwest Medicine,* 1969, *68,* 537–541.
Levendusky, P., & Pankratz, L. Self-control techniques as an alternative to pain medication. *Journal of Abnormal Psychology,* 1975, *84,* 165–168.
Lewis, S. R., Goolishian, H. A., Wolf, C. W., Lynch, J. B., & Blocker, T. G. Psychological studies in burn patients. *Plastic and Reconstructive Surgery,* 1963, *31,* 323–332.
Liebeskind, J. C., & Paul, L. A. Psychological and physiological mechanisms of pain. *Annual Review of Psychology,* 1977, *28,* 41–60.
Lipowski, Z. J. Delirium: Clouding of consciousness and confusion. *Journal of Nervous and Mental Disease,* 1967, *154,* 227–255.
Meichenbaum, D. A self-instructional approach to stress management. A proposal for stress inoculation. In C. D. Spielberger & I. G. Sarason (Eds.), *Stress and anxiety* (Vol. 1). Washington, D.C.: Hemisphere, 1975.
Meichenbaum, D. *Cognitive-behavior modification.* New York: Plenum Press, 1977.
Meichenbaum, D., & Turk, D. The cognitive-behavioral management of anxiety, anger, and pain. In P. Davidson (Ed.), *Behavioral management of anxiety, anger, and pain.* New York: Brunner/Mazel, 1976.
Melzack, R., & Wall, P. D. Pain mechanisms: A theory. *Science,* 1965, *150,* 971–979.
Melzack, R., & Wall, P. D. Psychophysiology of pain. In M. Weisenberg (Ed.), *Pain: Clinical and experimental perspectives.* St. Louis: C. V. Mosby, 1975.
Miller, W. C., Gardner, N., & Mlott, S. R. Psychological support in the treatment of severely burned patients. *Journal of Trauma,* 1976, *16,* 722–725.
Mlott, S. R., Lira, F. T., & Miller, W. C. Psychological assessment of the burn patient. *Journal of Clinical Psychology,* 1977, *33,* 425–430.
Morris, J., & McFadd, A. The mental health team on a burn unit: A multidisciplinary approach. *Journal of Trauma,* 1978, *18,* 658–663.
Novaco, R. W. Treatment of chronic anger through cognitive and relaxation controls. *Journal of Consulting and Clinical Psychology,* 1976, *44,* 681.
Novaco, R. W. A stress inoculation approach to anger management in the training of law enforcement officers. *American Journal of Community Psychology,* 1977, *5,* 327–346.
Noyes, R., Andreasen, N. J. C., & Hartford, C. E. The psychological reaction to severe burns. *Psychosomatics,* 1971, *12,* 416–422.
Rybstein-Blinchik, E. Effects of different cognitive strategies on chronic pain experience. *Journal of Behavioral Medicine,* 1979, *2,* 93–101.
Schultz, J. H., & Luthe, W. *Autogenic training.* New York: Grune & Stratton, 1959.
Scott, D. S., & Barber, T. X. Cognitive control of pain: Effects of multiple cognitive strategies. *Psychological Record,* 1977, *27,* 373–383.
Simons, R. D., Green, L. C., Malin, R. M., Suskind, D. A., & Frank, H. A. The burn victim: His psychosocial profile and post-injury career. *Burns,* 1978, *5,* 97–100.
Simons, R. D., McFadd, A., Frank, H. A., Green, L. C., Malin, R. M., & Morris, J. L. Behavioral contracting in a burn care facility: A strategy for patient participation. *Journal of Trauma,* 1978, *18,* 257–260.
Spanos, N. P., Horton, C., & Chaves, J. F. The effects of two cognitive strategies on pain threshold. *Journal of Abnormal Psychology,* 1975, *84,* 677–681.

Spanos, N. P., Radtke-Bodorik, H. L., Ferguson, J. D., & Jones, B. The effects of hypnotic susceptibility, suggestions for analgesia, and the utilization of cognitive strategies on the reduction of pain. *Journal of Abnormal Psychology,* 1979, *88,* 282–292.

Spielberger, C. D., Gorsuch, R. L., & Lushene, R. E. *The state-trait anxiety inventory.* Palo Alto, Ca.: Consulting Psychologists Press, 1970.

Steiner, H., & Clark, W. R. Psychiatric complications of burned adults: A classification. *Journal of Trauma,* 1977, *17,* 134–143.

Stone, C. I., Demchik-Stone, D. A., & Horan, J. J. Coping with pain: A component analysis of Lamaze and cognitive-behavioral procedures. *Journal of Psychosomatic Research,* 1977, *21,* 451–456.

Tellegan, A., & Atkinson, G. Openness to absorbing and self-altering experiences ("Absorption"). *Journal of Abnormal Psychology,* 1974, *83,* 268–277.

Trent, J. T. *Cognitive relaxation as a treatment of chronic pain: A single care experiment.* Paper presented at the annual meeting of the Southeastern Psychological Association, Washington, D.C., March 1980.

Turk, D. C. Cognitive behavioral techniques in the management of pain. In J. P. Foreyt & D. P. Rathjen (Eds.), *Cognitive behavior therapy.* New York: Plenum Press, 1978. (a)

Turk, D. C. *The application of cognitive and behavioral skills for pain regulation.* Paper presented at the Annual Meeting of the American Psychological Association, Toronto, August 1978. (b)

Turk, D. C., & Genest, M. Regulation of pain: The application of cognitive behavioral techniques for prevention and remediation. In P. C. Kendall & S. D. Hollon (Eds.), *Cognitive-behavioral interventions: Theory, research, and procedures.* New York: Academic Press, 1979.

Turk, D., Meichenbaum, D., & Genest, M. *Pain and behavior medicine.* New York: Guilford Press, 1983.

Weisenberg, M. Pain and pain control. *Psychological Bulletin,* 1977, *84,* 1008–1044.

Weisz, A. E. Psychotherapeutic support of burned patients. *Modern Treatment,* 1967, *4,* 1291–1303.

Wernick, R. L. *Pain management in severely burned adults: A test of stress inoculation.* Unpublished doctoral dissertation, North Texas State University, 1980.

Wernick, R. L., Taylor, P. W., & Jaremko, M. E. *Assessment and treatment manual for the use of stress inoculation with burn patients.* Unpublished manuscript, Medical University of South Carolina, 1978.

Wernick, R. L., Brantley, P. J., & Malcolm, R. Behavioral techniques in the psychological rehabilitation of burn patients. *International Journal of Psychiatry in Medicine,* 1980, *10,* 145–150.

Zide, B., & Pardoe, R. The use of behavior modification therapy in a recalcitrant burned child. *Plastic and Reconstructive Surgery,* 1976, *57,* 378–382.

7

A Cognitive-Behavioral Approach to Psychophysiological Disorders

KENNETH A. HOLROYD, MARGRET A. APPEL,
and FRANK ANDRASIK

When applied to the treatment of psychophysiological disorders, cognitive-behavioral interventions seek to modify physiological symptoms indirectly by altering the way the individual responds cognitively and behaviorally to symptom-related stresses (Holroyd, 1979). Utilization of this treatment often requires not only a familiarity with cognitive-behavioral treatment techniques but also an understanding of the pathophysiology of the disorder being treated and of the ways coping can influence and be influenced by physiological processes. Therefore, we will begin with a general discussion of stress and coping, emphasizing the ways coping can influence psychophysiological symptoms. We will then discuss the treatment of three specific disorders chosen because they illustrate issues and problems that are likely to arise in the treatment of disorders with different etiologies and pathophysiologies.

A Framework for Intervention

The current diagnostic and statistical manual (American Psychiatric Association, 1980) acknowledges that stress can be a contributing factor

---

KENNETH A. HOLROYD and MARGRET A. APPEL • Department of Psychology, Ohio University, Athens, Ohio 45701 and FRANK ANDRASIK • Department of Psychology, State University of New York, Albany, New York 12222. Preparation of this chapter was supported in part by NIMH Fellowship IF32MH08327-01 to the senior author.

in a wide range of physical disorders, not just the subset of psychophysiological disorders recognized in the previous manual (DSM-II). It is unfortunate that the current manual provides few guidelines for determining when and how stress might contribute to a particular disorder. The clinician is simply instructed to evaluate whether symptoms are preceded by "intense affect," obviously stressful life events, or an "excessive number" of smaller life changes (Looney, Lipp, & Spitzer, 1978, p. 307). No guidelines are provided for this assessment and the difficulties of making such complex judgments appear to be minimized. In addition, the possibility that characteristic ways of responding to daily stress may contribute to disease processes in the absence of either the expression of intense affect or dramatic life changes (Glass, 1977) and the possibility that stress may be distally rather than proximally related to symptom formation (see later discussion of essential hypertension) are ignored. Thus, the manual is likely to prove of limited use in evaluating the effects of stress on physiological symptoms or in planning treatment.

We feel that the model of stress articulated by Richard Lazarus and his colleagues over the past 15 years (Coyne & Holroyd, 1982; Coyne & Lazarus, 1980; Holroyd & Lazarus, 1982; Lazarus, 1966, 1980, 1982; Lazarus, Cohen, Folkman, Kanner, & Schaefer, 1980; Lazarus & Launier, 1978) provides a more useful framework for viewing cognitive–behavioral interventions with stress-related disorders than does the model implicit in the current diagnostic and statistical manual. Lazarus's model and cognitive behavioral interventions are similar in their emphasis on the active role of the individual in shaping stress experiences and on the importance of cognitive processes both in determining stress responses and in guiding efforts to manage and control stress. The model thus provides useful categories for discussing psychological factors that influence stress responses and for analyzing interventions designed to alter these processes.

According to this formulation, psychological stress exists when there is recognition by the individual of an imbalance between environmental or internal demands and the individual's resources for coping with them. When this imbalance occurs, stress responses are assumed to be determined psychologically by reciprocally interacting appraisal and coping processes. Appraisal refers to ongoing evaluations of events in terms of their significance for the person's well-being (primary appraisal) or in terms of available resources or options the individual possesses for responding (secondary appraisal). Coping refers to both intrapsychic and behavioral efforts to manage or tolerate stress. Whereas early research focused primarily on appraisal as a determinant of stress responses, current work increasingly emphasizes coping (Lazarus, 1980, 1982).

Coping and Somatic Functioning

Coping has emerged as an important construct in stress theory. There is a growing consensus that the way people cope with stress can be a more important determinant of physiological stress responses and somatic functioning than are the frequency and character of the stressful situations they confront. Rapid social change and developmental crises of adulthood regularly confront people with demands that cannot be managed routinely (e.g., Levinson, 1978; Toffler, 1970). As a result, effective coping rather than the absence of stress is increasingly seen as a major deterrent to illness (Antonovsky, 1979; Henry & Stephens, 1977; Roskies & Lazarus, 1980). Workers in disciplines such as epidemiology and sociology emphasize that the impact of stressful environments on health can be understood only when environmental demands are viewed in the context of the resources available to the individual for coping (Cassel, 1976; Henry & Stephens, 1977; Jenkins, 1979; Kaplan, Cassel, & Gore, 1977; Rahe & Ranson, 1978). Evidence that physiological stress responses are, in part, determined by the coping activity of the individual has been available for some time in psychophysiology and psychosomatic medicine (Lazarus, 1966), although the exact ways coping shapes physiological stress responses remains unclear (Mason, 1970). Evidence that coping efforts influence symptom formation (Glass, 1977; J. M. Weiss, 1977) and the outcomes of disease processes is more recent (Weisman & Worden, 1975).

Coping can affect somatic functioning through at least four general pathways, and each of these pathways requires the attention of the therapist considering cognitive-behavioral intervention. First, by influencing the frequency, intensity, and character of the stressful transactions the individual experiences, coping efforts influence the mobilization of physiological stress responses and, thus, the effects of this mobilization on health. The damaging effects of the prolonged or repeated elicitation of neuroendocrine stress responses were recognized by Cannon (1932) 50 years ago. More recently, Selye (1956, 1976) has argued that this mobilization plays a significant etiological role in a large number of disorders. However, it is becoming increasingly evident that stress-related fluctuations in neuroendocrine activity affect somatic functioning in complex ways. On the one hand, hemodynamic control mechanisms may be disregulated in the early stages of hypertension (Kaplan, 1979) or immune mechanisms may be disrupted in some cases of Graves' disease and asthma (Bowers & Kelly, 1979; Morillo & Gardner, 1979; Rodgers, Dubey, & Reich, 1979). On the other hand, stress hormones may enhance the effectiveness of the immune response and act protectively against disease processes (Amkraut & Solomon, 1974). Consequently, straightforward notions about the therapeutic effects of reduced arousal (Stoyva, 1976) probably are, if not incorrect, at least overstated.

At present, we lack the precise understanding of the effects of coping on physiological stress responses that could facilitate the development of empirically based interventions. Laboratory paradigms in the biological sciences have tended to isolate stress responses from their psychological context. As a result, the potent role that psychological variables play in eliciting neuroendocrine stress responses has been acknowledged only recently by researchers in the biological sciences (Mason, 1975), and we know relatively little about the types of transactions that elicit pathogenic patterns of response in naturalistic settings.

It is fortunate that behavioral scientists are beginning to examine integrated biobehavioral responses to stress, and their research promises to provide empirical guidelines for therapeutic intervention. For example, Glass (1977; Glass, Krakoff, Contrada, Hilton, Kehoe, Manucci, Collins, Snow, & Elting, 1980) has argued that fluctuations in catecholamines sufficiently dramatic to influence the pathogenesis of coronary heart disease are elicited by a coping style that alternates between intense efforts to control stressful transactions and helplessness when coping efforts fail. Similarly, Obrist (Obrist, Light, Langer, Grignolo, & McCubbin, 1978) has contrasted cardiovascular responses associated with active and passive coping and has presented evidence that only active coping is accompanied by sympathetic stimulation of the heart and is thus likely to be associated with the hemodynamic changes pathogenic for essential hypertension.

Second, actual physiological symptoms may be learned or maintained because of their effectiveness as coping responses. Whitehead, Fedoravicius, Blackwell, and Wooley (1979) have argued that only readily perceptible physiological symptoms, likely to come under the control of environmental contingencies, will be learned in this manner. However, drawing on research indicating that baroreceptor stimulation inhibits reticular formation activity and thereby produces sedative-like effects, Dworkin (Miller & Dworkin, 1977) suggests that even nonperceptible symptoms such as essential hypertension might be learned as coping responses. Dworkin speculates that genetically predisposed individuals who lack more effective coping responses may learn to cope with stressful situations by elevating blood pressure because this response will be reinforced by sedative-like effects. Although this hypothesis is speculative, it does illustrate one way in which physiological activity and cognitive or behavioral coping responses may not only serve similar functions but be highly interdependent.

Illness behavior (i.e., reporting symptoms and/or seeking treatment) can also be a way of coping with stress rather than a rational effort to obtain symptom relief. Thus, illness behavior may be maintained by secondary gains and reinforcements or may serve a stabilizing function in conflicted families. Reviewing a substantial body of epidemiological research, Mechanic (1968) concluded that illness behavior should be seen "as part of a coping repertory, an attempt to make an unstable challenging situation more manageable for the person who is encountering difficulty" (p. 117). It is important for the therapist to know whether illness behavior or physiological symptoms are serving as coping responses. In such instances, the therapist may focus on helping the client to evaluate the costs and gains of a particular coping strategy, teaching more effective or less costly ways of coping with symptom-related stresses or attempting to alter the behavior of others in the individual's environment so that this coping response is less effective.

Third, coping efforts may contribute to disease through associated changes in health behaviors that expose the individual to injurious agents such as alcohol, tobacco smoke, or allergens. For example, Katz, Weiner, Gutman, and Yu (1973) reported that in 60% of their patients, gout was reactivated by the excessive consumption of food and alcohol in response to job-related stress. Others have reported that a significant number of peptic duodenal ulcer sufferers increase their consumption of alcohol (which stimulates acid secretion by the stomach) in response to stress (Weisman, 1956) and that stressful events are associated with increased smoking in men at risk for coronary heart disease (Horowitz, Hulley, Alvarez, Reynolds, Benfari, Blair, Borhani, & Simon, 1979). Therefore, even when symptoms appear to covary in a systematic manner with stressful events, it is important to evaluate the role that stress-related changes in health behavior play in aggravating symptoms.

Finally, accumulating evidence suggests that the way the individual copes with the threat of acute illness (Gentry, 1975; Pancheri, Bellaterra, Matteoli, Cristofari, Polizzi, & Puletti, 1978; Pranulis, 1975) or with the demands of chronic illness (Cohen & Lazarus, 1979; Moos & Tsu, 1977) can be an important determinant of the course of the illness and of the medical care that is received. For example, the asthmatic who responds to the threat of airway obstruction with helplessness will often be prescribed more steroid medication than the patient who is more persistent in efforts to cope with this threat, even when objective measures indicate similar levels of pulmonary function (Dirks, Jones, & Kinsman, 1977; Kinsman, Dahlem, Spector, & Staudenmayer, 1977). Moreover, Dirks, Kinsman, Horton, Fross, and Jones (1978) have observed that these styles of coping with symptoms will influence a patient's self-medication and this in turn may influence the course of the illness. Therapeutic efforts to teach skills for the self-management of symptoms, therefore, must take into account not only primary symptoms, but also the patient's own efforts to regulate and control the disorders.

Although the above discussion serves to draw attention to issues that may be important in planning cognitive-behavioral interventions, the biological processes involved in symptom formation and the psychological processes involved in coping are greatly simplified in such a discussion. Actually, stress-related symptoms are likely to be influenced by a mosaic of interacting biological, psychological, and environmental factors that exert etiological and maintaining influences (Weiner, 1977). These multiple variables can probably best be viewed from the vantage point of systems theory as interacting elements in a dynamic system where concepts of linear causation are supplanted by those of systems operating in cyclical fashion through positive and negative feedback loops (Schwartz, 1979; Von Bertalanffy, 1968). As therapists, we would do well to keep in mind Pinkerton's (1973) admonition that "no single factor is of overriding importance in symptom production [in psychosomatic illness]. The clinical outcome is always determined by a complex etiological sequence, so that the key to successful management lies in correctly evaluating each factor's importance in any given case" (p. 462).

In the next sections, we discuss some of the issues and problems likely to arise in the treatment of three specific disorders—chronic headache, bronchial asthma, and essential hypertension. In each case, a discussion of the disorder will provide a groundwork for our discussion of therapy. With each disorder, we then discuss how characteristics of the disorder affect treatment strategy.

CHRONIC HEADACHE[1]

Symptoms and Epidemiology

Headache is one of the top 14 problems mentioned by outpatients seeking medical attention (DeLozier & Gagnon, 1975). Surveys reveal that approximately 50% to 70% of all people have headaches at some time (Andrasik, Holroyd, & Abell, 1979; Hurley, 1969; Kashiwagi, McClure, & Wetzel, 1972; Lance & Anthony, 1971; Waters & O'Connor, 1975), and that 10% to 12% of these individuals are prompted to seek medical attention (Hurley, 1969). Of the 15 classes of headache identified by the American Medical Association's Ad Hoc Committee on Classification of Headache

[1]An extended discussion of the material in this section can be found in Holroyd and Andrasik (1982).

(1962), the two most common types—tension and migraine—will be discussed here. Tension headache, also termed muscle-contraction, psychogenic, or nervous headache, occurs most frequently and accounts for about half of all forms of headache. Although migraine occurs less frequently, there are approximately 12 million migraine sufferers in the United States.

Tension Headache Symptoms

The Ad Hoc Committee (1962) described tension headache as an "ache or sensation of tightness, pressure or constriction, widely varied in intensity, frequency and duration, sometimes long-lasting and commonly sub-occipital" (p. 718). In practice, key inclusion and exclusion features are used to diagnose tension headache. Inclusion features consist of pain that is persistent, vice- or band-like, dull and drawing, and slow in onset and resolution. Exclusion features include the absence of vascular features (unilaterality, auras, nausea and vomiting, throbbing sensations, and photophobia), underlying organic factors, and association with climate changes, allergies, or sinus involvement.

Migraine Headache Symptoms

The Ad Hoc Committee (1962) identified five types of migraine; features common to all are "recurrent attacks of headache, widely varied in intensity, frequency, and duration. The attacks are commonly unilateral in onset; are usually associated with anorexia and, sometimes, with nausea and vomiting; in some are preceded by, or associated with, conspicuous sensory, motor, and mood disturbances; and are often familial" (p. 717). The two major types of migraine are classic and common. Classic migraine is vascular headache "with sharply defined transient visual, and other sensory or motor prodromes or both." Common migraine, in contrast, is "without striking prodromes and less often unilateral." (p. 717).

As with most diagnostic categories, symptom overlap occurs between tension and migraine headache (Ziegler, Hassanein, & Hassanein, 1972). In addition, it is not unusual for one type of headache to occur in combination with another type of headache. For example, it has been estimated that as many as one-quarter of all tension headache sufferers actually consist of a group intermediate between migraine and tension headache and that a small percentage of tension sufferers also suffer from classic migraine. Despite the existence of symptom overlap, data from a recent investigation that compared the diagnoses made by a board-certified neurologist with those of graduate students in clinical psychology revealed agreement in 86.4% of 66 consecutive patients

(Blanchard, O'Keefe, Neff, Jurish, & Andrasik, 1981). Over half of the disagreements occurred because patients conveyed different information to the two independent assessors or gave different emphasis to the same information.

Pathophysiology

Tension Headache

The dominant model of the pathogenesis of tension headache attributes head pain to the "sustained contraction of skeletal muscles" usually occurring "as part of the individual's reaction during life stress" (Ad Hoc Committee on Classification of Headache, 1962, p. 128). Head pain is thought to result from (1) the stimulation of pain receptors in the contracted muscles and (2) ischemia resulting from the compression of intramuscular arterioles. The latter effect often persists for days after the muscles relax (Haynes, 1981; Raskin & Appenzeller, 1980).

Migraine Headache

Migraine headache appears to be primarily of vascular origin, with vasoconstriction in both the intra- and extracranial arteries occurring during the prodromal phase and vasodilation occurring during the pain associated with a migraine attack (Adams, Feuerstein, & Fowler, 1980; Raskin & Appenzeller, 1980). Although these two phases usually occur sequentially, they may also occur concurrently. The high incidence of migraine in close blood relatives of migraine sufferers (as high as 50% to 70% in some investigations) suggests that an inherited defect in vasomotor regulation may provide a predisposition to migraine (Raskin & Appenzeller, 1980).

Two Distinct Pathophysiologies?

The widely held view that tension headaches are of muscle-contraction origin and migraine headaches are of vascular origin has little empirical basis. Thus (1) tension headache sufferers do not appear to show larger increases in EMG activity than do nonheadache sufferers in response to stress (e.g., Andrasik & Holyrod, 1980a); (2) intensive case study of tension headache sufferers reveals minimal relationship between pain reports and EMG levels (Epstein, Abel, Collins, Parker, & Cinciripini, 1978; Harper & Steger, 1978); and (3) in treatment studies, improvements in reported head pain and changes in EMG activity are often markedly desynchronous (e.g., Andrasik & Holroyd, 1980c; Epstein & Abel, 1977; Holroyd, Andrasik, & Westbrook, 1977). There is also evidence suggesting that vascular processes are operative in tension as well as migraine headache (Ostfeld, Reis, & Wolff, 1957; Tunis & Wolff, 1954). Muscle contraction may thus be a consequence and not a cause of tension headache, and the two disorders may be "quantitatively different clinical manifestations of vasomotor instability" (Raskin & Appenzeller, 1980, p. 174).

The vascular changes that characterize migraine, and possibly severe tension headache as well, have been studied in considerable detail. However, the mechanism by which these vascular alterations are produced remains poorly understood. The release and subsequent depletion of vasoactive substances that produce a passive distension of the arterial wall and reduced pain threshold appear to play an important role in migraine (Fanchamps, 1974). In particular, the modulation of sympathetic serotonin at the central level (altered reactivity of brain stem serotonergic neurons) and at the peripheral level (regulation of the synaptic turnover of serotonin) may be an important pathogenic mechanism in the disorder.

Stress and Headache

Tension Headache

It is generally accepted that tension headache occurs in conjunction with life stress. However, descriptions of the types of stresses that most frequently precipitate or aggravate tension headache symptoms are rare. In a sample of 72 nonmigrainous patients (apparently exhibiting tension headache symptoms), Howarth (1965) found an obvious association between stressful life events and headaches in 54% of the sample. For the most part, headaches did not appear to be triggered by dramatic life events, but rather by the everyday but personally meaningful stresses that may occur chronically. For example, in 27.7% of the cases, headache appeared to be precipitated by domestic or social problems and in 19.4%, by problems at work.

Migraine Headache

Stress is also the most frequent precipitant of migraine (Henryk-Gutt & Rees, 1973; Selby & Lance, 1960). Data collected by Henryk-Gutt and Rees (1973) from a sample of migraine patients over a two-month period revealed that over half of the headache attacks were associated with stressful events. There is a striking tendency for migraine symptoms to appear not at the peak of stress, but during a period of relaxation immediately following stress, e.g., on April 16 for tax accountants and at the end of the school year for teachers.

Migraine may also be precipitated by a large range of stimuli that are not directly stress related. These include diet (particularly items containing nitrate, glutamate, tyramine, or salt), oral contraceptives, physical exertion, menstruation, alcohol consumption, and excessive glare from light. Attempts to avoid these precipitants appear to be helpful in a small minority of cases (Medina & Diamond, 1978; Raskin & Appenzeller, 1980). Because chronic headache can occasionally be cured in this manner, the therapist should be familiar with all possible headache precipitants.

Relaxation and Biofeedback

During the last 10 years, biofeedback and relaxation training have been used extensively in the treatment of tension and migraine headache. Existing evidence indicates that relaxation training, EMG biofeedback from frontal muscle placements, and the combination of these two interventions are effective in reducing tension headache symptoms, with from 40% to 90% of clients rated much improved by the end of treatment. Relaxation training, peripheral skin-temperature biofeedback, autogenic training, and various combinations of these interventions appear also to be effective in reducing migraine symptoms, with from 40% to 80% of clients showing at least moderate improvement following treatment. Analytical reviews and meta-analysis of existing studies further indicate that these various treatments are equally effective (see discussions by Adams *et al.*, 1980; Andrasik, Coleman, & Epstein, 1982; Blanchard, Ahles, & Shaw, 1979; Blanchard, Andrasik, Ahles, Teders, & O'Keefe, 1980; Haynes, 1981; Turk, Meichenbaum, & Berman, 1979).[2]

Because similar results have been obtained with different treatments, it has been suggested that these various treatments may operate through a common mechanism, usually assumed to be relaxation. There is, however, no clear empirical support for this hypothesis and there are a number of findings that this explanation cannot easily accommodate. For example, the ability to reduce EMG activity following biofeedback is often unrelated to headache improvement (e.g., Andrasik & Holroyd, 1980c; Epstein & Abel, 1977; Holroyd *et al.*, 1977). Investigations of cerebrovascular responses to hand-warming have produced inconsistent results (Largen, Mathew, Dobbins, Meyer, & Claghorn, 1978; Mathew,

[2]A recent, relatively large-scale evaluation of relaxation training (Blanchard, Andrasik, Neff, Ahles, Arena, Jurish, Pallmeyer, Teders, & Rodichok, 1981) calls this conclusion into question in finding that relaxation training is somewhat less effective with migraine and mixed headaches than with tension headaches. This finding has treatment implications but has little implication for the models of headache discussed above because it is consistent with both the syndrome and severity models.

Largen, Dobbins, Meyer, Sakai, & Claghorn, 1980). Further, peripheral temperature changes during thermal training have been found, in some cases, to correlate negatively with independent indices of physiological arousal (Freedman, 1979; Freedman, Lynn, Ianni, Hale, & Michael, 1978).

Elsewhere (e.g., Holroyd, 1979), we have suggested that biofeedback and relaxation therapies may be effective because they indirectly induce patients to alter their transactions with the environment, not because they enable patients to directly control problematic physiological responses. A recent study (Andrasik & Holroyd, 1980c) provides some support for this contention. In this study, tension headache sufferers were led to believe that they were learning to reduce muscle tension while actually being provided one of the following: feedback for decreasing frontal muscle tension (the standard biofeedback treatment); feedback for increasing frontal muscle tension; or feedback from an irrelevant muscle group, the forearm flexor, so that frontal muscle tension remained constant. Since clients in all three groups received contingent "success" feedback, they were provided with the opportunity to attain a sense of mastery over the feedback task that false or noncontingent feedback control groups fail to provide.

Although clients in the three groups learned self-control of frontal muscle activity in the intended direction (decrease, increase, or no change; see Figure 1), all groups showed similar reductions in headache activity relative to a headache recording only group (Figure 2).[3] Thus symptom improvement was not mediated by the learned control of EMG activity. Other results from our laboratory (Holroyd, Andrasik, & Noble, 1980) suggest that the outcomes obtained with biofeedback cannot be dismissed as resulting simply from exposure to a credible treatment. Exposure to a highly credible treatment does not necessarily result in symptom improvement when clients are discouraged from changing the ways they cope with headache-eliciting situations.

Interview data from the Andrasik and Holroyd (1980c) study indicated that clients in all three biofeedback groups made major changes in the ways they coped with headache-related stresses during treatment. Clients reported rationally reevaluating headache-related stresses, behaving more assertively, avoiding stressful situations, and numerous other changes in their responses to situations that had previously elicited headache. These changes in coping rather than the learned control of EMG activity may therefore have mediated improvements in headache symptoms. One may speculate that (1) the enhanced awareness of muscle

[3]This pattern of results was still evident at three year follow-up (Andrasik & Holroyd, 1982) and has recently been replicated in a somewhat more elaborate study (Holroyd, Penzien, Tobin, Hursey, Rogers, Marcille, & Holm, 1982).

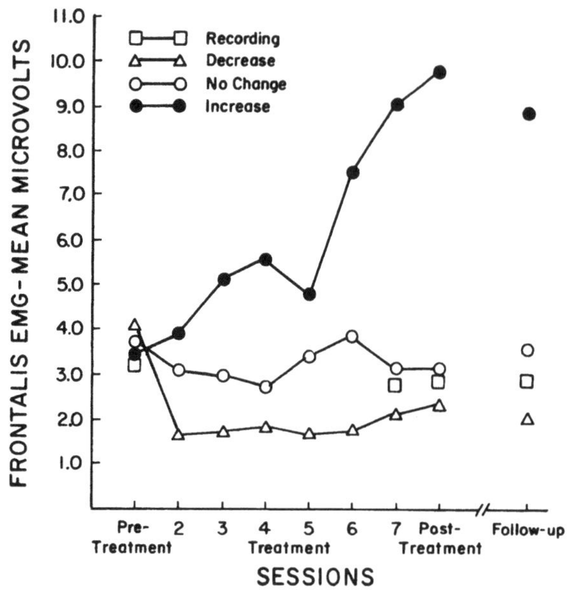

Figure 1. Integrated EMG activity during self-control periods (from Andrasik & Holroyd, 1980c).

tension resulting from biofeedback training sensitized clients to tension preceding headache symptoms, and (2) the contingent success provided during training increased participants' confidence in their ability to control their headaches. This sensitivity to cues antecedent to the headache and enhanced self-efficacy may have then led clients to initiate new ways of coping with headache-related stresses (Holroyd & Andrasik, 1980c).

Cognitive-Behavioral Therapy

Cognitive-behavioral interventions focus on indirectly altering symptom-related physiological activity by changing the way clients cope with headache-eliciting stresses. Treatment focuses directly on such cognitive and behavioral changes as those reported spontaneously by clients receiving biofeedback in the Andrasik and Holroyd (1980c) study.

This treatment approach has three potential advantages that biofeedback and relaxation approaches do not. If stress responses are embedded in the context of the individual's interaction with the environment, as we have argued, people will have difficulty controlling particular physiological responses while they continue to interact with the environment

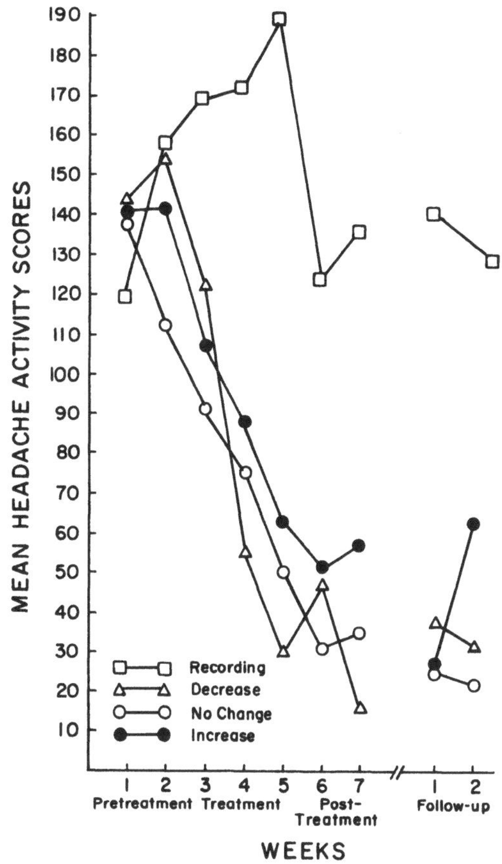

Figure 2. Mean weekly headache activity (from Andrasik & Holroyd, 1980c).

in ways that generate the very responses they are attempting to control. Therefore, treatment might be productively focused not solely on physiological stress responses but also on the cognitive and behavioral variables that influence these stress responses. Secondly, biofeedback and relaxation training provide clients with only a single coping response (relaxation), while the complex demands of everyday life often require flexible coping skills. Relaxation may simply not be an effective method of coping with many of life's stresses and alternate strategies will be required. Finally, cognitive-behavioral interventions appear better suited than relaxation and biofeedback therapies to combating the negative affect (e.g., depression) that can be both a precipitant and a consequence of chronic headache.

Cognitive-behavioral treatment can be divided roughly into three phases: education, self-monitoring, and problem-solving or coping-skills training. Before treatment is initiated, clients are instructed in recording the occurrence of headaches and rating the severity of head pain throughout the day. This can be done on a pocket-sized card that also provides space for recording efforts to manage head pain (both medication usage and psychological coping strategies) and the circumstances surrounding the headache.

Global retrospective reports of headache symptoms are only weakly correlated with daily headache recordings, so these two assessment methods cannot be considered equivalent (Andrasik & Holroyd, 1980b). Because daily recordings provide detailed information about the circumstances in which headaches occur, they are, in our experience, preferable to global reports. Occasionally, someone will report that headaches are exacerbated by daily recording. Often these individuals have learned to minimize head pain by deliberately not attending to their headache, so that recording disrupts an established although only partially effective strategy of coping with head pain. Although clients can be warned of this possibility, it is usually sufficient to explain that the information generated by daily recording is needed if more effective ways of controlling their headaches are to be devised.

Educational Phase

The educational phase has four goals: to educate the client about the pathophysiology and precipitants of headache, to explain the treatment process, to combat the demoralization and depression that often characterize chronic headache sufferers, and to convey to clients that they will be expected to take an active role in the control of their symptoms. Because headache sufferers often attribute their symptoms to overwhelming external pressures or global personal inadequacies, the therapist's task is to present convincingly an alternative framework emphasizing headache precipitants that are potentially under the client's control. The therapist and client discuss in detail both the ways stress can precipitate headache and the ways cognitive processes shape stress responses. Written materials, didactic examples, and the therapist's personal experiences are used to illustrate how psychological processes can influence stress responses and, thereby, headache symptoms.

Self-Monitoring

Once the treatment process has been explained, clients are taught to monitor their responses to stresses in their lives. The goal is to enable clients to identify patterns of covert and overt events that precede, accompany, and follow stressful transactions. In our experience, therapists who are most effective elicit finely detailed accounts of the client's response to stress, rather than global retrospective reports. We therefore encourage clients to record their feelings, thoughts, and behavior prior to, during, and following stressful events so they do not have to rely on their memory during the treatment sessions themselves. Detailed information is also elicited by having clients imagine stressful situations they have identified, reporting their perceptions and experiences in a stream-of-consciousness fashion. As the client becomes familiar with this self-monitoring, the therapist assists the client in identifying relationships among situational variables (e.g., criticism from spouse); thoughts (e.g., "I can't do anything right"); and emotional, behavioral, and symptomatic responses (e.g., depression, withdrawal, and headache).

Coping Skills and Problem-Solving

Therapy then begins to focus on preventing headaches by altering the psychological and behavioral antecedents the client has identified. Changes in environmental stimuli (e.g., elimination of possible chemical precipitants) or in diet may occasionally become a focus of treatment. Primary attention, however, is given to changing the way the client copes with headache-related stresses.

Beck and Emery (1979) have provided a detailed description of useful therapeutic techniques and we draw heavily on this work. Thus, clients are encouraged to identify expectations and beliefs that might explain their stress responses to a variety of situations (e.g., "In each of these situations where you made a mistake, you criticized yourself harshly, became depressed, and ended up with a headache. It appears you expect yourself to do everything perfectly."). They are then pushed to examine the behavioral and emotional consequences of these beliefs (e.g., "This requirement that you perform perfectly prevents you from attempting to learn new skills on the job, leads you to suffer unnecessary anguish over simple human errors, and contributes to your headaches and your having to leave work early to go home to bed.").At this point, the client and therapist cooperatively generate alternative coping strategies, the therapist helping the client rationally to evaluate options.

Once alternative courses of action are identified, didactic instruction, modeling, and graduated practice can be used to develop and practice coping skills. Signs of impending stress are then used as cues to implement strategies designed to alter stressful transactions or to manage or control emotional responses. Such strategies may primarily involve changes in behavior (e.g., more assertive behavior or withdrawal from the situation) or changes in thinking (e.g., attributional changes or changes in internal dialogue); although these coping processes are likely to be proposed initially by the therapist, the primary goal of treatment is to enable the client to develop effective problem-solving skills for managing everyday life stresses without therapeutic assistance.

Evaluation of Cognitive-Behavioral Interventions

In contrast to the large literature on the use of biofeedback and relaxation training in the treatment of chronic headache, there are only a handful of controlled studies evaluating cognitive-behavioral interventions. In the first of these studies (Holroyd *et al.*, 1977), 31 chronic tension headache sufferers received either eight sessions of cognitive therapy or eight sessions of EMG (frontal) biofeedback, or were assigned to a wait-list control group. Cognitive therapy was conducted essentially as described above except that only cognitive and not behavioral coping skills were taught. An index of headache activity obtained from daily recordings is presented for each of the treatment groups and the wait-list control group in Figure 3. It can be seen that cognitive therapy proved highly effective in reducing headaches and that these gains were maintained at the 15-week follow-up evaluation. On the other hand, only about half of the clients who received biofeedback showed improvement in headache symptoms.

At a recent two-year follow-up of participants in this study (Holroyd & Andrasik, in press), clients in the cognitive therapy group were still significantly improved, with over 80% still showing fairly substantial

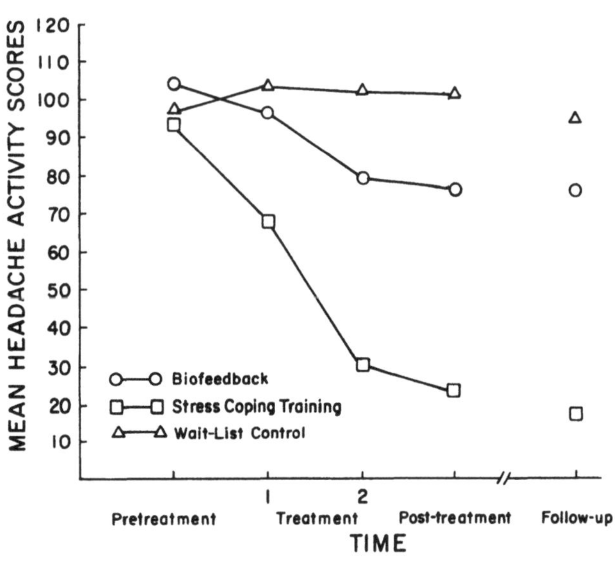

Figure 3. Mean weekly headache activity scores in two-week blocks (from Holroyd *et al.*, 1977).

(greater than 45%) reductions in headache activity from pretreatment levels. Clients in the cognitive therapy group were also significantly more likely than those in the biofeedback group to report use of cognitive coping strategies to control headache symptoms, suggesting that the impressive maintenance of therapeutic gains may have been facilitated by the problem-solving skills taught during treatment. The mixed outcomes observed in the biofeedback groups at the 15-week follow-up were still evident at the two-year follow-up, with the result that the number of clients who improved following biofeedback was too small to compare the maintenance of improvements produced by cognitive therapy with those of biofeedback. However, a comparison of the results of this follow-up with other reported findings (Budzynski, Stoyva, Adler, & Mullaney, 1973; Reinking & Hitchings, 1976) suggests that clients treated with cognitive therapy were somewhat more likely to maintain treatment gains than those treated with biofeedback or relaxation training. This suggests that cognitive therapy may be of particular value in facilitating the long-term maintenance of therapeutic gains.

In a second study (Holroyd & Andrasik, 1978), 39 chronic headache sufferers were assigned to one of three treatments differing in the coping skills taught or to a wait-list control group. All three treatments included educational and self-monitoring components similar to those previously described. Clients in all three groups were taught to identify the covert and overt events that preceded symptom onset. One group of clients was then taught cognitive coping skills in the same manner as in the Holroyd *et al.* (1977) study. A second group was taught both cognitive coping skills and the use of self-control relaxation as a coping skill (Goldfried & Trier, 1974). The third group was taught no specific coping skill; clients in this group were told that their headaches would improve if they understood the "underlying cause" of their symptoms. Therapist interventions for the latter group were designed both to increase the client's self-confidence and self-esteem and to provide plausible interpretations of material generated during self-monitoring in terms of historical events in the client's life.

Clients in each of the three treatment groups showed substantial improvements in headache symptoms that were maintained at one-month follow-up. In the two groups taught cognitive coping or cognitive combined with relaxation coping skills, clients reported during posttreatment interviews that they had used the skills they were taught during treatment to control their headaches. However, all but one of the participants in the group not taught specific coping skills reported they had devised and implemented specific techniques for controlling their headaches as well. Moreover, the one exception showed only minimal improvement in headache activity. These results suggest that it may be less crucial to provide clients with particular coping skills than to insure that they monitor the insidious onset of symptoms and can devise methods for interrupting the chain of overt and covert events that precipitate and aggravate symptoms.

Mitchell and White (1976, 1977) have used a treatment approach with migraine sufferers similar to the cognitive-behavioral intervention described here. They taught clients to monitor cognitive and behavioral responses to stressful situations and to employ a number of strategies for coping with the stressful situations they identified (e.g., self-instruction, thought-stopping, and assertion training). In the only controlled evaluation of their treatment, Mitchell and White (1977) assigned 12 migraine sufferers to either audiocassette versions of this treatment or relaxation training or to one of two control groups. Both treatments produced significant improvements in migraine symptoms, with the coping skills treatment producing more improvement than relaxation training (73% versus 44.9% improvement). Subjects in the control groups showed no reduction in symptoms. Although these findings are promising, conclusions about treatment effectiveness should be tempered because of the small number of people who were treated in this study.

Bakal is conducting an ongoing evaluation of cognitive-behavioral therapy with chronic headache sufferers. In a preliminary analysis of data from 45 treated tension, migraine, and mixed headache sufferers, Bakal, Demjen, and Kaganov (1980) found highly significant reductions in headache symptoms that were maintained at a six-month follow-up. Moreover, all three types of headache sufferers appeared to be equally responsive to this treatment approach.

The above findings appear sufficiently promising to justify the further evaluation of cognitive-behavioral treatment techniques in the management of chronic headache. In particular, it would be helpful to determine to what extent cognitive-behavioral interventions increase the effectiveness of relaxation training or are effective with patients who do not respond to relaxation training. Most therapists are likely to begin the treatment of chronic headache sufferers with relaxation training because it is not only frequently helpful in reducing headache symptoms but is also simple and straightforward to teach. Therefore, cognitive-behavioral interventions are likely to prove particularly valuable if they enhance the effectiveness of relaxation training or help individuals who cannot be assisted with relaxation training.

More information is also needed concerning the long-term maintenance of gains obtained with relaxation training, biofeedback, and cognitive-behavioral therapy. Because the goal of cognitive-behavioral intervention is to enable clients to draw on a flexible set of coping skills when they are confronted with stressful events, these treatment techniques may prove valuble in promoting the long-term maintenance of treatment gains (Lynn & Freedman, 1979), and Holroyd and Andrasik's (in press) results are promising in this regard. Even if cognitive-behavioral interventions prove no more effective than relaxation training in producing the immediate reduction of headache symptoms, they may prove helpful in promoting the long-term maintenance of treatment gains.

BRONCHIAL ASTHMA

Symptoms and Epidemiology

Bronchial asthma is a reversible obstructive pulmonary disorder characterized by hyperreactivity of the airways to a variety of stimuli. Asthmatic individuals experience recurrent episodes of wheezing or dyspnea associated with increased resistance to airflow. Resistance to airflow occurs as a result of changes in the bronchi or bronchioles involving some combination of constriction or spasm of bronchial smooth muscle, submucosal edema, hypersecretion of mucus, and tenacious mucus plugs. During an asthmatic episode, airflow is reduced to less than 50% of the predicted normal level, whereas improvement to more than 80% indicates that the individual is symptom free (Reed & Townley, 1978).

Asthma is a highly variable disorder. Asthmatics are heterogeneous in regard to variables such as severity of attacks, factors responsible for precipitating attacks, location of major areas of obstruction, and response to medication (Farr & Spector, 1975; Reed & Townley, 1978). Variability is also characteristic of individual asthmatics from one episode to another (Creer, 1979).

Clinically, asthma is classified into two types: extrinsic and intrinsic. In extrinsic asthma, attacks can be clearly attributed to the immunologic response of an atopic individual to exposure to a specific allergen. Asthmatic symptoms are mediated by the action of antigens such as pollen, mold, or animal dander on the immunoglobin-E (IgE) reagin. Intrinsic asthma is asthma of unknown etiology: Although causal relationships may be identified between a precipitant and asthmatic symptoms, the symptoms are not mediated by a known immunologic mechanism. Intrinsic asthma may follow a viral respiratory infection, or it may be caused by abnormal sensitivity to drugs such as aspirin or to various other stimuli including exercise, airway irritants such as cold air and chemicals, and psychosocial stimuli. Most asthmatics have a mixed form of asthma, with both an extrinsic and intrinsic component (Farr & Spector, 1975). More detailed discussions of definition and classification of asthma may be found in Farr and Spector (1975), Reed and Townley (1978), Scadding (1976), and Welch (1977).

The prevalence of asthma reported in the National Health Survey in 1970 is approximately 3% of the population (U. S. Department of Health, Education, and Welfare, 1973). However, estimates of prevalence range from 1% to 4% (Creer, 1979), while incidence estimates range from 2% to 20%, with 5% being most likely (Alexander, 1981). Onset of asthma may occur at any age, but about half of all asthmatics have an onset prior to age 15 (Creer, 1979), and most children develop the disease in the first 5 years of life (Siegel, Katz, & Rachelefsky, 1978). Prognosis is most favorable for those individuals who develop asthma after age 2 and before puberty (Siegel *et al.*, 1978), remission occurring for many childhood asthmatics during adolescence or early adulthood (Weiner, 1977).

Pathophysiology

The pathogenesis of asthma is incompletely understood, but it is most likely due to defects in one or more of the physiologic processes that regulate the airways (Reed & Townley, 1978). Much of the research has focused on the interrelationships between neural and humoral systems that control bronchial smooth muscle, with relatively less attention to the submucosal glands and other mechanisms. Bronchoconstriction and mucus production are under the control of vagal cholinergic innervation, whereas bronchodilation is influenced by beta-2-adrenergic sympathetic activity. The humoral bronchoconstriction system consists of primary mediators such as histamine and SRS-A released from submucosal mast cells and secondary mediators such as kinins and prostaglandins from other cells. The humoral bronchodilator is primarily epinephrine.[4]

A number of mechanisms have been suggested to account for airway hyperreactivity. Bronchoconstriction may occur due to vagal reflexes initiated by stimulation of receptors in the airways. This mechanism may be responsible for mechanically induced bronchoconstriction resulting from stimuli such as coughing, cold air, hyperventilation, crying, and laughing. Asthmatics may also have an autonomic imbalance involving blockage of beta-2-adrenergic receptors with a resulting preponderance of alpha-adrenergic or cholinergic activity or both. This imbalance would result in bronchoconstriction and would also enhance the release of humoral mediators. The adrenergic system is also implicated by the suggestion that asthmatics have decreased availability of epinephrine due to faulty release of epinephrine from the adrenal medulla or from altered uptake and metabolism. An inherited allergic state or inherited organ

[4]Knapp *et al.* (1976) note a paradox in the facts that symptoms arise in situations of stress which presumably result in increased sympathetic activity and that symptoms may be effectively controlled by sympathomimetic agents. "The troublesome question arises: Why do not such aroused asthmatic patients 'cure' themselves?" (p. 1060). To answer this question, Knapp *et al.* suggest that an adrenergic defect plays a role in asthma. They note that in psychophysiological studies, asthmatics respond selectively to laboratory stress. In particular, asthmatics fail to show stress-induced elevations in urinary epinephrine.

vulnerability may provide a predisposition for asthma. Discussions useful in understanding the physiology and pathogenesis of asthma may be found in Knapp, Mathe, and Vachon (1976); Middleton, Reed, and Ellis (1978); Welch (1977); and Weiner (1977).

Stress and Asthma

A number of studies have found that stress and emotion can affect respiratory functioning and the clinical course of asthma in asthmatic individuals (see reviews by Creer, 1978, 1979; Knapp *et al.*, 1976; Purcell & Weiss, 1970; Weiner, 1977). Although there is no evidence to support the viewpoint that psychological factors have primary etiological significance for the disorder (Alexander, 1980, 1981; J.H. Weiss, 1977), they may be important in the precipitation and aggravation of attacks, once asthma has developed.

Stress may come from many sources, but problems that occur as consequences of asthma are likely to be major stressors (see, e.g., Alexander, 1980, 1981; Creer, 1978; Graham, Rutter, Yule, & Pless, 1967). Both Alexander (1981) and Creer (1979) provide excellent descriptions of the many ramifications of the asthmatic condition, including activity restriction, school- and job-related stress, effects on self-esteem and affect, problems in symptom and environmental management, medication side effects, and financial burdens of the disorder. Interventions based on dealing with the psychological stresses of asthma are likely to be helpful to a wide range of asthmatics. However, when asthmatic individuals experience stresses independent of the asthmatic condition, these stresses may also have significant effects on the course of the disorder and must be considered in planning therapy.

Psychological factors may precipitate or aggravate asthma either directly or indirectly. At one level, coping may be an important mediator of the effects of psychosocial stimuli on asthmatics. Purcell and Weiss (1970) observed that in interpersonal situations, "the kinds of behavioral antecedents most immediately relevant to asthma are emotional or affect states" (p. 598), which might be elicited by interpersonal acts or by cognitions. Emotions may affect asthma through several different mechanisms, including neuroendocrine responses, or behaviors, such as crying or yelling, that lead to airway narrowing.

At a more indirect level, psychological factors may not be precipitants or aggravants *per se* but may "lead to symptoms via mediating events that are the 'real' precipitants or aggravants" (Weiss, 1977, p. 170). The "real" precipitants or aggravants may be behavioral (e.g., a child who fears peer rejection may react by engaging in excessive athletics and induce exercise-related asthma), or they may be nonbehavioral (e.g., due to a parent's inability to control an allergic child's behavior, the child comes in contact with an allergen and asthma results).

Psychological reactions to an actual attack may also serve to aggravate or reinforce symptoms. For example, the asthmatic may panic at attack onset and this emotional reaction may aggravate the attack. Panic reactions of those observing the attack may also be aggravants. The likelihood of recurrence may increase when reinforcement such as attention or release from an undesirable activity is given contingent on symptom occurrence.

Considerable research attention has been given recently to psychological variables associated with the experience of breathing difficulty in asthmatics. Dirks and his colleagues (Dirks *et al.,* 1977, 1978; Dirks, Kinsman, Staudenmayer, & Kleiger, 1979; Jones, Kinsman, Dirks, & Dahlem, 1979; Kinsman *et al.,* 1977) have devised a measure of coping style, Panic-Fear symtomatology, that assesses anxiety focused specifically on breathing difficulties. Individuals with high Panic-Fear symptomatology are greatly concerned about their illness and are vigilant about breathing difficulty, whereas low Panic-Fear symptomatology individuals show little concern about their illness and often appear to not perceive or to disregard breathing difficulty. Panic-Fear symptomatology may either enhance or worsen medical outcome depending on the individual's relative standing on a second measure, Panic-Fear personality. This measure relates to individuals' anxiety, dependence, and coping styles in a variety of situations and appears not to be dependent on or specifically directed toward breathing difficulties in asthma. Dirks *et al.* (1979) found that high Panic-Fear symptomatology combined with high Panic-Fear personality resulted in very poor medical outcome, whereas high Panic-Fear symptomatology with moderate Panic-Fear personality resulted in very good medical outcome. Presumably, the asthma-specific vigilance assessed by Panic-Fear symptomatology functions like signal anxiety and mobilizes the individual to react; style and effectiveness of coping are determined by characterological anxiety, which is assessed by the Panic-Fear personality measure.

Behavioral Interventions in Asthma

A wide range of behavioral techniques have been used in treating asthmatics, particularly asthmatic children (see reviews by Alexander, 1980, 1981; Creer, 1978, 1979; Knapp & Wells, 1978). Behavioral interventions have been generally more successful in changing behavior problems in asthmatics such as malingering (Creer, 1970), lack of appropriate academic behaviors (Creer & Yoches, 1971), and asthma panic (Miklich, 1973; Miklich, Renne, Creer, Alexander, Chai, Davis, Hoffman, & Danker-Brown, 1977) than they have been in altering respiratory functioning. Techniques such as relaxation training, biofeedback, and systematic desensitization have produced improvements in pulmonary function, but the changes are often not clinically significant, leading some investigators to question their utility in the treatment of asthma (e.g., Alexander, 1980, 1981; Alexander, Cropp, & Chai, 1979; Miklich *et al.,* 1977). Obviously, more work must be done to find effective treatments. Cognitive-behavioral interventions may prove useful in helping asthmatics to manage their disorder and to decrease asthma-related stresses.

Cognitive-Behavioral Treatment of Asthma

Goals of cognitive-behavioral treatment of asthma are to give clients a better understanding of the disorder and to teach coping strategies that will decrease the frequency and severity of attacks and alter the behavioral and emotional sequelae of the disorder. Clients are encouraged to accept responsibility for their own health and to develop skills for making critical decisions about management of the disorder (Clark, Feldman, Freudenberg, Millman, Wasilewski, & Valle, 1979; Creer, 1980a). In the long run, more effective self-management should reduce stress and decrease needs for medical and psychological services. For example, if a child learns to discriminate symptom onset quickly and to make an effective intervention before the attack worsens, the need for more vigorous intervention such as hospitalization or the use of corticosteroids will be reduced. The resulting decrease in both stress and cost can be expected to have positive effects on both the child and family.

The cognitive-behavioral treatment described here draws heavily on the self-management programs for asthmatic children and their families developed by Creer (1979, 1980a,b) and Feldman and his colleagues (Clark *et al.,* 1979). Readers interested in more detail on particular techniques should consult these sources. In addition, Creer's (1979) book provides useful information about the antecedents, concomitants, and consequences of asthma. Clark *et al.* (1979) have provided a detailed assesssment that is helpful in setting priorities for intervention.

Educational Phase

Clients are first given basic information about their disorder. Topics include symptoms and physiology of asthma, precipitants and aggravants of attacks, medications and their side effects, and nonpharmacologic methods of controlling symptoms. Treatment procedures and goals are then explained. In some cases, providing information will produce beneficial effects. Gaining an understanding of the disorder may be particularly helpful in relieving the guilt and frustration of intrinsic asthmatics because significant etiological variables for their asthma may be unknown and response to medical treatment may be poor. These factors can lead to the mistaken and potentially harmful attribution that the asthma is "all in the head" (Alexander, 1981).

Self-Monitoring

Clients are next taught to self-monitor their asthma and asthma-related behaviors. The most useful information is provided by a daily asthma diary. Clients are asked to record several types of information about their asthma, such as daily occurrence of attacks, a rating of attack severity, morning and evening peak flow, and amounts and schedule of medication taken. In addition, they should note the situations in which attacks occur, emotional reactions, and steps taken to manage the attack. Creer (1980a) has found that children as young as 6 years of age can be trained to provide reliable observations about their symptoms. In the case of young children, it may be helpful to have parents record the daily information about asthma as well as their own emotional reactions and management efforts. These daily recordings provide valuable information about asthma symptomatology, precipitants and aggravants of attacks, and coping skills. This information is used later to determine treatment foci.

Since attacks can intensify quickly, asthmatics must recognize onset rapidly so that they can initiate intervention while the attack is relatively mild. Individuals may be taught to discriminate attack onset by attending to physiological symptoms such as chest tightness or they can be shaped to relate subjective feelings of pulmonary function with an objective pulmonary measure such as that provided by the Wright Mini Peak Flow Meter (Creer, 1979). Taplin and Creer (1978) found that self-monitoring of peak expiratory flow data enabled some asthmatics to predict episodes with increased accuracy. When other family members assume at least partial responsibility for management of symptoms, they can be taught to recognize changes in the child's physical appearance that may precede attacks.

Coping Skills and Problem-Solving

Initial intervention efforts should focus on management of the attack and its emotional concomitants. In consultation with the physician, a sequence of coping behaviors is developed that can be used to abort or terminate attacks (see Creer, 1980a,b, for examples of such response chains). Clients are taught specific skills required at various points in the chain, such as relaxation, breathing exercises, and postural drainage. Cognitive restructuring and self-control relaxation can also be used to reduce maladaptive panic-fear. Parents of asthmatic children may also need assistance in handling their own emotional reactions to attacks. When insufficient vigilance is a problem, it can be treated by intensified training in early symptom perception and, where necessary, by confronting clients with the consequences of disregard of symptoms. Some clients may need to learn more effective skills for communicating with health care providers and for utilizing medical services.

Intervention next focuses on how asthmatics cope with precipitants and aggravants of attacks. In some cases, the therapeutic task may be to anticipate the occurrence of certain allergens and take measures to avoid them, or clients may be taught skills to cope with interpersonal situations that regularly elicit emotional responses leading to an attack. In other cases, the problem may be excessive restrictions aimed at curtailing exposure to precipitants. For example, Alexander (1981) notes that in some families, asthma may become a central focus with decisions about even simple family activities resting on consideration of their effect on the asthmatic. Some families may so restrict the child's activity that psychosocial and educational development is seriously delayed. In such cases, the therapist may intervene by helping the family evaluate the restrictions placed on the child and teaching parent and child how to negotiate realistic limits on the child's activity. When the disorder has led to psychosocial and educational delays, intervention can be directed at increasing requisite skills (see, e.g., Creer & Yoches, 1971; and Creer, Weinberg, & Molk, 1974).

Therapists should also pay attention to maladaptive behavioral and emotional patterns that develop in the course of coping with the disorder (e.g., helplessness, manipulativeness, and depression). Parents and others may compound these problems by their emotional reactions to the asthmatic or by reinforcing inappropriate behaviors. Intervention in such cases includes disrupting reinforcement contingencies that maintain the maladaptive behaviors, helping clients to evaluate the adequacy of their current coping behaviors, and developing more appropriate coping responses.

Evaluation

Both Creer and Feldman (personal communications) are currently involved in large-scale evaluations of self-management with asthmatic children and their families. Outcome data on these two programs were not yet available at the time of this writing.[5]

[5] Since this section was written, outcome data have become available and are highly promising. Creer (personal communication) found significant changes in respiratory functioning, self-concept, locus of control, attitudes about asthma, school absenteeism, and health care expenditures.

ESSENTIAL HYPERTENSION

Although several researchers have suggested that cognitive-behavioral interventions be evaluated as a treatment for essential hypertension (Holroyd, 1979; Novaco, 1975; Seer, 1979) to our knowledge not only has no outcome study been conducted, but no systematic description of treatment procedures exists. Therefore, in this section we will review selected literature on essential hypertension and attempt to answer questions that are likely to confront researchers interested developing cognitive-behavioral strategies for the treatment of essential hypertension. We will also make suggestions for conducting treatment. Until clinical trials demonstrate the effectiveness of this treatment, however, cognitive-behavioral therapy should be considered an experimental intervention to be evaluated preventively or as an adjunct to pharmacotherapy.

Symptoms and Epidemiology

Hypertension (elevated arterial blood pressure) of unknown cause is called essential or idiopathic hypertension. This disorder is diagnosed by exclusion when there is no evidence that elevated arterial pressure results from specific organ dysfunction (e.g., kidney disease, dysfunction of the adrenal or parathyroid glands, or constriction of the aorta), pregnancy, or oral contraceptives. About 90% of all identified cases of hypertension are diagnosed as essential hypertension.

Essential hypertension occurs in 10% to 20% of the adult population and substantially increases the individual's risk of cardiovascular disease. Over a 10-year period, it has been estimated that almost two million hypertensives aged 35–64 will die from the consequences of this disorder (Kaplan, 1978). Even infrequent large increases in blood pressure may be associated with a shortening of the life span (Merrill, 1966).

Stress and Essential Hypertension

The evidence implicating stress in the etiology of essential hypertension is largely circumstantial (see reviews by Gutman & Benson, 1971; Henry & Cassel, 1969; Page, 1976; Shapiro, 1978; and critique by Syme & Torfs, 1978). Stressful living and working environments have been associated with an increased incidence of hypertension in epidemiological studies, and stressful laboratory environments have been devised that induce hypertension and its cardiovascular sequelae in animals. For example, an increased incidence of hypertension has been observed in stressful urban neighborhoods (Harburg, Erfurt, Chape, Hausenstein,

Schull, & Schork, 1973; Harburg, Blakelock, & Roeper, 1979), taxing occupations such as that of air traffic controller (Cobb & Rose, 1973; Rose, Jenkins, & Hurst, 1978), and following natural disasters (Ruskin, Beard, & Schaffer, 1948) or prolonged combat duty (Graham, 1945). Hypertension and many of its cardiovascular sequelae can also be induced in mice if they are first raised in isolation so they do not learn to cope with the intricate dominance–submission hierarchy that characterizes social colonies, and then are placed in a living situation requiring territorial competition and continuous social interaction (Henry, 1976; Henry & Stephens, 1977). Environments capable of inducing hypertension in susceptible individuals have been characterized as posing constant threat and uncertainty (Henry & Stephens, 1977) and requiring coping responses that involve "continuous behavioral and physiologic adjustments" (Gutman & Benson, 1971, p. 550).

Pathophysiology

Blood pressure is primarily a function of the amount of blood pumped by the heart (cardiac output) and the resistance of the vesels to this blood flow (peripheral resistance). These two variables are embedded in a complex network of reciprocally interacting regulatory systems influencing blood vessel caliber and responsiveness, fluid volume, and cardiac function (see, e.g., Brown, Lever, Robertson, & Schalekamp, 1976); however, if blood pressure is elevated, either cardiac output or peripheral resistance must be increased. Frequently, cardiac output is elevated early in the course of the disorder but is normal at a later point when peripheral resistance is elevated (Kaplan, 1978).

Stress-related fluctuations in sympathetic activity may disregulate hemodynamic control systems producing essential hypertension along lines illustrated in Figure 4. Initially, increases in circulating levels of catecholamines and renin alter kidney function so sodium and water are not excreted appropriately in response to blood pressure elevations (alteration of pressure–natriuresis curve). The resultant relative excess fluid volume in concert with transient elevations in blood pressure during stressful transactions produces an adaptive thickening of the small arterioles increasing peripheral resistance. Hypertension and the continued relative fluid excess may then trigger a decrease in renin release. At this point, blood pressure remains elevated even though cardiac output and renin levels may return to normal. Evidence supporting this model of the pathogenesis of essential hypertension has been reviewed by Brown *et al.*, 1976; DeQuattro and Miura (1973); Julius and Esler (1975); and Kaplan (1979).

Genetically susceptible individuals who are overwhelmingly stress-

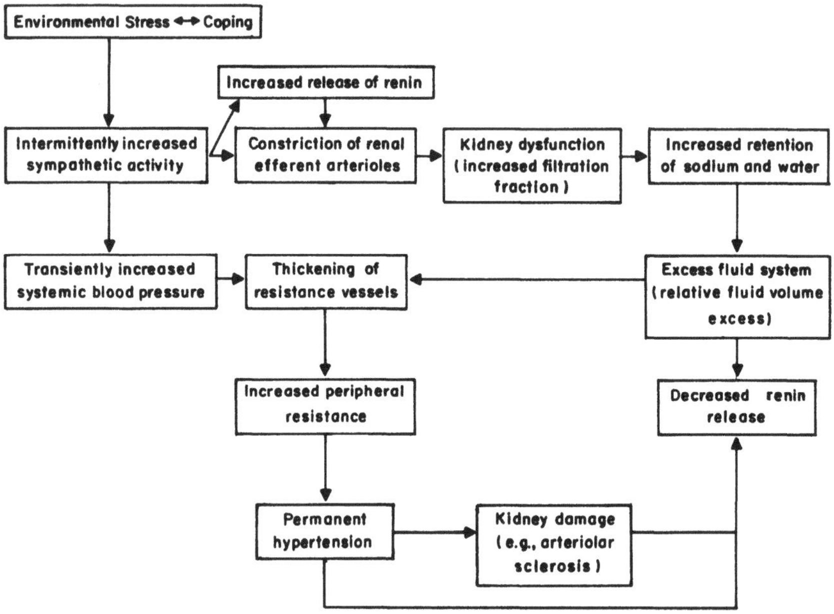

Figure 4. Model of the pathogenesis of essential hypertension (adapted from Kaplan, 1979).

ed or who cope with stress in ways that repeatedly stimulate sympathetic activity would be most likely to proceed down the hemodynamic path illustrated in Figure 4. High dietary sodium intake and obesity increase fluid volume and peripheral resistance through alternate mechanisms and thus, when present, may further potentiate the effects of stress.

Psychological Factors in Essential Hypertension

Results obtained by Obrist and his colleagues (Obrist, 1976; Obrist, Gaebelein, Teller, Langer, Grignolo, Light, & McCubbin, 1978; Obrist, Light, Langer, Grignolo, & McCubbin, 1978) suggest that sympathetic influences on the heart are maximized and heart rate and blood pressure are primarily under sympathetic control when the individual is, in Obrist's terms, actively coping with stress; during passive coping, heart rate and blood pressure are primarily under vagal control and sympathetic influences on the heart are minimized. Fluctuations in sympathetic activity initiating the hypertensive disease process might thus be elicited by a specific style of coping with stress.

The coping style that has most frequently been hypothesized as a risk factor for essential hypertension is a style of responding to interpersonal conflict and the resultant arousal of anger (e.g., Alexander, 1939; Alexander, French, & Pollock, 1968; Appel, Holyrod, & Gorkin, 1982; Harris & Forsythe, 1973; Thomas, 1967). At-risk individuals are hypothesized to cope with conflict by suppressing feelings of anger and then expressing anger explosively when this coping mechanism fails. Since this coping style is likely to leave unresolved or to exacerbate interpersonal conflicts, stressful transactions may occur repeatedly in a wide range of interpersonal situations. Physiological responses that may be either specific to the arousal of anger or more generally associated with the stress emotions are assumed to initiate the hypertensive disease process in genetically susceptible individuals.

Although research on the anger hypothesis has been conducted sporadically for 40 years, until recently studies have been so methodologically flawed as to be readiy dismissed (see reviews by Davies, 1971; Glock & Lennard, 1957; Harrell, 1980; Weiner, 1977). It is only during the last decade that well-designed epidemiological and longitudinal studies have promised to revive this hypothesis. For example, in an epidemiological study of hypertension in Detroit, Harburg *et al.* (1979) categorized responses to hypothetical conflict situations as oriented toward reflective problem-solving or resentment. Resentment included hostile actions, expressions of anger, and denying or ignoring conflict. Resentment was associated with higher age- and weight-adjusted blood pressures than reflective problem-solving in both black and white respondents. Similar results have been obtained in a 5-year prospective study of hypertension in 10,000 Israeli civil service workers (Kahn, Medalie, Neufeld, Riss, & Goldbourt, 1972) and in a 20-year prospective study of Harvard graduates (McClelland, 1979).

Evidence implicating psychological variables in the hypertensive disease process is, at present, only suggestive. One hopes that recent positive findings will stimulate investigators to specify these psychological variables more completely, to identify subgroups of hypertensives for whom psychological variables play a significant etiological role, and to elucidate physiological mechanisms of action (see e.g., Appel, Holroyd, & Gorkin, 1982; Esler, Julius, Zwelfer, Randall, Harburg, Gardiner, & DeQuattro, 1977; Holroyd & Gorkin,in press). Meanwhile, existing evidence seems sufficient that the management of anger should be addressed during treatment.

Implications for Cognitive-Behavioral Treatment

By the time hypertension is maintained primarily by an adaptive thickening of the small arterioles, psychological interventions may yield only modest reductions in blood pressure. Earlier in the disease process, treatments that reduce environmental stresses or teach skills for more effective coping with stress may help prevent the hemodynamic cascade toward essential hypertension illustrated in Figure 4. Therefore, psychological interventions need to be evaluated not only as treatments for established hypertension, but also as preventive interventions for individuals at risk for this disorder. Relevant criteria for selecting subjects for preventive intervention might include a family history of essential hypertension (which doubles the individual's risk), borderline high blood pressure, cardiovascular reactivity to laboratory stresses such as those used by Obrist (Obrist, Gaebelein, Teller, Langer, Grignolo, Light, & McCubbin, 1978), occupations associated with greater than average risk for essential hypertension, race (black), and sex (male).

Educational Phase

There are no perceptible symptoms associated with hypertension and, therefore, no discomfort to motivate clients to cooperate with demanding treatment procedures. As a result, it is particularly important in the case of essential hypertensives that clients understand the rationale and potential advantages of treatment. The model of the pathogenesis of essential hypertension described above, when presented in nontechnical terms, may be helpful in this regard. Educational materials available from the American Heart Association and from other sources (e.g., Galton, 1973; Kaplan, 1976) can also be useful. Adams (1981) has found that young males identified as at risk for essential hypertension (both having a positive family history of this disorder and showing cardiovascular hyperreactivity during laboratory stress) can be successfully recruited into and maintained in a preventive treatment program when care is taken to involve them in treatment.

Self-Monitoring

Blood pressure and other indices of cardiovascular reactivity are only weakly related to self-reports of anxiety and distress. Therefore, self-assessments of stress are likely to be poor indices of cardiovascular activity. It is unclear at this point whether treatment should be focused on teaching clients to cope with self-identified stresses or on modifying cardiovascular hyperreactivity, or should include both targets. Until this is determined, clients should probably record events that are experienced as stressful and should monitor heart rate and blood pressure periodically. Patel (1977) teaches clients not only to monitor personally stressful events, but also to use frequently occurring cues as a signal to monitor their stress levels. For example, a red dot can be attached to the client's wristwatch so that looking at the watch becomes a signal to self-monitor tension rather than to hurry. Sounds of doorbells and telephones or other stimuli such as traffic lights are similarly used as cues to monitor pulse rate and blood pressure. More elaborate automated recording equipment is also available for both research and clinical use.

Coping Skills and Problem-Solving

Existing studies have largely limited coping-skills training for hypertensives to teaching relaxation. For example, Taylor, Farquhar, Nelson, and Agras (1977) assigned 31 hypertensives to self-control relaxation, supportive psychotherapy, or medical treatment only. The self-control relaxation treatment involved five sessions of relaxation training and instruction in the use of relaxation as a coping skill. However, coping-skills training was limited to the instruction "to take a deep breath, hold it momentarily, and to imagine they were in a peaceful place; then to think the word 'relax' as they exhaled" (p. 340). Self-control relaxation training resulted in significantly larger reductions in blood pressure (13.6/4.9 mm Hg) than either of the other treatments. Although this improvement appeared to be maintained at six-month follow-up, attrition and improvements in the other groups prevented the differences from reaching significance at follow-up. Other studies are consistent with these findings in suggesting that at least moderate reductions in blood pressure result from the regular use of relaxation as a coping skill (see reviews by Agras & Jacob, 1979; Blanchard & Miller, 1977; Shapiro, Schwartz, Ferguson, Redmond, & Weiss, 1977).

It seems reasonable to expect that treatments focusing more comprehensively on altering cognitive and behavioral responses to stress might prove more effective than relaxation training alone if the latter treatment ignores the way cognitive and behavioral responses to environmental demands influence stress responses. For example, treatment might also focus on helping the client to recognize and monitor anger-engendering conflict, identify characteristic styles of responding, and, where appropriate, experiment with alternative ways of managing conflict. Cognitive-behavioral interventions for teaching skills to manage anger and conflict have been described by Novaco (1975).

CONCLUSION

Coping is increasingly emphasized as a determinant of the psychological and somatic costs of stress in theoretical formulations of stress, and self-management is increasingly emphasized as the therapeutic goal of behavioral medicine. At the same time that transactional models of stress have focused on the role cognitive processes play in shaping stress responses and in guiding coping efforts, cognitive-behavioral therapists have drawn attention to the role cognitive processes play in self-management and therapeutic change. Thus, there has been a convergence of developments in stress theory, behavioral medicine, and behavior therapy. One hopes that, in the coming years, the treatment of psychophysiological disorders will reflect each of these developments, drawing on advances in stress theory and behavioral medicine for a more sophisticated understanding of the ways in which psychological factors influence disease processes and on advances in behavior therapy and psychotherapy for treatment techniques appropriate to particular disorders and individuals.

Psychological approaches to the treatment of psychophysiological disorders have frequently lumped different disorders together, ignoring the fact that disorders included in such categories may have little in common. In our discussion, we have emphasized that the goals and techniques of cognitive-behavioral treatment must be tailored to the characteristics of particular disorders. For example, in the case of essential hypertension, where stress may be primarily of etiological significance in the early stages of the disorder, treatment may prove most useful when it is preventive. However, in the case of chronic headache, where readily perceptible symptoms tend to be triggered by stressful transactions, treatment may teach clients to control symptom onset by altering the ways they cope with symptom-related stresses. In the case of bronchial asthma, where stress may be neither an etiological nor a precipitating factor, treatment may focus on teaching skills for the management of the stressful consequences of the disorder. In each instance, treatment strategy must be shaped by the psychobiology of the disorder being treated.

In contrast to the large body of research on biofeedback and relaxation therapies with psychophysiological disorders, there has been only a trickle of research on cognitive-behavioral interventions with these disorders. One reason for this discrepancy may be that investigators interested in biofeedback are frequently psychophysiologists, whereas investigators with interests in cognitive-behavioral therapy are frequently clinical psychologists and are likely to be intimidated by the complexities of working with problems at the interface of physiology and psychology. However, cognitive-behavioral interventions may not only complement biofeedback and relaxation therapies in important ways, but also may have significant advantages that these treatments do not have. We hope that our discussion of the issues and problems involved in developing treatment strategies for particular disorders will interest other clinical researchers in developing and evaluating the potential of this treatment approach.

ACKNOWLEDGMENT

Appreciation is expressed to Richard Lazarus for comments on an earlier draft of this chapter.

REFERENCES

Ad Hoc Committee on Classification of Headache. Classification of headache. *Journal of the American Medical Association*, 1962, *179*, 717–718.

Adams, H. E., Feuerstein, M., & Fowler, J. L. Migraine headache: Review of parameters, etiology, and intervention. *Psychological Bulletin*, 1980, *87*, 217–237.

Adams, N. *Relaxation and self-control interventions to lower psychological responsiveness to stress in college students at risk for hypertension.* Unpublished doctoral dissertation, Ohio University, 1981.

Agras, S., & Jacob, R. Hypertension. In O. F. Pomerleau & J. P. Brady (Eds.), *Behavioral medicine: Theory and practice.* Baltimore: Williams & Wilkins, 1979.

Alexander, A. B. The treatment of psychosomatic disorders: Bronchial asthma in children. In B. B. Lahey & A. E. Kazdin (Eds.), *Advances in clinical child psychology* (Vol. 3). New York: Plenum Press, 1980.

Alexander, A. B. Asthma. In S. N. Haynes & L. Gannon (Eds.), *Psychosomatic disorders: A psychological approach to etiology and treatment.* New York: Holt, Rinehart, & Winston, 1981.

Alexander, A. B., Cropp, G. J. A., & Chai, H. Effects of relaxation training on pulmonary mechanics in children with asthma. *Journal of Applied Behavior Analysis*, 1979, *12*, 27–35.

Alexander, F. *Psychosomatic medicine.* New York: Norton, 1939.

Alexander, F., French, T., & Pollock, G. *Psychosomatic specificity.* Chicago: University of Chicago Press, 1968.

American Psychiatric Association. *Diagnostic and statistical manual of mental disorders* (3rd ed.). Washington, D. C.: Author, 1980.

Amkraut, A., & Solomon, G. F. From the symbolic stimulus to pathophysiologic response: Immune mechanisms. *International Journal of Psychiatry in Medicine*, 1974, *5*, 541–563.

Andrasik, F., & Holroyd, K. A. Physiologic and self-support comparisons between tension headache sufferers and nonheadache controls. *Journal of Behavioral Assessment*, 1980, *2*, 135–141.(a)

Andrasik, F., & Holroyd, K. A. Reliability and concurrent validity of headache questionnaire data. *Headache*, 1980, *20*, 44–46.(b)

Andrasik, F., & Holroyd, K. A. A test of specific and non-specific effects in the biofeedback treatment of tension headache. *Journal of Consulting and Clinical Psychology*, 1980, *48*, 575–586.(c)

Andrasik, F., & Holyrod, K. A. *Three-year follow-up of EMG biofeedback and biofeedback control procedures: What mediates outcome?* Paper presented at the meeting of the Association for the Advancement of Behavior Therapy, Los Angeles, November 1982.

Andrasik, F., Holroyd, K. A., & Abell, T. Prevalence of headache within a college student population: A preliminary analysis. *Headache*, 1979, *19*, 384–387.

Andrasik, F., Coleman, D., & Epstein, L. H. Biofeedback: Clinical and research considerations. In D. M. Doleys, R. L. Meredith, & A. R. Ciminero (Eds.), *Behavioral psychology in medicine: Assessment and treatment strategies.* New York: Plenum Press, 1982.

Antonovsky, A. *Health, stress and coping.* San Francisco: Jossey-Bass, 1979.

Appel, M. A., Holyrod, K. A., & Gorkin, L. Anger and the etiology and progression of physical illness. In C. VanDyke & L. Temoshok (Eds.), *Emotions in health and illness: Foundations of clinical practice.* New York: Academic Press, 1982.

Bakal, D. A., Demjen, S., & Kaganov, S. Cognitive behavioral treatment of chronic headache. *Headache,* 1980, *20,* 163. (Abstract)

Beck, A. T., & Emery, G. *Cognitive therapy of anxiety and phobic disorders.* Philadelphia: Center for Cognitive Therapy, 1979.

Blanchard, E. B., & Miller, S. T. Psychological treatment of cardiovascular disease. *Archives of General Psychiatry,* 1977, *34,* 1402–1413.

Blanchard, E. B., Ahles, T. A., & Shaw, E. R. Behavioral treatment of headaches. In M. Hersen, R. M. Eisler, & P. M. Miller (Eds.), *Progress in behavior modification* (Vol. 8). New York: Academic Press, 1979.

Blanchard, E. B., Andrasik, F., Ahles, T. A., Teders, S. J., & O'Keefe, D. Migraine and tension headache: A meta-analytic review. *Behavior Therapy,* 1980, *11,* 613–633.

Blanchard, E. B., O'Keefe, D., Neff, D., Jurish, S., & Andrasik, F. Interdisciplinary agreement in the diagnosis of headache types. *Journal of Behavioral Assessment,* 1981, *3,* 5–9.

Blanchard, E. B., Andrasik, F., Neff, D. F., Ahles, T. A., Arena, J. G., Jurish, S. E., Pallmeyer, T. P., Teders, S. J., & Rodichok, L. D. *The short-term effects of relaxation training and biofeedback on three kinds of headaches.* Paper presented at the meeting of the Association for the Advancement of Behavior Therapy, Toronto, November 1981.

Bowers, K. S., & Kelly, P. Stress, disease, psychotherapy, and hypnosis. *Journal of Abnormal Psychology,* 1979, *88,* 490–505.

Brown, J. J., Lever, A. F., Robertson, J. I., & Schalekamp, M. A. Pathogenesis of essential hypertension. *Lancet,* 1976, *1*(7971), 1217–1219.

Budzynski, T. H., Stoyva, J. M., Adler, C. S., & Mullaney, D. J. EMG biofeedback and tension headache: A controlled outcome study. *Psychosomatic Medicine,* 1973, *6,* 509–514.

Cannon, W. B. *The wisdom of the body.* New York: Norton, 1932.

Cassel, J. The contribution of the social environment to host resistance. *American Journal of Epidemiology,* 1976, *104,* 107–123.

Clark, N. M., Feldman, C. H., Freudenberg, N., Millman, E. J., Wasilewski, Y., & Valle, I. *Developing education for asthmatic children through study of self-management behavior.* Paper presented at the meeting of the American Public Health Association, New York, November 1979.

Cobb, S., & Rose, R. Hypertension, peptic ulcer, and diabetes in air traffic controllers. *Journal of the American Medical Association,* 1973, *224,* 489–492.

Cohen, F., & Lazarus, R. S. Coping with the stresses of illness. In G. C. Stone, F. Cohen, & N. E. Adler (Eds.), *Health psychology: A handbook.* San Francisco: Jossey-Bass, 1979.

Coyne, J. C., & Holyrod, K. A. Stress, coping and illness: A transactional perspective. In T. Millon, C. Green, & R. Meagher (Eds.), *Handbook of health care clinical psychology.* New York: Plenum Press, 1982.

Coyne, J. C., & Lazarus, R. S. Cognition, stress, and coping: A transactional perspective. In I. L. Kutash & L. B. Schlesinger (Eds.), *Pressure point: Perspectives on stress and anxiety.* San Francisco: Jossey-Bass, 1980.

Creer, T. L. The use of a time-out from positive reinforcement procedure with asthmatic children. *Journal of Psychosomatic Research,* 1970, *14,* 117–120.

Creer, T. L. Asthma: Psychologic aspects and management. In E. Middleton, Jr., C. E. Reed, & E. F. Ellis (Eds.), *Allergy: Principles and practice* (Vol. 2). Saint Louis: C. V. Mosby, 1978.

Creer, T. L. *Asthma therapy: A behavioral health care system for respiratory disorders.* New York: Springer Publishing, 1979.

Creer, T. L. *Asthma: Self-management.* Paper presented at the National Jewish Hospital/National Asthma Center Conference on Asthma, Keystone, Colorado, January 1980.(a)

Creer, T. L. Self-management behavioral strategies for asthmatics. *Behavioral Medicine,* 1980, *7,* 14–24.(b)

Creer, T. L., & Yoches, C. The modification of an inappropriate behavioral pattern in asthmatic children. *Journal of Chronic Diseases,* 1971, *24,* 507–513.

Creer, T. L., Weinberg, E., & Molk, L. Managing a hospital behavior problem: Malingering. *Journal of Behavior Therapy and Experimental Psychiatry,* 1974, *5,* 259–262.

Davies, M. Is high blood pressure a psychosomatic disorder? *Journal of Chronic Diseases,* 1971, *24,* 239–258.

DeLozier, J. E., & Gagnon, R. O. *National ambulatory medical care survey: 1973 summary, United States, May 1973–April 1974* (DHEW Publication No. HRA 76-1772). Washington, D. C.: U. S. Government Printing Office, 1975.

DeQuattro, V., & Miura, Y. Neurogenic factors in human hypertension: Mechanism or myth. *American Journal of Medicine,* 1973, *55,* 362–378.

Dirks, J. F., Jones, N. F., & Kinsman, R. A. Panic-fear: A personality dimension related to intractibility in asthma. *Psychosomatic Medicine,* 1977, *39,* 120–126.

Dirks, J. F., Kinsman, R. A., Horton, D. J., Fross, K. H., & Jones, N. F. Panic-fear in asthma: Rehospitalization following intensive long-term treatment. *Psychosomatic Medicine,* 1978, *40,* 5–13.

Dirks, J. F., Kinsman, R. A., Staudenmayer, H., & Kleiger, J. H. Panic-fear in asthma: Symptomatology as an index of signal anxiety and personality as an index of ego resources. *Journal of Nervous and Mental Disease,* 1979, *167,* 615–619.

Epstein, L. H., & Abel, G. G. An analysis of biofeedback training effects with tension headache patients. *Behavior Therapy,* 1977, *8,* 37–47.

Epstein, L. H., Abel, G. G., Collins, F., Parker, L., & Cinciripini, P. M. The relationship between frontalis muscle activity and self-reports of headache pain. *Behavior Research and Therapy,* 1978, *16,* 153–160.

Esler, M., Julius, S., Zwelfer, A., Randall, O., Harburg, E., Gardiner, H., & DeQuattro, V. Mild high-renin essential hypertension: Neurogenic human hypertension? *New England Journal of Medicine,* 1977, *296,* 405–411.

Fanchamps, A. The role of humoral mediators in migraine headache. *Canadian Journal of Neurological Sciences,* 1974, *1,* 189–195.

Farr, R. S., & Spector, S. L. What is asthma? In the Upjohn Company, *The asthmatic patient in trouble.* Greenwich, Conn.: CPC Communications, 1975.

Freedman, R. *Evaluation and treatment of Raynaud's phenomenon.* Paper presented at the meeting of the Biofeedback Society of America, San Diego, March 1979.

Freedman, R. R., Lynn, S. J., Ianni, P., Hale, P. A., & Michael, D. *Biofeedback treatment of Raynaud's disease and phenomenon.* Paper presented at the meeting of the Biofeedback Society of America, Albuquerque, March 1978.

Galton, L. *The silent disease: Hypertension.* New York: Crown, 1973.

Gentry, W. D. Preadmission behavior. In W. D. Gentry & R. B. Williams, Jr. (Eds.), *Psychological aspects of myocardial infarction and coronary care.* St. Louis: C. V. Mosby, 1975.

Glass, D. C. *Behavior patterns, stress, and coronary disease.* Hillsdale, N.J.: Lawrence Erlbaum, 1977.

Glass, D. C., Krakoff, L. R., Contrada, R., Hilton, W. F., Kehoe, K., Manucci, E. G., Collins, C., Snow, B., & Elting, E. Effect of harassment and competition upon cardiovascular and plasma catecholamine responses in Type A and Type B individuals. *Psychophysiology,* 1980, *17,* 453–463.

Glock, C., & Lennard, H. Psychologic factors in hypertension: An interpretative review. *Journal of Chronic Diseases,* 1957, *5,* 174–185.

Goldfried, M. R., & Trier, C. S. Effectiveness of relaxation as an active coping skill. *Journal of Abnormal Psychology,* 1974, *83,* 348–355.

Graham, J. High blood pressure after battle. *Lancet,* 1945, *1,* 239–246.

Graham, P. J., Rutter, M. L., Yule, W., & Pless, I. B. Childhood asthma: A psychosomatic disorder?—Some epidemiological considerations. *British Journal of Preventive and Social Medicine,* 1967, *21,* 78–85.

Gutman, M., & Benson, H. Interaction of environmental factors and systemic arterial blood pressure: A review. *Medicine,* 1971, *50,* 543–553.

Harburg, E., Erfurt, J., Chape, G., Hausenstein, L., Schull, W., & Schork, M. Socio-ecological stressor areas and black-white pressure: Detroit. *Journal of Chronic Diseases,* 1973, *26,* 595–611.

Harburg, E., Blakelock, E., & Roeper, J. Resentful and reflective coping with arbitrary authority and blood pressure: Detroit. *Psychosomatic Medicine,* 1979, *41,* 189–202.

Harper, R. G., & Steger, J. C. Psychological correlates of frontalis EMG and pain in tension headache. *Headache,* 1978, *18,* 215–218.

Harrell, J. Psychological factors and hypertension: A status report. *Psychological Bulletin,* 1980, *87,* 482–501.

Harris, R., & Forsyth, R. Personality and emotional stress in essential hypertension in man. In G. Onesti, J. Kim, & J. Moyer (Eds.), *Hypertension: Mechanisms and management.* New York: Grune and Stratton, 1973.

Haynes, S. N. Muscle-contraction headache: A psychophysiological perspective of etiology and treatment. In S. N. Haynes & L. R. Gannon (Eds.), *Psychosomatic disorders: A psychological approach to etiology and treatment.* New York: Holt, Rinehart & Winston, 1981.

Henry, J. Understanding the early pathophysiology of essential hypertension. *Geriatrics,* 1976, *30,* 59–72.

Henry, J., & Cassel, J. Psychosocial factors in essential hypertension. *American Journal of Epidemiology,* 1969, *90,* 171–210.

Henry, J., & Stephens, P. *Stress, health and the social environment: A sociobiologic approach to medicine.* New York: Springer Publishing, 1977.

Henryk-Gutt, R., & Rees, W. C. Psychological aspects of migraine. *Journal of Psychosomatic Research,* 1973, *17,* 141–153.

Holroyd, K. A. Stress, coping, and the treatment of stress related illness. In J. R. McNamara (Ed.), *Behavioral approaches in medicine: Application and analysis.* New York: Plenum Press, 1979.

Holroyd, K. A., & Andrasik, F. Coping and the self-control of chronic tension headache. *Journal of Consulting and Clinical Psychology,* 1978, *46,* 1036–1045.

Holroyd, K. A., & Andrasik, F. Self-control of tension headache. In F. J. McGuigan, W. E. Sime, & J. M. Wallace (Eds.), *Stress and tension control.* New York: Plenum Press, 1980.

Holroyd, K., A. & Andrasik, F. A cognitive-behavioral approach to recurrent tension and migraine headache. In P. C. Kendall (Ed.), *Advances in cognitive-behavioral research and therapy* (Vol. 1). New York: Academic Press, 1982.

Holroyd, K. A., & Andrasik, F. Do the effects of cognitive therapy endure: A two-year follow-up of tension headache sufferers treated with cognitive therapy or biofeedback. *Cognitive Therapy and Research,* in press.

Holroyd, K. A., & Gorkin, L. Young adults at risk for hypertension: Effects of family history and anger management in determining responses to interpersonal conflict. *Journal of Psychosomatic Research,* in press.

Holroyd, K. A., & Lazarus, R. A. Stress, coping and somatic adaption. In L. Goldberger & S. Breznitz (Eds.), *Handbook of stress.* New York: Free Press, 1982.

Holroyd, K. A., Andrasik, F., & Westbrook, T. Cognitive control of tension headache. *Cognitive Therapy and Research,* 1977, *1,* 121–133

Holroyd, K. A., Andrasik, F., & Noble, J. A comparison of EMG biofeedback and a credible pseudotherapy in treating tension headache. *Journal of Behavioral Medicine,* 1980, *3,* 29–39.

Holroyd, K. A., Penzien, D., Tobin, D., Hursey, K., Rogers, L., Marcille, P., & Holm, J. *Psychological vs. physiological learning mediating tension headache improvements following biofeedback.* Paper presented at the meeting of the Association for the Advancement of Behavior Therapy, Los Angeles, November 1982.

Horowitz, M. J., Hulley, S., Alvarez, W., Reynolds, A. M., Benfari, R., Blair, S., Borhani, N., & Simon, N. Life events, risk factors, and coronary disease. *Psychosomatics,* 1979, *20,* 586–592.

Howarth, E. Headache, personality and stress. *British Journal of Psychiatry,* 1965, *111,* 1193–1197.

Hurley, F. E. *Practical management of headache in office practice.* Paper presented at the meeting of the Chicago Medical Society, Chicago, March 1969.

Jenkins, C. D. Psychosocial modifiers of response to stress. *Journal of Human Stress,* 1979, *5,* 3–15.

Jones, N. F., Kinsman, R. A., Dirks, J. F., & Dahlem, N. W. Psychological contributions to chronicity in asthma: Patient response styles influencing medical treatment and its outcome. *Medical Care,* 1979, *17,* 1103–1118.

Julius, S., & Esler, M. Autonomic nervous system cardiovascular regulation in borderline hypertension. *American Journal of Cardiology,* 1975, *36,* 685–696.

Kahn, H. A., Medalie, J. H., Neufeld, H. M., Riss, E., & Goldbourt, U. The incidence of hypertension and associated factors: The Israeli ischemic heart disease study. *American Heart Journal,* 1972, *84,* 171–182.

Kaplan, H. B., Cassel, J. C., & Gore, S. Social support and health. *Medical Care,* 1977, *15,* 47–58.

Kaplan, N. M. *Your blood pressure: The most deadly high.* New York: Krieger, 1976.

Kaplan, N. M. *Clinical hypertension* (2nd ed.). Baltimore: Williams & Wilkins, 1978.

Kaplan, N. M. The Goldblatt Memorial Lecture Part II: The role of the kidney in hypertension. *Hypertension,* 1979, *1,* 456–461.

Kashiwagi, T., McClure, J. N., & Wetzel, R. D. Headache and psychiatric disorders. *Diseases of the Nervous System,* 1972, *33,* 659–663.

Katz, J. L., Weiner, H., Gutman, A., & Yu, T. F. Hyperuricemia, gout and the executive suite. *Journal of the American Medical Association,* 1973, *224,* 1251–1257.

Kinsman, R. A., Dahlem, N. W., Spector, S., & Staudenmayer, H. Observations on subjective symptomatology, coping, behavior, and medical decisions in asthma. *Psychosomatic Medicine,* 1977, *39,* 102–119.

Knapp, P. H., Mathe, A. A., & Vachon, L. Psychosomatic aspects of bronchial asthma. In E. B. Weiss & M. S. Segal (Eds.), *Bronchial asthma: Mechanisms and therapeutics.* Boston: Little, Brown, 1976.

Knapp, T. J., & Wells, L. A. Behavior therapy for asthma: A review. *Behavior Research and Therapy,* 1978, *16,* 103–115.
Lance, J. W., & Anthony, M. Thermographic studies in vascular headache. *Medical Journal of Australia,* 1971, *1,* 240.
Largen, J. W., Mathew, J. R., Dobbins, K., Meyer, J. S., & Claghorn, J. L. Skin temperature self-regulation and non-invasive regional cerebral blood flow. *Headache,* 1978, *18,* 203–210.
Lazarus, R. S. *Psychological stress and the coping process.* New York: McGraw-Hill, 1966.
Lazarus, R. S. The stress and coping paradigm. In C. Eisdorfer, D. Cohen, A. Kleinman, & P. Maxim (Eds.), *Theoretical bases for psychopathology.* New York: Spectrum, 1980.
Lazarus, R. S. Coping and adaption. In W. D. Gentry (Ed.), *The handbook of behavioral medicine.* New York: Guilford Press, 1982.
Lazarus, R. S., & Launier, R. Stress-related transactions between person and environment. In L. A. Pervin & M. Lewis (Eds.), *Perspectives in interactional psychology.* New York: Plenum Press, 1978.
Lazarus, R. S., Cohen, J. B., Folkman, S., Kanner, A., & Schaefer, C. Psychological stress and adaptation: Some unresolved issues. In H. Selye (Ed.), *Selye's guide to stress research* (Vol. 1). New York: Van Nostrand Reinhold, 1980.
Levinson, D. J. *The seasons of a man's life.* New York: Knopf, 1978.
Looney, J., Lipp, M., & Spitzer, R. A new method of classification for psychophysiologic disorders. *American Journal of Psychiatry,* 1978, *135,* 304–308.
Lynn, S. J., & Freedman, R. R. Transfer and evaluation in biofeedback treatment. In A. P. Goldstein & F. Kanfer (Eds.), *Maximizing treatment gains: Transfer enhancement in psychotherapy.* New York: Academic Press, 1979.
Mason, J. W. Strategy in psychosomatic research. *Psychosomatic Medicine,* 1970, *32,* 427–439.
Mason, J. W. Clinical psychophysiology. In M. F. Reiser (Ed.), *American handbook of psychiatry* (Vol. 4). New York: Basic Books, 1975.
Mathew, R. J., Largen, J. W., Dobbins, K., Meyer, J. S., Sakai, F., & Claghorn, J. L. Biofeedback control of skin temperature and cerebral blood flow in migraine. *Headache,* 1980, *20,* 19–28.
McClelland, D. Inhibited power motivation and high blood pressure in men. *Journal of Abnormal Psychology,* 1979, *88,* 182–190.
Mechanic, D. *Medical sociology: A selective view.* New York: Free Press, 1968.
Medina, J. L., & Diamond, S. The role of diet in migraine. *Headache,* 1978, *18,* 31–34.
Merrill, J. P. Hypertensive vascular disease. In J. V. Harrison, R. D. Adams, I. J. Bennett, W.H. Resnik, G. W. Thorn, & M. M. Wintrobe (Eds.), *Principles of internal medicine.* New York: McGraw-Hill, 1966.
Middleton, E. Jr., Reed, C. E., & Ellis, E. F. (Eds.). *Allergy: Principles and practice* (Vol. 1). Saint Louis: C. V. Mosby, 1978.
Miklich, D. R. Operant conditioning procedures with systematic desensitization in a hyperkinetic asthmatic boy. *Journal of Behavior Therapy and Experimental Psychiatry,* 1973, *4,* 177–182.
Miklich, D. R., Renne, C. M., Creer, T. L., Alexander, A. B., Chai, H., Davis, M. H., Hoffman, A., & Danker-Brown, P. The clinical utility of behavior therapy as an adjunctive treatment for asthma. *Journal of Allergy and Clinical Immunology,* 1977, *60,* 285–294.
Miller, N. E., & Dworkin, B. R. Critical issues in therapeutic applications of biofeedback. In G. E. Schwartz & J. Beatty (Eds.), *Biofeedback.* New York: Academic Press, 1977.
Mitchell, K. R., & White, R. G. Control of migraine headache by behavioral self-management: A controlled case study. *Headache,* 1976, *16,* 178–184.

Mitchell, K. R., & White, R. G. Behavioral self-management: An application to the problem of migraine headaches. *Behavior Therapy,* 1977, *8,* 213–221.

Moos, R. H., & Tsu, V. D. The crisis of physical illness: An overview. In R. H. Moos (Ed.), *Coping with physical illness.* New York: Plenum Press, 1977.

Morillo, E., & Gardner, L. Bereavement as an antecedent factor in thyrotoxicosis of childhood: Four case studies with survey of possible metabolic pathways. *Psychosomatic Medicine,* 1979, *41,* 545–555.

Novaco, R. W. *Anger control: The development and evaluation of an experimental treatment.* Lexington, Mass.: Lexington Books, 1975.

Obrist, P. The cardiovascular-behavioral interaction—As it appears today. *Psychophysiology,* 1976, *13,* 95–107.

Obrist, P., Gaebelein, C., Teller, E., Langer, A., Grignolo, A., Light, K., & McCubbin, S. The relationship among heart rate, carotid dP/dt, and blood pressure in humans as a function of the type of stress. *Psychophysiology,* 1978, *15,* 102–115.

Obrist, P., Light, K., Langer, A., Grignolo, A., & McCubbin, J. Behavioral-cardiac interactions: The psychosomatic hypothesis. *Journal of Psychosomatic Research,* 1978, *22,* 301–325.

Ostfeld, A. M., Reis, D. J., & Wolff, H. G. Studies in headache: Bulbar conjunctival ischemia and muscle contraction headache. *Archives of Neurological Psychiatry,* 1957, *77,* 113–119.

Page, L. Epidemiologic evidence on the etiology of human hypertension and its possible prevention. *American Heart Journal,* 1976, *91,* 527–534.

Pancheri, P., Bellaterra, M., Matteoli, S., Cristofari, M., Polizzi, C., & Puletti, M. Infarct as a stress agent: Life history and personality characteristics in improved versus not-improved patients after severe heart attack. *Journal of Human Stress,* 1978, *4,* 16–22; 41–42.

Patel, C. H. Biofeedback-aided relaxation and meditation in the management of hypertension. *Biofeedback and Self-Regulation,* 1977, *2,* 1–41.

Pinkerton, P. The enigma of asthma. *Psychosomatic Medicine,* 1973, *35,* 461–462.

Pranulis, M. Coping with acute myocardial infarction. In W. D. Gentry & R. B. Williams, Jr. (Eds.), *Psychological aspects of myocardial infarction and coronary care.* St. Louis: C. V. Mosby, 1975.

Purcell, K., & Weiss, J. H. Asthma. In C. G. Costello (Ed.), *Symptoms of psychopathology: A handbook.* New York: Wiley, 1970.

Rahe, R. H., & Ranson, R. J. Life change and illness studies: Past history and future directions. *Journal of Human Stress,* 1978, *4,* 3–15.

Raskin, N. H., & Appenzeller, O. *Headache*. Philadelphia: Saunders, 1980.

Reed, C. E., & Townley, R. G. Asthma: Classification and pathogenesis. In E. Middleton, Jr., C. E. Reed, & E. F. Ellis (Eds.), *Allergy: Principles and practice* (Vol. 2). Saint Louis: C. V. Mosby, 1978.

Reinking, R., & Hutchings, D. *Follow-up and extension of "Tension headaches: What method is most effective?"* Paper presented at the meeting of the Biofeedback Research Society, Colorado Springs, February 1976.

Rodgers, M., Dubey, D., & Reich, P. The influence of the psyche and the brain on immunity and disease susceptibility: A critical review. *Psychosomatic Medicine,* 1979, *41,* 147–164.

Rose, R., Jenkins, C., & Hurst, M. *Air-traffic controller health change study: A prospective investigation of physical, psychological, and work-related changes.* Report to the Federal Aviation Administration on research performed under contract DOT-FA73WA-3211, 1978.

Roskies, E., & Lazarus, R. S. Coping theory and the teaching of coping skills. In P. Davidson & S. Davidson (Eds.), *Behavioral medicine: Changing health life styles.* New York: Brunner/Mazel, 1980.

Ruskin, A., Beard, O., & Schaffer, R. Blast hypertension: Elevated arterial pressure in victims of the Texas City Disaster. *American Journal of Medicine,* 1948, *4,* 228–236.

Scadding, J. G. Definition and clinical categorization. In E. B. Weiss & M. S. Segal (Eds.), *Bronchial asthma: Mechanisms and therapeutics.* Boston: Little, Brown, 1976.

Schwartz, G. The brain as a health care system. In. G. C. Stone, F. Cohen, & N. E. Adler (Eds.), *Health psychology: A handbook.* San Francisco: Jossey-Bass, 1979.

Seer, P. Psychological control of essential hypertension: Review of the literature and methodological critique. *Psychological Bulletin,* 1979, *86,* 1015–1043.

Selby, G., & Lance, J. W. Observations on 500 cases of migraine and allied vascular headache. *Journal of Neurology, Neurosurgery, and Psychiatry,* 1960, *23,* 23–32.

Selye, H. *The stress of life.* New York: McGraw-Hill, 1956.

Selye, H. *The stress of life* (rev. ed.). New York: McGraw-Hill, 1976.

Shapiro, A. Behavioral and environmental aspects of hypertension. *Journal of Human Stress,* 1978, *4,* 9–17.

Shapiro, A. P., Schwartz, G., Ferguson, D., Redmond, D. P., & Weiss, S. M. Behavioral approaches to the treatment of hypertension: Clinical status. *Annals of Internal Medicine* 1977, *86,* 626–636.

Siegel, S. C., Katz, R. M., & Rachelefsky, G. S. Asthma in infancy and childhood. In E. Middleton, Jr., C. E. Reed, & E. F. Ellis (Eds.), *Allergy: Principles and practice* (Vol. 2). St. Louis: C. V. Mosby, 1978.

Stoyva, J. Self-regulation and the stress-related disorders: A perspective on biofeedback. In D. Mostofsky (Ed.), *Behavior control and modification of physiological activity.* Englewood Cliffs, N. J.: Prentice-Hall, 1976.

Syme, S., & Torfs, C. Epidemiologic research in hypertension: A critical appraisal. *Journal of Human Stress,* 1978, *4,* 43–48.

Taplin, P. S., & Creer, T. L. A procedure for using peak expiratory flow data to increase the predictability of asthma episodes. *Journal of Asthma Research,* 1978, *16,* 15–19.

Taylor, C. B., Farquhar, J. W., Nelson, E., & Agras, W. S. Relaxation therapy and high blood pressure. *Archives of General Psychiatry,* 1977, *34,* 339–342.

Thomas, C. The psychological dimension of hypertension. In J. Stamler, K. Stamler, & T. Pullman (Eds.), *The epidemiology of essential hypertension.* New York: Grune & Stratton, 1967.

Toffler, A. *Future shock.* New York: Random House, 1970.

Tunis, M. M., & Wolff, H. G. Studies in headache: Cranial artery vasoconstriction and muscle contraction headache. *Archives of Neurological Psychiatry,* 1954, *71,* 425–434.

Turk, D. C., Meichenbaum, D. H., & Berman, W. H. Application of biofeedback for the regulation of pain: A critical review. *Psychological Bulletin,* 1979, *86,* 1322–1338.

U. S. Department of Health, Education, and Welfare. *Prevalence of selected chronic respiratory conditions, United States—1970* (DHEW Publication No. HRA-74-1511, Series 10, No. 84). Rockville, Md.: Health Resources Administration, 1973.

Von Bertalanffy, L. *General systems theory.* New York: Braziller, 1968.

Waters, W. E., & O'Connor, P. J. Prevalence of migraine. *Journal of Neurology, Neurosurgery, and Psychiatry,* 1975, *38,* 613–616.

Weiner, H. *Psychobiology and human disease.* New York: Elsevier, 1977.

Weisman, A. A study of the psychodynamics of duodenal ulcer exacerbations with special reference to treatment and the problem of specificity. *Psychosomatic Medicine,* 1956, *18,* 2–42.

Weisman, A. D., & Worden, J. W. Psychosocial analysis of cancer deaths. *Omega: Journal of Death and Dying,* 1975, *6,* 61–75.
Weiss, J. H. The current state of the concept of a psychosomatic disorder. In Z. J. Lipowski, D. R. Lipsitt, & P. C. Whybrow (Eds.), *Psychosomatic medicine: Current trends and clinical applications.* New York: Oxford University Press, 1977.
Weiss, J. M. Ulcers. In J. D. Maser & M. E. P. Seligman (Eds.), *Psychopathology: Experimental models.* San Francisco: Freeman, 1977.
Welch, M. H. Obstructive diseases. In C. A. Guenter & M. H. Welch (Eds.), *Pulmonary medicine.* Philadelphia: Lippincott, 1977.
Whitehead, W. E., Fedoravicius, A. S., Blackwell, B., & Wooley, S. A behavioral conceptualization of psychosomatic illness: Psychosomatic symptoms as learned responses. In J. R. McNamara (Ed.), *Behavioral approaches to medicine: Application and analysis.* New York: Plenum Press, 1979.
Ziegler, D. K., Hassanein, R., & Hassanein, K. Headache syndromes suggested by factor analysis of symptom variables in a headache prone population. *Journal of Chronic Disease,* 1972, *25,* 353–363.

8

Stress Management for Type A Individuals

ETHEL ROSKIES

INTRODUCTION

Since 1976 my colleagues and I have been engaged in the paradoxical task of seeking to develop a treatment program for apparently healthy men. The individuals who are the target of our therapeutic efforts neither consider themselves sick nor are they so regarded by their families, co-workers, and even doctors. On the contrary, these men are so full of energy and activity that they give the impression of being super-healthy. Even a short interview reveals their mental alertness, emotional expressiveness, and rapid pace of thought and speech. Their ability to fulfill valued social roles is also noteworthy. All hold responsible managerial positions, and most add to their job demands a host of family obligations and community activities. In spite of these multiple pressures, there are remarkably few complaints of anxiety and depression. Some of the men go so far as to state that they thrive on challenge and tight deadlines—the more the better. Even when a man does experience malaise, be it in the form of tight shoulder muscles or difficulty in falling asleep, the usual tendency is to minimize the degree of discomfort and to accept it as a necessary part of the "stress of modern life."

ETHEL ROSKIES • Department of Psychology, University of Montreal, Montreal, Quebec, Canada H3C 3J7. The work reported in this chapter was supported by grants from Health and Welfare, Ottawa; Conseil de la Recherche en Sante du Quebec; and CAFIR, Universite de Montreal.

Seeking to intervene in the lives of men as well-functioning as these would be patently irresponsible unless there were strong evidence of health risk serious enough to outweigh the psychological and social dangers inherent in upsetting an existing equilibrium. The requisite evidence of serious health risk is all too available. By now it will not surprise most readers to learn that the men we have been describing are commonly categorized as type A and that individuals manifesting the type A behavior pattern bear a significantly increased risk of developing and dying from coronary heart disease (CHD) compared with their more relaxed, easygoing type B counterparts. We shall review the evidence for considering type A to be an important coronary risk factor below.

Even if the establishment of type A behavior as a health risk qualifies it for therapeutic intervention, it nevertheless remains a very different health problem from those discussed in the rest of this volume. In contrast to headache, hypertension, and chronic pain, which serve no social goals and only neurotic psychological ones, the type A behavior pattern possesses considerable social and personal value. To be competitive, ambitious, and hard working may increase one's chances of suffering a heart attack, but it also augments the likelihood of rapid job promotion (cf. Mettlin, 1976). To exert maximum effort to master a challenging situation not only increases wear-and-tear on the coronary arteries, but it also enhances the person's feelings of self-esteem and self-efficacy (Bandura, 1977). This complex blend of positive and negative features in the type A pattern creates some unusual methodological, motivational, and ethical problems for the would-be therapist. In this chapter we shall first describe these problems and then trace the development of our efforts to resolve them during two separate treatment studies.

TYPE A AS RISK FACTOR FOR CORONARY HEART DISEASE

The observation that heart patients are distinctive for their hyperalert, impatient, aggressive manner has been made repeatedly by clinicians during the course of the last 100 years (Dunbar, 1943; Gildea, 1949; Kemple, 1945; Menninger & Menninger, 1936; Osler, 1892). What distinguished the work in the early 1950s of two San Francisco cardiologists, Meyer Friedman and Ray Rosenman, was the recognition that this coronary behavior pattern could be elicited under appropriate conditions even in individuals who had not yet manifested any signs of heart disease. On the basis of a standardized 15-minute challenge interview, a trained interviewer could, by carefully attending to the style as well as the content of responses, classify a person as coronary-prone (type A) or non-coronary-prone (type B). With trained interviews, interrater reliability ranged from 0.74–0.84 (Caffrey, 1968; Jenkins, Rosenman, & Friedman, 1968) and, after 1½ years, test–retest reliability was 0.80 (Rosenman, Friedman, Straus, Wurm, Kositchek, Hahn, & Werthessen, 1964). This development of a simple classification system and a reliable measuring instrument means that, for the first time, the role of personality factors in heart disease could be studied prospectively, rather than in the traditional post-hoc fashion.

The largest prospective study of the association between type A behavior and heart disease is the Western Collaborative Group Study (WCGS) in which 3,100 initially well, middle-aged, middle-class white men were followed for 8½ years. In this study individuals classified at intake as type A were twice as likely as those classified as type B to develop and die from CHD (Rosenman, Brand, Jenkins, Friedman, Straus, & Wurm, 1975). More important, the increased risk associated with type A remained almost as great even when the possibly confounding interrelationships between type A and increased levels of traditional risk factors (e.g., smoking, serum cholesterol) were statistically controlled (Rosenman, Brand, Sholtz, & Friedman, 1976). Type A individuals who suffered a myocardial infarction and survived continued to demonstrate a significantly increased risk for future coronary events compared with type B cardiac patients; in fact, a questionnaire measure of the behavior pattern (the Jenkins Activity Survey) was the strongest single predictor of recurring heart attacks from among a set of variables that included smoking and serum cholesterol (Jenkins, Zyzanski, & Rosenman, 1976). These findings of the WCGS have recently been confirmed in another larger prospective investigation based on the Framingham sample. Even though the Framingham study used still another measure of type A behavior (the Framingham A scale), a very similar pattern of increased risk emerged (Haynes, Feinleib, & Kannel, 1980).

Type A has also found to be associated with morphological factors and physiological processes that are considered pathways to coronary artery disease. Compared with type Bs, type As show both more severe coronary artery blockage (Blumenthal, Williams, Kong, Thompson, Jenkins, & Rosenman, 1978; Zyzanski, Jenkins, Ryan, Flessas, & Everist, 1976) and faster progression of this blockage (Krantz, Sanmarco, Selvester, & Matthews, 1979). They also show greater autonomic and endocrine reactivity than type Bs, responding to stressful or challenging situations with greater increases in systolic blood pressure, heart rate, and epinephrine and norepinephrine levels (Dembroski, MacDougall, & Shields, 1977; Dembroski, MacDougall, Shields, Pettito, & Lushene, 1978; Dembroski, MacDougall, Herd, & Shields, 1979; Friedman, Byers, Diamant, & Rosenman, 1975; Glass, Krakoff, Contrada, Hilton, Kehoe, Mannucci, Collins, Snow, & Elting, 1980; Manuck, Craft, & Gold, 1978; Van Egeren, 1979).

The CHD risk associated with type A behavior takes on added importance because the pattern is widespread and affects some of the most productive members of society. The WCGS classified 50% of its sample of middle-aged, mainly middle-class males as type A; a study by Howard of senior Canadian managers found a prevalence rate of 75% (Howard, Cunningham, & Rechnitzer, 1976). In general, the prevalence of type A behavior is positively correlated with occupational status, particularly high concentrations being found in samples of individuals in high-stress occupations, such as cardiologists and NASA executives (Mettlin, 1976; Zyzanski, 1977). Women at large show a lower prevalance than men at large, but when women and men at the same occupational level are compared, this sex difference largely disappears (Shekelle, Schoenberger, & Stamler, 1976; Waldron, 1977; Waldron, Zyzanski, Shekelle, Jenkins, & Tannenbaum, 1977). Samples in the mainland United States shows a higher prevalence than do European samples, which in turn are higher than a sample of Japanese-Americans living in Hawaii (Cohen, Syme, Jenkins, Kagan, & Zyzanski, 1979; Zyzanski, 1977). When individuals as young as 20–25 years are included in samples, there is an inverse relationship between type A prevalence and age (Mettlin, 1976; Shekelle *et al.*, 1976). The highest concentration of type A individuals, therefore, is likely to be found in young and early middle-aged males working in highly demanding white-collar occupations and living in competitive societies such as the United States.

No risk factor for CHD is completely beyond controversy and there are still many unanswered questions concerning the role of type A in coronary heart disease. We do not know the mechanisms by which type A exerts its pathogenic effects nor even the relationship of type A to other psychological factors that have been implicated in the onset of coronary heart disease (Shapiro, 1979). Nevertheless, the accumulation of converging evidence from epidemiological, morphological, biochemical, and physiological sources has led to the gradual acceptance of type A as an important risk factor. In fact, a distinguished panel convened by the (U. S.) National Heart Lung and Blood Institutue to evaluate the evidence concerning the association between type A and CHD concluded that type A did indeed constitute an important and independent risk factor, the increased risk being of the same magnititude as that associated with age, systolic blood pressure, serum cholesterol, and smoking (The Review Panel on Coronary-Prone Behavior and Coronary Heart Disease, 1981).

TYPE A AS AN ATYPICAL THERAPEUTIC TARGET

Since 1974 when Friedman and Rosenman first raised the possibility of modifying type A behavior to reduce coronary risk, interest in this area of therapeutic effort has grown rapidly. There are at least seven published reports of treatment studies (Blumenthal, Williams, Williams, & Wallace, 1979; Jenni & Wollersheim, 1979; Rosenman & Friedman, 1977; Roskies, Spevack, Surkis, Cohen, & Gilman, 1978; Roskies, Kearney, Spevack, Surkis, Cohen, & Gilman, 1979; Suinn, 1975; Suinn & Bloom, 1978) and a number of studies are currently in progress (Friedman, 1978; Roskies, 1979; Roskies & Avard, 1982). Recent annual meetings of the American Psychological Association, the American Psychosomatic Society, the American Public Health Association, and the Association for the Advancement of Behavior Therapy have all contained papers on type A treatment, and the Society of Behavioral Medicine chose this topic as a major program feature of its first annual meeting. In the most recent *Annual Review of Behavior Therapy,* the editors discuss the available treatment studies in detail and predict "greatly increased research activity in this important area of behavioral medicine in the next few years" (Franks & Wilson, 1979, p. 382).

It is easy to understand why health psychologists working in the newly emerging area of behavioral medicine have seized on type A intervention with such enthusiasm. Eager to prove to our medical colleagues that the new behavioral technology can be of practical value in the prevention and treatment of disease, we are in search of medical problems responsive to behavioral input. The type A pattern is not only an unusually clear demonstration of the etiological importance of behavior, successfully and independently predicting the future emergence of a major somatic disease, but is is also an excellent example of the type of medical problem for which traditional pharmaceutical and surgical remedies have little relevance. A treatment approach anxious to prove its mettle has indeed found an appropriate challenge in the type A behavior pattern.

Unfortunately, the fact that type A constitutes a "hot" treatment area has led us to gloss over the problems involved in designing treatment studies that are clinically meaningful, methodologically sound, and ethically responsible (Roskies, 1980). Many of the design problems of the early studies, such as unrepresentative samples and inadequate control groups, are those likely to occur in any new area of therapeutic endeavor and will probably correct themselves in the course of time. Far more serious is the conceptual weakness characterizing most of the studies to date. Rather than developing a rationale to guide the choice of treatment techniques and outcome measures, the tendency instead has been to apply, more or less haphazardly, a variety of currently fashionable therapies (anxiety management, relaxation, psychotherapy, cognitive therapy, exercise training) to type A individuals in the hope that these treatments would change something in the person's physiological, emotional, or behavioral functioning that would somehow reduce his or her coronary risk. This failure to specify treatment goals in advance, coupled with a heterogeneous collection of outcome measures, has permitted all researchers to claim at least partial therapeutic success, but has added little to our understanding of what has been changed and why (Roskies, 1979).

The major conceptual problem confounding the type A therapist is the confusion between coronary risk and type A behavior. Not all type A behavior is necessarily coronary-prone behavior, and not all coronary-risk behavior, even in type A individuals, is linked to their type A pattern. To reduce the rapidity and explosiveness with which a person speaks is to modify a significant characteristic of the type A pattern but, at this point anyway, there is no evidence that such a change will alter his or her coronary risk. Conversely, to reduce feelings of life dissatisfaction and helplessness in type A individuals may reduce their coronary risk, but these changes do not indicate any alteration of what we commonly conceive of as the type A pattern. The unclear distinction between coronary risk and type A becomes even more evident when we focus on the physiological level: A decrease in *resting* blood pressure level lowers coronary risk but is not indicative of an alteration in the type A pattern, while a decrease in blood pressure *lability* does signify a change in type A functioning but not necessarily in coronary risk status. Essentially, we are in a situation where we know that type A individuals bear increased coronary risk, but we still do not know what exactly about their behavioral, physiological, and emotional functioning makes them vulnerable, or which mechanisms effect that vulnerability.

The ambiguity of type A as a therapeutic target places a double burden on the would-be therapist. Before he or she can even consider specific treatment techniques, there is the prior responsibility of deciding what exactly in the type A pattern requires changing. Essentially every therapist is forced to build his or her individual conceptual model of the links between type A characteristics and the disease end point. This problem can be avoided somewhat by those who choose to work with heart disease patients and can therefore use decreased rate of recurrence as an indirect measure of successful type A modification (Friedman, 1978, 1979), but for researchers choosing to work in prevention, the challenge of explaining why one is seeking a particular type of change is almost as great as that of effecting the changes desired (Roskies, 1979).

A second major difficulty in designing a type A intervention program results from the pervasiveness of the pattern. The current view is that type A does not constitute a personality trait *per se* but rather a response to certain situations of threat, harm, and challenge. However in individuals classified as type A there seem to be a limitless number of stimuli, internal as well as external, that provoke manifestations of the pattern. Instead of working with a symptom localized in time and space (e.g., examination anxiety), the therapist is confronting a response set that affects all situations and all relationships. The process of therapy, therefore, necessarily involves entering into all aspects of the person's life while at the same time remaining within the boundaries of a limited therapeutic contract—a delicate and difficult task.

What further complicates the task of the would-be therapist is that for type A individuals, the motivation to change their style of life is likely to be rather weak. The health-belief model developed by Rosenstock (1974) suggests that individuals are most likely to engage in preventive action when they feel that the disease to be avoided is a serious one, that they are susceptible to it, and that the benefits of preventive action outweigh the cost. For type A individuals, only the first of these conditions is met. While few would deny the seriousness of heart disease, most do not see any connection between their general lifestyle and an increased risk of developing heart disease. They do not consider their rushed, competitive lifestyle as pathological; on the contrary, both they and the society in which they live tend to view this lifestyle as normal and even praiseworthy. In fact, for many type A individuals there is a fear that any attempt to modify type A characteristics will make them less alive and productive.

The intensity of the reluctance to change will vary depending on the health status and demographic characteristics of the clientele being treated. Individuals who have suffered heart attacks will, as a group, consitute the most receptive clientele for therapeutic intervention (Friedman, 1978, 1979), while healthy, busy, occupationally successful persons—the group we have chosen to work with—form the other end of the motivational continuum. The men in this latter group do not deny the vulnerability of middle-aged men to heart disease, or even the potentially harmful effects of what they term "high-stress" jobs, but they also believe that the alternative to their present lifestyle may be literally worse than death itself. In their view, a time-pressured, competitive lifestyle is a necessary condition for the achievement and rewards that make life meaningful.

The fact that type A individuals are likely to be ambivalent in their desire to change and experience little social pressure to undertake treatment creates definite constrictions for the types of therapeutic intervention that can be attempted. The initial low investment in change, even in type A individuals who agree to enter a treatment program, places the onus on the therapist of establishing from the outset a clearly favorable cost–benefit ratio. Unless the individual rather quickly experiences benefits that are greater than the time, effort, and discomfort involved, the risk of drop-out is extremely high. The margin for therapeutic error here is a low one.

Balancing the type A individual's own resistance to change are the ethical constraints faced by the therapist working in an area where the risks of change are better documented than the benefits. At this point, we can only hope that certain types of individual and/or environmental changes will reduce the coronary risk associated with type A behavior, but we have far more certain knowledge of the personal, familial, and social disruption that can follow any radical change in lifestyle. Under these circumstances there are obvious ethical restrictions on the type of change that the clinician can responsibly advocate.

DEVELOPING A CONCEPTUAL MODEL FOR TYPE A INTERVENTION

When we began our work, the only explanatory model of type A behavior extant was that formulated by David Glass (Glass, 1977; Glass, Snyder, & Hollis, 1974). According to his view, type A behavior is essentially a coping response used to counter the threat of actual or potential loss of control. In contrast to individuals who are unable or unwilling to adapt to social norms, type A individuals have internalized thoroughly Western society's emphasis on the ability to control one's environment. The positive side of this mastery orientation is enhanced self-esteem and increased social reinforcement. The negative side of this adaptive pattern, in contrast, is the threat experienced in any situation in which the individual cannot be sure of complete control. When signs of possible loss of control do occur, as inevitably they must, the initial response is an increased effort to regain control, involving greater mental and physical exertion, stepped-up pace, heightened competitiveness, and so on (Glass, 1977; Glass & Carver, 1980). Even in situations where control is not attainable, type A subjects tend to avoid recognition of this fact and continue active struggling. Only when the cues signifying absence of control are highly salient will the type A individual lapse into a state of learned helplessness (Krantz, Glass, & Snyder, 1974; Glass, 1977). Thus, the usual coping style of the type A person is one of psychological and physiological hyperresponsiveness interspersed with periods of helplessness and hyporesponsiveness.

Our understanding of the physiological and biochemical processes linking this behavioral-emotional pattern to cardiovascular pathology is still tentative, for research on the issue is only in its early stages. Glass nevertheless postulates that the cycle of behavioral hyperreactivity and hyporeactivity in type A individuals may be accompanied by an analogous cycle of rising and falling catecholamines (Glass *et al.,* 1980). High levels of catecholamines increase coronary risk directly by accelerating the rate of arterial damage and inducing myocardial lesions (Raab, Chaplin, & Bajusz, 1964; Raab, Stark, MacMillan, & Gigee, 1961). They also lead to heart disease indirectly, by increasing the aggregation of blood platelets which, in turn, foster atherogenesis and thrombosis (Ardlie, Glen, & Schwartz, 1966; Duguid, 1946; Theorell, 1974). In short, by repeatedly engaging the body's nonspecific reaction to aversive stimulation, the type A person literally increases the wear and tear on his coronary arteries.

Assuming this pattern of functioning in type A individuals, it should be possible to reduce type A behavior by (a) restructuring the environment to reduce threats of loss of control, (b) changing the meaning that the person attributes to potentially stressful situations, and/or (c) reducing the intensity of the physical and emotional upheaval that characterizes the stress experience. The literature provides support for each of these therapeutic approaches. The sensitivity of type As to variations in environmental pressure has been well documented. In most laboratory studies of physiological and endocrine reactivity, baseline values for As and Bs are similar; only when the experimental challenge is introduced do As manifest greater sympathetic arousal than do Bs (Dembroski *et al.,* 1977, 1978, 1979; Friedman *et al.,* 1975; Glass *et al.,* 1980). Outside the laboratory, dramatic differences in the prevalence of type A in different settings (75% in Howard's study of Canadian senior managers versus 15% in a sample of Japanese-Americans living in Hawaii) also attest to the importance of environmental factors in eliciting the pattern. Therefore, if the degree of pressure in the natural environment could be reduced, even individuals predisposed to type A behavior would have less reason to manifest it.

A second point of intervention is to attempt to change the individual's perception of threat in situations involving loss of control. As Lazarus has repeatedly emphasized, stress lies in the eye of the beholder as much as in the external event itself; it is the individual's evaluation of the demands of a given situation as well as of the resources available to meet these demands that determines whether the situation will call forth a stress response (Lazarus, 1966). In fact, type Bs are capable of the same elevations in blood pressure and catecholamines under stress as are type As, but they undergo physiological upheaval less frequently because, in the absence of a strong need to control their environment, they perceive fewer situations as threatening and requiring maximal coping efforts (Glass *et al.,* 1982). Thus, if type As could learn to relinquish this exaggerated need for control, they could continue to live in the same pressured environment but experience the pressures very differently. The basic change envisaged by this approach is a cognitive one.

A third point of intervention is in the intensity of the stress response itself. If type A individuals can be helped to diminish the degree of autonomic and endocrine arousal they experience in stressful situations, then presumably much of the wear and tear on their coronary arteries could be avoided. Pharmaceutically, this could be done by administering sedative-type drugs, or beta-adrenergic blocking agents such as propanolol (Sigg, 1974). Alternatively, the same goal could be attempted by teaching individuals to consciously lower their level of emotional and physiological arousal by means of self-control techniques such as relaxation, meditation, and biofeedback. In this approach the emphasis is on retraining the physiological responses to stress.

THE INITIAL TREATMENT PROGRAM: RELAXATION VERSUS PSYCHOTHERAPY

In considering the different treatment alternatives, we eliminated environmental manipulation first. Attractive as this possibility might be theoretically, it did not seem to be feasible in practice. For the present anyway, the interest of business organizations in reducing the coronary risk of their employees did not extend to redesigning the work environment so as to reduce pressure. And to counsel individuals to leave high-pressure jobs in order to save their hearts was to provide advice that, in the present state of our knowledge, was possibly unethical and almost certainly likely to go unheeded. Pharmaceutic modification of physiological arousal by means of sedatives or beta-adrenergic blockers was the second alternative to be rejected, because there were ethical objections to exposing individuals to the risks involved in long-term use of potent drugs, at least until other avenues had been thoroughly explored. Furthermore, the low rate of success in treating hypertension (Sackett & Snow, 1979) alerted us to the motivational problems involved in asking asymptomatic persons to take medication over a long period of time.

The approach of teaching type A individuals to relinquish their need for mastery was a more interesting therapeutic possibility. If type A behavior emanates from a deep-seated need to exert continuous control over the environment, then modifying this need would certainly attack the problem at its roots. Moreover, Rosenman and Friedman, who had the greatest clinical experience to date in treating type A patients, stressed the importance of this type of philosophical reorientation (Rosenbaum & Friedman, 1977). Here too, however, we had doubts about the feasibility of the approach. Change at the level of deep-seated needs necessarily required psychoanalytically oriented psychotherapy—or so we thought at the time. This was not only an expensive and time-consuming process, but it was hardly likely to appeal to action-oriented, impatient type As. Even more to the point, Rosenman and Friedman found in their pilot study that such a therapy experience did not by itself lead to changes in type A behavior (Rosenman & Friedman, 1977).

The remaining treatment approach—that of teaching type A individuals self-control strategies to reduce arousal—was the most promising of the four in that it promised a maximum effect for a minimum therapeutic investment. Rather than seeking to fight the type A's need for control, we should instead capitalize on this need, but redirect it from control of the outside world to control of self. Thus, type A persons would be trained to become aware of their level of muscular tension and to attribute importance to bodily cues of loss of self-control, that is, heightened tension. When confronted with a challenging situation (e.g., a tense business meeting, or a difficult project with a tight deadline), the usual coping pattern or frenzied activity could then be replaced or at least supplemented by efforts to regulate bodily tension. Even if he could not always control the situation, the type A person could control his reactions to it.

The technique chosen for tension regulation was progressive muscular relaxation. Compared with biofeedback, yoga, meditation, etc., relaxation possesses the twin advantages of being inexpensive and portable. That is, no special equipment is required and the person can learn to practice relaxation unobtrusively throughout the day, rather than reserving his exercises for a specific time and place. Most important, relaxation is the tension-reducing technique for which the strongest evidence of physiological benefit currently exists (Warrenburg, Pagano, Woods, & Hlastala, 1980).

To test the benefits of teaching tension regulation to type A individuals, we recruited 27 extreme type A, physically healthy, occupationally successful middle-aged males for participation in a pilot project (Roskies *et al.,* 1978). The method of recruitment was by a newspaper article describing the program and the criteria for entry. In keeping with our belief that it was more economical to capitalize on the type A's existing motivational pattern rather than seeking to change it, the newspaper article stressed the inefficiency of the type A pattern, as well as its harmful physiological effects. The analogy used was of an engine continously racing at full speed. The planned intervention would not seek to change the individual's need or capacity to accomplish, but only this undifferentiated expenditure of energy. By learning how to pace himself—the promise held out by the program—the individual was likely to accomplish more with less strain.

The original aim was to recruit 30 men. The nature of our recruitment campaign, as well as the stringent requirements for entry (age 39–59, salary $25,000 +, absence of CHD, full-time managerial or professional position, nonsmoker, agreement to attend at least 12 of 14 sessions, willingness to deposit $100), seemed to appeal to the competitive instincts of type As and we were deluged by a flood of applicants. The Standardized Interview (Rosenman, 1977) was used to screen for type A characteristics. In this 15-minute interview, the interviewer poses a series of questions concerning the respondent's reactions to waiting in lines, need to win at games, desire for occupational achievement, and so on. The attitude of the interviewer is a challenging one, rather than the traditional clinical stance of sympathetic listening. On the basis of voice stylistics (loud, fast), motor mannerisms (tapping fingers, ticks), interpersonal interactions (interruptions, hostile remarks), as well as response content, individuals are classified as fully developed As (type A_1), possessing A characteristics in a less extreme form (type A_2), non-As (type B), or an almost equal measure of A and B characteristics (type X). All individuals selected for this pilot program were fully developed As (type A_1).

Of the 27 individuals who passed the physical examination (6 of the 33 men initially selected as A_1 were later placed in a separate group because of cardiac abnormalities revealed on an exercise EKG), 13 were randomly assigned to a 14-week tension-regulation program. In this program, individuals were first taught how to quantify their level of tension using a 0–10 scale and then instructed for a period of a week to record hourly the activity currently in progress and the level of tension experienced. This self-observation permitted participants to become more aware of variations in their level of arousal and the situations associated with these changes. At the same time, a sequence of relaxation exercises designed to foster physiological self-control was introduced. A 15-minute modified version of Jacobsonian muscle relaxation (Jacobson, 1938) was presented and participants were asked to practice this exercise twice daily following recorded instructions, noting tension levels before and after each practice session. After a few weeks of this regime, the muscle-relaxation exercise was shortened to 5 minutes and specific neck, shoulder, and breathing exercises were added.

Eventually, participants reached a level of proficiency at which they both could detect early warning signs of physical tension and could relax on command. The task now became one of using these skills to maintain a comfortably low level of tension. Regularly occurring events in the daily routine (e.g., shaving, opening one's agenda book, driving the car) became signals to check tension level and adjust it if necessary. Even when unexpected or strong arousal did occur (e.g., a discourteous driver cutting in, an argument with one's superior), relaxation techniques could be used to lower the tension level.

Although we had previously rejected the possibility of using psychotherapy for nonclinical subjects, the necessity of finding a control condition that would be credible to these type A men led us to turn to the psychotherapy unit of the hospital in which the program was carried out. But instead of simply serving as an attention-placebo condition, the therapists concerned, experienced and enthusiastic practitioners of brief psychotherapy, utilized their 14 sessions to run an active treatment program. Based on their view of type A behavior as an initially useful solution to a conflictual family constellation in childhood, the aim of therapy became one of showing these men how their childhood perceptions and responses distorted their current behavior. The assumption here was that once the individual understood why he was behaving in a certain way, he would be free to change this automatic pattern. While there was no explicit instruction in behavior change, the male and female cotherapists did serve as role models for a more relaxed, less competitive behavior style.

The results of this study were encouraging in that without apparent change of their diet, exercise, or smoking habits, and while continuing to work the same hours per week and to carry the same type of responsibility, men in the behavior therapy group showed significant decreases on physiological (serum cholesterol, systolic blood pressure) and psychological (time pressure, life dissatisfaction) risk factors (Roskies *et al.,* 1978). Even more important, six months later, most of these changes had been maintained (Roskies *et al.,* 1979). However, contrary to our expectations, men in the psychotherapy group showed almost as good treatment effects immediately after treatment; although the drop in serum cholesterol was larger and more consistent for the relaxtion group, differences between the two treatment conditions were not statistically significant. They became so only at the follow-up (Roskies *et al.,* 1979).

FROM MUSCLES TO COGNITIONS

In spite of the fact that relaxation training had proved to be a potent method for regulating tension in type A men, we grew increasingly dissatisfied with its limitations as an all-purpose coping technique. There were too many stress episodes where simply relaxing muscles did not speak directly either to the subjective experience of the person or to the situation at hand. For instance, many of our participants did not experience stress primarily through muscle tension, but rather in such forms as obsessive worrying, racing thoughts, anger outburts, and so on. For these individuals, muscle relaxation was a circuitous route for regulating tension. The difficulty of teaching coping solely as relaxation became most apparent in situations where effective coping was not simply a question of reducing the immediate discomfort, but also involved taking action to modify the situation that produced the tension. The manager constantly suffering from the effects of too much to do in too little time could certainly benefit from learning to keep his cool under time pressure, but he was likely to benefit even more from learning to allocate his time more effectively, to refuse inopportune requests, and so on.

The problem here was not to find a more powerful coping technique to substitute for relaxation, but rather to deal with the fact that no single coping technique can adequately respond to the variety of situations in which stress is experienced and the many forms it takes. We were supported in this intuitive dissatisfaction with a program based on a single coping strategy by the findings of some recent studies on how normal people in the community actually cope with the stresses in their daily lives. These findings clearly indicate that, far from relying on one standard coping technique, well-functioning individuals tend to use a number of different strategies in any one situation and to vary strategies from one situation to another (Folkman & Lazarus, 1980; Ilfeld, 1980). To conform with this concept of effective coping, the treatment program would have to be radically redesigned. Instead of teaching the type A person to replace a harmful coping pattern (physiological arousal) with a less harmful one (muscle relaxation), it would be necessary to introduce a repertoire of coping strategies.

Furthermore, this new program would have to pay increased attention to the crucial role of cognitions in determining how much stress was actually experienced. In asking individuals to relax their muscles, we had tried to modify the physiological response to a given stimulus. In fact, we had altered as well the mental set with which the person approached a potential stress episode, and participants in the program reported that sometimes this changed focus was sufficient to prevent the stress from ever occurring. An individual who entered a business meeting prepared for the possibility of becoming tense but feeling confident in his ability to control tension through relaxation often did not perceive events in the same way and would find himself with less tension to regulate. This experience is consonant, of course, with Lazarus's view that cognitive appraisal is the key element in determining whether certain events or bodily changes do, in fact, become stresses (Lazarus, 1966; Lazarus & Launier, 1978).

The fact that we had inadvertently produced cognitive changes that led to beneficial results was rewarding, but it also presented the challenge of learning to make explicit that which had been implicit in the first program. A brief treatment program might not be able to significantly alter such global concepts as "need for mastery," but it could seek to alter some of the expectations and interpretations that the individual brought to the specific stress episodes. The unexpectedly good results of participants in the psychotherapy group, almost as good as those in the relaxation program, was another incentive for examining how techniques devoted to changing cognitions could be incorporated into a behavioral treatment program.

THE SECOND TREATMENT PROGRAM: A COGNITIVE-BEHAVIORAL APPROACH

By the late fall of 1978 we were ready to recruit a new sample to test a multifaceted cognitive-behavioral program. Instead of the very select, highly motivated, extreme type As that constituted the sample for the initial treatment study, this time we sought to recruit men more representative of the population of type As as a whole. With the cooperation of medical and personnel officers of three large Canadian companies, letters were sent to all men at a designated middle-management level inviting them to participate in a research stress management program. Entry criteria were much less stringent than for the previous program: All men at the designated occupational level who did not manifest overt signs of heart disease would be accepted. The degree to which participants had to commit themselves to the program was also considerably less. In contrast to the first study, there was no deposit and both the initial screening interview and the treatment program were held at the worksite.

Sixty-six men volunteered during the two week recruitment period in December 1978. Unlike the men in the first sample, all of whom had been English-speaking, 44% of this group was francophone. Because these men were chosen at the middle-manager level, rather than the senior-manager and professional levels of the first study, they were also considerably younger ($\overline{X}$ = 41.33 versus $\overline{X}$ = 47.6). In this study smokers were not excluded and, in fact, 30% of the sample were currently smokers. Most important of all, however, was the difference in type A status. In contrast to the first study, where all participants had been classified as extreme type As (A_1), here only 47% of the sample (31 men) were placed in that category. An additional 40% were less extreme As, while 13% were clıssified as non-As (types B and X).

Forty of these sixty-six men were randomly assigned to a 13-week immediate treatment program, while 26 constituted a waiting-list control. The men in the immediate treatment condition met weekly in groups of 10 (there were 2 anglophone and 2 francophone groups) for 13 1½ hour sessions between February and June 1979. Participants in the waiting-list control condition were offered the same treatment between October 1979 and February 1980.

There is no single criterion of success in modifying type A behavior, particularly in a nonclinical population where it is unfeasible to use cardiac morbidity and mortality as outcome measures. Based on our belief that it was the frequency, intensity, and duration of sympathetic arousal that constituted the pathogenic elements in the type A pattern, we attempted to measure change by charting a number of indices of this arousal, in both laboratory and field situation (Roskies, 1979). Prior to and immediately following the intervention, all participants were exposed to a standard stress situation in the laboratory, and fluctuations in systolic blood pressure, diastolic blood pressure, heart rate, plasma epinephrine, and plasma norepinephrine before, during, and after the task were recorded.

In the field situation, one working day every fortnight during the course of the project was designated as a monitoring day (a total of nine monitoring days). During this day, four types of measures were tracked: psychological state, blood pressure, urinary catecholamines, and serum cholesterol and testosterone. Participants were asked to record hourly levels of muscular tension, irritability, time pressure, and performance (using a 0-10 scale) and follow this by a blood pressure reading using an electronic machine—Labtronix 4000—designed for home use. Urine for analysis of catecholamine levels was collected for 24 hours divided into three time periods: the night before the working day, the working day itself, and the evening after.

Treatment Rationale

In opting for a multifaceted program, we did not intend to simply present a smorgasbord of coping strategies to be used *ad libitum*. On the contrary, if the specific coping strategies taught were to be used meaningfully, we felt that it was essential that program participants acquire an understanding first of the deficiencies in their present mode of operating and second, of how these individual coping techniques fit together to form a pattern of improved coping. The first step in the development of the program, therefore, became one of constructing a treatment rationale.

The starting point of this rationale was the view that instead of marking a disruption of normal routine, stress is an inevitable part of it (Roskies & Lazarus, 1980). Most of the threats and challenges we face are not in form of major tragedy but rather of minor irritation. It is the surly son at the breakfast table, the traffic light that won't turn green, the job project stagnating in a series of repetitious committee meetings, the co-worker who won't listen, and so on that account for most of the strain on the human system. But while the person cannot control, except to a limited degree, the demands, challenges, and threats that impinge on his daily life, he can play an active role in determining the impact of a potential stressor and in shaping the course of a stress episode. An individual who is mentally prepared to encounter these inevitable daily hassles, and who also has a well-developed repertoire of coping strategies as well as confidence in his ability to use them is much less likely to be thrown off balance by a potentially stressful episode. Even in those relatively rare occasions when the minor stressor becomes a major one and the banal is transformed into the tragic, such a person will be better equipped to handle the situation as adequately as possible (Benner, Roskies, & Lazarus, 1980).

The type A managers with whom we work are characterized by a hypersensitivity to the hassles of daily life and invest a maximum of effort and energy in combating them. That this type of coping response is effective, at least to a certain degree, is attested to by their occupational success and their ability to maintain family relationships and community activities. Where the type A pattern is deficient is in its stereotypy of perception and response. Instead of carefully evaluating the nature of a given stressor and the resources available to deal with it, and then selecting an appropriate coping strategy, the type A person tends to behave in an automatic "all or none" fashion. Thus, an inattentive waiter, an unfriendly co-worker, and an alienated child are all perceived at the same level of severe threat. Similarly, the same fighting response will be used indiscriminately whether the situation is one of gaining a desired job or mourning its loss. These frequent, intense, and undifferentiated mobilizations constitute a maximum expenditure of energy for what at times may be minimal results. The physiological cost, however, is consistently high.

In contrast to this automatic, stereotyped response pattern is the individual who is aware of his thoughts, feelings, and physical and behavioral reactions and exerts active control over them. The competent coper is no more able than the deficient one to completely avoid potentially stressful situations, but his mental preparedness for the possibility, his differentiated appraisals of events (internal and external) and his broad repertoire of coping techniques allow him to respond in a manner that maximizes impact and minimizes strain. The differential cost of effective versus ineffective coping is analogous to the economical use of energy expended by an experienced hiker climbing a mountain compared with the huffing and puffing of an out-of-condition person who inadvertently finds himself on the same trail.

Fortunately, effective coping is a learnable skill. The same motivation and practice that lead an individual to improve his tennis game or acquire proficiency in a foreign language can also be used to attain more differentiated evaluations of stress situations and more flexible responses to them. The type A person who follows our program may still choose to use his old pattern of coping responses in certain situations, but this will now constitute an informed choice rather than simply a reflexive response.

Treatment Content

The coping techniques chosen for this program were muscle relaxation (Bernstein & Borkovec, 1973), rational-emotive thinking (RET; Ellis & Grieger, 1977; Maultsby & Ellis, 1978) communication skills training (Stuart, 1974), problem-solving (D'Zurilla & Goldfried, 1971), and, in a special role, an adaptation of stress inoculation (Meichenbaum, 1977). While the treatment rationale emphasized the development of a broad repertoire of coping skills, there was nothing in the rationale itself that would guide us to select these specific techniques from the multitude of those available. Instead, the choice of specific techniques was influenced by a number of other considerations.

First among these considerations was a therapeutic model previously developed by Jacqueline Avard, a collaborator in this research project. According to this model, personal effectiveness is defined as the ability to function well in and maintain equilibrium among physical, emotional, social, and cognitive functioning. In designing the program, therefore, we included at least one technique for treating problems in each of these four areas. Relaxation was seen as particularly useful for problems of *physical* tension regulation, RET for modulation of irrational *emotional* outbursts, communication skills for reducing *interpersonal* friction, and so on.

A second consideration guiding the choice of techniques was their suitability for type A individuals. The literature contains a multitude of coping strategies, all of which seek either to regulate cognitive, emotional, and physiological distress; to reduce the trauma in interpersonal interactions; or to facilitate decision-making. Because of subtle differences in rationale and procedure, however, some are more obviously relevant to the coping problems of type A individuals and, equally important, are more congruent with their self-image. Thus it is easier for a type A individual to see himself as too frequently angry rather than as not loving enough, to accept that he argues abrasively rather than in a nonassertive manner, or to view his problems in decision-making as related to trying to do too much rather than having difficulty in getting started.

Using this criterion of acceptability, we chose communication skills training rather than assertion training, adapted RET to focus on the problem of anger, and chose time pressure as the prototypical problem for stress inoculation.

A final consideration governing choice was the ease with which specific techniques could become an integral part of the daily routine. Rather than having group members set aside a specific time period each day to practice stress reduction, the aim was to have them repeatedly monitor and reduce physical, emotional, and cognitive tension throughout the course of the day. Following this criterion, we eliminated "nonportable" techniques, such as jogging, yoga, and meditation, and concentrated instead on strategies that could be used during a heated business discussion or a confrontation with an untidy teen-aged son.

Once the specific strategies had been chosen, the next problem was to decide in what order to present them. In accordance with our belief that, in the absence of symptoms or social pressure as motivators, it was essential for the therapy itself to maintain a favorable cost–benefit ratio, we attempted to order the presentation of techniques according to their consumer acceptability. Progressive muscular relaxation was chosen as the first technique taught because it is among the easiest to use and the benefits are almost immediate. Although participants are likely to show slightly more resistance to the principles of RET, practice in the control of negative emotions, such as anger, anxiety, guilt, and depression, also brings an immediate increase in sense of well-being. For this reason, RET was the second technique presented. Communication and problem-solving skills, designed to reduce the stress associated with interpersonal conflict and decision-making, followed next in the sequence. Once participants were proficient in the use of each technique individually, a modified form of stress inoculation was introduced to help them learn how to combine techniques for maximum impact.

Teaching Methods

The process of learning to monitor and reduce tension is similar to the acquisition of any complex skill. Initially, the willing pupil is only likely to reproduce the model awkwardly and imperfectly, whether the instructor is demonstrating a new tennis stroke or muscular relaxation. With regular practice and instructor feedback, however, he or she will gradually increase in ability until the new skill can be executed with ease, and eventually it will become a smoothly functioning part of the total repertoire.

To facilitate this learning process, the various techniques were broken down into small units and taught as a series of steps. Initially, the person would simply be asked to observe and chart the behavior targeted for intervention. When the new coping strategy was formally presented, these previously recorded problem situations became the first practice material. The person would be asked to fantasize the stressful situation, with its accompanying discomfort, and then to fantasize using the new coping strategy to reduce tension. The next stage was the practice of the new strategy "after the fact." Following an upsetting experience, group members were instructed to mentally replay the scene and imagine how their emotional reactions to these events might have been changed by the application of this technique. The final stage was the use of the technique in the heat of battle itself, beginning with situations that were less upsetting or threatening, and progressing gradually to the use of tension-reduction even in the midst of a full-scale crisis.

Shaping through corrective feedback constituted an essential part of the learning process. Between weekly sessions, the men were assigned homework of which they were asked to keep written records. This material could then be used by the therapist to provide suggestions for improved performance. There was also actual practice of techniques during sessions under the supervision and correction of the therapist.

Practice between sessions was necessary if proficiency in the use of techniques was to be attained. To make this homework as palatable and as feasible as possible, we asked participants to take a few minutes at a time, several times a day, rather than concentrating practice in a few massed sessions. The longest single homework session was the 20 minutes required for the long version of the muscular relaxation tape and this was terminated after four weeks. To further increase adherence, we analyzed the homework records for general trends, such as the most frequently chosen relaxation cues, or the variety of situations to which problem-solving skills had been applied, and then fed this information back to participants.

The group format provided considerable therapeutic assistance in the acquisition of these new skills. Many of the stressful situations encountered were common to all the participants, and the discussion of problems was leavened by humor and camaraderie. Also, other group members were often quick to spot ways in which the effectiveness of the techniques could be improved, or at least the frequency with which they were used increased.

The actual steps used in the teaching of a coping strategy varied, of course, with the particular strategy under consideration (cf. Roskies & Avard, 1982). Nevertheless, the way in which RET was presented serves as a convenient illustration of the teaching process. In the week preceding the introduction of this coping strategy, individuals would be asked to chart situations with strong unpleasant feelings, noting both the details of the situation and the quality and intensity of the feelings experienced. In the treatment session following the observation period, the therapist would use these homework records as the basis for a discussion on the dysfunctional nature of blind anger and the advantages to be gained from learning to control negative emotions. The stage having been set, one would then present the postulates of RET—first, that it is individuals rather than situations that determine what feelings are experienced, and, second, that many of our overreactions to disappointing or irritating situations are caused by the irrational expectations we have of ourselves, other people, and the world in general.

Given the high intelligence and combative nature of the type A individuals participating in the program, it is not surprising that most did not acquiesce passively to the attempt to change familiar patterns of behavior. On the contrary, the therapist's presentation was usually followed by a multitude of objections. Participants questioned, for instance, whether blowing off steam is not necessary to maintain health, whether control of anger will not lead to emotional flatness, and so on. The therapeutic task here was the usual one of correcting false perceptions and providing support for embarking on the change process. More particularly, the therapist continuously emphasized that the ability to keep one's emotions in control would permit the person to take more effective action. Contrary to the type A's commonly expressed fear, the replacement of habitual type A behavior by alternative coping strategies need not diminish performance, and might even enhance it.

Finally, the actual procedures involved in using RET were described. In the adapted version used in our program, this involved teaching individuals to conduct their own debates to dispute irrational beliefs (Maultsby & Ellis, 1978). Specific examples of commonly held irrational beliefs were presented. Participants were then asked to recall one of the upsetting situations recorded during the previous week, to recreate as fully as possible the feelings experienced at that time, and then to try to shift the feelings into a lower key. For instance, irritation, annoyance, frustration, disappointment, and so on were suggested as more rational responses than fury. Once the person had modulated his feelings, he was asked to recall what he had said to himself to change his irrational thinking and thereby modify his feelings.

During the course of the session the men would as a group silently go through the steps of the exercise, and then two or three of them would share their experiences with the other members. In the period between sessions, men were asked to hold three short practice sessions daily in which the individual imagined two upsetting situations with accompanying negative feelings each time, modified them, and then recorded the self-statements used to produce the changes. Discussion of these group practices and homework assignments permitted the therapist to point out the irrational nature of many common beliefs, as well as providing an opportunity to suggest more rational self-statements.

Reduction of negative emotions in imagery gradually changed to modification of feelings on the spot. Initially, participants would use rational emotive thinking to calm down more quickly when they were already upset but, as the weeks progressed, group members increasingly reported success in attenuating the full force of the emotional storm, and sometimes even heading it off completely.

Stress Inoculation as an Integrative Technique

During the course of treatment, participants would often mention that they had spontaneously combined two or more techniques in a given stress situation. For instance, a man baited by a surly clerk would first use relaxation and RET to lower his internal thermostat and then invoke his communication skills to state his needs as clearly and calmly as possible. Where the problem was not helped simply by communication, problem-solving would be added to the list of coping strategies. To provide a formal rationale and procedure for this process of combining strategies, a modified form of stress inoculation (Meichenbaum, 1977) was added to the program as an "umbrella" technique.

The analogy used in presenting stress inoculation was that of playing tennis. Up to now, participants had learned and practiced individual strokes. To play a good game of tennis, however, the person must be able to put these strokes together into a smoothly flowing process. Expert players have the additional skill of being able to plot strategy in advance, but, if necessary, changing this strategy as the game proceeds.

Stress episodes can be divided into those that can be predicted in advance on the basis of past experience, and those that arise unexpectedly. The former are far more numerous than we commonly believe, if we are prepared to accurately examine patterns of behavior and interaction. To cite an example not usually associated with stress, the Christmas holiday is habitually visualized as a time of joy and good cheer. Accurate recollection of previous holidays, however, permits individuals to pinpoint the stresses that they personally experienced even during a good holiday. These can include the time pressure of buying and wrapping gifts, guilt and anxiety concerning money expended, physical and mental exhaustion from too many social gatherings, interpersonal tensions generated by the gathering of the clan, and so on. To be aware of the potential stresses inherent in the Christmas holiday is not to become a Scrooge, but rather permits the person to take steps in advance of the event to modify the situation and/or his reactions. By this preparatory coping, a good holiday becomes an even better one. This same procedure is even easier to use with regularly recurring situations that have more obvious negative connotations, for instance, family arguments about getting to the theatre on time, waiting in a bank line, and so on.

Even with the best of preparation, individuals will occasionally find themselves experiencing stress. There are also the stressful situations that are unanticipated and unexpected. Here it is important for the individual to be sensitive to and correctly label physical and cognitive signals of stress so that remedial action can be promptly initiated. Essentially, this involves recognizing the discomfort but using one's coping skills to manage the situation rather than catastrophizing or feeling overwhelmed. For example, the individual might defuse the upset by transforming negative self-statements into positive ones, by actively relaxing tense muscles, or by employing any other of the previously learned coping strategies that are appropriate to the present situation.

Because time pressure constituted a universal stressor for this group, we used it as an example on which to practice stress inoculation procedures. First, participants were instructed to monitor feelings of time pressure in the course of their week, noting the circumstances in which they occurred and the emotional and physical reactions they engendered. The next step was to consider procedures for changing the situation and/or the reactions. These could include allowing time for inevitable emergencies and interruptions in drawing up the daily agenda, assigning a priority order to tasks, and discussing unrealistic demands from supervisors or peers in a problem-centered manner. Should the individual find himself pressured by time in spite of these efforts, he could seek to reduce his distress by actively relaxing and emitting reassuring and positively reinforcing self-statements. The aim here was both to reduce the frequency with which the individual found himself under pressure of time, and to teach him to better cope with it when it did occur.

CONCLUDING COMMENTS

This chapter cannot discuss the data of the second treatment study because they are still being analyzed. Nevertheless some comments about the feasibility of this type of intervention and the clinical problems encountered might be useful at this time.

When we first began our work, we were concerned that type A individuals without overt heart disease would not be motivated to seek change. To overcome this anticipated reluctance, we launched what we considered to be a clever recruitment campaign. The fact that we immediately attracted our full quota of volunteers was testimony, so we thought, to the appeal of these specific recruitment procedures. To test the second program, in contrast, we launched a much more low-keyed appeal. Here too, however, we managed to attract almost a full quota (66 of the 80 originally wanted) in a two-week period just before Christmas. This suggests that recruitment is a less imposing hurdle than we initially imagined it to be. It appears that stress management is a topic that concerns healthy, occupationally successful, middle-aged men, and one for which they are prepared to accept professional guidance.

Where recruitment procedures do make a difference is in the type of sample that will be constituted. By imposing age limits, (39–59), health limits (nonsmokers), and language limits (all English-speaking) in the first study, we attracted a sample that was quite homogeneous in life situation. The second treatment program, in contrast, used occupational level as the sole demographic criterion for entry and this made for much more heterogeneity. Some of our middle managers, for instance, were in their early 30s and just beginning their occupational rise while others, in their late 50s, had long since plateaued and were marking time till retirement. Even more important, all participants in the first program had accepted prior to entry that they shared a common problem of extreme type A status. In contrast, participants in the second program knew that there was a range of A status present (from individuals classified as extreme type A to those classified as clear-cut non-As), and consequently, any individual could believe that the problems being discussed did not apply fully to him. Because of this heterogeneity in life situation and lack of a clearly defined common problem, it was much more difficult in the second program to form a cohesive group and to fully utilize the group as a source of social support.

The presence or absence of stringent selection criteria also affected the eventual level of commitment to the program. In the first program, all men had overtly to accept that they were of high coronary risk because of their type A status, they had to make the effort to come to the hospital for the initial interview, and, most important of all, they had to deposit $100 as a guarantee that they would attend at least 12 of 14 sessions. This screening procedure almost certainly eliminated a number of potential participants, but of those who did complete it, only 2 men dropped out and 85% of the total sample (23 of 27 men) attended the minimum 12 sessions. The second program, in contrast, did not require either overt acknowledgment of coronary risk, the deposit of $100, or even the effort of leaving the worksite for the initial interview. That participants in the second program were also genuinely interested is shown by the low drop-out rate (only 5 of 66) and by their compliance with the cumbersome evaluation procedures. But the difference in level of commitment is also shown by the fact that only 72% (29 of 40) met the much less stringent criterion of attending at least 8 of the 13 sessions.

In short, the first study chose a sample that was homogeneous, highly motivated, and probably unrepresentative of the population as a whole. The second sample was far more representative but less cohesive and less committed. Not surprisingly, the wider the net cast, the less select the catch. Researchers will have to weigh for themselves the relative advantages of different types of samples, but in view of the variance to be found within a type A population, the characteristics of the specific sample on which a treatment program is tested are almost as important as the content of the treatment program itself.

REFERENCES

Ardlie, N. G., Glen, G., & Schwartz, C. J. Influence of catecholamines on nucleotide-induced platelet aggregation. *Nature,* 1966, *212,* 415–417.

Bandura, A. Self-efficacy: Toward a unifying theory of behavioral change. *Psychological Review,* 1977, *84,* 191–215.

Benner, P., Roskies, E., & Lazarus, R. S. Stress and coping under extreme circumstances. In J. Dimsdale (Ed.), *Survivors, victims and perpetrators.* New York: Wiley, 1980.

Bernstein, D. A., & Borkovec, T. D. *Progressive relaxation training.* Champaign, Ill.: Research Press, 1973.

Blumenthal, J. A., Williams, R. B., Kong, Y., Thompson, L. W., Jenkins, C. D., & Roseman, R. H. Coronary-prone behavior and angiographically documented coronary disease. *Circulation,* 1978, *58,* 634–639.

Blumenthal, J. A., Williams, R. S., Williams, R. B., & Wallace, A. G. Effects of exercise on the type A (coronary-prone) behavior pattern. *Psychosomatic Medicine,* 1979, *42,* 583.

Caffrey, B. Reliability and validity of personality and behavioral measures in a study of coronary heart disease. *Journal of Chronic Diseases,* 1968, *21,* 191–204.

Cohen, J. B., Syme, S. L., Jenkins, C. D., Kagan, A., & Zyzanski, S. J. Cultural context of type A behavior and risk for CHD: A study of Japanese-American males. *Journal of Behavioral Medicine,* 1979, *2,* 374–384.

Dembroski, T. M., MacDougall, J. M., & Shields, J. L. Physiologic reactions to social challenge in persons evidencing the Type A coronary-prone behavior pattern. *Journal of Human Stress,* 1977, *3,* 2–10.

Dembroski, T. M., MacDougall, J. M., Shields, J. L., Pettito, J., & Lushene, R. Components of the Type A coronary-prone behavior pattern and cardiovascular responses to psychomotor performance challenge. *Journal of Behavioral Medicine,* 1978, *1,* 159–176.

Dembroski, T. M., MacDougall, J. M., Herd, J. A., & Shields, J. L. Effect of level of challenge on pressor and heart rate responses in Type A and B subjects. *Journal of Applied Social Psychology,* 1979, *9,* 209–228.

Duguid, J. B. Thrombosis as a factor in the pathogenesis of coronary artherosclerosis. *Journal of Pathology and Bacteriology,* 1946, *58,* 207–212.
Dunbar, H. F. *Psychosomatic diagnosis.* New York: Paul B. Hoeber, 1943.
D'Zurilla, T. J., & Goldfried, M. R. Problem solving and behavior modification. *Journal of Abnormal Psychology,* 1971, *78,* 107–126.
Ellis, A., & Grieger, R. (Eds.). *Handbook of rational-emotive therapy.* New York: Springer Publishing, 1977.
Folkman, S., & Lazarus, R. S. An analysis of coping in a middle-aged community sample. *Journal of Health and Social Behavior,* 1980, *21,* 219–239.
Franks, C. M., & Wilson, G. T. (Eds.). *Annual review of behavior therapy: Theory and practice.* New York: Brunner/Mazel, 1979.
Friedman, M. Modifying "type A" behavior in heart attack patients. *Primary Cardiology,* 1978, *4,* 9–13.
Friedman, M. The modification of type A behavior in post-infarction patients. *American Heart Journal,* 1979, *97,* 551–560.
Friedman, M., Byers, S. O., Diamant, J., & Rosenman, R. H. Plasma catecholamine response of coronary-prone subjects (Type A) to a specific challenge. *Metabolism,* 1975, *4,* 205–210.
Gildea, E. Special features of personality which are common to certain psychosomatic disorders. *Psychosomatic Medicine,* 1949, *11,* 273–277.
Glass, D. C. *Behavior patterns, stress and coronary disease.* Hillsdale, N. J.: Lawrence Erlbaum, 1977.
Glass, D. C., & Carver, C. S. Environmental stress and the type A response. In A. Baum & J. E. Singer (Eds.), *Advances in environmental psychology* (Vol. 2). *Applications of personal control.* Hillsdale, N. J.: Lawrence Erlbaum, 1980.
Glass, D. C., Snyder, M. L., & Hollis, J. F. Time urgency and the type A coronary-prone behavior pattern. *Journal of Applied Social Psychology,* 1974, *4,* 125–140.
Glass, D. C., Krakoff, L. R., Contrada, R., Hilton, W. F., Kehoe, K., Mannucci, E. G., Collins, C., Snow, B., & Elting, E. Effect of harassment and competition upon cardiovascular and catecholamine responses in type A and type B individuals. *Psychophysiology,* 1980, *17,* 453–463.
Haynes, S. G., Feinleib, M., & Kannel, W. B. The relationship of psychosocial factors to coronary heart disease in the Framingham study: III. 8 year incidence of CHD. *American Journal of Epidemiology,* 1980, *111,* 37–58.
Howard, J. H., Cunningham, D. A., & Rechnitzer, P. A. Health patterns associated with Type A behavior: A managerial population. *Journal of Human Stress,* 1976, *2,* 24–33.
Ilfeld, F. W. Coping styles of Chicago adults: Description. *Journal of Human Stress,* 1980, *6,* 2–10.
Jacobson, E. *Progressive relaxation* (2nd ed.). Chicago: University of Chicago Press, 1938.
Jenkins, C. D., Rosenman, R. H., & Friedman, M. Replicability of rating the coronary-prone behavior pattern. *British Journal of Preventive and Social Medicine,* 1968, *22,* 16–22.
Jenkins, C. D., Zyzanski, S. J., & Rosenman, R. H. Risk of new myocardial infarction in middle-aged men with manifest heart disease. *Circulation,* 1976, *53,* 342–347.
Jenni, M. A., & Wollersheim, J. P. Cognitive therapy, stress management training and the Type A behavior pattern. *Cognitive Therapy and Research,* 1979, *3,* 61–75.
Kemple, C. Rorschach method and psychosomatic diagnosis: Personality traits of patients with rheumatic disease, hypertension, cardiovascular disease, coronary occlusion and fracture. *Psychosomatic Medicine,* 1945, *7,* 85–89.
Krantz, D. S., Glass, D. C. & Snyder, M. L. Helplessness, stress level and the coronary-prone behavior pattern. *Journal of Experimental Social Psychology,* 1974, *19,* 284–300.

Krantz, D. S., Sanmorco, M. I., Selvester, R. H., & Matthews, K. A. Psychological correlates of progression of atherosclerosis in men. *Psychosomatic Medicine,* 1979, *41,* 467–476.

Lazarus, R. S., *Psychological stress and the coping process.* New York: McGraw-Hill, 1966.

Lazarus, R. S., & Launier, R. Stress-related transactions between person and environment. In L. A. Pervin & M. Lewis (Eds.), *Perspectives in interactional psychology.* New York: Plenum Press, 1978.

Manuck, S. B., Craft, S. A., & Gold, K. J. Coronary-prone behavior pattern and cardiovascular response. *Psychophysiology,* 1978, *15,* 403–411.

Maultsby, M., & Ellis, A. Techniques for using rational-emotive imagery. In A. Ellis & E. Abraham (Eds.), *Brief psychotherapy in medical and health practice.* New York: Springer Publishing, 1978.

Meichenbaum, D. *Cognitive behavior modification: An integrative approach.* New York: Plenum Press, 1977.

Menninger, K. A., & Menninger, W. C. Psychoanalytic observations in cardiac disorders. *American Heart Journal,* 1936, *11,* 10–26.

Mettlin, C. Occupational careers and the prevention of coronary-prone behavior. *Social Science and Medicine,* 1976, *10,* 367–373.

Osler, W. *Lectures on angina pectoris and allied states.* New York: D. Appleton & Company Inc., 1892.

Raab, W., Stark, E., MacMillan, W. H., & Grigee, W. R. Sympathetic origin and antiadrenergic prevention of stress-induced myocardial lesions. *American Journal of Cardiology,* 1961, *8,* 203–211.

Raab, W., Chaplin, J. B., & Bajusz, E. Myocardial necroses produced in domesticated rats and in wild rats by sensory and emotional stresses. *Proceedings of the Society of Experimental Biology and Medicine,* 1964, *116,* 665–669.

The Review Panel on Coronary-Prone Behavior and Coronary Heart Disease. Coronary-prone behavior and coronary heart disease: A critical review. *Circulation,* 1981, *63,* 1199–1215.

Rosenman, R. H. The interview method of assessment of the coronary-prone behavior pattern. In T. M. Dembroski, S. M. Weiss, & J. L. Shields (Eds.), *Proceedings of the forum on coronary-prone behavior.* Washington, D. C.: Dept. of Health, Education and Welfare. Publication No. (NIH) 78–1451, 1977.

Rosenman, R. H., & Friedman, M. Modifying Type A behaviour pattern. *Journal of Psychosomatic Research,* 1977, *21,* 323–333.

Rosenman, R. H., Friedman, M., Straus, R., Wurm, M., Kositchek, R., Hahn, W., & Werthessen, N. T. A predictive study of coronary heart diesease: The Western Collaborative Group Study. *Journal of the American Medical Association,* 1964, *189,* 15–22.

Rosenman, R. H., Brand, R. J., Jenkins, C. D., Friedman, M., Straus, R.,& Wurm, M. Coronary heart disease in the Western Collaborative Group Study: Final follow-up experience of 8½ years. *Journal of the American Medical Association,* 1975, *233,* 872–877.

Rosenman, R. H., Brand, R. J., Sholtz, R. I., & Friedman, M. Multivariate prediction of coronary heart disease during 8.5 year follow-up in the Western Collaborative Group Study. *American Journal of Cardiology,* 1976, *37,* 902–910.

Rosenstock, I. M. The Health Belief Model and preventive health behavior. *Health Education Monographs,* 1974, *2,* 354–386.

Roskies, E. Evaluating improvement in the coronary-prone (type A) behavior pattern. In D. J. Osborne, M. M. Gruneberg, & J. R. Eisler (Eds.), *Research in psychology and medicine* (Vol. 1). New York: Academic Press, 1979.

Roskies, E. Consideration in developing a treatment program for the coronary prone (type A) behavior pattern. In P. Davidson & S. M. Davidson (Eds.), *Behavioral medicine: Changing health lifestyles.* New York: Brunner/Mazel, 1980.

Roskies, E., & Avard, J. Teaching healthy managers to control their coronary-prone (type A) behavior. In K. Blakenstein & J. Polivy (Eds.), *Self-control and self-modification of emotional behavior*. New York: Plenum Press, 1982.
Roskies, E., & Lazarus, R. S. Coping theory and the teaching of coping skills. In P. O. Davidson & S. M. Davidson (Eds.), *Behavioral medicine: Changing health lifestyles*. New York: Brunner/Mazel, 1980.
Roskies, E., Spevack, M., Surkis, A., Cohen, C., & Gilman, S. Changing the coronary-prone (type A) behavior pattern in a non-clinical population. *Journal of Behavioral Medicine*, 1978, *1*, 201–215.
Roskies, E., Kearney, H., Spevack, M., Surkis, A., Cohen, C., & Gilman, S. Generalizability and durability of treatment effects in an intervention program for coronary-prone (type A) managers. *Journal of Behavioral Medicine*, 1979, *2*, 195–207.
Sackett, D. L., & Snow, J. C. The magnitude and measurement of compliance. In R. B. Haynes, D. W. Taylor, & D. L. Sackett (Eds.), *Compliance in health care*. Baltimore: Johns Hopkins University Press, 1979.
Shapiro, A., Non-A, non-B types: A parable for behaviorists (Editorial). *Psychosomatic Medicine*, 1979, *41*, 353–356.
Shekelle, R. B., Schoenberger, J. A., & Stamler, J. Correlates of the JAS Type A behavior pattern score. *Journal of Chronic Diseases*, 1976, *29*, 381–394.
Sigg, E. B. The pharmacological approaches to cardiac stress. In R. S. Eliot (Ed.), *Stress and the heart*. New York: Futura, 1974.
Stuart, R. B. Paper presented at the annual meeting of the Association des Specialistes en Modification du Comportement, Moncton, New Brunswick, June 1974.
Suinn, R. M. The cardiac stress management program for Type A patients. *Cardiac Rehabilitation*, 1975, *5*, 13–15.
Suinn, R. M., & Bloom, L. J. Anxiety management training for Pattern A behavior. *Journal of Behavioral Medicine*, 1978, *1*, 25–37.
Theorell, T. Life events before and after the onset of a premature myocardial infarction. In B. S. Dohrenwend & B. P. Dohrenwend (Eds.), *Stressful life events: Their nature and effects*. New York: Wiley, 1974.
Van Egeren, L. Social interactions, communications and the coronary-prone behavior pattern: A psychophysiological study. *Psychosomatic Medicine*, 1979, *41*, 2–18.
Waldron, I. Sex differences in the coronary-prone pattern. In T. M. Dembroski, S. M. Weiss, & J. L. Shields (Eds.), *Proceedings of the forum on coronary-prone behavior*. Washington, D.C.: Dept. of Health, Education and Welfare. Publication No. (NIH) 78–1451, 1977.
Waldron, I., Zyzanski, S. J., Shekelle, R. B., Jenkins, C. D., & Tannenbaum, S. The coronary-prone behavior pattern in employed men and women. *Journal of Human Stress*, 1977, *3*, 2–19.
Warrenburg, S., Pagano, R. R., Woods, M., & Hlastala, M. A comparison of somatic relaxation and EEG activity in classical progressive relaxation and transcendental meditation. *Journal of Behavioral Medicine*, 1980, *3*, 73–93.
Zyzanski, S. J. Associations of the coronary-prone behavior pattern. In T. M. Dembroski, S. M. Weiss, & J. L. Shields (Eds.), *Proceedings of the forum on coronary-prone behavior*. Washington, D.C.: Dept. of Health, Education and Welfare. Publication No (NIH) 78–1451, 1977.
Zyzanski, S. J., Jenkins, C. D., Ryan, T. J., Flessas, A., & Everist, M. Psychological correlates of coronary angiographic findings. *Archives of Internal Medicine*, 1976, *136*, 1234–1237.

III

Applications

Part B—Victims

When one thinks of individuals under stress, the picture of the victim often comes to mind. Whether the victim is living under the threat of potential violence; has been victimized by violence (e.g., terrorist attacks, rape); or has experienced stressful social conditions, the plight of the victim in each case calls for major efforts at coping. Two of our contributors share their treatment research programs for victimized individuals.

In the first chapter, Ofra Ayalon combines a fascinating journalistic account with a psychological analysis of the demands of coping with terrorism in Israel. In many ways Israel is a living laboratory for the study of stress. Since its birth in 1948, it has witnessed five major wars, mass immigration, triple-digit inflation, and, as Ayalon's chapter documents, numerous terrorist attacks. Between 1974 and 1980, there were 14 terrotist attacks in Israel in which hostages were taken. In 11 of those incidents, children were directly involved in terrorist actions. Ayalon provides the scenarios for 10 terrorist attacks and then considers the very important role that the social system or group processes play in influencing how individuals cope with stress. The structure and dynamics of the community prior to the stress of terrorist attacks had a major effect on how individuals coped. Thus, one could possibly identify high-risk groups or communities that could be the focus of stress prevention programs.

Ayalon's account reminds us that if one wants to help individuals cope with or avoid stress, then an important focus of our attention should be on influencing and mobilizing the group process. Insofar as the group can be viewed as a source of physical protection and emotional support; and insofar as the group can provide prior preparations for future stressors, allocate roles, facilitate communication, provide speedy means of recovery and a framework of traditional values and procedures to work through grief and sorrow; then the individual's ability to cope with stress will be enhanced and the likelihood of secondary victimization will be decreased. Clearly, any consideration of stress reduction and prevention programs must consider interventions at the group as well as at the individual level. Her chapter is more than a reminder to consider group processes, since she focuses her attention on children as victims of terrorist attacks. She challenges the would-be intervener to consider how one's intervention has to be tailored to the needs of children. The use of play and fantasy, the use of the ventilation of unspent feelings, the use of the peer group, and the role that teachers can play as trainers are each considered.

Finally, the Ayalon program indicates that having a program to reduce stress is only half the battle. The other half is convincing administrators that they should permit the training procedure to be employed. The discussion of patient resistance in Chapter 4 wanes in comparison to the type of resistance one may encounter from administrators. It has been our experience, however, that many of the clinical ploys, sensitivities, and conceptualizations that one employs with a resistant patient can also be used with a resistant administrator. There is a need to view the administrator's resistance from his or her perspective. One needs to anticipate and overcome such resistance in the initial presentation of the training program; one has to martial the data for the need for such a program; one may have to use a "soft-sell" approach; and one has to include objective evaluation of the training program in order to have it considered by the administrators. In short, Ayalon's chapter raises a number of very important issues that must be considered in setting up stress prevention and management programs.

The impact of traumatic events, such as terrorist attacks and rape, on vicitms is often long-term and calls for different types of intervention at different stages of the stress reaction. It is important to appreciate that the nature of the stress management program required immediately after the trauma may be different from the program required some years after the trauma.

Louis Veronen and Dean Kilpatrick describe a treatment program for rape victims. Their description of the stress reactions of the rape victims highlights the need for any stress management program to focus attention not only on the victim, but also on the significant others in the victim's life, such as a spouse or those professionals who deal with the victim (e.g., police, doctors, lawyers, and courts). In many instances the attitudes and behavior of significant others toward the rape victim may engender further stress rather than reduce it. As Holmstrom and Burgess (1978) note, stress related to rape does not end with the assailant's departure but is often increased by the treatment victims receive from hospitals and enforcement and judicial systems. Victims characteristically are herded through appointments and examinations; treated as objects, intimidated, pressured, and subjected to the stress of repeated confrontations with the memory of the assault. Through this ordeal, the social agents often convey disbelief in her story, suspicion of her motives, condescension, and at times outright disdain. Thus, stress prevention and reduction programs should be directed not only at the victim but also toward significant others and institutional systems. As Holmstrom and Burgess note, it is important to insure that institutions do not further harm the very people they are supposed to help.

REFERENCES

Holmstrom, L., & Burgess, A. *The victim of rape: Institutional reactions.* New York: Wiley, 1978.

9

Coping with Terrorism

The Israeli Case

OFRA AYALON

One aspect of terrorism that is often neglected is the existence of the terrorized. At a time when terrorism has been commonplace, it is appropriate to take a close look at those who have been personally affected by it.

Terrorist attacks against civilians have written a bloody chapter in the Arab-Israeli conflict since the turn of the century. On top of the long list of wars, armed clashes, and across-the-border shellings, noncombatant residents have been exposed to assaults of terrorists on schools, the seizing of hostages, and various instances of random injury and murder. As a result of these attacks, a large number of children have been victimized. Some have been killed or wounded, while others have witnessed the cold-blooded murder or wounding of their parents, siblings, and mates.

What happens to individuals who have been swept up in such a surge of violence? What sequence of responses, feelings, and behaviors unfold in such episodes of terror, when people suddenly awaken to discover bloodshed and murder in their own homes?

This paper is mainly a study of children who, through no fault of their own, became pawns in horrendous situations. Such child victims, whether they are actual survivors of direct terrorist attacks or "near-miss" victims, have often emerged from their plight carrying specific syn-

---

OFRA AYALON • Department of Education, University of Haifa, Haifa, Israel.

dromes, typical of other victims of massive psychic trauma. Some children have been resilient. What can account for the difference in the children's vulnerability to such stress? We will look to the children's social groups (e.g., family, peers, community), their cultural values as sources of coping attitudes, support from peers of shared fate, and the help in recuperation received from supportive intervention in the aftermath.

We will also be concerned with the sustained effects of the stress episode on both the individual and the group, and will suggest certain modes of stress inoculation to buffer prospective traumatic experiences of the same nature.

The paper presents a cumulative natural study of the ramifications of terrorist attacks in Israel over the period of 1974–1980. During the years 1974–1975, 10 terrorist raids that involved the capture and killing of hostages were launched on Israeli civilian populations. These events will be described in the following pages, in a series of detailed scenarios, as background to the analysis of individual and group responses to the assaults. During the preparation of this paper, four additional terrorist attacks took place in Israel. One of the latter attacks will be discussed in some detail because it illustrates an intervention program with children in the aftermath of the attack. The documentary data of the sequence of events were derived from news reports and from files of social agencies on "victims of hostile actions against the civilian population" (under the law issued in 1971). The study will focus on children's responses to the confrontation with terrorists, highlighting reaction patterns in three critical periods of stress endurance: throughout the event, immediately upon rescue, and in the long-term follow-up. The personal data came from a series of in-depth interviews and clinical observations of survivors and near-miss populations, conducted by the writer over a six-year period. Finally, intervention and preventive programs will be explicated.

This analysis will begin to provide the needed taxonomy of cognitive and emotional styles for handling extreme stress situations. The availability of such a descriptive system should prove valuable for devising appropriate interventions and for possible preventive programs in order to enhance the coping skill and resilience of populations at risk of hostile victimization.

FACE TO FACE WITH TERRORISTS

The process of terrorization is the exertion of irresistable force threatening annihilation (Fields, 1979). It uses brutal and sophisticated devices to project a sense of unpredictability and powerlessness on the target population. Since Freud's time (1950), there have been ample empirical data that confirm the erosive effects of the uncertainty of impending danger on the ability of the individual to hold up under stress (Rachman, 1978). Thus terrorization, as well as other militant acts, instigates extreme stress, which by definition is a state in which the demands of the situation exceed the resources of individuals or groups. According to Lazarus (1966), four basic threats influence an individual's appraisal of stress, all of which are present in the situation brought about by a terrorist attack. These include threats to one's life, one's physical integrity, one's emotional security anchored in one's kin, and one's self-image and value system. Any such threat may produce a temporary or chronic emotional shock, often referred to as traumatic neurosis, even in previously stable individuals (Hastings, 1944; Janis, 1951, 1971; Star, 1944). The individual's assessment of the stressfulness of an event is affected by situational factors such as one's proximity to the location of the stressor, the duration and ferocity of the assault, and the degree of ambiguity of the source and outcome, as well as by personal factors. The most salient among the personal factors seem to be resourcefulness, degree of anxiety, tolerance threshold for threat and pain, previous experiences (positive or negative) of exposure to danger, and confidence, or lack of it, in one's ability to mold the environment to suit one's purpose (Janis, 1958; Lazarus, 1966; Spielberger, 1966). Intermittent recurrence of stress situations and their cumulative effect may contribute to their bearers' gradual burn-out (Maslach, 1976) and reduce their resilience. Added to the recurring stress of confronting the violence of terrorist attacks is their irregularity, which precludes any prior warning. This unpredictability of terrorism, which increases the impact of the disaster, makes it an everpresent threat, in spite of its relatively low probability.

The target population of this study has been exposed to various warlike hostilities during peace-time. One group of events comprised artillery shelling and boobytrap explosions; and the other involved the capture and killing of hostages. Although both types of events are highly loaded with stress-producing threats, recent studies (Ophir, 1980; Zuckerman-Bareli, 1979) show that they elicit marked differences in the reactions of the potential victims (i.e., the near-miss population). Shellings and explosions, though more frequent and rather unpredictable, produce less morbidity and less lasting anxiety than do the random but very powerful direct attack of terrorists. Remote-control hostilities are perceived in a way similar to the view of natural disasters: The agent of destruction is anonymous and the blow is finite, whether or not it is impregnated with ill intention (Erikson, 1979; Fredrick, 1980). The alarm and protective system retain their credibility and so do the first-aid, repair, and compensation procedures. It is also probable that the recurrence of such events, with relatively low levels of damage, has made them commonplace.

The threat of direct confrontation with assailants transcends the probability of being hit or injured. It involves a dissonance of interpersonal perception that shatters the root of reasonable expectations in a person-to-person interaction, namely recognizing the other (opponent) as a human being. In kidnapping, hostage-taking, and other extortion tactis, terrorists abuse other people in an obnoxious, instrumentalistic manner that deprives the victims of their identity and individuality. The victim's dehumanized image affects his self-concept in an unpredictable manner, as is evident from studies of victims of violence (Ochberg, 1978; Symonds, 1975). The stress wrought upon a survivor of such direct face-to-face encounters with the aggressor is increased by the physical proximity and the immediacy of the threat, which reduce him to utter helplessness. The victim's illusion of invulnerability, sense of control over his own life, and his responsibility toward and protectiveness of others are irrevocably disrupted by the confrontation with the captors' ruthless, murderous intentions. This type of terrorization inflicts a morbid fright alien to ordinary human experience. Notwithstanding awareness of mankind's long history of wars, presecutions, and pogroms, the individual remains unprepared for the terrorist scenario, because there is no group memory to fall back on. The hostility that individuals encounter in their daily lives in the modern civilized world is seldom expressed as the intention to annihilate them utterly in cold blood, or to obliterate their humanity by reducing them to worthless objects. Survivors of airplane hijackings (Jacobson, 1975) and hostages (Fields, 1978) show signs of grave psychological damage that is analogous to the "massive psychic traumatization" observed in survivors of Nazi concentration camps (Krystal, 1968). The common features of their ordeal is the direct confrontation with the captors without any means of self-defense, completely devoid of the ability to predict the duration of their plight, the chances of survival or rescue, or the actual morbidity of their affliction.

One of the victim's major difficulties created by the suddenness of the confrontation with terrorists is the disruption of the cognitive functions of appraisal and decision. His chances for rescue may all depend on his ability to mobilize acute evaluation of the risks and alternatives of escape, resistance, or surrender. There is an urgent need to make hazardous decisions and act on them immediately. Critical choices must be made: Should one attempt to save oneself by fleeing? (Of those who did ignore the others and fled, quite a few stayed alive; yet others who decided to flee were killed on the spot.) Should one try to overcome the enemy by force? Again it is a decision that can be evaluated only by retrospective knowledge. Twice in our cases did resistance of captives eliminate the threat. At other times it was futile and tragic. Should one distract the captors and let others flee? The longer the interim period between the onset of the threat and its termination, the more crucial does the decision become. With the progress of time, other opinions arise; for example, should one try to make contact with the terrorists, disarming them by rehumanization?

Yet the process of decision-making is completely disrupted by the very threat that the victim is desperately trying to avoid. All avenues of escape are blocked, the time factor is unknown; and viable alternatives for action become unavailable, as a result of which the victim may succumb to defensive self-deception, loss of hope, and panic behavior (Janis & Mann, 1977). In this case panic behavior exacerbates rather than alleviates the crisis, and may range from wild flight to total paralysis of will and action (Schulz, 1964). In the final analysis, the very life of the victim may depend on whether, at this juncture of decision-making, his behavior is adaptive or not. How does this face-to-face confrontation with the attacker influence the victim's perception of the threat? What may this interaction with the victimizer mean to the children who as a rule are more dependent on others than are adults?

We will take a close look at the children's reactions to the exceptional events that have confronted them, in the light of their immediate social surrounding. Table I presents in sequence the terrorist attacks on civilian populations in Israel between April 1974 and November 1975. It includes the objective aspects of the stress situation, such as the duration of the attack, and its casualties. It also describes the population of each target according to certain group characteristics, such as the structure of the community and the socioeconomic level of the residents. An examination of those factors may begin to provide us with some informal guidelines relating to societal and individual coping processes. Table II brings the documentation of the terrorist attacks on Israeli settlements up to date. A brief description of each attack is provided in the next section.

Scenarios of Terrorism

April 11, 1974—Kiryat Shmona

The Community

This is a development town near the Lebanese border. Most of the residents came originally from Asia and North Africa after the found-

Table I. Table of Events

Date	Location	Type of settlement	Size of settlement	Type of population	Duration of attack	Number killed and wounded
April 11, 1974	Kiryat Shmona	Border development town	Large	Underprivileged	4–5 hours	18 dead; dozens wounded
May 15, 1974	Ma'alot	Development town	Large	Underprivileged	16 hours	4 dead; dozens wounded
May 15, 1974	Tzfat	Development town	Large	Underprivileged	12 hours	22 dead; 56 wounded
June 13, 1974	Shamir	Border kibbutz	Small	Established	Brief	3 dead; 1 wounded
June 25, 1974	Nahariya	City	Large	Established	2 hours	3 dead; 4 wounded
November 7, 1974	Beit She'an	Border development town	Large	Underprivileged	2½ hours	4 dead; 21 wounded
December 1, 1974	Rechanya	Circassian village	Small	—	1 hour	1 dead; 1 wounded
December 6, 1974	Rosh-Hanikra	Border kibbutz	Small	Established	Brief	no dead; 1 wounded
March 5, 1975	Savoy Hotel, Tel Aviv	City	Large	Mixed	6 hours	7 dead; 11 wounded
June 15, 1975	Kfar Yuval	Border village	Small	Underprivileged	2 hours	2 dead; 4 wounded
November 20, 1975	Ramat Magshimim	Religious border village	Small	Established	5 minutes	3 dead; 2 wounded

Table II. Additional Events (1978–1980)

Date	Location	Number killed and wounded
March 11, 1978	The coastal road bus hijacking	37 killed; dozens wounded
March 3, 1979	Ma'alot[a]	1 killed; 1 wounded
April 23, 1979	Nahariya[a]	4 killed
April 8, 1980	Misgav-Am (kibbutz)	2 killed; 7 wounded

[a]Second assault.

ing of the State of Israel and settled in Kiryat Shmona in the 1950s. Most of the public positions and better jobs are held by the locally born (Sabras) and Jews of European origin.

The town has been frequently shelled by terrorists based in southern Lebanon, perpetuating, in an atmosphere of tension, a constant threat to life and property. In spite of these constant threats, the community relies for its defense not on local elements but the IDF (Israel Defense Forces). To add to the already tense atmosphere, there is a scarcity of air raid shelters.

The Incident

A group of terrorists crossed the Lebanese border in the early hours of the morning. The terrorists broke into two buildings; they ransacked every apartment and shot everybody in sight. After the bloody massacre, they barricaded themselves on the top floors of the buildings.

Initial Reactions

Half an hour after the first shots were fired, the alarm was sounded and the inhabitants of a nearby building rushed into shelters. Curfew was enforced for 4½ hours, by the end of which period the security forces stormed the occupied building, killing all terrorists. Throughout this time, the wounded remain untended. Eighteen children and adults were killed, and dozens were wounded.

Subsequent Reactions

As a direct result of the incident, angry demonstrations erupted in the town. Residents burned the bodies of the terrorists. Funerals of the victims were interrupted by outcries and accusations against city and government authorities who failed to protect them. The community remained in an uproar for a time after the event. There were reports of sleepwalking, symptoms of physical malaise, anxieties, and absenteeism from work and school. Quite a few families moved from the area.

Remarks

The attack on Kiryat Shmona was the first in a series of similar terrorist invasions of civilian settlements. However, while terrorist raids across the border had been frustrated by the security defense network, the terrorists' success in Kiryat Shmona in breaching these defenses shook the residents' faith in the authorities and their protective measures, as well as in their own image as capable defenders of their homes and families.

May 15, 1974—(A) Ma'alot

The Community

This is a Western Galilee development town near the Lebanese border, surrounded by Israeli-Arab population. Residents are mostly recent immigrants from Moslem countries, still struggling with the effects of dislocation. Many families are orthodox and are heavily loaded with children, a blessing in accordance with their cultural and religious traditions. Low-placed on the economical and occupational scale, a substantial number of families are welfare clients. Large groups of children are considered "educationally disadvantaged" (Marx, 1970) and in need of specialized care in schooling.

The Incident

Three armed men who stole across the Lebanese border into Israel hit the town at midnight, shooting an old man on their way. Next they invaded an apartment, chosen at random, killing, in bed, the father, the pregnant mother, and a four-year-old child and gravely wounding their five-year-old girl. They next stopped at a local school, apparently intending to wait for the children to arrive in the morning. As fate would have it, over 100 teenagers with their teachers from another town (Tzfat) on a school outing were staying the night in this school building. On reaching the school grounds the terrorists encountered one of the teachers, whom they forced at gun point to take them inside the building. The terrorists occupied the school for 16 hours, holding up to 105 hostages. Seventeen pupils and most of the teachers fled from the very start, in addition to several other children who were released while negotiations were in process. The IDF stormed the building. All of the terrorists were killed. This rescue operation did not prevent the terrorists from first killing 1 soldier and 22 children and wounding 56 more children. Because of the large number of casualties, the incident is known as the Ma'alot Massacre.

Reactions to the Incident

The residents of Ma'alot reacted as near-miss survivors. In the first hours after the attack, the petrified population was in a state of shock to the extent of denying even first aid for the previous night's victims. The place was flooded by people: troops, senior commanders, government representatives, the hostages' relatives, and medical personnel and volunteers, highlighted by both the national and international news media. The town, holding its breath during the long hours of negotiation with the terrorists, broke in turmoil in the wake of the gory rescue operation.

Funerals of the local victims were disrupted by violence of a verbal and physical nature on displaced targets of aggression, such as national and local-level authorities. A leading member of the cabinet, attending the funeral, was beaten up by a number of frantic mourners. When the initial impact of the incident began to wane, the community went through a multifaceted crisis that lasted many months. Among the reported reactions were psychosomatic illnesses, complaints of anxieties and insomnia, and a growing incidence of miscarriages. A substantial number of children and adults required medical care. Some segments of the population, namely, preschool children and high-risk mothers, accepted extra care, paid for by the compensation money that trickled into the community. Typically, the surge of helping volunteers dwindled after a while, leaving an additional vacuum. No systematic stress intervention was initiated in Ma'alot during or following the crisis.

May 15, 1974—(B) Ma'alot–Tzfat

The Place

"Netiv Meir" school, Ma'alot.

The Incident

105 high school kids from Tzfat, camping in a school building, were trapped and most of them held hostages for 16 hours by three armed terrorists. The terrorists wired explosives around the building and, firing occasionally, used their hostages for sandbags at the windows, shooting between their legs, while negotiations went on. The captors' treatment of the hostages as a rule was relentless, except for a few hours when, unpredictably lenient, they allowed their captives some freedom of move-

ment. The crisis culminated toward the terrorists' decreed deadline, when armed troops launched their rescue operation. Before being killed, the terrorists managed to get in more shots and grenades at their hostages, of whom 22 were killed and more than 50 injured.

Reactions during Acute Crisis

The crisis constituted a 16-hour-long detainment bouncing between two catastrophes: the terrorists' attack at the onset, and the gory rescue operation at the end.

At the onset, most of the teachers, the guides and 14 of the students managed to escape, leaving the rest of the group to fate. Those on the spot kept stalling, first refusing to acknowledge the threat and eventually petrified into immobility. By then it was too late for any action. Panic and chaos took over during the rescue massacre as well.

For the greater part of their captivity, however, the hostages were mainly panicked, numbed, and impassive. There was much sobbing, and some fainting and involuntary wetting (precipitated by the limitation on the use of the toilets). Emotions vacillated among despair, self-blame, and bewilderment and the more positive states—hope, group-belonging, and altruism. Power was sought through prayer, vows, and omens, as well as in conjuring images of home and hearth. Activities were mainly limited to preoccupation with food or compulsive eating and vacating. Scant attempts were made to communicate with the captors and to initiate contact of any kind with possible allies outside.

Aftermath

For two years after the incident, 75% of the survivors kept suffering of insomnia, anxiety nightmares and psychosomatic complaints. One-third of these were ridden with depression, anxiety, enuresis, fear of people, and undefined psychic distress. More than half of them dreaded the recurrence of the trauma (Gal, 1980).

May 15, 1974—(C) Tzfat

The Community

This ancient city, now a summer resort, is located in the central Galilee and is known as the Cradle of the Cabbalah. The affected population was that of immigrants from Asia and North Africa, ethnically and demographically of a background similar to that of the residents of Ma'alot. Most of the victimized families were of the same run-down neighborhood and thus were in some way interrelated. The disaster consequently shattered the whole of their social network. Also, they were isolated from the town's mainstream in a way.

Reaction to Crisis

The agony of the young hostages' close relatives began with the news coverage of the terrorists' attack on Ma'alot. More than 100 such families underwent 12 hours of this agony, not knowing what would happen to their children. The shocking announcement of the many deaths and casualties added outbursts of rage and violence to a mourning, directed at government institutions and the ministry of education, which were held responsible for the disaster. In this hunt for scapegoats, the bereaved families expressed acute feelings of deprivation, transformed into demands for material compensation at a later stage.

No attempt was made to unite for any common goals or to assist one another. The affected families, relatively isolated from the wider urban community, experienced no communal support except for formal contacts with welfare and rehabilitation officials. Feelings and expressions of bitterness were kept alive for a long time.

November 7, 1974—Beit She'an

The Community

This is a development town in the Beit She'an Valley about 5 km west of the Jordanian border. The population consists primarily of Asian and North African immigrants. Most families are large and of the low-income bracket.

The Incident

At 4:45 A.M., four terrorists made their way into an apartment building, shooting and killing at sight. Breaking into an apartment, they murdered the family's mother.

Initial Reactions

The remaining members of the family leaped out the window, as did their neighbors on hearing shots. Two hours later, a security task force stormed the apartment, killing the terrorists. Four residents of that apartment building were killed and 21 wounded, mostly as a result of leaping to safety. Many people, consequently, went into shock with manifested symptoms of panic for hours.

Subsequent Reactions

The town went into chaos, residents ran amuck, rampaging through the streets and burning the terrorists' bodies. In the pandemonium, the body of the one of the victims was burned as well.

Some of the residents took to helping with wounded, others volunteering for civil guard duty—a typical case of altruism. Different groups were, at the same time, shocked into rage, hurling accusations at the town's authorities, a process that climaxed during the victims' funerals.

Comments

These victimized populations share several common denominators, all of which render them most vulnerable to crises of that kind. Mass dislocation and immigration, the stress of acculturation, involving the destruction of traditional and religious values and habits, have put a heavy burden on individuals and families. On top of present stress and strain, the toll of murders in three out of these four communities was enormous and especially difficult to sustain because it hit children.

June 13, 1974—Kibbutz Shamir

The Community

A kibbutz about 5 km from Kiryat Shmona near the Lebanese border. Its 600 residents are either native Israelies or of European and American origin.

The Incident

Four terrorists invaded the kibbutz in the early hours of the morning, shooting and killing three women and one man.

Initial Reactions

A six-year-old boy who witnessed the shooting ran off to alert the guard, whereupon the internal predrilled defense procedure of the kibbutz was instantly put into operation. The ensuing close-range gun battle put all the terrorists to death. Except for their special defense squad, the kibbutz's residents stayed in the shelters equipped for emergencies of this kind. The whole area was thoroughly searched for additional terrorists. When none were found, vigiliance was restored to normal.

Subsequent Reactions

Mourning was restrained. Declarations of identification and the intention not to desert the place were made during and after the funerals. The community regained its composure and functionability. No further aftereffects were reported.

December 6, 1974—Kibbutz Rosh–Hanikra

A kibbutz on the seacoast of the Western Galilee, on the Lebanese border. Population similar to that of Kibbutz Shamir.

The Incident

A group of terrorists invaded the kibbutz from the Mediterranean, attacking a family at home. One man was injured.

Initial Reactions

Immediately the residents organized both for defense and pursuit. One terrorist was killed on the spot and the others were forced to escape, eliminating the threat. The residents, still agitated but safe, tried to resume their normal activities. They adamantly refused any outside interference by closing their doors on the security forces as well as the news media.

Subsequent Reactions

Within a short time the community dropped back into routine. It is the only incident in which no lives were lost.

November 20, 1975—Ramat Magshimim

The Community

A newly settled religious agricultural village, on the Lebanese border. Resident majority is of European or American origin, combining agriculture and religious study with army service in the village.

The Incident

Four terrorists overpowered five students as they were studying in their living quarters. The terrorists withdrew from the room, taking one hostage and hurling a grenade at the four students who remained in the room. The hostage escaped as they retreated. Result of the incident: three students were killed and two wounded. The incident lasted five minutes.

Initial Reactions

Thoroughly drilled security measures were put into immediate effect. The IDF combed the countryside for 12 hours looking for other terrorists.

Subsequent Reactions

Mourning for the victims turned into an opportunity to express religious solidarity in the community. Bereaved parents went to the extent of sending their younger sons to the village for Sabbath rituals as an expression of their allegiance and faith.

Common Denominators

The common denominators recognizable at the incidents of Kibbutz Shamir, Kibbutz Rosh–Hanikra and Ramat Magshimim are the readiness of the community to meet attack (through prior drill and effective role-allocation and communication), rate of recovery, and the working-out of grief through a framework of traditional values.

December 1, 1974—Rechanya

The Community

A small Circassian village, 1–2 km from the Lebanese border, consisting of and established by several of their traditional class. The Circassians, a tiny minority in Israel, are Moslem who left Russia at the end of the last century in the wake of religious persecution. The village structure is similar to that of a traditional Moslem Arab village. The young men serve in the Israeli army.

The Incident

The terrorists infiltrated the village at about midnight. Bursting into a home, they killed the head of the household and wounded his wife. In the course of the attack, the terrorists discovered they had by "accident" attacked Arab-speaking Moslems. Apologizing to their victims, they turned themselves over to the Israeli security forces. One of the terrorists was wounded.

Reactions

Immediate: The wounded mother protected her son (aged 8), sent her daughter (age 12) for help, and waited to be killed. The daughter did not lose her head. Tending to her mother while transmitting information in Circassian to her uncle, who subsequently called an army troop that captured the terrorists preventing further damage. Other residents of the village, while expressing outrage over the attack, failed to act.

Subsequent: The villagers expressed their solidarity with Israel, rejected the terrorists' "apology," and asked to be allowed weapons for future self-defense.

June 15, 1975—Kfar Yuval

The Community

A small cooperative farming village on the Lebanese border. After its founding, settlers had deserted the site 20 years earlier; then Indian and

Moroccan Jews resettled it. For a long time the settlement was threatened off and on by artillery bombardments.

The Incident

The terrorists penetrated the defense lines of the village at dawn, shot the watchman, took control in an occupied home, and opened fire in all directions. Security forces blocking the roads attacked the terrorists' position, killing them all. The incident lasted 2½ hours. During the fire exchange, the head of the captive family managed to join the IDF task force; he was killed in action. His wife and sons, kept hostage in the house, survived. The incident resulted in two killed and most of the hostages wounded.

Reactions

After the attack, many residents expressed a heightened sense of commitment to their community. Expressions of grief were moderate. Within hours, the community returned to normal.

June 25, 1974—Nahariya

The Community

A medium-size well-established community, situated on the coast not far from the Lebanese border.

The Incident

About midnight, a group of terrorists attacked an apartment building after shooting the watchman. Residents barricaded themselves in their apartments. One of the neighbors attempted to save his wife and daughters by lowering them to the ground through the window, but this proved fatal; they were shot and killed in the process.

Upon arrival, the IDF wiped out the terrorists without further casualties.

Reactions

In the beseiged building, neighbors took reasonable measures in self-defense when they barricaded the doors of their apartments. The attempt at safety by fleeing the building seems to have been based on a similar but successful attempt during a previous terrorist raid at Beit She'an. The community returned to normal after a brief period of restrained mourning.

March 5, 1975—Savoy Hotel, Tel Aviv

The Community

Tel Aviv is Israel's largest city. Located on the seashore but away from any hostile border, it is considered to be the safest place in the country.

Close to the beach in central Tel Aviv, the hotel is wedged in between the city's more affluent and more deprived neighborhoods.

The Incident

During the night, a group of terrorists penetrated Tel Aviv's beach area from the Mediterranean Sea. The infiltrators first attempted to take over a movie theatre next to their target, but were thwarted by an usher who blocked all exits and rushed the audience into the air-raid shelter. The terrorists took hold of the Savoy Hotel, herding into and keeping at gun point all hostages in one room. The security forces got to the scene shortly thereafter and began negotiating with the terrorists, using one hostage as mediator. Six hours later, security stormed the building, while the terrorists succeeded in killing 7 and wounding 11 hostages and soldiers.

Hostages' Coping Reactions

One of those wounded pretented to be dead, while another believed herself to be dying. A third person tried to sustain the other hostages' spirits by messages of an optimistic nature. A young woman hostage took charge of the group and acted as mediator between the terrorists and the army outside. According to her evidence, given later, she had discovered unsuspected resources in herself: physical stamina, first-aid skills, and fluency in Arabic for the negotiations she conducted between the IFD and the terrorists. She reported feeling strengthened by the sense of the commonality of destiny and the prevailing spirit of togetherness, though the group of hotel guests held hostage was random. Once it was over, she said she knew she would never be afraid again (Golan, 1979).

Reactions of Bystanders

Those without a clearly defined role: milling around the scene, or running away, or passively waiting for orders. Those with clearly defined roles: (a) the usher in the movie theatre barred the entrance exit doors; (b) an ambulance driver, having blocked the street, summoned help and; (c) doctors living in the area sped to the nearest hospital.

Subsequent Reactions

In no time, life in the affected area returned to normal. In the immediate area of the onslaught, residents remained agitated, but elsewhere in the city there was hardly any noticeable effect.

GROUP SUPPORT

When the individual is part of a group under attack his appraisal of that group as a source of physical protection or emotional support influences his estimation of the chances of survival and rescue. If the community outside the besieged area has in the past successfully protected or rescued victims of similar attacks, the threatened individual may look to that community for his salvation. But it is also likely that the individual will experience a feeling of desertion, of being left to his own fate, that may bring in its wake one of two contradictory reactions:

1. Social feelings of amicability and closeness to others, feelings of love and altruism (Bettelheim, 1961, 1979); or
2. Asocial feelings of isolation and loss of faith in others, egoism, and occasionally the willingness to sacrifice another to save one's own life (Orwell's *Nineteen Eighty Four* gives a stunning example of this).

The threatened individual may have an illusion of his centrality in the unfolding drama, failing to grasp what is actually occurring around him and see himself as the only endangered party (Wolfenstein, 1957). This sensation is fostered by the "news vacuum" that the victim tries to fill with scraps of information. As his awareness of the true extent of the disaster increases, his concern passes from himself to the group. The sobering realization of the actual situation may lead either to readiness to cooperate with other victims to effect release or to a distrust of all his companions. According to Caplan's ecological theory of mental health (1974), social support systems act as "buffers" to help the individual cope with stress by enhancing his trust in the continuation of emotional ties and by facilitating mastery of the environment. The supportive matrix includes family, peers, school, and religious and ethnic mutual-help groups. Mutual-help groups are created in times of stress to fill in the gaps between the domain of the family and that of professional agencies. But when the community at large is traumatized, the supportive matrix may crack. The attacked communities, as social systems, vary in the degree of vulnerability or immunity they provide to the individual. They may either fail their members and disintegrate under stress, or support afflicted members both during and after the event, turning the excessive demands into an opportunity for a higher degree of functioning (Caplan, 1974; Januv, 1976). These factors have an impact on the children of the community, since different modes of upbringing contribute to different ways of managing anxiety and stress.

The Snowball Effect in Communities Exposed to Stress

The communities involved in the 10 terrorist attacks just documented are a typical sample of social structures in Israel. The structure and dynamics of the community prior to stress has a dominant effect on the manner of coping of the population at large and of individuals in particular (Caplan, 1974). Although some generalized features appear in groups of victims and survivors, individual differences still account for a typical response, as will be evident from further analysis. The circumstances and outcomes in each case (e.g., the extent of the damage and number of the casualties, etc.) contaminate comparison of the different communities' approaches and reactions. In spite of this restriction, we can identify three groups of factors that may account for the differences in the stress-response:

1. Historical-cultural-demographic characteristics of a population, including previous experience of stress and loss, determine its orientation toward activity or passivity in handling morbid occurrences.
2. Systemic features of the community—its boundaries, transactions and interactions, leadership and role allocation, group cohesiveness, and channels of communication and support—may be regarded as predictors of the coping potential of the community (see discussion of systems analysis in Bertalanffy, 1968; see also Moldar, 1954).
3. The third group of factors involves the existence or absence of a vigilant approach and preparedness to meet unpleasant life eventualities, such as war, civil strife, or terrorist violence.

In the same way that pooling resources improves the chances of standing up to additional stress, the forces of disruption and confusion in a problem-ridden community can snowball and lead to its deterioration.

Four out of six raided towns, Kiryat Shmona, Ma'alot, Tzfat, Beit She'an—are small to middle-sized urban dwellings, inhabited by multiproblem, underprivileged immigrant populations. These populations have, over decades, endured the crises of forced migration and cultural transition, resulting in the loss or distortion of most of their communal, cultural, and family values. Low on occupational and educational scales (Smooha & Peres, 1974) and perpetually frustrated (Marx, 1970), their deprivation is carried over to second and third generations (Frankenstein, 1968, 1970). The structure of these communities is loose, and interactions are diffuse. No credible leadership has emerged and the overall orientation is passive. These features may contribute to the phenomena of general panic and hopelessness during the attack and displaced aggression against local authorities in the aftermath.

As immigrants from Arabic-speaking countries, such as Morocco, Tunisia, Syria, Iraq, and Yemen, and refugees of previous racial persecutions, these populations were doubly traumatized by the all-too-familiar threats from which they had tried to escape. Their frustration at the failure of the authorities to protect their dear ones was tremendously augmented by the massive bloodshed that they suffered during two of the attacks. For a culture with a very high investment in its children, the toll of children's deaths verged on the intolerable.

Small size and cohesive communities (like the Kibbutzim Shamir, Rosh–Hanikra, and Ramat Magshimim and the villages Rechanya and Kfar Yuval), with a high degree of awareness, credible leadership and role-allocation, and open channels of communication, seem to have fared much better in facing the threat and stress of the attacks. In the kibbutz, a selective society with a tradition of self-reliance and mutual responsibility, emergencies were handled promptly and efficiently, and care was given to casualties and survivors. Vigilance has paid off, leading to a continual readiness to meet emergencies and to deal with their consequences (see also Ginath & Krasilowsky, 1970; Kaffman, 1977; Ziv & Israeli, 1973).

The two cities in which terrorist attacks took place represent a mixed category, with heterogeneous populations and changing modes of operation under stress. In both cities (Tel Aviv and Nahariya) it was apparent that people who had pre-assigned roles and were trained to deal with emergencies (such as doctors, soldiers and psychologists) functioned adaptively both during and after the crisis. People with no well-defined roles, however, showed tendencies to mob and panic. Rumors spread and increased the level of anxiety. Nearby neighborhoods were more adversely affected than was the periphery.

A more rigorous analysis of the ameliorating and exacerbating factors that influence coping with extreme stress should be conducted. A small move in this direction is being made in a cross-cultural comparison of coping with stress of guerilla warfare and terrorism in violent environments such as Southern Lebanon and Northern Ireland (Mar'i, Ayalon, & Fields, 1980).

But even at this preliminary state of research, the conclusions that can be drawn indicate the need to nurture those social attitudes and community resources, described before, that were found to be most adaptive in dealing with stress. Stress-preventive intervention can be used as a level for promoting community involvement and for tapping potential for active coping.

FACTORS INFLUENCING THE MANNER OF COPING WITH TERROR

What behaviors, thoughts, or feelings in the face of the extreme stress of a hostage situation would be considered coping reactions rather than failure and disintegration?

The concept of *coping* has been obscured by undifferentiated usage, lumping together both adequate and inadequate stress reactions. However, the success of any coping reaction must be judged primarily by its results, namely by its contribution to survivor's well-being during the four critical phases of induced stress: the warning phase, the actual occurrence, the immediate recovery, and the long-range phase of adaptation.

Coping is a survival formula. As such, it is a process including any behavior that proves effective in canceling or reducing the physical or the psychological threat and that also leads to management of self and others in gaining control over the situation. The nature of coping lies in its flexibility to change with the changing circumstances and with the duration of each phase.

Lazarus (1976) has provided a classification of stress reactions, dividing them into five categories, which convey action, underlying emotions and defensive aims:

Flight in fear, the aim of which is the elimination of threat;
Fight in anger, which is geared to attacking the stressor or its representatives;
Immobility in panic, which takes the form of paralysis of thought and action, designed to avoid anxiety, often resulting from conflicting drives;
Resourcefulness, which through an active search for alternatives is sometimes successful in converting the threat into a challenge for change, growth, and achievement; and
Intra-personal palliative strategies, which are employed to moderate distress when action fails. These are mental acts that reduce the threat not in reality but in the mind of the individual.

The degree of adaptivity of any stress reaction is assessed according to the immediate circumstances and to its effectiveness over time. Coping reactions that prove adaptive at one phase may have deleterious aftereffects. In some of the cases described, when flight from captors was feasible, it turned out to be the most appropriate reaction for saving the lives of the fugitives. But for many, their flight, which terminated one stress, created a new one—the stress of long-lasting and unrelieved guilt for having abandoned their fellows and having been saved at their expense. Another example of this "boomerang" effect is evident in the shame and self-rejection experienced by some survivors who had initiated contact and conversation with their captors. They later considered this behavior as repellent and humiliating, in the light of retrospective knowledge of the terrorists' murderous acts.

The choice of stress reaction is partly determined by personal and ecological factors, directly influenced by situational characteristics.

While adaptive coping is nourished by intellectual resources and ego strength, its effects may be curbed by lack of social support, previous adverse experience, emotional disturbance, guilt feelings, high anxiety, and a sense of being dwarfed by authority (Wolfenstein, 1957). This last element was obvious in Ma'alot, when hostages were reduced to humiliating regression and complete dependency by the terrorists' utter control of such basic functions as their toilet practices. The psychological mechanism of denial may impede the emergence of adaptive coping reactions in some situations. Denial may bring about immobility and clinging to old forms of behavior through reluctance to break routine patterns. It creates an attitude of dependence on external forces and on fate, as was the case in Ma'alot where, according to their own report, the stunned teenagers refused to acknowledge the reality of the attack until it was too late for any protective activity. The very same mechanism of denial may have a palliative effect when threat cannot be removed. Denying the reality or its implication represents a way of coming to terms with an extremely obnoxious situation in which insanity seems the only sane reaction. Frankenthal (1969) reported that one woman imprisoned in a concentration camp, who was repeatedly sexually assaulted by her jailors, was able to survive only by denying the realistic implications of her situation and replacing them by a delusion of being harrassed by devils.

Along with regression and denial, the exposure to terrorists' brutality heightens the danger of emotional leakage, namely the spilling over of the unhindered aggression from offender to victim. The victim's psyche is flooded with aggressiveness erupting from three sources: frustration-induced aggression (Dollard, Doob, Miller, & Sears, 1939) over his lost opportunities for escape and rescue; perceiving the aggressor as a role model, an authority figure whose power is derived from his absolute physical advantage over his victims, from whom he exacts total submission and dependence; and the breaking down of acquired psychological barriers against aggressive behavior. The uninhibited and gruesome violence of the attacker serves as a strong provocation to the victim's own aggressive impulses. Because a direct outlet is completely denied to the victims, a vicious circle of increased anxiety, regression into irrational and magical thinking, and self-destructive behavior may ensue (Frankenstein, 1956, 1958).

In the long run, some survivors of terrorist attacks suffer guilt feelings and become chronically suspicious of or angry with others. Some have turned their unspent aggression inward, damaging themselves mentally or physically. In addition, anxiety—which can, during conditions of stress and danger, activate hidden resources and place the entire organism on the alert—may, after the danger has passed, rebound on the victim like a golem that rises against its maker and destroys him. The resulting pathological phenomena have been described in detail by Janis (1951), Selye (1956), Krystal (1968), Lifton (1967), Horowitz (1976), and Ochberg (1978).

The effectiveness of any particular response cannot be evaluated in isolation. Hence the difficulties in predicting how effective a specific reaction will be in determining one's success in coping. By analyzing and studying the response-repertoire revealed to us by the victims of terrorism, we can draw some guidelines for classifying coping patterns. We can learn how to improve coping skills, though we must be cautious in drawing up a blueprint for how people should cope with such extreme stress. We will consider implications of these conclusions in programs of services for survivors of violence and in training for stress prevention.

Patterns of Survival in Victimized Children and Adolescents

Very little is known about children's reactions to active, externally-induced crisis, in contrast to the ample evidence accumulated on intrapsychic trauma (Furst, 1967). Children may be oblivious to threats which are remote or abstract, such as war across the border, but will fully perceive and react to immediate physical danger. It is also true that children usually experience stress through their "meaningful adults" (Bowlby, 1952). However, in the case of such a trauma-induced situation, children may be directly exposed to a destructive imbalance in their ecological system that effects their cognitive, emotional, and physical well-being. A child who witnesses violence and/or who is physically violated may suffer a systemic shock, that transcends subjective evaluation.

Childhood is regarded as a most impressionable period, when events set a unique and permanent stamp on the future personality. When childhood experiences are overwhelming and stressful, an arrest of personality development may occur and a pattern of repetitive maladaptive behavior may be set in motion, with ensuing crippling effects on the growing child.

Clearly, children should be protected physically and emotionally, and are rightfully dependent on adult support and guidance. But in all the instances in which the hostages were children, a central stress-inducing feature was also the vulnerability of their adult protectors.

In most of the cases, children endured long periods of separation from their parents and in several instances, they even went through the harrowing experience of watching their parents being killed (in Kiryat-Shmona, Ma'alot, Beit She'an, and on the coastal road bus hijacking).

Since children are considered especially susceptible and are apt to suffer permanent damage, it is particularly important to evaluate their reactions in order to formulate ways of helping them deal constructively with the trauma.

Children's reactions should be viewed in light of their maturity. Victims as well as survivors ranged from infancy through adolescence. It is reasonable to assume that their reactions, both during the event and later, would depend on age-specific skills and needs. But the evidence, as well as survivors' reports, point to the trauma having been an equalizer: The recorded reactions in many ways resembled those of adults, both in the same situation and in other disasters (Erikson, 1979; Lindemann, 1944; Lifton, 1967). This may be due to the overpoweringly regressive effects of imminent threat and loss on adults and on older children.

Despite the similarities in reactions, some age-specific modes of responding appeared in the children's behavior, of which we will note a few: The very young infants who were held hostage in a kibbutz children's home cried helplessly during the night. One infant was shot and died. The captors received a supply of milk on request, but did not feed the babies. Thus, their crying went unrelieved. A follow-up assessment will be necessary to determine the full damage that such events inflicted on these babies. Four toddlers were also held hostage in the same room and had a narrow escape after the military rescue operation. Upon reunion with the families, their main complaint concerned their despair that pleas for their caretaker had gone unheeded. "Why didn't you come when we called you?" (Children in a kibbutz sleep in a separate home from their parents and are watched by a caretaker during the night and part of the day.) These insistent recriminations may signify a breach of the three-year-olds' developing trust.

School-age children were often ingenious in handling the situations, calling for help or rescuing themselves. One example is a girl of six who, after having been captured, freed herself, ran from the terrorist, and hid under a piece of furniture while the terrorist was pacing the room looking for her. She stayed in hiding until the danger had passed. More examples will follow.

In spite of the children's immediate resourcefulness, their experience took its toll, as expressed during the recovery phase by symptoms such as regressive bed-wetting, excessive fears and nightmares, aggressive and retaliatory fantasies, acting-out, or withdrawal behavior and compulsive and ritualistic play (cf. Terr, 1979).

Adolescents are particularly susceptible to stress that involves a threat of disfiguration and humiliation. The stress of being rendered totally helpless and exposed to violence thrusts the adolescent back into identity confusion, regressive submissiveness to authority, loss of trust, and blocking of affect, because he is struggling with issues of identity formation and independence. Earlier conflict over guilt and punishment were reactivated in some of the juvenile hostage group. Regression was enhanced by the fact that the captors held control over toilet procedures and the privilege to move, talk or eat. Given the fact that the group was leaderless and created no alternative supports, the damaging effect of isolation increased the need to cling to some external, even supernatural sources of rescue.

Facing Terrorists

As noted, the various phases of coping make different demands and require different interventions: the initial phase, during the event; the recovery phase, from one week to a couple of months later, and the long-range adaptive phase that can last a lifetime. In order to illustrate these various phases, we should consider the results of an interview study we conducted with child survivors of terrorist attacks. The following are examples of behaviors during each phase, as drawn from survivors' testimony. In this study, the followup of survivors extends up to six years following the event.

The main sources for data of the following response and coping profiles were interviews held with survivors and near-miss populations during 1978–1980. One series of interviews with exhostages was held 5–6 years after the event, the sample including noninjured, slightly injured, and severely injured young adults, who were 16–17 years old at the time of the victimization.

In more recent attacks, interviews and observation of victimized and near-miss child population were conducted directly at the termination of hostilities and have been going on ever since at timely intervals, to secure knowledge of short- and long-term coping behaviors. This immediacy reflects the growing awareness of victims' needs and the strict necessity for systematic evaluation. One limitation of this kind of naturalistic study is the amount of distortion that filters through in post hoc statements of highly charged activities under stress. To gain more credibility, indirect sources of data were used, such as officially collected testimonies, case reports, and diaries and letters written within a few weeks after the attack. A persistent feature of interviewees' reactions was their willingness to talk and their expression of relief for having been listened to.

The adaptivity of the specific behavior chosen by the individual is contingent on his perception of the threat and his immediate goals. When the perceived threat was that of being overpowered by gunmen and the immediate aim was the elimination of the threat, both fight and flight could be considered adaptive. Final assessments include the consequences of these behaviors. The degree of relief actually achieved by certain modes of operation is an indication of their supportive value. Paralysis and panic were often determined by the constraints of the situation as much as by personal tendencies.

Immediate Response to the Onset of the Disaster

Fight

Although scarce in our case reports, as in other reported terrorist attacks (Schrieber, 1978), fighting back appeared at Rosh–Hanikra and Shamir and during recurrent attacks on both Ma'alot and Na'hariya on the part of highly vigilant adults. Other attempts to overcome terrorists by fighting were reported by a few adolescents in Ma'alot, who planned a "suicide rescue operation" and managed to snatch a knife from a captor's bag. It is impossible to predict the adaptability of such plans, as they were nipped in the bud by the bewildered resistance of the rest of the group.

Flight

Flying from captors at the onset of attack was feasible in many cases, but was practiced by only a few. The decision to jump out of high-rise windows demanded a high degree of risk-taking. Most jumpers were saved, though for a few the jump was fatal.

Methods of flight varied from hiding in a closet to jumping from a high building. One eight-year-old girl at Kiryat Shmona overcame her initial confusion and paralysis and managed to escape her mother's and siblings' fate by hiding in a closet. A 16-year-old at Ma'alot hid in the bathroom, then found shelter under a corpse during the rescue raid, and finally threw herself from s second floor window, in spite of having been wounded. Seventeen students in Ma'alot escaped by jumping out of the windows, following their fleeing teachers. The same happened in Beit She'an, when a boy (15) who jumped from a third-floor window was followed by his brother (14), then by more children and adults. The decision to escape was also charged with a conflict between a life-preserving tendency and responsibility toward others. One example, which had many repercussions on later events, is the escape of the teachers in Ma'alot, at the cost of pushing others from the escape routes and depriving the rest of the pupils of reliable leadership and moral support. A contrary example on the same scene came from youngsters who reported later that their first inclinations to escape had been inhibited by consideration of responsibility for a younger sibling. Sometimes caring for others was incorporated in self-saving escape, as shown in the following example: While fleeing with her family from her home to safety, a 13-year-old girl from Nahariya disregarded her mother's urging to keep on running and stopped to wait for a small girl who was also running for her life. She remembers thinking, "This is a human being, who cannot be left alone in the middle of the night."

In all these cases, the children were on their own, the responsible adults being either missing or killed. Those who were actively engaged in a self-saving act not only survived, but, in the interview, appeared to have also preserved a positive self-image. Interviews after a couple of years with the same children revealed a mixture of a sense of self-reliance with shame and guilt over having been spared the hardship of their classmates, but less guilt was apparent than was admitted by those children who escaped totally unharmed after the rescue operation.

Flight from threat is a very basic reaction, but so is clinging to a parent. Was it lack of appraisal of the danger, in one case, and premature vigilance in the other that led to death of a five-year-old girl who insisted on following her father to his own death, while her six-year-old neighbor pulled herself away from her running father to hide and be saved?

Paralysis and Panic

A person in a stress situation might wildly thrust about or freeze up in stunned terror, losing whatever momentary opportunity there may have been to save himself. Both reactions were subjectively experienced as failure to respond. Among the overt manifestations of panic were screaming, crying and trembling fits, running around aimlessly, loss of bladder control, and fainting (Beit She'an, Ma'alot). The word "panic" was used repeatedly in the interviews to convey "unbearable horror." Freezing was described by survivors as a temporary loss of voluntary mobility of limbs or tongue, accompanied by total numbing of thoughts and feeling. For example, a five-year-old girl in Ma'alot who had witnessed the slaughter of her family and was severely wounded, described herself later as having been "turned to stone," unable to move or feel any pain. At Kiryat Shmona, one eight-year-old felt "stunned and unable to take even one step toward my dying mother and sister lying there on the floor crying for help." The shock and paralysis took quite a few minutes to wear off. Five out of six children from Beit She'an, on hearing cries of "Terrorists, help" and seeing their relatives bleeding, described themselves as greatly confused and petrified, not able to move until galvanized by one more active boy.

The Tzfat children (ages 15–16) recall their first reactions as disbelief and attempting to ward off warning cues: "I saw three terrorists and heard them shouting, then went on sleeping. . . ." This first response was followed by paralysis of will, confusion, and shock. "I sat quietly in the midst of all the crying, not feeling anything," one 16-year-old reported. One boy reported feeling "completely indifferent" and others dozed off for long periods when they heard the terrorists. Concomitant with emotional numbing is the loss of the physical sensation of pain, reported by several children who were wounded and others who trod on glass and thorns in their escape. When paralysis wore off, it gave way to various nonspecific responses that aggravated the situation.

Resourcefulness

Attempts to call for outside help are secondary reactions following the initial stage of paralysis and panic, and demand a realistic assessment of the danger and of the sources of rescue. In some of the cases, a wounded parent summoned enough strength to send the child to bring help (Kiryat Shmona, Rechanya), while in other places, for lack or loss or parents, the frightened children organized among themselves and sent for help (Beit She'an).

In Shamir, it was vigilance and a quick decision that sent a boy of six to alert the guard to the presence of armed strangers on the kibbutz grounds. In Rechanya, a 12-year-old succeeded, under the threatening guns of the terrorists who had just killed her father and wounded her mother, to contrive a method of communication with the army, using a different language to mislead the captors.

As stress lingered on, new patterns of active coping emerged, characterized by ***role-taking*** and ***altruistic behavior***. Some activities took much courage—serving as sandbags at the windows, shielding others from bullets, or even planning a suicidal rescue attempt. One girl (17), who in particular seems to have tried to gain more control than most, committed risky endeavors by shielding the terrorists against bullets from the outside while they were negotiating and by jolting the muzzle of one of their guns away from an outside negotiator. On other occasions she attempted to establish contact with the rescue forces.

Only a few individuals summoned enough energy to be active—caring for the wounded and comforting and nurturing the others. The activities seemingly served to distract them from the overwhelming fears as well as benefitting the others.

> I felt a raw, deep fear in my stomach. Looking around me I suddenly saw dry lips, wide and frightened eyes. It dawned on me that I had to help in some way. A girl fainted and then another. The terrorists ordered us not to move. What could happen to me? I would feel a bullet and that's all. I got up and stepping on the stretched bodies I went over to one of the girls, avoiding looking in the terrorists' direction. I heard their order to sit down but I went on. Then I

> turned and begged them, still not looking at them, to give me some water. I said that in Arabic. Their commander hesitated, then called in Hebrew to someone to go and bring water. Immediately one of the boys got up and went to the toilets, returning with a full bottle. (Gal, 1980, p. 11)

A few more kids shared these chores. One or two girls took responsibility for guiding others in prayer. Most hostages at Ma'alot, within the narrow confines of possible behavior, displayed a relatively low level of activitiy. Fearful and resentful, they thwarted more purposeful attempts at self-rescue planned by several boys. The few others who did not succumb to passive, apathetic behavior occupied themselves within the limited choice of actions, either by preparing food and perpetual eating, or by providing others with food and drink.

The benefit of activity under stress is paramount (Gal & Lazarus, 1975). Those who muster the energy to be active gain a sense of purpose, or at least succeed in distracting their thoughts from their ill fate. In spite of its obvious advantages, it seems that only a few people spontaneously initiate activity under extreme stress of this kind (see also Jacobson, 1973).

Contact with Captors

Deciphering the captors' facial expressions became vital to victims. Eyes and mouth became salient features for predicting potential dangers. The Ma'alot hostages were subjected to the effects of their captors' gazes: "I was overwhelmed by his terrible eyes, which looked through me, reducing me to nothing. I felt his looks could kill," or else, "I could not believe he would do me any harm after I had looked into his eyes." But prediction failed for one five-year-old survivor who watched an armed stranger smiling at her face while firing his bullets into her belly.

When the terrorists seemed less tense, a couple of hostages ventured to talk to them. One girl approached them boldly, challenging their murderous intentions as contradictory to their religion. Engaging in conversation with those "in utter control" seemed to have helped the girl to regain some feeling of security, especially since she was indulging in the illusion of "talking them out of it." Later she suffered self-deprecatory guilt feelings for "contaminating myself by contact with the murderers of my mates." No conversion signs of positive feelings toward captors were obvious or even conceivable in the situation where victims endured humiliation and abuse (cf. Fields, 1980).

Palliative Modes of Coping

When all avenues of escape were closed and the stress was prolonged over a period of time, other patterns arose of intra- and inter-psychic mechanisms for managing the erosive stress of exposure to danger and deprivation. Because almost no support was available from peers and very scant information came from the outside (which was quite hectic at that time), captives withdrew attention from the obnoxious reality into fantasies and memories of their childhood, parents, and friends back home. These served to distract their minds from the present misery and to provide the badly lacking warmth of trusted figures.

Support and solace were sought in applying to God for help and saying prayers, which was quite in tune with these children's religious upbringing. There were individual differences in the conviction with which religious rituals were followed and relied on. One girl, who found a prayer book in her pocket, urged others to pray. "Two girls refused to say their prayers and now they are among the dead," she concludes.

Parental dictums and warnings were elicited in half delusional states. One girl claims to have heard her father's voice in her dream, instructing her to say Thanksgiving to the Lord for saving her. She is convinced that this was an omen that predicted her rescue. Another teenager attributes her good luck to paternal instructions: "My father had told me always to sit in a corner when there is trouble. So I did, never moved from the wall." Some youngsters felt that they were being punished for some sins, particularly for disobeying their parents by going on that trip. Desperate attempts at repentance took the form of confessions and asking for absolution, bargaining and taking vows to reform, and promises for contribution to charity and for complete obedience to God and parents. Pleas for Divine support are a common phenomenon under threat of death, and in this specific group this may have been part of their coping socialization. (In other groups, repudiation of God was as common.)

Omens and portents, along with magical, superstitious thinking, can serve as mechanisms to "restore some order and logic to the disrupted world-image" (Terr, 1981). A diary, written in the hospital during the first week after the rescue, lists a number of such portents, recalled and registered by a 16-year-old wounded survivor.

> Sending the letter to my boyfriend, I had a passing thought: if I die he will still have my letter. A day before the trip I asked a friend (who was killed the next day) to draw me a picture to remember her by. . . . Sitting in the school bus everybody is singing but me. I feel some harm coming. . . I wish I could stop the bus and get out. . . . Climbing a steep rock, the same afternoon, I had to fight a drive to tumble and break a leg so I'd be sent back home (I wish I'd done that). . . . On arriving at school I felt a heavy weight on my chest. . . did not participate in the games, could hardly sleep. I was waiting for something to happen. . . ."

Such portents, having been consolidated by the turning of events, may easily be reinforced into a lifestyle of compulsive-obsessive worrying.

Recuperation

What can one do for victims of such violence? The period of recovery is impregnated with hazards. Acute symptoms of traumatic neurosis occur, at least temporarily, following the direct involvement in such disasters, even in the most stable personalities.

The symptoms that we found in the children who were interviewed or observed in this second phase of trauma coincided with Lindemann's (1944) profile of prolonged traumatic reaction: shock, bewilderment, partial loss of temporal and spacial orientation, preoccupation with catastrophic ideas and images, prolonged grief, crying spells, and lability of moods, loss of appetite, and sleep disturbances. The threshold for tolerating noises, darkness, and unexpected movements was temporarily lowered. Some survivors expressed a pronounced consciousness of carrying a special mark that set them apart from other people. This period of immediate recuperation was marked by a compulsive need for a repetitive recounting of the experience, as the survivors tried to master anxieties they could not cope with at the time by reliving the event in fantasy. Not heeded and treated, these symptoms may develop into a lasting acute neurosis (Horowitz, 1976; Janis, 1971).

Secondary Victimization

The survivor's plight does not terminate with actual rescue, as has been demonstrated by Klein (1968), Krystal (1968), Lifton (1967), Erikson (1979) and so forth. But what is common knowledge in the professional community is vehemently denied by survivors themselves, by their families, and by the community at large. This denial results in avoiding further treatment that could ameliorate future morbid dysfunctions. When post-traumatic intervention is not administered to the survivors and others in the community, as has been the case in most of the reported events, a process of secondary victimization is often set into motion.

Secondary victimization is a complex phenomenon in which social stigma adheres to the survivor, trapping him in the web of an antagonistic atmosphere. At the same time, this phenomenon contains the seed for prolonged or permanent personality injury that will affect the survivor's future chances and choices. Evidence of secondary victimization was revealed in our follow-up interviews, held from one to six yeas after the terrorist attack. We will examine the social stigmatization and rejection as observed by our subjects and then proceed to describe a condensed profile of the most dominant features found in survivors six years after the rescue.

Survivors' complaints and disappointment of the ways they were treated by the community are also affected by what Symonds (1980) called "second injury." The need of the survivor for an enormous amount of compassion and nurturance, to compensate for his crushed feelings of trust and self-esteem, is sometimes complicated by contradictory needs to express his pent-up rage and regain mastery and independence. They became harder to satisfy when coupled by rejection and scapegoating on the part of the community.

Hostility in different guises was experienced by the survivors of Ma'alot on their returning home and going back to school. The school authorities' demands for discipline and conformity to norms and regulations bluntly overlooked the special physical and emotional needs of the children. In one case, where the school had a rule against girls wearing pants, some female victims wore slacks to cover wounds on their legs. These youngsters were expelled from the class and prohibited from participation in the group process. In this way the work of a therapeutic group, initiated by a crisis team of social workers, was curtailed in its first steps. The students, who found concentration an impossible chore, were accused of taking advantage of the situation. On the whole, they were urged to "forget it all and come back to normal" as soon as possible. Peer society in school responded with a mixture of curiosity and rejection: "They looked at us as if we were pariahs," complained one of the girls.

Jealousy toward any possible prerogative was also prevalent in the outside circle and among the survivors themselves. Suspicion and accusations were hurled at them and extended to their families as well, accentuating the social isolation. Animosity of the bereaved families toward survivors took pathological forms. One of the examples concerns a bereaved family whose daughter had been killed. They took to cursing and throwing stones at her cousin who came back alive from the ordeal. This behavior, which persisted for two years, stopped only when this cousin's brother was killed in a military action.

Discrimination, real or imagined, against those who were crippled aggravated the feelings of ongoing victimization: "I wish they knew how it feels to be captured by terrorists, then maybe they would stop ridiculing and bullying me over my amputated arm," said one 23-year-old male survivor. "They only keep me in my job out of pity, they accuse me of trading my suffering for a car, although I paid for most of the cost myself," he continued.

Social pressures to exhibit the signs of mourning have been exerted on those who tried to shake off their grief: "Whenever I laughed aloud they criticized me," said one of the girls. Very similar responses were noticed among the schoolmates of the "near-miss" group of children in

Nahariya. Derisive remarks were made about their noctural flights, and accusations heard about their taking advantage of the event in order to skip lessons. These insinuations were shared by some of the teachers and children's parents. One 13-year-old complained about his teachers' ignoring his newly acquired fears: "They shouldn't have put me on guard duty at the gate so soon after what happened. I was shaking with fear." "Children call us names; they think that we are bragging whenever we try to talk about what happened," said a 14-year-old. She continued, "They call us 'chickens' when we show signs of fear. Had they been there. . . ."

Long-Term Personality Changes

One major transformation in the self-image noted among the interviewees was an emergence of a "survivor's identity." Whenever the new identity was adopted or denied, it became the scale and measure of all ensuing experiences. The most extreme manifestation was provided by a young man who began to sign correspondence using a self-administered title: "Survivor of Ma'alot." Others present themselves much in the same way in new social contexts. The event and publicity have bestowed a certain halo with which there is a reluctance to part. At the other extreme, we found a young woman who resented being reminded of the events and tried to alienate herself from the others because she "does not want to be considered a survivor."

The passing of time has not reduced the impact of the experience. Recurring events of a similar nature in other parts of the country evoke a strong sense of identification with the new victims and new traumatization. But even without such reminders, a catastrophic expectation of recurrence of the disaster lingers on. A 22-year-old related a fantasy: "Listening to the radio, I imagine hearing: 'A survivor of Ma'alot has again been rescued from yet another terrorist attack!' "

Probing into the personal meaning of holding onto the "survivor" image, two distinct interpretations have emerged that coincide with other optimistic or pessimistic attitudes toward life. The experience imprinted on a number of survivors leads them to a conviction of having been "chosen for life" by supernatural forces. This has been reinforced by their "good luck" in having survived the ordeal. They had a feeling of immunity, of being protected. For others, the very same experience has been registered as proof of being guilty and condemned, and consequently of being eligible for further persecution. A severly wounded survivor was thought to be dead and put in the morgue, to be pulled out and rescued by his father. He is depressed and listless most of the time and finds it difficult to believe that he is alive.

Long-range recuperation of the Ma'alot–Tzfat survivors has taken three different paths according to the nature or degree of physical injury.

1. Those who were ***severely wounded*** and ***crippled*** are obviously suffering at present from their losses. They are preoccupied with both their handicaps and their more or less successful attempts at rehabilitation. Hostility is displaced from the initiators of their troubles, namely the terrorists, to more recent causes of aggravation: society at large, disappointing social agencies, abandoning friends, and so forth.

2. Those victims harboring the most guilt feelings and the worst fears, anger, and vengeance are those who were ***saved unharmed.*** One of the hostages who, by volunteering to carry the terrorists' messages out of the building, was spared several hours of the ordeal and its harrowing termination, described a perpetual preoccupation with his guilt and a great need to act out his hostility. During a military action against the terrorists' bases in Lebanon, in which he participated as a regular soldier, it became well known that he was "carrying out a private war of revenge for his murdered mates." According to him, he succeeded in releasing an enormous personal pressure by being able to participate in this military operation. But he is still considerd an "angry young man."

3. Quite different is the fate of those who were ***slightly injured,*** not badly enough to become crippled, but who felt they still deserved and accepted the care and concern of those surrounding them. The partial injury seems to have helped them toward a more complete solution of their victimization than the other two groups. Their injury provided secondary gains and absolved them from the growing guilt of being "unharmed." Their injury served as an atonement to God, as if they too have paid their toll and are now exempt from further harm.

Other characteristic features found among the survivors concerned relations to others. Here too dichotomization was found between an attitude of resentment bordering on paranoid suspicion of others on one hand, and on the other, an altruistic, self-sacrificing attitude. The first attitude is probably a part of the syndrome of unspent aggressiveness projected on others. The second attitude seems to activate a need for reversing the image of "victim" into the image of the "rescuer," conveying a sense of mastery and control. There is more than a hint of a ritualistic "appeasement of the gods" ingrained in these behaviors. Religious beliefs and religious rituals showed an increasing hold over the survivors, though a minority among them denounced God in face of the atrocities to which they had been exposed.

The impact of the trauma, which in many different ways inhibits their capacity for enjoying life and for trusting themselves and others, featured prominently in the interviews of all the survivors. Another common feature was their strong need to talk and share their experiences, in spite of the time elapsed. This pattern of reactions suggests the need for some form of intervention following traumatic experiences. Intervention may be useful not only immediately following the event, but also, as the interviews indicate, many years later. The victimized children may pay the price of their trauma long after its termination.

Apart from short and erratic attempts at crisis intervention, no systematic stress prevention program has been implemented to help these young people to come to terms with their experience. Services for victims should be geared to reduce acute suffering among casualties and to preventing long-range adverse psychological repercussions. Moreover, stress inoculation for high-risk population could be of great preventive value.

INTERVENTION AND PREVENTION

The arena that seems at first glance to be most appropriate for conducting stress-preventive intervention with children, prior to or following a traumatic event, is the school. The school is a good choice since it encompasses vital peer-group interaction opportunities and the presence of qualified adults in an educational framework. But existing practices still lag behind the recommended ones, giving stress intervention a rather controversial status. Until recently, even postcrisis treatment was regarded as superfluous, if not downright harmful (e.g., Bellos, 1977).

There is little mystery behind rationales and rationalizations antagonistic to stress intervention, stemming from various political and social sources, and expressed by a reluctance to confront directly the responsibility for stress and its consequences. The social system at large, and the educational system in particular, are adamant in opposing the demands for the allocation of financial and personal resources that a large-scale preventive program would demand. The shift from instrumental leadership to an expressive-supportive orientation is strongly opposed by traditional school management. The teachers' basic training is also considered inadequate to deal with emotionally charged issues (Ayalon, 1979b). There is a prevailing tendency not to unbalance the system during relatively peaceful periods, and reservations exist about overloading the already burdened schedule.

At a less obvious level, the reluctance to invest in stress prophylactics stems from fear and guilt of violating social taboos that inhibit open discussion of loss and death (Feifel, 1971; Toynbee, 1969). These proceedings may raise atavistic apprehensions such as those expressed colloquially as "inviting in the devil," "casting an evil eye," and "stirring up trouble." Teachers discussing death in one of my courses on "Stress Education" claimed that since they opened up the issue, the death rate in their schools had increased remarkably (Ayalon, 1979b). With some effort, they were helped to see that it was their awareness that had become more acute. School children are often unaware of the need for extra input and have to be carefully motivated to engage in a preventive program without needless augmentation of their anxieties. Another objection is the controversy over the psychological cost of breaking down the denial of unpleasant facts or feelings. Denial in case of low probability and/or unavoidable threats is considerd an adaptive mechanism (Lazarus, 1982). Its absence may cause perpetual apprehension about danger and may release uncontrolled anxiety.

Examining the Israeli scene of stress and stress prevention can bring these contradictions to the fore and hint at possible solutions. The following are some of the controversial issues that arise following the introduction of a preventive intervention:

1. It is likely that the threat of a terrorist assault is so horrendous that it can hardly be mitigated by exposure to minor threats, in the form of inoculation.
2. Given the existing geopolitical situation, the mere rehearsal of forecasts can have deleterious effects on the subjects, unnecessarily augmenting their anxieties and enhancing phobic responses to minor threats.
3. Moral issues arise from the fact that such rehearsal may reinforce stereotypical dichotomization of "enemy figures." One must be cautious in how one uses such cognitive-behavioral techniques as imagery rehearsal, role-playing, and so forth.
4. Another moral and educational concern, which strongly projects on future development of childrens' interpersonal attitudes, stems from the danger of encouraging callous, if not ruthless, responses as is frequently apparent in children who learn to brace themselves against threats of a violent environment (cf. Coles, 1964; Fraser, 1973).

The Israeli scene demands a multifaceted method of intervention, adaptable to a variety of cultural-traditional response modalities, to personal coping styles, and to age-specific needs. Intervention should also be sensitive to both external and internal stresses, most of them unpredictable.

The dilemma of preventive intervention in situations of unpredictable violence against those who are the most vulnerable is delineated by conflicting pressures: the surfacing reluctance to take preventive measures, and the painful burden of neglect in cases of inflicted trauma.

With full consideration of all those conflicting issues and needs, a large-scale preventive program was developed in the University of Haifa School of Education. The program, called COPE (Community Oriented Preparation for Emergency) (Ayalon, 1978), is a loose-leaf package of structured, open-ended suggestions for coping activities. It was initially devised during the war of October (1973) and adapted by the Ministry of Education for dissemination in the Israeli educational system, giving priority to schools in vulnerable areas.

During the war and shortly afterwards, it became obvious to both the school authorities and mental health agents in schools that a crisis intervention, such as was often called upon in schools that had suffered losses, could not operate efficiently without prior preparation. Thus, the crisis created by the war both increased the need for a structural, well-guided intervention and facilitated its implementation. As reservations still exist against acknowledging the need for prevention during peaceful and nonproblematic periods, the program is more likely to be used during a crisis and in the aftermath. The implementation of COPE in the educational community was handled in a systematic approach in order to guarantee the expected changes in procedures and behaviors. An elaborate training format was introduced to key people from all strata of the educational hierarchy, such as principals, counselors, teachers, youth leaders, and volunteer workers. Winning them over to the idea of prevention by working through personal attitudes, memories, and hang-ups was an important guarantee for a responsible operation of the program. (For a detailed model of the community operation, see Ayalon, 1979a.)

Because this intervention was developed under conditions that had not been mentioned or tackled before in the stress and coping literature, it is quite intriguing to note similarities and differences to other stress inoculation procedures. Most of it is quite consistent with the cognitive-behavioral model of stress inoculation, as put forward by Orne (1968), Meichenbaum, Turk, and Burstein (1975), and Meichenbaum and Turk (1976, in press). Nevertheless COPE has some distinctive features. One difference, for example, arises from the notion that *mastery of mild stress creates future tolerance for stressful stimuli of greater intensity.* This notion does not find a counterpart in prevention work with such extreme stress as the encountering of terrorist violence. Such stress calls for a different approach, to develop skills "to grapple effectively with unexpected and temporarily insoluble problems and to persevere in this in spite of confusion, discomfort and frustration" (Caplan, 1979). In accordance with Caplan's suggestions, COPE provides training to acquire *generic skills* that operate effectively under stress, to develop self-trust and tolerance for distress, to find new solutions where the old ones have failed, and to develop and employ specific skills required by the situation.

The focus of COPE is ***affective education based on cognitive learning of discrimination and appraisal of threat cues.*** Essentially the program provides the children with opportunities to develop *cognitive-emotional maps* to guide them in different, unexpected threatening situations.

Consistent with the stress inoculation procedure, COPE programs involve an initial stage in which a conceptual framework of stress and coping is offered, followed by a stage of identification of social skills, and finally a stage focusing on the acquisition and training of coping skills within a supportive atmosphere. The training is carried out in small peer groups. One of the main ingredients of this approach is the emphasis on the social supportive network within which all activities are performed. Peer-group cohesion is encouraged throughout, within which identification, a sense of shared fate and open communication is enhanced. The small group is used to generate alternative solutions to complicated challenges that may be beyond the scope of individual capacity. Participants are encouraged to learn supportive behaviors, to receive support without humiliation, and to give support without becoming overprotective. By delegating such supportive roles to the children, the teacher, who is an indispensable adult source of support, can act as a facilitator to a great number of children when urgent needs arise, as will be described shortly.

It is proposed that a crucial determinant of the childrens' ability to cope with stress is the ability to ventilate "unspent emotions," either by talking, drawing, or reenacting. The techniques offered by COPE are varied, flexible, and amenable to change by the program leader. An extensive use is made of *in vitro* exposures, such as ambiguous pictures and photographs, used as triggers for role-playing and for expressive writing. Carefully chosen short stories and poems are used for the same purpose, in the spirit of bibliotherapy (Ayalon, 1979b). Several simulation games were specially devised and conveniently packaged into the program. On the whole, the child's language of play and fantasy, creative as well as communicative expressions, are carefully employed to help nurture and strengthen the children's ability to cope with unforeseen stress and also to handle previous grievances. The child is encouraged to work through his feelings using a variety of modes of expression and activities. The focus of training is not only the ventilation of emotion and the development of cognitive problem-solving skills, but also the prompting of a number of specific behavioral skills, such as relaxation, downgrading reactions to fearful stimuli, etc. Special attention is given to practicing relaxation techniques that, by the use of guided fantasy, become a most effective tool for handling fear cues.

Activity is regarded as a most adaptive and appropriate behavior under stress. The COPE program provides ample opportunities for the children to develop an active attitude toward stress, either as a direct attempt at reducing the stressor or using activity as a palliative device for the period of possible confinement.

The teachers' role throughout the process is mainly to disseminate relevant and reliable information, to stimulate and guide the various activities, and to provide reassurance by means of physical proximity and empathy. The program is packaged in an "Emergency Kit" in the form of a loose-leaf teacher's guide and resource book. The kit is constructed so it can be used by non- or para-professional facilitators, in cases of teachers' enforced absence (quite probable in a sudden alarm or during war-like situations).

Facilitators, whether teachers, parents, or substitutes, are provided with suggestions for implementing the stress-reducing activities. They are guided to help the children channel distress into constructive, growth-producing behavior. High motivation is achieved by adapting the training of coping patterns to individual ages, temperament, and previous life experience and by appealing to spontaneous and imaginative inner sources. For example, the use of projective techniques helps to solicit the children's suppressed worries that may be consequently allayed. The ultimate aim of the program is to encourage mastery through active coping that may contribute to a clearer assessment of the stressful situation, tapping the children's potential adaptive resources.

As a crisis intervention, the COPE program has been used in cases of distress caused by death in the family, separation and divorce, illness, and surgery and ensuing physical handicaps. Pain and loneliness can be mitigated by proper channeling of children's energies so that they may acquire greater control over their environment and new modes of expressing fears and worries, by transforming their passive role into one of activity.

The need for such a primary prevention program has been highlighted in several recent emergencies that will be discussed presently. Clearly, during the acute stress there is almost always too little time to make important decisions and too many issues to cope with. Such training aims at establishing beforehand workable routines and a clearly defined role-allocation. Producing a vigilant approach is a delicate art involving a balance between downgrading threatening cues, without becoming callous, and staying alert, without being overwhelmed by anxiety. The following case describes our attempt to affect such a balance.

A Case of Crisis Intervention

What follows is a short description of a crisis intervention "marathon" carried out by an ad hoc emergency team in Nahariya, the day after terrorists raided a house on the beach. Two men and two small girls were murdered, while the other residents of the immediate vicinity, under the impression of being persecuted, either hid or fled. A survey of the schools the next morning indicated that 54 children were absent. They were identified as the near-miss, high-risk group of school children. The list of complaints these children reported included descriptions of acute anxiety states, reawakening of early frightening fantasies, and fear of the dark, of noises, and of the beach (the scene of the crime). Haunted by images of the murdered girls, the children in this high-risk group found concentration impossible and were given to crying spells, headaches, stomach-aches, sleeplessness, and clinging to parents. These reactions are consistent with the syndrome of acute stress neurosis reported in adults (Janis, 1971). The treatment, however, was unique and prompt.

All the children (8–14 years old) were grouped according to age, to be observed and treated for the duration of the crisis. Each small group was conducted by a member of the crisis team for five consecutive days, four hours each day, within the school setting.

The treatment, which was later documented (Ben-Eli & Sella, 1980), proceeded through several distinct stages.

Initial Ventilation of Feelings

This stage was marked by a diffuse expression of the chldren's fear and anger, both verbal and non-verbal (in drawing and finger painting). Sighs and crying and feelings of misery and grief were dominant. Some children seemed flooded with frightening images of past and present experiences.

Abreaction

Role-play and excited narration interchanged as the children relived the traumatic events of the night. The cries, flights, and hidings, the sights and sounds were repeated until exhaustion. Some children have chosen to play the victims' roles or else the aggressors', imitating the terrorists' shouts and even letting themselves be "captured" and "killed." Minute descriptions of every move and thought, feelings of self and others were reanimated and produced discharge of excessive affect.

All expressions, even the most idiosyncratic, were granted full legitimation by the therapists and explained as "normal" for this stage of mourning.

Aggression Channeling

As violent emotions surged, they channeled themselves into scenarios of vengeance and retaliation against the aggressors, acted out through plays and puppet shows. First signs of relief were noticed in the children at the end of what had become a mimicked execution of the puppet terrorists.

At that stage, children ventured angry accusations against the coast guards who had failed them and exposed them to such horrid dangers. Because these feelings had apparently become too frightening, solutions were found in make-believe games, in which the guards or the children succeeded in eliminating the attackers before they had a chance to perpetrate their crime.

Gradual *in vivo* Exposure

It seems that overreaction to noises is one of the most persistent post-traumatic symptoms. The extinction of fear reactions to the beach was carried out with the parents' help. Much support and encouragement was needed until the prestress level of confidence was retrieved. One 14-year-old stated, "My father took me to the shore. I saw the terrorists' boat, the rocks on which they smashed the head of the little girl. I regret having seen the boat, it haunts me in my dreams. But I am not afraid of the sea any longer." In addition, gradual exposure to noises has been conducted during relaxation (i.e., desensitization). But those imagery procedures led only to partial relief. *In vivo* exposure was more effective.

Cognitive Reappraisal of the Experience

Road maps and clay models of the scene were created by the children, accompanied by detailed reconstruction of the sequence of events. Participants dwelt on their recollections, trying to evaluate each reaction in the light of retrospective knowledge: those who hid, others who fled, the girl who stopped to pick up another fleeing girl, the little one who summoned enough courage to push back her captor and to flee for her life. They were especially perturbed by what happened to one family while hiding: A mother smothered her little baby, trying to hush its crying while the terrorists killed her husband and other daughter. By reappraising this entire situation, they reached an understanding that enabled them to make a condolence visit to this bereaved young woman, having come to terms with their ambiguous feelings toward her act.

Working Through

At this stage, expression has become more structured. Children regained their writing skills and the use of rhyme and rhythm, and used these skills in their struggle to gain mastery over their stormy reflections. They became engaged in a "poetic dialogue," writing poems to each other. Later they published these poems in a memorial format. Drawings changed into illustrative portrayals of the scenery and of the victims. Erecting memorials signified the beginning of acceptance of the loss.

Mapping Alternatives

Provided with all the information about the event, participants engaged in suggestions for future encounters with threat and danger. The feelings that had been expressed in earlier phases were now channeled into a problem-solving mode designed to consider what could be done differently in future stressful events. By focusing both on working through their feelings about the past traumas and about the present and future eventualities, the children slowly "came to terms" with the stress of being near-miss victims.

During this period, families were counseled in how to respond to their children. The parents were encouraged to share their own feelings with their children and together to work through the difficult period of recuperation. The reactions subsided gradually and the children resumed their daily activities. The follow-up surveys, at two months and at eight months later, found no perseverence of symptoms in any of the children, with a few exceptions for whom treatment was resumed. Since the survey included a sample of the entire child population of the town, an interesting phenomenon became obvious: The impact of the trauma on the children changed depending on the actual physical distance from the scene of the event. The further the children lived from the site of the attack, the less they were affected (with the exception of a few vulnerable children, who had previously gone through a personal crisis that had been reactivated by the attack).

To illustrate a family approach to intervention in the same crisis, an abstract of the case treatment of a family with phobic reactions will be cited (reported by Maj. N. Alon, Military Mental Health Center, Israel Defense Forces).

> The family lived in a house in Nahariya which was severely assaulted by terrorists in April 1979. During the attack the father (aged 35) and his two daughters (8 and 6) were captured by the terrorists, had a narrow escape and lost each other, each one believing the others were dead. The mother (29) hid with the only survivor of another family, and witnessed the death of their baby. Stress reactions appeared a few days later, after another stressing event occurred in fathers' family. A marathon crisis-intervention session proved insufficient in overcoming the following: decay of family routines; father's depression; family isolation behind defensive hardware; severe fears, especially at nights; watching at the windows for terrorists; girls refusing to sleep anywhere except parents' bedroom; wife unable to stay without husband. All had severe sleep disturbances, violent startle reactions, especially to noises, and suspicions towards strangers. Parents' behavior led to intensification of the girls' problems, but it was felt that direct treatment would be too threatening.

> A brief behavioral intervention was agreed upon, in which the girls' difficulties were declared to be the focus. The underlying principles of the following intervention were: a) Mastery through activity. b) Psychological distance through humor. c) Desensitization. d) Personification of vague frightening fantasies. e) Mutual support. f) Paradoxical intention. Examples follow: Grading of rooms by level of fearfulness and signing girls' room with self-made poster: "The room of terrible fear." A "fear diary" to be written by the girls whenever fear arises. *In vivo* training for mastery reactions to natural fearful stimuli. Mothering of "frightened dolls" at fearful moments. After the girls returned to their room: mock escape to parents' bedroom. Re-definition of fear as legitimate essential to self-preservation, a "magic-word" was given for self-administration of deep relaxation to overcome anxiety. The girls' phobias disappeared after four 2-hours sessions. Marked decrease in parents' fears was achieved. (Alon, 1980)

The quest for tailor-made preventive approaches to fit a variety of conditions had prompted alternative intervention strategies. Two examples follow of polarized attitudes that try to cater to the need for vigilance and the need for confidence.

The national television designed a series of short dramatized features, warning the population against suspicious figures and objects. These exposures, although they contribute to anxiety, have been quite successful in leading to early detection of dangerous activities, saving many lives.

On the other hand, reported states of morbid anxiety among children in a previously attacked area have stimulated interventions in order to alleviate fears and restore confidence. In these cases the intervention intended to reassure the children of the low probability of a recurrent terrorist attack (calculated as 3 actual attacks to 100 across-the-border infiltration attempts thwarted by security forces).

Second, a simulated board-game, processing realistic information on terrorists maneuvers and security strategems, was made into a simplified chess-like format. Playing this simulation helped the participants to make a more realistic appraisal of the situation and to allay their anxieties (Ophir, 1980).

A NEED FOR EVALUATION

The dire need for such stress intervention and prevention programs can easily become a Sisyphian task. The continual tensions in the Middle East and the urgent need for stress intervention make the task of systematically evaluating such programs difficult. But, with patience and some luck, we are able to demonstrate in repeated trials the effectiveness of such stress-prevention programs.

One model program of coping training is being conducted in one of the schools of a previously mentioned town, Kiryat Shmona, a notoriously easy target for across-the-border shelling (Zuckerman-Bareli, 1979).

The effects of the training might not have become known, had it not been for the occurrence of a recent ultrasonic boom that sent the whole school running to the air shelter. A natural experimental design offered itself to the ready observer. More than 400 pupils, aged 6–12, panicked in the shelter in the same way they had done in previous shelling attacks, having learned no prior adaptive behavior through repeated experiences. Their teachers were helpless as well. But one large group of 50 children stood out as an organized island of peace amidst the commotion. These were the recipients of the coping training, who had already been well drilled in routines for peer-group support and peer leadership, and who were equipped with prearranged activity kits with tasks to be fulfilled in the shelter. For them, the event was a cue to rehearse their newly acquired behaviors.

A second group of 16 children, only half-way through their coping training, were rehearsing a simulated shelling attack when the alarm struck. Their behavior was more problematic. Initially they panicked, but they pulled themselves together in a very short while and joined the "experimental" group in modeling both mastery and ingenuity (reported by M. Lahad, program facilitator).

CONCLUDING REMARKS

At a time when social scientists and policy-makers argue about preferred strategies to curb world terrorism, we have chosen to shed some light on the fate of the victims. We have tried to understand what determines the behavior of a person who has become a pawn in a gory game not of his making. Can such behavior be predicted? Can it be channelled to assist the victims in regaining control over their threatened lives? Is there any feasible way to reduce the damage caused to survivors? Assessments of psychological damage have been used to determine the amount of compensation due (Eitinger & Strum, 1973; Lifton, 1976; Niederland,1968; Parkes,1976) and to initiate suitable treatment methods (Brill, 1974; Fields, 1977; Frankl, 1970; Fraser, 1973; Klein, 1968; Kliman, 1973). We suggest that such assessment be used for a study of *the potential prevention of the psychic trauma of victimization.* Stress prevention programs are in their preliminary stages of development and should be researched, modified and consolidated. As far as we know, no systematic evaluation of such programs has been undertaken with children. Both the challenges and needs are great. The present clinical description of our programs will, we hope, stimulate such research.

Life "under a volcano" certainly poses problems of mental health and burn-out that deserve further concern. Why is evidence so scarce and research so scant? Why do we know so little about the mechanisms of coping and surviving under threatening circumstances?

A unique report of survivors' reactions to their plight by Lieblich (1978) indicated the high price paid by individuals who tried to cope by maintaining a "stiff upper lip" approach that had been recommended as the most suitable for channelling vital energies away from stressful preoccupations. In contrast, quite different recommendations emerge from our present exploration. Our data lead us to reject this "ostrich" strategy. More research is needed to identify the best patterns of coping.

In summary, more than 10 communities were observed in their response to the onslaught of terrorism. Some structural characteristics were examined that contributed to the group's behavior and influenced individual responses in both short and long term. It appears that the most adaptive attitude was not avoidance and denial, nor anxious preoccupation with impending dangers, but rather vigilant awareness of the possibility of inherent threats, allowing for prophylactic measures. Individual patterns of survival were identified through interviews and observations. A preliminary stress prevention program was described. The need for a critical evaluation was emphasized.

The dilemma of children exposed to hostilities demands special attention. Can we prevent children from absorbing the violence and protect them from crippling anxiety? There is an urgent need for longitudinal follow-up of the survivors of the above-described man-induced disasters, mainly the children among them, in whom the future of society is invested.

ACKNOWLEDGMENTS

I am greatly indebted to all those young people who allowed me to share their pain and admire their courage. Thanks to Zichria Golan and Lila Namir for their indispensable help.

REFERENCES

Alon, M. *Treatment of a family with phobic reaction.* Paper presented at the meeting of the International Congress of Behavior Therapy, Jerusalem, 1980.

Ayalon, O. *Rescue! A teachers guide for coping with emergencies.* Issum Publishing Co. University of Haifa, 1978. (In Hebrew.)

Ayalon, O. Community Oriented Preparation for Emergency: COPE. *Death Education,* 1979, *3*(3), 227–245. (a)

Ayalon, O. Is death a proper subject for the classroom. *International Journal of Social Psychiatry,* 1979, *25*(4), 252–258. (b)

Bellos, S. Teachers ill-prepared to cope with emergency situation. *Jerusalem Post,* January 20, 1977.

Ben-Eli, Z., & Sella, M. Terrorists in Nahariya. *Journal of Psychology and Counselling in Education,* 1980, *13,* 94–101. (In Hebrew.)

Bertalanffy, L. von. *General system theory.* New York: George Braziller, 1968.

Bettelheim, B. *The informed heart.* New York: The Free Press, 1961.

Bettelheim, B. *Surviving and other essays.* New York: Knopf, 1979.

Bowlby, J. *Maternal care and mental health.* World Health Organization, 1952.

Brill, F. *On the way to a humanistic psychotherapy.* Tel-Aviv: Levin, Epstein, Modan, 1974. (In Hebrew.)

Caplan, G. *Support systems and community mental health behavior.* New York: Behavioral Publications, 1974.

Caplan, G. *Mastery of stress: Psychological aspects.* International Congress of Psychosomatic Medicine, Jerusalem, 1979.

Coles, R. *Children in crisis: A study of change and fear.* Boston: Atlantic Monthly Press, 1964.

Dollard, J., Dobb, L., Miller, N., & Sears, R. *Frustration and aggression.* New Haven: Yale University Press, 1939.

Eitinger, L., & Strum, A. *Morality and morbidity after excessive stress.* New York: Humanistic Press, 1973.

Erikson, K. *In the wake of the flood.* London: Allen & Unwin, 1979.

Feifel, K. The meaning of death in the American society: Implication for education. In B. Green & D. Irish (Eds.), *Death education: Preparation for living.* Cambridge, Mass.: Schenkman, 1971.

Fields, R. *Society under seige.* Philadelphia: Temple University Press, 1977.

Fields, R. *Hostages and torture victims: Studies in effects of trauma induced stress.* Paper presented at the Second International Conference on Psychological Stress and Adjustment to Time of War and Peace, Jerusalem, June 1978.

Fields, R. *Terrorized into terrorists.* Unpublished manuscript, Alexandria, Virginia, 1979.

Fields, R., Victims of terrorism: The effects of prolonged stress. *Evaluation and Change,* 1980, 76–83.

Frankenstein, C. Structural factors in the anxiety of children. *Acta Psychologica,* 1956, *12,* 321.

Frankenstein, C. The structural meaning of aggressiveness. *Acta Psychologica,* 1958, *14,* 253.

Frankenstein, C. *Psychodynamics of externalization.* Baltimore: Williams & Wilkens, 1968.

Frankenstein, C. *Impaired intelligence.* New York: Gordon & Breach, 1970.

Frankenthal, K. Autohypnosis and other aids for survival in situations of extreme stress. *The International Journal of Clinical & Experimental Hypnosis,* 1969, *27*(3), 153–159.

Frankl, V. *Man's search for meaning.* New York: Touchstone, 1970.

Fraser, M. *Children in conflict.* New York: Basic Books, 1973.

Fredrick, C. Effects of natural vs. human induced violence upon victims. *Evaluation & Change,* 1980, 71–75.

Freud, S. One problem of anxiety. In *Collected Papers* (Vol. 5). London: Hograth Press, 1950.

Furst, S. (Ed.). *Psychic trauma.* New York: Basic Books, 1967.

Gal, P. *Psychic trauma & support system.* M. A. Thesis, Tel-Aviv University, 1980.

Gal, R., & Lazarus, R. The role of activity in anticipating and confronting stressful situation. *The Journal of Human Stress,* 1975, *1,* 4–20.

Ginath, Y., & Krasilowsky, D. Adaptive changes of different social structures facing a common hostile situation. *Israel Annals of Psychiatry,* 1970, *8,* 146–162.
Golan, A. *The hostage city.* Tel-Aviv: Zemora, Bitan, Modan, 1979. (In Hebrew.)
Hastings, D. W. Psychiatry in 8th Air Force. *Air Surgeon's Bulletin,* 1944, *1,* 4–5.
Horowitz, M. *Stress response syndrome.* New York: Jason Aronson, 1976.
Jacobson, S. Individual & group responses to confinement in a skyjacked plane. *American Journal of Orthopsychiatry,* 1973, *43*(3), 459–469.
Jacobson, S. *Leadership patterns and stress adaption among hostages in three terrorist captured planes.* Paper presented at the International Conference on Psychological Stress and Adjustment in Time of War and Peace, Tel-Aviv, January 1975.
Janis, I. *Air war and emotional stress.* New York: McGraw-Hill, 1951.
Janis, I. *Psychological stress.* New York: Wiley, 1958.
Janis, I. *Stress and frustration.* New York: Harcourt, Brace, Jovanovich, 1971.
Janis, I., & Mann, L. *Decision making.* New York: The Free Press, 1977.
Januv, B. Short term intervention: A model for emergency services in a community crisis. *Social Security,* 1976, 5–18. (In Hebrew.)
Kaffman, M. Kibbutz civilian population under war stress. *British Journal of Psychiatry,* 1977, *130,* 489–494.
Klein, H. Problems in psychotherapeutic treatment of Israeli survivors of holocaust. In H. Krystal (Ed.), *Massive psychic trauma.* New York: International Universities Press, 1968.
Kliman, A. *The Cronin flood projects.* Subcommittee on Disaster Relief of the Community & Public Works, U. S. Senate, Sept. 1973.
Krystal, H. (Ed.). *Massive psychic trauma.* New York: International Universities Press, 1968.
Lazarus, R. *Psychological stress and the coping process.* New York: McGraw-Hill, 1966.
Lazarus, R. *Patterns of adjustment.* New York: McGraw-Hill, 1976.
Lazarus, R. The costs & benefits of denial. In Breznitz (Ed.), *Denial of stress.* New York: International Universities Press, 1982.
Lieblich, A. *Tin soldiers on Jerusalem beach.* New York: Pantheon, 1978.
Lifton, R. *Death in life.* New York: Touchstone, 1967.
Lifton, R. The human meaning of disaster. *Psychiatry,* 1976, *39,* 1–18.
Lindemann, E. Symptomatology & management of acute grief. *American Journal of Psychiatry,* 1944, *101,* 141–148.
Mar'i, S., Ayalon, O., & Fields, R. *The impact of defined environmental violence of prolonged fraternal strife on children of Southern Lebanon & Northern Ireland.* Manuscript submitted for publication, 1980.
Marx, E. Violence of individuals in development town. *Megamot,* 1970, *17*(1), 61–77.
Maslach, C., Burn-out. *Human Behavior,* 1976, *5,* 16–22.
Meichenbaum, D., & Turk, D. The cognitive-behavioral management of anxiety, anger and fear. In P. Davidson (Ed.), *The behavioral management of anxiety, depression and pain.* New York: Brunner/Mazel, 1976.
Meichenbaum, D., & Turk, D. Stress, coping & disease: A cognitive behavioral perspective. In R. Neufeld (Ed.), *Relations between psychological stress & psychopathology.* New York: McGraw-Hill, in press.
Meichenbaum, D., Turk, D., & Burstein, S. The nature of coping with stress. In J. Sarason & C. H. Spielberger (Eds.), *Stress and anxiety* (Vol. 2). New York: Wiley, 1975.
Moldar, M. The structure of communication, decision and group performance. In N. Ben-Ami (Ed.), *Social psychology.* Tel-Aviv: Am-Oved, 1954.

Niederland, W. The psychiatric evaluation of emotional disorders in survivors of Nazi persecution. In H. Krystal (Ed.), *Massive psychic trauma.* New York: International Universities Press, 1968.

Ochberg, F. The victim of terrorism: Psychiatric consideration. *Terrorism: An International Journal,* 1978, *1*(2), 147-167.

Ophir, M. Simulation games as treatment of situational anxiety. I A. Raviv, A. Klingman, & M. Horowitz (Eds.), *Children under stress and in crisis.* Tel-Aviv: Oztar-Hamoreh, 1980. (In Hebrew.)

Orne, M. Psychological factors maximizing resistance to stress with special reference to hypnosis. In S. Klauser (Ed.), *The quest for self-control.* New York: Free Press, 1968.

Parkes, C. M. Abarfan—Disaster and recovery. Unpublished manuscript, 1976. (Available from the Department of Psychiatry, London Hospital, London.)

Rachman, S. *Fear and courage.* New York: Pergamon Press, 1978.

Schrieber, J. *The ultimate weapon.* New York: Morrow, 1978.

Schultz, D. *Panic behavior.* New York: Random House, 1964.

Selye, H. *The stress of life.* New York: McGraw-Hill, 1956.

Smooha, S., & Peres, Y. Ethnic inequality in Israel. *Megamot,* 1974, *20,* 4–42.

Spielberger, C. (Ed.),*Anxiety and behavior.* New York: Academic Press, 1966.

Star, S. Psycho neurotic symptoms in the army. In S. Stouffer, A. A. Lamsdaine, R. Williams, M. B. Smith, I. L. Janis, S. A. Star, & L. Cotrelli, Jr. (Eds.), *The American soldier: Combat and its aftermath* (Vol. 2). N.Y. Princeton, 1944, 411–455.

Symonds, M. Victims of violence: Psychological effects and after effects. *American Journal of Psychoanalysis,* 1975, *35,* 19–26.

Symonds, M. The 'second injury' to victims of violent crimes. *Evaluation & Change,* 1980, 36–38.

Terr, L. Children of Chowchilla: A study of psychic trauma. *Psychoanalytic Study of the Child,* 1979, *34,* 552-623.

Terr, L. Psychic trauma in children: Observations following the Chowchilla schoolbus kidnapping. *American Journal of Psychiatry,* 1981, *138*(1), 14–19.

Toynbee, A. *Man's concern with death.* New York: McGraw-Hill, 1969.

Wolfenstein, M. *Disaster.* New York: The Free Press, 1957.

Ziv, A., & Israeli, R. Effects of bombardment on the manifest anxiety level of children living in kibbutzim. *Journal of Consulting and Clinical Psychology,* 1973, *40,* 287–291.

Zuckerman-Bareli, C. Effects of border tensions on residents of an Israeli town. *The Journal of Human Stress,* 1979, *9,* 29–40.

10

Stress Management for Rape Victims

LOIS J. VERONEN and DEAN G. KILPATRICK

INTRODUCTION

Overview

Our major objective in this chapter is to describe stress management procedures we have developed to be used with rape victims. We will discuss issues involved in the definition of rape, in the estimation of its incidence, and in the investigation of rape-related problems. We will briefly describe the Sexual Assault Research Project and review our findings and those of others regarding the aftermath of rape. Having substantiated our contention that rape is a stressful event that produces substantial, long-lasting problems for many of its victims, we will review other treatment procedures for rape-induced problems, describe our stress inoculation procedure, present assessment data on victims requesting treatment, discuss preliminary results regarding treatment efficacy, and provide information about the use of stress inoculation training with a victim. The chapter will conclude with some observations and speculations about general treatment issues.

Definition of Rape

How one defines rape obviously determines who one designates as a rape victim. As we have discussed elsewhere (Veronen & Kilpatrick,

---

LOIS J. VERONEN and DEAN G. KILPATRICK • Department of Psychiatry and Behavioral Sciences, Medical University of South Carolina, Charleston, South Carolina 29425 and People Against Rape, Charleston, South Carolina 29401. Data in this chapter are the result of research sponsored and funded by the National Center for the Prevention and Control of Rape of the National Institute of Mental Health through Grant No. RO1 MH29602.

in press), rape can be viewed from many perspectives, and one's definition of rape is largely determined by one's perspective. All perspectives are shaped by a general overlay of cultural beliefs that define rape quite narrowly and hold victims responsible for their own assaults. Many people believe that women like to be overpowered sexually, that women say "no" but mean "yes," that "nice" women don't get raped, and that many women make false rape reports to get even with a man or because they are pregnant (Burt, 1980). What effect would these cultural beliefs have on definitions of rape?

The first effect is that rape becomes defined narrowly. If the victim is of unquestioned virtue and if considerable physical force is used, the act is defined as "real" rape. The prototypic "real" rape occurs when a nun on her way to Mass is attacked, raped, and brutally beaten by a motorcycle gang. In contrast, a woman forced to have sex by a man she just met in a bar is not defined as a rape victim by many. A second effect is that there is a tendency to trivialize the impact of a rape experience. Since most victims are partially responsible anyway and like to be overpowered, how could unwanted sex cause major problems? As we shall discuss, rape is considerably more than unwanted sex. A third effect is that women whose rapes do not fit the pattern of a "real" rape may be considerably less likely to report their rapes.

It is our contention that rape should be defined broadly. Therefore, our definition is that rape is any form of nonconsensual sexual activity obtained through coercion, threat of force, or force. As clinicians, it is not our job to make judgments about whether rape legally occurred. If a woman considers herself to have had nonconsensual sexual activity, we consider her to be a victim. Clearly, this definition places heavy emphasis on the victim's perspective. As cognitive-behaviorists, we argue that this is where the emphasis should be since it is the victim's experience and interpretation of it that might be expected to have the greatest impact on her subsequent adjustment.

Incidence of Rape

Unfortunately, good data on the incidence of rape do not exist. What we know about the frequency of rape is based on official crime reports and victimization studies. As Chappell (1976) noted, there are numerous factors that influence official reporting rates. Nevertheless, FBI Uniform Crime Reports indicate that the rate of reported rapes doubled from 1970, when there were 37,900, through 1979, when there were 75,989. Victimization studies attempt to discover the extent of under-reporting by interviewing randomly selected samples about victimization experiences that were unreported. Chappell cited data from such studies indicating that the ratio of unreported to reported rapes ranged from 3.5:1 to 2.0:1. Application of these under-reporting rates to the 1979 FBI statistics suggests that somewhere between 151,978 and 265,962 rapes occurred during the year.

There are several factors to keep in mind when trying to estimate rape incidence. First, if someone is raped and never tells *anyone,* there is no way of detecting her rape and including it in estimates of rape incidence. Second, official crime reports *do not* incude data from women who report being raped but whose cases the police and/or prosecutor "unfound" (i.e., made a judgment that the evidence was insufficient to pursue the case). Nor do statistics include cases that do not meet the legal definition of rape and that are recorded as lesser charges (e.g., aggravated assault). Third, women are at the risk of being raped not just during one year but throughout their lifetimes, a factor that increases the odds that a given woman will be victimized. Fourth, as was previously noted, the narrow definition of rape generally adopted and the cultural biases against victims of more broadly defined rape have the net effect of reducing willingness to report, particularly for those women whose rapes do not fit the "real" rape stereotype. A final factor to consider is that rape affects not only the victim but also her family and friends.

It is reasonable to summarize by stating that we do not have good information on the true incidence of rape and that existing estimates underestimate the extent of the problem. However, we can state with certainty that rape occurs frequently and represents a major problem.

General Issues in Rape Victim Research

As we have discussed elsewhere (e.g., Kilpatrick, 1981), there are numerous difficulties involved in conducting methodologically adequate research on the effects of rape. A victim's mood, behavior, self-concept, and psychological symptomatology after the rape can be conceptualized as reflecting complex interactions of a variety of variables. Variables that might affect her postrape functioning include her prior history, level of functioning and coping skills, various aspects of the assault itself (e.g., amount of force or violence), her coping skills after the assault, various environmental events, the reaction of significant others, and her access to networks of social support. Most of these variables are difficult to measure singly, and measuring their interactive effects is exponentially more difficult. Considering the fact that there are natural fluctuations in mood state and behavior that occur in most people, regardless of their victim status, investigators might decide that the most prudent course of action is to throw up their hands in despair. When we attempt to superimpose treatment and evaluation of its efficacy on this already complex set of fluctuating variables, our problems are compounded. Our task is merely to identify all variables that affect the victim's behaviors, to devise ways of measuring those variables, to develop appropriate and effective treatment procedures, to identify appropriate outcome measures, and to determine the relative contribution of each variable! Additionally, many victims do not wish to participate in research (Veronen, Kilpatrick, & Best, 1978), and there are differences between participants and nonparticipants.

Given the complexity of the topic, it is not surprising that definitive research does not exist. Systematic research in the area is a recent development, and we must consider this as we evaluate this literature.

The Sexual Assault Research Project (SARP)

The Sexual Assault Research Project is a joint effort of the Medical University of South Carolina and People Against Rape, a Charleston, S. C., rape crisis center. It is funded by a five-and-a-half-year grant from the National Center for Prevention and Control of Rape, which opened in 1977. The project has several objectives, two of which are (1) longitudinal assessment of victim reactions to a rape experience, and (2) evaluation of the efficacy of treatment procedures for rape-induced fear and anxiety responses. To accomplish the former objective, recent rape victims and a comparison group of nonraped women, matched for age, race, and residential neighborhood, were assessed at the following postrape intervals: (1) 6–21 days, (2) 1 month, (3) 3 months, (4) 6 months, (5) 1 year, (6) 18 months, (7) 2 years, (8) 3 years, and (9) 4 years. Assessment measures are objective, standardized measures of anxiety, fear, mood state, psychological symptomatology, self-esteem, self-concept, and social adjustment. There is evidence that participation may have been therapeutic for victims. Therefore, we changed our design so that victims and nonvictims are now randomly assigned to one of three conditions: (1) Repeated Assessment (these participants are assessed at 6–21 days, 1 month, 2 months, and 3 months postrape),(2) Delayed Assessment (these are assessed at 6–21 days and 3 months only), and (3) Brief Behavioral Intervention Procedure (these are assessed at 6–21 days and 3 months, but also receive 4–6 hours of cognitive-behavioral, feminist treatment). The latter study, which is in progress, should provide data on the reactivity of assessment procedures and about the prophylactic value of early treatment.

Many victims experience considerable rape-induced fear and anxiety for months or even years after the rape. Therefore, a second thrust of our research has been to develop a cognitive-behavioral treatment for these rape-induced problems and to evaluate its efficacy. Designed for use with victims whose rape was at least 3 months prior to treatment onset, this stress inoculation training package is the major focus of the chapter. By October 1, 1980, more than 150 victims and 100 nonvictims had participated in the Sexual Assault Research Project.

The Aftermath of Rape—Empirical Findings

Prior to presentation of research findings, we would like to make one cautionary remark. We will be talking about how rape victims in general differ from nonvictims in general. However, we must remember not to fall prey to a uniformity myth by believing that all rape victims are alike and experience identical effects following a rape. We must appreciate individual differences as well as group similarities. Having made this point, let us consider the rape victim's perception of her rape experience. She reports experiencing considerable anxiety, fear, and helplessness during the rape (Veronen, Kilpatrick, & Resick, 1979). She views rape as a threat to life, as a situation that has gotten out of her control to the extent that she feels she may be killed or seriously injured. She feels degraded and violated (Veronen & Kilpatrick, in press).

During assessments 6–21 days and 1 month postrape, victims experience generalized distress and disruption of behavior (Kilpatrick, Veronen, & Resick, 1979a). Victims were significantly more disturbed than nonvictims on 25 of 28 measures. By three months postrape, generalized distress had diminished to the extent that victims scored significantly higher than nonvictims primarily on measures of fear and anxiety. This same finding was obtained at the six-month postrape assessment. At one year postrape, victims continued to experience significantly higher levels of fear and anxiety (Kilpatrick, Resick, & Veronen, 1981). Results of these two studies suggest that victims experience improvement in most areas assessed within three months after their assault. Their fear and anxiety improves somewhat but remains at rather high levels for at least a year postrape. Examination of the items and situations rated as most disturbing by victims but not by nonvictims using the Veronen–Kilpatrick Modified Fear Survey (Veronen & Kilpatrick, 1980a) revealed that such fears were rape-related (Kilpatrick, Veronen, & Resick, 1979b). Some were rape cues or conditioned stimuli acquired through association with the rape experience (e.g., darkness, a man's penis). Others were attack-vulnerability cues, or cues that might signal potential vulnerability to subsequent attack (e.g., darkness, strangers, being alone). Still others were rape-precipitated concerns, or direct outcomes of the rape that place the victim in stressful situations where she would not be were it not for the rape. Patterns of fear appeared to change so that attack-vulnerability cues became most salient with the passage of time.

It is predictable that rape might affect a woman's self-concept and/or self-esteem. Veronen (1978) found that victims' self-concepts were more negative than those of nonvictims and that victims rated themselves as having been changed negatively by rape. Using another measure of self-esteem, we found that victims experienced significantly less self-esteem than nonvictims for at least a year after their assault (Veronen & Kilpatrick, 1980b).

Two other research groups have focused primarily on depression. Calhoun, Atkeson, and Resick (1979) and Frank, Turner, and Duffy (1979) both reported on increased incidence of depression among victims. Additionally, two other groups of researchers investigated the impact of rape on subsequent sexual activity. Feldman-Summers, Gordon, and Meagher (1979) found that rape decreased victims' rated satisfaction with a variety of sexual behaviors, and Becker (1982) is finding substantial evidence that rape-induced sexual dysfunction exists.

To summarize, rape victims as a group do experience considerable anxiety, depression, fear, sexual dysfunction, and diminished self-esteem for at least a year following their assault. This suggests that rape is a life event that can produce extraordinary stress in many of its victims. However, as difficult as it may be for the reader or victim to believe, rape can be the precursor of positive as well as negative changes, and between 17% and 25% of the untreated victims in our study were found to be relatively symptom-free at one year postrape (Veronen & Kilpatrick, in press). Several case studies also demonstrated that significant positive changes were made subsequent to the assault experience (Veronen & Kilpatrick, in press). Frank and Turner (1981) found that some victims were asymptomatic two or three weeks after their rape. These findings suggest that all victims neither need nor require formal treatment intervention to recover from rape. Many victims have rape-induced problems that might benefit from appropriate treatment, however.

Having documented the existence of rape-induced fear and avoidance behavior in many victims, we then examined the impact of rape-induced fear and avoidance (Veronen & Kilpatrick, 1980c). Victims fear subsequent attack and are particularly fearful of being alone. We noted that rape-induced fear always has the net effect of reducing a woman's perceptions of her options. As she retrenches, assuming more traditional roles and behaviors, she often receives considerable social reinforcement for doing so. A society ambivalent about women entering nontraditional roles in the first place tends to greet the victim's retrenchment with some enthusiasm. Feminist authors, most notably Brownmiller (1975), argue that rape is a major way in which men control women and maintain the status quo. Our analysis suggests that here, feminists may be at least partially correct in that rape-induced fear restricts the lives of many victims. We also contend that this whole topic warrants considerable investigation. Although we do not know the extent or exact nature of the effects, we do know that rape-induced fear and avoidance behavior have major effects that require a broader perspective than the usual clinical focus.

The Role of Expectancies, Attribution Theory, and Cognitive Appraisal

The problems experienced by the rape victim may vary greatly depending on the cognitions, beliefs, and expectations of the people with whom she deals, as well as on her own cognitive framework. Just as the epileptic of the Middle Ages was regarded as a pariah, from the lack of information about the true nature of this medical disorder, the rape victim also has suffered. Through public education, treatment personnel as well as the victim herself are becoming increasingly aware of the actual nature of sexual assault and its impact on the victim. Our particular community has the unique advantage of having had an active rape crisis center providing public education, training, and service to the community since 1974. Largely due to the efforts of this organization, the awareness regarding the needs of victims has been increased and victim-blame myths have been dispelled. The stress inoculation treatment that we have designed is being conducted by treatment personnel who have sympathetic attitudes toward the victim. The cognitive variables that we believe may influence the victim and her reactions will be discussed. The three constructs particularly useful as theoretical underpinnings are (1) expectancy theory, (2) attribution theory, and (3) cognitive appraisal. After briefly defining these terms, we will examine implications of these concepts for understanding effects of rape and for treatment of rape-related problems.

Expectancy as generally understood pertains to the belief that something will happen in a particular way. Expectancies in the case of the rape victim relate to her actions or lack of actions when faced with the attack itself, her actions or behavior in response to the assailant, the circumstances preceding the assault, and her reactions following the assault.

The expectations that women have regarding rape *vis-à-vis* themselves are varied. As researchers and clinicians who have worked with a large number of women, it is our belief that the confusion between rape as a sexual act and rape as an act of violence creates the wide range of expectancies. Some women hold the belief that they could never be raped. They naively believe the myth that no woman can be forced to have sex against her will. This belief is based on the misconception that rape is sexual intercourse and that by holding their legs together, they can avoid being raped. The phrase uttered by some ignorant individuals, "You can't thread a moving needle," reflects the belief that a woman has the capacity to prevent rape. They do not consider or recognize the violence, force, and threat of force that is associated with rape, nor do they recognize their own fear response and vulnerability when confronted with a situation in which someone is threatening a life. For a woman who held the expectation that she was immune to rape, the reality of the rape creates a state of disbelief and shock. Many women indicate that they never thought rape could happen to them. These statements or beliefs are typically resolved before a victim begins treatment. The "it could never happen to me" issue usually arises immediately or within the first few days after the assault. It is our impression that the victims who hold the "it could never happen to me" belief also represent a large number of nonreporters.

Other expectancies that affect reactions of the victims are those regarding how a victim should have behaved in the threatening situation (i.e., how much resistance should she have used to ward off the assailant?). We suggest that the victim should be told that if she survived the assault, then she did the right thing in that situation. Some experts argue that women who have been raped should not be called "victims" but should be called "survivors" (Bart & O'Brien, 1980).

Victims also hold expectations as to how they should behave after the rape. Some victims expect to be capable of resuming their schedules and previous levels of activity immediately after the assault. Women who hold unrealistically high expectations for themselves often experience a period during which they become angry and frustrated at themselves and wonder if they are "going crazy." They find themselves crying, scared, having trouble sleeping, or exhibiting other behavioral disturbances typical of a person whose life has been threatened but is unaware that these are normal reactions for someone in that situation.

A comprehensive discussion of attribution is beyond the scope of this chapter. However, attribution theorists (e.g., Wortman & Dintzer, 1978) state the individuals have a compelling need to understand their experience and are constantly interpreting environmental events and attaching meaning to them. People feel more comfortable believing that the universe is predictable and lawful. Having a "reason" for why things happen brings events more under one's control than does a belief that things happen randomly and unpredictably. Attribution theory states that any attempt to understand human behavior must deal with the attributions, or explanations, people ascribe to events. From this perspective, it becomes important to examine not just what happens to a person *per se* but also why they think it happened and what they think it means. The whole attribution process can be viewed as a cognitive coping process by which individuals attempt to achieve some perceived control over what often appears to be a rather chaotic set of events. The term *cognitive appraisal* may be defined as the process by which an individual interprets and attaches meaning to events. From the perspective of attribution theory and cognitive appraisal, actual environmental events are less important than the way individuals perceive those events and the meaning they attach to them.

Given this emphasis, attribution theorists would argue that the proper approach for understanding rape would be to focus on the victim's perception of what happened, her appraisal of why it happened, and her interpretation of what it all means rather than on what actually happened.

It has long been noted that rape victims tend to blame themselves for their own assaults, and counseling approaches often focus on combating this self-blame (e.g., Burgess & Holmstrom, 1974; Veronen & Kilpatrick, 1980c). However, a recent application of attribution theory to the topic by Janoff-Bulman (1980) distinguishes between two types of self-blame in rape victims, behavioral and characterological. Behavioral self-blame consists of a victim believing that the rape occurred as the result of some action or behavior she either did or failed to do. Thus, she may believe that she was raped because she walked alone, hitchhiked, went to a bar, or failed to lock her door. In contrast, characterological self-blame occurs when a victim attributes the assault to some type of personality flaw or character trait of hers. She believes that she was raped because she was too naive, gullible, trusting, or passive.

In our opinion, the discrimination between behavioral and characterological self-blame is interesting theoretically but may have little practical or treatment significance. In our work, we see little characterological self-blame. Our approach to the self-blame issue with victims is quite different. We approach the issue of victim self-blame at two levels. Therapists, counselors, nurses, and physicians who interact with the victim have been trained to assume the attitude that no woman asks to be raped. The actions of the assailant were unwarranted despite the physical or emotional condition of the victim. At a second level, we acknowledge that, to some degree, women feel responsible for events that befall them. The treatment approach of the Brief Behavioral Intervention Procedure, the short-term treatment for victims (see p. 351, the Treatment Section) examines ways in which women are conditioned to feel responsible for rape. Through early childhood sex education, girls learn that they are the ones who must say "No" to sexual advances. Women bear the biological burden of intercourse. The news media portray women who act in independent fashions or in ways not acceptable for women as being likely to be punished. The tale of Little Red Riding Hood, who went out alone and was eaten by the wolf, is one of the first of a long series of societal messages that caution girls and women that they should not go places alone or unaccompanied by a man. The Freudian concept of female masochism and unconscious motivation has taught that women unconsciously desire to be raped. Women have also learned to accept responsibility for an assault through the experience of childhood punishment for wrongdoing. As a young child, one is physically punished or humiliated when one does something wrong. As an adult, if one is physically assaulted and humiliated, there may be a conditioned response to examine one's behavior to see what one did wrong.

Attributions regarding responsibility for the assault are important but so are attributions about the meaning of the assault, particularly with respect to victims' plans for their lives after they are raped. As we have noted elsewhere (Veronen & Kilpatrick, in press), rape can be the precursor of positive as well as negative changes. This is not to say that the rape itself is a positive experience, but rather that it is appraised as an important event—as a choice point at which the victim can redirect her life in a positive manner. We presented several models for promoting positive change which included: (1) the Life Threat/Life Appreciation Model, (2) the Rape as a Consciousness-Raising Model, and (3) the Rape as a Challenge Model. Each of these models, which can be summarized only briefly, places heavy emphasis on the victim's cognitive appraisal of her rape.

In the Life Threat/Life Appreciation Model, the victim responds to the threat of being killed inherent in rape by developing a greater appreciation for life, by giving the rape the attribution of an important crossroads in her life, by reprioritizing her goals, and by resolving to "make her life count." In the Rape as a Consciousness-Raising Model, the victim interacts with a counselor/advocate who analyzes rape from a feminist perspective, which stresses that victimization is not an isolated event and results from many sociocultural and political factors. The victim's cognitive appraisal of the rape changes as she views it from a feminist perspective, and she becomes encouraged to make changes in her life that increase her control over her own life. In the Rape as a Challenge Model, the victim expects rape to be a devastating event that causes victims to fall apart. She resolves to avoid this typical reaction, manages to function adequately, then sees herself as brave, strong, and capable. She experiences a sense of mastery in having successfully met the challenge.

Once victims cognitively appraise rape as a choice point or crossroads from which they can go in positive as well as negative directions, they can be encouraged to identify ways in which they can take control of their lives rather than restrict or limit themselves. As a part of treatment, we might say to victims:

> Now that you have been raped, you are at a crossroads. There are several things you can do. Some of these things restrict or limit your freedom. These include accepting subtle blame for the attack, limiting your physical movement (not going out at night, discontinuing a night course, never being alone), limiting yourself socially (not meeting new people, making yourself physically unattractive), and limiting your growth and positive potential. By doing other things, you can take control of your life. You can take an active role in the police investigation and court procedures of your case. You can set your own schedule. You can explore new avenues for personal growth. You can help other victims. You can overcome what has happened to you.

This cognitive reappraisal process is an important part of recovery.

TREATMENT OF RAPE-INDUCED PROBLEMS

Overview

Scant information exists in the literature about treatment of rape-induced problems. Even less information exists on data regarding treatment efficacy. Given the primitive status of the field, treatment procedures can be discussed only briefly. Results of assessment research previously reported indicates that victims experience different problems initially, when they are in a state of generalized distress, and at a later time, when their problems are more focused. Therefore, we prefer to divide treatments into those dealing with short-term problems of recent victims and those dealing with long-term problems of nonrecent victims.

Short-Term Approaches for Recent Victims

In a recent review (Kilpatrick & Veronen, in press), we noted that some modification of crisis intervention is the treatment procedure most frequently offered to recent victims. Sometimes provided by "professionals" such as nurses, counselors, and psychologists and sometimes by "paraprofessionals" such a rape crisis counselor/advocates, most crisis-intervention approaches are based on Burgess and Holmstrom's (1974) model. They describe the following basic principles for crisis intervention: (1) It is short-term and issue-oriented, (2) the counselor responds to crisis requests of victims, (3) the counselor deals primarily with rape-related problems, not with other problems, and (4) the counselor takes an active role in initiating follow-up contacts. Burgess an Holmstrom provide considerable data and counseling suggestions but have never described in detail the content of their treatment, the amount of treatment offered, or data on treatment outcome. Although crisis-intervention treatment based on their work is popular, its efficacy has never been systematically evaluated.

Ellen Frank, Sam Turner, Barbara Duffy, and their colleagues at the University of Pittsburgh are currently engaged in an evaluation of the efficacy of two behavioral treatment procedures with recent victims. Within one month of their rape, victims are randomly assigned to a systematic-desensitization or a cognitive-therapy treatment procedure; the latter treatment is based on Beck's (1972) work. Victims are assessed before and after the 14-hour treatment intervention. Preliminary findings indicate that both groups show substantial improvement (Frank, 1979; Turner, 1979). However, there are problems with this study that require us to interpret its findings with caution. Since the study includes no comparison or control group of untreated victims, it is difficult to determine whether improvement was due to effects of treatment, effects of normal postrape recovery, or some interaction between the two. Our research indicates that substantial improvement occurs without formal treatment somewhere between one and three months postrape, rendering interpretation of the Frank *et al.* findings difficult. (Frank and her colleagues are planning to obtain data from untreated victims.)

We are currently investigating the efficacy of a treatment for recent victims of rape, that is, victims less than one-month postassault. This treatment, called the Brief Behavioral Intervention Procedure (BBIP), is 4–6 hours in length and is conducted in two sessions. The treatment contains some elements that are strictly behavioral and others that are primarily cognitive. Among the elements included are relaxation training, an explanation of the origin and existence of rape-related fear and anxiety, an explanation of the feelings of self-blame and feelings of responsibility for the attack that a woman has subsequent to an assault, an abbreviated training session in self-talk, and a discussion of "reentry strategies" or ways to initiate or resume activities that may be avoided because of fear. The development of BBIP and the evaluation of its efficacy is still in progress so we have yet to examine outcome data; however, we are optimistic about it for several reasons. It has strong face validity. The treatment counselors conducting the treatment enjoy it. It is brief; victims have difficulty maintaining an extended treatment contract when they have so many other agencies and individuals with which to deal. It appears to be highly relevant. Victims' problems immediately after the assault include anxiety, fear, the reactions of people to them, depressive and negative thinking, and avoidance of activities and places reminiscent of the attack.

Treatment Approaches for Nonrecent Victims

Systematic research on the treatment of long-term problems of nonrecent victims is practically nonexistent. There have been two case reports describing treatment of rape victims by psychoanalytically oriented therapies (Factor, 1954; Werner, 1972), although both reports were impressionistic rather than data-based. Notman and Nadelson (1976) discussed the dynamics of the response to rape and discussed particular issues that victims may encounter at various life stages. They noted that a young woman at age 17–24 may have different concerns and problems precipitated by the assault than does a middle-aged woman, and they offered therapeutic suggestions for each life stage. However, the efficacy of these suggestions was not evaluated.

Except for our own work on treatment of long-term problems, the behavioral literature consists of two single case study designs. Blanchard and Abel (1976) used a heart-rate biofeedback procedure to reduce rape-induced tachycardia successfully. Forman (1980) used cognitive modification of obsessive thinking in a victim 34 months postassault. Additionally, Judith Becker, at Columbia University, is currently conducting a study investigating the efficacy of the behavioral treatment for rape-induced sexual dysfunction.

THE SEXUAL ASSAULT RESEARCH PROJECT TREATMENT EFFICACY STUDY

Overview

A major objective of our project is to evaluate the efficacy of treatment for rape-induced fear and anxiety in nonrecent victims (three months postrape or longer). Initially, the study design called for evaluation of three treatments: (1) stress inoculation training (SIT), (2) peer counseling, and (3) systematic desensitization. The explanations for treatment were offered by the co-principal investigator. A written explanation of each treatment was read to the victim.

The written descriptions of the treatment were all less than one typed page in length, and it took approximately five minutes to explain each treatment. The victim was told that, after the descriptions of the treatment were given, any questions she had would be answered. Finally, the victim made her treatment selection. Many victims attempted to get the co-principal investigator to make the treatment selection for her by asking "Which treatment do you think would be best for me?" In such instances, where this question was posed, the victim was again told to select the treatment she wanted.

Although random assignment to treatment conditions would have been more advantageous methodologically, victims were permitted to select treatment for two reasons, one ethical and one methodological. Ethically, allowing victims to select among treatments permitted them to regain some control at a time when they often feel powerless and lack control. Methodologically, this procedure provides information about the extent to which the three treatments are palatable to victims. With respect to treatment preference, SIT was by far the most popular. Since few victims elected other treatment procedures, the design of our study was modified so that SIT is now the only treatment procedure offered.

Determination of Treatment Eligibility

Victims must be at least three months postrape to be eligible for treatment. Other criteria for eligibility are (1) elevation of self-reported fear and anxiety as measured by psychometric tests, (2) presence of clearly defined target phobias, (3) presence of specific avoidance behaviors, (4) absence of other pathological behaviors that would interfere with treatment participation, and (5) willingness to participate in treatment. Determination of eligibility is accomplished by one of the co-principal investigators on the basis of an interview with each victim and an examination of evaluation data. Due to the nature of our research investigation, we are treating only victims whose primary problem is that of fear and anxiety. If a victim exhibits substantial depression, she is referred elsewhere for treatment. Once her depression improves, she is reevaluated for SIT eligibility. Although it is our belief that SIT could easily be adapted for use with the depressed victim, our research design specifies that fear and anxiety must be the predominant symptoms.

By October 1, 1980, 57 victims had been assessed for treatment eligibility. Thirty of the 57, or 52.6%, were judged eligible for treatment.

Victims judged ineligible for SIT were women who did not manifest fear and anxiety as their primary symptoms. Victims whose primary problem was depression were excluded, as were victims for whom interpersonal conflict was the primary problem. Another group of victims not included were those lacking sufficient mental ability to comprehend treatment. Such victims were those who were highly confused and disturbed for a variety of reasons ranging from poor intellectual development to thought disorder or major mood disturbance.

We rigorously applied our research criteria and have not attempted to conceptualize all victim problems as those of fear and anxiety. Those victims who are not accepted but who need treatment are referred and treated by private therapists. As noted, while we have not done so in this project, we believe that SIT could easily be adapted for use with depressed victims. Beck, Rush, Shaw, and Emery (1978) have discussed how cognitive therapy can be employed with depressed clients. There appears to be some overlap between cognitive therapy and SIT.

Target Behavior Assessment

Following agreement to enter treatment, three specific target phobias are identified. These are situations and/or events that (1) cause the victim subjective distress and (2) are the source of avoidance behavior. A target phobia must be assault-related and represent something the victim wishes to change; it is a fear that did not exist prior to the assault or was not of the high intensity that it is now. For example, being alone is a frequently identified target phobia. Subsequent to assault, many victims seek to be with other people at all times and are extremely uncomfortable alone. The onset of this phobia is directly attributable to the rape, and it is something that the victim wishes to change.

Assessment of Treatment Efficacy

A multiple criteria assessment procedure is used. Psychophysiological measures of responsiveness, fear thermometer ratings of target situations, and psychometric tests are administered before treatment. Psychophysiological and fear thermometer assessments are also obtained after treatment of the first target behavior. The physiological assessment involves the monitoring of skin conductance, skin resistance, and heart rate while the victim listens to an audiotaped recording describing a 15- to 20-second scene of her target fear. For example, a woman whose target fear is being alone might be asked to imagine herself in her home alone at night, hearing an unfamiliar noise or having someone come to the door. Assessment also occurs at the end of treatment and three months after treatment.

Procedural Aspects of Treatment

Each of the three treatments is conducted individually and is 20 hours in length. We attempt to schedule two sessions a week, two hours in length, but, occasionally, only one session per week is conducted. All treatment is conducted by one of our female members of the project staff, all volunteer rape-crisis counselors who have been trained in specific cognitive–behavioral therapy techniques. The content of each treatment is carefully specified to insure that a standard format is followed. Additionally, treatment sessions are tape-recorded, and counselors are supervised to insure that treatment techniques are being applied consistently and appropriately.

Stress Inoculation for Victims of Rape

Rationale for Development of Rape-Induced Fear and Anxiety

We have presented evidence that rape is stressful and that rape-induced fear and anxiety are problems for many victims. While it is generally accepted that the factors leading to the acquisition of a behavior are not necessarily the same factors that are important in the maintenance of that behavior, the ways in which fear and anxiety can be acquired by a rape experience present relevant questions. We have developed a theoretical model that attempts to answer these questions and that forms an important portion of the educational phase of stress inoculation training (Kilpatrick, Veronen, & Resick, 1977; Kilpatrick, Veronen, & Resick, 1982; Veronen & Kilpatrick, 1980a).

Briefly described, our social-learning theory model states that there is considerable theoretical justification for predicting the range of victim responses. We view rape as an *in vivo* classical conditioning situation in which the threat of death and/or physical damage, pain, and/or confinement evoke responses of cognitive, physiological, and behavioral fear and anxiety. We also recognize the role of cognitive variables as determinants of victim responses. The rape experience occurs to a woman who has particular expectancies about rape and rape reactions, holds particular beliefs about the causes of rape, and perceives the rape situation in her own unique way.

For women in our social milieu, rape has been linked with sexual passion. Some movies and books have portrayed women who have been raped as being overcome by a man who forces sex on them. Although initially the woman resists, she ultimately recognizes that her efforts are in vain and a passionate sexual encounter ensues. This portrayal does not reflect the reality of the situation.

For the victim, a rape experience means being powerless and in danger of serious physical harm or even death. This is true whether the rapist is a total stranger or an acquaintance. Rape is a situation that has gotten out of control, is perceived as a threat to physical and psychological safety, and is terrifying. When subjected to such a painful and dangerous situation, it is reasonable to assume that the rape victim would respond by experiencing high levels of fear and anxiety.

We found empirical support for this contention (Veronen *et al.*, 1979) in that 96% of victims reported feeling scared, 92% felt terrified, 96% felt worried, and 88% felt helpless during the rape. Moreover, a high percentage of victims experienced such physiological symptoms of anxiety as shaking or trembling (96%), heart racing (84%), pain (72%), tight muscles (68%), and rapid breathing (64%).

Stimuli associated with rape-induced unconditioned stimuli acquire the capacity to evoke fear and anxiety as well. Thus, neutral stimuli such as persons, situations, or events present at the time of the rape acquire the capacity to produce conditioned responses of fear and anxiety through their association with rape-induced terror. Some stimuli present in all rape situations, such as a man and cues associated with sexual behavior, should be conditioned stimuli for fear and anxiety for practically all victims. Other stimuli are more idiosyncratic to each specific case and will be conditioned stimuli only in those rape cases. Classical conditioning literature also suggests that fear and anxiety responses may generalize to other stimuli similar to conditioned stimuli present during the rape. The proposed classical conditioning model predicts that a victim's observed fears are related to the circumstances of her rape situation.

We also contend that cognitive events, such as thoughts, can become conditioned stimuli and are capable of evoking anxiety (Kilpatrick, Resick, & Veronen, 1981). Thus, thoughts or cognitions associated with the rape experience become conditioned stimuli for fear and anxiety. An example of this phenomenon is the victim who becomes distressed when she describes her rape experience to someone. In such a case, there are no physical stimuli to remind the victim of her rape. Rather, there are cognitive stimuli that evoke anxiety.

There is one final point about our theoretical model worth noting. We do not conceptualize the conditioning that occurs during rape as a simple S–R process. As cognitive behaviorists, we fully acknowledge the contributions of cognitive variables in conditioning. Thus, the victim's perception of the stimulus situation and her cognitive appraisal of it are quite important.

Description of Stress-Inoculation Training (SIT) Procedure for Rape Victims

Rationale and Educational Phase

One point must be made prior to beginning our description of our SIT for rape victims. The victims for whom this treatment was developed were those exhibiting fear, anxiety, and phobic avoidance. This is a specific set of problems, ones that we found were most significant for the victim. This is not to say that victims do not have other problems and, indeed, they do. Following our description of the SIT, we will describe the BBIP, which we believe has wider applicability and can be utilized with nearly all rape victims.

Stress inoculation training begins with a two-hour educational phase in which (1) SIT is described to the victim, (2) a rationale for treatment is given, and (3) an explanation of the origin of fear and anxiety is presented.

The treatment is described as a cognitive behavioral approach to the management of rape-related fear and anxiety. Coping skills, or ways to deal with anxiety, are taught.

The rationale for SIT includes several points. First, anxiety is discussed as an unavoidable aspect of life that must be managed. The goal of SIT is not the elimination of anxiety but the management of it. Second, SIT is described as a procedure that can be utilized in a number of situations and settings. Since a wide variety of stimuli and situations may be anxiety-provoking, a treatment that can be used trans-situationally is advantageous. Third, since rape victims are frequently troubled by negative, self-defeating thoughts as well as by flashbacks to the assault situation, SIT emphasizes an analysis of cognitions and internal dialogue and images. Fourth, SIT encourages active participation of the victim and allows the victim considerable latitude in electing which coping skills she will use.

The conceptual framework offered to the victim for the presence of her rape-related fear is twofold. The first portion is a tripartite explanation of the fear response (Lang, 1968) and an explanation of the stage-fear response. The second portion is the classical conditioning model of rape-induced fear and anxiety.

Fear and/or anxiety is explained as a normal, learned response that can occur in three channels: behavioral or motoric, cognitive or mental, and physical or autonomic. Anxiety experienced in the three channels may be related in different ways within one individual. All three channels may vary together (i.e., show changes at the same time) or an interaction may occur (i.e., one channel may dominate or influence the other channels). For many individuals, the cognitive or mental channel is the dominant one and influences the others. From one person to another, or even for the same person at different times, the pattern may be different.

Examples of manifestations of the fear response in each of the three channels are elicited from the victim in the following manner:

> In the physical or autonomic channel, one may feel her heart begin to pound; her throat may become dry; there may be ringing in the ears; a slight dizziness, flushing, trembling, or weakness in the knees. What physical or autonomic symptoms do you experience when you come in contact with or think about a particular feared situation?

Fear manifestations in the three channels are discussed in detail. The counselor obtains many examples from the victim to insure that she understands the three-channel framework.

In addition to discussing the fear response within the three-channel approach and the origin of her fears, the victim is given an explanation of a stage-fear response. The fear response occurs in stages and is not an all-or-none phenomenon. If one can identify the early indicators of the fear response, one can better control her reaction to it.

Following the tripartite and stage-fear response explanations, the counselor reviews the classical conditioning model of fear. Sexual assault is experienced by most women as a sudden traumatic event in which the woman fears that she will be killed. She may be overpowered, held down, restricted, or in some way made to feel powerless. Sex is then forced on her. Several aspects of this situation make the development of fear and anxiety very predictable. The victim is helped in understanding this development with the following explanation:

> Fear and anxiety following a rape are normal responses. The development of rape-related fear can be understood through a process called classical conditioning. Rape is an unconditioned stimulus that brings about the unconditioned response of pain or fear of being harmed or killed. Persons, situations, or events that are paired with the assault may also bring about fear and anxiety responses. Rape-related fears may also generalize; thus, persons, situations, or events that are similar to those present at the time of the assault may also bring about fear and anxiety responses. Now, let's look at your target fears and see in what way they are related to the process of classical conditioning.

Coping Skills: Acquisition and Application

Following the educational phase, which typically takes one to two sessions, instruction in the coping skills is begun. For each channel of fear, specific coping skills are taught. In order to manage fear expressed through the physical channel, the victim learns muscle relaxation and breath control. Management of fear expressed through the behavioral or motoric channel is accomplished through covert modeling and role-playing. Thought stoppage and guided self-dialogue are the coping skills used to counter cognitive expression of fear.

Each of the coping-skills sessions is conducted in a similar manner. The session begins with a review of the previous session's activity and an update on the utilization of coping skills in the victim's natural environment.

The format that the counselors use to teach coping skills to victims has been standardized. It includes a definition of the coping skill, the rationale and mechanism for the skill, a demonstration or explanation of the skill, and two applications of the skill. The first time the skill is applied, it is used with a non-target-related fear; the second time, it is used with a target fear.

An example of the format used for teaching role-playing to a 25-year-old military wife, raped in her home while she slept, is described below.

The counselor explained that role-playing is the "acting out of behaviors, rehearsing lines and actions. It is pretending to be in a particular situation or in a set of circumstances." Role-playing is explained as "a way to learn new behaviors and words for old ways of doing things. It gives you a chance to practice before the event occurs. It is a dress rehearsal. The repeated practice of a behavior reduces anxiety and makes it more likely that you will use the new behavior when it is called for."

The role-playing demonstration involved the counselor acting out the role of the victim in a problem area. The victim described her problem as being "put down" by a building contractor. For the demonstration of the skill, the counselor played the victim, and the victim played the building contractor. In the application, the victim played herself and the counselor acted the role of the building contractor. The victim felt put down, discounted, and dismissed by men with whom she tried to have business dealings. She felt that the contractor did not take her seriously; deferred to her husband, and did not follow her instructions. After one role-play, she criticized herself and received suggestions from the counselor. Feedback focused on voice, posture, and words used. She role-played the scene three times, each time becoming more confident in her request. Her homework assignment was to go home and tell the contractor what she wanted. During the next session, she role-played her first target behavior situation, which was staying alone by herself at night. She pretended that she was alone and role-played herself doing some cleaning, talking on the phone, writing a letter, reading, and listening to music. Following this session, she had as her homework assignment to stay alone for a few hours by herself during the afternoon, which was an approximation of the behavior of staying alone at night.

The six coping skills, a brief description of each, and the way in which each is utilized are given below.

Muscle Relaxation. The Jacobsonian (1938) tension-relaxation contrast training is used to teach muscle relaxation. In the third or fourth hour of SIT, relaxation training is begun. The first session includes a total relaxation of all major muscle groups. In addition, an audiotape of the peer therapist conducting the relaxation training and a tape recorder are provided for each victim so that she can practice relaxation between sessions. Additional sessions of relaxation training, using the "focusing" and "letting go" procedures, are conducted until the victim is capable of attaining a relaxed state in a relatively brief time. The victim is encouraged to practice relaxation skills during everyday activities such as driving the car, house-cleaning, or work-related tasks.

Breath Control. Exercises that emphasize deep, diaphragmatic breathing are taught subsequent to muscle relaxation exercises. This type of breathing is familiar to many women who have taken instruction in yoga or gone to Lamaze natural childbirth classes. Again, this skill is practiced both in therapy sessions and at home.

Role-Playing. The role-playing skill is the third skill to be taught and was described previously.

Covert Modeling. Covert modeling is described as "a skill similar to role-playing, except that it is done through your imagination." The victim visualizes or imagines scenes and situations in which she confronts and successfully works through fear- or anxiety-provoking situations. Training in this procedure is begun after the victim has experienced success with the three previous skills.

Thought Stoppage. Thought stoppage, a technique reported by Wolpe (1958), has been used to counter the ruminative or obsessive thinking characteristic of the rape victim (Forman, 1980). Although it was originally utilized to obliterate self-devaluative and negative internal dialogue related to social censure and criticism, its use in breaking up obsessional thoughts of being harmed illustrates a natural extension of the technique.

Thought stoppage was used with one victim who had a great avoidance of taking a shower. In the shower, with the water running, she could not hear what was going on outside the bathroom. An example of ruminative thinking is given in the following situation:

Cathy is in the shower; the bathroom door is closed, the water is beating down on her head, and she can't hear what is going on in other parts of the house. Her thoughts are, "Was that a noise I heard? Someone could be breaking in, and I can't hear him; I know someone will be waiting for me when I step out of the shower." If her husband was home, she would continue her thinking with, "Someone is holding Ted at gunpoint. I know he is going to get me."

Thought stoppage is taught by having the victim think the troublesome thoughts. After they have continued for 30–45 seconds, the therapist, in a loud, commanding voice, says, "Stop," and asks the victim what happened. She typically replies that the thought stopped. This process is repeated several times. The next step is to have the victim herself say "Stop" aloud when the thought begins. Finally, the victim is capable of stopping the thinking with a "Stop" verbalized silently.

Guided Self-Dialogue. This skill is perhaps the most important of the coping skills taught. For acquisition of this skill, the therapist teaches the victim to focus on her internal dialogue, or on what she is "saying" to herself. Irrational, faulty, or negative dialogue is so labeled, and rational, facilitative, or task-enhancing dialogue is substituted. The victim is instructed to ask and answer a series of questions or respond covertly to a series of statements. The framework for the guided self-dialogue is taken from Meichenbaum's (1974) examples in stress inoculation training. The four dialogue categories include statements for (1) preparation, (2) confronting and handling a stressor, (3) coping with feelings of being overwhelmed, and (4) reinforcement. For each category, victim and therapist generate a series of questions and/or statements that encourage the victim to (1) assess the actual probability of the negative event happening, (2) control self-criticism, (3) manage overwhelming avoidance behavior, (4) engage in the feared behavior, and (5) reinforce herself for attempting to engage in the behavior and for following the protocol. Examples of general self-statements that may be used by victims are presented in Table I. For each victim, the set of self-statements is tailored to fit her target fears, though some general statements are nearly always included in a particular victim's set of self-statements. Self-statements are written on 3 × 5-inch cards, and the victim takes them with her in order to practice them outside the treatment session.

As the victim acquires the coping skills, she is encouraged to utilize them in order to handle everyday problems and difficulties. Frequently, there are spontaneous endorsements on the part of the victim regarding the success of these coping skills.

An example of successful practice of coping skills and spontaneous use of coping skills occurred in the following situation:

Nettie, a 68-year-old black victim, had been given the task of practicing her covert modeling and role-playing coping skills with a written piece that she was to read as part of a church program. After the program, people came up to congratulate her, and one of them hugged her abruptly. One of Nettie's target fears had been being touched unexpectedly. She

Table I. Examples of Self-Statements

1. Preparing for a stressor
What is it you have to do?
What is the likelihood of anything bad happening?
Don't think about how bad you feel; think about what you can do about it.
Don't be so caught up in yourself; thinking only about your feelings won't help.
You have the support and encouragement of people who are experienced in helping you deal with these problems.
You have already come a long way toward handling the problem; you can go to the rest of the way easily.
2. Confronting and handling a stressor
One step at a time; you can handle the situation.
Don't think about being afraid or anxious, think about what you are doing. The feelings you are having should be a signal for you to use your coping exercises.
There's no need to doubt yourself. You have the behaviors to get you through.
Focus on the plan. Relax . . . take a deep breath, you are ready to go.
3. Coping with feelings of being overwhelmed
When feelings of being afraid appear, take a deep breath and exhale slowly.
Focus on what is happening now; what is it you have to do?
You can expect your fear to rise, but you can keep it manageable. Think to yourself, "This will be over soon." You can convince yourself to do it.
This fear may slow down, but you will not be incapacitated by it.
You may feel nauseated and want to avoid the situation but you can deal with it.
4. Reinforcing self-statements
It was much easier than you thought.
You did it—you got through it, each time it will be easier.
You had a plan and it worked.
There is nothing to it, you've got it together.
When you manage the thoughts in your head, you can manage your whole body.
You are avoiding things less and less. You are making progress.
One step at a time—easy does it.
Nothing succeeds like success.

immediately began using her breath-control coping skill. She reported back to her therapist that the unexpected touch didn't disturb her as much as past touches.

At the end of every SIT session, the victim is given some type of homework. This homework is either practicing a coping skill, confronting an everyday stressor, or completing an approximation of the target fear. For example, for one victim who feared sleeping alone in the dark in her home, her approximations to the target fear included darkening the room during the day and then turning out the light, turning out the lamp at night while her hand remained on the switch, turning out the lamp at night and placing her hand in her lap, turning out the lamp and lying in bed, and eventually sleeping with the light out.

RESULTS OF THE SEXUAL ASSAULT RESEARCH PROJECT'S TREATMENT EFFICACY STUDY

Overview

Because of the preliminary nature of our research, we are unable to present definitive data regarding treatment efficacy. Nevertheless, there are several issues related to SIT with rape victims that will be examined. The first issue is treatment preference. When victims are given a thorough description of three treatments, which do they select and why? A second issue is: What are the characteristics of victims who desire treatment? What is the nature of their complaints? A third issue is: What appear to be the effects of treatment intervention? The final portion of this section will illustrate the use of SIT through a single case-study format.

Treatment Preference

In traditional clinical practice, it is the therapist who makes the decision regarding what treatment the patient will receive. It is our impression that a great deal could be learned about face validity of treatment, placebo effects, and the plausibility of our explanations by making the patient a collaborator in the selection of treatment. Furthermore, it is our impression that in ordinary treatment facilities, motivation for treatment would be higher if the patients felt they had a role in determining which was the best treatment for them.

Prior to the change in procedure for this study providing SIT to all clients, a total of 15 victims were given descriptions of the three treatment procedures (peer counseling, systematic desensitization, and SIT) and were asked to select the one in which they wished to participate. One victim could not make a selection and was randomly assigned to SIT. Three selected peer counseling, and the remaining 11 selected SIT. None chose systematic desensitization.

The selection process was interesting. Nearly all victims viewed peer counseling as quite different from the two behavioral treatments. Peer counseling was presented to them as a treatment that involved the sharing of common experiences and problems with a peer counselor as well as examining societal reactions to women and their changing roles. It was described as a "talk" therapy or counseling. Victims either accepted or rejected this approach rather quickly. If peer counseling was rejected, considerable deliberation ensued over the relative merits of the two behavioral procedures. All victims who preferred SIT indicated that systematic desensitization was their second choice and that they had selected SIT because it seemed more comprehensive. The sentiment was expressed in the following statements made by victims: "It has more to it," "It is more thorough," "It covers more," and "I need to learn new ways to deal with things." The focus of SIT on self-dialogue was appealing to victims, some of whom said, "I need to learn to change the things I say to myself," and "My thoughts are sometimes very depressing."

Stress inoculation training was also the clear preference of the counselors conducting treatment. They enjoyed it because of its variability (i.e., a number of coping skills are taught), the level of victim participation required (i.e., the victim must be quite active), and the element of choice and perceived freedom afforded to the victim (i.e., she was taught a variety of coping skills and could choose to use any or all of them).

Characteristics of Treatment Candidates

Overview

If treatment is not appropriate for all victims, determining the characteristics of those for whom it is appropriate becomes important. Eventually, we hope to identify characteristics of those who respond positively to treatment, but at present, we will address the issue of what victims are like who meet our criteria for treatment eligibility. We will approach this topic from two perspectives. First, we will summarize the results of psychometric comparisons of treatment candidates with other victims at two postrape intervals. Second, we will examine the content of target phobias identified by treatment candidates.

Psychometric Characteristics of Treatment Candidates

The battery of psychometric measures used in our assessment study and described elsewhere (Kilpatrick *et al.,* 1979a) is also used to determine eligibility for treatment. Space limitations preclude a description of these measures or of the details of the experimental design and statistical analysis of data on which the following conclusions are based. However, the basic strategy was to compare the scores of treatment candidates with those of untreated victims obtained at 6–21 days postrape and at 3 months postrape. All treatment candidates had to be at least 3 months postrape. We hypothesized that those judged eligible for treatment might be experiencing greater distress than their counterparts not eligible for treatment. Since our assessment research had shown that most victims improved substantially at the 3-month-postrape assessment, we hypothesized that treatment candidates' scores would resemble the 6- to 21-day postrape normative scores of victims more than the 3-month postrape normative scores. In other words, we felt that treatment candidates might be those victims whose high levels of initial distress had not shown the improvement that usually occurs for most victims by the 3-month postrape period.

Analysis of the anxiety, fear, mood-state, and psychological symptomatology data from the assessment battery provided considerable support for our hypothesis. Psychological symptom and mood-state patterns of treatment candidates were much more similar to the distressed profiles of the 6- to 21-day victims than to the less distressed profiles of the 3-month postrape victims. Treatment candidates show particular elevations on measures of fear and anxiety, a finding not altogether surprising since the selection criteria place heavy emphasis on identification of anxious, phobic victims and the assessment battery is used in the determination of treatment eligibility.

In summary, psychometric evaluation of treatment candidates reveals them to be anxious and fearful. It appears that treatment can-

Table II. Target Phobias

Treatment candidate		Treatment candidate	
A.	1. Walking alone 2. Being talked about 3. Being dominated/protected by men	F.	1. Going out alone at night 2. Observing or reading about violence 3. Sleeping alone at home at night
B.	1. Being alone at night 2. Being approached by black men 3. Observing someone being confined, restricted, or made helpless	G.	1. Walking from the car to apartment or from apartment to car alone at night 2. Being alone in the car after dark 3. Being approached by a man/men
C.	1. Being alone at home at night 2. People behind me 3. People in authority	H.	1. Teenage boys 2. Going out alone at night 3. Being alone at home
D.	1. Waking up and being harmed or child being harmed 2. Night/darkness 3. Sleeping in the bedroom	I.	1. Not being able to get help 2. Being alone at night 3. Darkness
E.	1. Being alone at home at night 2. Being approached by men 3. Being observed or criticized	J.	1. Being alone at night 2. Unexpected movements of people 3. Watching violence on television or at the movies

Table III. Summary of Target Phobias for 25 Treatment Candidates

Being alone/going places alone	80%
Men who look like assailant/strange men	28%
Going out	20%
Sight of or hearing about violence	16%
Darkness[a]	16%

[a]Darkness or night was mentioned as a component of a target phobia by 72% of these candidates.

didates are those victims whose fear and anxiety remain at a high level instead of declining, as is the case for most victims.

Target Phobias

Another source of information regarding fears that victims experience subsequent to an assault is provided by the target phobias. Presented in Table II are the target phobias of 10 of 25 victims who have been accepted into our treatment study. The letter identifies the treatment candidate. Each candidate selected three phobias, and they are listed in order of greatest severity. The first fear listed is the most disturbing. According to our operational definition, a target phobia must be more than a self-rating of discomfort or fear. A victim must indicate that this fear results in avoidance behavior, by offering examples of ways in which this stated fear has prompted some change in behavior on her part. These victims are at a minimum of three months postassault, though several victims sought treatment for assaults that occurred several years ago and one, as long as seven years ago.

A summary of target phobias is presented in Table III. Listed are the most frequently appearing fears and the number of victims who endorsed each fear.

The data reveal that the mostfrequent and most intense fears that bring a victim to seek treatment are being alone, staying alone, or going places alone. Underlying all of the fears of being alone is a fear of subsequent attack—that someone may rape them again.

Effects of Treatment Intervention

Although several victims are now involved in SIT, six victims have completed this treatment procedure. Because of the small number of cases, we elected not to perform statistical analysis of the data obtained from these women. However, we shall summarize pre- and posttreatment assessment data of these victims to permit preliminary evaluation of treatment efficacy. Such data should obviously be interpreted with caution.

One assessment measure used in our evaluation was the Derogatis Symptom Check List (Derogatis, 1977; SCL–90R), a 90-item self-report symptom inventory designed to measure a variety of psychological symptom patterns. Examination of the mean symptom profiles of the six victims pre- and post-treatment indicates that victims improved on all scales. The largest improvements were observed on the phobic anxiety, hostility, and anxiety symptom scales. It is also interesting to note that even after treatment, victims remained at least a standard deviation above the mean for the normative group of "normal" females on 9 of the 12 scales.

Scores obtained before and after treatment on the Profile of Mood States Scale (McNair, Lorr, & Droppleman, 1971; POMS), a measure of six mood dimensions, also reflect what appear to be treatment-related improvements. Victims scored lower after treatment on all "negative" mood states and higher on the "positive" mood state of vigor-activity. Pretreatment mood states were characterized by elevations on the tension-anxiety, depression, anger, and fatigue dimensions, while heightened scores on the vigor-activity dimension characterized the post-treatment profile.

Both state and trait anxiety, as measured by the State-Trait Anxiety Inventory (Spielberger, Gorsuch, & Lushene, 1970; STAI), appeared to diminish following treatment. State anxiety scores were reduced from a pretreatment mean of 49.50 to a posttreatment mean of 36.67. The corresponding means for pretreatment and posttreatment trait anxiety scores were 47.83 and 41.67, respectively.

A similar pattern of improvement occurred on the Veronen-Kilpatrick Modified Fear Survey (Veronen & Kilpatrick, 1980a; MFS). Victims were less fearful after treatment on all but the Animal subscale. After treatment, victims were below the mean fearfulness level of nonvictims as well.

Stress Inoculation Training: A Case Study

Background Information

The victim, A. D., was a 22-year-old Caucasian woman of bright, normal intelligence from a middle-class background. She was raped a year prior to entering treatment by a young black man who broke into her apartment. Her assailant was never apprehended, and her rape-induced fear had become so great that her husband was forced to quit his night job to be at home with her at night. She experienced considerable discomfort entering and leaving her house. She was extremely fearful of black men and reported walking well out of her way to avoid meeting a black man on the street. She would become physically ill on seeing a depiction of rape or physical violence against women on television or in the movies. Particularly distressing to her were situations in which victims were restrained, confined, and/or made helpless through force or threat of force. Assessment revealed that her three target phobias were (1) being alone at night, (2) being approached by black men, and (3) observing somemeone being confined, restricted, or made helpless.

Treatment

Stress inoculation training (SIT) was conducted according to the previously described format. Following the tenth session, A. D. began staying alone. While initially quite anxious, she stated that utilizing the coping strategies she had been taught permitted her to become increasingly comfortable. Approach by black men also was markedly less anxiety-provoking. She related incidents in which she had greeted older black men as she quickly passed them on the street. The coping skill she found most useful was guided self-dialogue.

During the final week of SIT, she was hospitalized for a respiratory problem. After a week's hospitalization, during which numerous diagnostic tests were conducted, her physicians determined that she had a rare lung disorder. Shortly after her release from the hospital, her husband experienced a period of severe behavioral disturbance during which he (1) squandered their savings, (2) lost his job, (3) wrecked the family car, (4) had a psychiatric hospitalization from which he left against medical advice, (5) attempted suicide, and (6) was hospitalized for detoxification. Despite the magnitude of these stressors, she managed to cope rather well and stated that her capacity to deal with these problems was directly related to the skills she had learned in SIT. One may wonder whether SIT should not also be offered to members of the victim's family.

Stress Inoculation Training's Efficacy

Analysis of A. D.'s SCL–90R profiles before SIT, after SIT, and at three-month follow-up revealed the following findings: Her pretreatment profile was characterized by an extremely high score on the phobic anxiety scale. After treatment, decreases were apparent on several scales, most notably Anxiety and Phobic Anxiety. Interestingly, she scored somewhat higher on the Somatization, Depresion, and Hostility subscales. Experiencing increased symptomatology in these areas is not surprising given her health and family problems. These findings also suggest that the SCL–90R is an instrument sufficiently sensitive to pick up positive effects in some areas and negative effects in others. Examination of data obtained at follow-up reveals that treatment effects were maintained and even improved in some cases.

The corresponding mood-state data were measured by the POMS. Changes on this measure were less dramatic, but considerable improvement occurred on the tension-anxiety dimension. The decrease in the mood state of vigor-activity at the end of treatment and at follow-up may have been attributable to A. D.'s health problems. With the exception of Vigor scores, all mood changes were in a favorable direction.

With respect to performance on the Veronen–Kilpatrick Modified Fear Survey, a general pattern of improvement on all subscales was noted except for Animal and Tissue Damage fears. Particular improvement occurred on the measures of social–interpersonal, failure-loss of self-esteem, and rape fears. The 3-month follow-up data show that even greater improvement occurred on most measures.

A similar pattern was noted with respect to A-trait and A-state scores. The pretreatment, post-treatment, and follow-up A-state scores were 47, 39, and 37, respectively. The corresponding A-trait scores were 40, 37, and 35. At the end of treatment and at follow-up, both A-trait and A-state were within normal limits.

Summary

The use of stress inoculation training with A. D. appears to have been highly successful. In addition to the favorable changes observed on the psychometric measures, A. D. also reported considerable behavioral change. She became able to stay at home at night alone and no longer had to avoid black men. Although this specific target phobia was never treated, her fear of viewing violence in the media also diminished. Moreover, she attributed the skills she learned in SIT with helping her to cope successfully with her health and marital problems. It is also encouraging to note that the therapeutic gains observed at the end of SIT were maintained and even improved at follow-up assessment. Such a finding suggests that SIT teaches general problem-solving and coping skills that can be used to deal with a variety of problems.

CONCLUSIONS AND IMPLICATIONS

In this chapter, we have reviewed evidence suggesting that fear and anxiety can be acquired through a rape experience and that fear, anxiety, and avoidance behavior represent significant long-term problems for many rape victims. We noted the paucity of information available about treatment of rape-related problems and described our stress inoculation training (SIT) package and treatment efficacy research project. We presented preliminary data indicating that SIT is an attractive and preferred form of treatment for rape victims and that it appears to be an effective treatment as well. Data obtained for the single case study confirmed the efficacy of SIT and revealed that the victim appeared to learn coping skills that enabled her to deal with problems other than those specifically treated. Obviously, such a case study can prove only encouraging to us as we now undertake group and within-group comparisons.

What are the conclusions to be drawn from this material? What are our opinions as to implications for treatment of rape-induced problems?

First, we do not think that SIT is appropriate for all victims for several reasons. Both our own research and that of Frank and her colleagues identified some symptom-free victims, and these victims have little need for treatment. Most of the remaining victims experience high levels of distress the first few weeks and months after the assault, and we believe that high distress makes it extremely difficult for such victims to participate in treatment procedures that require repeated, sustained contact. Most victims have problems that could benefit from treatment but there is no evidence that sustained treatment is feasible for the majority of victims. Frank and her colleagues found that fewer than one-fourth of recent (one month postrape or less) victims completed a 14-hour treatment program, and our own data indicate that less than 50% of victims three-months postrape or longer, judged in need of treatment, agreed to participate in SIT. Rape so disrupts women's lives that it is hard for them to attend frequent, regularly scheduled appointments that are required for therapy. Recent victims' ability to attend to, comprehend, and implement the demanding components of a treatment such as SIT may be limited by problems in cognitive functioning caused by high levels of rape-induced anxiety.

Second, our best guess is that SIT would work best with those victims who have resolved most of their other rape-related problems but who remain fearful and anxious. Our assessment research shows that many other problems appear to be resolved within the first three months postrape without formal treatment, suggesting that SIT might be more appropriately used with long-term victims. Victims with well-developed and well-defined phobias should benefit most from SIT.

Third, the battery of asessment measures used in our research is quite sensitive to the effects of therapeutic intervention. Particularly encouraging were the specificity of findings and the way test results corresponded with clinical observations of behavior change.

Fourth, we must carefully acknowledge the limitations of our current knowledge about treatment. What is known is vastly exceeded by what is not known. However, we know more now than we did a few years ago, and ongoing research should clarify matters considerably. Moreover, preliminary findings are encouraging in that they suggest that SIT can help some victims.

Finally, let us speculate a bit about a few other issues. Clearly, a victim's cognitive appraisal of her rape and of the problems it produces is quite important. Providing her with information about the political and social context in which rape occurs, offering her general emotional support, gently confronting her about irrational self-blame, offering her a conceptual framework to explain how her rape-induced problems occur, and encouraging her to view her rape experience as a choice point are all actions that might help victims reappraise the rape in beneficial ways. It is also clear that the behaviors and attitudes of family, friends, and institutions (e.g., health care delivery and criminal justice systems) have impact on the victim. Much of the effort of the rape crisis center movement has been focused on educating individuals and institutions about the true nature of rape and how to deal with victims more humanely, and mental health professionals should join these educational efforts. Rape is stressful for family and friends as well as for victims, and there is definitely a role for the use of stress management procedures in this context. However, there are many cases in which family members of victims are having problems but refuse to get involved in treatment because, they say, it is the victim who has the problem, not them. A final area that requires additional attention is the development of early intervention strategies that are both feasible and effective prophylactically. Our work in this area should eventually provide useful information, but it would be premature at this time to discuss our findings.

In conclusion, we offer one observation and one invitation. The observation is that rape and its aftermath offer a fascinating opportunity to study a complex and interesting topic. The invitation is that we urge our cognitive-behavioral colleagues to join us in our quest to understand the aftermath of rape and to develop ways for helping victims cope with its effects.

REFERENCES

Bart, P. B., & O'Brien, P. *How to say no to Storaska and survive: Rape avoidance strategies.* Paper presented at the meeting of the American Sociological Association, New York, August 1980.

Beck, A. T. *Depression: Causes and treatment.* Philadelphia: University of Pennsylvania Press, 1972.

Beck, A. T., Rush, J., Shaw, B, & Emery, G. *Cognitive therapy of depression: A treatment manual.* Philadelphia: Aaron T. Beck, M. D., 1978.

Becker, J. V. *Sexual dysfunctions in rape victims.* National Center for the Prevention and Control of Rape, NIMH, Grant No. RO1 MH32982, 9/25/79–8/31/82.

Blanchard, E. B., & Abel, G. An experimental case study of the biofeedback treatment of a rape-induced psychophysiological cardiovascular disorder. *Behavior Therapy,* 1976, *7,* 113–119.

Brownmiller, S. *Against our will.* New York: Simon & Schuster, 1975.

Burgess, A. W., & Holmstrom, L. L. *Rape: Victims of crisis.* Bowie, Md.: Robert J. Brady Co., 1974.

Burt, M. R. Cultural myths and supports for rape. *Journal of Personality and Social Psychology,* 1980, *38,* 217–230.

Calhoun, K. S., Atkeson, B. M., & Resick, P. A. *Incidence and patterns of depression in rape victims.* Paper presented at the meeting of the Association for Advancement of Behavior Therapy, San Francisco, December 1979.

Chappell, D. Forcible rape and the criminal justice system: Surveying present practices and projecting future trends. In M. J. Walker & S. L. Brodsky (Eds.), *Sexual assault: The victim and the rapist.* Lexington, Mass.: D. C. Heath, 1976.

Derogatis, L. R. *SCL-90-R manual.* Author: Clinical Psychometrics Research Unit, Johns Hopkins University, Baltimore, 1977.

Factor, M. A woman's psychological reaction to attempted rape. *Psychoanalytic Quarterly,* 1954, *23,* 243–244.

Feldman-Summers, S., Gordon, P. E., & Meagher, J. R. The impact of rape on sexual satisfaction. *Journal of Abnormal Psychology, 1979, 88*(1), 101–105.

Forman, B. Cognitive modification of obsessive thinking in a rape victim: A preliminary study. *Psychological Reports,* 1980, *47,* 819–822.

Frank, E. *Cognitive therapy in the treatment of rape victims.* Paper presented at the meeting of the Association for Advancement of Behavior Therapy, San Francisco, December 1979.

Frank, E., & Turner, S. M. *The rape victim: Her response and treatment.* National Center for the Prevention and Control of Rape, NIMH, Grant No. RO1 MH29692, 4/1/78–3/31/81.

Frank, E., Turner, S. M., & Duffy, B. Depressive symptoms in rape victims. *Journal of Affective Disorders,* 1979, *1,* 269–297.

Jacobson, E. *Progressive relaxation.* Chicago: University of Chicago Press, 1938.

Janoff-Bulman, R. *Rape victims' behavioral/characterological self-blame.* National Center for the Prevention and Control of Rape, NIMH, Grant No. RO3 MH33402, 8/1/79–7/31/80.

Kilpatrick, D. G. The scientific study of rape: A clinical research perspective. In R. Green & J. Wiener (Eds.), *Methodology in sex research.* Washington, D.C.: DHHS Publication No. (ADM) 81–766, 1981.

Kilpatrick, D. G., & Veronen, L. J. Treatment for rape-related problems: Crisis intervention is not enough. In L. H. Cohen, W. Claiborn, & G. Specter (Eds.), *Crisis intervention.* New York: Human Sciences Press, in press.

Kilpatrick, D. G., Veronen, L. J., & Resick, P. A. Responses to rape: Behavioral perspectives and treatment approaches. *Scandinavian Journal of Behaviour Therapy,* 1977, *6,* 85.

Kilpatrick, D. G., Veronen, L. J., & Resick, P. A. The aftermath of rape: Recent empirical findings. *American Journal of Orthopsychiatry,* 1979, *49*(4), 658–669.(a)

Kilpatrick, D. G., Veronen, L. J., & Resick, P. A. Assessment of the aftermath of rape: Changing patterns of fear. *Journal of Behavioral Assessment,* 1979, *1*(2), 133–148.(b)

Kilpatrick, D. G., Resick, P. A., & Veronen, L. J. Effects of a rape experience: A longitudinal study. *Journal of Social Issues,* 1981, *37*(4), 105–122.

Kilpatrick, D. G., Veronen, L. J., & Resick, P. A. Psychological sequelae to rape: Assessment and treatment strateiges. In D. M. Doleys, R. L. Meredith, & A. R. Ciminero (Eds.), *Behavioral medicine: Assessment and treatment strategies.* New York: Plenum Press, 1982.

Lang, P. J. Fear reduction and fear behavior: Problems in treating a construct. *Research in Psychotherapy,* 1968, *3,* 90–102.

McNair, D., Lorr, M., & Droppleman, L. *Manual, profile of mood states.* San Diego: Education & Industrial Testing Service, 1971.

Meichenbaum, D. *Cognitive behavior modification.* Morristown, N. J.: General Learning Press, 1974.

Notman, M. T., & Nadelson, C. C. The rape victim: Psychodynamic considerations. *American Journal of Psychiatry,* 1976, *133,* 408–413.

Spielberger, C. D., Gorsuch, R. L., & Lushene, R. E. *The state-trait anxiety inventory.* Palo Alto, Calif.: Consulting Psychologists Press, 1970.

Turner, S. *Systematic desensitization of fears and anxiety in rape victims.* Paper presented at the meeting of the Association for Advancement of Behavior Therapy, San Francisco, December 1979.

Veronen, L. J. Fear response of rape victims (Doctoral dissertation, North Texas State University, 1977). *Dissertation Abstracts International,* 1978, *38*(7). (University Microfilms No. TSZ 77–29, 577.)

Veronen, L. J., & Kilpatrick, D. G. Self-reported fears of rape victims: A preliminary investigation. *Behavior Modification,* 1980, *4*(3), 383–396.(a)

Veronen, L. J., & Kilpatrick, D. G. *The response to rape: The impact of rape on self-esteem.* Paper presented at the meeting of the Southwestern Psychological Association, Oklahoma City, April 1980.(b)

Veronen, L. J., & Kilpatrick, D. G. *Transcending the effects of rape: Towards an integration of behavioral and feminist perspectives.* Paper presented at the meeting of the American Sociological Association, New York, August 1980.(c)

Veronen, L. J., & Kilpatrick, D. G. Rape: A precursor of change. In E. J. Callahan & K.A. McCluskey (Eds.), *Life span developmental psychology: Non-normative life events.* New York: Academic Press, in press.

Veronen, L. J., Kilpatrick, D. G., & Best, C. L. *The invisible woman: Characteristics of the rape victim who does not participate in research.* Paper presented at the meeting of the Southwestern Psychological Association, New Orleans, April 1978.

Veronen, L. J., Kilpatrick, D. G., & Resick, P. A. Treatment of fear and anxiety in rape victims: Implications for the criminal justice system. In W.H. Parsonage (Ed.), *Perspectives on victimology.* Beverly Hills, Calif.: Sage, 1979.

Werner, A. Rape: Interruption of the therapeutic process by external stress. *Psychotherapy: Theory, Research, and Practice,* 1972, *9*(4), 349–351.

Wolpe, J. *Psychotherapy by reciprocal inhibition.* Stanford: Stanford University Press, 1958.

Wortman, C. B., & Dintzer, L. Is an attributional analysis of the learned helplessness phenomenon viable?: A critique of the Abramson-Seligman-Teasdale reformulation. *Journal of Abnormal Psychology,* 1978, *87,* 75–90.

III

Applications

Part C—Specific Populations

Military recruit training and combat experience are replete with stressful events. Ray Novaco, Thomas Cook, and Irwin Sarason provide moving descriptions of the nature of the stressful environment n both combat and in marine corp training camp and of the resulting psychological and social sequelae. With a substantial attrition rate during recruit training and during the first term of enlistment, there is ample room for interventions designed to reduce stress. Their chapter indicates the value of conducting a behavior-analytic and social analysis in order to understand the factors that contribute to stress and attrition. Their analyses indicated that the nature of the training unit environment (e.g., group morale, quality of leadership, social climate) plays a key role in affecting attrition rates and stress levels.

As in the case of Ayalon's description of the importance of Israeli communities in influencing how well individuals cope with terrorist attacks, Novaco *et al.* report that the training unit environment or social climate is critical in preventing and reducing the stress level of military recruits. Thus, interventions can be focused at the group level as well as at the individual level. For example, such group procedures as the following can be used to reduce the level of stress: setting superordinate challenges and goals that foster group cooperation and an *espirit de corps,* setting up group competition that fosters subgroup coherence, and providing leadership and communication training.

At the individual level, Novaco *et al.* indicate the importance of expectation, appraisal, and social support processes in the stress reaction. They then consider the implications of these processes for a coping-skills training program. They emphasize the importance of the involvement and cooperation of drill instructors and military officers for any such program to be successful.

It is necessary to remember that any stress management program is offered in the context of a social milieu that can sabotage its effectiveness.

This point has been made by several contributors. All too often, program developers focus on those elements of their program that are tailored to the individual and they lose sight of how the social environment can be the focus of intervention and how significant others in that environment must be brought to the point of viewing themselves as collaborators. In the same way that the cognitive–behavioral therapist tries to have the patient become a collaborator (using the personal scientist metaphor), the trainer similarly must enlist the collaboration of significant others who can affect the training program.

In the previous chapters, the contributors have examined how individuals react to major life stressors such as traumatic events and medical disorders. Matt Jaremko shifts the focus of concern to the stress of social interactions. The incidence data reviewed by Jaremko indicate that social anxiety is a significant social problem. In considering social anxiety, it is important to appreciate the complexity of the problem. It is *not* merely a case of physiological arousal, negative self-statements, or inadequate social skills. There is a complex interrelationship of these processes; which are in turn affected by the individual's current concerns or personal attribution. As Jaremko notes, a stress-engendering cycle can be established involving these several processes. Jaremko describes how a cognitive–behavioral treatment approach can be used to help socially anxious clients recognize and interrupt this maladaptive pattern. There is a need to tailor the intervention procedures to the specific needs of the client (e.g., anxiety prone but relatively skillful, and so forth). Whatever the exact sequence of the intervention, it is necessary to insure that the treatment techniques are offered in an organized procedural package that follows from the treatment rationale.

Few social problems can induce more stress and havoc in a community than adolescent anger. The remarkable increase in juvenile crime, as reported by Feindler and Fremouw, underscores the grave need for effective treatment interventions for this population. After briefly reviewing the limitations of other treatment approaches, Feindler and Fremouw describe an innovative cognitive–behavioral intervention for adolescent offenders. As in the other projects reported in this volume, the Feindler and Fremouw study provides encouraging data that bear replication and extension. Two features of the program merit highlighting: (1) the use of *in vivo* training tasks (simulated and real-life social provocations), and (2) the training of child-care workers in the use of stress management procedures. The portability of such techniques across settings and personnel is one of the strengths of the cognitive–behavioral stress training program.

11

Military Recruit Training

An Arena for Stress-Coping Skills

RAYMOND W. NOVACO, THOMAS M. COOK, and IRWIN G. SARASON

The study of human stress has no better context for investigation than in military environments. The American soldier drew attention during the Second World War, because theaters of battle were naturalistic, albeit cruel, domains for the study of psychological trauma and adaptation to extreme environments (Stouffer, 1949). Unmistakably, research on human stress received a key impetus from investigations of psychological functioning in warfare.[1] Stress as regards the military, however, pertains to conditions and issues much broader than those of war. Problems of stress, coping, and adaptation are not only paramount in situations of combat but are also highly salient in recruit training and indeed remain so throughout the enlistment period.

[1]Just as World War I gave impetus to the study of human aptitudes, World War II set the stage for the study of attitudes and their association with behavior. Many behavioral scientists who have made significant contributions to the field of psychology had participated in wartime studies of adjustment among military personnel. In fact, many of the early formulations of stress, adaptation, and coping resulted from observations made by psychological researchers working with the military. Psychologists not of this era who are interested in stress might review the personal accounts of their forerunners (Doob, 1947).

RAYMOND W. NOVACO and THOMAS M. COOK • Program of Social Ecology, University of California at Irvine, Irvine, California 92717. IRWIN G. SARASON • Department of Psychology, University of Washington, Seattle, Washington 98195.

We have been engaged in a program of research that has been concerned with stress, coping skills, and adaptation among Marine Corps personnel. Our primary focus has been on the process of recruit training and the first term of enlistment. The nature of the research has been with regard to the complex interplay between environmental forces and the adaptation resources of individuals and groups as they function over time. We have specifically been intrigued by the social climates of training units as they are shaped by training personnel and how variation in training unit environments is associated with cognitive and behavioral outcomes.

Military recruit training, as an environmental context, has a particular significance for the cognitively oriented interventionist. The recruit is exposed to intense environmental demands continuously for several months and is isolated from all previous sources of social support, status, and self-esteem. There is a high degree of supervision of one's actions, and behavior is highly constrained. Coping with the demands of recruit training, particularly in the initial phases, is unmistakably a cognitive process. There is virtually no way to cope behaviorally, in the sense of modifying the environment or regulating one's exposure to stressors.

As stress researchers, we were naturally drawn to this environment as a prime naturalistic condition to which large numbers of young men and women are exposed. We quickly recognized the importance of cognitive coping skills for successful adaptation to the demands of the training environment. While trying to learn about coping strategies in this environment, we developed a cognitively based intervention that hypothetically would reduce stress among recruits. Using principles generic to the field of cognitive-behavioral interventions, we have now implemented an experimental program to augment stress-coping skills among recruits.

Viewing stress as a condition of imbalance between environmental demands and the person's resources for coping with those demands, stress can be reduced either by lowering the demands or stressors or by augmenting coping resources. Since the demands of recruit training are fixed, as established by formal policy regarding standard operating procedure, stress reduction in this environment can more readily be attempted by interventions aimed at increasing stress-coping skills.

This chapter will focus on the dimensions of stress associated with recruit training and the stress reduction intervention we have developed. In order to set the stage for the presentation of that work, we will first present an overview of some unique demands of military service. The nature of the training environment in the Marine Corps will then be described, along with the characteristics of those who enter it and those who shape it. Following a process analysis of the training experience, we will give a cognitive-behavioral assessment of psychological functioning in that environment and portray how we have attempted to improve adjustment by increasing stress-coping skills.

PROBLEMS OF STRESS AND ADAPTATION IN THE MILITARY

The challenges of adaptation *vis-à-vis* the military no doubt begin when one either entertains options of military enlistment and/or is confronted by the imminence of service obligations. The military receives wide media exposure, both journalistic and dramatic, and it is a fact that over one-third of the adult male population of this country are counted on the roles of the Veterans Administration. Surely, then, it can be assumed that most young people have formed initial impressions of military service before reaching the age of eligibility. These personal representations and their associated affect are key determinants of enlistment decisions. The perception of challenge and the opportunity to fulfill certain personal needs can be contrasted with the appraisal of service demands as beyond personal capability or simply as aversive. Nearly all recruits, however, enter military training with some measure of apprehension, which is invariably magnified by both routine and chance occurrences in the training environment.

For those who enlist, the potential discrepancy between the cognitions shaped by recruiting efforts and the realities encountered on entry into the training environment becomes a source of stress for both the individual and the organization. Each of the services recognizes that they must maintain an image consistent with current cultural values. Recruiting campaigns are designed to attract specific groups such as minorities and women and are pitched to appeal to yearnings for advanced education, technical training, upward social mobility, and the chance to overcome a history of personal failure. Traditional values such as patriotism and social responsibility have not been emphasized in the past decade. However, the reality encountered by the recruit during training does not always match expectations engendered by recruiting appeals.

In making the decision to enlist, the recruit expects the association with the military to be positive and personally beneficial. The military expects the individual tomake a contribution to the mission of the particular service branch. While both the individual and the service organization expect tangible rewards from the association, the new recruit is immediately taxed with the difficult demands of social, psychological, and physical adjustment inextricably entailed in basic training.

All military recruits are required to undergo a period of basic training that is 8–12 weeks in duration. The duration, intensity, and content of training varies considerably across services, as do the criteria used for recruit selection and evaluation. These variations are a function of the general organizational mission of the specific service and the anticipated demands of that service branch. Recruit training is designed to impart the basic skills, attitudes, and behavior deemed essential for mission performance, as well as to inculcate the language and demeanor characteristic of the service branch.

Despite the variations across services, the process of recruit training is relatively similar. Basic training is a period of rapid resocialization and enculturation occurring under conditions of relative isolation and confinement. In a few short weeks, a heterogeneous assemblage of young individuals are expected to develop new behavior that is confined to a narrow range of acceptability. In this regard, a staff of carefully selected training supervisors functions as the agent of change. In fact, supervisor performance is evaluated on the basis of their ability to teach the desired behaviors and eliminate unwanted behaviors and cognitions. The training process thus consists of an intense tutelage, marked by heavy doses of reward and punishment applied so as to shape desired behavior and positive cognitions about the system.

The transition from recruit training to the "real world" of service life is often accompanied by a personal sense of loss, disillusionment, and disappointment. The recruit departs from an intense environment in which personal behavior and one's very experience have been tightly regulated and proscribed. In most cases, recruits remember their supervisors as exemplary individuals and have fond reflections of unit cohesiveness. However, at the new duty station, the novice is quickly confronted with a new set of environmental contingencies. There is a noticeable difference in the degree of control, supervision, and discipline. The new arrival is expected to learn local rules quickly and to assimilate into the social structure with minimal guidance. Many individuals feel a deep sense of loneliness, finding it difficult to form new attachments and to locate sources of social and emotional support, especially in settings that are culturally dissimilar to those with which they are acquainted.

Although this transition is often difficult, successful adjustment is a prerequisite for service life. Military personnel must constantly be prepared to disengage from familiar surroundings and personal associations and to accept assignment to a new location, as dictated by the needs of the military, regardless of rank or experience. While all services consider individual desires in the making of assignments, in the final analysis, the needs of the service prevail. Sometimes service personnel will welcome assignment to new and unfamiliar locations. Frequent relocations can satisfy a need for adventure and may even become a way of life. Yet for some persons, especially those who are married, who have limited cross-cultural experience, or who must make a disproportionate number of relocations, the frequent readjustments can exert considerable strain.

The rigors of basic training, to be described later, are mainly intended to prepare recruits for combat. In a general sense, boot camp habituates the recruit to the kind of unpredictable stressors likely to be encountered in combat. Discipline, motivation, physical conditioning, and weapons skills are the goals of basic training. Yet there is considerable variance in the ease with which these objectives can be attained. Physical conditioning and competence with weapons are more readily achieved than are discipline and motivation. Conditions of war are unpleasant. Preparing soldiers for war inevitably involves a degree of nastiness. To an extent, boot camp is tacitly designed as an analog to the duress of combat.

STRESS ENGENDERED BY WARFARE

The demands of recruit training must be understood in terms of preparation necessary for survival in combat. The stress associated with exposure to the extreme environments of warfare has been studied extensively. Among the most notable works are those of Grinker and Spiegel (1945) on air combat units, Kardiner and Spiegel (1947) regarding traumatic neuroses, Bourne (1969, 1970) on psychological and physiological stress reactions in Vietnam, and Figley (1978) on combat-related stress disorders among Vietnam veterans. It is beyond the scope of our chapter to review the work in this area; our presentation here is therefore cursory.

Combat environments entail multiple sources of stress that have cumulative effects. Stress is engendered, in part, by exposure to elements of environmental fields that require an adaptive response from the organism or system (Novaco, 1979). Two principal classes of stress-inducing factors prevalent in warfare are ***harsh physical circumstances that affect tissue needs*** and ***the threatening psychological ambiance of combat.***

Deprivation, extreme stimulation, disease, and injuries are ever-present circumstances that threaten a soldier's well-being. The soldier is often constrained in the quantity and quality of food available. Beyond matters of nutrition, this can have significant effects on morale (cf. Kardiner & Spiegel, 1947). Sleep deprivation is a closely related factor. Fatigue can occur even when there is opportunity for sleep, because vigilance and anxiety preclude relaxation. Even air crews, whose living quarters are the envy of infantry, are likely to have their sleep interrupted by night briefings, early missions, and the tension of daily combat flights. Oxygen deprivation has also been a problem in high-altitude flying.

Extreme stimulation in combat most commonly involves unpleasant temperature and noise. Extreme cold and heat are ever-present stressors in theaters of war, as determined by geographic climate and by lack of insulation from the elements. Combat vehicles, such as tanks and planes, also have extreme temperatures associated with their use. While air temperature is a continuous condition, loud noise from exploding bombs, rockets, shells, etc. is an ever-present but often unpredictable stressor in the battlefield. Auditory hypersensitivity is the most common symptom of the traumatic neuroses and is linked with patterns of irritability and aggressiveness observed among psychological casualties of warfare (Kardiner & Spiegel, 1947).

Soldiers are often exposed to disease-engendering conditions. Poor hygienic conditions, inadequate diet, exhaustion, and limitations on medical care create propensities for illness. Infections range from diarrhea to malaria. Injuries and battle-inflicted wounds are obvious sources of combat stress and are the confirmation of the soldier's most basic fear. Moreover, wounds often induce trauma in the victim. This was tragically seen in Vietnam, where booby traps and mines were common causes of injury resulting in multiple amputations.

These harsh physical conditions constitute only ne dimension of the stress-inducing circumstances of warfare. The more pervasive dimension is the psychological ambiance of combat. This has several components: the continuous threat of death and injury, the loss of friends, and the recognition of one's own destructive capacity. Along with the harsh physical conditions of war, the psychological sources of strain summate over time to increase risk of psychological impairment. The recognition of these cumulative effects of exposure was in fact acted on in Vietnam, where the tour of duty was limited (365 days) and there were opportunities for brief periods of rest and relaxation. These factors, along with the application of modern military psychiatry, probably lowered the psychiatric casualty rate in Vietnam, although there are a number of reasons to question the reported statistics for that war.[2]

[2]A variety of psychological adjustment problems, such as drug abuse, assault on superiors, and insubordination occurred with considerably higher frequencies in Vietnam than in previous wars. These forms of "unconventional psychopathology" (Kormos, 1978) in many cases were not included in psychiatric casualty reports. These adjustment problems were typically handled by the military command structure, rather than by psychiatric staff. In our own research on recruit training, our analyses of the attrition process have found inconsistencies and variation in the use of discharge categories within the Marine Corps organization. Given the same behavior, recruits may be referred for a psychiatric evaluation

The business of war is the destruction of the enemy and of their will to fight. Every soldier must therefore cope with the fear of death. One of the early studies of fear in combat was undertaken by Dollard and Horton (1944). They found that the most common symptoms of fear were a pounding heart and rapid pulse, muscle tension, a sinking feeling in the stomach, dryness of the mouth and throat, trembling, and sweating (in that order of frequency). Fear was found to be greatest *before* going into action and was reported by 7 out of 10 men. Of importance to cognitive-behavioral interventions, they found that over 80% of their subjects said that it was better to admit fear and discuss it before battle. From the body of their findings, it can be inferred that the best way to regulate fear in battle is to expect to be afraid, to prepare for it in advance, and to counteract fear in battle by concentration on the tasks at hand. Analogously, we have utilized these ideas in our stress-coping skills intervention for recruit training.

All wars involve being immersed in a hostile atmosphere. The soldier is enveloped by the sights, sounds, and smells of destruction. The clandestine nature of the fighting in Indochina exacerbated the psychological strain of the combat ambiance. American troops developed "a sense of helplessness at not being able to confront the enemy in set piece battles. The spectre at being shot at and having friends killed and maimed by virtually unseen forces generated considerable rage which came to be displaced on anyone or anything availble" (DeFazio, 1978, p. 30).

One of the most important resources for coping with stress in combat is friendship. Beginning in basic training, the soldier learns the importance of teamwork and discovers reciprocity in helping others. The loss of friends in combat (due to death, injury, or transfer) is emotionally traumatic, since extremely close attachments are formed among the members of combat units. This loss of support is unquestionably stress-inducing (cf. Cobb, 1976; Heller, 1979). Yet, those in combat may not only suffer the bereavement but may also have witnessed the horrors of their buddy's death. The anguish can persist with images indelibly impressed in their memories.

Warfare is ugly and soldiers become tormented by the horror of their own actions. Being responsible for the death of others induces guilt, but it also creates apprehension about uncontrolled agressive impulses. In

---

or may be discharged administratively in a "training failure" category or in one of several ability or motivation deficit categories. For example, the recruit training depot at Parris Island, South Carolina, has registered during certain periods more than twice the frequency of "training failure" discharges than has the depot in San Diego. This does not mean that MCRD, San Diego, is twice as effective in training recruits. It simply reflects differential use of separation codes by the two depots.

building motivation for combat, the military indoctrinates soldiers to despise the enemy, who are labeled by assorted derogatory characterizations. It is as if the soldier must come to believe that those he is fighting are less than human. However, Grinker and Spiegel (1945) stated that "It is erroneous to consider that hatred of the enemy is necessary for a good fighting morale, for hatred and sadistic gratification from killing are sources of guilt to the hater and are not the best motivation for objective and successful combat" (p. 40). They maintained that until one is personally injured by the enemy or has experienced the loss of close friends, it is hard to escape the inner revulsion associated with killing the enemy.[3] Furthermore, the teamwork and coordination necessary in battle precludes giving vent to uncontrolled aggressive inclinations.

The psychological ambiance of combat associated with the Vietnam war has had a particular negative effect on veterans who are manifesting "delayed stress reactions." The common themes of the postcombat syndrome are guilt and self-punishment, feeling scapegoated, indiscriminate rage, "psychic numbing," alienation, and doubt about one's ability to love and trust others (Shatan, 1978). The inability to distinguish friend from foe, the necessary mistrust of villagers, the emphasis on body counts, and the political tensions of the war created an atmosphere in which indiscriminate killing occurred and dehumanizing conditions prevailed.

After this brief overview of the multiple stressors associated with combat environments, we will now turn to our principal subject, that of recruit training. We will delineate the objectives of the training procedure, describe the nature of the training process, and present a cognitive-behavioral analysis of recruit adaptation. We will then describe the coping-skills intervention that we are conducting with Marine Corps recruits.

MILITARY TRAINING: OBJECTIVES, FUNCTIONS, AND PROCESSES

All first-term enlistees in the Armed Forces are required to undergo a period of basic training that is normally 9–12 weeks in duration. Recruit training is designed to impart those skills, attitudes, and behaviors deemed essential by each service for mission performance. Since each service has a general mission assigned by Congress, recruit selection and training is thought to be directly related to the demands entailed in the assigned mission. For example, Navy training emphasizes seamanship

[3] This process is dramatically and tragically illustrated in Caputo's (1977) personal account of psychological and behavioral changes that occurred in response to the extreme and unusual conditions encountered by the Marines in Vietnam.

and adaptation to shipboard life, whereas Marine Corp training emphasizes physical fitness, personal/unit discipline, and marksmanship in anticipation of the demands of close combat. Because of the differences in the general missions of the services, recruiting standards vary, as do the duration, intensity, and content of recruit training.

For the military, it is the proper combination of recruit selection and systematic training that insures continuity and accomplishment of the assigned mission. This vital process of selection and training maintains the organization and increases the probability that assigned missions will be successfully carried out. For the individual, recruit training is intended to facilitate personal adjustment to the military way of life and to provide those skills necessary for adequate coping with future demands.

Few would question the logic of preparing members of the military for future assignments and life experiences. Since individual assignments vary greatly, from the operation of complex technology to participation in protracted, small-unit combat, it is reasonable to assume that training should be conducted so as to prepare the majority for the range of environments they may encounter. Not only is it necessary to train personnel in the technical aspects of their jobs, but it is also necessary to acquaint new enlistees with the organizational structure of the particular service and to instill in them those attitudes and behaviors valued by the organization.

The principal function of recruit training is to organize and indoctrinate young enlistees to insure that the military maintains a prescribed level of mission capability. An assumption underlying both the content and the process of recruit training is that society does not provide certain experiences and training that are thought necessary for survival in situations where the military might be deployed. Each service assumes that a recruit is relatively unprepared for military life. The new recruit is viewed initially as undisciplined, unkempt, and not adequately prepared for the responsibilities of adult life. It is not uncommon for training supervisors to attribute the recruits' lack of skill and preparation to some basic flaw in society.

However, it is useful to bear in mind the distinction made by Merton (1968) regarding manifest and latent functions. Manifest functions refer to intended objective consequences, whereas latent functions refer to unintended, unrecognized, but nevertheless identifiable consequences that result from a standardized practice. Military training clearly performs a collateral or latent function of providing education, employment, and opportunity otherwise not available to a segment of the adolescent population. In the structure of our society it is difficult, if not impossible, for educational institutions and industrial organizations to provide opportunity, education, and employment for everyone. Furthermore, there are subgroups within society (e.g., adventure seekers, risk takers) having distinctive needs and desires that are unsatisfied by established institutions. It can be argued that a significant latent function of military training is to provide alternative channels for social mobility for those who are otherwise excluded from the more traditional avenues for personal and social advancement. Additionally, military experience provides an opportunity for many to overcome a history of failure and maladjustment.

A significant number of those who enlist in the service do so for such benefits as education, travel, and the opportunity to prove to themselves and others that they have the ability to be productive and useful members of the community. For some individuals, the primary motivation to enlist comes from a need to be confronted with a challenge in which success constitutes an immediate and tangible reward. In this regard, recruit training can be viewed as an environment where individuals are tested on their social, psychological, and physical adaptation skills.

Before concluding this section, we would like to discuss some issues regarding the experience of the social scientist in the military training environment. It is often difficult for psychologists or social scientists, with little military exposure, to view recruit training as anything other than negative, aversive, and dehumanizing. The realities of the environment are indeed harsh, demanding, and often unpleasant. There are, in fact, few situations that equal these intense conditions, in which individuals are systematically exposed to extreme demands. At first glance, it appears that the sole purpose of training is to break individuals psychologically and physically and to render them helpless in the face of the system's desires.

These conditions may present some dilemmas for the research psychologist. There is no doubt that the systematic process of stress induction that occurs in basic training far exceeds what would or should be permitted in the laboratory. It is this contrast between the ethics of human research and the ethics of preparing individuals for difficult and unusual environments (e.g., combat and confinement) that may pose a problem for researchers who may be hesitant about involvement with an institution that ostensibly has little regard for human welfare.

The researcher entering the military setting should be prepared to confront the reality that people are being trained to win in combat through the total destruction of a politically defined enemy. Regardless of the content of training, the basic mission remains to project maximum resources in the theater of battle to destroy the opponent. All other considerations are secondary. The questions posed by an association with the military are not easy ones and demand that the researcher continuously evaluate both the nature and the level of participation, keeping in mind that the military is an institution that has a profound and far-reaching influence on present and future society.

Bearing in mind these issues, the recruit-training environment does afford the stress researcher a unique opportunity to study stress and adaptation. The organizational structure of the military training environment provides a degree of natural control not often found in field research settings. Record systems are systematic and comprehensive, allowing the researcher to incorporate archival data and training-process information at various levels of analysis. Naturally existing conditions allow the researcher who has adequate knowledge of the system to achieve an acceptable level of experimental control without having to resort to the artificial manipulation of persons or environmental conditions. Of particular importance is the fact that stress levels in recruit training are often quite high.

RECRUIT TRAINING IN THE MARINE CORPS

Each year, approximately 50,000 young men enlist in the Marine Corps, where recruit training is commonly acknowledged to be the most rigorous of all military branches. Marine recruits are trained in two locations—Parris Island, South Carolina, and San Diego, California—with approximately 25,000 recruits being trained in each of these recruit depots. Our research has been located at the training base in San Diego and the associated facilities at Camp Pendleton.

The training base is an austere environment that is adjacent to the San Diego Airport, Lindberg Field, from which the booming takeoffs of commercial jets regularly impede routine conversation. Incoming recruits arrive on commercial flights to Lindberg Field, where they assemble at a military liaison facility in the airport to await an anxiety-filled bus trip to the receiving barracks at the training base. When a sufficient number of recruits arrive at the receiving barracks to form a platoon (60–90 men), the first stage of recruit training, known as *processing,* will begin the 87-day training cycle.

Recruit training is conducted in four stages: processing and three training phases. The processing stage is a 4–6 day period that is designed to acquaint the individual with military life and the members of his training unit (platoon). This stage is an important period of transition from the civilian to the military life style. During this period, the recruit completes a number of administrative processing tasks, undergoes various tests, and has a thorough medical and dental evaluation. While the Marine Corps considers this time to be uneventful and "low stress," it is often quite traumatic for the young recruit.

From the moment he is ordered off the shuttle bus from the airport, he enters an alien environment composed of unfamiliar sights, sounds, faces, and rules. When first introduced to supervisory personnel (drill instructors), the recruit is confronted with an authority figure who is impeccable in bearing and dress and is in complete control of the situation. Immediately, it becomes clear that the only acceptable behavior is that prescribed by the drill instructor.

Disembarking from the bus, recruits quickly go to a warehouse, where they receive a tub of gear, and then promptly assemble in a formation at the rear of the receiving barracks. The position of the formation is precisely demarcated by rows of yellow footprints set at 45^0 angles to denote the position of attention. Following a roll call, each recruit inventories his recently issued gear, explicitly directed by the drill sergeant, whose instructions demand prompt and precise responses. Each piece of gear is inventoried and is then stuffed into a large dufflebag (sea bag). The recruits then are shown how to stand at attention, and the drill instructor recites in a booming voice key articles from the Uniform Code of Military Justice (laws governing the Armed Forces of the United States). The statements come at a pace that defies information-processing capacities, but the basic message is unmistakably clear: "Follow orders and respect your supervisors or you will be punished." The message that unacceptable behavior will be quickly followed by aversive consequences is one that is continuously reinforced.

Personal freedom, privacy, and individuality are lost. Within half an hour of getting off the bus, the recruits file through the rear door of the receiving barracks and receive their first Marine Corps haircut. The haircut takes about 30 seconds. They then file into a large room where they are issued military clothing. Promptly, they remove their civilian clothing and dress in a Marine Corps uniform. Sequentially, they move to another room, where they are issued toiletries and stationery and where, following a lecture on contraband, they have a period of amnesty to surrender any forbidden articles, ranging from matches to weapons or drugs. Various personal belongings, such as photographs of girlfriends, are collected, to be returned after training is completed.

Bourne (1967) characterizes this period as one of "environmental shock." His view is that past experience with remotely comparable events can ameliorate the high level of stress occasioned by the early stages of basic training. The recruit who has been away from home, has played sports, or perhaps has been in detention will, in Bourne's view, have a less severe reaction. Differential adaptation during the initial period is not related to preexisting psychopathology; with the exception of extreme cases. Furthermore, whatever factors facilitate adjustment during the first few days may not be related to later adjustment.

It is very likely that this introductory period constitutes the point of maximum stress for most recruits. Bourne (1967) noted that following the first 24-hours, men exhibited a picture of dazed apathy. In addition, he cited research indicating that this acute reaction is dramatically reflected in the 17-hydroxycorticosteroid levels of the men, comparable to those measured in schizophrenic patients during incipient psychosis. This is not surprising: Minutes after arrival, the recruit has been stripped of his personal freedom, has been denied expression of idiosyncratic behavior, and has had hair, clothing, and other personal belongings removed. Previously learned verbal and nonverbal responses are quickly found to be inadequate and inappropriate. All behavior is under the control of the drill instructor. Any display of emotion (fear, anger, disgust, crying, smiling) brings an immediate negative reaction from supervisory personnel. Any attempt by the recruit to exert personal control over the situation, other than responding to the task commanded, results in personal criticism. Through the use of a variety of carefully planned and executed aversive measures, training personnel are able to bring behavior of the group under their control. For the recruit, the first lesson learned in training is the avoidance of aversive stimulation by quickly and accurately responding to the directions of the staff. This basic lesson is continuously reinforced throughout the training cycle at both the individual and the group level.

Successful adaptation is in large measure contingent on the recognition that aversive stimulation decreases as the frequency and quality of desired behaviors increase. In the early days of training, virtually all reward involves negative reinforcement contingencies. Those who are either slow or unwilling to modify their behavior accordingly are singled out for increased attention, possible disciplinary action, or recommendation for discharge. Some recruits have acute stress reactions, resulting in referral for psychiatric screening. Our analyses of archival data revealed that approximately 58% of those failing to adjust psychologically or behaviorally are discharged within 17 days of the start of training (prior to the start of Phase II). One is led to speculate that failure of these individuals to adapt begins during the first 24 hours and increases progressively over time. The stress reduction interventions that we have developed are targeted on the recruits' psychological experiences during the processing period. Our intent has been to help him understand his reactions during these initial days, to prepare him cognitively for future experiences, and to offer some coping strategies for the challenges he is about to face.

After processing is completed, the recruit and his platoon are introduced to the drill instructor team that will supervise their entire training.[4] *Phase I* dramatically begins with an event known as "sea bag drag," in which the members of the platoon haul their sea bags, about three feet long and about 50 pounds in weight, from the receiving barracks to the training barracks, a distance of about one-quarter mile. The key elements of this event are that it is to be done at a quick pace, in accord with the drill instructors' urgings, and that the platoon is to move as a unit. Sometimes platoons are circled back to pick up trailing recruits.

Phase I is a two-week period of basic instruction in military skills and knowledge. Physical conditioning is given maximum emphasis, with the recruit quickly progressing from basic physical exercises to very strenuous tests of strength and endurance. The transition from Processing to Phase I requires adjustment to a new set of drill instructors who have been glorified by personnel in the processing phase. In essence, the recruits have been given a set of expectations regarding these new authority figures that is indeed anxiety-producing. There is little doubt in the recruit's mind that these drill instructors are in complete control of him. There is also no doubt that engagement with the demands of training has begun.

During this period, a concerted effort is made to increase performance and to instill discipline. As training moves into full gear, anxiety begins to decrease, and what appears is a process described by Goffman (1957) as "mortification." This process results from the sharp distinction between the recruit class and the supervisory class. The recruit comes to realize that he has no other identity within this environment other than that based on *performance* and *conformity.* Autonomous decisions are eliminated through the scheduling of daily activities. Most channels of communication with the outside world are broken or severely restricted.

Competition among individuals and units increases as pressure is applied to substandard recruits by drill instructors and fellow recruits. For those who have difficulty meeting minimum performance standards, the demands of the total environment increase disproportionally. The strain is likely to be felt most by those who have achieved or have been ascribed highest status in civilian life.

As training progresses, the recruit is expected to keep up with increasingly difficult physical training demands. He is also introduced to a

[4]Drill instructor teams are typically composed of from three to four Marine Non-Commissioned Officers who have been carefully screened and trained for their duties. Each team has a senior drill instructor who has had considerable experience training recruits and who is responsible for the conduct and performance of the platoon. The senior is also charged with providing close supervision and guidance to the juniors on his team.

new aversive event—"incentive training." When individuals or groups make mistakes, they are subjected to a series of exercises, with a prescribed number of repetitions, performed at a very rapid pace under close supervision. The incentive offered is removal of the threat of extra physical exercise, contingent on the satisfactory performance of tasks. Thus, the system relies on negative reinforcement to shape recruit behavior.

There is a distinct demarcation at the beginning of the second phase of training. ***Phase II*** is conducted at Camp Pendleton, which is located 40 miles of San Diego. This phase involves two weeks of training with the service rifle, one week of combat training, and one week of work duty (mess duty or grounds maintenance). It is important to note that this phase constitutes a period of attainment for the recruit. Marksmanship proficiency is an explicit result of individual effort and competition. Qualification tests, conducted at the end of two weeks at the range, represent the first occasion of tangible recognition of the individual by the system—silver badges are awarded according to levels of performance. Successful qualification is marked by exhilaration and a pronounced sense of efficacy.

After attaining proficiency with their rifles, recruits begin to internalize their new identity. They are then given one week of field combat training in which combat conditions are simulated. For most recruits, this is an enjoyable as well as a demanding time: While this is what many expect life to be like in the Marines, it stands in contrast to the following week of training which provides a glimpse of normal work life in the Marine Corps. The work details are fatiguing, but they do provide the first opportunity for recruits to have contact with someone other than fellow recruits and drill instructors. At this point in training, the recruit has "passed over the hump" and can now anticipate graduation as a Marine.

In ***Phase III*** the recruit prepares for various tests of military proficiency to be completed prior to graduation. These will consist of oral and written tests of military knowledge, physical fitness tests (PFT), and evaluation of the platoon's performance in drill. For obvious reasons, the Marine Corps places a strong emphasis on physical conditioning, and the recruits must not only perform on routine exercises (running, sit-ups, and pull-ups) but must also be able to succeed on the obstacle course, which involves many strenuous tasks of running, jumping, and climbing.

The environmental context is predominantly that of a "total institution." Goffman (1957) has portrayed the characteristic of "total institutions": (1) All aspects of life occur in the same place under the same authority, (2) each phase of daily functioning is carried out in the immediate company of others, with everyone treated alike and required to do the same thing, (3) activities are tightly scheduled and the scheduling is imposed by institutional authorities, and (4) all activities are part of an overall plan to fulfill the aims of the institution.

Although Goffman's concepts are distinctly applicable to the recruit training environment, there are certain aspects of recruit training that depart from his characterization of total institutions. For many recruits, as our longitudinal data have shown (Cook, Novaco, & Sarason, 1982), the training cycle provides an opportunity to learn that significant rewards result from personal effort. Many recruits have overcome ingrained negative self-perceptions and experience the enhancement of self-esteem as training progresses to the point at which graduation is in sight. One characteristic of the early phase of training is *equalization*. Those who have had minimal status in their past lives now have an opportunity for accomplishment. By meeting established performance criteria, positions of responsibility and other rewards can be achieved by those for whom reinforcement has been elusive. When recruits graduate, they are in excellent physical conditioning and are imbued with confidence. They are extremely proud of their accomplishments in the completion of training. Many feel they have now attained adulthood in society's eyes.

In order to understand fully the psychosocial demands of recruit training, it is important to keep in mind that the primary purpose of basic training is to prepare recruits for the stress of combat. The Marine Corps is strongly committed to the position that the methods and techniques used in training are necessary to provide a realistic test of stress tolerance. From this perspective, the Marine Corps believes that it is more prudent, and ultimately more humane, to provide this screening and learning under conditions in which the probability of death due to error is very low than it would be to send ill-prepared trooops into combat. This assumption underlies both the process and content of training and is one often overlooked in discussion of the efficacy of methods used by the military.

ATTRITION IN RECRUIT TRAINING

Of all the recruits who begin basic training ("boot camp"), 88% successfully complete the training cycle. The remaining 12% are discharged (attrite) for a variety of medical, psychological/behavioral, and other reasons. Attrition has proven to be a perplexing problem fo the military, ranging up to 40% during the first term of enlistment. Given that approximately 3,000 recruits fail to complete training at each of the Marine Corps' training bases each year, it is not surprising that attrition is a problem that receives organizational attention and has been extensively researched (Hand, Griffeth, & Mobley, 1977).

Our attention to attrition in recruit training has been guided by our ideas about stress-coping skills. Conservatively estimated, about 45% of attrition in recruit training is psychological/behavioral in nature. Because the recruit cannot simply opt for a discharge to escape the stress of training, attrition can be viewed as a breakdown in performance under stress. However, this is not to say that attrition is primarily due to the individual. Our research on attrition, in fact, departs from most previous investigations by its attention to objective properties of the organizational environment and its analysis of attrition in terms of the interrelated components of the system (Novaco, Sarason, Cook, Robinson, & Cunningham, 1979).

We sought to map rates, forms, and patterns of attrition to understand its nature and to determine the degree to which attrition results from factors or conditions that are psychologically related and therefore might potentially be influenced by a psychological intervention. We pursued these objectives beginning with an analysis of archival data on attrition over a one-year period. We then conducted a case analysis of psychologically related discharges. These efforts then led to an extensive study of a month cohort (those entering training in October 1978) of recruits through the training cycle, which we are now tracking through the entire enlistment period. A second cohort study (June 1979) was conducted as a replication. In these investigations, we assessed the influence of demographic, aptitude, personality, and training-unit factors on attrition and performance.

The most important findings that have emerged in our research concern the variations in training-unit[5] environments that are linked to patterns of recruit attrition (Novaco *et al.*, 1979). In conducting the analyses of archival data, we noticed that attrition rates varied significantly among the three battalions of the training regiment. Since this analysis involved over 2,925 attriters and a total accession of 24,481 recruits, our finding of a 5% difference in attrition rate between battalions suggested the operation of nonrandom factors. We then found in a study of randomly selected cases discharged for psychological/behavioral reasons that one battalion, which accounted for 37.9% of the total accessions, accounted for 49.3% of the psychological/behavioral discharges in our sample (N = 205). These findings consequently led us to track attrition at the platoon level to further examine the operation of training-unit differences. This was done in a study of the October 1978 cohort. In that investigation, we studied a one-third random sample (N = 597) of recruits through the

[5] The organizational structure for recruit training breaks down as follows: the *regiment* is the basic organizational unit for the administration of training. Within the regiment, there are three training *battalions* consisting of three to four *companies*. Each company is composed of two *series* which contain four *platoons*. Our analyses of training units have focused primarily on platoons, but we have examined effects at all organizational levels.

training cycle, collecting extensive measures on demographic, aptitude, personality, and training performance variables. A total of 15 platoons were involved in the study.

The training-unit variation was pronounced. Attrition varied from 0% to 28% across platoons. The question of course is what factors are responsible for such variation? Our hypothesis, generated by informed observations of the training process, was that the variability in attrition rate is associated with the manner in which the drill instructor team operationalizes the training regimen. That is, despite the highly routinized and specified procedures for the conduct of training (activities are scheduled down to the minute), the social environment created by drill instructor teams may vary nonetheless. Our belief was that the variations in social climate were not related to recruit attainment of skills.

There are several competing explanations to our hypothesis about the social environment of training units. First, the variation in attrition rates might be due to a variety of pretraining variables, such as demographic, aptitude, or personality factors, that are not evenly distributed across platoons. Another possibility is that the differences in attrition are a function of differences in the performance standards of unit leaders. This rival explanation asserts that attrition is direcly correlated with performance. High attrition rates are seen as resulting from the exclusion of low-achieving recruits from high-achieving units. Conversely, low-attrition training units reflect laxity in achievement standards. Furthermore, this view maintains that low attrition during the training cycle constitutes a suppression of attrition that will inevitably occur after graduation, during the enlistment period.

In order to test the alternative hypothesis, we constructed a three-level classification (ATTRITVAR) of platoons according to their attrition rate, thus generating low, medium, and high ATTRITVAR groupings. Our data have shown that there is no support for the belief that variation in attrition is due to differences in the initial composition of platoons or to the performance standards hypotheses. Remarkably, no demographic, aptitude, or personality factor differentiates the ATTRITVAR groups at the 0.05 level of significance. This is striking because, given the sample size, small differences that account for little variation and have no practical significance can attain statistical significance. With regard to the performance outcomes, the results are particularly persuasive because the analysesare biased in favor of the performance standards hypothesis in that the performance measures are taken late in the training cycle—that is, when the vast majority of attrition has occurred. Consequently, if recruit attrition represents the exclusion of poor performers, then performance must surely be highest in the high-attrition condition. However, the results are that the high-attrition platoons do not produce higher performing recruits and that on certain measures (e.g., marksmanship and military knowledge) they are significantly *lower* in performance. These findings, obtained with the October 1978 cohort, were replicated with the June 1979 cohort.

The second aspect of the performance standards hypothesis concerned the possibility that low attrition in recruit training merely suppressed attrition that would consequently occur after graduation. In essence, high-attrition drill instructors are viewed as expediting the inevitable. However our recently obtained longitudinal data on the October 1978 cohort shows that at the two-year point in the enlistment period, the *postgraduation* discharge rate for the low and medium ATTRITVAR conditions is significantly *lower* than that for the high ATTRITVAR group. Training units having high attrition during the training period continue to have high attrition after graduation. The difference in total attrition from the start of training to the two-year point is striking when the two lowest attrition and the two highest attrition units are contrasted (17.6% and 15.6% versus 48.8% and 33.3%, respectively). It is unmistakable that recruit training is being operationalized in different ways by unit leaders and that these differences in the implementation of training are important from both practical and scholarly standpoints.

At present, we are studying the nature of the social environment of the training unit as shaped by the drill instructor team. This is being accomplished by repeated measurement of recruits over the training cycle to assess changes in cognitions and affective states, as well as the development of the social support network within the platoon. Some of the findings on cognitive changes will be discussed in the subsequent section. We are also conducting studies of drill instructors to determine the correlates of low-attrition versus high-attrition outcomes in cross-sectional investigations, and we are examining developmental processes in longitudinal studies beginning with the start of drill instructor school.

A COGNITIVE-BEHAVIORAL ANALYSIS OF RECRUIT TRAINING ADJUSTMENT

As stress researchers, we are drawn to this environment, with its multidimensional stressors, as a prime context for studying the dynamics of person–environment exchange over time. It was also evident that, given the environmental structure, the successful completion of training is highly dependent on the development of cognitive coping skills. We hoped to learn about the cognitive coping strategies that recruits adopt to make it through the rigors of training, and we sought to implement a stress-coping skills intervention based on theoretical models and on our field observations.

The discovery that the training-unit environment is the key factor in determining attrition has important implications for stress reduction interventions that are aimed at the recruit. The environmental demands in certain training units may override the beneficial influence that might otherwise be obtained from our coping-skills intervention. The fact that the exposure time for the intervention program will necessarily be short relative to the length of exposure to the environmental demands imposes an additional limitation. Nevertheless, many things point to the critical significance of the early stages of training and the importance of adaptive cognitive strategies during this period.

The process of adjustment to recruit training can be understood in terms of the cognitive-behavioral framework proposed by Novaco (1979) for conceptualizing human stress. This model identifies two classes of cognitive processes that function as mediators of stress, these being *expectations* and *appraisals*. The expectancies pertain to anticipated environmental demands and to the person's beliefs about performance capabilities in response to those demands. The appraisals refer to interpretations of the environmental demands and to judgments made about one's response to them. The historical and contemporary use of the concepts of expectancy and appraisal in various psychological theories (e.g., Arnold, 1960; Bandura, 1977; Lazarus, 1966; Rotter, 1954; Seligman, 1975) reflects the utility of these constructs for describing, explaining, and predicting behavior.

These two classes of cognition are viewed as interrelated and as having reciprocal-influence relationships to behavior. Expectations, as subjective probabilities about future events, are based on previous appraisals of related circumstances and on behavioral performance in those situations. Appraisals, which accompany or follow the exposure to environmental demands, are a function of expectations about demands, expectations of performance, and self-observation.

Related to the operation of these basic classes of cognitions is the role of private speech. Self-statements give representation in language to the expectation and appraisal structures. Thus, self-statements are seen as expressions of the dynamic cognitive operations, but they also act as internal stimuli that can incite, maintain, or regulate emotional arousal and can serve as cues for attention and for behavior. In the cognitive-behavioral therapy literature, much emphasis has been given to the use of coping self-statements, following the work of Meichenbaum (1974). In the recruit-training environment, where behavior is highly constrained, coping self-statements take on even greater significance.

We described earlier some of the routine events that recruits encounter as they enter and become immersed in the training environment. We will now portray these stressful experiences in terms of the expectations and appraisals of recruits. We will illustrate the changes in cognitions during the training cycle and discuss the role of social support in the adjustment process.

Expectations

Recruits indeed form definite expectations about basic training prior to their arrival at the training base. Virtually everyone has had someone tell them about boot camp and about drill instructors. The common expectations are that training will be intense and demanding and that drill instructors are harsh in their manner. However, although recruits expect training to be tough, their notions of this are primarily with regard to *physical* demands. And the vast majority of recruits are not prepared for them. They anticipate tests of physical strength and endurance, but their first dose of stress derives not from physical athletic-type challenges—rather, it is a matter of psychological ambiance.

When recruits arrive at the receiving barracks after an anxiety-ridden bus shuttle from the airport, they immediately find themselves immersed in an environment that envelops their daily lives. By design, the recruit experiences a definitive break from civilian life and a rapid exposure to the rigors of the Marine Corps. Ordered to perform many new tasks under time constraints coupled with pressures for perfection, removed from all previous sources of security, and continuously reminded of the consequences that will result from the failure to obey orders, the recruit is in a state of disequilibrium marked by anxiety and worry. One recruit who had a stress reaction on the second day of processing had this to say about his experience the first night:

> "Man, it was nothing like I expected. My nerves just crashed. I thought there would be some sort of break-in. I was psyched out. I was telling myself, 'what is going down, man?' You feel weird, really weird."

Some of his friends had told him boot camp "was a bitch," and there were others who said that it wasn't so bad, "just a lot of physical training." When he arrived at San Diego he tried to prepare himself for the experience, but despite his resolve, the uncertainty was evident.

"I was nervous. I kept wondering, always wondering, 'What will we do tonight?' I was thinking, 'Man, here I am; I better be ready. I hope I can handle it.' "

Despite his efforts to learn what he could about the training regime before his arrival, he found himself caught off balance.

"I just had to come to feel what it was like. I didn't expect it to be what it was. [I'd tell others] you'd better be more ready for this than anything in your life. You won't even expect half of what you get."

When experiences are discrepant from expectations, the person is in a state of disequilibrium and induced physiological arousal. This physiological activation is unmistakable during the first hours at the receiving barracks, where the recruit is bombarded by demands that require an immediate response, keeping him continuously off balance. Even successful recruits experience this stressful disorientation.

"It started at the airport desk [military liaison station]. You got your first taste of boot camp. No more chewing gum or touching your face. No talking, always stand at attention—all that hollering was a real shock. Everything was a shock."

"Everybody was standing in a corner not knowing what to expect, just too scared to talk. A lot of things are going through your mind."

"You're real, real nervous. You wonder, you want to ask a question, but are they going to holler at you? Are they going to call you stupid or something?"

What are some of the things that recruits say to themselves when they first get off the bus and encounter their drill sergeant?

"I want to go back home."
"Is this guy for real?"
"Why am I here? I could be home enjoying myself."
"Why did I do this? Why didn't I go to the Navy or the Air Force?"

The disorientation is nicely conveyed by one recruit, who subsequently graduated with honors:

"[The sergeant] was rattling things off so fast [that] it registered in your mind, but you didn't know what to do. That's the first taste of getting in trouble for a lot of recruits. I know because I was one of the first ones.

"I was carrying documents from the AFEES [Armed Forces Entrance and Enlistment Station], and I had to take them into the office building inside, and he was yelling off to go through this door and that door, and I was scared to death. I was even afraid to breathe. All I seen was a door, and I ran through it and up the stairs, but the Sergeant saw me and started hollering at me and called me down to the bottom floor. I was really scared. I didn't know what to do, how to answer him . . ."

This disorientation and the associated anxiety lead to mistakes, hesitations, and general confusion. Virtually every recruit feels the apprehension of making mistakes.

"It felt like being tied up in a knot; not knowing which way to turn."
"You're just confused, nervous, and shaky."
"You start tryng to do things so fast, you just screw things up worse."

The theme of unexpected events and ambiance is consistently conveyed by those we have interviewed and by our field observations. The disturbed affect associated with task demands and responding to the drill instructor stands in contrast to how recruits respond to the haircut (electric clipper shaving) that they receive shortly after arrival at the receiving barracks. The haircut, which can give shivers to an observer, really does not bother the recruit. It is a clearly defined event, and they expect it. They are psychologically prepared for it when it happens and commonly joke about it afterwards.[6]

Coupled with the exposure to unexpected demands is a low sense of efficacy. Especially during the initial days of training, the recruit finds that he cannot do anything right. This sense of incompetence is exacerbated by the absence of positive reinforcement from the training personnel. There is virtually no praise, complements, congratulations, or any other form of verbalized encouragement in the utterances of drill instructors during the early phase of training. At best, the recruit strives to perform so as to avoid or escape criticism and punishment. When recruits fail to meet their drill instructor's performance expectations, they are punished by having to do intensive physical exercise (known as "incentive training"), the length and pace of which is regulated in accord with how far the recruit is in the training cycle. Thus, reward largely consists of negative reinforcement contingencies. It is noteworthy that this low sense of efficacy experienced and, to be sure, induced during the initial part of training will be dramatically altered as the recruit progresses through training.

Appraisals

The focus of the recruit's appraisal processes is the drill instructor. His voice, which booms from beneath a Smokey-the-Bear hat, unfailingly captures the recruit's attention. His impeccable dress and self-assured manner stands in sharp contrast to the recruit's sense of personal awkwardness and ineffectuality. He is very much in control of the recruit, a fact that elicits a full gamut of emotional responses.

[6] An almost universal experience is that, when going to sleep that first night, recruits are sensitized to their head being cold. They can vividly recall trying to keep their head warm as they lay in bed, trying to shield it from the cold air coming in from the open windows in the squad bay.

The recruits' reactions to their drill instructors during the early periods of training are a mixture of fear and anger, with anxiety reactions being the most prevalent. Their appraisals commonly refer to them being recipients of a "shock treatment" that continues throughout the training cycle:

> "You're always in shock . . . I believe that's what they wanted to accomplish—to test you mentally, see what you are made of. They still try to do that, they've done that since T-1 [training day one]. They test ya all the time."
> "You really never wear off the initial shock; they keep you on edge. All they have to do is snap their fingers. They can work you and put you back into shock."

Coupled with the obvious anxiety is a modicum of anger arising from the drill instructor's manner:

> "I wanted to lay him out."
> "I didn't like his attitude. He felt we were the lowest meat on the counter—worms."
> "I'd be sayin', 'Get off my case man, give me some slack.' "
> "I cussed in my sleep."
> "It wasn't the haircut, it was they way they handled my head."

The antagonistic appraisals that lead to anger must be kept in balance if the recruit is to adjust successfully. Expressions of anger, even the slightest hint of annoyance, are not tolerated by training personnel. Any verbal or nonverbal behavior by the recruit that suggests annoyance with training personnel or tasks will promptly result in aversive consequences. Thus, to the extent that a recruit feels angry, he must control it, and direct the anger toward constructive outcomes, perhaps using it to energize his behavior (Novaco, 1976).

Disappointment and depression are also among the stress-related affects that arise in conjunction with training demands. For many recruits, there is a recurrent worry of being set back in the training cycle either because of failing on performance tasks (e.g., the obstacle course) or because of interrupting circumstances (e.g., health problems). A high value is attached to being able to complete training with one's original platoon (the importance of social support is discussed below), and recruits do experience considerable disappointment when they are recycled. Organizational leaders have been particularly sensitive to the possibility that recruits who are set back will form failure appraisals and will experience loss. Consequently some commanders have given explicit attention to recruits in these circumstances during the transition period when they await joining a new platoon.[7]

COGNITIVE CHANGES ASSOCIATED WITH TRAINING

Over the course of training, marked changes occur in the recruit's expectations and appraisals. With each new achievement, the recruit develops increased confidence in his ability to take on new challenges. The changes in efficacy expectations and their relationship to performance are currently being examined. We have found that locus of control expectancies shift according to training unit environments, particularly in combination with the pretraining expectancies and life experiences of recruits (Cook *et al.*, 1982). Those who are trained in units having low-attrition or medium-attrition rates become more internal in locus of control. This is particularly true for recruits who begin training categorized as externals and who have had negative life experiences, as indexed by the Life Experiences Survey (Sarason, Johnson, & Siegal, 1978) and by failure to complete high school. In contrast, training in high-attrition rate platoons results in shifts toward externality, particularly for those who begin training as internals. Our hypothesis about these findings is that they reflect the reinforcement contingencies in the training unit as engineered by the drill instructor team.

The changes that occur in the appraisals of recruits who successfully complete training result from both (1) *exposure to the environmental elements over time* and (2) *the coping efforts utilized by recruits.* Quite obviously, recruits learn from experience and reappraise environmental circumstances accordingly. For example, as training proceeds, they begin to recognize that tasks and drills that may have seemed to be irrelevant nuisances at first later turn out to have had a purpose.

> "Everything they try to teach you has a purpose."
> "There is basically a reason for everything."
> "All the stuff that they made us do back in receiving [processing] that you thought was a bunch of bull, it all turns out to have a reason."

The prime case of reappraisal occurs with regard to the drill instructor. Recruits will commonly view him with high admiration, especially as the day of graduation nears.

[7] One of our early ideas was that recruits who have been set back may be a high risk group for adjustment problems. A coping skills intervention might be targeted specifically on such recruits. However, we found that being set back in training had no particular relationship to attrition.

> "You think he is the meanest man in the world at first."
> "After a while, you get feelings of respect. They grown on ya."
> "After you've been with him awhile, you'll find out [that] they're understanding. They know what you're going through."
> "If you behave in a military manner, they'll treat you in a military manner and will give you privileges—not a lot, just enough to keep us in line, with the understanding [that] there will be more."

To be sure, there are distinct differences in the personalities of drill instructors, who would all not be the object of encomium. We are now conducting longitudinal studies of drill instructors, beginning with their own training for this organizational role. One focus of this work is on the cognitive and behavioral attributes of drill instructors as associated with their performance as unit leaders.

Reappraisal also occurs as a result of coping efforts. In order to adapt to the manifold demands of the training environment, recruits must learn to alternatively construe the harsh circumstances to which they are exposed. Some of these coping reappraisals concern interactions with drill instructors and their patented high-volume supervision:

> "Ya wonder, did I really do all that bad to make him yell in my ear? Why is he yelling? But then you think, if I try harder the next time, then he won't be yelling at me."
> "Yelling is just part of it, you couldn't have screwed up that bad. You just get accustomed to it."
> "You try hard not to make mistakes, but you're gonna make them, because you're a recruit."

One of the best illustrations of coping reappraisals occurs in conjunction with physical training and its associated pain. The intense regimen of calisthenics, long-distance running, the obstacle course, and even the shooting positions at the rifle range all involve the endurance of pain and discomfort. Recruits must learn to cope with this pain, and their efforts reflect the strategies advocated by Turk (1978) for pain regulation:

> "Pain is always gonna be there, you just fight it."
> "It isn't going to last forever, you know it's going to end."
> "You keep telling yourself you gotta do it, because if you quit it going to be a lot worse."
> "Just let it hurt, because later on it won't, and it will be good for me."
> "I keep my mind loose and keep happy thoughts."
> "It's kind of mind over matter."
> "You never know how long the run is going to be, so I think about the scenery—keep your mind off your legs."

As competence and conditioning improve, pain and discomfort inevitably diminish. An irony in this regard is that the punitive "incentive training'' exercises must be intensified in order to serve their intended function. Phase III recruits would barely work up a sweat doing the "IT" administered to Phase I recruits.

At this point in the training cycle, recruits have developed all of the psychological resources required for successful coping. They will be exposed to an intensification of demands that they have already encountered (e.g., physical conditioning tests) and to several new stressful circumstances, such as those in field combat training.[8] But they have now learned what to expect from their drill instructions and how to constructively appraise the routine stressors of the training regimen. Having successfully qualified at the rifle range, many of their performance anxieties have thereby been allayed. Although they will worry about succeeding on other tests of performance, they now know that they can succeed.

Coping self-statements are actively utilized by recruits in many aspects of training and particularly in regard to performance demands. Some of these self-statements have been included above as representations of the expectation and appraisal processes. However, recruits actively engage in self-instruction as a way to prime their motivation, especially when endurance is an issue, as it is for long-distance running:

> "I tell myself, 'I can keep going.' You gotta motivate yourself."
> "Just one more mile, and we'll be home."
> "I keep telling myself, 'I'll get better.' "
> "You tell yourself, 'If I don't make it, you might as well forget it.' "

Another key use of coping self-statements is with regard to maintaining a task orientation. Recruits commonly will instruct themselves to "Concentrate on the task," "Stay alert," "Listen to the D.I.," and "Just do it right, and keep your cool."

When recruits go to Camp Pendleton for the second phase of training, their primary agenda concerns instruction in marksmanship and field combat techniques. The experience at the rifle range is an important one psychologically, because it is the recruits' first structured opportunity to receive positive reinforcement and to strive for personal achievement. We have observed that recruits become enthusiastically engaged in attaining the best possible performance. Their mood is generally positive during this period, and there is distinct bonding of the platoon members.

[8] After approximately five weeks in the training environment, recruits undergo one week of intensive field training designed to acquaint them with the realities of infantry life. They are exposed to such experiences as weapons training (hand grenades, small artillery, etc.) and to the fatigue that comes from long hours in rough terrain. For most, this time appears to be most enjoyable in spite of the difficult physical demands. After this experience most recruits can realistically look forward to graduation.

Their group performance is tabulated and so it reflects on the quality of the platoon. Drill instructors, invested in the performance of their platoon, begin to supply encouragement to the recruits who are actually trained by special teams of range instructors. After two weeks, recruits undergo marksmanship qualifications tests, during which much comraderie, enthusiasm, and determination can be observed. This is reflected in comments made by two recruits just prior to going to the firing line:

> "This takes all the stress off."
> "Put this on record, today's 007 (platoon number) day; everybody's shooting for our PMIs (marksmanship instructor) and our drill instructors."
> Interviewer: "So it's important for you guys to take the range?"
> "Yes, sir. Real important."

Qualification at the rifle range is a milestone achievement on the road to graduation, and recruits are noticeably elated when they pass this hurdle. These self-instructions direct their attention to the task at hand and, importantly, function to prevent disruptive cognitions. Learning how to remain task-oriented is a central part of coping during circumstances that have the potential of arousing anxiety or anger (Novaco, 1975; Sarason, 1978).

Related to being task-oriented is the idea of sequential coping—taking each test and each day as it comes. Particularly during the early weeks of training, recruits are very nervous about the unknown things they will have to face. As they learn to cope day-to-day, taking one step at a time toward the goal of graduation, the process of coping becomes more manageable. The sense of gradual, successive progress spurs perserverance:

> "You tell yourself, 'Well I've made it this long, you might as well go all the way with it.' "

Making it through boot camp can seem like an overwhelming task, but by taking the view of day-to-day chunks rather than a massive challenge, coping can be facilitated. This is a central theme of the intervention module.

SOCIAL SUPPORT

Considerable research has now shown that the impact of stressful events can be moderated by the presence of supportive social conditions that protect the person from debilitating forces (Cobb, 1976; Heller, 1979). Social support has been a rubric for studies otherwise identified as investigations of social networks, social isolation, social participation, loss of support, and psychological assets. The common denominator in this research has been the concern with psychosocial factors that mitigate the consequences of stressful conditions. Nevertheless, the heterogeneity of research programs has produced considerable variation in the way social support has been construed and operationalized. Cobb (1976) viewed social support as "information leading the subject to believe that he is cared for and loved, esteemed, and a member of a network of mutual obligations" (p. 300). This definition confounds social support as a preexisting condition, with its effects on the person. In contrast, Caplan (1974) construes social support as "continuing social aggregates that provide individuals with opportunities for feedback about themselvs and for validations of their expectations about others" (p. 4). Caplan further emphasizes the reciprocity of need-satisfaction in relationships persisting over time, and his view is suitable for characterizing social support phenomena in the recruit-training environment.

For the Marine recruit, social support has a prominent role in the adjustment process. The support has two basic origins: (1) family and loved ones, and (2) fellow platoon members. Many recruits will drive themselves through the demands of training by conjuring images of graduation day. And associated with such images is the expected pride of their family and friends. As they struggle through the hardships of training, recruits often cope by thinking about those whom they love. However, thoughts about home must be kept in balance, if the recruit is to succeed. Preoccupation with matters extraneous to training tasks, particularly when news from home is disconcerting, can seriously interfere with performance. Nevertheless, when asked about what "keeps them going," recruits commonly mention letters from home as being a major source of motivation. Knowing that there is someone back home who cares about them ameliorates the daily duress.

In addition to support from distal environment sources is that which emerges within the proximal environment. The nature and progression of training are inherently suited for the forming of social bonds among platoon members. Recruits turn to each other for validation of the concatenation of emotions and cognitons they experience during the early days. They are relieved to find that everyone else has been scared, nervous, worried, and angry. As time goes on, they discover that getting singled out for criticism is a routine but universal experience. They discover that few individuals are good in all aspects of training and that there is reciprocity in helping others.

> "Everybody's scared. If you act big and tough, you won't make friends. And everybody will think you are a coward."

Through the sharing of their experiences, recruits develop an adaptive perspective on the harsh realities of training. They discover that many recruits have felt distressed, just like themselves, but that the vast majority of recruits do successfully complete training.

Intrinsic to the training objectives is the development of teamwork. Recruits must often work with each other on training tasks, and the platoon itself develops a unit identity. Platoon leaders work to instill pride (*espirit de corps*) among unit members, which is invoked throughout training, especially during performance tests where there is much competition between platoons. A strong sense of togetherness is formed, which impels recruits to encourage and inspire one another.

The development of the social support network within the platoon is currently being investigated in our research. It is hoped that what we learn about social support relationships will also inform us about the attrition-related variations among the training units.

FACILITATING ADJUSTMENT TO STRESS

Our field observations and analyses of archival data have indicated that the most stressful aspects of recruit training occur during the early stages of training. We therefore sought to develop a stress reduction intervention aimed at augmenting stress-coping skills that would be implemented during the processing period at the receiving barracks, through the use of videotape modules.

There have been two previous efforts to facilitate adjustment to recruit training by using intervention films. Datel and Lifrak (1969) developed an experimental film for the purpose of creating realistic expectations among recruits in Army basic training. Their own research had indicated that recruits highly underestimate the level of distress that they will experience during training, as measured by the Multiple Affect Adjective Check List (Zuckerman & Lubin, 1965) on repeated testings. Heavily influenced by the ideas of Janis (1958) in his work on stress experienced by surgical patients, Datel and Lifrak reasoned that stress during basic training is a function of emotional preparedness. They hypothesized that those who are prepared to expect severe, prolonged stress will report less distress during the training cycle.

To create realistic expectations, Datel and Lifrak utilized an existing Army training film, entitled "This Is How It Is," editing portions of the film that portrayed gratifying or rewarding aspects. This resulted in a 20-minute experimental film, and a control film was also included in their design. The MAACL results demonstrated an elevation in expected distress following the experimental film; however, the film had no effect on measured distress during training. The authors' discussion of their negative results is instructive:

> Perhaps in other words, all *E* film did was to make *Ss* momentarily anxious . . . perhaps to give them a cognitive structure on which to focus their anxieties. Maybe the "work of worrying" has no preparatory value if one is not taught specifically what one should worry about. Or, maybe *E* film's message told *S* to worry about the wrong things.
>
> How does one adequately prepare the new recruit for the stress of basic training? Apparently it is not done by a one-shot film which, while it does scare him, fails to arm him. (1969, p. 879)

Datel and Lifrak speculate that their experimental film was not successful because it did not include content related to the "culture shock" or "stripping process" (Goffman, 1957) inherent in basic training. However, it is unclear to us that a portrayal of "stripped identity" phenomena would reduce stress. Rather, recruits must be presented with suggested ways of coping. It is the absence of information about coping techniques that would seem to be the key ingredient missing from the Datel and Lifrak intervention.

An intervention effort analogous to that of Datel and Lifrak has been undertaken with Marine Corps recruits at Parris Island. Horner, Meglino, and Mobley (1979) developed an instructional film, called "PIRATE" (Parris Island Recruit Assimilation Training Exercise), which aims to give recruits a realistic preview of recruit training experiences. Their intervention is also directed at recruit expectations, but the impetus for their program comes from research on organizational management and employee turnover. More specifically, it is guided by a role-choice model that is a variation of the generalized expectancy models used in the study of organizational behavior (Lawler, 1973; Mitchell, 1974; Porter & Steers, 1973; Vroom, 1964). Mobley, Meglino, and their associates have been studying the relationships of values, expectations, and intentions to organizational problems such as attrition. The Horner *et al.* study used an 80-minute videotape that acquaints recruits with training situations and does offer some advice for new recruits. They report an experiment consisting of a treatment, placebo, and control condition, finding reductions in attrition both prior to and following graduation that they attribute to the experimental film. Serious methodological problems, however, weigh against their interpretation. Recruits were not randomly assigned to conditions, which are badly confounded with training-unit effects that go unnoticed by the investigators. Critically, no significant effects were obtained on any manipulation check variables, yet Horner *et al.* ignore this elementary and essential issue in explaining differential group outcomes. Furthermore, although presenting recruits with a realistic preview of training experiences indeed seems like a worthy intervention it is quite implausible that viewing an 80-minute videotape could result in the 14% reduction in attrition that they report for the postgraduation enlistment period.

Our intervention program was developed independently of the Paris Island program. We began by conducting the archival investigations referred to earlier, and then a series of process-monitoring activities were initiated to gather the raw material for the intervention modules. Since two members of the research team[9] are former Marine Corps officers, we were well-informed about the training environment. However, it was still necessary to systematically observe the training process in terms of our theoretical models, as well as to obtain audio and video material.

The raw material for the intervention videotape was obtained by several procedures. We first selected, by a near-random process, 10 recruits to be subjects for an audio-visual catalogue of training experiences, concentrating on the first five days and on events at the rifle range. These recruits were tracked from the moment they deplaned at San Diego Airport. A photographer and two assistants with tape recorders accompanied these subjects through all aspects of the first five days on the base, thus compiling an extensive record of events and reactions. It must be noted here that because of the intensity and multiplicity of training demands, the recruits rapidly became oblivious to the presence of the research team. It is fair to say that in less than 30 minutes after their arrival at the receiving barracks, the recruits paid no attention to the camera and microphones.

The next step in the recording procedure consisted of studio interviews with these same recruits conducted just after the marksmanship qualifications test. At this point in training, three of the ten recruits had attrited, and one was set back to be recycled. The remaining six recruits were first brought to a viewing room, where they had a most unusual experience—by assembling hundreds of slides and tapes, we recreated their first days in boot camp. The slides and the coordinated sound track presented them with a psychologically powerful documentary of those unforgettable early days and thus served as a powerful stimulus for the studio interviews that we conducted with them over the next two days.

Our "stars" were interviewed on camera in groups of three. The interviews probed into their experiences throughout training and sought to learn how they coped with the various adversities. Segments of the videotaped interviews are incorporated in the intervention module, and some of the sound track is also used as voice-overs for other video

[9]Thomas M. Cook and Francis J. Cunningham.

material. The voice-overs are useful to convey stress-related cognitions and coping strategies in juxtaposition with videos of training circumstances.

A third procedure by which audiovisual material was gathered involved "minicam" footage of training events such as physical-conditioning exercises, close order drill, and grauation ceremonies. All of the raw material was subsequently edited in a studio located on the base in accord with a script that we composed.

The module begins with a brief preview of the various aspects of training somewhat like the "realistic job preview" approach. However, in our module this is an abbreviated presentation and is intended primarily as introductory material to get the viewer's attention. There are two key themes in the intervention module: *the self-control regulation of emotion* and *task performance effectiveness.* The coping skills related to these targeted concerns are introduced by instructional inscriptions that are superimposed on the screen and are modeled in conjunction with specific training situations.

The messages related to the regulation of emotion begin with validation of the recruits' experiences during the initial days. It is conveyed that fear, anger, disappointment, and worry are perfectly normal and quite common reactions among recruits. They are presented with the circumstances that have induced this distress and are told that despite their worry and confusion, thousands of recruits have felt the same way yet have ultimately succeeded in training.

In order to minimize the occurrence of disruptive emotions, several steps are taken to develop an adaptive cognitive orientation. Specific information is imparted about the roles of training personnel and what is to be expected of them. For example, in addition to describing troop handlers and drill instructors in terms of characteristics routinely recognized by the military organization (e.g., being an example of physical conditioning, military proficiency, bearing, and devotion to duty), the viewer is told:

> "You may have had trouble understanding the language used by the troop handler. Some of his words may seem strange. He does not come across as being friendly. He does not hand out praise when tasks are completed."

Detailed information is also given about what is generally expected of recruits and the general ingredients of successful performance. Thus, consistent with many cognitively based treatment interventions and, in particular, with the educational phase of the stress inoculation approach, recruits are cognitively prepared for the acquisition of coping skills.

Efforts are then made to influence the expectation and appraisal structures of recruits so as to prevent disruptive emotions and to promote adaptive behavior. For example, recruits must learn to perform under time pressures and to constructively deal with their inevitable mistakes. They must expect to be sharply criticized for mistakes and learn not to appraise such criticism antagonistically or in a self-derogating manner. Very importantly, they must learn how to remain *task-oriented* when confronted by threat or provocation. Novaco (1975) and Sarason (1975), respectively for anger and anxiety, have emphasized the value of maintaining a task orientation as an important stress-coping skill.

The regulation of emotion theme is thus intertwined with the task-performance theme. In order to do well on demanding training tasks, recruits must learn to control self-defeating emotional stages and to tune out self-preoccupying cognitions that engender such emotions. They must also process information efficiently, exercise good judgment, attend to detail, endure duress, learn from mistakes, and develop teamwork. We will attempt to transmit this obviously complex set of skills by illustrating them in conjunction with a simple task (making a rack) and then generalizing their application to other tasks in training.

The presentation is structured according to a task-performance framework having the following components: (1) a cognitive orientation, (2) information input, (3) meaning analysis, (4) response execution, and (5) feedback consequences. This scheme is exemplified in a role-play enactment in which two recruits must make and remake a "rack" (bed) under the close and highly energetic supervision of a drill instructor. So as to convey this more clearly, excerpts from the script are given below. The italicized words appear as characters superimposed on the video.

> "Let's take a look at two recruits performing a task that will be part of your everyday experience in training—making a rack. Watch carefully and notice that the task is being done under difficult conditions.
>
> There is a *time limit.*
>
> They must pay close *attention to details,* and
>
> the drill instructors are providing very *close supervision and correction.*
>
> Pay close attention to how these recruits react. It is obvious that these recruits are under pressure. They must
>
> *Be ready to respond.*
>
> *Listen carefully* to directions and know what is being asked of them.
>
> *Perform quickly* and make as few mistakes as possible.
>
> *Correct* their *mistakes* smoothly and accurately.
>
> Not let their personal feelings interfere with their performance (*control feelings*).
>
> *Work as a team,* making sure each knows what the other is doing.
>
> In order to help you understand not only what goes into doing well in making a rack, but also on other tasks you will be given in training, we are going to break down the task performance into its working parts. These parts or components of task performance are *mental attitude, input, judgment, response,* and *results.*"

Each task-performance component is then illustrated by some additional training task, alternately referring back to the rack-making scene to reinforce the message.

The module, in summary, attempts to augment the stress-coping skills of recruits by acknowledging the presence of distress, providing useful information about the environment, promoting an adaptive cognitive orientation, offering suggestions about coping techniques, and modeling successful coping behaviors. The second and third modules, which focus on the regulation of emotion and task performance respectively, are designed to elaborate and reinforce these two key themes. They are currently being developed, and when completed will be implemented on the second and third day of the processing period. Supplementary printed material to be included in the recruits' *Handbook of Essential Knowledge* is also being developed to further reinforce the intervention program.

EXPERIMENTAL EVALUATION

The effects of the first coping skills module are being examined as part of a larger investigation of recruit-training factors and outcomes. We are conducting a longitudinal analysis of cognitive and performance measures in order to learn more about the social environment of training units, as well as to explore various other topics. The measurement time points are the first and third days of processing, midway through training, and just prior to graduation.

In conjunction with this larger study, we sought to evaluate the impact of the first coping-skills module. To be sure, viewing one 35-minute videotape may not have much influence on measures distant in the training cycle, but we do expect exposure to the one module to affect cognitions during the processing period. We thus implemented an experimental design that would test for such effects and here report some preliminary findings on this evaluation.

The experimental evaluation was conducted by randomly dividing 530 recruits among five conditions. One group (MI) saw the coping-skills module ("Making It"); another group (BG) saw a comparison film ("The Beginning"), which was the San Diego version of the "PIRATE" film developed at Parris Island, with some additional material[10]; a third group saw both films, viewing the coping-skills module first (MI + BG); a fourth

[10] The San Diego version of "PIRATE" was made while we were in the process of producing our coping skills module. The San Diego film, "The Beginning," differs from the Parris Island version in that it devotes more attention to the processing period of recruit retraining, makes reference to coping with stress, and utilizes a role play. While these additions were made in the San Diego production, the thrust of the film is the realistic job preview.

group saw both films in reverse order (BG + MI); and the fifth group was in a no-film control condition. The experimental design is a 2 × 2 factorial (viewing or not viewing each film) with an additional control group (BG + MI) to counterbalance order of viewing.

The films were shown in large classrooms. After completing the questionnaire instrument containing various sets of self-report scales, recruits were sent to classroom locations corresponding to the treatment conditions. Importantly, *the randomization was done within platoons.* The procedure was implemented for each of 6 platoons in the September 1980 cohort. These platoons had formed on successive days and were thus tested separately. The retest was administered two days later to each platoon sequentially. The entire procedure was conducted over a period of two weeks.

The dependent measures consist of ratings of perceived difficulty and efficacy expectations for particular training tasks, perceptions of control, adjustment problems, social support, locus of control (IE), and other stress-relevant indices. Performance measures and archival data pertaining to disciplinary action and sick call are also utilized in our analyses. The results of the evaluation are forthcoming, and here we present only a few preliminary findings to illustrate the impact of the intervention. The complexity of the analyses, particularly insofar as they involve moderator variables such as locus of control, demographic factors, and training-unit conditions, precludes presentation here.

Regarding the effect on cognitions during the processing period, we have found that viewing the coping-skills module ("Making It") resulted in a significant increase in efficacy expectations across training tasks. Using a 2 × 2 × 2 ANOVA design (MI × BG × IE)[11] applied to a composite index of changes on 11 task expectancy ratings, we obtained a significant MI main effect, $F(1,236) = 5.26$, $p < 0.02$, and the triple interaction approached significance ($p < 0.07$). No other main effects or interactions resulted on this composite index. Examination of the analyses for individual task ratings shows that the MI main effect on the composite index in particular results from the efficacy ratings for marksmanship, physical training, endurance under stress, controlling emotions, learning essential knowledge, and living up to drill instructor expectations. The groups that see "Making It" subsequently have higher expectations of how they will perform on these tasks than do the groups that do not see the coping-skills module. In addition, recruits in the MI conditions report significantly less trouble adjusting to the demand of drill instructors, $F = 3.85(1,251)$; $p < 0.05$.

[11] The IE condition is a two-level factor consisting of the upper and lower tertiles of the IE distribution. The analyses reported in the text thus involve a reduced sample as reflected in the degree of freedom for the statistical tests.

The triple interaction on the composite index results from significant three-way effects on drill, military appearance, physical training, and endurance under stress. Most simply described, this interaction results from the MI condition effects on externals and the BG condition effects on internals. The strongest gains in efficacy occur for external locus of control recruits who see "Making It." But, while "Making It" primarily enhances the efficacy expectations of externals when it is shown by itself, in the combined condition with the comparison film, internals gained more than did externals. The differential effect of the MI condition on externals is also reflected in significant two-way interactions (MI × IE) on several individual task efficacy ratings.

The composite index for a set of six personal control items also had a significant MI × IE interaction, $F(1,246) = 6.38$, $p < 0.01$, with no other effects being significant. This result is due to particular personal control beliefs for grades and job success, emotional state, and problems at home. For each of these variables, in the conditions shown the coping-skills module, external locus of control recruits increase more in their perceptions of control than do internals (who basically do not change); whereas, in those conditions not shown the coping-skills module, internals increase more in perceptions of control than do externals (who basically do not change). As with the composite index, no effects other than the MI × IE interactions are significant.

These findings thus indicate that the coping-skills module has a significant positive effect on the cognitions of recruits during the stressful processing period. Viewing the experimental intervention videotape increased the efficacy expectations of recruits with regard to a number of specified training tasks and also increased their personal control beliefs concerning several sources of stress. Moreover, the inclusion of a comparison film in the experimental design strengthens the significance of the obtained effects, particularly since the comparison film was made for the purpose of helping recruits to adjust.

The analyses of the intervention also indicate that the coping-skills module has differential effects according to locus of control orientation. Externals gain the most from the intervention. In addition to the dependent measures described above, the results on other indices show that externals in the intervention conditions increase in the belief that good performance on various designated training tasks will determine success as gauged by drill instructors. This is in contrast to various control conditions in which externals either decrease or show no gain in such beliefs.

These results for external locus of control recruits are important in light of our previous findings that externals have a higher rate of attrition (17%) than do internals (7%), as well as being more negative in their self-appraisals (Cook *et al.,* 1982). Those having an external orientation are less likely to succeed in training and, even when advancing to graduation, still increase in levels of anger provocation. In this regard, the coping-skills intervention module seems to be positively affecting those who are most in need of help. Further analyses will sharpen our understanding of these effects, particularly as they combine and/or interact with the influences of the platoon environments.

SUMMARY AND PROSPECTIVE ISSUES

The Marine Corps recruiting training environment is a highly stressful arena in which cognitive coping skills are of the utmost importance. The intensity, duration, and multiplicity of the environmental demands, occurring in a context where overt coping behavior is highly constrained necessitate the early acquisition of cognitive restructuring capabilities. The successful completion of training is actually determined in the early stages of the training cycle, when recruits must make rapid adjustments.

For many recruits, there unfolds a "natural mastery of stress" (cf. Epstein, Chapter 3, this volume) by which the individual gradually assimilates representations of threat and initially high levels of resting-state arousal subside. Some recruits are not at all successful in this natural mastery process and manifest stress reactions that result in discharge. Others who do manage to complete training may nonetheless experience distress which impairs their performance in training and may have residual effects after graduation.

To facilitate the coping resources of recruits, we have developed and have begun to implement[12] a cognitive-behavioral intervention designed to increase stress-coping skills. The first of three videotape modules has been experimentally evaluated, and the results indeed support the effectiveness of the intervention in producing adaptive cognitive changes among recruits. We expect that the additional modules will add significantly to the positive results.

While results of the preliminary evaluation are encouraging, several issues emerge regarding the use of group-administered video presentations in the recruit environment. First, recruits take a passive role with no opportunity to request additional information and clarification or to demonstrate understanding of the concepts and required behaviors. Second, there is little opportunity for the recruit to receive feedback from peers and supervisors concerning cognitive or behavioral coping styles and problem-solving strategies once training has begun.

[12]The coping skills module actually had been incorporated into the Processing schedule at MCRD, san Diego, by the base command prior to our conducting the experimental evaluation.

Since drill instructors play such an important role in the creation and maintenance of training-unit environments, it is both prudent and logical that they be given an active part in the stress-coping intervention. If any intervention is to be successful in this environment, it must receive the support of drill instructors and junior officers (e.g., series officers and company commanders). Including these supervisors in some meaningful way would serve to increase acceptance of the program and boost the external validity of module content.

Drill instructors could be included in the intervention in the following ways. Those responsible for both the processing and the training phases would be introduced to the rationale for the intervention and given available data regarding the potential for recruit adjustment and performance. All drill instructors responsible for the processing phase, and selected drill instructors from training platoons, would then receive a short training period in the techniques of guided discussions, with emphasis on those issues raised by the modules. The use of guided discussions is thought to be particularly effectual since all Marine leaders are trained early in their career in such techniques as part of the Marine Corps Leadership Program. Thus, discussions designed to reinforce the content of the video modules could be implemented with a minimum of administrative and educational cost.

Such discussions could be held at the platoon level for the purpose of clarifying concepts or issues and to provide a forum where fears, concerns, and behavioral options may be openly expressed and discussed. Drill-instructor discussion leaders would then be able to provide valuable feedback to recruits regarding the efficacy of various cognitive strategies or behaviors and to suggest alternatives based on personal experience and the theoretical model.

Discussions could be scheduled immediately following the viewing of each of the modules during the processing period and at several selected points during the training cycle. The content of the discussions would be derived from module content during processing and from a demand analysis of later phases of training (e.g., how to cope with the anxiety of rifle qualification) and platoon-specific issues could be selected by the drill instructor.

The implementation of these additional procedures is expected to enhance the impact of the stress-coping modules by providing the opportunity for transfer and generalization across training phases and situations. In addition, the inclusion of drill instructors in the process is expected to increase program support and convey the subtle message to recruits that the information is important because their leaders are actively involved.

The coping-skills intervention is only one part of our research on the stress associated with recruit training. Moreover, the augmentation of coping skills is only one component of our stress reduction perspective. Viewing stress as a condition of imbalance between environmental demands and coping resources signifies that stress can be mitigated by modifying environmental demands as well as by boosting coping skills. Achieving changes in military training environments is, of course, a complex and exceedingly difficult undertaking, yet our research on training-unit influences holds considerable promise for organizational interventions.

To elaborate briefly on the prospect of environmental change, we contend that the environmental demands during recruit training are determined not only by the rigorous tasks and challenges specified by Marine Corps training standards but also by the particular way in which the training regimen is operationalized by training personnel. Drill instructor teams, in particular, vary in the manner in which they conduct training, so that there is variation in the social environments of platoons. The demands to which recruits are exposed are not uniform. This is manifested in variation in attrition rates, as well as on the cognitive structures of platoon members, such as locus of control. Our ongoing longitudinal studies of recruits and drill instructors will, we hope, provide a body of information that might contribute to organizational policy decisions in the interest of optimizing training environments.

Related to our interest in environmental determinants are some difficulties that have arisen with regard to the "stress inoculation" approach to stress reduction that has been advocated by several authors in this volume (Epstein, 1967; Jaremko, 1979; Meichbaum, Turk, & Burstein, 1975; Novaco, 1976). Far too often, as can be seen in the studies reviewed by Jaremko (1979), attempts to implement the stress inoculation approach have consisted of little more than the use of coping self-statements anteceded by some didactics about the problem state (anxiety, pain, or anger). Typically, in such instances, the investigators use the stress concept merely as a convenient surrogate for other topic labels such as "emotion," "disorder," or "problem." Stress is induced by environmental demands, cognitively mediated, to be sure, and the implementation of the "stress inoculation" approach must pay explicit recognition to these environmental circumstances. The utilization of the stress inoculation model presented by Novaco (1979) emphasizes that environmental demands, ostensibly unrelated to anger provocation, can function to predispose persons to anger problems by elevating their levels of arousal.

Cognitive-behavioral interventionists who are concerned with stress reduction must attend to the contextual determinants of stress reactions and must design interventions that heed the environmental sources of stress. Our research on recruit training proceeds in that direction, and we hope to have generated interest in such agendas. Beyond this concern, we believe that the coping-skills intervention represents a significant extension of clinically based treatment methods to an uncommonly intense stress context.

REFERENCES

Arnold, M. B. *Emotion and personality.* New York: Columbia University Press, 1960.

Bandura, A. Self-efficacy; Toward a unifying theory of behavior change. *Psychological Review,* 1977, 191–215.

Bourne, P. G. Some observations on the psychosocial phenomena seen in basic training. *Psychiatry,* 1967, *30,* 187–196.

Bourne, P. G. *The psychology and physiology of stress.* New York: Academic Press, 1969.

Bourne, P. G. *Men, stress, and Vietnam.* Boston: Little, Brown, 1970.

Caplan, G. *Support systems and community mental health.* New York: Behavioral Publications, 1974.

Caputo, P. *A rumor of war.* New York: Ballantine Books, 1977.

Cobb, S. Social support as a moderator of life stress. *Psychosomatic Medicine,* 1976, *38,* 300–314.

Cook, T. M., Novaco, R. W., & Sarason, I. G. Military recruit training as an environmental context affecting expectancies for control of reinforcement. *Cognitive Theory and Research,* 1982, *6,* 409–427.

Datel, W. E., & Lifrak, S. T. Expectations, affect change, and military performance in the army recruit. *Psychological Reports,* 1969, *24,* 855–879.

DeFazio, V. J. Dynamic perspectives on the nature and effects of combat stress. In C. R. Figley (Ed.), *Stress disorders among Vietnam veterans: Theory, research and treatment.* New York: Brunner/Mazel, 1978.

Dollard, J. & Horton, D. *Fear in battle.* New York: AMS Press, 1977. (Originally published, 1944.)

Doob, L. W. The utilization of social scientists in the overseas branch of the Office of War Information. The American Political Science Review, 1947, *41,* 649–667.

Epstein, S. Natural healing processes of the mind. In H. Lowenheim (Ed.), *Meanings of madness.* New York: Behavioral Publications, 1976.

Figley, C. R. (Ed.). *Stress disorders among Vietnam veterans: Theory, research and treatment.* New York: Brunner/Mazel, 1978.

Goffman, E. *Asylums.* New York: Doubleday, 1961.

Grinker, R. R., & Spiegel, J. P. *Men under stress.* Philadelphia: Blakiston, 1945.

Hand, H. H. Griffeth, R. W., & Mobley, W. H. *Military enlistment, reenlistment, and withdrawal research: A critical review of the literature* (TR-3). South Carolina, Center for Management and Organizational Research, December, 1977.

Heller, K. The effects of social support: Prevention and treatment implications. In A.V. Goldstein & F. H. Kanfer (Eds.), *Maximizing treatment gains: Transfer enhancement in psychotherapy.* New York: Academic Press, 1979.

Horner, S. O., Meglino, B. M., & Mobley, W. H. *An experimental evaluation of the effects of a realistic job preview on Marine recruit affect, intentions and behavior* (TR-9).

South Carolina, Center for Management and Organizational Research, September 1979.
Janis, I. *Psychological stress.* New York: Wiley, 1958.
Jaremko, M. A component analysis of stress inoculation: Review and prospectus. *Cognitive Therapy and Research,* 1979, *3,* 35–48.
Kardiner, A., & Spiegel, H. *War stress and neurotic illness.* New York: Paul B. Hoeber, 1947.
Kormos, H. The nature of combat stress. In C. R. Figley (Ed.), *Stress disorders among Vietnam veterans: Theory, research and treatment.* New York: Brunner/Mazel, 1978.
Lawler, E. E. *Motivation in work organizations.* Monterey, Calif.: Brooks-Cole, 1973.
Lazarus, R. S. *Psychological stress and the coping process.* New York: McGraw-Hill, 1966.
Meichenbaum, D. *Cognitive-behavior modification.* New York: Plenum Press, 1977.
Meichenbaum, D., Turk, D., & Burnstein, S. The nature of coping with stress. In I. Sarason & C. D. Spielberger (Eds.), *Stress and anxiety* (Vol. 2). Washington, D. C.: Hemisphere, 1975.
Merton, R. K. *Social theory and social structure.* New York: Free Press, 1968.
Mitchell, J. C. Social networks. *Annual Review of Anthropology,* 1974, *3,* 279–299.
Novaco, R. W. *Anger control: The development and evaluation of an experimental treatment.* Lexington, Mass.: D.C. Heath, 1975.
Novaco, R. W. The function and regulation of the arousal of anger. *American Journal of Psychiatry,* 1976, *133,* 1124–1128.
Novaco, R. W. The cognitive regulation of anger and stress. In P. Kendall & S. Hollon (Eds.), *Cognitive behavioral interventions.* New York: Academic Press, 1979.
Novaco, R. W., Sarason, I. G., Cook, T. M., Robinson, G. L., & Cunningham, F. J. *Psycholocigal and organizational factors related to attrition and performance in Marine Corps recruit training* (AR-001). Seattle: University of Washington, November 1979.
Porter, L. W., & Steers, R. M. Organizational, work, and personal factors in employee turnover and absenteeism. *Psychological Bulletin,* 1973, *80,* 151–176.
Rotter, J. P. *Social learning and clinical psychology.* Englewood Cliffs, N.J.: Prentice-Hall, 1954.
Sarason, I. G. Anxiety and self-recognition. In I. G. Sarason & C. D. Spielberger (Eds.), *Stress and anxiety* (Vol. 2). Washington, D. C.: Hemisphere, 1975.
Sarason, I. G. The test anxiety scale: Concept and research. In C. D. Spielberger & I. G. Sarason (Eds.), *Stress and anxiety* (Vol. 5). New York: Wiley, 1978.
Sarason, I. G., Johnson, J. M., & Siegel, J. M. Assessing the impact of life changes: Development of the Life Experiences Survey. *Journal of Counseling and Clinical Psychology,* 1978, *46,* 932–946.
Seligman, M. *Helplessness: On depression, development and death.* San Francisco: W. H. Freeman, 1975.
Shatan, C. F. Stress disorders among Vietnam veterans: The emotional content of combat continues. In C. R. Figley (Ed.), *Stress disorders among Vietnam veterans: Theory, research and treatment.* New York: Brunner/Mazel, 1978.
Stouffer, S. *The American soldier: Combat and its aftermath.* Princeton, N. J.: Princeton University Press, 1949.
Turk, D. C. Cognitive behavioral techniques in the management of pain. In J. P. Foreyt & D. P. Rathjen (Eds.), *Cognitive behavior therapy.* New York: Plenum Press, 1978.
Vroom, V. H. *Work and motivation.* New York: Wiley, 1964.
Zuckerman, M., & Lubin, B. *The Multiple Affect Adjective Checklist.* San Diego, Calif.: Educational & Industrial Testing Service, 1965.

12

Stress Inoculation Training for Social Anxiety, with Emphasis on Dating Anxiety

MATT E. JAREMKO

The last decade has seen an increasing concern with the assessment and treatment of social anxiety (Arkowitz, 1977; Curran, 1977; Rehm & Marston, 1968). A major impetus for this increasing interest has been the recognition that social anxiety represents a problem of considerable daily concern to individuals (Borkovec, Stone, O'Brien, & Kaloupek, 1974). Such problems as shyness, lack of assertion, dating anxiety, and fear of others represent the most important referral source in university counseling services (Orr & Mitchell, 1975) while at the same time representing a major concern of clinically referred populations (Kanter & Goldfried, 1979). When speaking of social anxiety, it is important to note that this construct refers to a continuum from shyness to the extreme degree of social phobia perhaps evident in the behavior of an agoraphobic. The importance of social anxiety reduction programs will no doubt increase in the future as community-oriented outreach programs attempt to meet the needs of problems in living (Barton & Sanborn, 1977). For example, a significant percentage of college campuses already offer outreach pro-

MATT E. JAREMKO • Department of Psychology, University of Mississippi, University, Mississippi 38677.

grams that attempt to deal with social anxiety (Morrill & Oettuig, 1978). This chapter will review previous work on the assessment and reduction of social anxiety with specific emphasis on dating anxiety. Attention will be paid to presenting and evaluating various treatment approaches. In particular, the chapter will focus on treatment programs that view social situations as stressful events and that utilize stress prevention and management tehniques to deal with the troublesome aspects of social interactions.

THE NATURE OF SOCIAL ANXIETY

A common clinical example of social anxiety demonstrates the nature of this problem. A young man has occasion to be around a woman he would like to ask out for a date. In this situation, he experiences a racing heartbeat, sweaty palms, and "butterflies." He interprets these physiological phenomena as "anxiety." This global interpretation makes it likely that the young man will emit highly idiosyncratic negative self-evaluations and self-references. He may say to himself, "She will not find me attractive," or "She looks too old for me." These negative self-references lead to further physiological arousal, which keeps the cycle going. The young man may face the stressor by talking to the woman and, if he possesses social skills appropriate to the initiation stage of social interaction, his social anxiety will probably decrease when he judges the interaction successful. If he faces the stressor but is awkward and unskillful, he may have a failure experience and increase his social anxiety. Finally, the man can avoid talking to the woman (by procrastinating, devaluing her attractiveness, etc.). In this case it will probably be more difficult for him the next time he has occasion to talk with a woman. His social anxiety will only continue and may even get worse.

This example illustrates that social anxiety is a complex process in which three specific categories of behavior interact to make the situation aversive and the person less likely to engage in socially competent behavior. The tripartite model, offered by Lang (1971) and Rachman (1976), proposes that the three response systems of physiology, cognition, and behavior contribute to the stressful reactions. Data exist that support the notion that socially anxious individuals can manifest unwanted responses in any or all of these three systems. For example, Borkovec, Stone, O'Brien, and Kaloupek (1974) have shown that individuals high in social anxiety show higher heart rates in social situations. Cacioppo, Glass, and Merluzzi (1979) found that socially anxious males spontaneously generate more negative self-statements prior to a social interaction. And a number of workers have demonstrated specific behavioral differences between high- and low-anxiety individuals (see below for a brief overview of these data). For example, Fischetti, Curran, and Weissberg (1977) found that socially anxious males were deficient in the timing of their social interaction responses.

It thus appears that the assessment of social anxiety requires a thorough task analysis (Schwartz & Gottman, 1976) before treatment can be offered. For some clients, behavioral skills training will be required; for others, phsyiological responses require attention; and still others will require techniques designed to modify faulty cognitive processes and structures. In other words, a broad-based treatment program is required to deal effectively with all the aspects that can operate in social anxiety problems. This chapter will suggest that stress inoculation training provides such a comprehensive treatment program.

A model of social anxiety also needs to account for how the three response systems interact. Cognitive-behavioral writers have suggested a model of social competence in which the three component systems interact in a self-perpetuating cycle (Jaremko, 1979; Meichenbaum, Butler, & Joseph, 1982). When interacting in a social situation, the anxious person not only experiences physiological arousal but also brings certain "cognitive structures" (Meichenbaum *et al.,* 1982) to the interaction. These cognitive structures operate automatically and provide the "scripts" for social interaction. The cognitive structures include the individual's meaning system or "current concerns" about the situation (Meichenbaum *et al.*, 1982), negative perceptual processes (Mahoney, 1974), and simple and/or higher-order rules that define the social situation as possibly leading to negative outcomes (Rathjen, Rathjen, & Hiniker, 1978). In a discussion of social competence, Meichenbaum *et al.* (1982) illustrate the role of cognitive structures by describing the meaning individuals might attach to social contacts at a party. For some, the party represents a pleasant social event; for others, it is a chance to impress people; while for some it is a "trial" in which all are being judged. The nature of one's cognitive structures influences how one appraises social situations, what one says to him- or herself, and how one behaves. Any treatment program for social anxiety requires attention to these thematic, global cognitive phenomena (Lazarus, Kanner, & Folkman, 1980).

Jaremko (1979) proposed a model of stress responding that bears on the foregoing discussion. In his model, Jaremko suggested that physiological responses (emotions) trigger cognitive appraisals (cognitive structures) that in turn trigger a variety of negative self-statements and images. These self-statements and images perpetuate and augment the physiological activity that, in turn, maintains the global cognitive activity.

A cycle of unpleasant physiological arousal, global cognitive appraisal, and specific negative self-communications sets up a strong potential for avoidance behavior. The individual's behavioral responses will help determine the course of the cycle.

If this description of social anxiety is valid, it suggests that the cycle can be broken at several points. For example, the person can face the stressful social interaction and produce appropriate social skills, thus reducing the associated fear responses (Greist, Marks, Berlin, Gournay, & Noshirvani, 1980). Such a successful experience contributes to what Bandura (1977) has called "self-efficacy expectations" or enhanced self-confidence about producing the desired behavior. Such success reduces the likelihood of the cycle operating, thus making it easier to face similar social stressors in the future.

The importance of breaking the cycle is highlighted by the role of avoidance behavior in social situations. When an individual escapes or avoids a social situation, the detection of anxiety cues is made more likely because it is associated with anxiety reduction (Jaremko, 1980a). In similar situations in the future, the person is more likely to perceive the unpleasant cues of the stress cycle. In other words, it will take less threat to set off the cycle. Such avoidance behaviors are probably greatly responsible for the development of the anxiety problem (Jaremko, 1980b). In treating social anxiety it is important to insure that escape or avoidance is precluded so that fear responses can extinguish and self-efficacy expectations can develop.

As previously stated, a major implication of this tripartite model is the need to develop treatment programs that are comprehensive enough to focus on the interdependent cycle described above. Specifically, clients must first become aware of the cycle and second they must learn skills that can interrupt and/or stop the cycle as well as skills that insure successful interaction. Comprehensive programs will thus need to include the training of physical, cognitive, and behavioral skills to combat social anxiety. The remainder of this chapter will consider the assessment and treatment of social anxiety with these implications in mind.

THE INCIDENCE OF SOCIAL ANXIETY: THE DATING ANXIETY EXAMPLE

Data bearing on the incidence of dating anxiety in college populations can illustrate that social anxiety is a problem experienced by a large number of people. Orr and Mitchell (1975) surveyed 988 college students and found that 34% report high levels of anxiety in opposite-sex situations, 34% report avoidance behavior of opposite-sex situations, and 38% perceive themselves as lacking in social competence. Data from a survey at the University of Richmond, in which 845 subjects responded, are equally revealing. The following are the percentages of students who reported problems in each area: Faulty relationships—11%, feeling ill at ease with others—8%, shyness—16%, feeling left out—19%, submissiveness—15%, sexual attractiveness—7%, dating—19%, loneliness—19%, and feeling distant from others—35%. It thus appears that social situations present a problem to a great many people.

Klaus, Hersen, and Bellack (1977) report data that are of interest to the question of the incidence of social interaction problems. These researchers report that the mean number of dates per month in college students is 5.58. It was found that finding dating partners and initiating sexual activity while on dates were the two aspects of the situation associated with the greatest difficulty. Freshmen reported more difficulty in these areas than did upperclass students. Females reported more difficulty than did males in finding dates, feeling at ease on dates, making conversation, ending the date, and obtaining a second date with the same partner. Males had more problems in initiating contact on the telephone. Klaus *et al.* (1977) also found that some aspects of dating seem to covary, for example, obtaining a second date covaries with making conversation and feeling at ease. While the foregoing data are of interest, it is noteworthy that they are obtained with college students. No acceptable norms on social problems exist for noncollege adults, but Kanter and Goldfried (1979) suggest that heterosocial problems in community populations may be more severe than those found in college populations. If that is the case, we may expect the college population data to be a minimum from which one can work upward in estimating the incidence of the problem of social anxiety.

THE ASSESSMENT OF SOCIAL ANXIETY

In assessing social anxiety, it is important to use the tripartite model as a guide for such assessment. The major thrust of assessment in social anxiety should be a thorough task analysis of the behaviors involved in or required for successful or unsuccessful social interaction. According to the tripartite model, assessment should include the three areas of physiology, cognitive activity, and overt behavior. This section will present data from each of the three areas, suggest possible additional techniques for assessment, and discuss problems in each assessment area.

Physiological Assessment

While some writers have found psychophysiological differences between individuals high and low in social anxiety, overall there have been relatively few studies addressing the issue. As mentioned previously, Borkovec, Stone, O'Brien, and Kaloupek (1974) found that high socially anxious males showed higher heart rates than did nonanxious males when interacting in a social situation. Twentyman and McFall (1975) found that pulse rates of shy males were higher than those of confident males when engaging in a series of standard social situations. In both these studies, all subjects manifested physiological increases prior to and during social interaction, but the socially anxious individuals manifested even higher rates of arousal than did the nonanxious people.

A few studies evaluating treatment programs have used physiological measures as indices of improvement. Geary and Goldman (1978) found that subjects treated with behavioral rehearsal and systematic desensitization had lower pulse rates and respiration rates during social interaction than did untreated subjects. Keane and Lisman (1978) found that heart rate increased and skin resistance decreased for both treated and untreated groups during presentation of socially relevant slides. Finally, Kanter and Goldfried (1979) found that clients treated with either cognitive restructuring or self-control desensitization showed less heart-rate increase in response to a social interaction after treatment than before treatment.

These data suggest that there are physiological differences between individuals who differ in social anxiety. In assessing problems of this nature, it is worthwhile to determine the exact physiological pattern of the client prior to treatment. Data exist to suggest that different clients tend to respond in different physiological systems, with varying response specificity (Lacey, 1967), and with different reactions to different situations or situational stereotypy (Lacey & Lacey, 1970). These issues need to be taken into account when conducting a task analysis of the socially anxious client (Kallman & Feuerstein, 1977). For example, in treating a socially anxious male, it would be helpful to know that the client responds to interactions with females by a racing heart rate but responds to assertion conflicts with greatly reduced respiration. The treatment of these two specific instances of social anxiety might proceed differently based on this information. Physiological responses may be an integral part of social anxiety problems in some clients (Borkovec, Wall, & Stone, 1974), and their proper assessment and treatment can aid amelioration of difficulties in this area.

In fact, physiological assessment would be maximally effective if it proceeded along the lines of a *cognitive-functional* approach (Meichenbaum, 1977) in which the functional relationship among cognitive activity, physiological responding, and behavioral responses were mapped out. Information derived from this approach readily suggests treatment programs and renders assessment and treatment essentially one process. There is an emerging set of data relevant to the relationship of cognitive activity and physiological responding (e.g., Bauer & Craighead, 1979; May, 1977). A consideration of these interrelationships would greatly aid the development of treatment programs.

Cognitive Assessment

There are an increasing number of studies that demonstrate the role of specific cognitions in social anxiety. Cacioppo *et al.* (1979) used a thought-listing procedure to tap the cognitive activity of high and low-anxious subjects while waiting for a social interaction. These researchers found that high-anxious subjects spontaneously generate more negative self-statements that did low-anxious subjects. Schwartz and Gottman (1976) found that low-assertive individuals engaged in equal amounts of negative self-statements and positive self-statements, whereas high-assertive subjects say many more positive self-statements than negative ones. Schwartz and Gottman characterized these data as indicating that the low-assertive subjects experienced an internal dialogue of conflict in which positive and negative self-statements competed against one another and interfered with interpersonal behavior. One can easily conjure up visions of a socially anxious individual debating the relative merits of approaching an opposite-sex stranger, thinking of possible approaches and then negating each in turn. Such cognitive activity readily interferes with social competence and is likely to render a social interaction unsuccessful.

Related to the above, Fiedler and Beach (1978) found that the individual's expectancies about the consequences of being assertive were the best predictor of behavior in a social situation. Interestingly Rehm (1977) reviewed data showing that depressed and nondepressed individuals also differ in self-evaluation and self-reinforcement processes. Social anxiety may be characterized by similar deficits in cognitive activity.

Not only do data support the existence of cognitive differences between high- and low-anxious individuals, through the contrasted groups approach, but also, experiments in which negative self-statements are manipulated show the relationship of cognitive activity to emotional arousal. For example, Goldfried and Sobocinski (1975) demonstrated that having subjects imagine negative self-statements regarding social rejection increased their feelings of anxiety and anger. Sutton-Simon and Goldfried (1979) found that generalized social anxiety was closely related to irrational thinking, but a specific anxiety condition of acrophobia was closely related to both irrational thoughts and negative self-statements. These data and those presented earlier highlight the important role that negative ideation plays in social anxiety. Assessing this cognitive activity will help support specific approaches to treating social anxiety.

A number of different assessment approaches have been used to measure cognitive activity. Meichenbaum (1977) has described several of these. They include interviewing, imagery procedures, behavioral assessments, postperformance videotape reconstruction, TAT-like tests, homework assignments, and *in vivo* group assessments. Each of these sources can be used to conduct a functional analysis of the client's self-statements, behaviors, and physiological responses. These relationships can be used in developing tailor-made treatments for a particular client's situation. Kendall and Korgeski (1979) and Meichenbaum and Butler (1980) suggest other techniques for cognitive assessment, which incude postperformance questionnaires, thought listing, think-aloud procedures, thought sampling, and spontaneous production of private speech. Cognitive assessment is a very active and potentially useful focus for future research. As more sophisticated assessment procedures become available, more complicated aspects of the cognitive component of social anxiety will become evident.

Overt Behavior

Perhaps the greatest amount of research in social anxiety has been devoted to assessing the respective skills of individuals high and low in social anxiety. In the area of heterosocial anxiety, the results of this research are equivocal. Several extensive reviews of these data have been offered (Curran, 1977; Hersen & Bellack, 1977; Arkowitz, 1977). The following behavioral aspects have been found to differ in high and low socially anxious individuals: talk time, (Arkowitz, Lichenstein, McGovern, & Hines, 1975), talk latencies (Pilkonis, 1977), number of silences (Borkovec, Stove, O'Brien, & Kaloupek, 1974), and amount of attention to the other person (Kupke, Calhoun, & Hobbs, 1979). Curran, Little, and Gilbert (1978) found that socially anxious males were less likely to respond to the approach cues of women than were nonanxious subjects. However, many of these findings have not been replicated and several methodological problems exist in the research in this area (Farrell, Mariotto, Conger, Curran, & Wallander, 1979).

Apparently, aspects other than overt social skill play a role in successful social interactions. Curran (1977) suggested that the timing of the skills is more important than their presence or absence. Fischetti *et al.* (1977) echo these findings. Further, Jaremko, Myers, and Daner (1980) found that the dating frequency of the partner with whom one interacted either facilitated or debilitated social performance by affecting the appropriateness of one's voice and emotional characteristics. The physical attractiveness of the people involved also seems to account for a good deal of the performance variance (Greenwald, 1977; Mitchell & Orr, 1976). Additionally, Keane and Lisman (1978) found that alcohol debilitated social interaction, while Lipton and Nelson (1980) found that the developmental stage of the social relationship was an important factor. It thus appears that the skills of social interaction are very complex, and the reliable demonstration of specific skills-differences has not yet been demonstrated. Given the equivocal nature of the findings, one should be cautious in prescribing treatment and preventative programs. This caveat applies to treatment programs of stress inoculation training as well. Perhaps Curran's (1977) advice that a wide and diverse range of skills should be taught is to be heeded. With appropriate mindfulness of the problems in this area, general guidelines for intervention can be drawn.

TREATMENT OF SOCIAL ANXIETY

Thus far, social anxiety has been shown to involve some forms of deficits and/or excesses in three areas: physiology, cognition, and overt behavior. Even though the knowledge base in each of these areas is limited, this has not restricted attempts to intervene. There have been a large number of treatment studies for social anxiety. These studies will be reviewed briefly along the lines of the tripartite model of social anxiety proposed earlier. It will be shown that previous treatments have focused on only one or two of the three classes of response involved in social anxiety. A call will be made for programs that cover all three aspects of social anxiety and their interrelationships. The stress inoculation approach will be considered as an attempt to do this.

Emotional Approaches

Systematic desensitization has been the treatment of choice that theoretically focuses on the physiological component of social anxiety. A number of studies have shown that desensitization can decrease social anxiety. For example, Orr, Mitchell, and Hall (1975) treated 31 socially anxious males using traditional desensitization (6 sessions), short-term desensitization (4 sessions), and no treatment. Results showed that the desensitization groups were more improved on self-report anxiety, social competence, and avoidance behavior than were the relaxation procedure and the no-treatment group. Short-term desensitization was somewhat more effective than the extensive desensitization. Curran and Gilbert (1975) compared desensitization to a skills-training approach. The desensitization group improved on self-report measures but *not* on behavioral measures, whereas the skills training group improved on both. Curran (1975) also found that desensitization did not influence the behavioral component of social anxiety as much as it influenced the self-report measures. A similar result was found by Geary and Goldman (1978). It is important to note, therefore, that systematic desensitization is effective more in reducing self-reported social anxiety than the behavioral component. Desensitization would thus appear to be a restricted and limited treatment procedure for social anxiety. Treatments for social anxiety need to include procedures designed to deal with all three components of the problem.

Behavioral Skills Training

A large number of studies have shown that the training of overt behavioral skills will decrease anxiety and enhance social skills (Curran, 1977). While there are methodological difficulties in this research, the data generally support the conclusion that skills-training can help socially anxious individuals *on a short-term basis.* Data are either equivocal or, in some cases, not available concerning the long-term effectiveness of this approach in treating social anxiety. Behavioral skills-training has included a wide ranging set of procedures. Twentyman and McFall (1975) successfully used behavioral rehearsal feedback, coaching, and modeling in training the skills of telephone talking and face-to-face conversation with an opposite-sex stranger. Curran, Gilbert, and Little (1976) used general discussion, videotaped presentation of inappropriately and appropriately modeled skills, role-playing, and homework to train giving and receiving compliments, nonverbal communication methods, feeling (emotion-related) talk, handling silences, planning dates, physical intimacy, and enhancing physical appearance. Melnick (1973) found that videotape self-observation enhanced the use of skills-training similar to the training used by Curran *et al.* (1976). MacDonald, Lindquist, Kramer, McGrath, and Rhyne (1975) showed the effectiveness of training skills such as smiling, initiating conversation, communicating interest in another, judging receptivity, planning dates, and initiating physical contact. It has also been shown that practice or arranged dating is effective in reducing social anxiety (Christensen & Arkowitz, 1974).

While all of these studies show that behavioral training is effective, there are methodological problems that cloud interpretation (Curran,

1977). Curran (1977) offered five areas of deficiency that need improvement in these studies: subject selection (making sure subjects are seriously troubled by social anxiety), assessment (using valid, reliable, and multiple assessment), transfer measures (establishing the generalizability of the treatments), follow-up, and attention to treatment–subject interactions. Additionally, some recent studies have shown that behavioral skills-training results in improvement only on behavioral measures (Elder, Edelstein, Fremouw, Lively, Walker, & Womeldorf, 1978; Jaremko, Myers, & Jaremko, 1979) and not in the other components of social anxiety. It is therefore difficult to conclude that behavioral skills-training is the most adequate treatment for social anxiety. As with approaches focusing only on emotional components, skills-training by itself may not be enough. More attention to other components is needed.

Cognitive Behavior Modification Approaches

Recently, a number of studies have evaluated the use of cognitive behavior modification procedures in the control of social anxiety. These approaches have had two purposes: (1) to treat the cognitive component of social anxiety directly and (2) to extend the generalization of treatment effects to nontreatment settings (Meichenbaum, 1977). These goals have been met with varying amounts of success. Glass, Gottman, and Shmurak (1976) compared a cognitive restructuring group, a behavior skills-training approach, and the combination of the two. Meichenbaum (1977) described the study by noting that the authors

> compared the relative effectiveness of coaching and rehearsal versus cognitive self-statement modification in enhancing dating skills in girl-shy college males. They found that the cognitive self-statement intervention caused the greatest transfer effects to untrained, laboratory, role-playing situations and to ratings made by females whom the subjects called for dates.
>
> The subjects in the studies were trained to become aware of the negative self-statements that they emitted, for such recognition was the signal to produce incompatible self-statements and behaviors. The training included a coach who presented the situation and then acted as a cognitive-coping model, verbalizing what he would say to himself as if he were actually in the situation. This self-talk began negatively, continued with the model's realizing that he was being negative, and then switched to positive self-talk. Finally, the coach modeled giving himself verbalized reinforcement for changing his self-talk from negative to positive.
>
> Following is an example of the training. . . .
>
> 1. *Situation.* Let's suppose you've been fixed up on a blind date. You've taken her to a movie and then for some coffee afterwards. Now she begins to talk about a political candidate, some man you've never heard of; she says, "What do you think of him?" You say to yourself:

2. *Self-talk.* An example of self-talk might be: "She's got me now. I'd better bullshit her or she'll put me down. I hate politics anyway so this chick is obviously not my type. . . . Boy, that's really jumping to conclusions. This is only one area and it really doesn't show what type of person she is. Anyway, what's the point of making up stuff about somebody I have never heard of? She'll see right through me if I lie. It's not such a big deal to admit I don't know something. There are probably lots of things I know that she doesn't."
3. *Self-talk reinforcement.* "Yeah, that's a better way to think about it. She's just human, trying to discuss something intelligently. I don't have to get scared or put off by her." (1977, pp. 131–132)

Thus, cognitive behavior modification appeared to be a promising approach to an area of treatment that requires more comprehensiveness. However, Curran (1977) questioned the utility of the Glass, *et al.* (1976) study since subjects were not selected by a rigorous screening process. Other authors have, therefore, attempted comparisons similar to those of Glass *et al.* (1976). Kanter and Goldfried (1979) compared cognitive restructuring, self-control desensitization, their combination, and a waiting-list control in reducing interpersonal anxiety. Clients were 18 males and 50 females from a university community (though not college students *per se*). Most of the subjects were homemakers with an average age of 35.6. These subjects were similar to the kinds of people who would be seen in private practice or a mental health setting.

Assessment included behavioral, self-report, and physiological measures. A five-minute interaction with two confederates (one male and one female) was videotaped and rated on a 15-item anxiety checklist. The self-report measues included the State-Trait Anxiety Inventory (Spielberger, Gorsuch, & Lushene, 1970), the Social Avoidance and Distress Scale and the Fear of Negative Evaluation Scale (Watson & Friend, 1969), S-R inventories of anxiousness with four generalization situations (Endler, Hunt, & Rosenstein, 1962), and the Jones (1968) irrational beliefs test. The physiological measure was 30-second pulse counts taken prior to telling a subject about the interaction, immediately before the interaction, and after it. All of these measures were taken before the interaction, after it, and at a nine-week follow-up.

Treatment involved seven weekly group sessions each lasting one and one-half hours. A standard hierarchy of 12 anxiety-arousing social situations constituted the content of the treatments. Self-control desensitization clients were given a rationale for the use of desensitization as a coping skill (Goldfried, 1971). Clients were taught progressive relaxation and given imagery practice. Sessions involved the basic desensitization format with the instruction to use any anxiety that was experienced as a signal to relax away tensions. Clients also were asked to record relaxation experiences and tension levels before and after visualizing each scene. After the presentation of the third scene, a group discussion of the client's experiences in imagining the scenes took place. Homework was also included and involved practice relaxation in social and nonsocial situations.

Cognitive restructuring involved helping the clients recognize their unrealistic and self-defeating thoughts and images and replacing them with coping strategies (Goldfried, Decenteceo, & Weinberg, 1974). In order to achieve this, imagery training was used. The clients were asked to visualize the hierarchy of social scenes and instructed to note any feeling of anxiety and the accompanying anxiety-engendering thoughts (e.g., "I'm going to say something foolish to these people, and they're going to think I'm really dumb"). The clients were taught to challenge these thoughts, and to substitute coping, anxiety-reducing thoughts (e.g., "Chances are I won't say anything foolish. Even if I do, it really doesn't mean I'm a dumb person"). Since the treatment was conducted on a group basis, group discussion about the ways to challenge anxiety-provoking thought was interlaced in the imagery training. Homework assignments involved recognizing and implementing the coping strategies. In subsequent sessions, the outcomes of these homework assignments were discussed.

The treatment group who received the combined training engaged in the same procedural process as the other treatment groups but they used anxiety as a signal to relax as well as to identify anxiety-engendering thoughts and to replace them with coping strategies.

The results indicated that the three treated groups showed more improvement than did the waiting-list control. The cognitive restructuring group produced many more within-group differences than did desensitization or the combination group, but these were limited to self-report measures. Thus, cognitive restructuring represents one potential procedure for use in treating social anxiety.

Another study demonstrating the relative effectiveness of a cognitive restructuring approach was reported by Linehan, Goldfried, and Goldfried (1980), in which unassertive women were treated. Cognitive restructuring, behavioral rehearsal, and a combination of the two were compared. Cognitive restructuring focused on the role of emotional responses and beliefs in assertion as well as on anxiety-reducing thoughts (e.g., "The fact that someone said 'No' does not mean that I shouldn't have asked in the first place."). Cognitive coping strategies were modeled by the therapist and rehearsed imaginally and behaviorally by the subject. Subjects received feedback on their performance. The results showed that the combination treatment was the most effective. The two separate programs of cognitive restructuring and behavioral rehearsal were not different from each other but they were more effective than a relationship control group and an assessment control. Meichenbaum, Gilmore, and Fedoravicius (1971) have also shown a similar combination treatment to be most effective. Several stress management programs have also used a combination procedure to treat social anxiety.

Stress Management for Social Anxiety

Two such illustrative studies will be considered in this section. Frisch, Elliott, Atsaides, Salva, and Denney (1979) compared social skills training with and without stress management in the enhancement of Veteran Administration patients' interpersonal competencies. The patients, 34 males in a day hospital, were more severely disturbed than the subjects used in many of the studies already considered, thus posing a difficult test for the treatments being studied. The patients' social competence was assessed by means of a taped rehearsal test of their responses to problematic social situations (both treated and generalization situations). The subjects' responses to these taped social situations were rated by graduate students using a behavioral skills checklist. Subjects' scores were the sum of skills present on either or both of the treated items and generalization items. A simulated interaction was also used in which the patient engaged in a 10-minute interaction with a confederate. The confederate was instructed to "test" the patient by asking him to tell more about himself, criticizing some aspect of the patient's appearance, requesting a monetary loan, and making excuses for missing an arranged date between the two. The interaction was taped and rated for social skills. Additionally, the confederate rated the patient's skill and comfort.

Self-report measures included the Social Avoidance Distress Scale, (Watson & Friend, 1969), an assertion inventory (Gambrill & Richey, 1975), and an assessment of one's feelings of inadequacy (Hovland & Janis, 1959).

The treatment program for the skills training involved 22 relevant and anxiety-provoking social situations encompassing five response classes: (1) initiating and maintaining conversation, (2) making and refusing requests, (3) giving and receiving criticism, (4) giving and receiving compliments, and (5) interpreting nonverbal cues in others' behavior. Specific skills were listed in each of these classes and were the focus of training. Additionally, the training was assisted by nine color videotapes that exemplified inappropriate and appropriate ways of dealing with social situations.

The process of training involved presentation of a rationale followed by role induction practice in the behavioral rehearsal procedures that would be used later in the treatment (Garfield, 1971). Six procedural steps constituted the bulk of the skills training. (1) Patients viewed the videotape focusing on the demonstrated skill; (2) a social situation relevant to the skill was chosen for practice; (3) patients were instructed to visualize the social situation, experience any anxiety associated with it if they were involved in it, and imagine using the specific skill under consideration in a successful coping manner; (4) each patient then continued to role-play the scene with the therapist until a satisfactory performacne was obtained; (5) the patient received feedback from the other patients and therapist; and finally (6) homework assignments related to the social skills practiced were given. In subsequent sessions, the outcome of the homework assignments were discussed.

The combined skills and stress management group received a similar treatment regimen with the addition of relaxation as self-control skill, cognitive restructuring, and an expanded treatment rationale—the rationale included the potential use of relaxation as a skill and a cognitive–behavioral view of stress. This was followed by the role-induction procedures, which included relaxation training and discussion of the role of maladaptive beliefs and thoughts on behavior. The training sequence then included the following components: (1) viewing a tape segment; (2) choosing a scene; (3) role-playing the scene; (4) giving corrective feedback; (5) evaluating the role that one's thoughts and feelings play in contributing to stress; (6) imagining the situation, experiencing anxiety, relaxing and verbalizing coping strategies, and then imagining dealing with the situation (covert rehearsal with relaxation and cognitive restructuring and rehearsal); (7) integrating skills during a second role-play; and (8) doing homework assignments. Table I is a flow chart comparing the treatments.

The results reveal that the two treated groups showed significant improvement at posttest and follow-up on all behavioral measures. No behavioral and self-report differences were obtained between the skills group and combined group. Results on the taped rehearsal test showed that subjects diagnosed as psychotic did better in the skills group, whereas those diagnosed as neurotic did better in the combined group. However, the limited sample size when this subsample analysis was conducted limits interpretation of these interactive effects.

In attempting to explain why no difference was obtained between the two treatment groups, the authors offered three hypotheses. First, the social skills group may have had a stress-control component already in it.

Table I. Treatment Component Sequence For Groups in Frisch et al. (1979)

Skills training	Combined group
Skills rationale	Skills, relaxation, cognitive restructuring rationale
Role induction: Behavior rehearsal	Role induction: Behavior rehearsal and cognitive restructuring, relaxation training
View videotape scene	View videotape scene
Choose social situation	Scene chosen by therapist
Covert rehearsal	Overt rehearsal
Overt rehearsal	Feedback
Feedback	Evaluate impact of cognitions and feelings on behavior
Homework	Covert rehearsal with relaxation and cognitive restructuring
Feedback and discussion of homework	"Integrative" overt rehearsal
	Homework
	Feedback and discussion of homework

This is probably true because the covert rehearsal aspect of treatment contained procedures very similar to other cognitively oriented anxiety reduction techniques (Kazdin, 1974, 1975; Meichenbaum, 1972). Second, the combined treatment may have been too unwieldly and complex; some subjects in this group complained of that. Inspection of Table I shows clearly that the two groups differ in terms of amount of treatment content. Third, the patients studied in the Frisch *et al.* (1979) study likely have more skill deficits than do other subjects (e.g., college students). In fact, the differential responsiveness of psychotics and neurotics to treatment may indeed reflect this difference. Frisch *et al.* suggest that subject variables be taken into account when conducting skills-training, and that we individually tailor treatments. If one is working with a skills-deficient population, skills-training is likely to be the most effective treatment. But if one is working with an anxiety-prone but relatively skillful population, stress-control procedures may be the most effective treatment. The approach of combining skills-training and stress management is worthy of additional attention, and Frisch, Atsaides, and Elliott (1977) present a detailed treatment manual for that purpose. The Frisch *et al.* study was reported in some detail for two reasons: It is one of the first studies to use a clinical population, and the treatment regimen is consistent with a cognitive-behavior modification stress inoculation framework.

Another study in which stress management was evaluated was Jaremko *et al.* (1979). These authors compared stress inoculation training to a behavioral skills-training program patterned after MacDonald *et al.* (1975). Clients were self-referred from a university community and represented a population that was more severely debilitated by social anxiety than are subjects normally chosen for social anxiety or who have volunteered for analog studies. A total of 48 clients were treated in four waves of outreach workshops conducted in four different school terms.

The design was a groups (stress inoculation training and skills training) by subjects (high and low frequency of dating groups) by trials (pretreatment, post-treatment, and two-month follow-up) factorial design. Assessment measures included a variety of self-report inventories and a social interaction diary. Self-report inventories consisted of the Social Avoidance and Distress scale, and Fear of Negative Evaluation Scale (Watson & Friend, 1969), a measure of self-efficacy in dating situations (Bandura, 1977), a modified S-R inventory using 10 common social situations (Mitchell & Orr, 1976), and a dating and assertion questionnaire (Levenson & Gottman, 1978). The behavioral diary was of the same form as that used by Wheeler and Nezlek (1977) in establishing an epidemiology of college student social interactions. The self-referred clients were required to record every social interaction of over five minutes, indicating the nature of the relationship, the length of the interaction, an intimacy rating of the interaction, the pleasantness of the interaction, and the nature of the interaction (a date, business, party, etc.).

Treatment took place in four two-hour sessions in groups of 4–10. The behavioral skills-training involved a rationale for behavioral rehearsal and practiced role-playing using nonheterosocial situations. Within this context, various skills were then presented, discussed, role-played, critiqued, and role-played once again. The skills that were trained included grooming skills, detecting positive approach cues, functional opening lines, smiling, giving compliments, what to do on a date, development of prospective dates, and initiating a conversation. At the end of session two, three, and four, each client practiced the skills by interacting with an opposite-sex stranger for five to ten minutes. These three interactions allowed the clients to practice the skills in a lifelike situation and to experience a prolonged-exposure type of treatment for social anxiety (Emmelkamp, Kuipers, & Eggeraat, 1978). Since the stranger was different for each session, the client received a fairly strong dose of "practice dating." This exposure is comparable to the application phase of stress inoculation training.

The stress inoculation training included the following: initially, a conceptual model of dating behavior was offered to the clients. It included four stages of relationship development, namely initiation, development, maintenance, and termination (Lipton & Nelson, 1980). The clients were told that the workshop would focus on the initiation process, especially overcoming the anxiety associated with interacting with strangers. This aspect of social interaction received most attention since it was deemed that clients frequently escaped or avoided potential social interactions, thereby making their reactions to social stress worse. The discussion of dating stress was conducted in the context of a self-perpetuating model of stress (see Figure 1) (Jaremko, 1979).

Figure 1 is a diagram that was used to illustrate the model of stress for the clients in the stress inoculation group. Talking to an opposite-sex person may be quite a stressful event that in turn leads to a readily predictable cycle of internal and external behavior. If the cycle continues unabated, it is likely that the person will further avoid interacting with people, which serves to make it more difficult to interact in future situations. Thus, the goal of treatment is to make subjects aware of this cycle, especially at the incipient stages where prodromal cues are evident, and then interrupt and break the cycle with the consequence of encouraging social interaction. In short, the cycle involved a repeating process in which the stressor may set off uncomfortable physiological activity that contributes to the appraisal process of the situation as potentially harmful. This negative

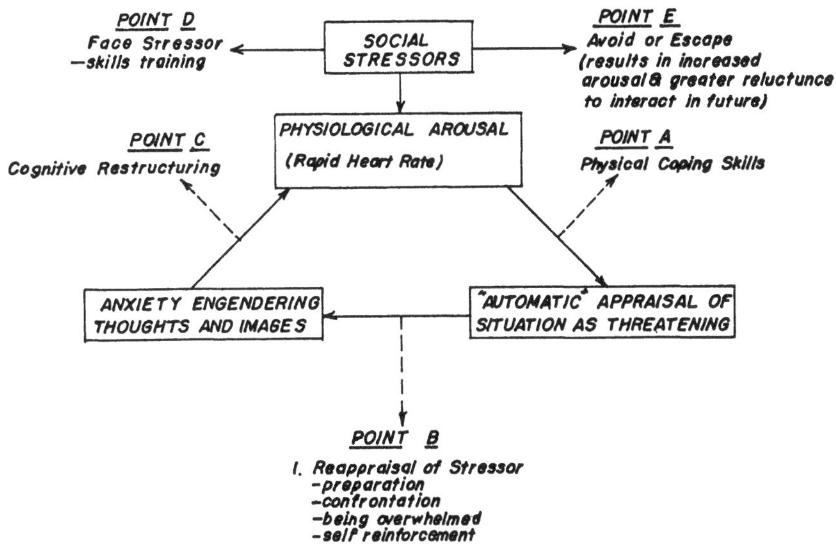

Figure 1. Educational model for stress inoculation of social anxiety.

appraisal engenders a series of negative self-statements and images that in turn cause the physiological processes to increase, triggering the cycle once again. Thus, social anxiety is viewed as a consequence of several ongoing streams of behavior, thoughts, feelings, and physiological responses that intimately and interdependently "feed" on one another in a manner that engenders anxiety and avoidance.

The discussion then focused on how, by means of stress inoculation, clients could break the cycle. Three sets of skills were used at Points A, B, and C (see Figure 1) to combat and control the negative cycle and make it more likely that the client would be able to cope. Clients were given a copy of Figure 1 for their own use in remembering the dynamics of social stress.

Given that social anxiety is so complex and that clients differ in exactly what they need, the training package was offered in such a manner that the client could choose "cafeteria-style" from a number of procedures. For use at Point A, the physical skills of reducing idiosyncratic physical tension (e.g., chewing gum for dry mouth, toweling sweaty palms, warming up cold hands, tightening and loosening specific muscle groups, etc.), breathing slowly and deeply, reducing general muscle tension, and "mental" relaxation (e.g., autogenic training; Jencks, 1973) were introduced and practiced. At Point B, the clients were taught how to reappraise the stressor as a four-stage process of preparing the self, confronting the problems, handling intense moments, and reflecting on how things went (Meichenbaum & Turk, 1976). In collaboration with the therapist, the group generated a sequence of coping self-communications that were rehearsed and eventually practiced *in vivo* in order to overcome the automatic nature of their negative appraisal. Systematic cognitive restructuring, similar to that used by Kanter and Goldfried (1979), was used at Point C to replace negative self-statements and images. Clients individually identified the negative self-statements they emit in social situations. They then generated positive coping statements, and imagined three times per session a sequence of social situations, negative self-statements, coping replacement statements, and appropriate social behavior.

These skills were discussed and practiced a number of times during the four sessions. A treatment manual is available that describes the exact sequencing and amount of time spent on these skills-training procedures. At the ends of the last three sessions, each client practiced the coping skills in the application phase of stress inoculation. Prior to interacting with an opposite-sex stranger, the client went through an imagery "coping-sequence" (Jaremko, Hadfield, & Walker, 1980) in which the various coping skills were organized. The coping imagery sequence involved each client planning and implementing a step-by-step skills sequence while confronting the social stressor. At first, the coping imagery sequence was initiated and controlled by the therapist's instructions. At subsequent sessions, the therapist did less prompting until, at the last session, the client went through the entire coping imagery sequence on his or her own. This fading process was facilitated by the fact that all clients observed each other engaging in the coping sequence and provided constructive feedback. By the time all clients had gone through the practice interaction three times, the coping sequence was a well-learned response chain.

In the four sessions, therefore, the client received a comprehensive model of heterosocial stress and the attendant rationale for how coping can be achieved, repeated exposure to and practice with three sets of anxiety-reduction skills (namely, relaxation, cognitive reappraisal, and cognitive restructuring), and imaginal and *in vivo* practice applying the skills to real interactions with three opposite-sex strangers. Table II diagrams the aspects of this stress inoculation treatment as well as the behavioral skills-training treatment to which it was compared.

The results showed that both the behavioral skills group and the stress inoculation training group improved on all self-report measures except the assertion questionnaire (Levinson & Gottman, 1978). The stress inoculation training group showed greater improvement on the fear of negative evaluation scale, S-R inventory, and state-anxiety inventory. The behavioral skills group showed more improvement on the self-efficacy measure. The behavioral diary results showed that the behavioral skills group had a greater number of interaction than did the stress inoculation

Table II. Treatment Component Sequence for Both Groups in Jaremko et al. (1979)

Skills training	Stress inoculation
Behavioral rehearsal rationale ↓	Dating stress rationale Dating process Stress cycle Negative reinforcement of avoidance Break cycle at three points ↓
Role-playing practice ↓	Presentation and practice of physical skills ↓
Present skill ↓	Presentation and practice of reappraisal skills ↓
Discuss skill ↓	Cognitive restructuring ↓
Role-play skill ↓	Imaginal and behavioral practice of integrated application of skills using a "coping sequence" ↓
Critique role-play ↓	Three practice interactions ↓
Three practice interactions ↓	Discussion and feedback of practice interactions
Discussion and feedback of practice interactions	

group. The stress inoculation group, however, showed higher ratings of intimacy and pleasantness in opposite-sex interactions.

Taken together, the self-report and behavioral data show that behavioral skills-training resulted in improvement on behavioral measures (number and length of interactions, self-efficacy to perform dating behaviors) whereas the stress inoculation training resulted in improvement in measures of anxiety, social evaluation, and interaction valence. In other words, the result of the Jaremko *et al.* (1979) study reveal that skills-training improves aspects of the behavioral component of heterosocial anxiety, and that stress management improves aspects of the cognitive and emotional component. Once again it is apparent that what is needed is a broad-based treatment that attempts to treat directly all three components of social anxiety. The only study that has attempted to combine physiological, cognitive, and behavioral techniques has been Frisch *et al.* (1979), but their results regarding the superiority of a comprehensive treatment approach were only suggestive. The results of Linehan *et al.* (1979) and Meichenbaum *et al.* (1971), indicating that a combined cognitive approach is superior to either approach in isolation, also suggests the value of a combined comprehensive approach. What might such a comprehensive approach include? The remainder of this chapter will briefly review the variety of successful techniques that may be used for each of the three components of social anxiety, physiological, cognitive-affective, and behavioral. Suggestions will be provided for how these procedures could be combined within a model of stress inoculation training.

THE COMPREHENSIVE TREATMENT OF SOCIAL ANXIETY

The studies considered so far in this chapter have suggested some important implications for treating social anxiety. In addition, there have been a number of specific techniques used successfully in treating this problem. A listing of these implications and treatment techniques can set the stage for suggesting a possible comprehensive treatment program.

One implication is that any treatment approach should be preceded by a thorough behavioral and task analysis in which the idiosyncratic aspects of each client's social anxiety are identified. This information can be collected through the assessemnt procedures considered earlier in the chapter. This information provides the basis for individually tailoring treatment programs. In this way, one can focus on the various response elements (physiological, cognitive, behavioral) that make up social anxiety. Providing clients with a plausible and comprehensive understanding of their own stress reactions will lay the groundwork for such interventions. Such an understanding by the client provides the basis for the training of a wide variety of skills and coping techniques. Jaremko, Hadfield, and Walker (1980) provide evidence that treatments are more effective when they possess such a rationale or conceptualization phase. Another implication is that treatment programs should possess a wide range of skill and coping procedures so that the clients can choose "cafeteria style" those procedures that will work best for them. This procedural diversity should aid in producing treatment tailor-made to each client's need.

Given these characteristics of a desirable treatment program, there are a large number of specific techniques that can be included in a comprehensive treatment program. Each of the techniques to be described has been included in successful or partially successful programs, but very few of them have been isolated as being contributory on their own. Their inclusion in any comprehensive treatment program is obviously limited by the restraints of practicality. The following techniques could be considered the procedural specifics that are to be used to serve the needs of the implications cited earlier. These techniques are listed and briefly described in Table III.

For treatment of the physiological component of social anxiety, a number of skills have been used. These include muscle-relaxation training, autogenic exercises, reducing idiosyncratic physical arousal, diaphragmatic breathing, and mental imagery. One might also be able to prescribe prophylactic physical exercise regimens to reduce and/or prevent untoward stress responses (Goldstein, Ross, & Brady, 1977).

The large number of cognitively oriented techniques for treating social anxiety attests to the increasing realization of the importance of this factor in social problems (Meichenbaum *et al.,* 1982). These procedures include covert modeling and rehearsal, cognitive restructuring, and the coping reappraisal of social stress. Rathjen *et al.* (1978) suggest a lengthy list of cognitive procedures that might prove useful in treating social anxiety, including identifying cognitive distortion patterns, double- and triple-column techniques, testing cognitions, role reversal, and coaching other socially anxious people.

The behavioral skills-training procedures that have been used in treating the dating anxiety aspect of social anxiety have involved behavioral rehearsal, role-playing, performance feedback, videotape self-observation, coaching, and observing appropriate and inappropriate models. The skills that have been taught include telephone talking, face-to-face conversation, giving and receiving compliments, nonverbal communication, description of feelings, handling silences, planning dates, physical appearance enhancement, smiling, initiating conversation

Table III. Procedures Useful in Treating Social Anxiety

Technique	Source	Description	Target
A. Physical			
1. Muscle relaxation training	Bernstein and Borkovec (1973)	Tensing and allowing various muscle groups to limp and relax.	Physiological arousal
2. Autogenic exercises	Jencks (1973)	Imagine relaxation inducing self-instructions (e.g., "My arms are heavy and warm").	Physiological arousal
3. Reducing idiosyncratic arousal	Jaremko, Hadfield, and Walker (1980)	Identifying and counteracting individually peculiar types of arousal (e.g., tensing and releasing tension in muscles around eyes).	Physiological arousal
4. Diaphragmatic breathing	Harvey (1978)	Slow deep breathing in which the diaphragm pulls and pushes air in and out of lungs (stomach moves out on inhale, in on exhale).	Physiological arousal
5. Physical exercise	Goldstein *et al.* (1977)	Standard daily physical exercise (jogging, calisthenics, etc.).	Physiological arousal
B. Cognitive-Affective			
6. Covert modeling	Kazdin (1975)	Imagine anxiety-engendering scene in which initial worry and reticence is overcome by effective coping behavior.	General coping

7. Cognitive restructuring	Kanter and Goldfried (1979)	Imagine anxiety-engendering scene in which person makes negative self-evaluation which is replaced by a positive coping self-statement.	Negative self-talk
8. Coping reappraisal	Meichenbaum and Turk (1976)	Internal dialogue program in which client talks to self about how to deal with a stressor. Self-talk centers on preparing for stress, confronting it, coping with intense moments, and self-evaluation.	Negative/self-defeating appraisal of social situations
9. Identifying cognitive distortion patterns	Beck, Rush, and Kovacs (1976)	After collecting negative thoughts and images, the client looks for underlying trends and themes (e.g., feeling unfairly treated).	Negative self-evaluations
10. Double and triple column techniques	Beck *et al.* (1976)	The client writes down in columns next to one another a negative cognition, a rational thinking alternative, and a reinterpretation.	Faulty and negative cognitions
11. Testing cognitions	Beck *et al.* (1976)	The client devises experimental tests of whether a cognition truly represents reality.	Faulty cognitions
C. Behavioral			
12. Role reversal	Rathjen *et al.* (1978)	The client plays the role of the other person in an anxiety-evoking social situation.	Inaccurate social perception

Continued

Table III (Continued)

Technique	Source	Description	Target
13. Coaching an anxious person	Fremouw and Harmatz (1975)	The client works with another person who is socially anxious, trying to enhance that person's social skill.	Social avoidance
14. Behavioral rehearsal	Lazarus (1971)	The client practices a specific social interaction sequence until it is overlearned.	Lack of social skill
15. Performance feedback	Melnick (1973)	The client is provided with specific feedback about a social performance.	Lack of social skill
16. Observing appropriate and inappropriate models	Curran *et al.* (1976)	The client views models who demonstrate appropriate and inappropriate skills.	Social skill
17. Skills training	Numerous	The skills that have received focus are conversation, feeling talk, handling silences, planning dates, physical enhancement, smiling, opening lines, communicating interest, judging receptivity, initiating physical intimacy, practice with feedback.	Lack of social skill
18. Coping sequence	Jaremko, Hadfield, and Walker (1980)	A set sequence of coping skills is individually constructed, organized, and overlearned.	General coping integration of skills
19. Practice dates/ interactions	Christensen and Arkowitz (1974)	Clients go on dates or interact with other people (nonconfederates).	Social avoidance

(opening "lines"), communicating interests, judging receptivity, and initiating physical intimacy. The specific skills used for types of social anxiety other than heterosocial dating problems differ to some extent, and it would be worthwhile for an interested investigator to compile a list in the specific area of focus. Before training these skills, it is important to demonstrate that such behavioral deficits in fact exist. Also, one must be cautious to take into consideration cultural and situational differences that influence the functional value of any one of the behavioral acts.

Two other techniques that can be suggested for comprehensive treatments in helping the client integrate the various treatment components are the use of imaginal and behavioral rehearsal, and *in vivo* practice by using practice dates and/or interactions. The imagery coping sequence procedure (Jaremko, Hadfield, & Walker, 1980) may act as a memory-enhancing organizational device in order to help the client structure and use the coping devices to which he or she has been exposed. The laboratory-based interactions and *in vivo* practice dating procedures may help to insure that the client will use the skills and coping devices in the presence of the social stressor. Such practice also provides a component of graduated exposure or participant modeling to the treatment package. Success in such social situations provide the needed feedback, the "evidence" to change one's cognitive structures and behavior.

The many techniques recounted above need to be organized in a procedural package that will allow them to be presented in a smooth and effective manner. The model offered earlier (see Figure 1) provides a way to integrate the various techniques that may be required in treating social anxiety.

Since one of the goals of stress inoculation training is to make it more likely that the client will not avoid or escape social situations, the existence of effective behavioral skills is very important. As described in the previous model (Figure 1), clients are offered a stress model describing the importance of effective interpersonal skills at Point D. Skills-training would then take place, along with physical and cognitive skills that are taught in stress inoculation training. Further, the client is made aware that avoidance or escape behavior will lead only to further social anxiety, as is shown at Point E in Figure 1. By appealing to the client's own ability to control anxiety and skills difficulties, one employs a model of therapy more likely to be generalized to real-world settings (Mahoney, 1980). By helping the client adopt a "personal scientist" view in the prediction and control of social behavior and anxiety, we impart skills that can be used in a variety of settings. The comprehensive treatment program of stress inoculation training is designed to enhance a personal science view in those with social anxiety problems. Thus, if a client tries a specific skill and *it does not work,* this should be the occasion to conduct a task and behavior analysis. In fact, in training, the therapist can anticipate with the client what problems may occur and what can be done about them. Will such failures be occasions for further negative thinking and avoidance, or will they prompt the client to employ the "personal scientist" perspective by changing behavior and cognition accordingly? Given that the array of different techniques can overwhelm both the client and trainer, it is suggested that the "personal scientist" perspective will provide an important integrative framework. Stress inoculation training is designed to instill this perspective.

SUMMARY

A model was presented that viewed social anxiety as consisting of activity in three sometimes interactive and sometimes independent categories of behavior: physiology, cognition, and overt behavior. A review of previous research on the assessment and treatment of social anxiety reveals that clinical work that comprehensively deals with all three components has not been conducted. The organization and implementation of assessment and treatment techniques in all three areas is proposed. Specific examples of techniques are presented and an overall conceptual model to integrate these techniques is proposed as a way to enhance a "personal scientist" view in treating social anxiety.

REFERENCES

Arkowitz, H. Measurement and modification of minimal dating behavior. In M. Hersen, R. M. Eisler, & P. M. Miller (Eds), *Progress in behavior modification* (Vol. 5). New York: Academic Press, 1977.

Arkowitz, H., Lichtenstein, B., McGovern, K., & Hines, P. The behavioral assessment of social competence in males. *Behavior Therapy,* 1975, *6,* 3–13.

Bandura, A. Self-efficacy: Toward a unifying theory of behavioral change. *Psychological Review,* 1977, *84,* 191–125.

Barton, W., & Sanborn, C. *An assessment of the community mental health movement.* Lexington, Mass.: Lexington Books, 1977.

Bauer, R. M., & Craighead, W. E. Psychophysiological responses to the imagination of fearful and neutral situations. *Behavior Therapy,* 1979, *10,* 389–403.

Beck, A. T., Rush, A. J., & Kovacs, M. *Individual treatment manual for cognitive/behavioral psychotherapy of depression.* Philadelphia: University of Pennsylvania, 1976.

Bernstein, D. A., & Borkovec, T. D. *Progressive relaxation training: A manual for the helping professions.* Champaign, Ill.: Research Press, 1973.

Borkovec, T. D., Fleischmann, D. G., & Caputo, J. A. The measurement of social anxiety in an analogue social situation. *Journal of Consulting and Clinical Psychology,* 1973, *41,* 157–161.

Borkovec, T. D., Stone, N. M., O'Brien, G. T., & Kaloupek, D. G. Evaluation of a clinically relevant target behavior for analog outcome research. *Behavior Therapy,* 1974, *5,* 503–513.

Borkovec, T. D., Wall, R. L., & Stone, N. M. False physiological feedback and the maintenance of speech anxiety. *Journal of Abnormal Psychology,* 1974, *83,* 164–168.

Cacioppo, J. T., Glass, C. R., & Merluzzi, T. V. Self-statements and self-evaluations: A cognitive-response analysis of social anxiety. *Cognitive Therapy and Research,* 1979, *3,* 249–262.

Christensen, A., & Arkowitz, H. Preliminary report on practice dating and feedback as treatment for college dating problems. *Journal of Counseling Psychology,* 1974, *21,* 92–95.

Curran, J. P. Social skills training and systematic desensitization in reducing dating anxiety. *Behavior Research and Therapy,* 1975, *13,* 65–68.

Curran, J. P. Skills training as an approach to the treatment of heterosexual-social anxiety: A review. *Psychological Bulletin,* 1977, *84,* 140–157.

Curran, J. P., & Gilbert, F. S. A test of the relative effectiveness of a systematic desensitization program and an interpersonal skills training program with date anxious subjects. *Behavior Therapy,* 1975, *6,* 510-521.

Curran, J. P., Gilbert, F. S., & Little, L. M. A comparison between behavior replication training and sensitivity training approaches to heterosexual dating anxiety. *Journal of Counseling Psychology,* 1976, *23,* 190–196.

Curran, J. P., Little, L. M., & Gilbert, F. S. Reactivity of males of differing heterosexual social anxiety to female approach and nonapproach cue and conditions. *Behavior Therapy,* 1978, *9,* 961.

Elder, J. P., Edelstein, B., Fremouw, W., Lively, L., Walker, J., & Womeldorf, J. *A comparison of response acquisition and cognitive restructuring in the enhancement of social competence in college freshmen.* Paper presented at the meeting of the Association for the Advancement of Behavior Therapy, Chicago, 1978.

Emmelkamp, P. M. G., Kuipers, A. C. M., & Eggeraat, J. B. Cognitive modification versus prolonged exposure *in vivo*: A comparison with agoraphobics. *Behavior Research and Therapy,* 1978, *16,* 33–41.

Endler, N. S., Hunt, J. M., & Rosenstein, A. J. An S-R inventory of anxiousness. *Psychological Monographs,* 1962, *76* (17, Whole No. 536).

Farrell, A. D., Mariotto, M. H., Conger, A. J., Curran, J. P., & Wallander, J. L. Self-ratings of heterosexual social anxiety and skills: A generalizability study. *Journal of Consulting and Clinical Psychology,* 1979, *47,* 164–175.

Fiedler, D., & Beach, L. R. On the decision to be assertive. *Journal of Consulting and Clinical Psychology,* 1978, *46,* 537–546.

Fischetti, M., Curran, J. P., & Weissberg, H. W. Sense of timing: A skill deficit in heterosexual-socially anxious males. *Behavior Modification,* 1977, *1,* 179–195.

Fremouw, W. J., & Harmatz, M. A helper model for behavioral treatment of speech anxiety. *Journal of Consulting and Clinical Psychology,* 1975, *43,* 652–660.

Frisch, M. B., Atsaides, J. P., & Elliott, C. H. *Social skills and cognitive stress management program: Therapist manual.* Kansas City, Mo.: Veterans Administration Medical Center, 1977.

Frisch, M. B., Elliott, C. H., Atsaides, J. P., Salva, D. M., & Denney, D. R. *Social skills and stress management training to enhance interpersonal competencies.* Paper presented at the meeting of the American Psychological Association, New York, 1979.

Gambrill, E. D., & Richey, C. A. An assertion inventory for use in assessment and research. *Behavior Therapy,* 1975, *6,* 550–561.

Garfield, S. L. Research on client variables in psychotherapy. In A. E. Bergin & S. L. Garfield (Eds.), *Handbook of psychotherapy and behavior change.* New York: Wiley, 1971.

Geary, J. M., & Goldman, M. S. Behavioral treatment of heterosexual social anxiety: A factorial investigation. *Behavior Therapy,* 1978, *8,* 971–972.

Glass, C., Gottman, J., & Shmurak, S. Response-acquisition and cognitive self-statement modification approaches to dating skills training. *Journal of Counseling Psychology,* 1976, *23,* 520–527.

Goldfried, M. R. Systematic desensitization as training in self-control. *Journal of Consulting and Clinical Psychology,* 1971, *37,* 228–235.

Goldfried, M. R., & Sobocinski, D. The effect of irrational beliefs on emotional arousal. *Journal of Consulting and Clinical Psychology,* 1975, *43,* 504–510.

Goldfried, M. R., Decenteceo, E. T., & Weinberg, L. Systematic rational restructuring as a self-control technique. *Behavior Therapy,* 1974, *5,* 247–254.

Goldstein, D. S., Ross, R. S., & Brady, J. V. Biofeedback heart rate training during exercise. *Biofeedback and Self-Regulation,* 1977, *2,* 107–126.

Greenwald, D. P. The behavioral assessment of differences in social skills and social anxiety in female college students. *Behavior Therapy,* 1977, *8,* 925–937.

Greist, J. H., Marks, I. M., Berlin, F., Gournay, K., & Noshirvani, H. Avoidance versus confrontation of fear. *Behavior Therapy,* 1980, *11,* 1–14.

Harvey, J. R. Diaphragmatic breathing: A practical technique for breath control. *The Behavior Therapist,* 1978, *1,* 13–14.

Hersen, M., & Bellack, A. S. Assessment of social skills. In A. R. Ciminero, K. S. Calhoun, & H. E. Adams (Eds.), *Handbook of behavior assessment.* New York: Wiley, 1977.

Hovland, C. I., & Janis, I. L. (Eds.). *Yale studies in attitude and communication: Personality and persuadability.* New Haven: Yale University Press, 1959.

Jaremko, M. E. A component analysis of stress inoculation: Review and prospectus. *Cognitive Therapy and Research,* 1979, *3,* 35–48.

Jaremko, M. E. *Cognitive-behavior reflections on some dimensions of personality.* Washington, D. C.: University Press of America, 1980. (a)

Jaremko, M. E. The application of signal detection theory to anxiety perception. *Journal of Behavior Therapy and Experimental Psychiatry,* 1980, *11,* 112. (b)

Jaremko, M. E., Myers, E., & Jaremko, L. L. *A comparison of social skills training and stress inoculation training for treating dating anxiety.* Paper presented at the meeting of the Southwestern Psychological Association, San Antonio, 1979.

Jaremko, M. E., Hadfield, R., & Walker, W. E. Contribution of an educational phase to stress inoculation of speech anxiety. *Perceptual Motor and Skills,* 1980, *50,* 495–501.

Jaremko, M. E., Myers, E., & Daner, S. *Differences in daters: Effects of sex, dating frequency, and dating frequency of partner.* Unpublished manuscript, University of Mississippi, 1980.

Jencks, B. *Exercise manual for J. H. Schults's standard autogenic training.* Salt Lake City: Alphagraphics, 1973.

Jones, R. G. *A factored measure of Ellis' irrational belief system, with personality and maladjustment correlates.* Unpublished doctoral dissertation, Texas Technological College, 1968.

Kallman, W. M., & Feuerstein, M. Psychophysiological procedures. In A. R. Cimenero, K. S. Calhoun, & H. E. Adams (Eds.), *Handbook of behavioral assessment.* New York: Wiley, 1977.

Kanter, N., & Goldfried, M. R. Relative effectiveness of rationale restructuring and self-control desensitization in the reduction of interpersonal anxiety. *Behavior Therapy,* 1979, *10,* 472–490.

Kazdin, A. E. Effects of covert modeling and model reinforcement on assertive behavior. *Journal of Abnormal Psychology,* 1974, *83,* 240–252.
Kazdin, A. E. Covert modeling, imagery assessement, and assertive behavior. *Journal of Consulting and Clinical Psychology,* 1975, *48,* 716–724.
Keane, T. M., & Lisman, S. A. *Behavioral, cognitive, and physiological effects of alcohol on heterosocial anxiety.* Paper presented at the meeting of the Association for the Advancement of Behavior Therapy, Chicago, 1978.
Kendall, P., & Korgeski, G. Assessment and cognitive-behavioral interventions. *Cognitive Therapy and Research,* 1979, *3,* 1–22.
Klaus, D., Hersen, M., & Bellack, A. S. Survey of dating habits of male and female college students: A necessary precursor to measurement and modification. *Journal of Clinical Psychology,* 1977, *33,* 369–375.
Kupke, T. E., Calhoun, K. S., & Hobbs, S. A. Selection of heterosocial skills. II. Experimental validity. *Behavior Therapy,* 1979, *10,* 336–346.
Lacey, J. I. Somatic response patterning and stress: Some revisions of the activation theory. In M.H. Appley & R. Trumbull (Eds.), *Psychological stress.* New York: Appleton-Century-Crofts, 1967.
Lacey, J. I., & Lacey, B. C. Some autonomic-CNS interrelationships. In P. Black (Ed.), *Psychological correlates of emotion.* New York: Academic Press, 1970.
Lang, P. J. The application of psychological methods to the study of pyschotherapy and behavior modification. In A. E. Bergin & S. L. Garfield (Eds.), *Handbook of psychotherapy and behavior change: An empirical analysis.* New York: Wiley, 1971.
Lazarus, A. A. *Behavior therapy and beyond.* New York: McGraw-Hill, 1972.
Lazarus, R., Kanner, A., & Folkman, S. Emotions: A cognitive-phenomenological analysis. In R. Plutchik & H. Kellerman (Eds.), *Theories of emotion.* New York: Academic Press, 1979.
Levenson, R. W., & Gottman, J. M. Toward the assessment of social competence. *Journal of Consulting and Clinical Psychology,* 1978, *49,* 453–462.
Linehan, M. M., Goldfried, M. R., & Goldfried, A. P. Assertion therapy: Skill training or cognitive restructuring. *Behavior Therapy,* 1980, *11,* 59–67.
Lipton, D. N., & Nelson, R. O. The contribution of initiation behaviors to dating frequency. *Behavior Therapy,* 1980, *11,* 59–67.
MacDonald, M. L., Lindquist, C. U., Kramer, J. A., McGrath, R. A., & Rhyne, L. L. Social skills training: The effects of behavior rehearsal in groups on dating skills. *Journal of Counseling Psychology,* 1975, *22,* 224–230.
Mahoney, M. J. *Cognition and behavior modification.* Cambridge, Ma.: Ballinger, 1974.
Mahoney, M. J. Psychotherapy and the structure of personal revolutions. In M. J. Mahoney (Ed.), *Psychotherapy process.* New York: Plenum Press, 1980.
May, J. R. Psychophysiology of self-regulated phobic thoughts. *Behavior Therapy,* 1977, *8,* 150–159.
Meichenbaum, D. Cognitive modification of test anxious college students. *Journal of Consulting and Clinical Psychology,* 1972, *29,* 370–380.
Meichenbaum, D. *Cognitive-behavior modification: An integrative approach.* New York: Plenum Press, 1977.
Meichenbaum, D., & Butler, L. Cognitive ethology: Assessing the streams of cognition and emotion. In K. Blankstein, P. Pliner, & J. Polivy (Eds.), *Advances in the study of emotion communication and affect* (Vol. 6). *Assessment and modification of emotional behavior.* New York: Plenum Press, 1980.
Meichenbaum, D., & Cameron, R. *Stress inoculation: A skills training approach to anxiety management.* Unpublished manuscript, University of Waterloo, 1973.

Meichenbaum, D., & Turk, D. The cognitive-behavioral management of anxiety, fear, and pain. In P. O. Davidson (Ed.), *The behavioral management of anxiety, depression, and pain.* New York: Brunner/Mazel, 1976.

Meichenbaum, D., Gilmore, B., Fedoravicius, A. Group thought vs. group desensitization in treating speech anxiety. *Journal of Consulting and Clinical Psychology,* 1971, *36,* 410–421.

Meichenbaum, D., Butler, L., & Joseph, L. G. Toward a conceptual model of social competence. In J. Wine & M. Smye (Eds.), *The identification and enhancement of social competence.* Washington, D.C.: Hemisphere Publications, 1982.

Melnick, J. A comparison of replication techniques in the modification of minimal dating behavior. *Journal of Abnormal Psychology,* 1973, *81,* 51–59.

Mitchell, K. R., & Orr, F. E. Heterosexual social competence, anxiety, avoidance, and self-judged physical attractiveness. *Perceptual and Motor Skills,* 1976, *43,* 553–554.

Morrill, W., & Oettuig, E. Outreach programs in college counseling. *Journal of College Student Personnel,* 1978, *19*(4), 51–54.

Orr, F. E., & Mitchell, K. R. *The problem of social isolation in the university community.* Paper presented at the Sydney Metropolitan Tertiary Counselor's Conference. University of Wollongong, Wollongong, N.S.W., Australia, 1975.

Orr, F. E., Mitchell, K. R., & Hall, R. G. Effects of reduction in social anxiety on behavior in heterosexual situations. *Australian Psychologist,* 1975, *10,* 139–148.

Pilkonis, P. A. The behavioral consequences of shyness. *Journal of Personality,* 1977, *45,* 596–605.

Rachman, S. The passing of the two-stage theory of fear and avoidance: Fresh possibilities. *Behavior Research and Therapy,* 1976, *14,* 125–131.

Rathjen, D. P., Rathjen, E. D., & Hiniker, A. A cognitive analysis of social performance: Implications for assessment and treatment. In J. P. Foreyt & D. P. Rathjen (Eds.), *Cognitive behavior therapy.* New York: Plenum Press, 1978.

Rehm, L. A self-control model of depression. *Behavior Therapy,* 1977, *8,* 787–804.

Rehm, L. P., & Marston, A. R. Reduction of social anxiety through modification of self-reinforcement: An instigation therapy technique. *Journal of Consulting and Clinical Psychology,* 1968, *32,* 565–574.

Schwartz, R., & Gottman, J. Toward a task analysis of assertive behavior. *Journal of Consulting and Clinical Psychology,* 1976, *44,* 901–920.

Spielberger, C. D., Gorsuch, R. L., & Lushene, R. E. *The state-trait anxiety inventory (STAI) test manual for form X.* Palo Alto, Calif.: Consulting Psychologists Press, 1970.

Sutton-Simon, K., & Goldfried, M. R. Faulty thinking patterns in two types of anxiety. *Cognitive Therapy and Research,* 1979, *3,* 193–204.

Twentyman, G. T., & McFall, R. M. Behavioral training of social skills in shy males. *Journal of Consulting and Clinical Psychology,* 1975, *43,* 384–395.

Watson, D., & Friend, R. Measurement of social-evaluative anxiety. *Journal of Consulting and Clinical Psychology,* 1969, *33,* 448–457.

Wheeler, L., & Nezlek, J. Sex differences in social participation. *Journal of Personality and Social Psychology,* 1977, *35,* 742–754.

13

Stress Inoculation Training for Adolescent Anger Problems

EVA L. FEINDLER and WILLIAM J. FREMOUW

INTRODUCTION

Adolescent aggression and antisocial behavior represent a significant clinical and social problem. Although youths between the ages of 13 and 18 form only 11% of the population, in 1977 people under 18 years of age constituted 41% of the arrests for the Crime Index offenses of homicide, rape, robbery, aggravated assault, burglary, and auto theft (Webster, 1979). Furthermore, the rate of arrests for violent juvenile crime increased by 98% between 1967 and 1976 compared with a 65% increase in arrests for people over 18 years of age (Federal Bureau of Investigation, 1977). These aggressive acts are not just transitory adjustment problems. After review of 16 longitudinal studies, Olweus (1979) concluded that aggressive behavior is not situation-specific, but is a relatively stable, individually consistent reaction pattern to many situations. In fact, temporal stability of aggressive behavior almost equals that typically reported for intellectual and cognitive processes. While some aggression is instrumental in securing external rewards, much of adolescent aggression represents rapid, unplanned, impulsive reactions to provocations (Saunders, Reppucci, & Sarato, 1973).

Anger is commonly associated with adolescent impulsive and ag-

EVA L. FEINDLER • Department of Psychology, Adelphi University, Garden City, New York 11530. WILLIAM J. FREMOUW • Department of Psychology, West Virginia University, Morgantown, West Virginia 26505.

gressive behavior. Rule and Nesdale (1976) reported that the arousal of anger facilitates aggressive behavior, especially toward the perceived source of the anger state. While anger arousal does not always produce aggression and not all episodes of aggression are preceded by anger (Konecni, 1975a,b), the treatment of anger problems is one approach to reducing adolescent aggressive and antisocial behavior.

Anger is typically conceptualized as an affective response to stress during which a person experiences high levels of physiological arousal (Konecni, 1975b; Schacter & Singer, 1962). The stressful situations are usually perceived as frustrations, annoyances, insults, or assaults and often occur in social situations. The combination of one's perception of frustration or insult and a high level of arousal leads to the labeling of this state as anger (Konecni, 1975b, Schacter & Singer, 1962). Novaco (1975, 1979) has amended this two-component view of anger to include a behavioral determinant of anger. He states that one's behavior during provocation, not just one's type of cognitions and level of physiological arousal, can affect the level of anger. Aggressive response to provocation can increase the level of anger because it may escalate the situation and elicit further provocations from others. Conversely, coping responses such as appropriate assertiveness or leaving the situation may decrease the degree of provocation being experienced and lower the anger. In this model, the level of anger is the result of the continual interaction of cognitions, physiological arousal, and behavioral reactions. Changes in each component affect the other two components and the degree of anger produced.

Historically, Witmer (1908) reported the first successful treatment of anger for an 11-year old boy. The boy was described as having "mean moods" and "unreasoning anger," and he was treated by means of an educational, problem-solving procedures. Approximately half a century later, Redl and Wineman (1951, 1952) popularized a neoanalytic conceptualization and treatment program for aggressive adolescents in their classic books *Children Who Hate* and *Controls from Within*. Their residential program was designed to strengthen ego functioning by providing the youths with a consistent, structured, group-oriented environment.

CURRENT INTERVENTIONS

Behavioral Treatments

The development of behavioral treatments has provided an alternative to Redl and Wineman's analytic view of anger and aggression as the manifestation of intrapsychic conflicts. Many early programs extended the successful application of operant token-reinforcement procedures, from modifying academic work (Tyler & Brown, 1968) and interpersonal behaviors (Hobbs & Holt, 1976) to the treatment of anger and aggression among adolescents. Programs have manipulated the consequences of the aggressive behavior through reinforcement (Hobbs & Holt, 1976), contracting (Weathers & Liberman, 1975), and response cost and time out (Kaufman & O'Leary, 1972). Although initially effective, Kazdin (1977) concluded that the behavioral improvements from the operant-token programs "usually extinguish when the program is withdrawn" (p. 175). Generalization of improvement across situations and maintenance of change over time do not occur. Furthermore, the selection of effective reinforcers for adolescents is very difficult.

Anger problems have also been treated through systematic desensitization to decrease the physiological arousal that precedes and accompanies anger. This approach focuses on the respondent-conditioned component of anger instead of the consequences. While deeply relaxed, clients are instructed to imagine themselves in an anger-provoking situation without experiencing anger. Research demonstrates that systematic desensitization is effective relative to control conditions (Rimmm, deGroot, Boord, Heiman, & Dillow, 1971) and maintains effectiveness six months after treatment (Evans & Hearn, 1973). Although promising, systematic desensitization has not been widely researched beyond these few initial studies and has not been applied for adolescent anger problems.

Cognitive Behavior Modification

In addition to operant and respondent procedures, new treatments have been developed to integrate the cognitive dimension with behavioral treatment (Mahoney, 1974; Meichenbaum, 1977). Cognitive factors are very relevant for the ànalysis of anger problems. Bandura (1973) suggested that the absence of verbal skills to cope with stress often leads to aggression. Experimental data also suggest that insufficient cognitive mediation may lead to anger and aggression. Camp (1977) found that young aggressive boys are deficient in the use of language skills to control their behavior. They respond impulsively instead of responding after reflection. When they were trained to increase their self-verbalizations, their prosocial behaviors increased and their aggressiveness decreased (Camp, Blom, Herbert, & Van Doornick, 1977). Shure and Spivack (1972) also report that poor cognitive skills are associated with aggressive behavior. They found that youths in special schools, when compared with those in regular schools, were deficient in problem-solving skills and that their solutions to problems were impulsive and aggressive. Hospitalized adolescents in comparison with a control group were also deficient in their ability to generate alternative solutions and to articulate a sequential plan to solve a problem (Platt, Spivack, Altman, Altman, & Peizer, 1974).

Based on these findings, Meichenbaum (1977) concluded that impulsive youths do not routinely and spontaneously analyze stimuli in a cognitively mediated manner and they do not formulate or internalize rules that may help control their behavior in new situations. Thus, an extremely stressful situation, which requires a variety of cognitive coping responses to control both emotional arousal and aggressive responding, would be very difficult for adolescents with deficient cognitive skills or faulty labeling processes.

Stress inoculation training was first developed by Meichenbaum (1975) to treat anxiety, and later was applied to pain (Turk, 1976) and then to anger (Novaco, 1975). This three-step procedure attempts to help the individual acquire a repertoire of more effective skills for managing the stress that can lead to anger. The first phase is to educate clients about the cognitive, physiological, and behavioral components of anger; the positive and negative functions of anger; the antecedents of their anger; and the alternative coping skills that they can use. During the second phase, clients learn cognitive and behavioral coping skills, which are then practiced in increasingly stressful situations of the final application phase (Novaco, 1979).

The gradual exposure of the clients to stressful situations while applying newly learned coping skills is the inoculation procedure that prepares them to cope successfully with similar situations outside of the training sessions. Thus, these steps teach the client to discriminate the antecedents for anger, to insert coping statements in the chain between the antecedent stimuli and previously automatic emotional response, and to practice these alternative responses during increasingly stressful situations.

In his initial research, Novaco (1975, 1976) trained 34 adults with anger-control problems to use either cognitive coping procedures, relaxation, or the combination of these components. In the coping-skills procedure, clients were instructed to generate self-statements specific to the different temporal stages surrounding a potential provocation. The stages are (1) preparing for a provocation, (2) initial confrontation and its impact, (3) coping with arousal, and (4) subsequent reflection after resolved or unresolved conflict. Relative to an attention-control condition, the combination procedure led to significant improvement, while the two components each produced some reduction of anger. In a subsequent case study of a hospitalized depressed subject with severe anger problems, Novaco (1977a) revised the earlier procedure to include the rehearsal of the coping skills during increasingly stressful situations—

the practice phase of stress inoculation. Both self-report and behavioral ratings demonstrated the effectiveness of the treatment program. Novaco (1977b) also used stress inoculation of anger in training police officers to cope with the conflict and provocations encountered in their work. In a related study, probation counselors were trained to administer stress inoculation training to their clients (Novaco, 1980).

Recently, Schlichter and Horan (1979) applied stress inoculation for treatment of anger problems among institutionalized juvenile delinquents. Thirty-eight male adolescents received either stress inoculation training; a treatment elements condition, in which the subject practiced relaxation and role-played successively stressful situations but omitted the educational and the self-instructional training components of the standard stress inoculation procedure; or a no-treatment control condition. While both active treatments lowered anger responses on an imagined provocations test, only the stress inoculation group produced significant reductions in verbal aggression during role-played provocations. Neither treatment affected self-report or pre–post staff ratings of verbal or physical aggression. These tentative results need further replication and demonstration that stress inoculation training affects *in vivo* behaviors and not just role-played analog assessments.

A few other case studies have reported the successful treatment of adults with anger problems through such techniques as humor (Smith, 1973) and rational restructuring therapy (Hamberger & Lohr, 1980). However, with the exception of Schlichter and Horan (1979), a case study by McCullough, Huntsinger, and Nay (1977), and the results described later in this chapter, stress inoculation techniques have *not* been systematically applied and evaluated for the treatment of adolescent anger problems. The remainder of this chapter will detail (1) assessment procedures to evaluate anger control problems, (2) a stress inoculation training program specifically for adolescents, (3) experimental results from three applications of these procedures, and (4) directions for future research and development.

ADOLESCENT ANGER-CONTROL TRAINING

Assessment Procedures for Anger-Control Problems

Prior to the implementation of an anger-control program, the anger problem requires description and measurement (1) to determine whether the problem exists, (2) to identify individual patterns of responding, and (3) to provide a pretreatment measure from which the treatment's effectiveness can be evaluated. Because anger includes cognitive, physiological, and behavioral dimensions (Novaco, 1975), a comprehensive assessment should evaluate each of these. This section will review briefly some of the devices available for the measurement of adolescent anger and aggression.

Self-Monitoring

Self-monitoring procedures can be used for the individual to record the situational, physiological, and cognitive stimuli antecedents to anger and to note the topography and consequences of the anger episode. Through an individual's self-monitoring of the specific antecedent and consequences of anger, the person completes a functional analysis of the anger problem that can be used in the training program and can provide a continuous self-report of anger problems. This can be used to evalute the intervention's effectiveness.

Table I represents a sample data sheet used for the self-monitoring of anger experiences by residential delinquents in the Feindler (1979) study. This "Hassle Log," which was to be completed following each hassle or conflict in which the adolescent was involved, required a minimal response, yet remained open-ended for spontaneous recording of data. Through this data-collection procedure, adolescents learned discrimination of situational variables such as time, place, other persons, and antecedent provoking stimuli that may have influenced the aggressive response. The Hassle Log also included an enumeration of all responses exhibited and the individual's rating of performance and level of emotional arousal experienced. The resulting data enable the clinician to evaluate the frequency and severity of anger incidents, antecedent stimulus and response patterns, and the client's self-observations and evaluations of internal and external events. In addition to covering situational antecedents, this type of self-monitoring form could be expanded to include enumeration of self-statements antecedent to the anger. However, preliminary efforts with adolescents to monitor these covert events indicated that they had little awareness of their self-statements preceding anger outburst until they had received extensive training. Instead, they were able to monitor situational events that did provoke anger. Thus, the Hassle Log focuses on those types of antecedents.

Results from a three-week self-monitoring treatment phase (Feindler, 1979) demonstrated that self-monitoring itself does not reduce aggressive acts. In fact, based on data from teachers, anger episodes slightly increased. The adolescents did comply with the procedure and recorded both resolved and unresolved conflicts. Based on this experience, self-monitoring procedures are a promising tool for anger assessment and warrant further development.

Self-Report Inventories

There are a few paper-and-pencil inventories designed specifically to assess adolescent anger. The Rathus Assertion Schedule (Vaal, 1975), the

Table I. Hassle Log—Conflict Situations

Date: ____________

Morn.____ Aft.____ Even. ____

Where were you?

Class ____	Specialty class ____	Off campus ____
Cottage ____	Dining ____	Other ____
Gym ____	Outside/on campus ____	____

What happened?

Somebody teased me.......... ____
Somebody took something of mine.......... ____
Somebody told me to do something.......... ____
Somebody was doing something I didn't like.......... ____
Somebody started fighting with me.......... ____
I did something wrong.......... ____
Other: ____________ ____

Who was that somebody?

Another student ____	Teacher ____	Counselor ____
Parent ____	Another adult ____	Sibling ____

What did you do?

Hit back ____	Told supervising adult ____
Ran away ____	Walked away calmly ____
Yelled ____	Talked it out ____
Cried ____	Told peer ____
Broke something ____	Ignored ____
Was restrained ____	Other: ____

How did you handle yourself?

1	2	3	4	5
Poorly	Not so well	Okay	Good	GREAT

How angry were you?

1	2	3	4	5
Burning mad	Really angry	Moderately angry	Mildly angry but still okay	Not angry at all

Adolescent Anger Inventory (Schlichter & Horan, 1979); the Jesness Behavior Checklist Self Appraisal (Jesness, 1966), which contains a four-item anger control subscale; and the Buss-Durkee Hostility Inventory (1957) have been used in research with adolescents. Data from aggressive adolescents on the Anger Inventory indicated no change following a cognitive-behavioral anger-control intervention (Schlichter & Horan, 1979), and data from the self-appraisal form of the Jesness Behavior Checklist indicated insignificant increases in prosocial behaviors following intervention (Feindler, Marriott, & Iwata, 1980). The sensitivity to change, reliability, and social desirability of these measures requires further investigation. Although the Novaco Anger Inventory (Novaco, 1975) had demonstrated sensitivity to change with adult respondents, the self-report measures used with adolescents have not reflected improvements occurring on other measures of anger. Further work is needed to refine assessment in this area.

Cognitive Measures

Many of the investigations of adolescent impulsivity and problem-solving have employed cognitive assessment devices that have been sensitive to behavior change resulting from cognitive-behavioral interventions. These measures have included Porteus Maze tasks (Meichenbaum & Goodman, 1971) and the Matching Familiar Figures Test (Anderson, Fodor, & Alpert, 1976; Kendall & Wilcox, 1979). Error rates and response latencies improve on these measures following self-control interventions related to cognitive tasks and following cognitive-behavioral self-control training, (e.g., Feindler, 1979; Feindler, Marriott, & Iwata, 1980). The improvement on these performance measures is encouraging and suggestes the effectiveness and maintenance of treatment.

Another cognitive task that has received some attention is problem-solving. Shure and Spivack (1972) have offered several paper-and-pencil problem-solving measures designed to assess adolescent means–ends sequential thinking and the generation of alternative responses to problem situations. Problem-solving measures are being further developed to increase their utility. (See Butler & Meichenbaum, 1980, for a review.)

Ratings and Direct Observations

Pre- and post-treatment ratings by teachers or counselors are the most common form of evaluation for adolescent anger-control programs. The Jesness Behavior Checklist observer form is a reliable assessment of social-emotional skill levels, yet indicated little change in teacher and counselor ratings as a result of anger-control training (Feindler, Marriott, & Iwata, 1980). The Self-Control Rating Scale (Kendall & Wilcox, 1979), a 33-item inventory designed to assess a teacher's or parent's evaluation of the child's impulsivity and self-control responses, may become a reliable and valid instrument for the assessment of explosive adolescents. Unfortunately, initial investigations (Feindler, Marriott, & Iwata, 1980) indicate minimal changes in teachers' ratings for both treatment and control groups during an 18-week treatment study. Similar to the self-report inventories, rating scales do not appear to be highly sensitive to the levels of improvement produced by the current cognitive-behavioral treatments.

A more sensitive and stringent measure of treatment impact is the continuous monitoring of the adolescent's behavior *in vivo,* where the adolescent is confronted with provocations and consequences that maintain aggressive behaviors. These data reflect the rate of specific problem behaviors and are not a general summary across time of behaviors that self-report inventories or checklists represent.

A continuous direct-observation system was designed for the Feindler (1979) study to assess the frequency, severity, and topography of aggressive behaviors occurring at specified times outside the training environment. The Aggressive Behavior Observation System (ABOS) includes seven categories of aggressive behavior: tease, argue, threat, hit, start fight, infight, and property damage (see Table II for operational definitions). In addition to recording the frequency of these behaviors during half-hour intervals throughout the day, observers rated the severity of each aggressive behavior on a three-point scale (1 = mild, 2 = moderate, 3 = severe). Following training, the teachers and counselors were able to use the rating scale to monitor reliably the behaviors of the target student. The ABOS provided a severity rating, an overall aggressive behavior frequency count, and frequencies for each subcategory of aggression.

The comprehensiveness of this system provided several types of data that are useful in evaluating the effectiveness of the anger control training. First, aggressive behavior patterns can be mentioned across settings by different observers to evaluate the generalization of the treatment effects. Second, the frequency and severity assessments of aggressive responses across time and situations enable the trainers to individualize the training regimen. Feindler (1979) found that each adolescent had relatively stable patterns of aggressive responses, which were reduced by means of the stress inoculation training. However, the categories of aggressive behaviors remained proportional. Finally, the continuous recordings also provide a sensitive evaluation of which treatment techniques are more effective.

Anger-Control Techniques for Adolescents

Several cognitive-behavioral treatment techniques that were developed to manage anger arousal in adults and impulsivity in children have

Table II. Aggressive Behavior Observation System (ABOS): Definitions

TEASE:	Provocative statements directed toward another student or adult. Include ridiculing, name calling, taunting, picking on and other nagging or provoking verbal responses. Exclude friendly, playful teasing and other statements accompanied by smiles and laughter by both students. Do *not* include threats to harm another person or another's property. EXAMPLES: 1. "Hah, hah, you got in trouble." 2. "Man, you are really a cry baby." 3. "You ugly S.O.B."
ARGUE:	A three-statement sequence of negative verbal provocation. Mark this category if you observe or hear a verbal fight or screaming match involving two or more students and including the target student. Include any verbal provocations that occur in sequence, such as teases, ownership statements, refusals, denials, and other verbal responses with negative affect and meaning. Exclude threats, playful arguing and true debates. EXAMPLES: 1. "Get lost." "No, I won't." "Just leave me alone." 2. "You jerk." "Don't call *me* names." "I'll do what I want." 3. "Give it back." "It's mine, go lay off." "You liar. You stole it out of my room."
THREAT:	A verbal statement or physical gesture to hurt another person or destroy something belonging to another. Verbal statements must include a behavioral referrent to aggressive responding, such as "I'm gonna break your arm." Gestures may include fist swinging, a raised belt or stick, etc. If physical contact is made to other person or property, mark both THREAT and HIT or DAMAGE categories. Exclude playful, good-natured threats ("I'll get the boogie man after you!") and threats that are unrealistic in terms of the behavioral repertoire of student (I'll crush your mother with my foot.") Include any threat that the student may be able to carry out. EXAMPLES: 1. "I'm gonna let the air out of your tires." 2. "I'll smack your face if you do that." 3. "I'm gonna break every bone in your body." "I'm gonna kill you."
HIT:	Aggressive behaviors toward another person that may produce pain or injury. Physical contact must be made with a part of the target student's body or an object with which he has contact. Mark only if you actually observe the aggressive act. Includes shoving, hitting, slapping, punching, kicking, pinching, throwing objects at, etc. Exclude playful or friendly contact performed in a

Table II (Continued)

	HIT *(continued):* positive context (smiles and laughter). If several behaviors occur in rapid sequence, mark as one episode but use greater severity rating. If behaviors are separated by 10 seconds or more, mark as two episodes. If the victim responds, and the target student HITS again, do not mark this category, but move to FIGHT category. EXAMPLES: 1. A swift kick in the butt. 2. Several punches in the arm. 3. A rapid succession of blows to the head with a fist or a 2 × 4.
IN FIGHT:	Mark only if you observe the target student engaged in an exchange of physical and agressive behaviors. This requires two or more students including the target student and at least a three-response sequence of behaviors from the HIT category. Exclude playful fighting or wrestling that is done in a positive context and/or is accompanied by smiles and laughter. Still mark this category if one of the students involved in the exchange is only making weak attempts to fight and is less aggressive. EXAMPLES: 1. Student A throws a pencil. Student B throws it back. Student A kicks B. 2. Student A slaps student B on the back. Student B turns and kicks A. Student A punches B's face. 3. Student A hits Student B in the face. Student B punches A's head. Student A kicks B powerfully in the groin.
START:	Mark this category only if you are certain that the target student started the fight (see above definition)—you must observe the initial physical contact. Do not mark both the START and IN FIGHT categories for the same fight episode.
DAMAGE:	Unauthorized destruction of personal or school property. Includes breaking, ripping, tearing, cutting, shredding, smashing, burning, shattering, etc. Exclude appropriate disposal of items such as stomping on a used milk carton and throwing it in the trash. Include marking or marring. 1. Writing obscenities on the walls. 2. Tearing someone's shirt. Stepping on ping pong ball. 3. Smashing windows, punching through walls or fire setting.

been tailored for application to adolescent anger and aggression problems. Described below and summarized in Table III are individual cognitive and behavioral self-control methods that have been successfully used with individuals and with groups of adolescents to control explosive behavior.

Table III. Summary of Anger-Control Procedures for Use with Aggressive Adolescents

I. Assessment and analysis of provocation cues and anger responses

Self-monitoring techniques

1. Identification of aggressive responses to provocation, antecedent provoking stimuli, and consequent events.
2. Self-rating of anger components
3. Training in self-recording and compilation of own data.
4. Analysis of provocation sequences and behavioral patterns.

II. Training of alternative responses to external provoking stimuli

A. Self-instructions

1. Definition and generation of relevant self-instructions (termed, REMINDERS).
2. Modeling and role-playing of *how* and *when* to use self-verbalizations to guide overt and covert behaviors.
3. Training both generalized and specific self-instructions.

B. Self-evaluation skills

1. Determination of individual self-evaluating statements that currently function as reinforcers or punishers.
2. Definition of self-evaluations as a form of self-instruction that provide feedback and guide performance in both resolved and unresolved provocation incidents.

C. Thinking-ahead techniques

1. Presentation of problem-solving strategy designed to help client use the estimation of future negative consequences for misbehavior to guide current responses to provocation.
2. Modeling and role-playing of *how* and *when* to use self-generated contingency statements concerning negative consequences.

D. Relaxation techniques

1. Presentation of arousal-management techniques to aid in the identification of physiological responses to provocation and to control muscle tension during or in anticipation of conflicts.
2. Deep breathing as a time delay and an alternative response.
3. Deep muscle relaxation training.

III. Techniques to Control Own Provocation Behaviors

Table III (Continued)

E. Angry behavior cycle

1. Discrimination of own behaviors that may act as provocation cues to others and of escalating sequences of aggression.
2. Contracting for change in frequency and/or intensity of nonverbal (voice volume, tone, threatening gestures) and/or verbal (threats, teases, arguments) aggressive behaviors that may provoke others.

F. Assertion without aggression

1. Examination of peer pressure, conformity, and conflict with authority issues.
2. Enumeration of personal rights and responsibilities.
3. Modeling and role-playing of assertion techniques including empathetic assertion, fogging, broken record, confrontation, minimal assertive response.

Behavioral Controls

The initial focus of treatment is usally the immediate suppression of both verbal and nonverbal aggressive responding by the adolescent to the variety of antecedent anger cues that have been identified through self-monitoring procedures. Conceptually, simple impulse-delay techniques are easy for the adolescent to understand and to transfer to *in vivo* provocations. However, developing the skill of sequencing the components of the provocation cycle—namely, antecedent anger cues or external provocations, aggressive responses, and consequent events—is necessary first.

After adolescents are able to discriminate antecedents to aggression and anger expression, they can begin to learn self-control by inserting a time delay between the provoking stimulus and the automatic response. Teaching adolescents to stop and either remove themselves from the provoking stimuli or ignore the external provocation for a few seconds will lay the groundwork for the development of cognitive controls. These "time-out" responses help the adolescent to slow down the behavior chain and to better evaluate the provocation situation and allow time for the substitution of alternative responses.

In addition to the adolescent's learning *not* to respond are other techniques aimed at training more appropriate behavioral response to provocations. For those adolescents who are able to discriminate physiological anger-arousal cues and for whom this heightened level of arousal interferes with adaptive responding, relaxation techniques seem applicable. Responding with a few slow, deep breaths during the time delay between the provoking stimulus and the subsequent response helps to reduce the arousal level. Although actual deep-muscle relaxation may not be the appropriate response to an aversive and threatening stimulus, some adolescents who evidence anxiety and agitation will readily respond to increasing their control of physiological arousal. A shortened version of the relaxation sequence that involved tightening and relaxing selected, unobtrusive muscle groups such as the jaw, fists, and stomach was employed, along with slow, deep breathing, during conflict situations for those adolescents able to discriminate their own arousal levels. Another component of the behavioral control techniques centers around the training of appropriate assertion and problem-solving skills. Until recently (Feindler, Marriott, & Iwata, 1980; Lee, Hallberg, & Hassard, 1979), assertion training for aggressive delinquents was not explored. However, if we are to assume a possible skill deficiency in assertion or problem-solving (Platt *et al.,* 1974), then appropriate verbal and nonverbal assertive responses designed to replace aggressive responding must be taught concurrently with anger-control skills. Observations during role-play and videotape feedback of brief conflict scenes can help to identify the excesses and deficiencies in the verbal and nonverbal components of assertive and aggressive responding. Through behavioral rehearsal of conflict scenes, behaviors such as direct eye contact, appropriate gestures, modulated tone of voice, and requests for another's behavior change can replace the aggressive responses of staring, threatening gestures, a harsh tone, and demands. A reduction in the use of threatening body posture or in voice volume, for example, may result in others perceiving the adolescent as less aggressive and as providing fewer provoking stimuli. The techniques of *broken record,* which involves calm repetitions of the adolescent's original request or assertion until the problem is solved; *fogging,* which entails an agreement with another's direct criticism in such a manner as to confuse the other; and *minimal effective response,* which entails a gradual escalation of assertive demands, beginning with the least forceful and ending in a direct demand, can all be modeled and practiced through role-plays of interpersonal conflicts. Teaching the common assertion techniques detailed in popular literature (Smith, 1975) will broaden the adolescent's repertoire and enable him or her to obtain desirable reinforcers in a more appropriate manner.

Finally, problem-solving strategies similar to those suggested by D'Zurilla and Goldfried (1971), which aid the adolescent in identifying the problem situation and enumerating and evaluating alternative solutions, are useful with impulsive aggressors. Each problem-solving skill (problem specification, enumerating alternative responses, listing consequences of each response and rank ordering alternatives, implementing an alternative, and evaluating the outcome) is presented verbally to the adolescent with accompanying examples from typical school and home conflicts. Verbal rehearsal of these skills, accomplished by prompting an analysis of numerous relevant problem situations and the identification of each component step, teaches the adolescent to conceptualize problems in this sequenced manner and to use these skills to guide overt responding. These problem-solving responses, which can be either situation-specific or generalizable, provide the adolescent with yet another set of alternative behaviors to emit following the discrimination of aversive or provoking external stimuli.

Cognitive Controls

Incorporated into training programs for impulsive and aggressive adolescents are specific cognitive techniques that provide the adolescent with alternative mediating responses to provocations. Self-instructional training, which entails the generation of specific covert self-verbalization to guide overt behavior, has been effective in increasing self-control (Camp *et al.,* 1977; Hamberger & Lohr, 1980; McCullough *et al.,* 1977; Schlichter & Horan, 1977; Snyder & White, 1979). The content of the self-statement can vary from specific strategies for solving particular types of tasks to general instructions such as "stop and think" or to coping responses relevant to the adolescent's emotional response (e.g., "I'm going to ignore this guy and keep my cool"). Overall, a self-instruction sequence seems most effective if it (1) includes the inhibition of the first impulsive response of the adolescent, (2) enumerates and guides the selection of alternative responses to provoking stimuli, and (3) connects the verbalizations with subsequent behavior (Fuson, 1979). In this manner, self-instructions can be used to help prepare the adolescent for aggression-eliciting events, to "remind" the adolescent of other behavior controls learned, and to reduce the intensity of emotional responding while increasing self-control. The Six-Step Coping Strategy outlined by Schlichter and Horan (1979), in which different self-instructions are utilized in a sequence of anger management, is presented in Table IV.

In teaching the adolescent to incorporate various self-statements and to use them to guide overt behavior, several procedures have proven helpful. Following the developmental sequence used with children (Meichenbaum & Goodman, 1971), desirable self-statements are modeled first aloud by the trainer *during* a role-played conflict situation. The adoles--

Table IV. Six-Step Coping Strategy[a]

1. Recognition of aggression-eliciting situations in one's history.
2. Preparation for such events through self-instructions to remain calm.
3. Continuation of self-instructions to remain calm when actually confronting the provocation.
4. Utilization of autonomic responses as cues to employ coping skills to reduce the intensity of angry feeling (e.g., relaxation, backward counting, pleasant imagery).
5. Exhibition of an assertive (not aggressive response).
6. Self-reinforcement for effectively handling the situation.

[a]Schlichter and Horan (1979).

cent should attend not only to the content of the self-instruction but also to the precise timing of its occurrence relative to the behavioral sequence of the interaction. Next, the roles are switched and the adolescent is prompted to respond aloud with an appropriate self-instruction. Discussion following role-play should focus on the differing content of before, during, and after self-instructions for conflict situations; the timing of implementation; and the evaluation of both internal and external outcome. Finally, role-plays can be conducted in which self-statements are rehearsed covertly by both the trainer and the adolescent and subsequently discussed in terms of the parameters outlined above. Some adolescents require visual cues, such as self-statements on index cards or specified signals from the trainer, in the early stages of covert rehearsal of the self-instruction procedure.

Other cognitive techniques that focus on the client's attributions and appraisals of the anger-eliciting situation have been proposed by Novaco (1976, 1977a) and are readily incorporated into coping self-instructions. In light of recent research suggesting that aggressive adolescents frequently misconstrue social stimuli as being hostile or provoking (Nasby, Hayden, & DePaulo, 1980), what seems primary is the modification of the adolescent's interpretations of aggression-eliciting antecedents. The inclusion of calming, reinterpretative, and coping statements—"This kid is jealous that I did well in my test," "My brother is frustrated because...or "He must have one hell of a hang-up if he has to go around teasing everyone"—will help to regulate respondent emotional arousal and enable the adolescent to substitute more appropriate responses. This modification of attributions and appraisals of social stimuli is accomplished through modeling and discussion of alternate interpretations and through reinforcement of the incorporation of these appropriate attributes into self-statements to guide responding.

Finally, self-instructional training should include skills in the self-evaluation of performance during conflict situations, of ability to manage anger arousal, and of effective goal attainment. Aggressive adolescents seem quite deficient in accurate appraisal of their performance in the area of self-control and they require modeling and coaching in the process of providing feedback to themselves. The sequence used to teach self-instructions can be used to teach self-reinforcement statements. The trainer can model positive reinforcement statements by directly praising the adolescent's desirable behaviors during a role-played scene or while viewing videotape feedback. The trainer can also praise his own behavior and thus model the procedure of self-reinforcement. The adolescent may need prompting in the identification of discrete and desirable behaviors and in the verbal praise of his own performance. Questions such as "What things were good about how you asked John to return your radio?" "How did you keep yourself from yelling at him?" "How did the situation turn out?" "How did you handle yourself?" etc. are useful prompts. Self-statements that include self-reinforcement for appropriate behavior and constructive feedback for inappropriate responses should be used folllowing both resolved and unresolved conflict situations.

A related cognitive control technique is a thinking-ahead procedure that targets the deficient sequential-thinking skills of problem adolescents (Platt *et al.,* 1974). This strategy is designed to help the adolescent use the estimation of future negative consequences for misbehavior to guide current responses to provocation. Several steps are required in teaching the adolescent to anticipate contingencies and incorporate them into self-control behaviors. First, an outline must be made of a range of predictable punishers for inappropriate behavior, from least to most severe. Next, the adolescent is given self-contingency statements such as "If I (misbehave) now, then I will get (future negative consequences)." and is asked to complete the statement by inserting a frequent inappropriate behavior and one of the negative consequences that will result. After practicing the generation of these contingency statements, tie-ins to specific conlfict situations are then made explicit. The trainer can prompt recollection of recent conflict situations in which the adolescent exhibited a specific aggressive response and received a specific negative consequence. At this stage it is important to focus on both short-term and long-term consequences *and* observable (extra homework, staying after school) and covert consequences (teacher trusts student less, bad reputation with peers). A sample chart used to prompt sequential thinking during parent conflicts is presented in Table V (Feindler, Marriott, & Iwata, 1980) in the same sequence outlined above. During a role-played conflict scene, the trainer and then the adolescent will model aloud the appropriate contingency statement before responding. Discussion of the implementation of this Think-Ahead procedure should focus on the timing of the contingency statement and the process of using anticipated negative consequences as deterrents to present inappropriate responding. Some imagery training designed to increase attention to the actual parameters of the eventual punishing stimulus may be helpful also.

Methods of Training: Packaging Stress Inoculation Techniques for Anger Control

All of the specific behavioral and cognitive control techniques outlined above can be presented in a systematic training sequence. The following steps are offered as a workable package in both individual and group sessions: (1) The trainer should first present the control technique in a didactic manner and then model its implementation: (2) the structuring of a behavioral rehearsal, using an actual conflict incident so that the adolescent can practice each alternative response to provocation, is then indicated; (3) the use of peer model and actual authority figures in these practice role-plays will enhance generalization of skills by providing closer approximations to actual provoking stimuli; and (4) the Barb technique (Kaufman & Wagner, 1972), which provides unplanned, intense, aversive stimulation and the enactment of powerful situations, such as encounters with police officers (Weiner, Minkin, Minkin, Fixen, Phillips, & Wolf, 1975), should be introduced after the adolescent has learned to handle mild, anger-arousing stimuli.

The Barb technique entails the graduated presentation of specific provocation statements to the adolescent while decreasing warnings or prompts to "get ready." For example, an adolescent who reliably responded with intense anger to statements about "his mother" would receive these provocations repeatedly in order to inoculate him to the intensity of this provoking stimuli and to enable him to display increasing self-control.

Adolescents usually enjoy role-playing conflict situations, but at times, certain teaching aides may be necessary. The trainers or other group members may need to coach or prompt the target adolescent during role-plays. Some impulsive adolescents also require extra visual cues

Table V. Control of Responding in Making Requests[a]

A. Stimulus control

1. Probe to determine if there are any competing stimuli.

   a. Is/are the adult(s) busy?
   b. Is/are the adult(s) in a "bad mood"?

B. Anticipate contingencies

1. Determine if there are any uncompleted responsibilities.
2. Determine if there are any conditions associated with granting the request.

C. If A and B are followed and response is "No," then determine if there are any points of negotiation.

D. Points to remember

1. Consideration of parents' previous behavior.
2. Careful listening.
3. Shaping parents' approval by starting with approximations to ultimate request.
4. Reinforce parents' behavior.
5. No fighting. This will result in counteraggression.

[a]Feindler, Marriott, and Iwata (1980).

as to which coping strategy to employ and when to implement it. Flashcards presented by the trainer during role-plays provide a spontaneous cuing procedure that prompts the adolescent to review the alternative rsponse repertoire. Sequential worksheets and cartoons are also useful in helping to sequence visually the antecedent, response, and consequence components of a conflict situation. Some of these audiovisual aids are available from the authors.

Finally, the transfer of training must be programmed to any anger-control training program. Treatment techniques that enhance generalization of behavior change include homework assignments prompting the use of self-control skills in a variety of problem situations (e.g., academic, social, and sports situations).

These homework assignments require the adolescent to practice each skill between training sessions, and to document this practice in some fashion. For example, the adolescent may be directed to generate three contingency statements incorporated into the thinking-ahead procedure and to use these statements in three problem situations. If students continue to self-monitor conflict situations, these new responses can readily be recorded. Other homework assignments include twice-weekly practice of relaxation, observation of a "target other's" anger cues, listing of coping statements to use before a conflict situation, or the use of the broken record technique in a peer and in a family situation. Completion of these concrete assignments will ensure some transfer of training to natural environments.

Also useful is the establishment of simple cues for anger control, such as little "keep cool" stickers placed on a notebook or pocketbook easily transferred across environments. *In vivo* role-plays, in which persons provoking anger in the adolescent are prompted to reinforce increased self-control, and follow-up booster sessions should also aid long-term maintenance of behavior change. Further, each adolescent in the training program should receive systematic preparation for nonreinforcement or punishment of increased anger control. Behavioral and cognitive changes occurring in adolescents as a result of this training program may not be supported in the natural environment and may in fact result in increased provocation and aggression by others. Preparatory role-plays and the application of relevant coping statements will serve to strengthen the individual's self-regulatory responses in these stress situations.

Role-plays in which the target adolescent, for example, responding in a controlled manner, ignores the teasing of another student and in turn gets ridiculed by his peers for being a "wimp" should be conducted toward the end of training. Self-statements relative to the adolescent's increased self-control and reappraisals of the other students' teasing will be instrumental in maintaining the anger-control responses in such situations. Other potential problem situations involve loss of "macho" status, increased aggression from others, loss of property, physical danger, teasing, ridicule, and failure to obtain desired outcomes or reinforcers immediately. Preparing the adolescent to deal with these sometimes harsh punishers through behavioral rehearsal and self-evaluative statements will certainly help promote generalization and maintenance of training.

A final note must be included on the adolescent who is resistant to participation in the program or to change in aggressive responding. We have found that it is critical to have adolescents voluntarily consent to participate in treatment and to involve them in the planning of in-session role-plays and homework assignments. This initial commitment may be prompted through a discussion of the negative consequences for aggressive, out-of-control behavior that exist in the adolescent's environment. Enumerating examples of short-term and long-term punishers, such as frequent in-school detentions, suspensions, extra assignments, loss of privileges, possible incarceration, or repeated court contacts, may prompt a desire to control behavior. However, the potential reduction of the adolescent's aggressive behaviors provide the primary sources of resistance—for certain cultures and environments, aggressive behavior may be adaptive. We have found it helpful to "sell" the anger-control package as a way to increase self-control, control of others, and personal power. Impulsively aggressive adolescents are often targets of another's manipulation or teasing, since they respond quickly and reliably to provocation. The notion of being "harder to get" or increasing self-control and detachment can be presented as an enhancement to the adolescent's powerful self-image. Finally, resistance and uncooperativeness may be circumvented by providing some tangible reinforcers for participation in training sessions and completion of homework assignments. Free time, leaving early, learning to work the videotape equipment, or role as actors in the role-played scenes are all potential in-group reinforcers that we have employed to maintain attention to and participation in the group. Caution should be used when using reinforcers for behavior change, because the concept of self-control and individual commitment to controlling anger and aggression may be undermined.

Illustrative Case Study

Lybie P. was a 16-year-old adolescent who had resided at a minimum security treatment facility for 22 months. Her prior history included numerous foster placements following her removal from an abusive family of eight siblings, and numerous court contacts for incorrigibility, elopment, and petty theft. Lybie had a measured IQ of 72 and was functioning at the fifth-grade level in reading and math skills, but was considered to be quite "streetwise." The staff described Lybie as pleasant to interact with when things were going her way. However, Lybie was easily provoked by the teasing of other residents and by directives and limits posed by authority figures. During these explosive incidents, Lybie would become extremely aggressive and unable to control herself. The behavior sequence consisted of screaming, crying, property damage, self-abuse, and finally attack on others. Typically, isolation or physical restraints were invoked to stop her outbursts.

Following her consent to receive anger-control training, Lybie completed many conflict data sheets. Inspection of these anger patterns indicated some reliable covert antecedents, such as increased rates of negative self-statements about herself and her environment, subvocal cursing, a "sick" feeling in the pit of her stomach, and a more general physical agitation. (She "felt like slamming something.") External antecedents that were direct provocations by authority figures or disliked peers, included teasing, trespassing on her property or privacy without permission, and an injustice leveled against a friend. Lybie discriminated these internal and external anger cues through self-observation and self-recording in her natural environment and was prompted by the therapist to categorize them (observable-covert; physiological-cognitive-motoric; before-after conflict) and identify patterns of antecedent cues. She also identified her usual responses, which included initial verbal attack, then escalation into physical aggression, and finally withdrawal and depression.

Lybie learned the relaxation sequence and deep-breathing response quite readily. Use of her physiological arousal as a cue to take herself out of the situation and to RELAX helped Lybie to delay her automatic aggressive response. During this brief time delay, Lybie was taught to substitute alternative coping responses through modeling and in-session response practice. These procedures involved the therapist providing Lybie with examples of appropriate coping responses and then acting these out in role-play scenes generated by Lybie. Following modeling, the alternative behaviors were discussed and consequences were evaluated. Finally, Lybie practiced the target responses in simulated situations, progressing from overt practice of verbal responses to covert practice of deep breathing and self-instructions. These responses included concrete and brief self-instructions such as "Keep calm," "Just ignore this," "I'm not going to get myself off," and "This isn't a big deal," which were effective in changing her interpretations of external provoking stimuli and in increasing her self-control.

Since continued explosive incidents would result in long-term residential placement, the Thinking Ahead and Self-Evaluation procedures were also effective with Lybie. Reminders that increased self-control ("Keeping Cool") would indicate her appropriateness for community placement further served to reduce the severity of Lybie's outbursts. Also effective were her self-instructions to accept calmly small punishers (such as an extra chore or early bed) so that extended punishment or escalation of the conflict would not occur. Finally, due to the depressive quality of Lybie's negative self-statements, positive statements for keeping calm and for controlling her anger and impulsive aggression were modeled and rehearsed. These statements included, for example, "I'm much better at keeping calm," "I did a good job ignoring her threats," "I thought first before I opened my mouth, and he listened to me." These self-reinforcement responses served to maintain the other newly acquired self-control responses and to help Lybie maintain an assertive rather than an aggressive style.

Following eight sessions of anger-control training, reductions in major categories of classroom and cottage aggression were recorded. Lybie became skilled at controlling her impulsive verbal responses to mild provocations and at discriminating those provoking stimuli that she should avoid and ignore. This increased anger control resulted in a reduction in severe punishers (isolation and restraint) and an increase in social reinforcers from peers and adults. Lybie P. is now living in a small community group home and is successfully attending a vocational training program.

Empirical Support for Adolescent Anger-Control Trraining

The cognitive-behavioral stress inoculation techniques that have been described as effective in reducing the occurrences of anger and aggressive responding in explosive adolescents have been evaluated in separate research projects. Each project extended the treatment methodology to other settings and other target populations; a summary of the data is presented below.

A Single-Subject Evaluation

Feindler (1979) evaluated the effects of self-monitoring and cognitive-behavioral modification techniques on the reduction of angry and aggressive behaviors of residential, delinquent adolescents ranging in age from 13 to 16½ years of age. These male and female students were selected on the basis of staff ratings of the most aggressive residential adolescents and on the basis of the highest frequencies of aggression for one week of direct classroom observation. Using a modified multiple baseline design across students, in which introduction of treatment was staggered, each subject was matched with a comparison subject. The aggressive behaviors of four students and four yoked, untreated, control students were monitored with the ABOS direct observation system. All eight students received pre- and post-test batteries, consisting of the Raven's Progressive Matrices (Raven, 1958), the Jesness Behavior Checklist and self-appraisal and observer forms (Jesness, 1966), and the Means–Ends Problem Solving Inventory (Shure & Spivack, 1972). During 14 twice-biweekly, 50-minute session, students received individual training in identifying critical self-monitoring and in using cognitive strategies as self-instructions, coping statements, self-evaluation of one's behavior, thinking ahead about future consequences, and also in relaxation. The self-monitoring training was evaluated alone during an initial three-week phase following baseline. A seven-month follow-up assessement was conducted with the two treatment and the two control subjects still at the residential facility.

The results indicated that self-monitoring and cognitive-behavioral modification techniques were effective in reducing both the frequency

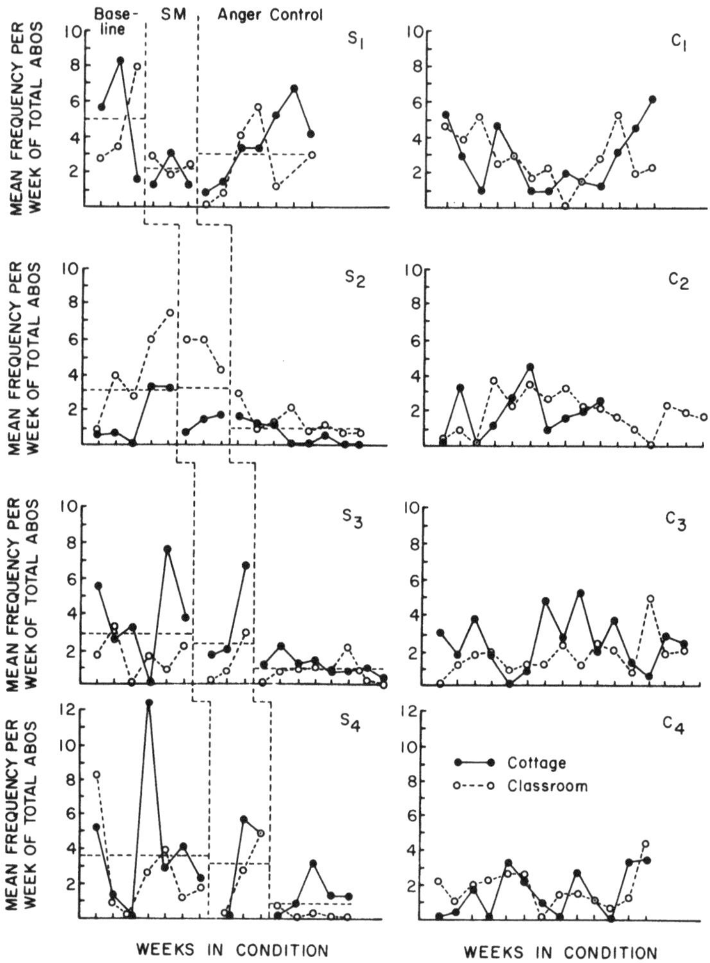

Figure 1. Mean daily frequency per week of total aggressive behavior during all phases of treatment and comparison subjects (Feindler & Fremouw, 1980).

and the intensity of aggressive, explosive behavior in the treatment group, compared with little or no change in matched control. Figure 1 demonstrates that all subjects had different patterns of aggressive behavior in each observation setting and that the frequency of aggressive behavior showed great variability over time. During the self-monitoring phase, decreases in aggression were noted for Treatment Subjects 1, 3, and 4, while a slight increase was noted for Subject 2. All treatment subjects showed decreases in the mean daily frequency of aggressive behavior from baseline to anger-control training levels. Individual anger-control phase means for treatment subjects were 3.0, 1.0, 0.96, and 0.88

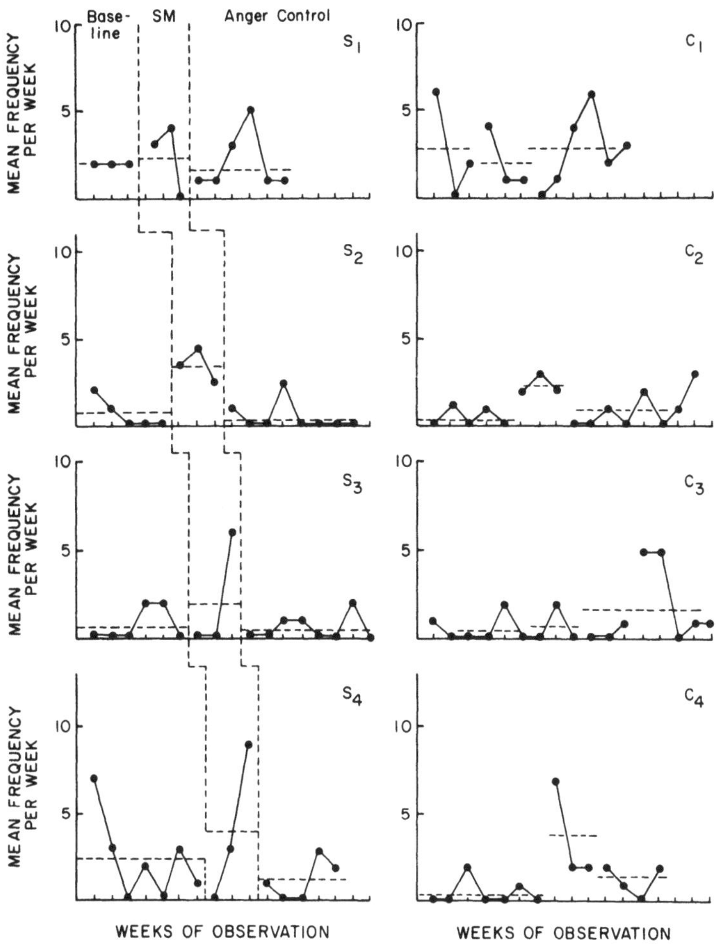

Figure 2. Mean frequency per week of critical incidents for treatment and comparison subjects during three conditions (Feindler & Fremouw, 1980).

occurrences of aggression per day for Subjects 1, 2, 3, and 4, respectively, while individual means for control subjects were 2.61, 3.5, 2.71, and 2.24 occurrences per day during this training phase.

Figure 2 presents the rates of severe aggression designated as critical incidents and indicates a reduction in frequency from a baseline mean of 3.6 incidents per week to an anger-control training mean of 2 per week. All subjects showed improvement except for Subject 1. Although the frequency ranges were low, interesting effects were noted during the self-monitoring phase, when the frequencies of critical incidents—the major focus of treatment—increased for all subjects. The reactive effects may be due to the increased attention to episodes of explosive behavior and the lack of more appropriate coping responses to aversive stimulations.

Results from the pre- and post assessments show a similar pattern of slight improvement in the treated subjects. The number of problem-solving responses on the Means–Ends Problem Solving Inventory increased from a pretreatment mean of 1.69 responses per story to 2.17 [$t(3) = 2.06, p<0.10$] responses for treatment subjects. Compared with the problem-solving means of a normal adolescent population reported by Platt *et al.* (1974), these results reflect the initial deficiency of problem-solving skills in explosive adolescents and the subsequent improvements of cognitive problem-solving. Response latencies on the Raven's Matrices increased for treatment subjects and decreased for control subjects, indicating a reduction in impulsivity on a cognitive task. Finally, improvement on subscales relevant to aggression on the Jesness Behavior Checklist were greater for treatment subjects. This initial evaluation of the anger-control training demonstrated a modest reduction in impulsive and aggressive responding to provoking stimuli across settings for the treatment subjects, and increases in the generation of solutions to problems and in reflectivity on cognitive tasks, compared with untreated controls.

Group Training with Junior High School Delinquents

The implications of modest treatment success in three of the four subjects in the Feindler (1979) study were severely limited by the small subject pool, and further replication of the Anger Control Training program was required. The self-control techniques were slightly modified to be delivered in a group format for twice-weekly 50-minute sessions at a public junior high school. For this research project (Feindler, Marriott, & Iwata, 1980), 36 adolescents were chosen from an in-school sample of 100 students in a behavior modification program for multiply suspended delinquents. Selection criteria were based on high rates of classroom and/or community disruptions evidenced in monthly school records. Students were randomly assigned to one of three treatment groups (six students each) or to three non-contact control groups (six students each) in two equivalent public schools. All subjects received a pre- and post-test battery including the Means–Ends Problem Solving Inventory, the Jesness Behavior Checklist, and the Self-Control Rating Scale (Kendall, 1979) completed by teachers and teachers' aides. Continuous measures recorded daily throughout the study included school suspensions and fines for disruptive behavior in the already existing behavior management contingency program.

During the 12-session training program, students were taught both general self-control strategies and strategies specific to anger/disruptive incidents. Sessions included information on relaxation techniques, self-instructional training, evaluating consequences of behavior, ignoring, and remaining task-oriented. Students learned to observe, sequence, and analyze their own response patterns through flow charts and homework assignments.

Analyses of the results revealed significant change in scores for treatment subjects on several dependent measures. The number of Means provided on the Means–Ends Problem Solving Inventory increased significantly [$t(17) = 2.26 p<0.05$] for the treatment group and decreased for the control group. Increases in response latency on the Raven's Matrices, in the overall percentile score and in selected subscales of the Jesness Inventory were also noted for the treatment group only. On the Self-Control Rating Scale, the treatment group did not receive improved ratings by teachers, whereas the control group did. This may be related to the chance pretreatment difference that was found between the groups. Although not statistically significant, the treatment group had a higher frequency of disruptive behavior during baseline compared with control adolescents. Figure 3 presents the changes in mean daily frequencies of fines for disruptive behavior (single demerits) and for severe aggression resulting in expulsion from school (double demerits). Examples of behavior resulting in a single demerit include yelling, threatening adults, refusal to comply with rules, walking out of class, teasing others, throwing things, etc. Examples of behavior resulting in a double demerit include hitting and other physical assault, destroying property, stealing, and a tantrum requiring restraint or removal. The mean daily frequency of single demerits for the treatment group changed from a baseline level of 7.8 per day to 6.8 per day during the seven-week training program and finally to 7.2 per day during the five-week follow-up phase. Although this change is statistically insignificant, a comparison with the changes in frequencies of single demerits for the control group supports the effectiveness of the intervention. During the 18-week data collection, the control-group mean changed from a 6-week baseline mean of 5.2 single demerits per day to 7.5 during the treatment phase and finally to 7.84 per day during the follow-up phase.

Figure 3 also presents the mean daily frequencies of double demerits, which were fines for severe and continued disruptive or aggressive behavior in school. The mean daily frequency for the treatment group changed from a baseline level of 1.45 per day, to 1.0 per day during the seven weeks of anger control training, to 0.72 double demerits per day during the follow-up. Again the comparsion with the control group daily means of 1.37, 1.2, and 1.1 for the three phases further supports the effectiveness of the intervention.

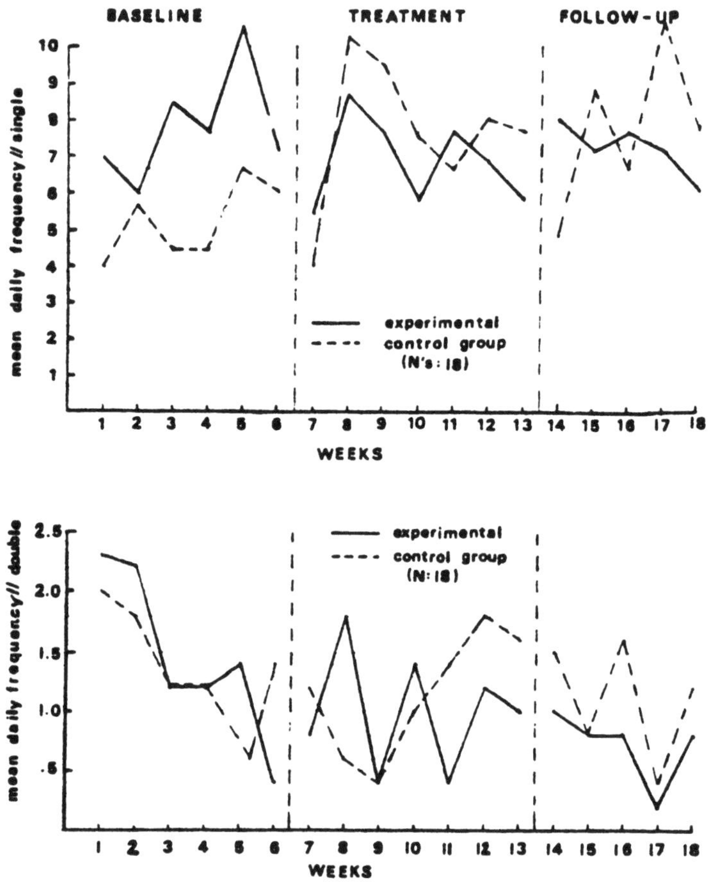

Figure 3. Group changes in mean daily frequencies of single and double fines for disruptive classroom behavior.

Although caution is advised when interpreting continous data that reflect institutional contingencies, the anger-control training appeared effective in reducing the frequency of severe occurrences of disruptive and aggressive behavior and the resulting school expulsions. The slight decrease in single demerits for the treatment group suggests a training effect when compared with the initially less disruptive control group, in which the frequency of single demerits showed an increase. Due to the nature of these data, it is not possible to determine actual changes in aggressive responding; however, the increase in response latency on a cognitive task and problem-solving skills indicates generalization of training across response categories.

Anger-Control Training for Child-Care Workers in a Residential Facility

A further extension of the stress inoculation program involved training child-care workers in a residential, adolescent facility to use these procedures (Feindler, Latini, Nape, Romano, & Doyle 1980). Recently, Novaco (1980) indicated the usefulness of stress inoculation training for probation counselors because of frequent contact with aggressive clients and because of the high levels of stress induced by the position. With this dual objective, the anger-management skills that child-care workers were trained to use with target adolescents could also be used by the workers to control their own stress, thereby serving as models to the adolescents.

Treatment subjects included 12 child-care workers and their 19 male adolescent clients taken from a ward considered the most difficult to manage at a residential treatment facility. The ages of the residents ranged from 12 years to 15½ years. A group comparison design was employed in which the unit targeted for intervention was matched with a comparable, no-contact control unit. Dependent measures consisted of collecting existing unit data and school data on the number of restrictions for physical aggression and disruptive classroom behavior that occurred daily for each resident.

Following the stress inoculation outline proposed by Meichenbaum (1977), the anger-control program was divided into three phases. In the initial phase of the program, didactic presentation of anger-management skills was followed by small group discussions in which child-care workers applied these skills to specific provocation incidents involving adolescents on the unit. One psychologist and two male graduate students were available on the unit five hours a week, for five weeks during the second phase to model appropriate intervention and anger management techniques. They observed, coached, and gave feedback to the child-care workers.

The results indicate that the anger-control training program for child-care workers reduced the frequency of on-ward fines for physical aggression from a baseline level of 29.2 per week to 17.1 per week for the target unit [$t(15) = 2.9$, $p<0.01$]. By comparison, the control unit evidenced only 21 restrictions per week during baseline and showed a small reduction to 18 restrictions per week during the comparison intervention period [$t(15) = 0.43$, NS].

Additional data analyses included the changes in frequencies of school infractions incurred by subject from the treatment and no-contact control units. The mean number of exclusions, which included expulsions, dismissals, and suspensions from school, imposed on target subjects prior to treatment was 18 per week. The post-treatment mean of 11.3 exclusions per week [$t(17) = 2.85$ $p<.01$] can be considered significant especially when compared with the control group, which showed a reduction in school exclusions from a baseline mean of 10 per week to 8 exclusions per week during the intervention period [t(17) = 0.107, NS]. A final class of school infractions, which included unit- and living-area restrictions as well as restrictions on attending classes and other activities, provided less encouraging results. For the target unit, the pretreatment mean was 16 restrictions per week, and a small reduction in the number of restrictions during and after training reduced this mean to 11 [t(17) = 1.28, NS]. These same data also showed a reduction for the control unit from 12.7 restrictions to 11 per week during the comparison treatment phase [t(17) = 0.76, NS].

In summary, it appears that brief in-service training with child-care workers from in-patient units housing the most aggressive adolescents is effective in reducing the frequency of unit fines imposed for physical aggression. An estimate of the generalization of treatment effects is available from the analysis of school exclusions and restrictions data, which also showed modest reductions. Although the implementation of specific stress inoculation techniques was not monitored, it seems that the child-care workers were effective in reducing on-ward conflicts and in modeling anger-management skills for the adolescents, but were less effective in focusing on school-related provocations.

FUTURE DIRECTIONS

The preliminary empirical support for a stress inoculation, anger-control training program is promising. Several areas related to anger-treatment research invite further investigation. Perhaps the formulation and description of these clinical research questions will stimulate interest in the area of adolescent anger-control and will ultimately result in increased effectiveness and efficiency of the self-control treatment techniques.

Assessment Issues

Both clinicians and researchers in the field of adolescent anger would benefit from the evaluation of existing assessment methodology and the development of more reliable and valid methods of assessing anger. Comprehensive validational research is needed for the variety of structured inventories (Anger Inventories, Jesness Behavior Checklists, Self-Control Rating Scale, etc.) as well as measures such as direct observation of aggression, analog role-play measures, and self-monitoring.

Because of the great potential of self-monitoring procedures, the reliability of self-monitoring and validity of self-report of anger incidents are particularly important to determine. Unfortunately, little research on reactive effects of self-monitoring and on the correspondence of verbal behavior and motor behavior in the area of adolescent aggression has been conducted.

The indirect methods of assessing adolescent anger also require further clinical and psychometric investigation. Measures such as monitoring existing institutional contingencies and frequency of fines or other punishments contingent on aggressive behavior may prove to be valuable for evaluating treatment programs. However, since such institutional data reflect primarily the staff behaviors of observing, recording, and providing consequences for adolescents' aggression, questions about their reliability and validity are certainly of paramount importance. Comparisons of institutional measures and more direct observation during the implementation and evaluation of treatment are warranted.

A final assessment issue involves the much-needed development of analog assessment methods for adolescent anger. The "Barb" treatment technique, described by Kaufman and Wagner (1972), involves the presentation of a known provoking verbal stimulus and the observation and recording of the subject's subsequent verbal and nonverbal responses to this provocation. This technique could readily be developed to approximate the Behavioral Assertive Test for Children (Bernstein, Bellack, & Hersen, 1972), in which peer models provide verbal prompts and assertive behaviors are rated for frequency and duration. The use of actual provoking models, such as school and authority figures and certain peers, would increase the comprehensiveness of this type of assessement device. The development of an analog assessment procedure would be an efficient means to measure an adolescent's anger but would require validation with the more direct methods of aggression assessment and with the standardized inventories.

Treatment Methodology

Although the initial results with stress inoculation training for anger are encouraging, the major need now is for the replication of substantial treatment effects in studies with adequate control groups. If the stress inoculation procedure is effective in more rigorous evaluations, then research could be directed at dismantling the treatment components. Precisely which components of the treatment technology are most effective has not been determined. Many of the individual techniques incorporated, such as self-monitoring, behavioral rehearsal, self-instructional training, self-reinforcement, and relaxation, have been documented as effective with child and adult populations. Which techniques and which sequence of techniques are most effective for adolescents with anger control problems remains unclear. The delivery of cost-efficient and optimally effective treatment requires careful component analysis and a final clarification of the best treatment package.

In addition, further delineation is needed on individual subject variables that may predict appropriateness for self-control treatment or account for differential responses to treatment. Variables such as age, length of residential treatment, nature of aggressive acts, attributional style, cognitive ability, level of social skills, family stability, and degree of peer involvement in antisocial acts may all help to predict adolescent responsiveness to treatment.

Finally, adolescents experiencing difficulties in controlling their anger may have other behavioral problems that require more immediate behavior change efforts. Severe problems of self-abuse, depression, phobic behaviors, addictive behaviors, and other maladaptive responses may inhibit the development of self-control responses related to anger outbursts. Given the complexity of the problems of anger control in adolescents, it is naive to expect any *one* treatment approach—stress inoculation, contingency contracting, or social skills training—to be effective for all youths. Perhaps it is the recognition of this fact that is the most important consideration for future research attempts. The present description of a cognitive-behavioral approach is intended to increase the clinician's ability to deal with the important social problem of anger.

SUMMARY

Adolescent anger control has been presented as a critical problem in self-control that appears amenable to cognitive-behavioral treatment techniques. A number of treatment techniques, including self-monitoring, self-instructional training, behavior rehearsal, and sequential thinking, were effective in reducing aggressive responding in natural environments and transferring to performance on cognitive tasks. Data from three research studies provide preliminary support for the effectiveness of the anger-control package with in-patient and public school populations. More data from a variety of sources are still needed to evaluate this relatively new application of self-control techniques. The authors have proposed several future directions in hopes of stimulating both research and clinical activity.

REFERENCES

Anderson, L., Fodor, I., & Alpert, H. A. A comparison of methods of training self-control. *Behavior Therapy,* 1976, *7,* 649–658.

Bandura, A. *Aggression: A social learning analysis.* Englewood Cliffs, N.J.: Prentice-Hall, 1973.

Bernstein, M., Bellack, A., & Hersen, M. Social skills training for unassertive children: A multiple baseline analysis. *Journal of Applied Behavior Analysis,* 1977, *5,* 443–454.

Buss, A. H., & Durkee, A. An inventory for assessing different kinds of hostility. *Journal of Consulting Psychology,* 1957, *21,* 343–349

Butler, L., & Meichenbaum, D. The assessment of interpersonal problem-solving skills. In P. C. Kendall & S. D. Hollan (Eds.), *Cognitive-behavioral interventions: Assessment methods.* New York: Academic Press, 1980.

Camp B. Verbal mediation in young aggressive boys. *Journal of Abnormal Psychology,* 1977, *86,* 145–153.

Camp, B., Blom, G., Herbert, F., & Van Doornick, W. "Think Aloud": A program for developing self-control in young aggressive boys. *Journal of Abnormal Child Psychology,* 1977, *8,* 157–169.

D'Zurilla, T., & Goldfried, M. Problem solving and behavior modification. *Journal of Abnormal Psychology,* 1971, *78,* 107–126.

Evans, D. R., & Hearn, M. T. Anger and systematic desensitization: A follow-up. *Psychological Reports,* 1973, *32,* 569–570.

Federal Bureau of Investigation. *Crime in the United States, 1976.* Washington, D. C.: U.S. Government Printing Office, 1977.

Feindler, E. L. *Cognitive and behavioral approaches to anger control training in explosive adolescents.* Unpublished doctoral dissertation, West Virginia University, 1979.

Feindler, E. L., & Fremouw, W. *Cognitive and behavioral approaches to stress inoculation training in explosive adolescents.* Paper presented at the Annual Convention of the Eastern Psychological Association, Philadelphia, April 1979.

Feindler, E. L., Marriott, S. A., & Iwata, M. *An anger control training program for junior high delinquents.* Paper presented in symposium entitled "Issues in anger assessment and management" at 14th Annual Convention of Association for Advancement of Behavior Therapy, New York, November 1980.

Feindler, E. L., Latini, J., Nape, K., Romano, J., & Doyle, J. *Anger reduction methods for child-care workers at a residential delinquent facility.* Paper presented at 14th Annual Convention of Association for Advancement of Behavior Therapy, New York, November, 1980.

Fuson, K. D. The development of self-regulating aspects of speech: A review. In G. Zivin (Ed.), *The development of self-regulation through private speech.* New York: Wiley, 1979.

Hamberger, K., & Lohr, J. M. Rational restructuring for anger control: A quasi-experimental case study. *Cognitive Therapy and Research,* 1980, *4,* 99–102.

Hobbs, T. R., & Holt, M. M. The effects of token reinforcement on the behavior of delinquents in cottage settings. *Journal of Applied Behavior Analysis,* 1976, *9,* 189–198.

Jesness, C. *Jesness inventory.* Palo Alto, Calif.: Consulting Psychologists Press, 1966.

Kaufman, K. F., & O'Leary, K. D. Rewards, cost, and self-evaluation procedures for disruptive adolescents in a psychiatric hospital school. *Journal of Behavior Analysis,* 1972, *5,* 292–309.

Kaufman, L., & Wagner, B. Barb: A systematic treatment technique for temper control disorders. *Behavior Therapy,* 1972, *3,* 84–90.

Kazdin, A. E. *The token economy: A review and evaluation.* New York: Plenum Press, 1977.

Kendall, P. On the efficacious use of verbal self-instructional procedures with children. *Cognitive Therapy and Research,* 1977, *1,* 331–341.

Kendall, P., & Wilcox, L. F. Self-control in children: Development of a rating scale. *Journal of Consulting and Clinical Psychology,* 1979, *6,* 1020–1028.

Konecni, V. J. Annoyance, type, and duration of post annoyance activity and aggression: The "cathartic effect." *Journal of Experimental Psychology,* 1975, *104,* 76–102. (a)

Konecni, V. J. The mediation of aggressive behavior: Arousal level versus anger and cognitive labeling. *Journal of Personality and Social Psychology,* 1975, *32,* 706–712. (b)

Lee, D. Y., Hallberg, E. T., & Hassard, H. Effects of assertion training on aggressive behavior of adolescents. *Journal of Counseling Psychology,* 1979, *26,* 459–461.

Mahoney, M. *Cognition and behavior modification.* Cambridge, Mass.: Ballinger, 1974.

McCullough, J., Huntsinger, G., & Nay, W. Self-control treatment of aggression in a 16 year old male: Case study. *Journal of Consulting and Clinical Psychology,* 1977, *45,* 322–331.

Meichenbaum, D. A self-instructional approach to stress management: A proposal for stress inoculation training. In C. Spielberger & I. Sarason (Eds.), *Stress and anxiety* (Vol. 2). New York: Wiley, 1975.

Meichenbaum, D. *Cognitive-behavior modification: An integrative approach.* New York: Plenum Press, 1977.

Meichenbaum, D., & Goodman, J. Training impulsive children to talk to themselves. *Journal of Abnormal Psychology,* 1971, *77,* 115–126.

Nabsy, W., Hayden, B., & DePaulo, B. M. Attributional bias among aggressive boys to interpret unambiguous social stimuli as displays of hostility. *Journal of Abnormal Psychology,* 1980, *89,* 459–468.

Novaco, R. W. *Anger control: The development and evaluation of an experimental treatment.* Lexington, Mass.: D. C. Heath, 1975.

Novaco, R. W. Treatment of chronic anger through cognitive and relaxation controls. *Journal of Consulting and Clinical Psychology,* 1976, *44,* 681.

Novaco, R. W. Stress inoculation: A cognitive therapy for anger and its application to a case of depression. *Journal of Consulting and Clinical Psychology,* 1977, *45,* 600–608. (a)

Novaco, R. W. A stress inoculation approach to anger management in the training of law enforcement officers. *American Journal of Community Psychology,* 1977, *5,* 527–346. (b)

Novaco, R. W. The cognitive regulation of anger and stress. In P. C. Kendall & S. D. Hollon (Eds.), *Cognitive-behavioral interventions: Theory, research, and procedure.* New York: Academic Press, 1979.

Novaco, R. W. The training of probation counselors for anger problems. *Journal of Counseling Psychology,* 1980, *27,* 385–390.

Olweus, D. Stability of aggressive reaction patterns in males: A review. *Psychological Bulletin,* 1979, *83,* 852–875.

Platt, J. J., Spivack, G., Altman, N., Altman, D., & Peizer, S. B. Adolescent problem-solving thinking. *Journal of Consulting and Clinical Psychology,* 1974, *42,* 787–793.

Raven, J. C. *Advanced progressive matrices.* London: H. K. Lewis, 1958.

Redl, F., & Wineman, D. *Children who hate.* New York: Free Press, 1951.

Redl, F., & Wineman, D. *Controls from within: Techniques for the treatment of the aggressive child.* New York: Free Press, 1952.

Rimm, D. C., deGroot, J. C., Boord, P., Heiman, J., & Dillow, P. V. Systematic desensitization of an anger response. *Behavior Research and Therapy,* 1971, *9,* 273–280.

Rule, B. G., & Nesdale, A. R. Emotional arousal and aggressive behavior. *Psychological Bulletin,* 1976, *83,* 851–863.

Saunders, J. T., Reppucci, N. D., & Sarato, B. P. An examination of impulsivity as a trait characterizing delinquent youth. *American Journal of Orthopsychiatry,* 1973, *43,* 789–795.

Schachter, S., & Singer, J. E. Cognitive, social, and physiological determinants of emotional state. *Psychological Review,* 1962, *69,* 379–399.

Schlichter, K. J., & Horan, J. J. *Effects of stress inoculation on the anger and aggression management skills of institutionalized juvenile delinquents.* Paper presented at the meeting of the Educational Research Association, San Francisco, 1979.

Shure, M. B., & Spivack, G. Means-ends thinking, adjustment, and social class among elementary school-aged children. *Journal of Consulting and Clinical Psychology,* 1972, *38,* 348–353.

Smith, R. E. The use of humor in the counter-conditioning of an anger response. *Behavior Therapy,* 1973, *4,* 576–580.

Smith, R. E. *When I say no, I feel guilty.* New York: Bantam Books, 1975.

Snyder, J., & White, M. The use of cognitive self-instruction in the treatment of behaviorally disturbed adolescents. *Behavior Therapy,* 1979, *10,* 227–235.

Turk, D. *An expanded skills training apprach for the treatment of experimentally induced pain.* Unpublished doctoral dissertation, University of Waterloo, 1976.

Tyler, V. O., & Brown, G. D. Token reinforcement of academic performance with institutionalized delinquent boys. *Journal of Educational Psychology,* 1968, *59,* 164–168.

Vaal, J. J. The Rathus assertive schedule: Reliability at the junior high school level. *Behavior Therapy,* 1975, *6,* 566–567.

Weathers, L., & Liberman, R. Contingency contracting with families of delinquent adolescents. *Behavior Therapy,* 1975, *6,* 566–567.

Webster, W. *Crime in the United States, 1978.* Washington, D.C.: U.S. Government Printing Office, 1979.

Weiner, J. S., Minkin, N., Minkin, B., Fixen, D. L., Phillips, E. L., & Wolf, M. M. Intervention package: An analysis to prepare juvenile delinquents for encounters with police officers. *Criminal Justice and Behavior,* 1975, *2*(1), 55–70.

Witmer, L. The treatment and cure of a case of mental and moral deficiency. *The Psychological Clinic,* 1908, *2,* 153–179.

Concluding Comments

The chapters in Section I of this volume, by Leventhal and Nerenz, Epstein, and Janis, reviewed the stress literature and concluded that the following factors all play an important role in determining how successfully individuals cope with stress:

1. flexibility in one's coping repertoire;
2. graduated exposure, or what Epstein calls "proactive mastery" of stressful events by assimilating threat in small doses;
3. use of cognitive strategies or what Epstein calls "constructive defenses";
4. use of preparatory information and contingency planning;
5. predictability, personal commitment, and social support.

The chapter in Section II, by Meichenbaum and Cameron, described how a cognitive-behavioral stress inoculation training regimen could be developed to take into consideration the complexities of the stress and coping processes described in Section I. The need for *caution* in determining an effective way to cope with stress is worth underscoring once again. One should be cautious about prescribing coping techniques. Instead, a flexible collaborative "personal-scientist" self-evaluative approach should be established between client and trainer in order to determine the best ways for that particular individual to cope with stress. Stress inoculation training recognizes that coping with stress is a dynamic process that changes with time and circumstances. Indeed, stress inoculation training may be successful, in part, because of the flexibility afforded due to its wide range of techniques and its focus on individually tailored procedures.

The chapters in Section III on "Applications" illustrate the procedural diversity and clinical flexibility in being able to individually tailor stress inoculation training to the needs of specific populations. While there is some diversity in the application of stress inoculation training across populations some common features are apparent. These include the important role placed on developing a reconceptualization of the client's stress reactions and stressful circumstances, the training of direct action and palliative coping modes of responding, and the use of performance-based procedures. Each of these elements can be altered to meet the time-frame of the specific intervention, the level of experience of the trainer, the needs of the clients, and the goals of the intervention.

Although the results reported in Section III are encouraging, they are preliminary. In many ways, the ideas in this book are ahead of the data, and the objective of the book is to narrow this gap. The present volume is designed to stimulate research that will critically evaluate stress inoculation training. There is an urgent need to evaluate these procedures with stressed populations using comparison control groups matched for treatment credibility, and using a variety of different levels of dependent measures, assessed over time (i.e., including long-term follow-up assessments). Once a robust effect has been established, one can then conduct subject-by-treatment interaction studies and dismantling studies.

The contributors to Sections II and III have described many of the "how-to" features in order to convey the complexity of the interventions, to illustrate the clinical sensitivity required, and to encourage replication and extension. In implementing such stress prevention and management programs, it is necessary to anticipate and plan accordingly for the resistance one will encounter from clients, staff, and administrators. One must recognize the social context in which the particular training program is imbedded.

Intervention designed to prevent and manage stress reactions needs to be *multileveled.* While most of the contributions to this volume have focused on the level of the individual (that is, the medical patient, the victim, the client), the cognitive-behavioral perspective can be extended to interventions at the level of the group, community, or society, as suggested by Novaco *et al.,* Ayalon, and others. A fuller consideration of such group interventions must await another volume. It is also important to remember that training individuals to cope with stress should *not* be viewed as a substitute for social change, especially with structurally rooted social problems. We can reduce and avoid stress by teaching better coping skills, by raising self-esteem, by helping people identify and establish support groups, and also by reducing preventable and unnecessary forms of stress.

Author Index

Subject Index